Withdrawn

For Reference

Not to be taken from this room

U.S. Military Records

U.S. Military Records

A Guide to Federal and State Sources, Colonial America to the Present

By

James C. Neagles

Neagles, James C.

U.S. military records : a guide to federal and state sources, Colonial America
to the present / by James C. Neagles.

p. cm.

Includes bibliographical references and index.

ISBN 0-916489-55-8

1. United States—History, Military—Archival resources—Directories.
2. United States—Genealogy—Archival resources—Directories. I. Title.

Z1249.M5N43 1994

[E181]

929'.3'0973—dc20   94-3848

Copyright 1994
Ancestry Incorporated
P.O. Box 476
Salt Lake City, Utah 84110-0476

First printing 1994
10 9 8 7 6 5 4 3 2 1

Printed in the United States of America

Contents

CHAPTER 1

Types of Records: Records Created During Military Service

CHAPTER 2

Types of Records: Post-Service Records and Records Relating to Civilian Affairs

CHAPTER 3

Resources of the National Archives Microfilm Room

CHAPTER 4

Resources of the National Archives Reference Branches

CHAPTER 5

Resources of the National Archives Repositories
Outside Washington, D.C.

CHAPTER 6

Resources of the History and Research
Centers in Washington, D.C.

CHAPTER 7

Resources of the History and Research Centers
Outside Washington, D.C.

CHAPTER 8

State Resources

CHAPTER 9

Published Sources: Works That Pertain
to More Than One State

APPENDIX

America's Military Conflicts: A Brief History   393

INDEX   413

Foreword

Occasionally, there is a contribution to American genealogical research that is destined to become a classic. James Neagles' *U.S. Military Records* is such a work. The product of much patient research and collaboration with one of genealogy's leading publishers, this volume will be a standout in the field.

Military and pension records are among the most useful sources available to genealogists because of the detail they offer. These records are important because they may provide an ancestor's date of birth, place of residence, the names and addresses of family members, and other details that can round out a picture of his or her life. Because nearly all families have members who have served in the military, these records are valuable to a broad range of researchers.

Researching among military records is not unlike a detective's task. Many clues, published and unpublished, await discovery in a myriad of government and private institutions. The search begins at home with an examination of such sources as family stories, photographs, letters, diaries, newspapers, medals, discharge papers, and cemeteries, among others. After the search has begun and precise research questions have been formulated, Neagles' guide provides an indispensable outline to resources that are most likely to be helpful in providing answers.

Here, Neagles assembles not only a new base of research information that draws on his expertise, he also provides an approach that will open access to these important but often underused records to researchers in many disciplines. Nine chapters describe the general types of records that exist; resources available at the National Archives in Washington, D.C., and other repositories around the nation; and published sources pertaining to each state and to the United States in general. A useful summary of America's military history is provided in an appendix. This information, together with a solid index, makes this volume both useful and easy to use.

Given the abundance of available resources and the complexity of military records research, the value and magnitude of Neagles' contribution are enormous. *U.S. Military Records* provides mountains of detail essential to the military researcher. In doing so, it fills a nearly complete void in genealogical research literature; there is nothing like it elsewhere. This book will appeal not only to genealogists but to anyone engaged in military history research. Simply put, it is one of the best genealogical research aids to come along in some time, and it will be regarded as one of the most important works in the field.

Judith P. Reid
Reference Specialist
Local History and Genealogy
Library of Congress

Preface

By James C. Neagles

A history of America might be characterized as a history of its military experiences. Certainly, anyone who attempts to reconstruct the life of any American must eventually consider the possibility that the person was associated with the military somehow during his or her lifetime. Fortunately, all branches of the military hierarchy have maintained voluminous records, and government agencies also have collected many records pertaining to veterans and their families. The key to using these records is to first learn what they are and where they can be found. That is the purpose of this guide.

Family and academic historians are aware that various types of military records, rich in personal information, are available for research. However, identifying and locating particular records can be difficult. Library catalogs and specific guides are a means of locating some sources but, in too many cases, finding needed facts has been a matter of luck or browsing aimlessly through books on library shelves. Selective guides and library catalogs point to only a small portion of the military documentation that is scattered across the nation. To the frustration of many, there has been no single, comprehensive guide for locating important military records sources. It is hoped that this volume will clearly define the vast and fascinating body of military records and lead the way to efficient and enjoyable research. It is also hoped that librarians and archivists will find this guide useful as they furnish information and assistance to patrons.

This guide could not have been completed without the generous assistance and advice offered by dozens of federal and state archivists and directors of research centers, too numerous to mention here. Archives and libraries are universally short-handed because of budget restrictions, and it is to the credit of their staffs that they somehow found time to help me when I visited their facilities or corresponded with them.

Special thanks are due Virginia Steele Wood, reference librarian in the Local History and Genealogy Reading Room, Library of Congress, who helped accumulate much of the data used to prepare the summaries of America's military engagements and who provided the majority of the bibliographical material.

Thanks are also due several National Archives officials who offered personal assistance. Among these are William E. Lind and Michael T. Meier of the Military Reference Branch, who provided considerable information and assistance in identifying useful collections of military records, and Jerry Wallace of the Office of National Archives Regional Archives. The following persons, who read appropriate parts of the manuscript and offered helpful suggestions and information, are also much appreciated: JoAnne Williamson, chief, Military Reference Branch, and military reference consultants Stuart Butler, Richard Von Daenhoff, and Ken Schlessinger for reading those portions of the draft manuscript that relate to the National Archives and who pointed out corrections needed and suggested additions.

Others who read the draft manuscript and provided valuable information were Ken Nelson of the LDS Family History Library in Salt Lake City, Judith Reid of the Library of Congress, and David Thackery of the Newberry Library in Chicago. The staff of Ancestry were meticulous in their editing and consultation functions. Recognition is also due Robert Welsh, formerly of Ancestry, who first conceived the idea and general format for this publication and suggested that I be the one to bring his idea to fruition.

Any errors or omissions are my sole responsibility.

Introduction

By Loretto Dennis Szucs

Military records are an abundant and fascinating resource for obtaining first-hand accounts of the military activities that have shaped this country. Whether created in time of war or in time of peace, these records, which have originated at the federal, state, and local levels, provide unique facts and insights into the lives of men and women who have served in the armed forces of the United States.

Almost every American family, in one generation or another, has seen one or more of its members serve in America's armed forces. From regimental histories, which provide blow-by-blow accounts of a unit's participation in military actions, to the personal details contained in the service and pension files of individual men and women, military records provide valuable information concerning a large and significant portion of the American population. And because military records have been preserved and made available at and through a number of research institutions, much information awaits the well-prepared researcher.

Some caveats are in order: As is the case with other government documents, military records have not been created with genealogists and historians in mind; rather, they have been intended to provide a record and to facilitate the everyday business of the federal government and state and local governments. For every government-created record that is replete with personal details, there are probably several thousand that are

not. Because certain types of military records contain much personal information and are heavily relied upon, some have been indexed and microfilmed to meet user demand. In fact, some of the best military sources are available in libraries all over the country. Unfortunately, however, a greater number of military records exist only in their original form, making it necessary for researchers to travel some distance to archives and other historical collections to examine them. To add to these difficulties, many collections are not indexed.

Before a researcher sets out to use any archives, library, museum, manuscript, or other collection, it is important to plan ahead. Records may be open to researchers only on certain days of the week or during certain hours of the day, and research policies may differ significantly from one research institution to another. Hours of operation and research policies tend to change over time. Before a research trip is made, therefore, it is important to understand what resources are available and when and how they can be used.

To the lament of many a librarian and archivist, and ultimately the researcher, an astounding number of persons, eager to include military records in their research, arrive at research institutions completely unprepared to use them. These would-be genealogists and historians, having only vague knowledge of the military subject they intend to research, frustrate themselves and those who are there to help them. It is hoped that this volume will serve as a major step in the direction of eliminating that problem.

Where to Begin

To locate military records for any individual, it is essential to know when and where in the armed forces he or she served and whether that person served in the enlisted ranks or was an officer. For those researchers who do not have that identifying information, there are some potential solutions.

As in any research project, it is important to study carefully whatever is already known about the subject of interest. Families and communities frequently pass down stories of military "heroes" from generation to generation. In most cases, these stories retain some fact, but, with the passage of years and in the process of retelling, accuracy fades. At any rate, family stories should not be overlooked for clues at the start of a military research project.

When and where did the individual live? Did the family keep evidence of military service? Certificates, letters, journals, diaries, scrapbooks, newspaper clippings, photographs, medals, swords and other memorabilia kept in private collections may also provide the basic facts needed to begin searching military records.

Creating a historical time line can be especially useful in determining if and when the subject might have served in the military. By compiling a chronological list of the known dates and places of residence of an individual from birth through adulthood, it is frequently easy to discover the possibility of military service. Was the subject of your interest the right age to be eligible for the draft or to serve voluntarily in the Civil War? Is it likely that this person served on the Northern rather than the Southern side, or vice versa? The appendix of this book briefly summarizes some of the many military engagements in which Americans have participated. A family historian who becomes aware that an ancestor lived in a specific region during a certain time might consult this chronologically arranged appendix for possible leads to further searching.

The researcher may look for records that describe military engagements that occurred in that region at that time. Conversely, the researcher may uncover some scrap of evidence of an ancestor's involvement in a specific war or battle or a vague event such as "the Indian wars." It would be logical, then, to learn something more about those particular military events. The appendix provides a quick

reference point from which further study in published histories is recommended.

Evidence of Military Service in Public Records

There are a number of public records that are potentially valuable in discovering the military history of an individual. It has been a long-standing American tradition to foster patriotism by honoring local sons and daughters who have defended the ideals of their country. Hometown war heroes are frequently noted on public monuments, and local newspaper files may yield surprisingly detailed accounts of the community's well-known and less-famous military personnel and veterans.

Commercial enterprises and historically-oriented groups and institutions have regularly published local histories. As a rule, these histories will include glowing accounts of the area's involvement in military activities. Some of the volumes provide biographical sketches of military leaders, while others attempt to list all of the community's participants in various military conflicts. The *History of Cook County, Illinois . . .* (Andreas 1884) is typical of the local history publications that were churned out around the turn of the century. A chapter in that volume titled "Early Military History" includes the history of Chicago, which, like so many other American cities, began as a military fort. From the 1812 Fort Dearborn Massacre to lists of Cook County's military companies and leaders in the Civil War, Andreas' volume provides solid facts that could be very useful for beginning a military research project. A large number of other state and local publications augment Andreas' volume. Histories printed in later years, of course, have the advantage of describing the county's involvement in military engagements long after the Civil War. Locally focused histories have been published at various times for virtually every state and county in the United States. They should not be overlooked as an important research aid. *A Bibliography of American County Histories* (Filby 1985) is a list of five thousand such sources.

In addition to the standard histories, local public libraries and historical societies usually preserve and make available other types of publications that document the military involvement of the geographical area served. Historical agencies collect biographies, letters, diaries, journals, and all sorts of memorabilia from local military units and servicemen and -women. The personal accounts found in some collections are a fascinating means of stepping back in time. First-hand accounts afford a better understanding of the day-to-day drudgery, loneliness, fears, and satisfactions of military life.

Cemeteries provide yet another local source of information regarding individuals who served in the armed forces. Almost every cemetery in the nation contains some evidence of military events and veterans. Cemetery records and grave markers frequently identify military dead by name, rank, and unit designation. When a man or woman died elsewhere while in the service of the country, the body was frequently brought home for burial; cemetery records often note the place and date of death. Chapter 2, Post-service Records and Records Relating to Civilian Affairs, provides important details on military burials.

Military Identified in Census Records

While they are not completely reliable sources, some federal and state censuses solicited special information regarding those who had served in the military. Since many of the schedules are well indexed, a quick check of census records may provide enough information to begin an in-depth search of military records. The 1840 federal census, for example, solicited the names and ages of military pensioners. The federal census form for 1850 and all of the federal census forms thereafter inquired about the occupations of all males over fifteen years of age.

A special census of Union veterans and widows of veterans was taken in 1890; however, a fire in the Commerce Department destroyed the special census schedules for the states having names that begin with the letters *A* through *K*. Approximately half of the special census for the state of Kentucky and the rest of the states from *K* through *W*, as well as those for Washington, D.C., survived, and many of those have been indexed. The 1900 census included separate military schedules and indexes for military personnel, including those at U.S. bases overseas and on navy vessels.

In 1910, the census inquired if individuals were survivors of the Union or Confederate army or navy. Military bases in the United States were supposed to have been enumerated and indexed separately in the 1920 census but, for unexplained reasons, some bases were not included in that grouping. When military individuals or bases cannot be located under the 1920 census microfilm heading "Military and Naval," they can sometimes be found combined with the regular state and county enumerations and indexes. Two separate rolls of microfilm

cover the 1920 enumeration of "Overseas Military and Naval Forces."

Using Court Records to Track Military Service

Court records can be yet another source for identifying those who served in the military. Some counties formally recorded and indexed the names of their citizens who were discharged from the military. In some local courts, "military discharges" will be found indexed separately, and in others the military records may be oddly interspersed with deeds, naturalizations, or other categories of documents. The contents of military records may vary greatly from courthouse to courthouse. Some will provide biographical information, while others may simply list names and the event or names and the date of certificate issue.

Naturalization records may be especially useful in pinpointing details of military service. In *American Naturalization Processes and Procedures 1790–1985* (Newman 1985), the author notes that "Special considerations regarding the naturalization process were given veterans." Legislation enacted in 1862 permitted any alien twenty-one years or older who had been honorably discharged from the armies of the United States to become a citizen of the United States by petition, without any previous declaration of intention. The 1862 act required veterans to prove only one year's residence in the United States. The legislation, designed to induce aliens to enlist for the Civil War, was then applied to other wars.

Naturalization documents may vary greatly from county to county and from state to state prior to 1906, when the process of becoming a U.S. citizen came under the jurisdiction of the Immigration and Naturalization Service. Most naturalization documents created prior to 1906 contain little of genealogical value. However, discharge from military service is generally noted together with rank and the name and number of the specific military unit in which the individual served. With this identifying information, it is relatively easy to follow through with research in records in the custody of the National Archives, state repositories, or county courts. For naturalizations that took place after 1906, contact the Immigration and Naturalization Service, 425 Eye Street NW, Washington, D.C. 20536. For a detailed description of naturalization records, see *The Archives: A Guide to the National Archives Field Branches* (Szucs and Luebking 1988).

Effective Research Strategies

As in any other phase of family history research, it is wise to become acquainted with efficient research strategies. Recommended are general guides to research such as *The Source: A Guidebook of American Genealogy* (Eakle and Cerny 1984); *The Researcher's Guide to American Genealogy*, 2nd ed. (Greenwood 1990); and *Guide to Genealogical Research in the National Archives* (National Archives Trust Fund Board, rev. 1985).

The Military Records

Fortunately, the armed forces have always required detailed records from their various units and organizations. Also, other government agencies collected many records pertaining to veterans and their families. The primary purpose of this book is to provide information about those records.

What Types of Records Are Available?

Once a researcher has determined when and where in the armed forces the subject of interest served, the next phase of research is to discover what types of military records are available. Chapters 1 and 2 of this guide describe some surprising and seldom-used information sources concerning the various branches of America's military. In these chapters, records such as unit muster rolls and rosters and those for prisoners of war, medical patients, casualties, and others in special categories are discussed. Also described are records of those who were otherwise related to military activity such as students in military institutions and civilians associated with the armed forces. A lengthy and important description of veterans' records, including pensions, assistance to veterans' families, soldiers' and sailors' homes, and military burial records, can be found in chapter 2.

Where Are the Records?

After gaining a general knowledge of the available records, the next step is to determine where such records can be found. Toward that end, this guide provides such detail. Chapters 3 through 7 list and describe the specific records (original and reproduced) held by various federal repositories and a few noteworthy private repositories. Arranged alphabetically by state, chapter 8 lists and describes, for each state, specific records (original and reproduced) available at state archives and libraries and selected state historical societies. The place to begin the search for military records may depend on the researcher's proximity to a records repository, whether it is a public or private library, historical society, county courthouse, local or state archives, or a national research center in Washington, D.C.

The primary repository of state and local records is a state archives or state historical society, while the primary repository of federal military records is the National Archives. However, large numbers of federal military records are available on microfilm not only at the National Archives and its regional centers but also at state archives and historical societies, public libraries, and at the Family History Library of The Church of Jesus Christ of Latter-day Saints, Salt Lake City, Utah. See chapter 7 for a description of U.S. military holdings in the Family History Library, which has the world's largest collection of family history-related materials.

Published Works

Complementing the original military records (or copies of them) are thousands of volumes of published works. Authors, abstractors, compilers, and editors have provided researchers with an abundance of published material describing America's military experiences and have transferred important data from official records to the printed page. Works pertaining primarily to particular states are included in chapter 8. Chapter 9 is a selected bibliography of published works that pertain to more than one state.

Regimental histories are probably unsurpassed in recreating the daily activities and operations of the individual units within the armed forces. When used with other sources, these accounts can be of great help in assembling a meaningful history.

A poignant example comes from a collection of letters written by an eighteen-year-old soldier. The letters, dated from December 1917 to November 1918, are full of good humor and describe life as it was for a "doughboy" in the American Expeditionary Force during World War I. "Somewhere in France" was the only return address the soldier could use on a letter he wrote to his father on August 21, 1918. "Well I guess we got 'Jerry' on the run now and it won't be long before he will realize it. I came out of the trenches Sunday night and during the time I was in, I tried to make it as uncomfortable for him as I could." A letter written eight days before the 11 November armistice with a return address of "Over There" had a more somber tone. The soldier noted the death of the chaplain, a wounded friend, and another in the hospital "suffering from gas poisoning." The letter-writing soldier was himself silenced by death shortly thereafter, so we have no more of his personal accounts to fill in the missing information. But by reading *A Record of Events of the 105th Machine Gun Battalion, 1st Cavalry, 27th Division, New York*, we can assemble a clearer picture of where he was and what he must have seen and experienced. A reading of the unit history puts into perspective the role played by this soldier's regiment and identifies events and places that could not be mentioned in letters for security reasons.

However, it is impossible to generalize about unit histories. As David Thackery of Chicago's Newberry Library notes, ". . . they can be dull, self-serving, whitewashing, as well as engrossing, honest, and perceptive. Sometimes all of these elements are present. In brief, they are subject to the strengths and weaknesses that we find in all history and memoir."

The history book provided the dry and impersonal calendar of a military unit's operations. It presented critical facts, chronicling the unit's departure from Fort Wadsworth, its training with British forces in Picardy and Flanders, the fierce fighting in the Meuse-Argonne Operation, and the unit's post-armistice activities in the vicinity of Verdun. Without the cold and factual unit history, one could not understand fully the very warm and human letters of a young soldier writing from "over there."

Technology and the Publication of Military Records

Recent technology has encouraged and hastened the publication of military and military-related materials. The ever-expanding number of new books, periodicals, microform material, and computer data bases are providing exciting research opportunities. Periodicals published by genealogical and historical organizations, as well as those published by genealogical publishing companies, make it possible for researchers to keep up with rapid developments in this area of interest. The Federation of Genealogical Societies, a not-for-profit organization, is outstanding in keeping its members up to date through its quarterly publication, *The Forum* (FGS Forum, P.O. Box 3385, Salt Lake City, UT 84110-3385).

State Military Collections

James Neagles personally visited most of the state archives and historical societies described in chapter 8. In those cases where he was unable to travel to a particular location, correspondence and telephone conversations were the means of gathering information. Authorities at each repository were asked to provide collection descriptions and policy statements as they would prefer to have them listed in this guide. After all pertinent data had been

combined and formatted for this guide, authorities at each repository were given the opportunity to review their respective sections for accuracy and completeness.

The National Archives

Federal military documents that have been classified as archival material are in the custody of the National Archives and Records Administration (NARA). It should be understood that not all records created by military agencies are judged to be permanently valuable. Considering the cost and space limitations, it is easy to understand that it would be impossible for the government to retain every scrap of paper created by every federal agency. Generally, only records of historical or administrative importance are kept.

Offices Within the National Archives

Two offices within the National Archives are responsible for the custody of records created by federal agencies:

The Office of the Federal Records Centers operates a system of fourteen federal records centers throughout the United States. These centers provide economical interim storage of non-current records of federal agencies pending their transfer to the Office of the National Archives or other disposition authorized by law. Records in the custody of a federal records center continue to be under the legal control of the federal agency that created them.

The Office of the National Archives, including the twelve regional archives, maintains the permanent (archival) records of federal government agencies. Once records are transferred to the Office of the National Archives from the originating agency, NARA assumes legal responsibility for them, regulates access to them, and assures their protection. The schedule shows how long records will be kept in a federal records center and whether they will eventually be transferred to the Office of the National Archives or destroyed (Szucs and Luebking 1988).

So while many military records, including a large number of Department of Veterans Affairs (formerly the Veterans Administration) records, are physically housed in National Archives facilities, they cannot be accessed through the National Archives. These records can be accessed only through the Department of Veterans Affairs or other agency that created them.

Accessing Federal Records From Outside Washington, D.C.

For most researchers, it is highly desirable to conduct research personally at the National Archives in Washington, D.C. But the wonderful array of federal records described in this volume is not entirely out of reach for those who are unable to arrange a trip. Many of the military indexes and published records described in this volume are available in major libraries and archives and through microfilm rental programs.

With sufficient identifying information, researchers may request a search of the registers of enlistments or the compiled military service records. The minimum information required for a search is 1) the soldier's full name, 2) the war in which he or she served or period of service, and 3) the state from which he or she served. For the Civil War, you must also indicate whether he served in the Union or Confederate forces. A separate copy of the form must be used for military service, pension, and bounty-land warrant applications. Requests for information about individuals who served in the military before World War I should be submitted on NATF form 80 (Order for Copies of Veterans Records). Write to the National Archives and Records Administration, General Reference Branch, Washington, D.C. 20408 to obtain copies of NATF form 80.

Requests for information about U.S. Army officers separated from the service after 1916 and army enlisted personnel separated after 1912 should be made on standard form 180 (Request Pertaining to Military Records) and sent to the Military Personnel Records Center, 9700 Page Boulevard, St. Louis, Missouri 63132.

In some cases, hiring a professional genealogist may be the best way to obtain desired information from military collections. The National Genealogical Society, 4527 Seventeenth Street North, Arlington, Virginia 22207-2399; The Association of Professional Genealogists, 3421 M Street NW, Suite 236, Washington, D.C. 20007-3552; and the Board for Certification of Genealogists, P.O. Box 5816, Falmouth, Virginia 22403-5816 can provide lists of researchers in every state. Similar lists may be furnished by state archives or state historical societies.

Sources Cited in the Introduction

Andreas, A.T. *History of Cook County, Illinois, From the Earliest Period to the Present Time.* Chicago: A.T. Andreas Publisher, 1884.

Eakle, Arlene, and Johni Cerny, eds. *The Source: A Guidebook of American Genealogy.* Salt Lake City: Ancestry, 1984.

Filby, P. William. *A Bibliography of American County Histories.* Baltimore: Genealogical Publishing Company, 1985.

Greenwood, Val D. *The Researcher's Guide to American Genealogy.* 2nd ed. Baltimore: Genealogical Publishing Co., 1990.

National Archives Trust Fund Board. *Guide to Genealogical Research in the National Archives.* Washington, D.C.: National Archives Trust Fund Board, rev. 1985.

Newman, John J. *American Naturalization Processes and Procedures 1790–1985.* Indianapolis: Indiana Historical Society, 1985.

Szucs, Loretto Dennis, and Sandra Hargreaves Luebking. *The Archives: A Guide to the National Archives Field Branches.* Salt Lake City: Ancestry, 1988.

1

Types of Records: Records Created During Military Service

1

Types of Records: Records Created During Military Service

Foresight and necessity have bequeathed to the researcher a vast accumulation of records concerning individuals who have served in America's armed forces. In most cases, particular record collections (or copies of collections) are available at more than one repository; in some cases, they can be found at only one location. This and the following chapter are intended solely to make the researcher aware of the types of military records that are available, wherever they may be found. Subsequent chapters must be consulted to learn where specific records are located. Chapters 1 and 2, therefore, should be used as a descriptive source only—not as a location source. Categories of records are described in these chapters either according to their general content or to the organization that created or gathered them. Some types of records are represented here in illustrations from samples found in various federal and state repositories.

Primary Sources

Data concerning an individual in uniform or otherwise closely involved with any branch of America's armed forces is best obtained from primary sources—those created during or near the time of the event. These sources are made up of official records generated or maintained by the war or navy departments or by state agencies. Most federal records, predominantly those from the Office of the Adjutant General, were eventually turned over to the National Archives. Federal records that were not turned over to the National Archives and state records that were not turned over to a state repository may often be found in the office of the agency that created or gathered them or in a history center maintained by one of the armed forces. Some records were retained by private individuals or by members of their families; these generally consist of original papers or copies of original papers—usually personal diaries, journals, etc., which the individuals possessed when they left a military or other government position.

Secondary Sources

There are several secondary sources of military information created from or based on data found in official records. Publications that contain lists of military personnel or lists of pensioners, especially the annual reports of the state adjutants general, are helpful because they are based on official data. There are also many published regimental or unit histories that are based on factual data or personal recollection. Censuses of veterans were taken by some of the states, and lists of veterans have been compiled by government and private organizations such as the National Society Daughters of the American Revolution (DAR) and by state and local historical and genealogical societies.

Town halls and county courthouses often possess records pertaining to local citizens who served in the military. These corroborate the federal and state records and often contain collateral data not found elsewhere. The National Archives, Work Projects Administration (WPA), state archives, and armed forces history centers have created many card indexes and have developed finding aids to assist the researcher in his or her search for ancestors or historical information.

Accessibility

In accordance with the federal Privacy Act (as amended in 1974), some information compiled during the past seventy-five years is not in the public domain. These laws permit the release of general information, but they restrict the release of personal information for the period of a normal life span. These restrictions protect veterans from intrusions upon their privacy and prevent use of their names and addresses by those who would use them for commercial purposes. Personal information is not kept from the veterans themselves or from their next of kin if the veteran is deceased or has given written permission for disclosure. "Next of kin" is defined as any of the following: unremarried widow or widower, son or daughter, father or mother, brother or sister. Because of the seventy-five-year moratorium, 1993 was the first full year in which all of the records generated during World War I became public. Many World War I records are available at the National Archives (RG 120), but individual personnel files are available only from the National Personnel Records Center, St. Louis, Missouri. In the meantime, some records pertaining to participants in all wars are available to the public—many of them in published form. These include published indexes and lists of individuals who served in the military, with respective dates, unit names, places stationed or served, medals and commendations awarded, casualties suffered, and place of burial. Other information, such as date of birth, social security number, home and work addresses, and other personal data, however, is withheld from public inspection. Some record collections cited in this volume might well be restricted currently, but they will be open in the future. Inquiries about availability can be answered by repository staff members.

Organization of This Chapter

Descriptions of official records are grouped in this chapter according to the following broad categories: a) militia and National Guard; b) U.S. Army; c) U.S. Navy; d) Marine Corps, Coast Guard, and Merchant Marine service; and e) military academies. Representative types of records found in each of these categories are listed and described below, usually accompanied by the name of the agency or individual by which they were created. Within each category, these descriptions are arranged generally according to time periods or by name of a war or armed conflict.

Records created after an individual was discharged from military service and records related to civilian affairs are discussed in the following chapter.

Records of Military Service: Militia and National Guard

The following are descriptions of the military records of persons who were not actually on active federal duty. These include individuals who served in local militias, the National Guard, or in reserve units.

Local militia units, now known collectively as the National Guard, are the oldest military organizations in America and provide the longest ongoing systems of records available to the military researcher. As early as 1636, militia units were organized and administered by colonial towns and counties. Able-bodied male citizens, generally those between the ages of sixteen and sixty, were organized into militia companies to defend against aggression from marauding Indians, foreign adventurers, criminals, and pirates. Militiamen were expected to provide their own weapons and ammunition and to report for regularly scheduled drills (usually on the town's common ground) or face the imposition of a fine. History shows the important role these units played when hostilities began to erupt between the American colonies and the regular armies of Great Britain. The importance of a militia was emphasized in the U.S. Constitution. The Second Amendment states: "A well regulated militia, being necessary to the security of a free state, the right of the people to keep and bear arms shall not be infringed." This amendment was adopted to protect the local militias from interference by a federal government—not necessarily to establish a "right" for every citizen to own or use a gun, except as an individual state might legislate such privilege or impose restrictions.

Militia companies were directed by a locally elected body of officers (figure 1) who were charged with supervising training and the use of arms, drilling, discipline, overseeing the construction of defense fortifications, and maintaining custody of the public supply of gunpowder. Fines for non-attendance at drills helped finance the purchase of supplies.

During the French and Indian War, some militia companies were assigned to serve under officers from other colonies but afterward were returned to local leadership and control. Subsequently, militia units were frequently transferred temporarily to federal control in time of military need. At the onset of the American Revolution the Continental Congress requested that Delaware, Maryland, and Pennsylvania raise a special force of ten thousand militiamen as a "flying camp" ready to move to any location on short notice. During the revolution a "Continental Line" was formed, frequently augmented by militia units pressed into service to replace Continental Line soldiers whose terms of service had expired.

In 1792 the United States authorized militias as part of the "organized militia." In 1784, during a visit to New York, the Marquis de Lafayette referred to them as the "Garde Nationale." One New York unit adopted the term to honor Lafayette, and the state of New York made the term formal by statute during the Civil War. (In other states these units continued to be referred to as militias until 1903.)

Some state militia units were organized during the Civil War, primarily for service only within the organizing state's borders. Regiments of "state guards" and "home guards" were also created, sometimes with conflicting loyalties—either to the governor or to the Confederate or Union governments. Political authority over such units often led to bitter conflict between state leaders and officials of the Confederate Army when calls were made for militia or guard units to leave their states and serve under Confederate control. When seeking records of these units, it is important to search state, federal, and Confederate records.

Local militia units continued to exist until 21 January 1903, when President Theodore Roosevelt signed the Act to Promote the Efficiency of the Militia, more commonly referred to as the Dick Militia Act because the legislation was introduced by Ohio Congressman Charles Dick, who was also president of the National Guard Association. That act gave federal status to the organized militias and led to federal appropriations and uniform standards for units in the various states. Since that time these units have been referred to as National Guard units.

Each National Guard unit specializes in a certain aspect of warfare or defense (Air National Guard, medical detachments, engineers, etc.). Membership in a National Guard unit often exempts an individual from federal military service, but complete units may be called up in times of national emergency, when all members automatically become subject to federal duty. National Guard units are required to meet regularly for training, and their personnel are reimbursed for time spent in training. Failure to comply may result in court-martial and appropriate punishment. Although operating under federal standards and ultimately under federal control, each state maintains its own National Guard that is subject to the orders of the governor. As such, National Guard units are often called upon to assist in quelling domestic disturbances or maintaining order in times of other emergency.

Records of militia and National Guard units consist largely of muster rolls, payrolls, and rosters. There is a personnel jacket (201 file) for each individual who is serving or has served. This file is personal and is closely controlled by each state's National Guard headquarters, especially those files less than seventy-five years old. Other documents, including indexes of names that do not contain personal information, may be viewed by researchers. In most instances, however, agency staff will review the index cards and provide basic information upon request, while withholding such personal information as date of birth, social security number, and other data of a private nature.

Militia records available at the National Archives or National Guard documents available at state facilities are generally arranged by name or number of the unit. Some have been microfilmed or photostated, but in many cases only the original documents are available. Name indexes are uncommon, and it is often necessary to identify a military unit to find the record of a particular individual. Rarely do militia or National Guard records contain any data other than name, unit, date of birth, enlistment or muster dates, discharge dates, promotions, and notations of other military history.

Figure 1. List of Officers Elected and Appointed in the Militia of the State of New York—Revolutionary War (courtesy National Archives).

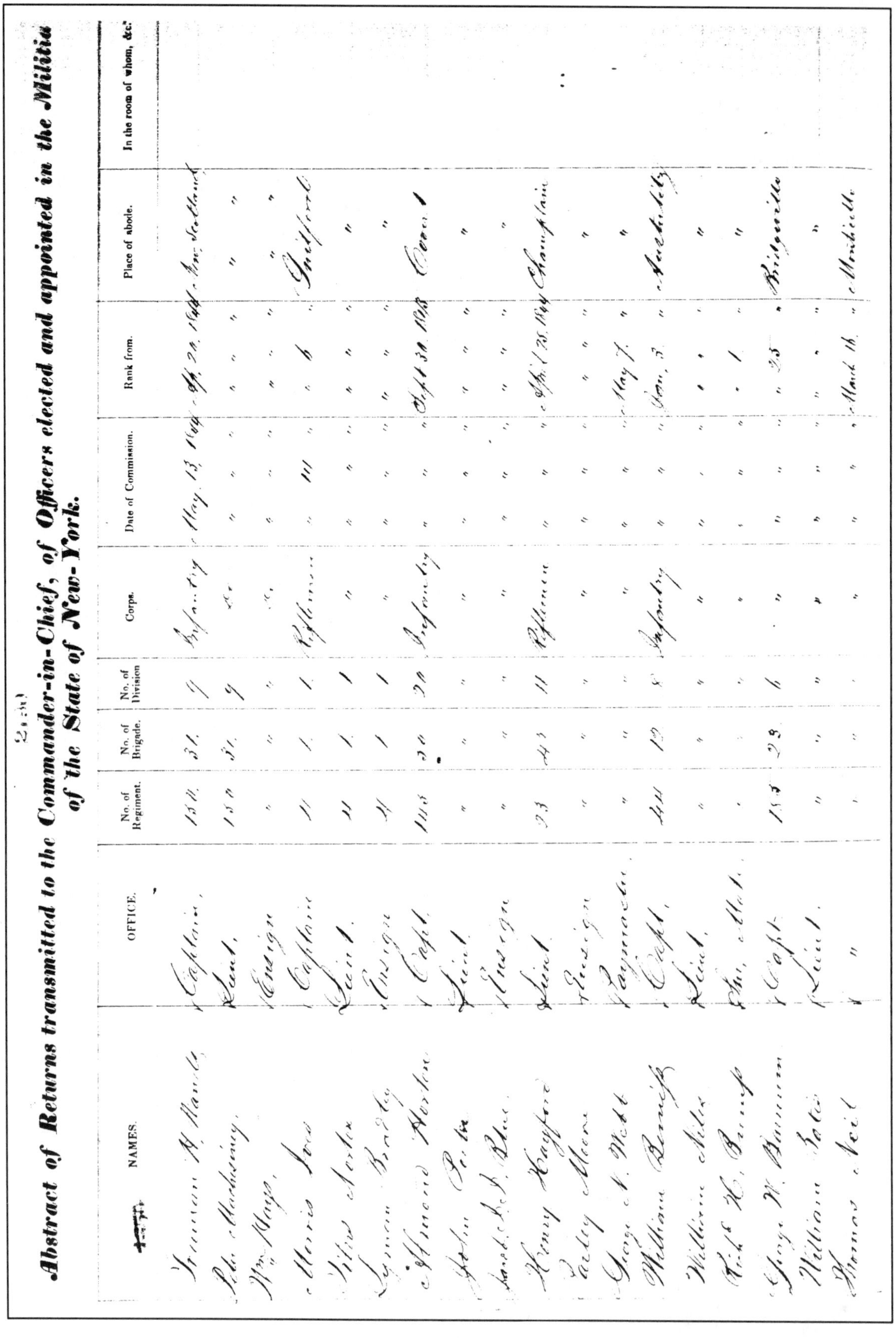

Records of Federal Military Service: Army

At the beginning of the American Revolution, the need for a national army was apparent in the aftermath of the initial clashes with British forces at Lexington, Concord, and Bunker Hill. On 14 June 1775, the Continental Congress adopted the so-called New England army—comprising volunteer forces from the New England states—as the nucleus of the Continental Army.

The Continental Army was disbanded on 24 September 1783, four days after the Treaty of Paris formally ended the revolutionary war. One infantry regiment and a battalion of artillery were retained. When Congress created the Department of War in August 1789, the nascent U.S. Army consisted of approximately 800 officers and men.

Records pertaining to regular army officers and enlisted men cover a wide range of collections, many of which are described in the National Archives publication *Preliminary Inventory Number 17, Records of the Adjutant General's Office*. Many of those collections consist mainly of correspondence between military units and their commanding officers. Reference is made to certain publications (cited later) that list regular army and navy officers, especially William H. Powell's *List of Officers of the Army of the United States From 1779 to 1900*. Another such source for the revolutionary war is Francis B. Heitman's *Historical Register of Officers of the Continental Army During the War of the Revolution*. Also helpful are several of Thomas H.S. Hamersly's registers containing lists of army and navy personnel (see chapter 9, Published Sources). Other sources of names are muster rolls and post returns, which routinely list the names of officers of each unit (figure 2).

Although incomplete, enlistment papers of enlisted personnel are maintained in the records of the Office of the Adjutant General. Although the actual papers are not available at the National Archives, registers of names pertaining to these papers are available there on microfilm: *Register of Enlistments in the United States Army, 1798–1914* (M233). These lists do not include registers for hospital stewards, quartermaster sergeants, or ordnance sergeants. The registers give name, place and date of enlistment, by whom enlisted, age, occupation, physical description, regimental assignment, and certificate of the examining surgeon and recruiting officer. There are two separate files, each arranged alphabetically by the first initial of the surname. One file covers the period 1798 through 17 May 1815, and the other covers the period 17 May 1815 through 30 June 1821. Other lists cover irregularly spaced periods of time through 1913.

The registers for the period 1798 through 30 June 1821 usually reflect the information on the document(s) from which the entries were made. The registers for the period 1 July 1821 through 1914 consist of two-page entries containing the same information found on the enlistment papers, along with data concerning termination of service as found in muster rolls and other records.

There are separate registers for mounted rangers, Indian scouts, post quartermasters, Philippine scouts, Puerto Rican provisional infantry, and certain classes of sergeants enlisted during the nineteenth century.

Officer Appointments and Commissions

Powell's *List of Officers of the Army of the United States From 1779 to 1900* provides lists of officers, both regular army and volunteers. In 1800, a fire at the War Department destroyed many documents pertaining to regular army officers who served between 1784 and 1800. Information concerning officers between 1800 and 1862 is best obtained from various documents maintained by the Office of the Adjutant General and in the custody of the National Archives (RG 94), which include papers pertaining to applications for commissions.

A Commission Branch of the Office of the Adjutant General was organized on 1 January 1863 to handle the administrative work involved in appointments, promotions, resignations, discharges, retirements, and assignments of officers. Officers who served in the regular army were volunteers, presidential appointees, veterinary surgeons, and officers of the militia of the District of Columbia. In 1871, the branch was redesignated the Appointment, Commission, and Personnel Branch. Officer appointments between 1871 and 1880 were made by the president, the secretary of war, and others. The National Archives has records of these actions; they are arranged chronologically by year and numerically thereunder. Records of the Appointment, Commission, and Personnel Branch include copies of commissions issued, original commissions that were never delivered, and copies of letters of appointment and promotion. Commissions signed by the president but not delivered are arranged chronologically for the years 1812 through 1902. The information usually found in the registers of commissions

Figure 2. Names and Description of a Company of the Regular Army—War of 1812 (courtesy National Archives).

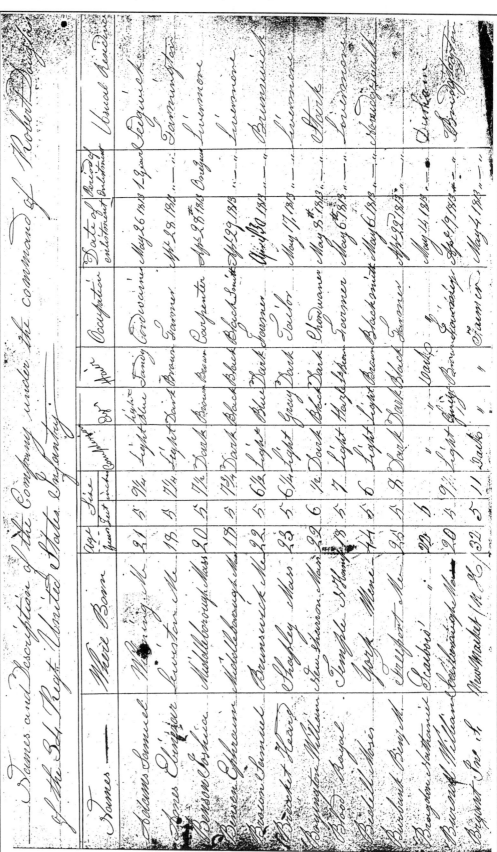

includes the name of the officer, rank, date of commission, date of acceptance, and remarks. Registers of appointments include name, rank, residence, organization, and date of appointment. The National Archives has three volumes of registers of commissioned officers: Vol. 1 covers the period 1799 through 1860; vol. 2, 1861 through 1900; vol. 3, 1901 through 1915. There is an additional volume containing a roster of officers, 1783 to 1826, that is arranged by initial letter of the surname. Also available at the National Archives is a set of alphabetically arranged records created in 1816, when every officer was required to furnish his place of birth, and a 1917 set of registration cards containing information relating to individuals who were qualified for appointment as officers in time of war. The cards give name, address, occupation, date of birth, race, qualification, previous military training, and other data.

The National Archives has an alphabetical card index, prepared by the United States Office of the Adjutant General, of each officer appointed to the Confederate Army. The cards give information about the appointment and the officer's subsequent military history, including promotions.

Muster Rolls

Muster rolls are lists, usually prepared bimonthly, of the names of soldiers assigned to any military unit—militia, National Guard, regular army or navy, or volunteer army or navy. Usually these refer to a company, but they often refer to a regiment, a special detachment, or a band. Rolls for personnel on board ships were referred to either as crew lists or muster rolls. The rolls were made at the time a unit was created (muster-in rolls), when a unit was reorganized, when two or more units were merged, and when a unit was disbanded (muster-out rolls). Names appearing on a muster roll indicate those who were present or accounted for on a given date, at which time a review of the troops and an inspection of their weapons and accoutrements was conducted (figure 3).

This roll was used as the basis for pay due the soldiers. Names of commissioned officers were listed first, followed by names of noncommissioned officers and then privates. Shown on the form are the date and place of enlistment of each individual, by whom enrolled and for what period of time, date of muster into service, and date of last payment. Remarks might include information about any individuals absent or deceased. Prior to 1918, muster rolls

sometimes also contained a "record of events" column describing the activities engaged in by the unit.

Payrolls

Muster rolls were frequently converted to payrolls for use by paymasters (figure 4). The payroll was used to indicate the amount of money due each individual and the date and amount of his last payment. It also served as a checklist to record each payment as made. Often available are receipts showing payments for expenditures made by individuals or units, as are records of such payments, which were recorded in journals and ledgers kept by an adjutant, paymaster, or other military fiscal officer.

Other Lists and Rosters

A simple list of names of the personnel assigned to a military unit was termed a roster (figure 5). These lists were made as needed for field units, detached units, and special groups, such as medical officers or other medical personnel, patients of a hospital or other medical unit, band members, prisoners confined in a stockade, and any other category of soldiers not active in a field unit undergoing training or actually taking part in military actions. Some such rosters are descriptive in nature (descriptive rolls) and as such often contain information concerning place of birth, age, previous occupation, physical description, bounty paid and amounts due, clothing and equipment issued or lost, and payments for horses furnished by the soldier. In many instances the data contained in these rosters and other sources, including the lists of discharges from service, forms the basis for an index card, usually referred to as a "service card," arranged in alphabetical or chronological order for easy reference (figure 6). These cards often give considerable information relative to each individual, and copies were often made and furnished to state archives.

Returns

Company clerks or their equivalent were responsible for preparing a daily "morning report" showing the personnel strength (by rank) of their units on that date. Other than special mentions of incidents, absences, casualties, or transfers, names of individual soldiers or sailors were not reported. The unit reports were submitted to the adjutant

MUSTER ROLL of Captain *Wm E Wallace* Company, ("E"), of the (Colonel *Elijah L Higdon*), from the *Thirtieth* day of

NO.	NAMES. PRESENT AND ABSENT. (Commissioned and Non-commissioned Officers according to rank. Privates in alphabetical order.)	RANK.	ENLISTED.				NAMES. PRESENT.
			WHEN.	WHERE.	BY WHOM.	PERIOD. YEARS.	
1	Wallace Wm E	Capt	May 1-98	Mobile Ala	O Kyle	2yrs	Wallace Wm E
1	Pride Mitchell N	1st Lieut	May 1-98	Mobile Ala	O Kyle	2yrs	Pride Mitchell N
2	Webb Wm J	2nd Lieut	May 1-98	Mobile Ala	O Kyle	2yrs	Webb Wm J
1	Marks Caesar E	1st Sgt	May 1-98	Mobile Ala	O Kyle	2yrs	Marks Caesar E
2	Albes John H	Sgt	May 1-98	Mobile Ala	O Kyle	2yrs	Albes John H
3	McCoy James H	Sgt	May 1-98	Mobile Ala	O Kyle	2yrs	McCoy James H
4	Joplin James W	Sgt	May 1-98	Mobile Ala	O Kyle	2yrs	Joplin James W
5	Banks Graham	Sgt	May 1-98	Mobile Ala	O Kyle	2yrs	
6	Hawkins Philip P	Sgt	May 1-98	Mobile Ala	O Kyle	2yrs	Hawkins Philip P

First Regiment of *Alabama U S Vol Infty* Army of the United States,
June, 1898, to the *Thirty First* day of *August*, 1898.

REMARKS.	LAST PAID.		YEAR OF CONTINUOUS SERVICE.	DUE U. S. FOR CLOTHING.			
	BY PAYMASTER.	TO WHAT TIME.		Dolls.	Cts.	Dolls.	Cts.
Absent on furlough Aug 9 to Aug 31- Ord Gen Brigader Wheeler. Returned to duty Aug 31-98	Maj Jno Krause	July 31-98					
	Maj Jno Krause	July 31-98					
	Maj Jno Krause	July 31-98					
	Maj Jno Krause	July 31-98					
	Maj Jno Krause	July 31-98					
	Maj Jno Krause	July 31-98					
	Maj Jno Krause	July 31-98					
Fined five (5.00) Dollar by G O C July 3- Case no-25 Absent on furlough ten days Aug 28 to Sept 4 By order Maj Gen Kiefer	Maj Jno Krause	July 31-98.					

Figure 3. Muster Roll for a U.S. Volunteer Infantry Company, June–August 1898–Spanish-American War (top: left-hand page; bottom: right-hand page) (courtesy National Archives).

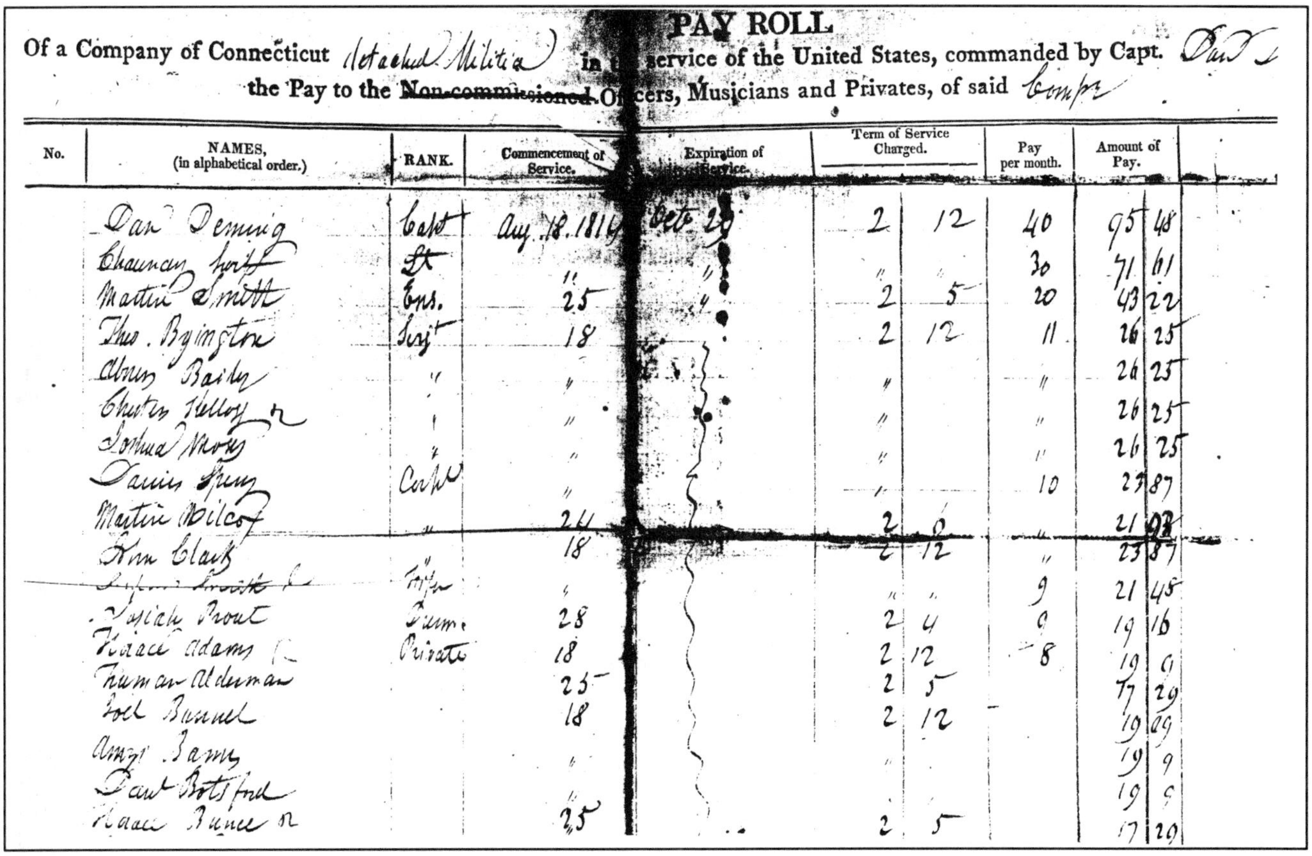

PAY ROLL

Of a Company of Connecticut Detached Militia in the service of the United States, commanded by Capt. Dan'l ... the Pay to the ~~Non-commissioned~~ Officers, Musicians and Privates, of said Company

No.	NAMES, (in alphabetical order.)	RANK.	Commencement of Service.	Expiration of Service.	Term of Service Charged.		Pay per month.	Amount of Pay.	
	Dan'l Deming	Capt	Aug. 18. 1814	Oct. 2	2	12	40	95	48
	Chauncey Loritt	Lt	"	"	"		30	71	61
	Martin Smith	Ens.	25	"	2	5	20	43	22
	Thos. Byington	Serjt	18		2	12	11	26	25
	Almon Bailey	"	"		"		"	26	25
	Chester Kellogg		"		"		"	26	25
	Joshua Mosey		"		"		"	26	25
	Darius Spry	Corpl	"				10	23	87
	Martin Wilcox	"	24		2	6		21	08
	Wm Clark		18		2	12	"	23	87
	[illegible]	Fifer	"		"	"	9	21	48
	Josiah Trout	Drum.	28		2	4	9	19	16
	Isaac Adams	Private	18		2	12	8	19	9
	Truman Alderman		25		2	5		17	29
	Joel Bunnel		18		2	12		19	09
	Amzi Barnes		"		"			19	9
	Dan'l Botsford		"					19	9
	Isaac Bunce		25		2	5		17	29

Figure 4. Payroll for a Company of Connecticut Detached Militia—War of 1812 (courtesy National Archives).

for compilation into similar reports for the entire battalion, regiment, corps, or division.

Based on the morning reports, each military post or military command was required to submit periodic strength reports to the adjutant general (figure 7). These were usually filed monthly (but sometimes quarterly) on special forms devised for this purpose. Included was data relative to the place where the unit was stationed, number of personnel, and the names and numbers of commissioned officers and their duties. The form was revised occasionally, so the information included varied over time. From 1873 a "record of events" section reported engagements, changes of station, distance marched, and other significant occurrences. The National Archives finding aid *Preliminary Inventory of the Records of the Adjutant General's Office* (RG 94) lists several collections of returns by the name of the unit. The National Archives microfilm *Returns From United States Military Posts, 1800–1916* (M617—1,550 reels) are valuable research sources, as is National Archives microfilm *Historical Information Relating to Military Posts and Other Installations, ca. 1700–1900* (M661).

Correspondence

Before the era of the telephone and the fax machine, communication between military commanders and between government leaders and commanders in the field was accomplished by horse-mounted couriers, by telegraphed messages, and by written letters, memorandums, and reports sent by U.S. mail or by military conveyances. This tremendous volume of correspondence was generally logged in at the government offices that received it. These logs were often converted to indexes to facilitate the later finding of a particular missive. Both the indexes and the actual papers can now be found in archival holdings. The National Archives numbered and otherwise classified many of them before they were microfilmed, and they are found as numbered memoranda or "manuscript files."

Following the Civil War, official military correspondence and reports were compiled to form the 128-volume *Official Records of the Union and Confederate Armies in the War of the Rebellion* (U.S. War Department. Washington, D.C: Government Printing Office, 1880-1900) and the 31-volume *Official Records of the Union and Confederate Navies in the War of the Rebellion* (U.S. War Department.

Figure 5. Regular Army Roster, 1850s (top: left-hand page; bottom: right-hand page) (courtesy Maine Archives).

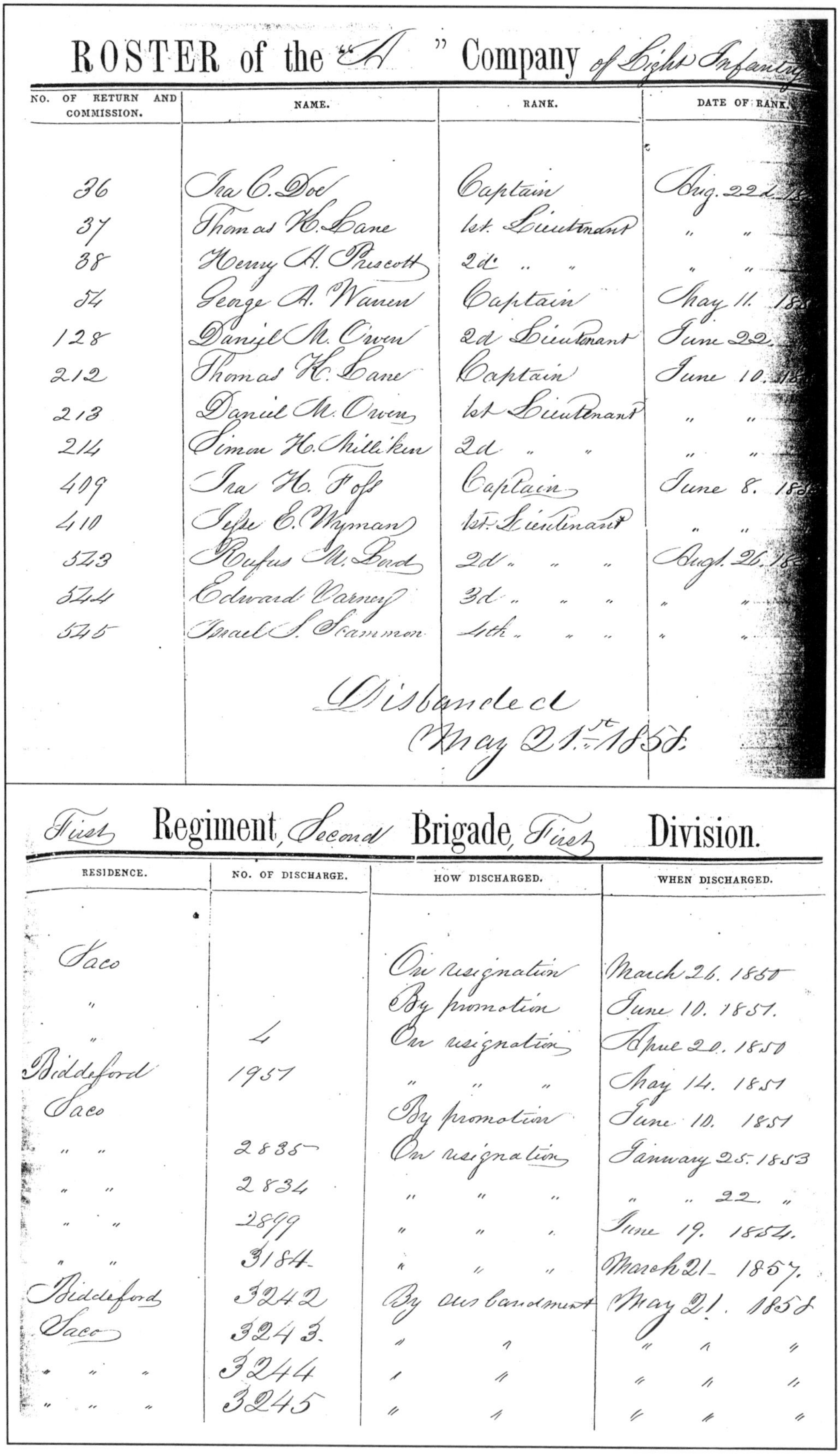

ROSTER of the "A" Company of Light Infantry

NO. OF RETURN AND COMMISSION.	NAME.	RANK.	DATE OF RANK.
36	Ira C. Doe	Captain	Aug. 22. 18..
37	Thomas H. Lane	1st Lieutenant	" "
38	Henry A. Prescott	2d " "	" "
54	George A. Warren	Captain	May 11. 185.
128	Daniel M. Owen	2d Lieutenant	June 22.
212	Thomas H. Lane	Captain	June 10. 18..
213	Daniel M. Owen	1st Lieutenant	" "
214	Simon H. Milliken	2d " "	" "
409	Ira H. Foss	Captain	June 8. 185.
410	Jesse E. Wyman	1st Lieutenant	" "
543	Rufus M. Lord	2d " " "	Aug. 26. 18.
544	Edward Varney	3d " " "	" "
545	Israel S. Stammon	4th " " "	" "

Disbanded
May 21st 1858.

First Regiment, Second Brigade, First Division.

RESIDENCE.	NO. OF DISCHARGE.	HOW DISCHARGED.	WHEN DISCHARGED.
Saco		On resignation	March 26. 1850
"		By promotion	June 10. 1851.
"	4	On resignation	April 20. 1850
Biddeford	1951	" " "	May 14. 1851
Saco		By promotion	June 10. 1851
" "	2835	On resignation	January 25. 1853
" "	2834	" " "	" " 22. "
" "	2899	" " "	June 19. 1854.
" "	3184	" " "	March 21. 1857.
Biddeford	3242	By disbandment	May 21. 1858
Saco	3243.	" "	" " "
" " "	3244	" "	" " "
" " "	3245	" "	" " "

Figure 6. Military Service Cards, Regular Army Medical Corps (courtesy National Archives).

MEDICAL DEPARTMENT U. S. ARMY. FORM 130.

153273

HAGOOD, Rufus Hanson, Jr.

FIRST LIEUTENANT, MEDICAL CORPS.

Appointed. May 22, 1915.

Accepted. July 30, 1915.

Born. November 21, 1886.

Residence. Pendleton, Oreg.

Previous service. M. R. C., July 27, 1912, to date.

Since July 1, 1915, assigned to duty with 2d Division, Texas City, Tex., with station at Ft. Ethan Allen, Vt.

July 19, 1915, reports arrival for duty.

Field Hospital 3, Galveston, Tex. 1-7, on duty at Army Med.School. 8-16, on leave of absence, per Par. 5, S.O. 147, W.D. June 25. 17-18, en route to Texas City. 19-31, on duty with F.H. 3, Galveston, Tex.

Texas City, Tex., Aug. 14, 1915, reports arrival for duty with Cantonment Hospital, 2d Div., per Memo. 2d Div.-g. 11. Left Galveston, Tex., same day.

Houston, Tex., Aug. 31, 1915: 1-13, on duty with F.H.3, Galveston, Tex. 14-27, asst. to C.O., Cantonment Hospital, 2d Div., Tex. City, Tex. 28-31, on temporary duty at Houston, Tex., at Houston Infirmary as attending surgeon for families of

officers and enlisted men removed to Houston for shelter in consequence of storm of Aug.16-17,1915.

Sept. 1-30, on duty at Houston Tex., as attending surgeon for families of officers and enlisted men.

Oct. 9, 1915, Par. 14, S.O. 235, W.D., directs 1st Lt. Hagood, on demobilization of 2d Div., to proceed to Nogales, Ariz., and report to C. O., 12th Inf., for temporary duty.

Oct. 13, 1915, Par. 3, S.O. 238, W.D., grants 1 month leave of abs. Oct. 18, 1915, Par. 35, S.O.242, W.D., directs 1st Lt. Hagood to report in person to commanding general 5th Brig., for duty until he avails himself of leave of absence granted by Par. 3, S.O. 238, W.D.c.s.

Oct. 20, one copy of above orders mailed to 1st Lt. Hagood, 12th Inf., Nogales, Ariz.

Texas City, Tex., Oct. 26, reports on duty with 2d Bn. Engrs., since Oct. 19, per V.O., Maj.Gen. Bell, in pursuance of tel.W. D. Oct. 18. Left Houston, Tex.,Oct.15.

Texas City, Tex., Oct. 31: 1-15, on duty as attending surgeon to families of officers and enlisted men at Houston, Tex. 16-19, on duty as asst. to C.O., Cantonment Hosp., 2d Div., Tex.City. 20-31, surgeon, 2d Bn. Engrs., Texas City.

Nov. 3, reports departure on leave of absence for 1 month. Address: 1008 S. Saint Bernard St., Philadelphia, Pa.

Nov. 29, 1916, Par. 5, S.O. 277, W.D., extends leave of absence 15 days. Same extension (15 da.) by 12 S.O. 276, H.S.D. Nov. 30.

Write nothing above this line.

On Leave of Absence, Nov. 30, 1915: 1-3, on duty with 2d Bn. Engrs. Texas City, Tex. 4-30, on leave of absence.

Dec. 6, 1915, Par. 25, S.O. 283, W.D., relieves 1st Lt. Hagood from temporary duty in Southern Dept., and further station at Ft. Ethan Allen, Vt., and directs him to proceed from San Francisco, Cal., on March 5, 1916, transport to Manila, P.I.

Dec. 15, 1915, acknowledges receipt of Par. 35, S.O. 242, W.D.c.s. Dec. 18, 1915, Par. 10, S.O.294, W.D., further extends leave of abs. granted in S.O. 238, W.D.c.s. and extended in S.O. 277, W.D.c.s., 15 days.

Dec. 21, two copies of Par. 10, S.O. 294, W.D.c.s. mailed to R.H.H., 1008-S. Saint-Bernard St., Philadelphia, Pa.

Dec.24, acknowledges receipt of Par. 10, S.O. 294, W.D.c.s. Reports change of address from 1008-South St.Bernard-St., Phila. to 312 Tuscaloosa, Av., Birmingham, Ala.

Dec. 1-31, on same leave of abs. 1916.

Jan. 1-31, on duty as asst. to surgeon, Camp Stephen Little, Nogales, Ariz.

En Route to San Francisco, Cal. Feb. 29, 1916: 1-27, on duty as asst. to surg. Nogales, Ariz., Camp S. Little. 28, left for P.I.

29, en route to San Francisco. San Francisco, Cal., Mar. 1, reports arrival.

Mar. 6, 1916, reports departure via U.S.A.T. "Sherman" for Manila, P.I.

En Route to P.I., March 31: 1-6, in San Francisco, and awaiting transportation to P.I. 7-31, en route to P.I.

Camp Stotsenburg, P.I., Apr.30: 1-2, en route from U.S. to P.I. 3-4, en route to station. 5, joined station, Camp Stotsenburg, P.I., per Par. 2, S.O. 75, H.P.D. Mar. 30, 1916. 6-30, on duty at station.

May 31, same.

June 30, same.

July 31, same.

Aug. 31, same.

Sept. 30, same.

Oct. 31, same.

Nov. 30, same.

Dec. 31, same.

1917

Jan. 31, same.

Feb. 17, reports depart. from Camp Stotsenburg, with 9, Cav. V.O. Post Comm. Feb 16, 17., reports arrival at Capas. P.I per order abov

Feb.1-16 on duty as asst. S to Surg.Camp Stotsen. B1.?PP2, SO:N5 3/30/16.

17-28 on duty as asst. Surg. 9,Cav. per VO. Post Comm, at Capas.

Mar. 2, reports deprt. from Capas, and arrival at Camp

W. D. STANDARD FORM 94.

Figure 7. U.S. Army Hospital Corps Return, 1911–12 (courtesy National Archives).

RETURN OF THE HOSPITAL CORPS

at Field Hospital No.3, Walter Reed General Hospital, Takoma Park, D.C.
(Here insert name of post or station, and department, or, in the field, name of camp and nearest town, also the field army, division, and regiment or command to which attached)

for the period from November 30th., 1911, to January 31st., 1912.

Enlisted strength of command on last day of period: 137.

LINEAL NO. BY GRADES (Designate colored men by a "C.")	NAMES (SURNAMES FIRST) (See Instruction 2)	RANK (Use ditto marks when applicable)	NO. OF HOURS OF INSTRUCTION DURING PERIOD	REMARKS
1	Wood, Richard A.	Sgt.1.Cl.		In general charge. Single.
2	Anderson, Cecil H.	"		Asst.Instructor in Materia Medica and Pharmacy. In charge of instruction records. Married.
3	Donovan, Thomas F.	"		In charge of property. Asst.Instructor in clerical work. Single.
1	Hester, Thomas G.	Sergeant		Asst.Instructor in Anatomy and Physiology and company drills.
2	Burke, Edmund	"		Asst.Instructor in First Aid and Diet Cooking and Company Drills. Relieved from duty as Mess Sergeant Jan.9th.1912 per Ord.#10, Field Hosp.No.3.Jan.8,1912
3	Chamberlin, Frank L.	"		Asst.Instructor in Equitation,Packing and Driving and Identification Work, and company drills.
4	Mitchell, Edward H.	"		Asst.Instructor in Nursing and Ward Management and company drills. Absent sick at Ft.Myer,Va., from Dec.19th.,1911 to Jan.8th.,1912, In line of duty.
5	Abernethy, Welborn B.	"		Appointed Mess Sergeant Jan.10th. 1912 per Ord.#10,Field Hosp.No.3. Jan.8,1912.
1	Brink, Hobart D.	Corporal.		Asst.Instructor in Bandaging and Company Drills. Absent sick at Ft. Myer, Va., Dec.19th.1911 to Jan. 2nd.1912. In line of duty.

Washington, D.C.: Government Printing Office, 1894–1927). Although these are historical treasure troves, they seldom include the names of enlisted soldiers or junior officers. Examples of correspondence collections are included in this volume to illustrate the variety of material available to the serious researcher. It may help to inquire of library reference staff how to use the indexes to these volumes.

Compiled Service Records

In modern times, a personnel file has been kept for each serviceman or -woman in the National Guard, reserve units, regular army and regular navy, marines, Coast Guard, and air force, and for those in volunteer units of all military branches. Historically, the only records kept were the various rolls described above and other similar rolls and lists. Thus, to learn the facts related to a particular person, a researcher was required to conduct an exhaustive search of all such rolls, lists, and reports filed by officers and clerks, and of voluminous correspondence among departments and divisions of the military, government officials, and private citizens. It became evident that, insofar as possible, all such records should be brought together and used as a basis for compiling individual records of service. The project encompassed the American Revolution, beginning in 1775, and all other wars up to and including the Philippine Insurrection of 1899 to 1902. Compiled service records pertaining to each war or period of time varied according to the amount and type of source documents available. The character and general content of each compilation for each war is described below.

Revolutionary War Period (1775–83)

Many valuable revolutionary war documents were destroyed in a fire at the War Department in 1800 and when the British captured and burned Washington, D.C., in 1814. At the beginning of the twentieth century, the War Department instituted a course of action to locate substitutes for the lost material. The result was the National Archives collection *War Department Collection of Revolutionary War Records* (RG 93). These files were used to expedite searches to validate military service and medical records of veterans who had applied for pensions or made other claims based on their military service. Documents used to make up this collection included the following:

- Private papers of Timothy Pickering, adjutant general and quartermaster general under George Washington

- Papers transferred to the War Department from other agencies of the government

- Lists of persons found on various pension rolls

- Copies of commissions, resignations, enlistment papers, orders and accounts, and correspondence

- Records loaned by the states of Virginia, North Carolina, and Massachusetts

- Records of the Continental and Confederated congresses and the Constitutional Convention

- *Receipt Books of John Pierce and Joseph Howell, Paymaster General and Commissioner of Army Accounts, 1783–85; 1787–90* (two volumes).

Since there were existing records relating to regular army personnel and to personnel in state militia units, it was determined that individual records should be compiled for the "volunteer" soldiers who were not in regular army units and for those in militia units that were not transferred to the Continental Army. Researchers should be mindful of the fact that compiled service records do not exist in the National Archives' collections for some revolutionary war participants. In such instances the records of the regular army and the militia records of the appropriate states can be searched.

The method used to compile the records was to examine each paper, extract data pertaining to each individual, and place the data on a nine- by four-inch "abstract card." There is one card for each entry located in a document that contained more than one name (such as a muster roll, payroll, etc.). When a document referred to only one individual, a transcription of that document, in lieu of an abstract card, was made. All abstract cards and copies of single-name papers were placed in a jacket-envelope bearing the soldier's name, rank, and military unit. This became his compiled military service record. Later, in preparation for the microfilming of these records, the jacket-envelopes were unfolded and laid flat.

After all the records were compiled they were arranged according to whether the units were a part of the "Continental Troops" or a unit raised in only one state. Other state units that were either transferred to the Continental Army or raised from more than one state were placed in the Continental Troops category. In either category, the jackets were further arranged by name of unit and thereunder alphabetically by name of soldier. In those cases where a soldier served in more than one military unit, there might be more than one jacket. Also, where there was confusion about the correct spelling of a surname, there might be more than one jacket under different spellings.

The National Archives has microfilmed indexes and copies of these compiled service records (figure 8).

Post-Revolutionary War Period (1784-1811)

The period 1784 to 1811 was characterized by various Indian campaigns, insurrections, and disturbances requiring the use of military force. In the same manner as for the revolutionary war period, compiled service records were created for volunteer soldiers. These are arranged by organization, including the First and Second Regiments of the United States Levies, and then alphabetically by name of state and territorial organization. Under each such classification the records are arranged according to military unit and thereunder alphabetically by name of the soldier. The National Archives has microfilmed indexes and copies of these compiled service records.

War of 1812 (1812-15)

At the outset of the War of 1812, Congress authorized the president to raise units of Rangers to protect the frontier (then the Mississippi River) and units of Sea Fencibles (as part of a Flotilla Service) to protect ports, harbors, and the coastline. There also was authorization to raise special volunteer units to fight the British. Because of confusion over which of these new units were part of the regular army or regular navy or were volunteer units, compiled service records were created to include all of them. Also serving in military capacities at that time were state militias and volunteer army units engaged in fighting Indians (1812 to 1815). Personnel in the units that confronted the Seminole Indians in Florida (1812), the Peoria Indians in Illinois (1813), and the Creek Indians in Alabama (1813 to 1814) are represented in the group of compiled service records created for personnel who fought in the War of 1812. Since many volunteers enlisted for brief periods (six, nine, or twelve months), some served more than once. In such cases there may be more than one compiled service record for the same individual. Many individuals who fought during this period also fought in the post-American Revolution period or in other Indian wars after the 1812 era. Some had additional service either in the American Revolution or in the Civil War. In such cases, multiple compiled service records might have been created.

The records are arranged by state or territory and thereunder by unit; others not identified by a single state or territory are arranged by units. Among the latter are: U.S. Rangers; Sea Fencibles; Cherokee, Chickasaw, Choctaw, and Creek Indian regiments; First U.S. Volunteers (Louisiana); First Regiment U.S. Volunteers (Mississippi Territory); Second Regiment Artillery (New York); and

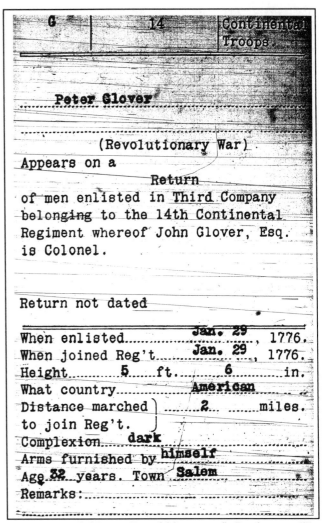

Figure 8. Compiled Service Record (abstract card)—Revolutionary War (courtesy National Archives).

Captain Booker's Company, U.S. Volunteers (Virginia). For each unit the records are arranged alphabetically by surname.

Indian Wars (1816-58)

Compiled service records for this period pertain to volunteer units that served independently or assisted regular army units in the Seminole "Florida" Wars (1817 to 1818, 1835 to 1842, 1855 to 1858), the Winnebago War (1827), the Sac and Fox War (1831), the Black Hawk War (1832), the Creek War (1836 to 1837), various Indian wars in Texas (1849 to 1851), the Indian Removal (1835 to 1841), and various other skirmishes and conflicts not classified as wars. In addition to those made up of American citizens, there were units made up wholly of allied Indians who served alongside white soldiers. Abstract cards (1815 to 1858) that make up these records indicate the name of the war or military action involved (figure 9). Indexes to these

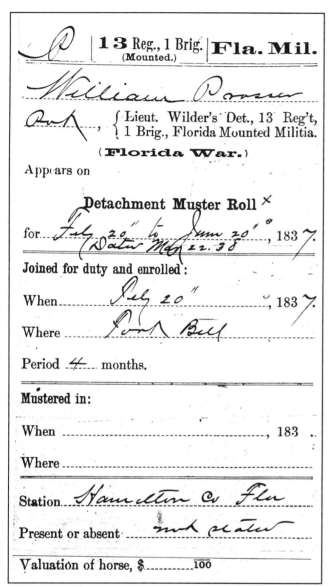

Figure 9. Compiled Service Record (abstract card), Florida Militia–Florida Indian Wars (courtesy National Archives).

records are arranged by state, but it must be remembered that state boundaries were not properly defined, and the possibility of residence in neighboring states should be considered when researching a soldier involved in any of these actions.

Patriot War (1838)

This war involved groups of American citizens and Canadian rebels who planned to attack the British armies along the U.S.-Canadian border and eventually establish an independent republic. The United States passed a neutrality act in March 1838 and sent federal troops to join local militias in suppressing the planned uprising. Compiled service records have not been microfilmed, but there are two microfilm indexes at the National Archives,

one listing the Michigan military personnel and one listing the New York military personnel.

Mexican War (1846-48)

Volunteer units from twenty-four states, California, and the District of Columbia served in the Mexican War. Although war was not officially declared by Congress until 13 May 1846, one unit from Louisiana and five units from the new state of Texas were in action during 1845. Units were also formed in New Mexico Territory. One unit was composed of Indians, and one–the Mormon Battalion–was composed of approximately five hundred members of The Church of Jesus Christ of Latter-day Saints (LDS church).

Compiled service records pertaining to this war are arranged alphabetically by state or territory, followed by the Mormon Battalion. Further breakdowns are by unit and then alphabetically by the name of the soldier.

Civil War–Union (1861-65)

The Union Army was made up of regular army soldiers, regular navy seamen, volunteer units from each loyal state and territory, volunteer units from most of the seceding states (most especially Tennessee and Arkansas), militia units pressed into federal service, and soldiers drafted into federal service beginning in 1863 (at which time state or territorial draft organizations were superseded). Early enlistments were for short periods of time up to one year; many were for only thirty or sixty days. Reenlistments sometimes resulted in more than one compiled service record for the same individual. In addition to personnel serving in local or state units, some were assigned to special units such as the U.S. Sharpshooters, Army Marines, U.S. Colored Troops, Balloon Corps, and others. Soldiers serving in the special unit "Mississippi Ram Fleet" were transferred to the navy in 1862. Although African-Americans and Indians sometimes served in predominantly white units before 1863, separate units composed of African-American or Indian soldiers were organized thereafter–usually with white commanding officers (figures 10 and 11).

There are compiled service records for volunteer soldiers who served during the period 1861 to 1865, including militiamen assigned to the Union Army. Compiled service records for soldiers engaged in Indian warfare during this period are filed along with the Civil War participants. Indexes of the compiled service records are arranged by state or territory (for all states except South Carolina, which officially provided no white soldiers to the Union). There

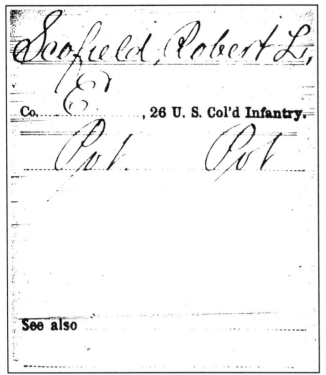

Figure 10. Compiled Service Record (abstract card), U.S. Colored Infantry—Civil War (courtesy National Archives).

are separate indexes for those who served in special units not associated with a particular state or territory. These include the U.S. Colored Troops (names of white officers may be found among the personnel of these soldiers), U.S. Volunteers (former Confederate soldiers), and others. There is no general name index to Union soldiers, so the researcher must have some knowledge of which state or states to search, bearing in mind that many individuals crossed state borders to join—especially those from border states.

Civil War—Confederate (1861-65)

There being few records pertaining to Confederate soldiers found in federal offices, the War Department used various Confederate records captured by Union forces. Many such records were transported to Charlotte, North Carolina, where they were turned over to a Union officer following the evacuation of Richmond, Virginia, in April 1865. Records of the U.S. provost marshal were also used, especially those concerning prisoners of war. In 1903, governors of the Southern states were requested to lend any Confederate records in their states to the War Department for use in compiling service records, after which they were returned to the states (figure 12).

In addition to the usual information on compiled service records, the Confederate records often contain informa-tion concerning capture, prison experience, and parole. When completed, the service records were arranged according to the units raised directly by the Confederate government or merged with other units, with the records arranged thereunder alphabetically by surname. Other records were arranged to include officers who occupied staff positions (as opposed to line positions) and the enlisted men in staff positions who were not a part of a regular field regiment. A consolidated index (chapter 3) includes all of the records for each state, including these special groups. Separate indexes were prepared for each state. There is a collection of unfiled papers that were never integrated into a compiled service record; they are available on National Archives microfilm *Unfiled Papers and Slips Belonging in Confederate Compiled Service Records* (M347–442 reels). Also see the section on National Park Service battle sites (chapter 7).

Spanish-American War (1898-99)

During the Spanish-American War, volunteer soldiers served in state or territory units, including militia units. They also served in federal units not identified with any particular state or territory. These included three regiments of U.S. cavalry, three regiments of U.S. engineers, ten regiments of U.S. infantry, and a Signal Corps. Regular army soldiers also served, but there are no compiled service records for them.

When the compiled service records were completed by the National Archives, they were arranged in four sections: state units (alphabetically), territory units, federal volunteers, and Puerto Rican volunteers. Access to these records is by a general index. There are also separate indexes at the National Archives for each state militia unit, and there is a separate index of all U.S. volunteer units (except Puerto Rico). There is also a separate collection of personal papers that never became part of the compiled service records. Cross-references in the service records indicate their presence (figures 13 and 14).

Philippine Insurrection (1899-1902)

For service in this military campaign, the federal government recruited volunteers and assigned them to federal regiments. The compiled service records at the National Archives are arranged numerically by regiment and then by unassigned infantry, two battalions of Philippine scouts, and a squadron of Philippine cavalry. There is a general name index at the National Archives and a separate collection of personal papers that never became part of the compiled service records. Cross-references in the service records indicate their presence.

Figure 11. Descriptive List Entry for a Former Slave Who Enlisted in the Union Army—Civil War (top: left-hand page; bottom: right-hand page) (courtesy National Archives).

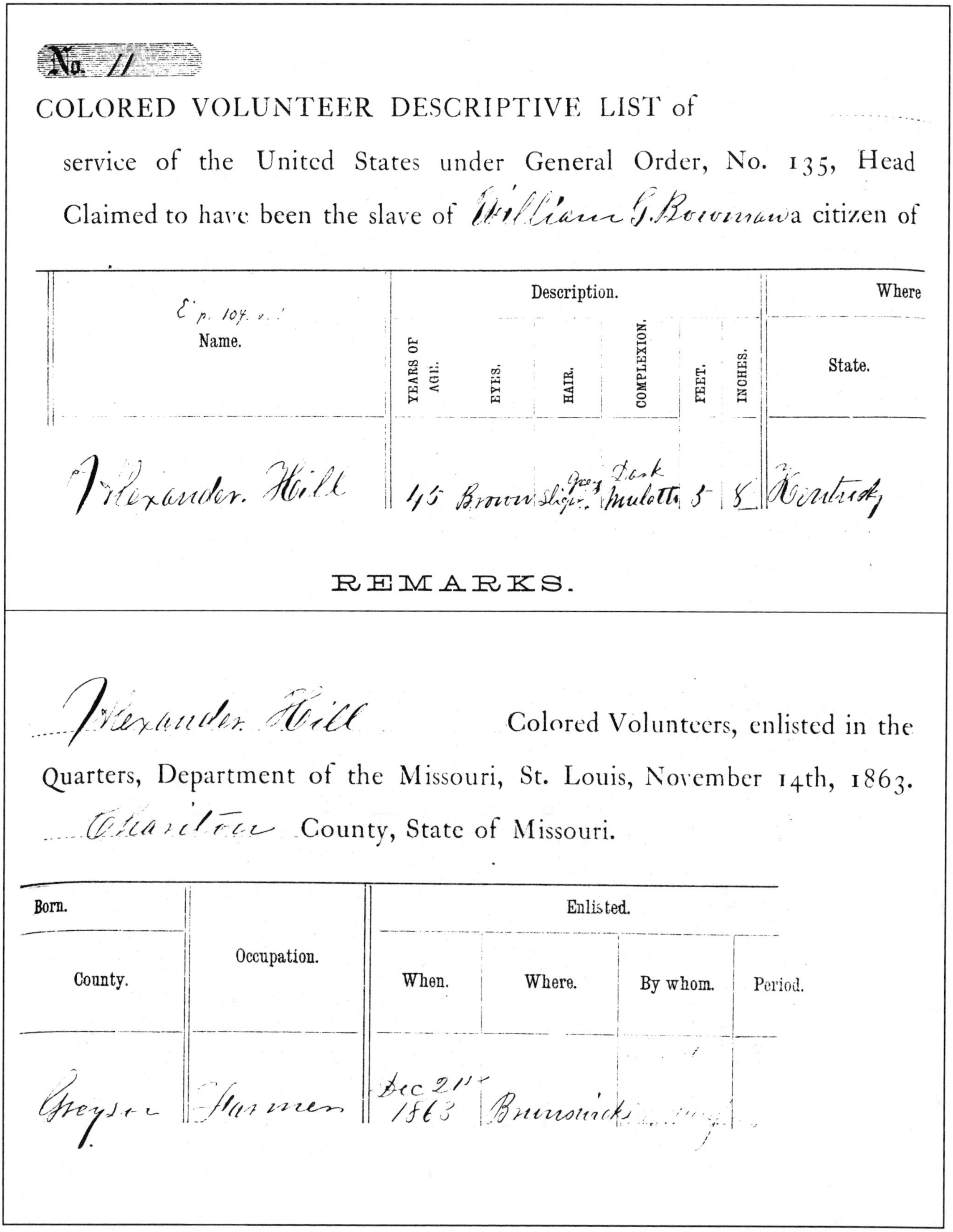

No. 11

COLORED VOLUNTEER DESCRIPTIVE LIST of

service of the United States under General Order, No. 135, Head

Claimed to have been the slave of *William G. Bowman* a citizen of

| Name. | Description. | | | | | | Where State. |
	YEARS OF AGE.	EYES.	HAIR.	COMPLEXION.	FEET.	INCHES.	
Alexander. Hill	45	Brown	Slight Grey	Dark Mulatto	5	8	Kentucky

REMARKS.

Alexander Hill Colored Volunteers, enlisted in the

Quarters, Department of the Missouri, St. Louis, November 14th, 1863.

Chariton County, State of Missouri.

| Born. | | Enlisted. | | | |
County.	Occupation.	When.	Where.	By whom.	Period.
Grayson	Farmer	Dec 21st 1863	Brunswick		

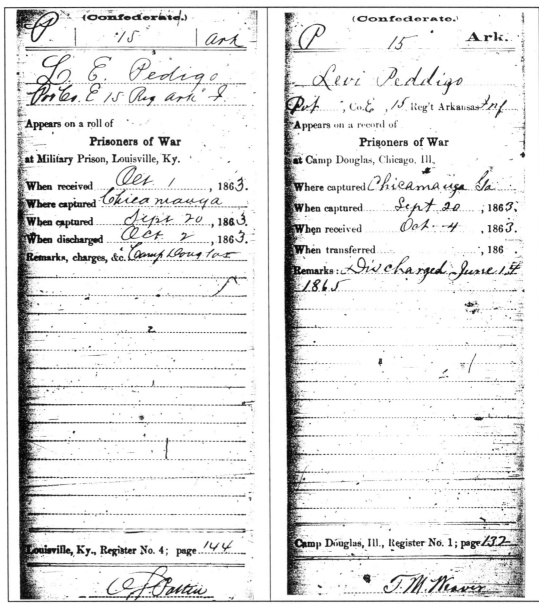

Figure 12. Compiled Service Record (abstract cards) for a Confederate Soldier (courtesy National Archives).

Battle Reports and Events

Once a soldier's record has been studied, a researcher is naturally interested in learning something of the soldier's experiences while in uniform. A way to ascertain this is to learn something of the history of his regiment or company during the time he served in it (figure 15). Regimental returns are often found with the muster rolls of volunteer and regular army units; regiments are arranged by unit in seven series of microfilm at the National Archives. In this regard it is important that the events and actions of particular companies be scrutinized, because certain companies were often split off, at least temporarily, from their regiments. Therefore, the combat history of a particular company does not necessarily coincide with that of its regiment.

From early times the periodic "returns" of regiments and companies, as well as of detached units, provided information concerning the units' whereabouts at certain times. The return forms that provide space for a "record of events" supply descriptions of daily activities, battles engaged in, and other activities. Returns were also required from military posts, camps, and stations. These always listed the names of the officers and the number of enlisted men, and usually contained a record of events. Although a separate form for post returns was developed, the data gathered was very similar to that gathered by off-post

No.   272   𝔖𝔱𝔞𝔱𝔢 𝔬𝔣 𝔐𝔞𝔦𝔫𝔢.

ADJUTANT GENERAL'S OFFICE.

Augusta,   March   11,   190 14.

𝔍𝔱 𝔦𝔰 𝔥𝔢𝔯𝔢𝔟𝔶 𝔠𝔢𝔯𝔱𝔦𝔣𝔦𝔢𝔡, *that it appears from the records of this office, that*

BERT W. ABBOTT   *a*   Private   *in Company*   D   ,

First Regiment of Infantry, Maine Volunteers, enlisted on the   2d

day of   May   *, 1898, and was mustered into the United States Service as a*

Private   *at*   Augusta,   Maine   *, on the*   13th   *day of*

May   *1898, for Two Years, unless sooner discharged. Mustered out and*

honorably discharged, as a   Private   *, the*   1st   *day of*

November   *, 1898, at*   Norway,   Maine   *by reason of*

Orders War Department mustering out the organization.

Said   Bert W. Abbott   *was born in*   Milton

County of   Oxford   *State of*   Maine   *a resident of*

So. Paris,   Maine   *, age*   19   ,   5   *feet*   11¼   *inches high,*

light   *complexion,*   blue   *eyes,*   lt.brown   *hair, and by occupation, when enlisted, a*

Student

Remarks "Absent sick on Surgeon's certificate. Discharge and final statements sent him at South Paris, Me. Physical examination waived."

Albert Greenlaw

Adjutant-General of Maine.

Figure 13. Certificate of Service—Spanish-American War (courtesy Maine State Archives).

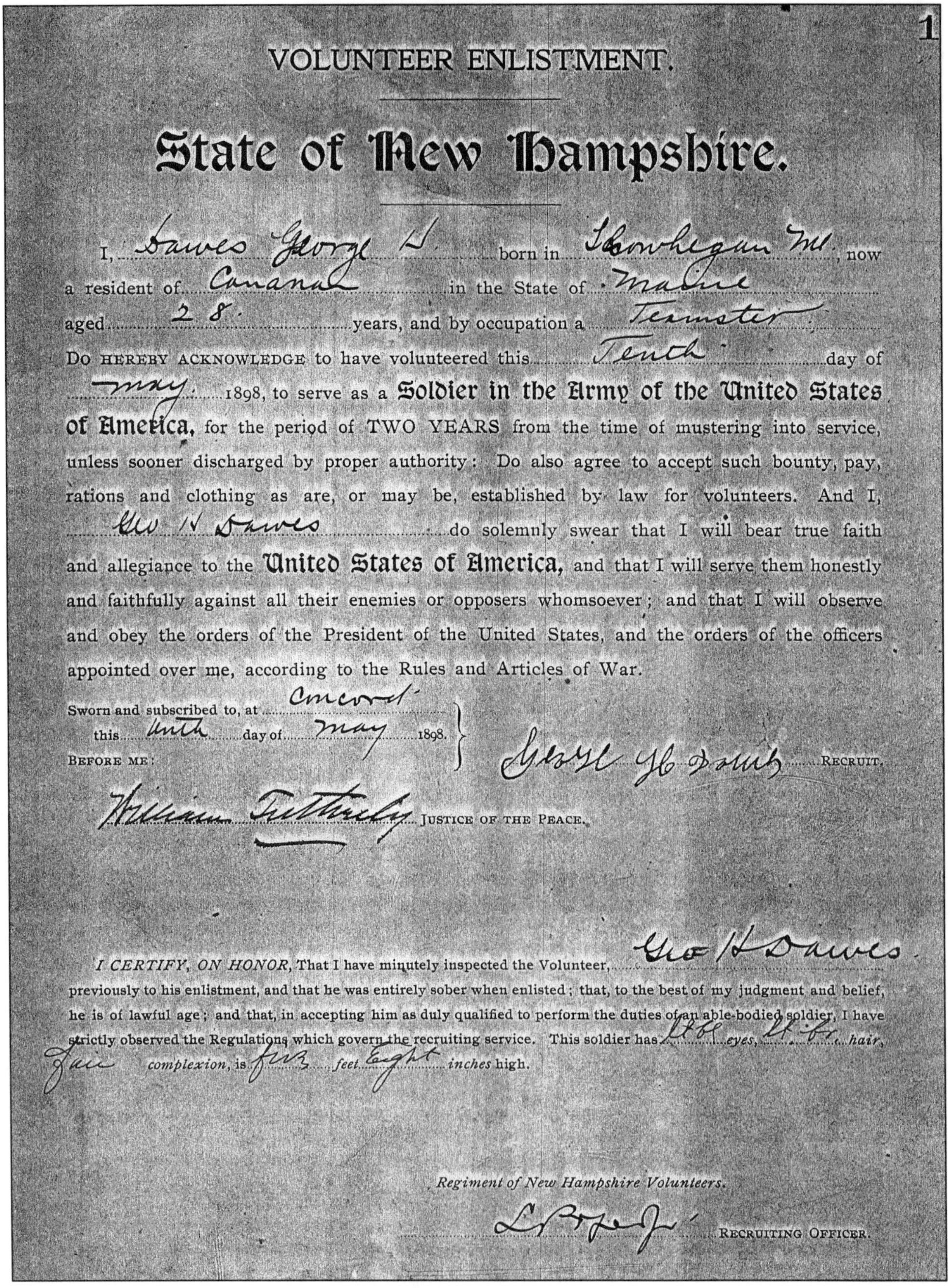

VOLUNTEER ENLISTMENT.

State of New Hampshire.

I, *Dawes George L* born in *Skowhegan Me* ; now a resident of *Canaan* in the State of *Maine* aged *28* years, and by occupation a *Teamster* Do HEREBY ACKNOWLEDGE to have volunteered this *Tenth* day of *May* 1898, to serve as a **Soldier in the Army of the United States of America,** for the period of TWO YEARS from the time of mustering into service, unless sooner discharged by proper authority : Do also agree to accept such bounty, pay, rations and clothing as are, or may be, established by law for volunteers. And I, *Geo H Dawes* do solemnly swear that I will bear true faith and allegiance to the **United States of America,** and that I will serve them honestly and faithfully against all their enemies or opposers whomsoever ; and that I will observe and obey the orders of the President of the United States, and the orders of the officers appointed over me, according to the Rules and Articles of War.

Sworn and subscribed to, at *Concord* this *Tenth* day of *May* 1898.

BEFORE ME :

George H Dawes .... RECRUIT.

William Tetherly JUSTICE OF THE PEACE.

Geo H Dawes

I CERTIFY, ON HONOR, That I have minutely inspected the Volunteer, previously to his enlistment, and that he was entirely sober when enlisted ; that, to the best of my judgment and belief, he is of lawful age ; and that, in accepting him as duly qualified to perform the duties of an able-bodied soldier, I have strictly observed the Regulations which govern the recruiting service. This soldier has *Blue* eyes, *Lt Br* hair, *fair* complexion, is *five* feet *Eight* inches high.

.... Regiment of New Hampshire Volunteers.

L Pope Jr RECRUITING OFFICER.

Figure 14. Enlistment Certificate, New Hampshire–Spanish-American War (courtesy New Hampshire State Archives).

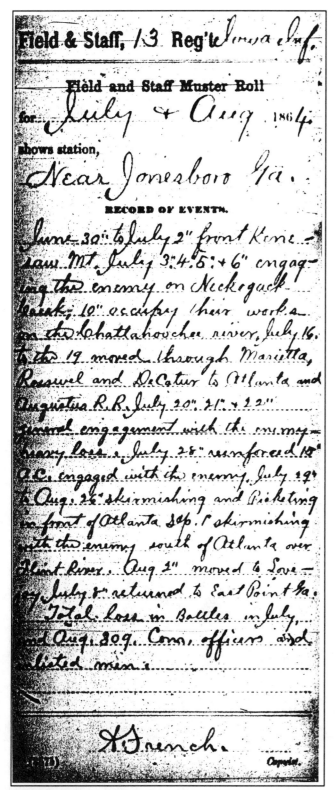

Figure 15. Record of Events for a Union Unit—Civil War (courtesy National Archives).

al Archives Military Reference Branch lists them and the time period covered. Regimental returns are arranged by the number of the regiment and thereunder chronologically. Similar records are available for regular army units of cavalry, artillery, coast artillery, regular army engineer battalions, and the Corps of Engineers. Time periods covered vary, but they range from the early 1800s to 1916.

In 1890, the War Department compiled historical information concerning volunteer military organizations that served in the Union forces during the Civil War. Separate jacket-envelopes labeled "Record of Events" contain pertinent papers of each military unit. These records include information found in the record-of-events sections of original muster rolls and returns. Although few names other than those of commanding officers are mentioned, these files deal with troop movements such as marches, boat transportation, and engagements (figure 16). The files detail losses, strength numbers, dates of the units' organization, and their disbandment or merger with other units. The jackets are arranged by state and thereunder by type and number or name of unit. In 1902 the Office of the Adjutant General prepared a bound volume (available at the National Archives) that consists of typescript summaries relating to the histories of various regular army units from the date of each unit's organization through 1902. These summaries include a chronological list of engagements and companies that participated.

Another source of Civil War unit historical data is the previously cited *Official Records of the Union and Confederate Armies in the War of the Rebellion* and similar collections pertaining to the navies. Using the indexes and names of commanding officers, it is possible to ascertain some of the activities in which specific units were engaged.

For the modern wars, unit histories are available in major libraries and in the military history centers in the Washington, D.C., area and at Maxwell Air Force Base in Montgomery, Alabama, and Carlisle, Pennsylvania. These centers may also hold after-action reports prepared immediately after an incident. (Also see citations in chapter 9 regarding military unit histories and bibliographies of such histories.)

Court-Martial Cases and Deserters

Evolving from the time of the American Revolution to the outbreak of the Civil War, there were four major levels of army court-martial proceedings: general courts-martial, regimental courts-martial, garrison courts-martial, and

regiments, companies, and detached units. Post returns are arranged alphabetically by name of the post, camp, or station, and a descriptive pamphlet available at the Nation-

Figure 16. Battle Lists for Union Cavalry Units—Civil War (courtesy National Archives).

BATTLE LIST OF *Seventh Iowa Cavalry*

NAME OR LOCATION AND DATE.		KILLED. OFFICERS.	KILLED. ENLISTED MEN.	WOUNDED. OFFICERS.	WOUNDED. ENLISTED MEN.	MISSING. OFFICERS.	MISSING. ENLISTED MEN.	AGGREGATE.	COMPANIES ENGAGED OR IN WHICH CASUALTIES OCCURRED.
Niobrara, N.T.	Dec 4 1863								
Tos-cha-owah-Koo-tah.	July 28-29 1864								
Smoky Hill Crossing, Kas.	Aug 16, 1864		4					14	H.
Fort Cottonwood, N.T.	Aug 28, 1864								
Fort Cottonwood, N.T.	Sept 18, 1864		2					2	C.
Julesburg, Col Ty.	Jany 7, 1865		14		2			16	F.
Rush Creek, I.T.	Feb 8, 1865		1					1	D.
Boyds Station, N.T.	June 3, 1865		1					1	E.
Cow Creek, Kas.	June 12, 1865				2			2	G.
Horse Creek, D.T.	June 14, 1865	1	3					4	B D.
Tongue River, D.T.	Aug 29, 1865								

Eighth Iowa Cavalry

NAME OR LOCATION AND DATE.		KILLED. OFFICERS.	KILLED. ENLISTED MEN.	WOUNDED. OFFICERS.	WOUNDED. ENLISTED MEN.	MISSING. OFFICERS.	MISSING. ENLISTED MEN.	AGGREGATE.	COMPANIES ENGAGED OR IN WHICH CASUALTIES OCCURRED.
Luville Varnells or Varnells Station, Ga.	May 7, 1864				2			3	E.
Buzzard Roost, Ga.	May 9, 1864				1			1	E.
Near Tilton, Ga.	May 13, 1864		1				1	2	C M.
Cassville, Ga.	May 19, 1864		1		1		1	3	G M.
Burnt Hickory, Ga.	May 24, 1864								
Burnt Church, Ga.	May 26-30, 1864							1	
Ackworth, Ga.	June 3, 1864				1			1	M.
Powder Springs, Ga.	June 20, 1864		1					1	F.
Newnan, Ga.	July 30, 1864		2		3	23	257	285	
Pulaski, Tenn.	Sept 27, 1864			1	2			3	B.
Raccoon Ford, Ala.	Oct 30, 1864		2		10	5	17	B E F G I	
Franklin, Tenn.	Nov 30, 1864		1		1			2	C M.
Pleasant Ridge, Ala.	Apl 6, 1865						30	30	

Ninth Iowa Cavalry

NAME OR LOCATION AND DATE.		KILLED. OFFICERS.	KILLED. ENLISTED MEN.	WOUNDED. OFFICERS.	WOUNDED. ENLISTED MEN.	MISSING. OFFICERS.	MISSING. ENLISTED MEN.	AGGREGATE.	COMPANIES ENGAGED OR IN WHICH CASUALTIES OCCURRED.
West Point, Ark.	June 16, 1864		1					3	
Clarendon, Ark.	June 26, 1864								
Ashly Station, Ark.	Aug 24, 1864								
Brownsville, Ark.	Aug 25, 1864								
Searcy, Ark	Sept 6, 1864		2		1		10	15	
Brownsville, Ark	Oct 30, 1864						2	2	A B

First Iowa Battery

NAME OR LOCATION AND DATE.		KILLED. OFFICERS.	KILLED. ENLISTED MEN.	WOUNDED. OFFICERS.	WOUNDED. ENLISTED MEN.	MISSING. OFFICERS.	MISSING. ENLISTED MEN.	AGGREGATE.	COMPANIES ENGAGED OR IN WHICH CASUALTIES OCCURRED.
Pea Ridge, Ark.	Mch 7, 1862		2		14				
Chickasaw Bayou, Miss.	Dec 28, 29-30 1862								
Arkansas Post, Ark.	Jany 11, 1863								
Port Gibson, Miss.	May 1, 1863				1			1	

summary courts-martial. (The latter were often referred to as "drum-head" courts-martial.) Only a general court-martial could try officers or impose a sentence of death, dismissal from service, forfeiture of more than three months' pay, or incarceration exceeding three months. In times of emergency a drum-head court-martial was authorized, so called because a unit's drummer was historically responsible for administering punishment (usually lashing). Drum-head courts-martial were characterized by speed and informality and were followed immediately by charges of guilt or innocence. The punishment was then agreed upon by the panel and administered without delay.

Playing a part in the military criminal justice system are courts of inquiry (investigative bodies without power to impose punishment) and special courts-martial for investigation and trial of military personnel and private citizens. Such proceedings are presided over by an officer acting as a trial judge advocate, who serves as the government's prosecutor.

During the revolutionary war, courts-martial were recorded among the daily entries in unit orderly books. A survey of such courts-martial, as found in the orderly books (originals, copies, or microfilm), is available at the National Archives—*Numbered Record Books* (M853)—or at the Manuscript Division of the Library of Congress. A survey of such courts-martial can also be found in James C. Neagles' *Summer Soldiers: A Survey and Index of Revolutionary War Courts-Martial* (Salt Lake City: Ancestry, 1986).

Beginning around 1829, clerks in the War Office began sorting and labeling court-martial papers received since 1809; they prepared registers according to the name of the defendant. These registers were placed in one volume, with each entry recording trial and sentence data. After 1829, the records of general courts-martial were registered as they were received, with batches of records bound into separate volumes as the numbers of records increased, especially with the onset of the Civil War. The National Archives has seventeen volumes of these registers covering the years 1809 to 1890: *Registers of the Records of the United States Army General Courts-Martial, 1809–1890* (M1105). The National Archives also has a separate set of records (taken out of a larger series for microfilming) pertaining to the cases of 267 soldiers who were executed by military authorities between 1861 and 1866 following findings of guilt by court-martial: *Proceedings of the United States Army Courts-martial and Military Commissions of Union Soldiers Executed by United States Military Authority, 1861–1866* (M1523). Also available at the National Archives are reference cards relating to courts-martial for the period 1861 to 1865; they are arranged alphabetically by state.

Records of the Office of the Judge Advocate General, also available in the National Archives (RG 153), include lists of various courts-martial and inquiries during the time period 1809 to 1938 (figures 17 and 18).

Occasionally, lists of deserters were prepared based upon returns and reports from various military units. Some Selective Service System boards kept notations of names and physical descriptions of deserters reported by the Office of the Provost Marshal, as well as of individuals who were classified as deserters for not complying with the draft laws (figure 19).

Prisoners of War

War of 1812

The Office of the Adjutant General received lists of names submitted by the Treasury Department and the Department of the Navy containing names of prisoners of war for the period 1812 to 1815; some are indexed. The lists include names of American prisoners held in Canada and the West Indies who died in British custody; who were held in the West Indies and Bermuda (indexed for names beginning with A through S only); and who were captured or held in England, Canada, and various locations in the United States. Also there are incomplete crew lists for the USS *Essex* and the brig *Vixen*, both captured by the British (these have only the names beginning with A and B). Most records indicate name, rank, organization, date and place of capture, and date of release.

Civil War

During the time the War Department was preparing compiled service records for Confederate soldiers and

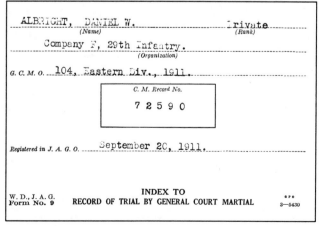

Figure 17. Index to Trial by Court Martial, 1911 (courtesy National Archives).

Figure 18. Summary Court-Martial Record for Headquarters, First Alabama U.S. Volunteer Infantry, 1898 (courtesy National Archives).

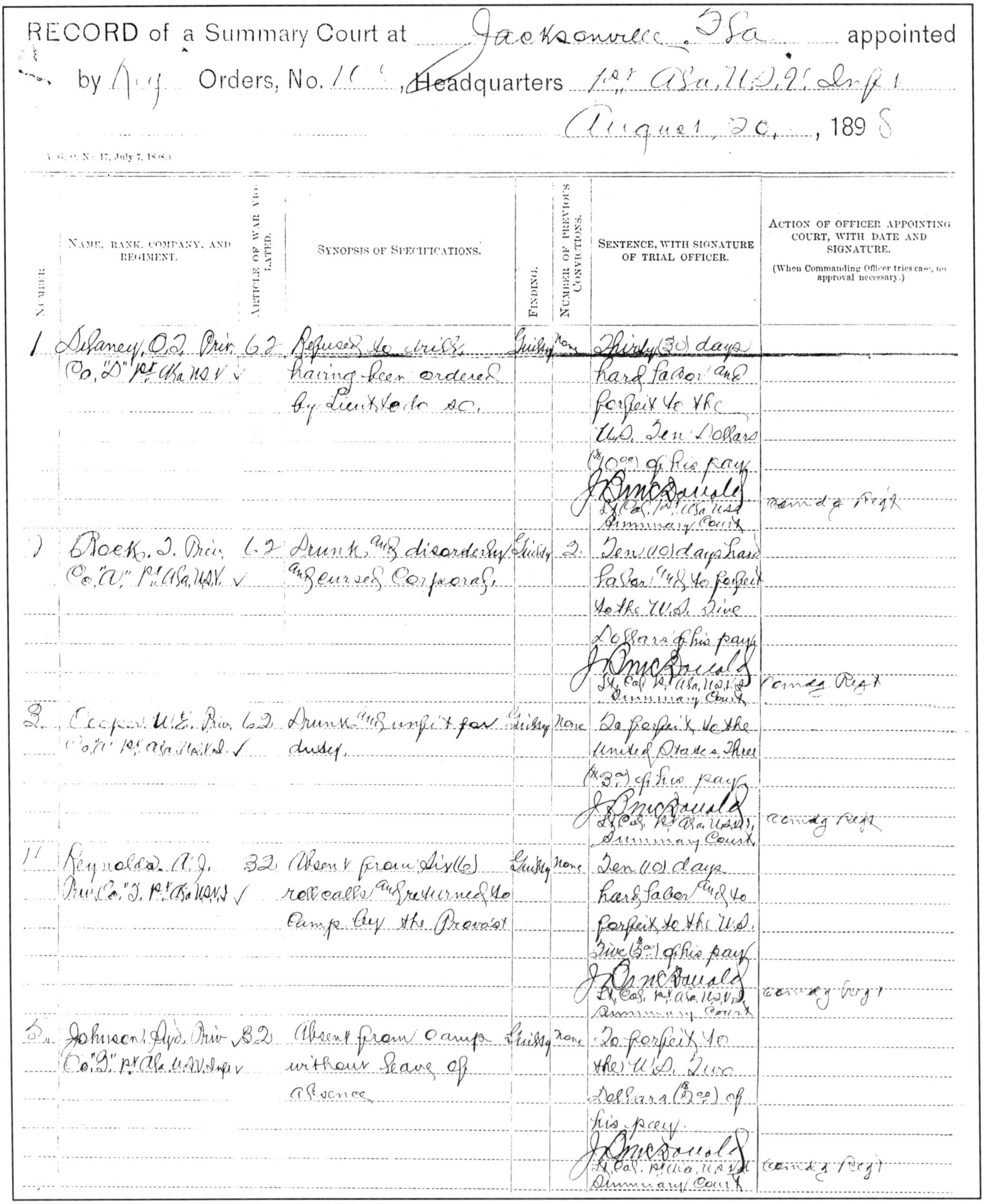

RECORD of a Summary Court at _Jacksonville, Fla._ appointed by _Aug_ Orders, No. _10_, Headquarters _1st Ala. U.S.V. Inf._ _August 20_, 189 8

A. G. O. No. 17, July 7, 1890.

NUMBER.	NAME, RANK, COMPANY, AND REGIMENT.	ARTICLE OF WAR VIOLATED.	SYNOPSIS OF SPECIFICATIONS.	FINDING.	NUMBER OF PREVIOUS CONVICTIONS.	SENTENCE, WITH SIGNATURE OF TRIAL OFFICER.	ACTION OF OFFICER APPOINTING COURT, WITH DATE AND SIGNATURE. (When Commanding Officer tries case, no approval necessary.)
1	Delaney, O.J. Priv. Co. "D" 1st Ala. U.S.V.	62	Refused to drill, having been ordered by Lieut. to do so.	Guilty	None	Thirty (30) days hard labor and forfeit to the U.S. Ten Dollars ($10.00) of his pay J.D. McDonald 1st Lt. Col. 1st Ala. U.S.V. Summary Court	approved Regt
2	Roeck, J. Priv. Co. "A" 1st Ala. U.S.V.	62	Drunk and disorderly and cursed Corporal.	Guilty	2	Ten (10) days hard labor and to forfeit to the U.S. Five Dollars of his pay J.D. McDonald 1st Lt. Col. 1st Ala. U.S.V. Summary Court	approved Regt
3	Cooper, W.E. Priv. Co. "A" 1st Ala. U.S.V.	62	Drunk and unfit for duty.	Guilty	None	To forfeit to the United States Three ($3.00) of his pay J.D. McDonald 1st Lt. Col. 1st Ala. U.S.V. Summary Court	approved Regt
4	Reynolds, A.J. Priv. Co. "I" 1st Ala. U.S.V.	32	Absent from Six (6) roll calls and returned to Camp by the Provost	Guilty	None	Ten (10) days hard labor and to forfeit to the U.S. Five ($5.00) of his pay J.D. McDonald 1st Lt. Col. 1st Ala. U.S.V. Summary Court	approved Regt
5	Johnson, Wd. Priv. Co. "D" 1st Ala. U.S.V. Inf.	32	Absent from camp without leave of absence	Guilty	None	To forfeit to the U.S. Two Dollars ($2.00) of his pay. J.D. McDonald 1st Lt. Col. 1st Ala. U.S.V. Summary Court	approved Regt

Figure 19. List of Deserters, Marine Corps (courtesy National Archives).

No.	Name	Rank	Co	Regt.	Date of Des.	Remarks
1	Pollard David O.	Private	"A"	2nd	Mch '63	
2	Kimball P. H.	"	"	"	" "	
3	Cushman W. H.	"	"	"	" "	
4	Condon W. D.	"	"	"	" "	
5	Leavitt Dudley H.	"	"	"	" "	
6	Sanborn Joseph W.	"	"	"	" "	
7	Marden J. W.	"	"	"	" "	
8	Hayes J. S.	"	"	"	" "	
9	Taylor Jno	"	B.			
10	Billings David F.	"	"	"	" "	
11	Gilman Charles W.	"	"	"	" "	
12	Herrick Daniel B.	"	"	"	" "	
13	Fox William G.	"	"	"	" "	
14	Smalley Augustus	"	"	"	" "	
15	Young Michael	"	"	"	" "	
16	Reene R. E.	"	C.	"	" "	
17	Robinson Zebulon	"	"	"	" "	
18	Lovejoy Ira	"	"	"	" "	
19	Lombard N. W.	"	"	"	" "	
20	Lowell Saml. O.	"	"	"	" "	
21	Cushing Franklin	"	"	"	" "	
22	Nickerson Chas. F.	"	"	"	" "	
23	Goodwin Saml. S.	"	"	"	" "	
24	Babbitt F. R.	"	"	"	" "	

military units, it kept a separate group of bound volumes containing records of military prisoners of war and the prisons in which they were confined (RG 109). Some of the records in these volumes were created by the Office of the Commissary General of Prisoners and others by the Surgeon General's Office, as well as by specific army commands. Most of the reports were originally submitted by officials of the Union prisons where Confederate prisoners were kept. They are arranged generally according to the offices that supplied the records and by state, but specifically by the name of the Union prison. These reports are available on National Archives microfilm *Selected Records of the War Department Relating to Confederate Prisoners of War, 1861–1864* (M598–145 reels). Reel 1 lists the contents of the remaining reels in this series. Usually it is not necessary to search these reels for prisoner-of-war data, since these records have been abstracted and placed on abstract cards that form part of an individual soldier's compiled service record and can be more easily located there.

A related collection grew out of federal legislation authorizing the location and marking of graves of Confederate soldiers who died in Northern prisons and who were buried there. Since there is no general name index, it is necessary to know the name or location of the grave of a Confederate soldier who died to find his record in this collection.

World War II

The Office of the Adjutant General maintains a card index that refers to war crimes investigations. Some refer to interviews with U.S. soldiers and airmen who were prisoners of war, including some who were victims of or witnesses to atrocities committed during their imprisonment in Europe and the Far East. The military history centers at Bolling Air Force Base, Washington, D.C., and at Maxwell Air Force Base, Montgomery, Alabama, contain detailed reports for nearly six thousand incidents in which air crews were missing as a result of action in World War II (figure 20). (Many of them were taken prisoner.)

Casualties and Deaths

There are several lists and card indexes of servicemen who suffered wounds or died in action. For example, there is a collection of "final statements" pertaining to regular army personnel for the period 1862 to 1899 (RG 127). These papers contain a record of death and burial, an inventory of personal effects, cause and place of death, and data concerning the deceased's financial affairs. Related to these papers is a register of deaths for the regular army, 1860 to 1889; it contains name, rank, organization, age, race, place of birth, length of service, cause of admission to a hospital, where death occurred in line of duty, disposition of the case, and date of death.

There are a card list and registers of casualties of marines dating from 1776 to 1930, with separate lists for the War of 1812, the Civil War, the Spanish-American War, and several subsequent wars and expeditions in which marines were involved. There are also separate lists showing those who died in explosions and earthquakes, 1924 to 1937, and showing casualties from miscellaneous causes, 1889 to 1945. There is also an incomplete list of deaths in naval service for the Civil War (figures 21, 22, and 23).

There are general death registers of soldiers who fought in particular wars, such as the Florida War (1835 to 1842), and for Union volunteer soldiers who died in the Civil War, 1861 to 1865, with an index of casualties (RG 94). A government-authorized *Roll of Honor* (twenty-seven volumes), published by the Office of the U.S. Quartermaster General, covers Union deaths during the Civil War. These rolls are arranged by location and by the name of the cemetery in which the deceased was buried.

Available in many libraries and archives are similar lists of casualties and deaths and *Rolls of Honor*, in book form, arranged by state, county, and cemetery (figure 24). They provide name, rank, unit, date of death, etc. Such rolls have been prepared for each war since the Civil War, up to and including the Vietnam War. *Vietnam Veterans Memorial. Directory of Names* (cited in chapter 9, Published Sources) serves as a location index to the names engraved on the Vietnam Memorial in Washington, D.C. Scrapbooks containing newspaper obituaries, often accompanied by photographs furnished by families, are also available in many local libraries and historical or genealogical societies.

Another source of information on U.S. Army and U.S. Army Air Force personnel who became casualties since 1939 (including those listed as missing in action) is the Mortuary Affairs and Casualty Support Services, U.S. Total Personnel Command, HQDA (Tape-PED-F), Alexandria, Virginia 22331-0482.

Medical Reports and Lists

Medical practice has always required meticulous record keeping, and this practice has resulted in a plethora of

Figure 20. Roster of Men Received and Transferred From Palawan Prison (Japanese prison camp)—World War II (courtesy National Archives).

A-1 ✓	MC NALLY, Theodore	C.M.M.		
	6821 Montgall Ave., Kansas City, Mo.			
A-2	GIBSON, Donald Clay	P/Sgt. 24 82 84	Marine C 4th Marines	
	1010 Miami Ave. Kansas City, Kansas			
A-3	HOUGH, Hubert Dwight	Y.1c 321 25 67	Navy C CINCAF	
	204 North C St., Oskaloosa, Iowa.			
A-4	MC AFOOS, Charles B.	S.M.2c 336 99 17	Navy C USS FINCH	2
	707 E. Burkett St., Benton, Ill.			
A-6	HODGE, Allen J.	Cox.	Navy C USS CANOPUS	2
	Dyersburg, Tennessee RFD # 1			
A-7	BULLARD, Delmar A.	Cox. 356 12 96	Navy C CINCAF	2
	Ft. Worth, Texas % Worth Mills			
A-8	WILSON, Earl Vance	M.M.1c	Navy C USS MINDANAO	
	414 W Monroe St., Delphi, Ind.			
A-11	BARNES, Carl Ellis	W.T.2c 375 78 63	Navy C USS OAHU	
	2525 Brundage Lane, Bakersfield Californ			
A-14	WILLIAMS, George Rudd	C.Q.M. 214 67 32	Navy C USS NAPA	2
	57 Standish Road, Milton Mass.			
A-15	SMITH, Juluo Forest	M.M.1c 3291 54 84	Navy C USS CANOPUS	2
	729 N. Illinois, Indianapolis, Ind.			
A-17	LOWMAN, Ralph Seaton	S.C.3c 337 14 16	Navy C USS MINDANAO	
	514 So. Russell St., W. Frankfort Illinois			
A-18	INGRAMS, Osburn F.	Sea.1c	Navy C USS PROPOISE	
	1301 Madison Ave., Memphis Tenn.			
A-19	PETERS, James Orval	Sea.1c 337 49 28	Navy C USS PIGEON	
	1012 So. Maple St., Centralia, Illinois			
A-22	DIMEO, Carmen Mario	P.F.C. 289947	C 4th Marines	
	705 S. Marshfield Ave., Chicago Ill.			
A-24	PARRISH, Francis Marion	B.M.2c 382 03 55	Navy C. USS LUZON	2
	Rt. # 1 Box 1096A, Downey Calif.			
A-25 ✓	ADKINS, Robert Arthur	Corp.	Marine C 4th Marines	2
	17 North Main St., Greenville, S.C.			
A-26	JAQUIN, Howard Frank	M.M.1c 238 55 58	Navy C. USS CANOPUS	
	339 Douglas St., Syracuse, N.Y.			
A-27 ✓	PRICE, Dillard	P.F.C. 279503	Marine C	
	2734 Mich. Ave., Dallas, Texas			
A-28	ANDERSON, Victor Samuel	Corp 278895	Marine C	
	Dassel, Minn RFD # 1			
A-29	DE BLASIO, John Joseph	Corp. 279333	Marine C	2
	173 W. Fulton St., Long Beach, N.Y.			
A-30 ✓	WALKER, George Murray	Corp. 230063	Marine C	2
	1305 Berkley Ave., Columbia, So. Carolina			
A-31	PIKE, Donavan Sanky	Corp. 281466	Marine C	20
	Oxnard, California			
A-32 ✓	WARREN, John Otis	P.F.C. 2922 02	Marine C	2
	Dekalb Mississippi Route # 2			
A-33	ANDERSON, Ralph Wilmer	P.F.C. 28 36 03	Marine C	2
	878 Pascal St. North, St Paul, Minn.			
A-34 ✓	LINDSEY, Kenneth Clyde	P.F.C. 27 49 73	Marine C	2
	Gillette, Wyo.			
A-36	WILLS, Alexander	Pvt 19002109	Army C 60th	
	129 Railroad Ave., Fresno, California			

Figure 21. Page From a Register of Deaths, Marine Corps, 1838–1906 (courtesy National Archives).

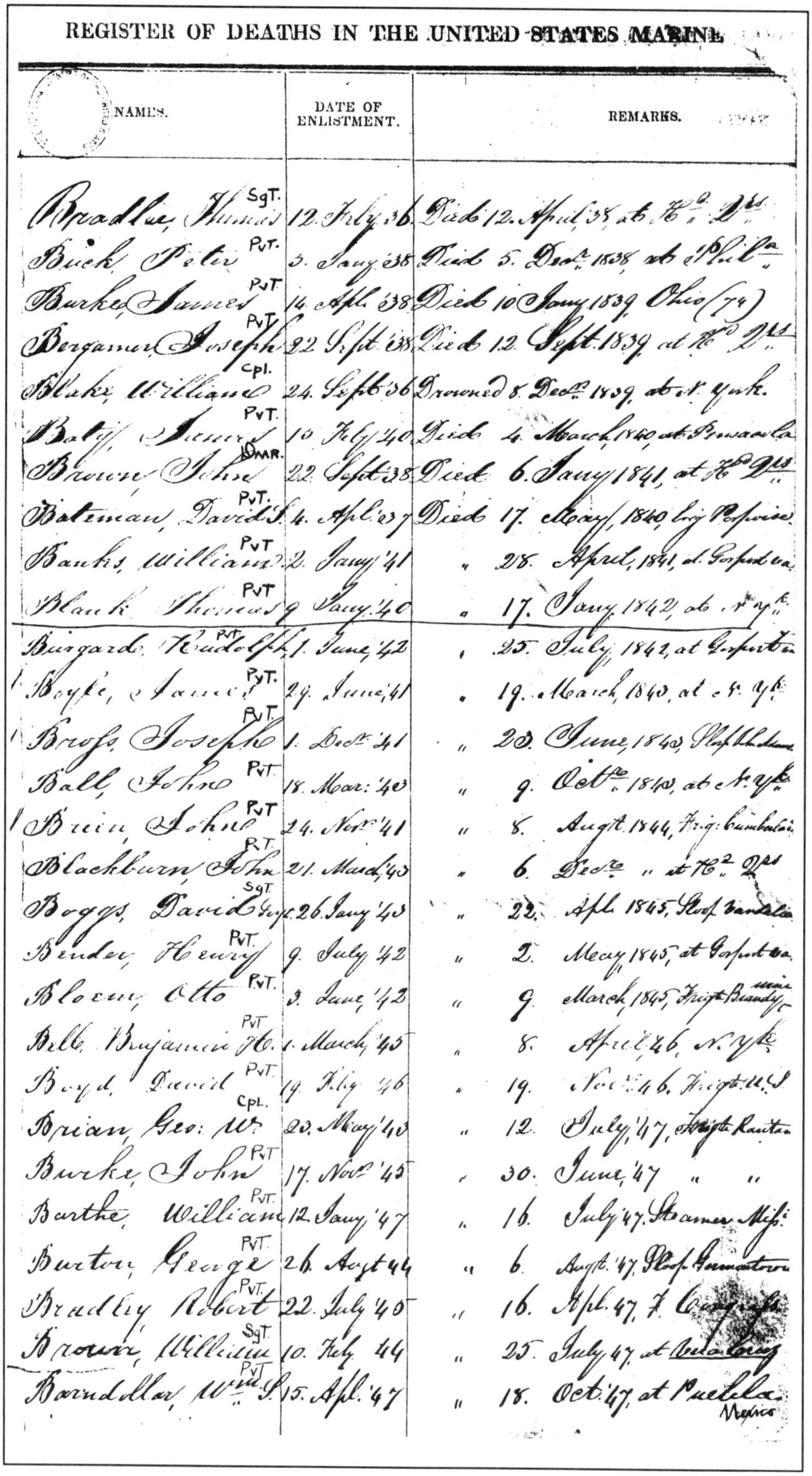

REGISTER OF DEATHS IN THE UNITED STATES MARINE

NAMES.	DATE OF ENLISTMENT.	REMARKS.
Bradlie, Thomas *SgT.*	12. Feby '36	Died 12. April 38 at Hd. Qrs.
Buck, Peter *PvT.*	5. Jany 38	Died 5. Decr. 1838 at Phil. Pa
Burke, James *PvT.*	14. Apl. '38	Died 10 Jany 1839 Ohio (74)
Bergamer, Joseph *PvT.*	22. Sept '38	Died 12. Sept. 1839 at Hd. Qrs.
Blake, William *Cpl.*	24. Sept '36	Drowned 8 Decr. 1839 at N. York.
Baty, James *PvT.*	10. Feby '40	Died 4. March 1840, at Pensacola
Brown, John *Dmr.*	22. Sept '38	Died 6. Jany 1841, at Hd. Qrs.
Bateman, David S. *PvT.*	4. Apl. '37	Died 17. May, 1840, brig Porpoise
Banks, William *PvT.*	2. Jany '41	" 28. April, 1841, at Gosport Va.
Blank, Thomas *PvT.*	9. Jany '40	" 17. Jany 1842, at N. Yk.
Burgard, Rudolph *PvT.*	1. June '42	" 25. July 1842, at Gosport Va.
Boyle, James *PvT.*	29. June '41	" 19. March, 1843, at N. Yk.
Brofs, Joseph *PvT.*	1. Dec '41	" 20. June, 1843, Sloop Albany
Ball, John *PvT.*	18. Mar: '40	" 9. Octr. 1843, at N. Yk.
Brun, John *PvT.*	24. Nov '41	" 8. Augt. 1844, Frig. Cumberland
Blackburn, John *R.T.*	21. March '43	" 6. Decr. " at Hd. Qrs.
Boggs, David *SgT.*	26. Jany '43	" 22. Apl. 1845, Sloop Vandalia
Bender, Henry *PvT.*	9. July '42	" 2. May 1845, at Gosport Va.
Bloem, Otto *PvT.*	3. June '43	" 9. March, 1845, Frig. Brandywine
Bell, Benjamin H. *PvT.*	1. March '45	" 8. April 46, N. Yk.
Boyd, David *PvT.*	19. Feby '46	" 19. Novr. 46, Frig. U.S.
Brian, Geo. W. *Cpl.*	23. May '40	" 12. July '47, Frigate Raritan
Burke, John *PvT.*	17. Nov '45	" 30. June, 47 " "
Barthe, William *PvT.*	12. Jany '47	" 16. July 47, Steamer Miss.
Burton, George *PvT.*	26. Augt 44	" 6. Augt. '47, Sloop Germantown
Bradley, Robert *PvT.*	22. July 40	" 16. Sept. 47, F. C...
Brown, William *SgT.*	10. Feby 44	" 25. July 47, at Vera Cruz
Barudelle, Wm. S. *PvT.*	15. Apl. '47	" 18. Oct. 47, at Puebla, Mexico

Figure 22. Casualty List, U.S. Navy—Spanish-American War (courtesy National Archives).

Address Bureau of Medicine and Surgery, Navy Department,
and refer to No.

/MP/

WASHINGTON, D. C.,

·January 23, 1903.

NAMES AND NATIVITIES OF THOSE WHO DIED FROM CASUALTIES
OF BATTLE DURING SPANISH-AMERICAN WAR, 1898, U.S.NAVY.

-----oooOooo-----

NAME.	RATE.	NATIV-ITY.	WHERE ENLISTED.	DATE OF DEATH.	PLACE OF DEATH.
BAGLEY,Worth	Ensign.	N.C.	------	May 11.	"WINSLOW".
BLAKELY,Frank I.	1-Cl.App.	Mass.	Phila.Pa.	Jun.22.	"TEXAS".
BOARDMAN,Wm.H.	Cadet.	Mass.	------	Aug.10.	"AMPHITRITE"
D'NEEFE,John	1-Cl.Fire.	Ireland.	Boston, Mass.	May 11.	"WINSLOW".
DUMPHY, Wm.	Private.	Mass.	Boston, Mass.	Jun.11.	Engagements at Guantanamo.
ELLIS,Geo.Henry	Ch.Yeo.	Ill.	New York.	Jul. 3.	"BROOKLYN".
GIBBS,John Blair	A.Surg.	Va.	------	Jun.12.	Engagements at Guantanamo.
GOOD,Henry	Sergt.	Ireland.	"CHICAGO"	Jun.13.	"
KOULOURIS,E.N.	C.P.	Greece.	"BANCROFT"	Aug. 2.	"BANCROFT".
McCOLGAN,J.P.	Private.	Mass.	Boston.	Jun.11.	Engagements at Guantanamo.
MEEK, Geo. B.	1-C.Fire.	Ohio.	N.Y.	May 11.	"WINSLOW".
REAGAN,Patrick	Private.	Ireland.	Brook-lyn.	May 11.	"MARBLEHEAD"
SMITH,Charles H.	Sergt.	Maryland.	New York.	Jun.11.	Engagements at Guantanamo.
SUNTZENICH,Ernest	1-C.App.	N.York.	N.York.	May 14.	"MARBLEHEAD".
TAURMAN,Goode	Private.	Va.	Ports-mouth,Va.	Jun.13.	Engagements at Guantanamo.
TUNNELL,E.M.	S.Cook, 1st.cl.	Va.	League Island.	May 11.	"WINSLOW".
VARVERES,John	Oiler.	Austria.	N.York.	May 11.	"
WIDEMARK,Frank	Sea.	Finland.	N.York.	May 12.	"NEW YORK".

Figure 23. Casualty List by State and Organization–Civil War (courtesy National Archives).

A list of the killed and wounded of General Pillow's command, in action at La Fayette Ga. June 24th 1864.

Armistead's Brigade.

Names	Rank	Regiment	Company	Killed	Wounded	Remarks
Armistead, C. G.	Col.	Comdg. Brigade.			Shoulder + Side	1 Severely –
Robbins, J. Q.	Corpl.	Armistead's	A	Killed		
Staunton, H. G.	Private	Do	"	"		
Barries, A. G.	"	"	"		Shoulder	! Slightly
Conley, R. W.	"	"	C	Killed		
Malone, D. L.	"	"	"	"		
Gibson, Wm.	"	"	"	"		
Bryan, R. B.	"	"	D	'		
Harper, T. P.	"	"	"		Leg	– Slightly
Wharton, J. M.	"	"	"		Neck	Mortally – prisoner.
Foster, T. T.	"	"	E	Killed		
Megee, W. F.	"	"	"	"		
Fulton, C. W.	Lieut	"	F		Hand	2 Severely.
Gladney, R. A.	Sergt.	"	'		Face	4 Slightly.
Vaughan, W.	"	"	G		Finger	5 "
Bryant, J. M.	Prvt.	"	H	Killed		
Lynch, J. D.	Capt	"	I		Leg	3 Slightly.
Shotwell, C. H.	Prvt.	"	"		Arm	4 " –
Holt, H.	Sergt.	"	K	Killed		
Culpepper, E. G.	Prvt.	"	"	"		
Bradshaw, J. W.	Lieut	'	"		Abdomen	4 Severely.
Evans, R. A.	Sgt.	"	"	do		
Davis, J. W.	Prvt.	"	"		Unknown	7 Captured.
Purdy, P.	"	"	"		Face	8 Slightly.
Miller, D. H.	"	"	I		Shoulder	9 "

Figure 24. Roll of Honor, Delaware—World War II (courtesy Delaware State Archives).

☆ **BASTOGNE** ☆ **GERMANY** ☆ **PHILIPPINES** ☆

MICHAEL JOSEPH SAFIAN, JR., Seaman Second Class, U. S. Navy, of 203 West Seventh Street, Wilmington, Delaware, son of Mrs. Victoria Ellis. Killed in action October 13, 1943, while serving on the U. S. S. BRISTOL when it was torpedoed and sunk in the Mediterranean Sea off the coast of Algeria. He served one year, eleven months.

BIAGIO JOHN SAIENNI, Private, U. S. Army, of 812 South Franklin Street, Wilmington, Delaware, son of Quindilio and Domenica Saienni, husband of Dorothy Ann (McDermott) Saienni. Killed in action October 11, 1944, in Italy while serving as a rifleman with the 351st Infantry Regiment, 88th Division, Fifth Army. He served one year lacking one day.

FRANK SANBORN, Seaman First Class, U. S. Navy, of 131 South Chapel Street, Newark, Delaware, son of Nicholas and Mary Anne (Charamella) Sanborn. Died April 16, 1946, at Newport, Rhode Island of accidental injuries suffered March 22 while awaiting discharge after returning from sea duty in the Pacific area. He served three years, eight months.

GEORGE LEROY SANDERS, JR., Private First Class, U. S. Marine Corps, of 39 Spruce Avenue, Elsmere, Wilmington, Delaware, son of George Leroy and Margaret (Curran) Sanders. Killed in action June 15, 1944, at Saipan while serving with Company G, 8th Regiment, 2nd Marine Division. He served one year, four months and was decorated with Presidential Unit Citation.

BENJAMIN FLOYD SANFORD, Ship's Cook Second Class, U. S. Navy, of Seaford, Delaware, son of Mrs. Carmen P. Sanford. Killed in action April 16, 1945, off Okinawa while serving as a U. S. Naval Reserve. He served two years, one month.

GEORGE EDWARD SAVAGE, Gunner's Mate Third Class, U. S. Navy, of Ocean View, Delaware, son of Archie F. and Gretchen (Wainwright) Savage. Killed in action March 26, 1945, when the U. S. S. HALLIGAN, to which he was assigned, was destroyed off Okinawa. He served two years, three months and was decorated with the Purple Heart.

JOHN FRANCIS SCHISLEY, Corporal, U. S. Marine Corps, of Kirkwood, Delaware, son of Stanley Joe and Stella (Bosak) Schisley. Killed in action November 20, 1943, at Tarawa while serving with a Marine Corps unit. He served three years and was decorated with the Purple Heart.

AMERICAN THEATRE ☆ **NORTH AFRICA** ☆ **ITALY** ☆ **FRANCE** ☆

PACIFIC THEATRE ☆ **LEYTE** ☆ **IWO JIMA** ☆ **OKINAWA** ☆ **CHINA**

☆ **SICILY** ☆ **CASSINO** ☆ **NORMANDY** ☆ **ANZIO** ☆

patient lists, certificates of disability, physical examination reports, and case study reports. Also numerous are rosters of physicians, nurses, and other hospital or medical unit personnel (RG 94). Some examples are the field hospital reports, 1821 to 1912 (11,000 volumes), available at the National Archives. These contain registers of sick and wounded, clothing and descriptive books, account books, rosters, and prescription and case books, the majority being from the Civil War. The books are arranged under "States and Territories," "Army Corps," "Departments," and "United States Army Regimental." Also at the National Archives is a collection of Mexican War hospital records, 1846 to 1848 (twenty-five volumes with indexes), and a similar collection of four thousand volumes for the Spanish-American War. Each military post submitted reports pertaining to its medical activities to the Surgeon General of the Army; there is a collection of 908 volumes for the years 1868 to 1913. In addition to the medical material, some volumes added records of births, marriages, and deaths. For the period 1886 to 1912 there are similar reports submitted by army hospitals in the United States and several overseas locations. There are also muster rolls and payrolls of medical personnel who served in these hospitals.

Rosters and lists of medical officers at certain posts or who served in certain wars can be found in separate National Archives collections. Also, there are reports of sick and wounded for the years 1820 to 1912; these provide personnel strengths and statistical accounting and also lists of patients' names, place of hospitalization, and miscellaneous personal data. Related sources are the so-called "B" books, which consist primarily of registers of patients in hospitals from the 1860s to 1919. Related are a set of "B Medical Cards" for individuals; these show name, rank, organization, hospital to which admitted, cause of admittance, whether injured or wounded in the line of duty, register number, and disposition of the case. An index is available.

Several types of reports of physical examination pertaining to recruits, officer applicants, and candidates for disability furlough, leave of absence, or discharge are available at the National Archives. There are also registers of deaths that include date, place, and cause of death, with remarks (figures 25 and 26).

Army medical officers who treated unusual cases or who believed a case merited special description submitted written case reports, often accompanied by physical specimens from the deceased, to the surgeon general. These now comprise the collection at the National Museum of Health and Medicine in Washington, D.C. (chapter 6).

Photographs

The physical description of a soldier or sailor can be ascertained by inspecting records that list a person's height, weight, color of hair and eyes, and any scars or disfigurements. A more revealing method is to locate a photograph taken during or near the time of military service. The development of the photographic process during the Civil War era enabled photographers, including those of a firm owned and led by the well-known photographer Mathew B. Brady, to make photographic records of battle and camp scenes. Union (and sometimes Confederate) officers and enlisted men were photographed as individuals or in groups. Thousands of these photographs are in the collections of the Still Pictures Branch of the National Archives (chapter 5) and of the Prints and Photographs Division of the Library of Congress (chapter 6). This practice continued during all subsequent wars and conflicts, and large photo collections are also available in such places as the history centers maintained by the military branches. Insofar as possible, group photos are identified by the unit name, and occasionally the individuals are named, although officers are more likely to be identified than are enlisted personnel. Regardless of personal identification, these photographs illustrate the uniforms, tentage, equipment, and other articles associated with military life in the field. Similar collections pertaining to nearby camps and posts may also be found in state archives or in historical society collections.

The National Museum of Health and Medicine has an extensive collection of photographs of patients with various disabilities and physical conditions, all identified by name and unit (see illustration in chapter 6). There are thousands of photographs of U.S. Navy ships (and vessels of other nations) at the U.S. Naval Historical Center, Washington, D.C., and there are also thousands of photographs of identified airplanes at the Air Force Historical Research Agency at Maxwell Air Force Base, Montgomery, Alabama (see chapters 6 and 7).

Published honor rolls of deceased military personnel often contain portraits, usually supplied by family members. Newspaper accounts of local men participating in battle, being awarded medals, or killed or wounded in action are frequently accompanied by photographs. Many of these find their way into scrapbooks created by or donated to local libraries, historical societies, or state or local agencies.

Figure 25. Surgeon's Certificate of Disability, 1863 (courtesy National Archives).

I HEREBY CERTIFY, That *Frank A. Kelly* a *private* in the U. S. ~~Navy~~ *Marine corps* attached to the (a) *U. S. Marine barracks, Boston Mass* and holding the rank above mentioned, *is* rendered unfit for the performance of his duty by reason of (b) *Deafness*, as set forth in the record in his case, of which the following is a copy: *Surgeon's Office, Navy Yard, Boston Mass. May 29th 1863 Frank A. Kelly, Marine 22. Vermont. Has been hard of hearing for two years; the deafness increases, so that now he hears with difficulty the tick of a watch one inch from the ear.*

and therefore, in the opinion of the undersigned, the interests of the service require that he should be discharged. *His disease did not originate in the line of duty.*

W.I.W. Ruschenbayer
Surgeon.

The above named *Frank A Kelley* was born at *Chambly* in the State of *Canada*; is *23* years of age; *5* feet *7½* inches high; *Fair* complexion; *Grey* eyes; *Lt Brown* hair. He entered the U. S. Naval service at *Boston Mass* on the *12* day of *August*, 186*1*, and discharged (d)

Paymaster.

APPROVED: *Jno Geo Reynolds.*
Comd'g U. S. *Marine Corps Charlestown Mass*

DISCHARGED *from the U. S. Naval service on the .... day of ...., 186 .*

Fourth Auditor.

(a) If at a navy yard, ship, or hospital, insert name and place.
(b) Wound, casualty, or disease.
(c) The record of the case need not include details of medical treatment. It is only necessary to state the circumstances under which the disease or injury occurred, as far as a claim for pension is involved.
(d) Insert whether final, or to hospital, or ship for passage home; in which cases the final discharge must be furnished by the Auditor.

REGISTER No. **13**

NAME **Kelly, Timothy** 34/W/1re./7-9/12

RANK **Cpl .** , Co. 5th , REGIMENT **Rec., G.S.I.**

ADMITTED **May 1, 1909.** (#1,G.O.70,W.D.,c.s.)

DISCHARGED the service of the United States, May 3,1909, on S.C.D.on account of Pott's fracture with backward dislocation of right foot, irreducible. Incapacitates for duty because of inability to bear weight of body on right foot; marked restriction of flexion and extension of right ankle joint; right ankle edematous. Disability incurred by slipping on station steps at R.R.Station,Sprigfied,Mass.,Dec.22,1908,while returning to Ft.Slocum from detached service. Soldier was not under the influence of liquor on the day of the receipt of injury (above are soldier's statements). In line of duty. Degree of disability: Three-fourths.
Diagnosis per transfer card U.S.A.General Hospital,Washington,D.C.,dated April 30,1909:"'Per transfer card Ft.Slocum,N.Y. dated April 14,1909:'Unreduced '"posterior dislocation,right foot and union of Pott's fracture,right leg in '"bad position,result of injury accidentally incurred at R. R. Station, Springfield, '"Mass.,Dec.22,1908,by slipping on station steps,while returning from detached "service to Fort Slocum, N.Y.In line of duty.' Original admission Feb.25,1909. "Diagnosis on transfer card confirmed."

   Diagnosis on transfer card confirmed.

   CAPTAIN, MEDICAL CORPS
   SIGNATURE OF WARD OFFICER.

STATION   WALTER REED ARMY GENERAL HOSPITAL
         WASHINGTON, D. C.
         3—1168

Figure 26. Case Summary, Walter Reed Army Hospital, Washington, D.C. (courtesy National Museum of Health and Medicine).

Records of Federal Military Service: Navy

The Continental Navy had its beginnings in October 1775, when the Continental Congress authorized Gen. George Washington to acquire several small ships to be used to attack and capture British transport vessels. Encouraged by the successes of these raiders, the Congress soon authorized the construction of more ships. The Continental Navy, along with privateers and ships of the states' navies, operated against British shipping throughout the American Revolution.

With the end of the war, the Continental Navy effectively ceased to exist. However, pirate attacks on American merchant shipping in the Mediterranean Sea and European hostility underlined the need for a permanent navy. On 27 March 1794, President Washington signed an act that allowed for the purchase of six new warships, thus officially creating the U.S. Navy. The Department of the Navy was established in 1798.

The compiled service records described earlier—for the American Revolution and Confederate forces in the Civil War—include U.S. Navy personnel as well as those of other branches of the military. In some instances navy, marine, Coast Guard, and Merchant Marine service records are arranged separately and have their own indexes, which may or may not duplicate general indexes. These naval personnel service records contain abstract cards from the records of several ships, lists of sailors, and other naval sources. There are no compiled military service records for navy personnel of the nineteenth century other than for the American Revolution and the Civil War.

A large collection of unbound papers assembled by the navy since the American Revolution is available in the National Archives' "area files." These papers date from the time of the American Revolution; they are arranged by the part of the world to which the papers relate. The content of these papers varies widely; they can be searched successfully only by those willing to spend considerable time and careful effort. Other papers are in bound volumes or collections, many with indexes.

The navy has created several card indexes relating to papers of the revolutionary war era: persons confined as prisoners of war at the Forton and Old Mill prisons in England, and prize money due the heirs of John Paul Jones.

Navy and Marine Officers

An early list of navy officers is available at the Naval Historical Center (see chapter 6). It is an alphabetical register for the period May 1815 to June 1821. Each entry gives name, rank, date of appointment to the rank, age, and remarks of superiors regarding potential for promotion. An indexed series consisting of two volumes contains statements of service submitted by the officers in the 1842-to-1844 period in response to a navy questionnaire. In 1861, each navy and marine officer was required to submit a certificate of age. Each certificate was signed by the officer and shows rank and date of birth.

Abstracts of service for most navy and marine officers (and a few others) were prepared and filed chronologically in fifteen volumes dating from 1798 to 1893. Thus, to locate these records it is helpful if the researcher has some idea when a certain officer was in service. These abstracts are available in National Archives microfilm *Abstracts of Service Records of Naval Officers ("Records of Officers") 1798–1893* (M330—nineteen reels). Other abstracts, primarily of officers of the regular navy for the years 1846 to 1902 (and a few of a more recent date), are available in numbered volumes that are now on microfilm for the years 1829 to 1924 (M1328). They can be found by referring to a loose-leaf index at the National Archives. In addition to other information, entries for those in service since 1908 show names of beneficiaries. There are a few miscellaneous

record collections such as registers, letters, etc., that refer to the Civil War era. Last, there is a set of personnel record cards of officers of the Naval Auxiliary Service, 1907 to 1917.

Navy Enlisted Personnel

The National Archives has muster rolls of ships and shore establishments of the navy (similar to the muster rolls and payrolls of the army). Muster rolls of vessels, 1860 to 1900 (366 volumes), are arranged chronologically and thereunder alphabetically by name of the vessel. There are 154 additional volumes of muster rolls of ships and stations, 1891 to 1900, composed of records from naval stations, torpedo boats, and vessels of the U.S. Coast and Geodetic Survey (figures 27 and 28).

Muster rolls of ship and shore establishments, 1898 to 1939, comprise 3,539 volumes arranged chronologically and thereunder alphabetically by name of the ship or shore establishment. Those for the years prior to 1930 are arranged alphabetically, and those of 1931 to 1939 are arranged by type of vessel. These rolls show names of those on board, periods of service, and data concerning transfers, discharges, desertion, and death. Those for the period 1939 to 1956 are indexed by name of vessel or unit. These latter include quarterly reports, alphabetical lists showing changes in rating or transfer, names of any passengers on board, and recapitulation and summary sections.

Registers of enlistment and rendezvous returns for the period 1845 to 1854 show name, date and place of enlistment, place of birth, and age. An index was prepared and incorporated into a larger National Archives microfilm series: *Index to Rendezvous Reports, Before and After the Civil War, 1846–31 and 1865–84* (T1098). Supplementing the above-cited records for enlisted men are weekly and quarterly returns, service certificates, personnel record cards for the Naval Auxiliary Service, and card abstracts of World War I service records.

Records of naval apprentices (all between the ages of sixteen and twenty-one) include collections of certificates of consent, apprenticeship papers, and a few registers of apprentices (RG 24).

Court-martial records of navy and marine personnel similar to those for other branches of the service are also available, as are lists of agents of the Office of Naval Intelligence (RG 25).

Figure 27. Muster Roll of the USS *Adams*, 1892 (top: left-hand page; bottom: right-hand page) (courtesy National Archives).

MUSTER-ROLL OF THE

Number of Continuous-Service Certificate.	Entitled to Hon. Dis. or not.*	NAMES. (Alphabetically arranged, without regard to ratings, with the surnames to the left. Appointed petty officers to be included.)	RATING.	DATE OF ENLISTMENT.			WHERE ENLISTED.	TERM OF ENLIST-MENT.	PLACE OR VESSEL FROM WHICH RECEIVED.
				YEAR.	MONTH.	DAY.			
-120	Yes	Roskey, Michael Joseph.	2d Cl.	1891	June	10th	Buffalo, N.Y.	Oct. 1st	Independence
	Yes	Reilly, John.	C.I.C.	1890	Aug.	27th	New York, N.Y.	3 years	U.S.S. Pensacola
	Yes	Rangoal, Martin	Cpt. Top.	1891	April	13th	Valparaiso, Chile	3 years	U.S.S. Pensacola
	No	Rosenberg, Gustav.	Sea.	1892	Mrch.	2nd	Mare Island, Cal.	3 years	Independence
	No	Reros, George A.	C.H.	1892	Jan.	27th	Mare Island, Cal.	3 years	Independence
	Yes	Ridge, Edward James	Sea.	1891	July	6th	Mare Island, Cal.	3 years	Independence
	Yes	Ramspurger, Frederick	Lds.	1892	Jan.	14th	Mare Island, Cal.	3 years	Independence
	No	Rainford, Samuel.	Sea.	1892	Febry.	15th	Mare Island, Cal.	3 years	Independence
	Yes	Reid, John.	1st C.F.	1890	Jan.	9th	Mare Island, Cal.	3 years	Independence
	Yes	Rangoal, Martin	Cpt. Top.	1891	April	13th	Valparaiso, Chile	3 years	Independence
	Yes	Reid, John	Mech.	1893	Jany.	18th	Mare Island, Cal.	3 years	Independence
	No	Lilly, John	C.H.	1892	Apl.	7th	Mare Island, Cal.	3 years	Independence
	No	Rugg, Jacob H.	Lds.	1893	June	7th	Mare Isl. Cal.	3 years	Independence
	Yes	Roberts, John	2d Cl.M.	1893	April	25	Mare Island, Cal.	3 years	Independence
10,131	Yes	Raynor, George	Sea.	1892	Dec.	9th	Honolulu H.S.	3 years	Boston

U.S.S. *Adams,* 3rd Rate.

	WHEN RECEIVED ON BOARD.	WHERE BORN.		PERSONAL DESCRIPTION.					HEIGHT		T. Dis. R. D.D.	REMARKS. (Date of transfer, discharge, desertion, or death. To what vessel or station transferred. Where and why discharged. Note against the names of deserters and stragglers the amount "due" or "overpaid." Where died and cause of death.)
		CITY, TOWN, OR COUNTY.	STATE.	AGE. Years.	OCCUPA-TION.	EYES.	HAIR.	COM-PLEXION.	Feet.	In.		
1	March 28 92	Albany	N.Y.	16 3/12	Baker	Blue	Brown	Fair	5	8 7/8	T	Nov. 10/94 to U.S.R.O. Independence
2	April 2nd 92	Boston	Mass.	46 7/12	Mariner	Gray	Gray	Fair	5	2 3/4	T	April 30 1893 to U.S.S. Mohican
3	April 1 92	Bodoe	Norway	34 7/12	Mariner	Blue	Chestnut	Dark	5	7 1/2	T	Transferred to U.S.R.S. Independence Jan. 25/93. Naval Hospital, Mare Isl. Cal.
4	March 28 92	Bremen	Germany	27 4/12	Mariner	Blue	Brown	Fair	5	9	R	Dec. 25 1892 at Mare Island, Cal.
5	March 28 92	San Francisco	Cal.	21 7/12		Blue	Brown	Fair	5	9 1/4	Dis.	at Mare Island Cal. Feb'y 7 1893, pr. ordrg. Bureau dated Jan'y 21 1893
6	March 28 92	Albany	N.Y.	29 1/12	Mariner	Hazel	Black	Fair	5	8	T	June 3/94 at Pitka, Al. to U.S.R.S. Independence for discharge
7	March 28 92	Hohenzollern	Germany	35 1/12	Carpenter	Hazel	Brown	Ruddy	5	6 7/8	T	Nov. 10/94 to U.S.R.S. Independence
8	March 28 92	Sydney	Australia	31 7/12		Blue	Brown	Florid	5	7	R	at Mare Island Cal. Dec. 28 1892
9	April 2 92	Essex	N.Y.	32 7/12	Fireman	Brown	Brown	Sallow	5	8	Dis.	at Mare Island Cal. Jan'y 8 1893 exp. Term of service. more Island Cal. For discharge
10	Jan'y 20 1893	Bodoe	Norway	34 7/12	Mariner	Blue	Chestnut	Dark	5	7 1/2	T	Nov. 3/94 at Honolulu H.S. to U.S.R.O. Independence at
11	Jan'y 1 1893	Essex	N.J.	35 1/2	Mech.	Yellow gray	Brown	Ruddy	6	7 3/4	T	Nov. 10/94 to U.S.R.S. Independence
12	Aug 25 93	Lubin	Ireland	21 1/12		Blue	Brown	Florid	5	7	R	at Mare Island Cal. Aug. 29 93 more Island Cal. for discharge
13	July 2 1/93	Tiblingen	Switz'l'd	24 1/12	Store	Brown	Black	Florid	5	2 3/4	T	May 29 1894 at Pitka, Alaska to U.S.R.O. Independence at
14	Aug 8 93	Beaumaris	England	23 1/12	Mariner	Brown	Brown	Ruddy	5	8 3/8	T	Nov. 10/94 to U.S.R.S. Independence
15	Sept. 25/93		England	34 11/12	Mariner	Green	Light	Fair	5	4 1/2	T	Nov. 10/94 to U.S.R.S. Independence

Figure 28. Shipping Articles (enlistments) of the USS *Adams*, 1890s (top: left-hand page; bottom: right-hand page) (courtesy National Archives).

Confederate Navy

After the Civil War, Confederate navy and marine corps records similar to those created by the Union forces were collected by the War Department. While service records were being compiled for individual Confederate soldiers and sailors, the extant papers pertaining to Confederate ships, hospitals, and prisons were arranged into collections. A few shipping articles for 1861 to 1865, containing a signature of the enlistee and enlistment data, comprise one bound volume with an index.

Deck Logs

Navy ships and shore stations are required to keep a continuous log of activities and events, including weather conditions at sea. The logs provide a day-by-day, chronological account of a ship's operation. These logs are available for ships dating from 1801 to 1961. A published index is available at the National Archive (*Special List 44*). Arranged by name of ship, it shows the period of time for which logs are available for each. Officers aboard are listed, but names of seamen, except in cases of their injury, death, court-martial, or other unusual event, are rarely given. They are available as bound volumes at the National Archives (figure 29).

War Diaries

For the period 1941 to 1953, each U.S. Navy vessel maintained a war diary in which daily (and sometimes hourly) events were recorded for historical purposes. These provide a complete and detailed history of each ship, and they are useful when studying the complete background for the time a sailor served on a ship. These are available at the Operational Archives of the Naval Historical Center, Washington, D.C. (figure 30).

Navy Correspondence

A series of reports known as the "Captains' Letters" consists of reports from rear admirals, commodores, and captains of ships or shore stations submitted to the secretary of the navy. They comprise 413 bound volumes and are available on the National Archives microfilm *Letters Received by the Secretary of the Navy From Captains ("Captains' Letters"), 1805–1861; 1866–1885* (M125).

The letters from ships at sea were concerned primarily with matters of shipboard discipline and the repair and supply of the vessels. Commanding officers filed monthly returns of numbers of officers and men present or absent, lists of passengers, and certificates of death. The letters also contained reports of special incidents, observations, and other information, especially any involving conflicts or disagreements with foreign governments.

As letters and reports were received they were sequentially numbered before binding. Most volumes contain two indexes, the first being an alphabetical list of the "captains" and the second being brief abstracts of the contents of each letter or report. It is important that the researcher have a general idea of the time period and the name of a vessel or shore installation in which a particular individual served.

Historical and Manuscript Collections

Useful as a source for the history of naval ships is the nine-volume *Dictionary of American Naval Fighting Ships* (Washington, D.C.: Government Printing Office, 1909–90), which contains histories of most commissioned ships of the Continental and U.S. navies. This work gives much technical information about each vessel, often accompanied by a photograph.

Manuscript collections and historical writings pertaining to the navy are available nationwide. In 1979 the U.S. Naval History Division published a guide to such holdings: *U.S. Naval History Sources in the United States* (Washington, D.C.: the division, 1979).

Records of Federal Military Service: Other Branches

Marine Corps

Continental marine units served during the revolutionary war, mainly to take part in close combat at sea. Congress

Figure 29. Deck Log of the USS *Fomalhaut*, December 1943 (courtesy National Archives).

BNP186

~~XPAROXIII~~

CONFIDENTIAL

Page 370

UNITED STATES SHIP   FOMALHAUT   Saturday   11   December , 19 43

Zone description   -12

Position	0800	1200	2000
Lat.			
Long.			

ADMINISTRATIVE AND
OPERATIONAL REMARKS
~~XVXXDXAXXX~~

0 to 4

Anchored in Suva Harbor, Viti Levu, Fiji Islands, in 13 fathoms of water with 60 fathoms of chain to port anchor on the following bearings: Beacon 320°(T), Beacon 254°(T). Ship darkened. Battle Condition III set. No. 2 generator in use for auxiliary purposes.

T. Hicks,
Lieut.(jg), USN.

4 to 8

Anchored as before. 0500 Made preparations for getting underway. 0524 Observed sunrise. Lightened ship. Set Modified Condition Yoke. 0529 Pilot, Comdr. Nasmyth, R.N.Z.N., came aboard. 0538 Underway for King's Wharf. Commenced steaming on various courses and speeds to conform to channel. Pilot conning. Captain and Navigator on the bridge. 0602 Moored port side to the Southern Berth of King's Wharf, Suva, Viti Levu, Fiji Islands.

A. W. Carlson,
Lieut., D-V(G), USNR.

8 to 12

Moored as before. 0820 Transferred the following named officers and enlisted men of the Fiji Military Forces ashore, transportation completed:

Officers

Major C.W.H. Tripp, 71394
Lieut. R.G. Adair, 48481
2nd Lieut. K.W. Dane, 63634
2nd Lieut. P.E. Holmes, 17620
2nd Lieut. L.R. Taylor, 62258

Enlisted Personnel

ASAILI, N., 6337, Pte
ASHBY, A.G., 24884, T/Sgt.
ASIVENI, N., 6315, Pte
ASTON, J.S., 64306, Cpl.
AKUILA, B., 5326, Pte
APENAI, R., 5372, Pte
APENAIA, T., 6248, Pte
APENIAS, V., 6141, Pte
APEROSA, T., 6111, Pte
AMANI, V., 5597, Pte
ANANAIASA, K., 5436, Pte
ATANIO, S., 6307, Pte
AVAKUKI, N., 6142, T/L/Cpl.
AVAROSA, B., 6181, T/L/Cpl.
BASITUKA, F., 6278, Pte
BOKAKA, J., 6145, Pte
BOLTON, F.W., 67802, T/L/Cpl.
BRIGHT, J.C., 64327, T/Sgt.
BURNETT, L.B., 69142, Cpl.

Approved:

PAUL L.F. WEAVER,
Commander, USN.,   *Commanding Officer.*

Examined:

Carter Garthright,
Lieut., USN.,   *Navigator.*

To be forwarded direct to the Commander in Chief, U. S. Fleet, either at end of an operation or at the end of the calendar month

☆ U. S. GOVERNMENT PRINTING OFFICE : 1943   16—33079-1

passed a law creating a semi-autonomous Marine Corps on 11 July 1798. The Marine Corps Act of 1834 placed the Marine Corps in the Navy Department. An act of 1952 recognized the Marine Corps as a separate service. The primary duty of the Marine Corps is to provide amphibious combat forces. Marine detachments also serve on navy ships and protect the property of naval units.

Records of service in the Marine Corps are similar to those of navy personnel. Separate registers for marine personnel, both officers and enlisted personnel, are available at the Marine Corps Historical Center (see chapter 6). Size rolls, 1798 to 1901, contain name, rank, age, place of birth, date and place of enlistment, physical description, and occupation of enlisted men. Descriptive lists, 1879 to 1906, contain much the same information as do the size rolls. Death registers exist for the period 1838 to 1942. Basic personnel record collections are muster rolls, certificate books showing military service, and a card list of casualties, 1776 to 1945 (figure 31).

Coast Guard

The U.S. Coast Guard is an amalgamation of five separate agencies that evolved into the present organization. Revenue cutters, vessels that were used in military and law enforcement roles, were put into use in 1790 and supervised by the Customs Service until 1843, when they were assigned to the Department of Justice. This force was returned to the supervision of customs collectors in 1849, and then it became the Revenue-Cutter Service in 1894. A Life-Saving Service, primarily a civilian organization, was established in 1848 within the Treasury Department. It merged with the Revenue-Cutter Service in 1915 to form the U.S. Coast Guard.

Figure 30. Portion of the War Diary of the USS *Tennessee*, 1941 (courtesy U.S. Naval Historical Center).

SUMMARY OF EVENTS PRIOR TO APRIL 1, 1942

1. Before the declaration of war, which was preceded by the Japanese attack on Pearl Harbor on December 7, this ship was regularly operating as the flagship of Commander Battleship Division TWO, as a part of what was then Task Force ONE. This task force had returned to Pearl Harbor on Friday, November 28, and the battleships had moored alongside the interrupted quays surrounding Ford Island. The TENNESSEE was in Berth F-6, starboard side to, with the WEST VIRGINIA moored along her port side. About 75 feet astern, in Berth F-7, was the ARIZONA with the VESTAL alongside her; the former was undergoing tender overhaul. Ahead of the TENNESSEE in Berth F-5, was the MARYLAND with the OKLAHOMA alongside.

2. The events of December 7th have been covered elsewhere. A copy of the detailed report submitted by the Commanding Officer to the Commander-in-Chief is attached and a brief of the damages sustained by this ship may be found in TENNESSEE letter to the Chief of the Bureau of Ships, file BB43/A16-3/L11-1/(020) of February 11, 1942.

3. During the battle, it was found that the WEST VIRGINIA in sinking had wedged the TENNESSEE between her and the forward pier of the interrupted quay so that this ship could not be moved. Two days after the battle, the MARYLAND was released from her position between the capsized hulk of the OKLAHOMA in Berth F-6 and was taken out to a berth in the Navy Yard. At the same time, it was decided that the TENNESSEE could be gotten clear if the forward pier was blown away, and this was accomplished several days later. On December 16, the pier was cleared and the ship taken out ahead by Navy Yard tugs. The ship was then moored in Berth 17 in the Navy Yard, where some battle damages were repaired. A brief of the repairs and alterations effected follows:

  (a) Made a strength weld of approximately 1500 of cracked seams. Welded points of approximately 2000 rivets.
  (b) Blanked off all airports below the main deck, with exception of about 20.
  (c) Patched top of turret with S.T.S.

4. About 1600, December 20, a force composed of the USS MARYLAND, PENNSYLVANIA, TENNESSEE and 4 destroyers got underway under the command of Rear Admiral W. S. Anderson, Commander Battleships, Battle Force, and proceeded to a position off the West Coast, where the PENNSYLVANIA and 2 destroyers was detached to go to San Francisco, while the remainder of the force proceeded to Bremerton. At 1456, December 29, the ship moored in Berth 6C in the Navy Yard Puget Sound for completion of damage repairs.

5. The ship remained at the Navy Yard from December 29 to

- 1 -

3

As early as 1716, individual colonies created lighthouse services to guide coastal ships. The Treasury Department maintained lighthouses between 1789 and 1852, when the Light-House Board was created within the Treasury Department. The Light-House Board was transferred to the Department of Commerce and Labor in 1903, and in 1913 it was placed in the Department of Commerce—a new, separate agency. In 1939 the Light-House Board was consolidated with the Coast Guard.

Figure 31. Papers From the Personnel File of Private Timothy O'Brien, U.S.M.C., 1895 (courtesy National Archives).

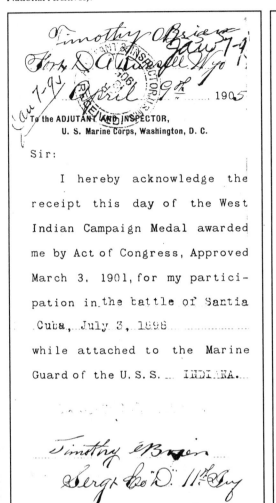

The Coast Guard assumed the functions of the Bureau of Marine Inspection and Navigation in 1942. The Coast Guard became part of the Department of Transportation in 1967 and remains there today. During World War I (1917 and 1918) and the World War II period (1941 through 1946), the Coast Guard was part of the U.S. Navy, but it reverted to its former status at the end of hostilities. Thus, those who served in the Coast Guard performed military duties during the two wars and at the same time were responsible for enforcing the maritime laws involving safe operation of vessels and importation of banned cargo or substances into the United States.

Service records, including muster rolls, payrolls, and "shipping articles" (agreements to serve), are similar to those pertaining to the

DESCRIPTIVE LIST

Name: *O'Brien Timothy* ; Rank, *private*

Born *1 March*, 18*69*, at *Cork. Ireland*

Complexion: *florid* ; Hair: *brn* ; Eyes: *gry*

Other personal characteristics: (permanent marks, scars, &c.) *no marks*

Former residence: *East Cambridge. Mass.*

Former occupation: *laborer*

Family history: —

When and where last examined: *1st Examination*

AGE.		WEIGHT.	HEIGHT.		THORAX.			VISION. (Snellen.)	STATE OF HEALTH SINCE EXAMINATION.
			VERTEX TO GROUND.	VERTEX TO PERINEUM.	MEAN CIRCUMFERENCE.	EXPANSION.	SPIROMETER.		
Years.	Mos.	Pounds.	Inches.	Inches.	Inches.	Inches.	Cu. inches.		
25	10	169	6 9/4	—	37 1/2	3	—	20/20	—

F. B. Stephenson. Surgeon, U. S. N.

Signature of Senior Medical Officer.

REMARKS.

Enlisted *7 January*, 18*95*, at *Boston Mass*, by *Major R. L. Meade U.S.M.C.*

for *five* years. Joined *by Enlistment*, 18___

Shore service, — yrs. — mos. — days. Sea service, — yrs. — mos. — days.

Expiration of last cruise, —, 18___ . Enlistment *First*

Character: ___

Robt. L. Meade

Major, U. S. M. C.,

Commanding, Marine Officer.

4—115

Figure 31. Marine Corps Personnel File (continued).

CONDUCT RECORD of *Timothy O'Brien Private*, U.S.M.C.,
While serving *On board the U.S.S. Indiana* from *Nov 20th 95 Nov 7th 98*

OFFENSE, AND DATE.	PUNISHMENT.	OFFENSE, AND DATE.	PUNISHMENT.
Dec 3rd 1895 Late hammock	2 hrs Ex. duty		
Mch 1st 96 13 hrs over time	2 Mo. Restriction		
July 7th 96 84 hrs over time	4 Mo. "		
Nov. 29th 96 63 hrs over time	3 " "		
Aug 29th 97 17 hrs over time	2 " "		
Aug 29th 98 108 hrs over time	3 " "		
		W.C. Dawson, 1st Lieut M.S.M.C. Comdg Guard.	

Figure 31. Marine Corps Personnel File (continued).

navy and the marines. Shipping articles cover the period 1863 to 1915. Registers of officers and seamen are available in published form.

Merchant Marine

Privately owned vessels crewed by civilian seamen have always transported goods and personnel for the military branches, both in peacetime and during armed conflict. In such capacity they are under the logistical control of the armed forces and are subject to attack by enemy vessels. (See chapter 5 for information concerning documents that show Merchant Marine service during World War II.)

Beginning around 1794 and continuing until at least 1817, seamen of Britain and other seagoing countries customarily boarded American ships and seized any

seamen who could not prove they were American citizens, pressing them into forced service on foreign ships. This practice was one of the major causes of the War of 1812, but it was not restricted solely to that era. The State Department amassed a collection of letters from the Customs Department and from individual citizens; these letters request various forms of relief from the practice. There are also bound registers of applications made for the release of captured seamen, dated 1793 to 1802. In 1816, President James Madison furnished the House of Representatives with three lists containing the names of almost two thousand Americans who had been pressed into British service.

To partially prevent this practice, American seamen could apply for and receive "seamen's protection certificates" to prove their identity when challenged. The certificates showed name, certificate number and date of issue, age, place of birth, how citizenship was obtained (by birth or naturalization), and a detailed physical description. Few certificates are on file because they were in the possession of the seamen. However, a few ports have applications and some supporting documents (see chapter 5).

Congress required the masters of U.S. ships to transmit to the Secretary of State an abstract of all the protests of impressments, which he in turn reports to Congress. The reports are found in Records of the Department of State (*Record Group* 59) and have been published in *American State Papers*.

Indexes to Seamen's Protection Certificate Applications for the Port of Philadelphia: 1776–1823 and 1824–1861 have been prepared by Ruth Priest Dixon, and published by Clearfield Company, Baltimore, Maryland.

Beginning in 1803, masters of American vessels leaving the United States for foreign ports were required to file crew lists with the collectors of customs. Crew lists for various ports are available for inspection. They are arranged by port and in chronological order. These may be seen in various National Archives microfilm series (see chapter 5). The principle ports covered are New York (1803 to 1919), New Orleans (1803 to 1902), Philadelphia (1803 to 1899), and San Francisco (1851 to 1899). The San Francisco lists are available at the National Archives regional archives (Pacific Sierra region) at San Bruno, California (near San Francisco).

Various other records (licenses, hiring lists, oaths of citizenship, etc.) pertaining to seamen employed in such inland ports as Duluth, Minnesota; Dubuque, Iowa; Galena, Illinois; St. Louis, Missouri; and St. Paul, Minnesota, are available. Similar records exist for seamen employed on U.S. Army transport vessels.

Shipping articles (contracts between seamen and vessel owners) were required as early as 1798 until about 1940 and were filed with the collectors of customs. These are arranged by port and chronologically through 1938. To locate these, the researcher must know where and when a merchant seaman was hired. However, records for the ports of New York, Philadelphia, Boston, Baltimore, and San Francisco are indexed by ship in rough alphabetical order.

Records of the Military Academies

Military training academies provide a college degree as well as training for leadership in military service to their graduates. The United States Military Academy at West Point, New York, and the United States Naval Academy at Annapolis, Maryland, are the principal academies insofar as genealogical research material is concerned. The Coast Guard, the Merchant Marine, and the Air Force also operate academies, but those institutions possess only minimal amounts of such material.

UNITED STATES MILITARY ACADEMY
West Point, New York

On 20 June 1777, Congress created a Corps of Invalids to serve garrison duty and "to serve as a military school." By 1782 eight companies had been assigned to that corps, which was stationed at West Point, where a library and school facilities were provided. After the revolutionary war, most of the Continental Army, including the Corps of Invalids, was dissolved, but a plan was put forward to create a military school at West Point. In 1794 the rank of cadet was established, and two cadets were assigned to each of the sixteen companies of a newly organized Corps of Artillerists and Engineers stationed at West Point. Progress was slow until 16 March 1802, when Congress created the U.S. Military Academy. The first class graduated in October 1802. At that time, the academy conducted a one-year training course for officers. In 1921 a four-year curriculum was established, and in 1933 the Association of American Universities authorized the conferring of the bachelor of science degree upon the academy's graduates. After graduation the graduates are commissioned into the U.S. Army.

Official records of the academy comprise National Archives RG 404, but the records are maintained at the academy's West Point archives. These records are arranged according to the administrative entities of the academy; thus, they contain papers from the Office of the Superintendent, Office of the Dean of the Academic Board, Office of the Director of Admissions and Registrar, and so forth. Records of special importance to genealogists are the applications for admission, reports of adjustment and accomplishments while enrolled (grades earned, lists of demerits, periodic reports, etc.), and lists of graduates. Included in some records are data concerning the cadets' families and backgrounds. A separate index lists the names of individuals buried in the academy cemetery.

Many supplemental records created prior to 1838 were destroyed by a fire in the headquarters building. Those dating from 1950 were turned over to the federal records centers at St. Louis and Kansas City and to the National Archives for safekeeping. The academy library has a Special Collections Division, where information concerning its graduates may be found. Alumni files of the Association of Graduates, USMA, through the class of 1894, are also housed in the academy library.

Registers of cadets and cadet applicants, applications for admission, monthly rolls, merit rolls, and academy graduates are also available at the National Archives. These may be found in RG 94 (Office of the Adjutant General).

Several registers and lists are also available on microfilm (figure 32).

UNITED STATES NAVAL ACADEMY

Annapolis, Maryland

The U.S. Naval Academy was established in 1845 at the site of Fort Severn at Annapolis, Maryland. It began operating on 10 October 1845 for the purpose of training midshipmen for careers as naval officers. The academy operated for five years under the Office of the Secretary of the Navy. With the outbreak of the Civil War in 1861, the grounds were taken over by the army for use as a base hospital. The Naval Academy moved to Newport, Rhode Island, and was accommodated at Fort Adams. In September 1865, at the close of the war, the academy was reestablished at Annapolis and has remained there since. The academy once functioned under the direction of the Bureau of Navigation, but since May 1942 it has operated under the Bureau of Naval Personnel. Between 1866 and 1874 a two-year course was conducted. The curriculum was later enlarged to four years; however, during World War I and World War II, the program was accelerated to enable completion in three years. Graduates of the academy may opt for a commission in the Marine Corps or in the U.S. Navy.

Official records of the academy were placed in National Archives RG 405, but they are maintained at the academy at Annapolis. Most of the records cover the period 1845

REGISTER OF CADET WARRANTS.

Name HOUGLAND, JOHN MASON

Date of Warrant June 23, 1906.

Year of Independence 130th.

Date of Rank June 15, 1906.

Sec. of War WM. H. TAFT.

The Mily. Secy.
~~Adjt. Gen.~~ F. C. AINSWORTH.

Figure 32. Register of Cadet Warrants, U.S. Military Academy (courtesy National Archives).

to 1927. They consist mainly of papers of the Office of the Superintendent, the Reserve Training Groups (which met at the academy during both world wars), and the Office of the Commandant of Midshipmen or Cadets. Records of special importance to genealogists are applications for admission, records of adjustment (grades earned, lists of demerits, periodic reports, etc.), and lists of graduates. Included in some records is data concerning the cadets' families.

2

Types of Records: Post-Service Records and Records Relating to Civilian Affairs

2

Types of Records: Post-Service Records and Records Relating to Civilian Affairs

W
hile many record collections provide information about individuals' service in the nation's military branches, even more detailed information about an individual may often be obtained from records created after discharge from the military. These records include those that refer to payments of bonuses, bounties, pensions, claims for reimbursement, and hardship payments to family members. They also include records of residents of soldiers' or sailors' homes and patients of veterans' hospitals. Records of death and burial and grave markers are also helpful in completing the stories of former military men and women.

of the Secretary of War, the Office of Military Bounty Lands and Pensions, administered the program. This unit was eventually separated into the Land Warrant Bureau and the Pension Office, and in 1832 a commissioner of pensions was named. The Pension Office was transferred to the newly created Department of the Interior on 3 March 1849. Known as the Bureau of Pensions, the organization remained there until July 1930, when it was merged with other offices that were also involved in veterans' affairs. All such duties were then assumed by the newly created independent agency known as the Veterans Administration. This agency was elevated to the Department of Veterans Affairs on 15 March 1989.

Pensions

American colonial governments granted pensions for disabled soldiers and sailors long before the American Revolution. The practice was continued when the U.S. government was established and when benefits were expanded to include dependents of veterans. When the federal government assumed responsibility for military pensions, the secretary of war became responsible for administering the program. In 1818 a unit in the Office

Revolutionary War

Three principal types of pensions were authorized for revolutionary war veterans and their dependents: "disability" or "invalid" pensions for physical disabilities incurred in the line of duty; "service pensions" for service in a certain stated period of time; and "widows' pensions" to wives of servicemen who were killed in the war or who served a certain stated period of time. Major provisions of the pension laws are summarized below.

26 Aug 1776   Half pay for officers and men disabled in the service and who were in-

capable of earning a living, the pension to continue for the period of disability.

15 May 1778   Half pay for seven years after the conclusion of the war to all officers who remained in Continental service to the end of the war; a gratuity of $80 for all enlisted men who served to the end of the war.

24 Aug 1780   Half pay for seven years to widows and orphans of officers who qualified under the provisions enacted 15 May 1778.

21 Oct 1780   Half pay for life to officers (changed to five years on 22 March 1783).

Many pensions were paid by the states, especially Virginia, as an inducement for recruitment. On 29 September 1789, the federal government assumed the responsibility for paying pensions formerly paid by the states, and on 23 March 1790 provided that veterans not yet receiving pensions could apply directly to the federal government.

10 Apr 1806   Pensions were authorized to veterans of state troops and militias, rather than only to those who had served in the Continental Army or Navy.

18 Mar 1818   Pensions for life were authorized based on a period of service (in Continental service or in the U.S. Navy or the marines) of nine months or until the end of the war to those in need of assistance but regardless of whether a disability was present.

1 May 1820   Certified inventories of a pensioner's estate and income were required. Those not able to prove need were removed from the pension files. Upon further application and proof of need, many were restored to the rolls after a relaxation of the criteria was instituted on 1 March 1823.

15 May 1828   Full pay for life to officers and enlisted men who became eligible under the terms of the 15 May 1778 legislation.

7 June 1832   Full pay for life to officers and enlisted men who served two years in the Continental Line or state troops, volunteers, or militia. Naval officers and enlisted men were included. Those with service of less than two years but a minimum of six months were eligible for pensions of some amount less than full pay. Widows

and children were authorized to receive money due the pensioner if it had not been paid before his death.

24 July 1836   Widows were authorized pensions that would have been authorized to the veteran if he were still alive, provided the widow had married the veteran while he was still in service.

7 July 1838   Widows were authorized pensions for five years if they had married the veteran before 1 January 1794.

29 July 1848   Widows were authorized pensions for life if they had married the veteran before 2 January 1800.

3 Feb 1853   All restrictions relative to date of a widow's marriage were eliminated.

9 Mar 1878   Widows were authorized pensions for life if the veteran had served as few as fourteen days or participated in any engagement.

To obtain a pension, the applicant was required to appear before a court of record in the state of residence to establish proof of military service (figure 33). Widows were required to make a declaration and offer supporting documents, such as marriage records, property schedules, and witnesses' affidavits. The court certified the accuracy of the papers and forwarded them to the appropriate federal agency in charge of pensions. After approval (sometimes only after submission of further documentation), the applicant was placed on the pension list and began receiving checks as provided for by the then-current law. Often, applicants who were denied pensions reapplied later when requirements were relaxed.

The pension file is a ten- by fourteen-inch envelope that contains the application and all supporting papers. The number of pages in a file can run to two hundred or more, but they typically number approximately thirty pages. Papers pertaining to widows or other dependents are filed jointly with papers filed by veterans or in separate envelopes designated by the veteran's name. Documents relating to bounty-land claims (see below) are also filed in the same envelope with the pension documents. Each file has a number preceded by the letter S (survivor) or W (widow). Applications that were not approved have a number preceded by the letter R (rejected). In these latter cases, previously filed and approved applications may be found in the same envelope (figure 34).

A fire in the War Department in November 1800 destroyed almost all pension and bounty-land files submitted before that date. There are a few file envelopes, however, that relate to applications filed before that date.

These bear the demarcation "Dis. No Papers." These envelopes were created on the basis of pension claims submitted for Congressional approval between 1792 and 1795, when such claims required such approval. A list of these claims can be found in the publication *American State Papers, Class 9, Claims* (Washington, D.C.: 1834), available at the reading room of the National Archives, the Library of Congress, and other major libraries. Some other pension files were destroyed in another War Department fire in 1814, and envelopes for some of them were also created, again bearing the demarcation "Dis. No Papers." Some pension files submitted to the state of Virginia before the federal government assumed responsibility are also available in a separate collection titled Virginia Half-Pay.

Revolutionary war pension files are now in the custody of the National Archives. They are arranged alphabetically by the name of the veteran and are indexed; both files and index are available on microfilm.

"Old Wars"

A separate collection of pension files based on death or disability incurred in the service during the conflicts known as "Old Wars" refers to career or "regular" servicemen who filed pension claims during the period after the revolutionary war and before the Civil War. Some files, however, may have been consolidated with pension files for veterans of the War of 1812, the Mexican War, Indian wars, and the Civil War, especially if the veteran also served in volunteer units in any of those wars. These files are arranged alphabetically by the name of the veteran and are indexed. The index is available on microfilm (figure 35).

War of 1812

By acts of Congress in 1871 and 1878, pensions were authorized to veterans who served between 1812 and 1815, provided they did not later support the Confederate States of America. The legislation provided pensions to veterans who had served fourteen days in any engagement and to their widows. These files include papers such as declarations by the applicant and an official document from the Treasury Department containing a summary of the applicant's military service. Claims for bounty land are filed in the same jacket that holds the pension documents. The files are arranged alphabetically by the name of the veteran. An index of pensions and bounty-land warrants

is available on microfilm, and the original files are available at the National Archives.

Indian Wars

Pensions were authorized for those military personnel who participated in various Indian wars between 1817 and 1898. However, several of the files may be found in the Old Wars series or in the series for service in the War of 1812, the Mexican War, and the Civil War, especially if action against the Indians took place concurrently with other wars. In addition to the usual information found in pension files, applicants in this series were required to complete personal history questionnaires and also family questionnaires showing the maiden name of the veteran's wife, date and place of marriage, and the name of the person who conducted the ceremony. Also included are names of any former wife, date and place of her death or divorce, and names and dates of birth of living children. The files are arranged alphabetically by the name of the veteran. An index is available on microfilm, and the original files are available at the National Archives.

Mexican War

Pensions were authorized for those who served at least sixty days during the period 1846 through 1848. Widows who had not remarried were also authorized pensions. A part of the file included a family questionnaire similar to that found in Indian war files. Some files for service in this war may have been consolidated with "Old Wars" pension files. The files are arranged alphabetically by the name of the veteran. An index is available on microfilm, and the original files are available at the National Archives.

Civil War—Union

During the Civil War (1861 through 1865), pensions were authorized for veterans of the Union army, navy, and marines. Pensions were also authorized during later years through 1916, notably for service during the Spanish-American War, the Philippine Insurrection, the Boxer Rebellion, and for service as a regular (career) serviceman. The federal government did not authorize pensions for service in Confederate forces until 1959; by that time few veterans of the Civil War were still living.

Figure 33. State Court Papers Pertaining to Application for Revolutionary War Pension, State of Maine (courtesy Maine State Archives).

STATE OF MAINE.

Hancock ss.....At a Circuit Court of Common Pleas for the *third* Eastern Circuit, begun and holden at *Castine* within and for the County of *Hancock* on the *second tuesday of July* being the *eleventh* day of *July* ~~and by adjournment~~ from day to ~~day, on the~~ ~~day of~~ in the year of our Lord one thousand eight hundred and twenty, ~~before the Honorable~~ ~~Judge of said Court.~~

ON this *eleventh* day of *July* in the year 1820, personally appeared *in open court* the same proceeding according to the course of the common law, having jurisdiction unlimited in amount, keeping a record of their proceedings, and having " the power of fine and imprisonment," and being a Court of Record for said Circuit, *Courtney Babbidge* aged *Fifty nine* years, resident in *Vinalhaven* in said Circuit, who being first duly sworn according to law, doth on his oath declare that he served in the Revolutionary War as follows, viz. as a *Private* in the company commanded by Capt. *Lord* in the Regiment commanded by Colonel *Sprout* in the line of the State of *Massachusetts* on the Continental Establishment, as is more particularly mentioned and described in his original declaration, made on the *Sixth* day of *May* A. D. 181*8*, and on which said declaration his Certificate of Pension, numbered *13,719* was granted. And I do solemnly swear that I was a resident citizen of the United States on the 18th day of March 1818 ; and that I have not since that time by gift, sale, or in any manner disposed of my property, or any part thereof, with intent thereby so to diminish it as to bring myself within the provisions of an Act of Congress, entitled " An Act to provide for certain persons engaged in the land and naval service of the United States, in the Revolutionary War," passed on the 18th day of March, 1818 : and that I have not, nor has any person in trust for me, any property or securities, contracts, or debts due to me ; nor have I any income other than what is contained in the schedule hereto annexed, and by me subscribed ; that my occupation and ability to pursue the same, together with the number and other particulars of my family, are in fact and in truth as is particularly described on the back hereof, also subscribed by me.

Courtney Babbidge

Sworn to and declared, on the *11th* day of *July* A. D. 1820.

BEFORE *the court*

{ One of the Judges of the said Court.

attest *Meson Shaw Clerk*

SCHEDULE *of the real and personal estate, (necessary clothing and bedding excepted) belonging to me the subscriber, viz :*

Yoke oxen 40$ 2 Cows @14$ 10 Sheep 12$	$ 62.00
1 yearling 4$ 1 Swine 4$ Plough 6/ Chain 6/	10.00
Shovel 3/ Hoe 1/6 Scythe 3/ Rake 1/6 ax 3/ Saw 3/	2.50
Pot 6/ Kettle 3/ Tea Kettle 3/ Spider 1/6 Keg 1/6	2.50
6 Milk Pans 6/ Churn 3/ other Dairy furniture 6/	2.50
Tongs 3/ Chest 6/ Table 3/ Coffee Pot Tin Pail Funnel &c 6/	3.00
Sett Cups Bowls Tea Pot & other Crockery ware 12/	2.00
6 Knives & Forks 6/ Spoons 3/ 8 Chairs Bench & Stool 9/	3.00
Bible & lot Pamphlets 6/ Bush. Corn 4/6 20" Pork 12/	3.75
1 Cheese 6/ Basket Tub bbl & sundry small articles 12/	3.00
	94.25

Claim vs Abner Babbidge Estate doubtful worth probably from 15 to 20 Dollars see other side }

Annual Income by Labour — $ 20.00
Ditto from my wifes Property (see other side) 3.00 $23.00

Courtney Babbidge

SCHEDULE *of the family residing with me* Courtney Babbidge
who, by occupation am a Farmer *which I am un able to pursue by*
reason of lameness in my wrist except but partially

NAMES.	AGES.	Capacity of each to contribute to their support.
Catherine Babbidge	44	one half – Dropsical & Paralytic
Olive Smith (wifes daughter)	17	common capacity
Lydia Babbidge	14	Ditto
Bester Babbidge	10	weak & sickly
Melinda Stimpson (wifes children)	10	Ditto
Rebecca Stimpson	7	common ability
Walter Babbidge	4	nothing
Benjamin Babbidge	2	Ditto

Courtney Babbidge

Figure 34. Papers From Pension File for Revolutionary War Veteran Thomas Moore (courtesy National Archives). Below: Thomas Moore's application for a pension, 1819.

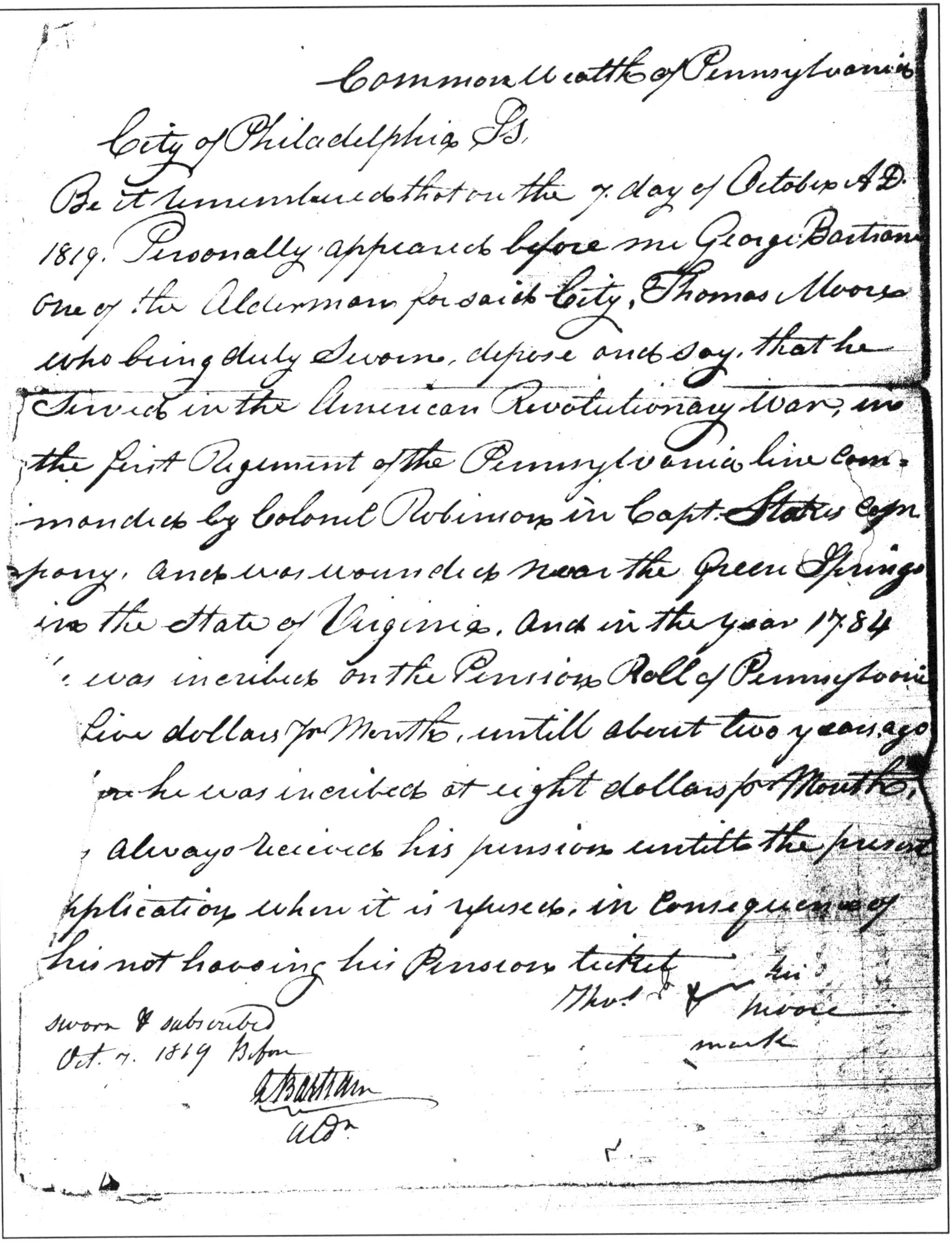

Commonwealth of Pennsylvania

City of Philadelphia SS.

Be it remembered that on the 7. day of October AD. 1819. Personally appeared before me George Bartram one of the Aldermen for said City, Thomas Moore who being duly Sworn, depose and say. that he Served in the American Revolutionary War, in the first Regiment of the Pennsylvania line commanded by Colonel Robinson in Capt. States company, and was wounded near the Green Springs in the State of Virginia. And in the year 1784 was incribed on the Pension Roll of Pennsylvania five dollars Pr Month, untill about two years ago or he was incribed at eight dollars Pr Month, always received his pension untill the present application when it is refused. in Consequence of his not having his Pension ticket

Thos. ✗ Moore
his mark

sworn & subscribed
Oct. 7. 1819 Before
G Bartram
Ald.

Military service statement for Moore, 1893.

BUREAU OF PENSIONS,

Washington, D. C., *May* , 189*3*

Sir

In reply to your request for a statement of the military history of

Thomas Moore , a soldier of the Revolutionary War, you will please find below the desired information as contained in his application for pension on file in this Bureau.

DATES OF ENLISTMENT.	LENGTH OF SERVICE	RANK.	OFFICERS UNDER WHOM SERVICE WAS RENDERED.		STATE.
			CAPTAIN.	COLONEL.	
March 1781	2 mo	Pri	Hugh Wardlaw	Anderson	S.C
May 1781	10 "	" Corp	Richard Johnson	Samuel Hammond	do
Served	2 "	"	Against Indians		

Battles engaged in, *Capture Fort Grayson Ga: Siege of 96 S.C. & Eutaw Springs*

Residence of soldier at enlistment, *District of 96 S.C*

Date of application for pension, *April 1833*

Residence at date of application, *Abbeville District SC*

Age at date of application, *born in Ireland in 1763 or 4 & came to America in*

Remarks: *Infantry*

Correspondence concerning Moore.

Mrs. Harry A. Hunt   Rev. & 1812 Wars Section
650 Riverview Avenue   ANF:MLB
Portsmouth, Virginia

Dear Madam:

    You are advised that it appears from the papers in the
Revolutionary War pension claim, S. 36169, that Thomas Moore
enlisted in Pittsburgh, Pennsylvania in January, 1777, and
served in Captains Benjamin Harrison's and Uriah Springer's
companies, Colonels Russell's and John Gibson's Virginia
regiments. He was in the battles of Brandywine and Germantown and served three years. He stated that he was out
under Colonel Brodhead against the Indians, also with
General A. Wayne in his Indian campaign.

    He was allowed pension on his application executed
November 2, 1818, at which time he was living in Bracken
County, Kentucky and was aged fifty-seven years.

    In 1820 he stated that his wife was aged fifty-eight
years, but did not give her name, and at this time he
referred to two children, twins, David and Jonathan as aged
fifteen years.

    The soldier died August 18, 1825.

        Very truly yours

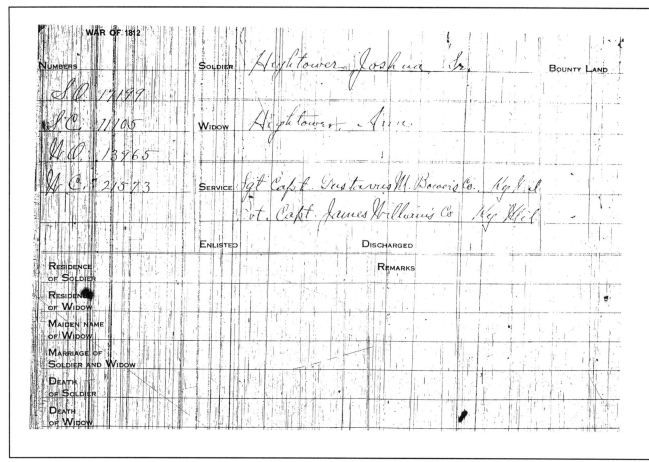

Figure 35. Index to War of 1812 Pension Files (courtesy National Archives).

Requirements for a pension varied according to congressional amendments after the original 1862 legislation. Each amendment extended the benefits by more liberal terms. Veterans, widows, parents, and minor dependents were eligible for pensions under certain conditions, and each was required to file an application. The files contain much military service and family information. Included are a declaration by the claimant, a statement of service from the War Department or the Navy Department, a personal history questionnaire, a family questionnaire, and affidavits by comrades-in-arms, relatives, and neighbors attesting to the validity of the claimant's declarations. Where disability and need were factors in the decision, medical reports of physical condition were included. Contrary to custom of several years ago, the medical documents were not withheld and are routinely part of the general file.

The *General Index to Pension Files, 1861–1934*, is available on microfilm (T288). The original files are available at the National Archives (figures 36 and 37).

Figure 36. Index to Civil War Pension Files–Union (courtesy National Archives).

Civil War–Confederate

The Southern states and the border states authorized pensions for Confederate service. These pensions were paid from state funds. Dates of enactment varied from state to state, and requirements for eligibility varied considerably, as did the amounts paid. One consistency among them, however, is the fact that veterans were permitted to

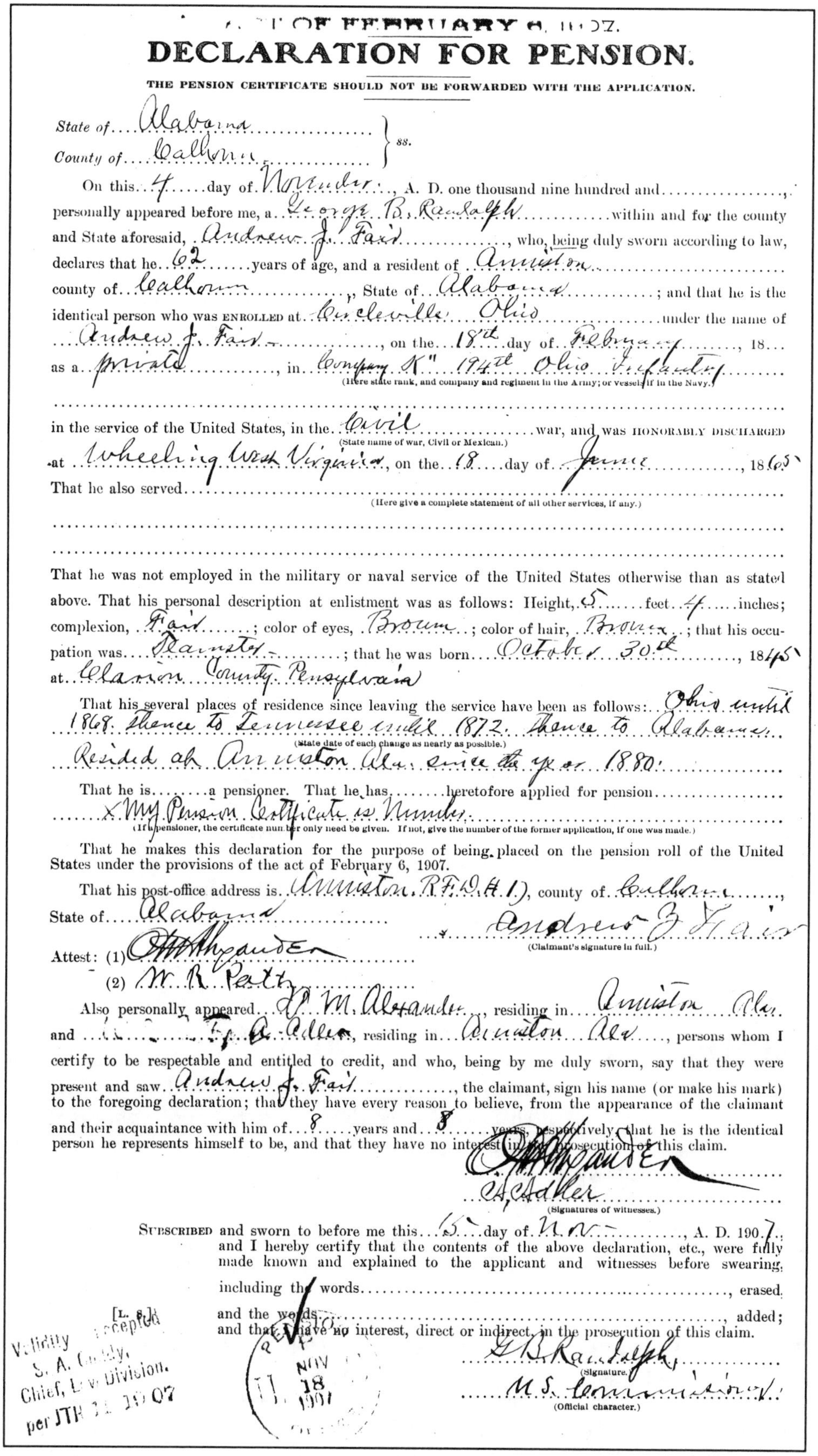

ACT OF FEBRUARY 6, 1907.

DECLARATION FOR PENSION.

THE PENSION CERTIFICATE SHOULD NOT BE FORWARDED WITH THE APPLICATION.

State of _Alabama_

County of _Calhoun_ } ss.

On this _4_ day of _November_, A. D. one thousand nine hundred and _____,
personally appeared before me, a _George B. Randolph_ within and for the county
and State aforesaid, _Andrew J. Fair_, who, being duly sworn according to law,
declares that he _62_ years of age, and a resident of _Anniston_
county of _Calhoun_, State of _Alabama_; and that he is the
identical person who was ENROLLED at _Circleville, Ohio_ under the name of
Andrew J. Fair, on the _18th_ day of _February_, 18__
as a _private_, in _Company "K" 184th Ohio Infantry_
(Here state rank, and company and regiment in the Army; or vessel, if in the Navy.)

in the service of the United States, in the _Civil_ war, and was HONORABLY DISCHARGED
(State name of war, Civil or Mexican.)
at _Wheeling West Virginia_, on the _18_ day of _June_, 18_65_
That he also served _____

_____
(Here give a complete statement of all other services, if any.)

_____

That he was not employed in the military or naval service of the United States otherwise than as stated
above. That his personal description at enlistment was as follows: Height, _5_ feet, _4_ inches;
complexion, _Fair_; color of eyes, _Brown_; color of hair, _Brown_; that his occu-
pation was _Teamster_; that he was born _October 30th_, 18_45_
at _Clarion County, Pensylvania_
That his several places of residence since leaving the service have been as follows: _Ohio until_
1868. thence to Tennessee until 1872. thence to Alabama.
(State date of each change as nearly as possible.)
Resided at Anniston Ala. since the year 1880.
That he is ____ a pensioner. That he has ____ heretofore applied for pension ____
X My Pension Certificate is Number
(If pensioner, the certificate number only need be given. If not, give the number of the former application, if one was made.)

That he makes this declaration for the purpose of being placed on the pension roll of the United
States under the provisions of the act of February 6, 1907.

That his post-office address is _Anniston, R.F.D.(H.1)_, county of _Calhoun_,
State of _Alabama_   _Andrew J. Fair_
(Claimant's signature in full.)

Attest: (1) _P.M. Alexander_

(2) _W. R. Rath_

Also personally appeared _P. M. Alexander_, residing in _Anniston Ala._
and _A. Adler_, residing in _Anniston Ala._, persons whom I
certify to be respectable and entitled to credit, and who, being by me duly sworn, say that they were
present and saw _Andrew J. Fair_, the claimant, sign his name (or make his mark)
to the foregoing declaration; that they have every reason to believe, from the appearance of the claimant
and their acquaintance with him of _8_ years and _8_ years, respectively, that he is the identical
person he represents himself to be, and that they have no interest in the prosecution of this claim.

P. M. Alexander
A. Adler
(Signatures of witnesses.)

SUBSCRIBED and sworn to before me this _5_ day of _Nov._, A. D. 190_7_,
and I hereby certify that the contents of the above declaration, etc., were fully
made known and explained to the applicant and witnesses before swearing,
including the words _____, erased,
and the words _____, added;
and that I have no interest, direct or indirect, in the prosecution of this claim.

G. B. Randolph
(signature.)
U.S. Commissioner
(Official character.)

[L. s.]

Validity
accepted
S. A. Grady,
Chief, Law Division.
per JTB 1907

NOV 18 1907

Figure 37. Declaration for Pension, Civil War—Union (courtesy National Archives).

apply for and receive a pension from the state in which they resided at the time of application, regardless of their state of residence before or during the time of military service. In some instances, however, a state imposed a minimum residency period, presumably to deter veterans from moving to a state where eligibility requirements or payment schedules were more liberal than the state in which they previously lived. In all cases, the veteran or widow was required to show financial need, and in some cases evidence of physical disability. The early pensions were granted solely to compensate for limbs lost in battle, but they were generally liberalized to include any later physical disabilities. For detailed summaries of pension laws and practices in the Southern states, see James C. Neagles' *Confederate Research Sources: A Guide to Archive Collections* (Salt Lake City: Ancestry, 1986.)

Confederate pension files are available only in state archives and may or may not be available on microfilm. Most have alphabetical indexes. The contents of pension records available in state archives are described in chapter 8, which details state records.

Wars of the Twentieth Century

Although bonuses were sometimes paid for military service during the twentieth century, no federal pensions were authorized. Bonuses or pensions were paid occasionally by certain states.

Navy Pensions

Before 1799, pensions for navy veterans were paid largely by the states. On 2 March 1799, Congress created the Navy Pension Fund, which was financed with money from the sale of prizes taken at sea. This fund was managed and directed by the secretary of the navy, the secretary of the treasury, and the secretary of war. In 1832 the fund was transferred to the treasurer of the United States. The secretary of the navy was made the sole trustee of the fund and was charged with receiving and approving pension applications and paying the amounts due. In 1840, Congress stipulated that the commissioner of pensions assume control over all pension funds, including the Navy Pension Fund, but the secretary of the navy was to remain trustee

of the fund until 1932, when the function was transferred to the Veterans Administration.

Before 1812, only invalid pensions were paid by the fund, but in 1813 half-pay pensions were authorized for five years to widows and children of navy officers and sailors who died in the line of duty. If the widow died or remarried during the five-year period, the children were entitled to a pension for the remainder of the five-year term. In 1817, eligibility was extended to widows and children of navy officers and seamen who died from disease or injury received in the line of duty. This eligibility was revoked in 1824 because of the expense, but it was reinstituted in 1834 with the possibility of extending the five-year period for an additional five years. That action also authorized half pay to widows and children regardless of the cause of the veteran's death, and it stipulated that the payments would be retroactive to the time the disability occurred. When the money in the fund was exhausted, payments were made from congressional appropriations.

With the outbreak of the Civil War, the amount of money realized from the capture of vessels and cargo enabled the fund to be reactivated. The surplus money thus obtained was invested in U.S. securities, and a separate navy account was continued until it was transferred to the Veterans Administration. Beginning at the time of the Civil War there was a general pension system that encompassed all military personnel and their dependents. Under that system disabilities were classified by degree and payments were scaled accordingly. Several changes regarding pensions for the widows and children of navy veterans were made before 1890, and the laws continued to be amended in future years through 1908.

Applications and supporting papers for pensions to navy veterans were kept separate from other service branches and were placed in two series: widows' (or other dependents') originals (NWO) and widows' (or other dependents') certificates (NWC). Each record was assigned a certificate or file number, and a card was created for each that showed the number along with the name of the veteran and his rank or rating. This system continued until around 1910, when the files were consolidated with army claims for the Civil War and later years.

Each approved navy pension application file (and the corresponding card) for the period 1861 through 1910 was reproduced on microfiche. (Sometimes more than one microfiche was needed to contain all of the data in the original file.) This microfiche series, referred to as "Navy Widows' Certificates," is available in the Microfilm Room of the National Archives.

A more-accessible source for navy pensions based on service during the Civil War and later is the microfilm *General Index to Pensions* (described in chapter 3).

Bounty-Land Grants

As an inducement to potential military recruits, the federal government offered free land in the public domain for military service. This procedure began with the revolutionary war and was continued until 1855. No bounty land was awarded thereafter, this incentive being replaced by the Homestead Act in 1862. Claimants were required to submit a claim to the appropriate federal agency and to support the claim with evidence of identity, military history, and family data. When an application was approved, a "warrant" for a specified number of acres was issued to the claimant. That document permitted the claimant to "locate" a desired plot in the public domain and then turn in his warrant in exchange for a "patent," which gave him title to the land. Usually, the transaction was then recorded at the county courthouse as a matter of public record. Those who received a land warrant but did not choose to relocate were permitted to sell their warrants, often to land developers who bought them for resale at a profit. Land entry papers contain the name of the person who eventually used the warrant to take title of the land. This person might be an heir to the veteran or someone unrelated. Exceptions are the warrants issued for service in the War of 1812, when warrants were not assignable.

Copies of warrants surrendered when the patents were issued, except some earlier ones (those numbered 1 to 6,912, which were destroyed in the 1800 and 1814 War Department fires), are available. The files are identified by the abbreviation "B.L.Wt," followed by a serial number, the number of acres granted, and the year of the enabling legislation—for example: B.L.Wt. 79615-160-55. The National Archives has an alphabetical list of warrants issued, but the bounty-land information has been incorporated into the pension file pertaining to the soldier.

Most revolutionary war warrants issued before 1855 were for land in the Military District of Ohio. Later, the warrants could be exchanged for scrip and used to purchase land in Ohio, Indiana, Illinois, and, by 1842, any land in the public domain.

The early War of 1812 warrants could be used only in designated tracts of 160 acres (double that amount in some instances) in Arkansas, Illinois, and Missouri. The actual warrant was sent to the General Land Office, and the veteran was notified of its presence. Later warrants could be exchanged for scrip that could be used to acquire land anywhere in the public domain. Alphabetical indexes of patentees in the three states mentioned above and also for warrants for use in any public domain land are available at the National Archives. However, the index for Illinois includes only those whose surnames begin with *C* or *D*. In each case a description of the land is given. A supplementary series of volumes, *Records of Land Warrants, Act of 1812*, serves as an additional index to the warrants (see chapter 9).

In 1847 Congress liberalized the bounty-land acts by granting eligibility to additional types of service personnel (wagonmasters and others) who had served as few as fourteen days. Originally, the amount of land granted varied according to the rank of the veteran, with high-ranking officers receiving the larger tracts. In accordance with the 1847 amendments, enlisted men who had received fewer than 160 acres were entitled to enlarge their holding up to 160 acres. Applications for warrants at the National Archives for the period after 1847 are arranged alphabetically, but the names of those to whom patents were issued are not indexed. There is little or no genealogical information in these applications.

State Bounty-Land Awards

For revolutionary war service of three years or more in a state or Continental unit, Virginia veterans or their heirs were offered bounty-land warrants that were exchangeable in the Virginia Military District of Ohio, which was then a part of Virginia. This land was located within the present bounds of Ohio and Kentucky, south of the Green River. Records relating to these warrants are available at the state archives of Virginia, Ohio, and Kentucky.

The state of Pennsylvania awarded "donation land" in the western part of the state in exchange for revolutionary war service, and related records are available at the state archives of Pennsylvania. The federal government awarded no bounty land in Pennsylvania because no part of the state was in the public domain. The state of Massachusetts awarded bounty land to revolutionary war veterans in the area that was later to become the state of Maine but which was then a part of Massachusetts. Related information is available at the Massachusetts state archives. New York also granted revolutionary war bounty land in its western areas (figure 38).

Bonuses and Family Assistance

In the mid-1930s, during the Great Depression, when the economy needed a boost and many citizens were destitute, the federal government awarded cash bonuses to all veterans of World War I.

No federal bonuses were paid to veterans of World War II or later wars or conflicts, but some states authorized bonuses for veterans of World War II, the Korean War, and the Vietnam War. In these instances, the state archives have index cards showing the name of the veteran, related military and personal data, and the amount paid.

In many states, separate state or county agencies were created to render financial aid to families of veterans. Generally, these agencies ceased to exist after state and federal public assistance programs were inaugurated during the 1930s, but a few continued for a time afterward. State archives and county courthouses have records of money paid to residents in need. Generally, these are in the form of minutes of actions taken by the members of the local agency, and they include the names of the recipients (figure 39).

Soldiers' Homes

United States Soldiers' Home

The United States Soldiers' Home, renamed the United States Soldiers' and Airmen's Home in 1972, is in Washington, D.C. This home, originally known as the United States Military Asylum, was created by Congress in 1851. At that time two other homes were established at East Pascagoula, Mississippi, and New Orleans. Later, another home was opened at Harrodsburg, Kentucky.

However, these three homes closed after brief periods of operation, leaving the Washington, D.C., home the only one still in operation. This home how accepts veterans and widows from any branch of the military.

Records at the National Archives consist of muster rolls, hospital registers (1872 to 1943), and death records (1852 to 1942) for all four homes. There are also case files for deceased members (residents of the home). These are alphabetically arranged and show the member's military and home history; date, place, and cause of death; and date and place of burial (figure 40).

National Homes for Disabled Volunteer Soldiers

In 1866 Congress established a series of national homes for needy veterans of the army, marines, and organized militia called into federal service, regardless of whether they were part of the regular establishment or of volunteer units—provided they were disabled by disease or wounds, were without adequate means of support, and were incapable of earning a living. Later, women who had served as nurses or in other capacities were also eligible for admission. After 1930 these homes became known as Veterans Administration Homes. Registers of residents for most of the homes are available at the National Archives. These include registers of deaths and registers of hospitalization. Burial registers are rare. Branch homes were founded in the following cities in the years shown.

Togus, Maine: 1866

Dayton, Ohio: 1867

Wood, Wisconsin: 1867

Kecoughtan, Virginia: 1870

Leavenworth, Kansas: 1885

Sawtelle, California: 1888

Marion, Indiana: 1888

Roseburg, Oregon: 1894

Danville, Illinois: 1898

Johnson City, Tennessee: 1903

Hot Springs, South Dakota: 1907

Bath, New York: 1929

St. Petersburg, Florida: 1930

Biloxi, Mississippi: 1930

Tuskegee, Alabama: 1933

Figure 38. List of Applications for Bounty-Land Granted by the State of New York for Civil War Service (courtesy New York State Archives).

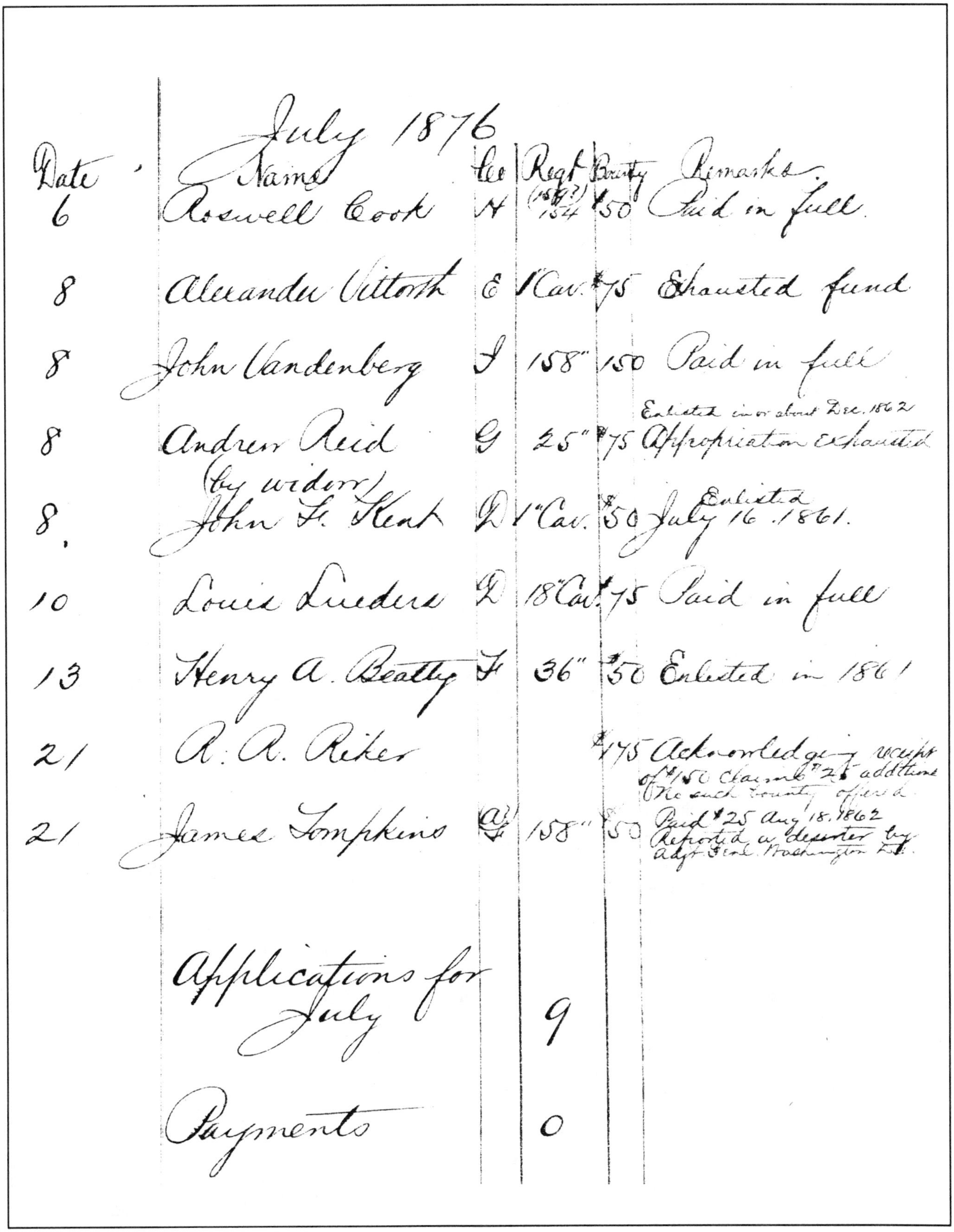

July 1876

Date	Name	Co	Regt	Bounty	Remarks
6	Roswell Cook	H	(159?) 154	$50	Paid in full.
8	Alexander Vittorth	E	1 Cav.	$75	Exhausted fund
8	John Vandenberg	I	158"	150	Paid in full
8	Andrew Reid	G	25"	$75	Enlisted in or about Dec. 1862 Appropriation exhausted
8	(by widow) John F. Kent	D	1 Cav.	$50	Enlisted July 16. 1861.
10	Louis Lueders	D	18 Cav.	$75	Paid in full
13	Henry A. Beatty	F	36"	$50	Enlisted in 1861
21	A. A. Riker			$175	Acknowledging receipt of $150 claims $25 additional No such bounty offered
21	James Tompkins	G F	158"	$50	Paid $25 Aug 18. 1862 Reported a deserter by Adjt Genl Washington D.C.

Applications for July 9

Payments 0

Figure 39. List of Persons Receiving Assistance Based on Civil War Military Service, New Hampshire, 1866 (courtesy New Hampshire State Archives).

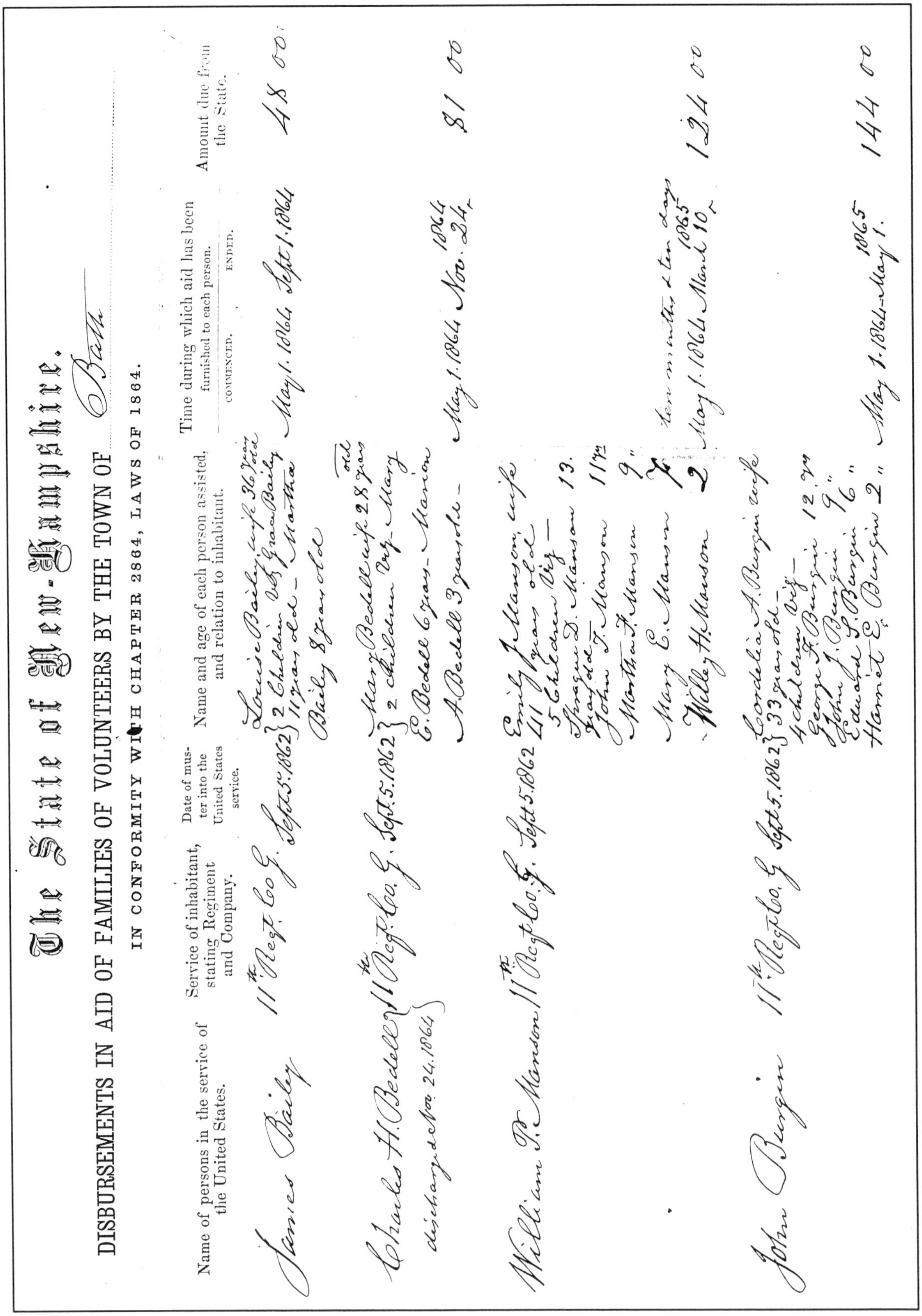

The State of New-Hampshire.

DISBURSEMENTS IN AID OF FAMILIES OF VOLUNTEERS BY THE TOWN OF Bath

IN CONFORMITY WITH CHAPTER 2864, LAWS OF 1864.

Name of persons in the service of the United States.	Service of inhabitant, stating Regiment and Company.	Date of muster into the United States service.	Name and age of each person assisted, and relation to inhabitant.	Time during which aid has been furnished to each person. Commenced.	Ended.	Amount due from the State.
James Bailey	11th Regt. Co G.	Sept 5. 1862	Louise Bailey wife 36 years old; 2 Children Viz Grace Bailey 11 years old – Martha Bailey 8 years old	May 1. 1864	Sept 1. 1864	48 00
Charles H. Bedell discharged Nov. 24. 1864	11th Regt. Co. G.	Sept. 5. 1862	Mary Bedell wife 28 years old; 2 children Viz – Mary E. Bedell 6 years – Marion A. Bedell 3 years old –	May 1. 1864	Nov. 24, 1864	81 00
William P. Manson	11th Regt Co. G.	Sept 5. 1862	Emily J. Manson, wife 41 years old; 5 Children Viz – Sprague D. Manson 13. years old; John T. Manson 11 yrs; Martha F. Manson 9 "; Mary E. Manson 7; Willey H. Manson 2	ten months & ten days; May 1. 1864	March 10, 1865	124 00
John Burgin	11th Regt Co. G	Sept 5. 1862	Cordelia A. Burgin wife 33 years old –; 4 children Viz – George F. Burgin 12 yrs; John J. Burgin 9 "; Edward S. Burgin 6 "; Harriet E. Burgin 2 "	May 1. 1864	May 1. 1865	144 00

Figure 40. Register of Persons Admitted to the United States Soldiers' Home, Washington D.C., 1902 (top: left-hand page; bottom: right-hand page) (courtesy National Archives).

REGISTER OF THE SICK TREATED at

No.	NAMES.	Age.	Nativity.	Regiment or Corps from Where Discharged.	Diagnosis.
8302	Fitch. Chas.	68	Ger	E 4 Cav	Musc Rheumatis
8303	Johnson, Wm C.	54	U.S.	Army Sur.	Otitis
8304	Cronin, Mich. P.	50	Irish	Ord.	Potts Fracture.
8305	Woods, John, S.	42	Eng	Eng	Indigestion
8306	Kaplan Louis	25	Rus	Hosp Corp	Retinitis Pigmentosa
8307	Morris, Geo, E.	56	U.S.	M 7 Cav.	Urethal Stricture
8308	Clausen Peter F.	50	Ger	H 20 Inf	Wound of Forehead
8309	Castor, Forest, L.	30	U.S.	M 2 Inf	Mitral Insufficiency

Barnes Hospital, U. S. Soldiers' Home, D. C.

Admitted.	Returned to Home.	Sent to Asylum.	Died.	REMARKS.
FEB 13 1902	FEB 20 1902			Recovered.
FEB 13 1902	MAR 23 1902			Recovered.
FEB 13 1902	FEB 18 1902			Recovered.
FEB 13 1902	FEB 18 1902			Improved.
FEB 14 1902	MAR 5 - 1902			Unimproved
FEB 14 1902	FEB 19 1902			Recovered
FEB 14 1902	MAY 10 1902			Recovered.
FEB 14 1902	FEB 20 1902			Improved.

United States Naval Home

The National Archives has records for the United States Naval Home, located in Philadelphia, Pennsylvania. (It was called the United States Naval Asylum until 1889.) These consist of personnel records of officers (1842 to 1885), beneficiaries of the home (1842 to 1885), and station logs (1838 to 1942). Also available are admission and discharge registers of the Naval Hospital, also located at Philadelphia, for 1855 to 1871. A similar home for retired navy and marine veterans now operates in Gulfport, Mississippi, and records may be found there.

State Soldiers' Homes

Many states operate soldiers' homes for state residents. Some of these have been converted into state/federal homes, reflecting a move to federal subsidization. Among the state homes are several Confederate homes established by the Southern states in the years following the Civil War. Registers of residents, hospital admissions, death lists (some have their own cemeteries), and related records are available at each of these homes or at the state archives. A list of the locations of these homes compiled during the 1920s includes the following:

California:	Veterans' Home—Napa County
	Womans Relief Corps Home—San Jose
Colorado:	Soldiers' and Sailors' Home
Connecticut:	Fitch's Home for Soldiers—Noroton Heights
District of Columbia:	Soldiers' and Sailors' Temporary Home—Washington, D.C.
Idaho:	Soldiers' Home—Boise
Illinois:	Soldiers' and Sailors' Home—Quincy
	Soldiers' Widows' Home—Wilmington
Indiana:	Soldiers' Home—Lafayette
Iowa:	Soldiers' Home—Marshalltown
Kansas:	State Soldiers' Home—Dodge
	Bickerdyke Annex—(presumably an annex of the State Soldiers' Home in Dodge)
Massachusetts:	National Soldiers' Home—Wollaston
	Soldiers' Home—Chelsea
Michigan:	Soldiers' Home—Grand Rapids
Minnesota:	Soldiers' Home—Minneapolis

Missouri:	Federal Soldiers' Home—St. James
Montana:	Soldiers' Home—Columbia Falls
Nebraska:	Soldiers' and Sailors' Home—Milford
	Soldiers' and Sailors' Home—Burkett
New Hampshire:	Soldiers' Home—Tilton
New Jersey:	Home for Disabled Soldiers—Arlington
	Home for Soldiers and Sailors, etc.—Vineland
New York:	Soldiers' and Sailors' Home—Bath
	Sailors' Snug Harbor—New Brighton
	Womans Relief Corps Home—Oxford
North Dakota:	Soldiers' Home—Lisbon
Ohio:	The Madison Home—Madison (for soldiers, wives, mothers, and nurses)
	State Soldiers' Home—Erie County
Oklahoma:	Union Soldiers' Home—Oklahoma City
	Confederate Soldiers' Home—Ardmore
Oregon:	Soldiers' Home—Roseburg
Pennsylvania:	Soldiers' and Sailors' Home—Erie
	Memorial Home—Brockville
	Home for Veterans and Wives—Philadelphia
Rhode Island:	Soldiers' Home—Bristol
South Dakota:	Soldiers' Home—Hot Springs
Vermont:	Soldiers' Home—Bennington
Washington:	Soldiers' Home—Orting
	Veterans' Home—Retail
Wisconsin:	Wisconsin Veterans' Home—Waupaca County
Wyoming:	Soldiers' and Sailors' Home—Buffalo

Burials

American war veterans are buried in a variety of cemeteries. Many are interred in federal military cemeteries or in national cemeteries located in various states. Others are buried in cemeteries located at soldiers' homes or in cemeteries located at military prisons. Thousands were interred in cemeteries in the foreign countries where they died. The vast majority, however, lie in private cemeteries, usually at or near their place of birth or place of residence at the time of death. Graves of some of these latter are marked to show military service. The Department of Defense operates a Graves Registration Service that compiles record cards containing data concerning military personnel who died while in service. The WPA surveyed countless cemeteries to record and compile lists of former military personnel buried in private cemeteries, and patriotic societies and historical societies have done and are doing likewise (figure 41). "Rolls of Honor," containing names of those who died in service, often provide considerable biographical information, and they sometimes provide portraits. Some of the sources and types of records available for burials in the above categories are described below.

Overseas Burials

The American Battle Monuments Commission maintains twenty-four permanent burial grounds in overseas locations, along with the National Memorial Cemetery of the Pacific in Hawaii. See chapter 6 for a description of the services offered by the commission. The War Department or Department of Defense Graves Registration Service has compiled record cards for all military personnel who died overseas, beginning with World War I. Each card shows the name of the soldier, unit, cause and date of death, date and place of burial, and name and address of next of kin or guardian.

Record cards were created for each individual connected with war crimes in Europe and the Far East during World War II. These cards serve as indexes to the case files and trial records available at the commission, and they may include the names of perpetrators, victims, or witnesses. Testimony of former prisoners of war often describes deaths that occurred in enemy prison camps.

Deaths at Soldiers' Homes

As described above, individual soldiers' homes or state archives have burial registers of residents who were patients in the hospitals and who died and were buried at the homes. The National Archives has four volumes of burials at the United States Soldiers' Home (1861 to 1863 and 1864 to 1868). There is also a separate list of Union soldiers buried at the United States Soldiers' Home (1861 to 1918).

Last Name	First	Middle Init.			Address			Serial No.
Abbott.	Jonathan.				Andover, (Oxford Co,) Maine.			

Date of Birth	At				War			
					Revolutionary.			

Date of Death	At		Cause	
Jan, 26, 1853				

Date of Burial	Cemetery		Section No.	Lot No.
	Woodlawn.		A	54

Grave No.	Book No.	Page No.	Next of Kin
82			

Date of Enlistment	At		Date of Discharge	Branch of Service
April, 19, 1775	Andover.		April, 21, 1775	Army.

Rank	Type of Marker or Stone
Sergeant.	Revolutionary Marker and Flag.

War Record

Capt. Asa Danforth's Co. Col. Converse's Regt. Capt Henry Abbotts Co. 1775

Additional Comments

2nd Enlistment Sept, 23, 1777. Oct, 15, 1777. Marched from Brookfield to join Gen. Gate's Army. Mass. S.S. of Revolutionary, Vol. 1. Page 10, 19.

Figure 41. Graves Registration Card—Maine (courtesy Maine State Archives).

Burials at Military Posts

Names of servicemen who are buried in cemeteries located at army posts, stations, or training academies are included in lists prepared by the quartermaster general or other federal agencies. The posts and academies often have lists pertaining to their own cemeteries. The Department of Veterans Affairs can provide information concerning burials at posts that are no longer in operation.

National Cemeteries

The Department of Veterans Affairs (formerly the Veterans Administration) operates a Cemetery Service, National Cemetery System, at its Washington, D.C., headquarters. Available there are alphabetically arranged record cards identifying practically all soldiers who have been buried in national cemeteries and other cemeteries under federal jurisdiction since 1861. Some cemeteries also have auxiliary lists of burials at their sites.

The Arlington National Cemetery, Arlington, Virginia, maintains its own list of burials with locations of the graves. Inquiries may be made there at a public information booth or at the Administration Building, Arlington National Cemetery, Arlington, Virginia 22211.

Headstones at Private Cemeteries

The Department of Veterans Affairs furnishes headstones for graves of military veterans buried in private or state cemeteries upon request from relatives, veterans' associations, local or state governments, or civic groups. Separate categories of such applications are arranged by state or foreign country, and a few pertain to burials at a branch of the National Homes for Disabled Volunteers (see above). Alphabetically arranged cards at Department of Veterans Affairs offices index the applications dated 1879 to 1903. Each card shows name, unit, name and location of cemetery, date and place of death, and date of the application. Included are some applications for Confederate veterans.

Civil War Burials

As part of the War Department project to create compiled service records for Civil War veterans, a separate category of records pertaining to Confederate soldiers who died in federal prisons and hospitals in the North was assembled. A register of the names of these soldiers is available in the National Archives microfilm *Register of Confederate Soldiers and Citizens Who Died in Federal Prisons and Military Hospitals in the North* (M918—one reel). This source is also available in printed form (see chapter 9).

The National Archives has a separate list of Union soldiers who were buried at the United States Soldiers' Home in the period 1861 through 1918. Other separate lists name Union soldiers buried in national cemeteries, 1861 to 1865, with a few as late as 1886. These are arranged by name of cemetery, by military organization, and, for certain states, by name of the soldier. The name indexes are available for Connecticut, Delaware, District of Columbia, Iowa, Maine, Maryland, Massachusetts, Michigan, New Hampshire, New Jersey, Pennsylvania, Rhode Island, Vermont, and Wisconsin.

The United States quartermaster published twenty-seven volumes of a *Roll of Honor*. These list Union soldiers buried in public and private cemeteries during the Civil War, and they provide rank, military unit information, date of death, and other information. These burials are arranged by name of the cemetery with an index of places.

State archives often have separate lists or collections of burial records pertaining to veterans. For example, Raymond W. Watkins, of Falls Church, Virginia, routinely locates and records Confederate soldiers' graves and submits this information to state archives and state libraries, some of which maintain a separate index of his submissions.

Censuses of Veterans

In addition to the federal 1890 Special Census (see chapter 3, Resources of the National Archives Microfilm Room), some states conducted censuses of veterans or pensioners residing in the state; these are available in state archives and state historical societies. They were in the form of questionnaires submitted to veterans for completion and return. These forms usually contained questions concerning family, social, and economic matters, as well as military history. Noteworthy among these are the censuses taken in Arkansas, Connecticut, and Tennessee.

Conscription

The first American conscription law was enacted by the Confederate Congress in April 1862, when it became evident that a sufficient fighting force could not be raised by relying exclusively upon volunteer enlistments or transfer of state militia and guard units to Confederate service. The primary purpose of that law was to entice soldiers whose one-year terms were expiring to reenlist rather than be stigmatized by being drafted. Those aged eighteen to thirty-five were affected. The law was amended on 27 September 1862 to include men aged eighteen to forty-five, and it was amended again in February 1864 to include men aged seventeen to fifty. Meanwhile, some of the individual states enacted their own conscription laws to fulfill their government-imposed quotas or to meet their own in-state military needs. The National Archives has some Union conscription records, most of them for the state of Virginia.

Exemptions from the draft were allowed to persons who were engaged in certain occupations or who held certain governmental positions. These included most government employees and most teachers, ministers, and druggists, and those with specified skilled trade experience. In the South, owners or overseers of more than twenty slaves (later reduced to fifteen) were exempted to avoid slaves being left unsupervised on plantations after young white males departed to fight. A drafted Southerner could pay a fee ranging up to $1,000 and hire a substitute to serve in his place. This provision was eliminated, however, in late 1863 because of its unpopularity among those who could not afford to pay such an amount and also because of the general inferiority of the substitutes.

Union forces were augmented by draftees beginning 3 March 1863, when Congress passed an act making all men aged twenty to forty-five subject to military duty. However, potential draftees could become exempt by paying a fee of $300, or they could directly purchase the services of a substitute who agreed to enlist and serve a term of three years (figure 42). Extant conscription records include lists created by enrollment districts. They are found in National Archives RG 110 (Records of the Provost Marshal General's Bureau). Similar records are sometimes included in naturalization records found in county courthouses or any American court. The records (consolidated lists and descriptive rolls) refer to individual men and give name, place of residence, age, occupation, marital status, place of birth, previous military service, and, occasionally, a physical description. Most are in bound volumes, some

with name indexes. It is important to be able to identify the congressional district in which the soldier lived in 1863. If the state and county of residence are known, one may ascertain the congressional district by referring to the *Congressional Directory for the Second Session of the Thirty-eighth Congress of the United States of America* (Washington, D.C.: U.S. House of Representatives, 1865). Case files of drafted aliens who intended to become naturalized citizens can be found in National Archives RG 59 (General Records of the Department of State) (figure 43).

When the United States entered World War I, Congress enacted legislation on 18 May 1917 to create a Selective Service System under the umbrella of the Office of the Provost Marshal. The system was largely managed by state and local boards of citizens who were given authority to register all eligible males in their jurisdiction, to classify them according to various criteria of ability to serve, to grant exemptions, and to call up men for service as needed. Each registrant completed a card upon which he entered his name, address, date of birth, age, race, citizenship, place of birth, occupation and employer, dependent relatives, marital status, father's place of birth, and name and address of next of kin. Each draft board maintained a docket book in which were listed the names of the registrants and the actions taken pertaining to each. Deferments and notations made when a potential draftee enlisted in the military are included in these records.

Following the war (by 31 May 1919), all draft boards were closed and further registration ceased. Registration cards for World War I are housed at the National Archives regional archives (southeast region) at Atlanta, Georgia (RG 163), where a request form for these records may be obtained. Recently, copies of these records were also made available at the National Archives regional archives (northeast region) at New York City. An ongoing project will soon make copies of these records available at other National Archives regional archives. Miscellaneous docket books and other papers of a regional or local nature may also be found in other National Archives regional archives. The LDS church Family History Library, Salt Lake City, Utah, has a complete set of the draft registration cards, and they may be seen there or through loan at any of the family research centers operated by the LDS church (see chapter 7). Miscellaneous papers created by or filed by some local draft boards may also be found in some state archives.

A draft administered by the Selective Service System was re-inaugurated during World War II. Until recently, the registration cards for this war were stored in federal records centers and were not generally accessible, but some National Archives regional archives are now processing them

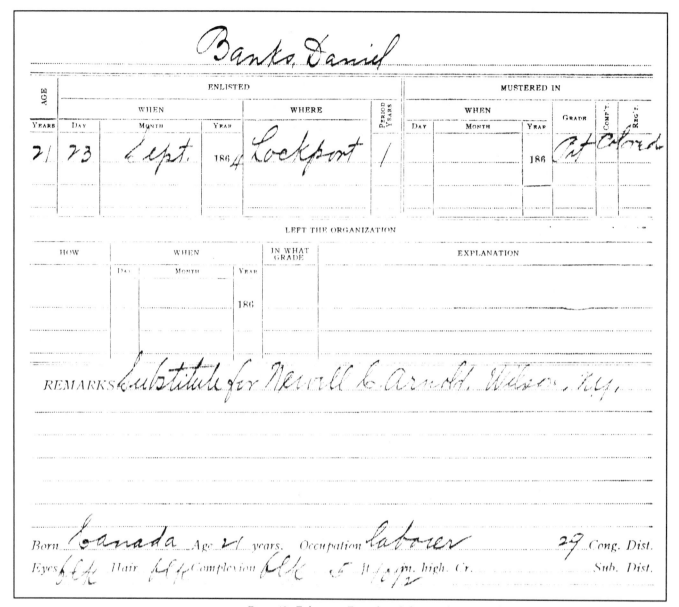

Figure 42. Enlistment Form for a Substitute for a Drafted Citizen, Civil War–Union (courtesy National Archives).

and making them ready for examination. For example, the National Archives regional archives (Great Lakes region) at Chicago already has processed and made available the cards for Illinois, Indiana, Michigan, Ohio, and Wisconsin. Inquiries should be made at the regional archives nearest the place where registration occurred (see chapter 5). Other Selective Service System documents of a local or regional nature, dating from 1940, may be found in some National Archives regional archives (RG 147), and sometimes fragments can be found among the holdings of state archives. Included in some of these holdings are lists of names of individuals who were sent to conscientious objectors' work camps in lieu of military service (figure 44).

The draft continued to be used to maintain a fighting force through the end of the Vietnam War, when the draft was suspended. However, President Jimmy Carter reinstituted draft registration, requiring all males to register for possible military service at age eighteen.

List of Persons drafted into the U.S. army from the Town of Cranston 2nd Cong. district R.I. July 8th 1863 and held to Service

Names of drafted Men	How disposed of
Zelotus R Corp	Paid Commutation
Albert C Cornell	" do
Jonathan S Potter	" do
Andrew J R Ralph	" do
Edwin W M Knight	" do
Joseph Carpenter	" do
Joseph H Cole	" do
Wm E Atwood	" do
Henry T Root	Furnished Substitute
Christopher Williams	Paid Commutation
Wm Marshal Potter	Furnished Substitute
Ambrose Nichols	Paid Commutation
Wm C Spencer	Furnished Substitute
Wm G Dearth	" do
Thomas B Mitchell	Paid Commutation
John B Gray	" do
Edwin C Gallup	" do
Asahel T Pierce	Furnished Substitute
James Campbell	Paid Commutation
George D King	" do
Samuel Gardner	" do
Henry W Haskell	" do
Jonathan L Kenyon	Furnished Substitute
Hillard Woodward	" do
Benjamin C Smith	Paid Commutation
Henry L Olney	" do
Geo W Hudson	" do
Peleg Rhodes	" do

Figure 43. List of Persons Drafted, Rhode Island, 1863 (courtesy Rhode Island State Archives).

Civilian Affairs

Many civilians have been associated with the armed forces, though they may never have entered the uniformed services. In such cases it is often helpful to search records sources for citizens associated with the military. Among others, these may include persons who were involved with the military establishment as employees, working under contract, or performing volunteer work. The records include those who submitted vouchers or received receipts, who filed claims for financial reimbursement for damage or services rendered, and who made a personal bond or took an oath of allegiance and petitioned for a pardon following the Civil War.

Employees and Contractors

At the National Archives there are various registers of applications and related papers, dated 1820 to 1903, pertaining to civilian employees of the War Department. Available are applications for positions as clerical workers, sutlers, Indian agents, scouts, surveyors, and others. There are similar registers for individual bureaus of the War Department, such as the offices of the quartermaster general, the chief of engineers, the surgeon general, the provost marshal general (Civil War), the paymaster general, the chief of ordnance, and the Freedmen's Bureau (post-Civil War).

Possibly the most valuable source of records of wartime civilian employees are the reports submitted monthly by quartermaster officers throughout the United States, in which were named all persons hired by them during the period 1818 to 1913. Indexes are few (there is one for 1861), so, in order to find a record, the name of the quartermaster must be known. Such names may be determined by searching post returns for the appropriate time period. Also valuable are similar records of the Army Transport Service (ships), which was formerly in the Quartermaster Department. These records are arranged generally by the name of a vessel.

During the nineteenth and early twentieth centuries, the military relied heavily on the services of civilian physicians and surgeons to complement regular army medical officers. A collection of personal papers concerning these professionals, both civilian and military, covers the period 1820 to 1917. Separate collections refer to hospital attendants, matrons, and nurses during the Civil War period.

Other sources are payrolls of civilians and slaves employed during the Civil War era at government installations such as shipyards and factories engaged in the manufacture of arms or military supplies. These are difficult to search because they are unbound and are not indexed.

Civilian Commerce and Service

Account books maintained by federal or state treasurers, auditors, and record keepers may provide records of reimbursements to civilians associated with any war. The most helpful collections are the Confederate papers relating to citizens or business firms. Assembled by the War Department, they consist of vouchers and other records that document business transactions between a citizen or business firm and the Confederate government, or between individuals, companies, or industries. These include transactions such as provision of food or forage, hauling and other transportation services, repairs, and grazing of livestock. Others include records of employment in or for the Confederacy and of civilian navy personnel at Confederate shore establishments.

The vast collection of papers described above, available in National Archives microfilm Confederate Papers Relating to Citizens or Business Firms (M346–1,158 reels), was compiled primarily to serve as a reference when processing claims for reimbursement filed by allegedly loyal Southern citizens who suffered incidental damages or losses arising from the Civil War. Evidence of loyalty to the Confederacy, as supported by one or more of the above-described papers, could disqualify an applicant.

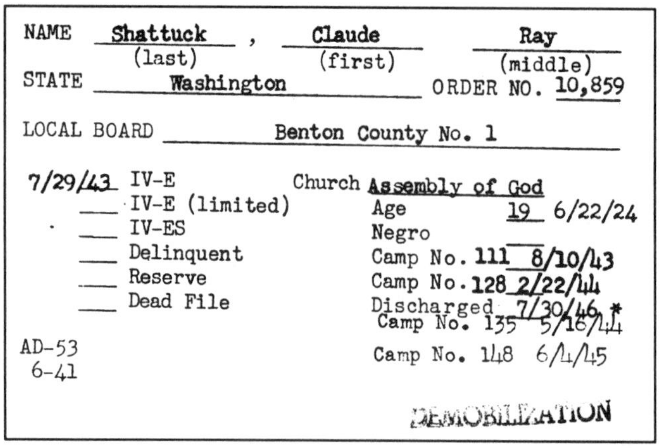

NAME Shattuck, Claude Ray
(last) (first) (middle)
STATE Washington ORDER NO. 10,859
LOCAL BOARD Benton County No. 1

7/29/43 IV-E
___ IV-E (limited)
___ IV-ES
___ Delinquent
___ Reserve
___ Dead File

Church Assembly of God
Age 19 6/22/24
Negro ___
Camp No. 111 8/10/43
Camp No. 128 2/22/44
Discharged 7/30/46 *
Camp No. 135 5/16/44
Camp No. 148 6/4/45

AD-53
6-41

DEMOBILIZATION

Figure 44. Index Card for Conscientious Objector Sent to Work Camp, 1941-47 (courtesy National Archives).

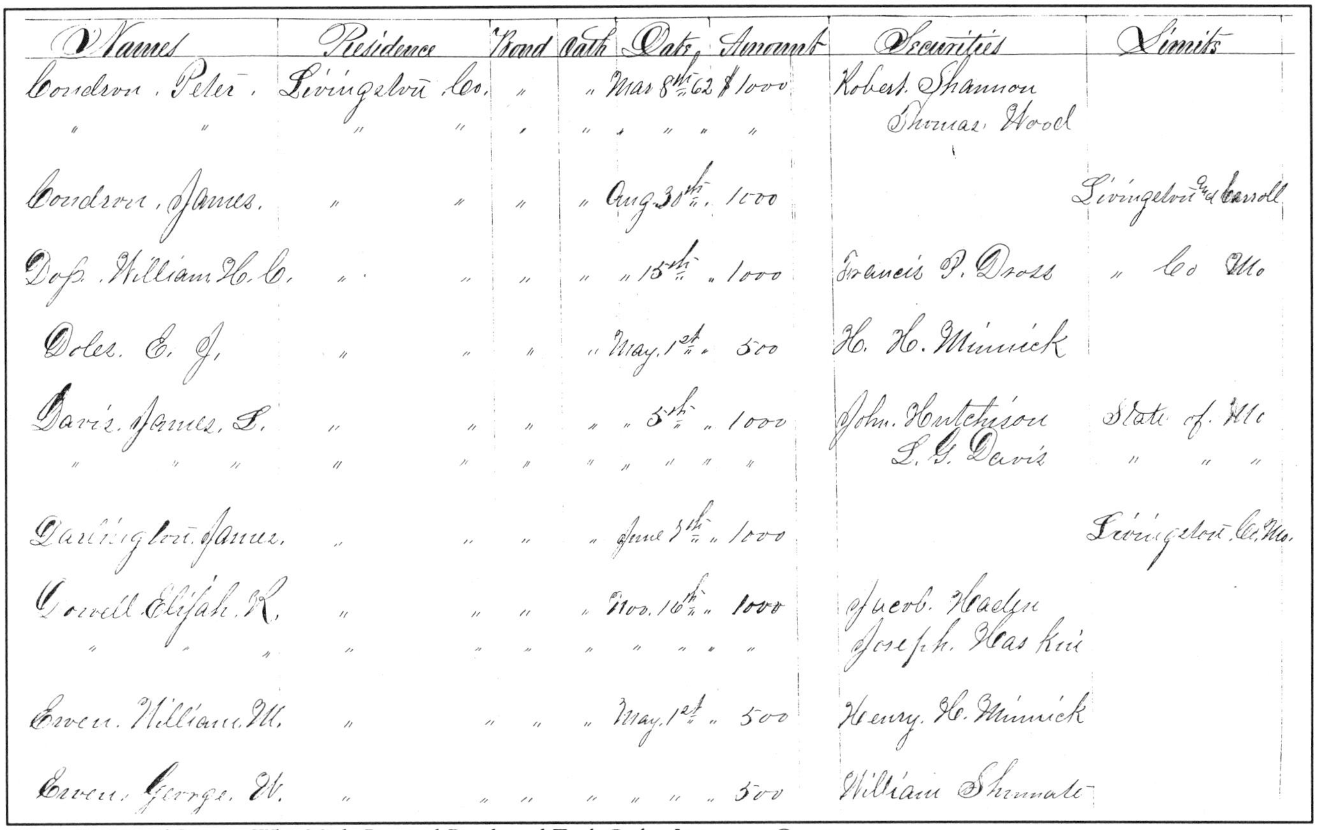

Names	Residence	Bond	Oath	Date	Amount	Securities	Limits
Condron, Peter,	Livingston Co.	"	"	Mar 8th 62	$1000	Robert Shannon	
" "	"	"	"	"	"	Thomas Wood	
Condron, James,	"	"	"	Aug 30th	1000		Livingston & Carroll
Doss, William H. C.	"	"	"	" 15th	1000	Francis P. Dross	" Co Mo
Doles, E. J.	"	"	"	May 1st	500	H. H. Minnick	
Davis, James L.	"	"	"	" 5th	1000	John Hutchison	State of Mo
" " "	"	"	"	" "	"	L. G. Davis	" "
Darlington, James,	"	"	"	June 5th	1000		Livingston Co. Mo.
Cowell, Elijah K.	"	"	"	Nov. 16th	1000	Jacob Haden	
" " "	"	"	"	" "	"	Joseph Haskin	
Erven, William M.	"	"	"	May 1st	500	Henry H. Minnick	
Erven, George W.	"	"	"	" "	500	William Shumate	

Figure 45. List of Citizens Who Made Personal Bonds and Took Oaths, Livingston County, Missouri, 1862 (courtesy National Archives).

Provost Marshal Reports on Civilians

The provost marshals, who served as military policemen, were concerned with Confederate and Union army deserters, spies, and citizens suspected of being disloyal to the Union. They investigated the theft of government property, arrested and detained both military and civilian prisoners, and maintained records of paroles and oaths of allegiance. They approved citizens' requests for travel between the states and within the border states, and they established courts to try civilians charged with violations of military laws and military personnel charged with violation of civil laws.

After the Civil War, the records of this office were separated into those that mentioned only one person and those that mentioned more than one person, including lists of names. The single-name collection is arranged alphabetically by name, and it can serve as a rough index to names found in the "two-or-more-name" collection. The latter collection is divided into five parts: geographical and subject; chronological and numbered; chronological and unnumbered; names of prisoners (civilian and military) arranged by name of the prison; and papers relating to confiscated or destroyed property. Lists of names of residents of certain counties or towns (especially in the border states), where there was some indication of possible disloyalty (as reported by neighbors), are often found in the first category. These records are available in National Archives microfilm *Union Provost Marshal's File of Papers Relating to Individual Citizens* (M345—three hundred reels) and *Union Provost Marshal's File of Papers Relating to Two or More Civilians* (M416—ninety-four reels) (figure 45).

Related to the cases investigated by provost marshal agents are the papers of the many investigations of U.S. Army Judge Advocate Levi C. Turner and Special Agent Lafayette C. Baker, who tried or investigated thousands of Confederate and Union civilians and military personnel involved in fraud, draft resistance, trading with the enemy, military desertion, and sea blockade running. These records are available in National Archives microfilm *Case Files of Investigations by Levi C. Turner and Lafayette C. Baker, 1861–1866* (M797—137 reels) (figure 46).

Claims

A total of 22,298 Civil War claims alleging damage or losses were filed by Southerners. The papers related to the claims and their disposition are arranged by state and county and thereunder by name of the claimant, with the amount of money involved. Following disposition, they were separated into those "allowed" or "disallowed" and a general index was prepared. Data found in these claims papers is available in National Archives microfilm *Records of the Commissioners of Claims (Southern Claims Commission) 1871–1880* (M87—fourteen reels). They are also available in printed form.

Among those who had business dealings with the Confederate military were owners of various types of river or sea-going vessels. These were much in demand by the Confederacy for use in internal waterway transportation of personnel and goods, as well as for eluding blockades set up by the Union navy outside Southern ports. Owners who were not willing partners in these schemes might well have had their craft confiscated. Following the war, many vessel owners filed claims with the United States for losses incurred. If no evidence indicating that the claimant was a willing participant or was loyal to the South was located, the claim was allowed. Papers collected for use by the government claims commission to determine such loyalty and the value of the property confiscated, referred to as "vessel papers," were alphabetically arranged according to the name of the vessel or the company that owned the vessel.

Petitions for Pardon

In 1863, President Lincoln issued an offer of amnesty to Southern "rebels" based on certain eligibility. After Lincoln's assassination, President Johnson reissued the offer but restricted one group from eligibility—those who owned more than $20,000 in property. As time went on, this exemption was modified until, on 25 December 1869, the offer was opened to all "unconditionally and without reservation." Approximately 14,000 applications were filed, primarily by propertied persons who were anxious to gain pardon and stave off possible confiscation of their lands and other assets. Most applications were approved. The applications are arranged by state in which they were filed. These files are available in National Archives microfilm *Case Files of Applications From Former Confederates for Presidential Pardons ("Amnesty Papers," 1865–1867)* (M1003—seventy-three reels) (figures 47 and 48).

Figure 46. Provost Marshal's Report Concerning Alleged Crime, 1862 (courtesy National Archives).

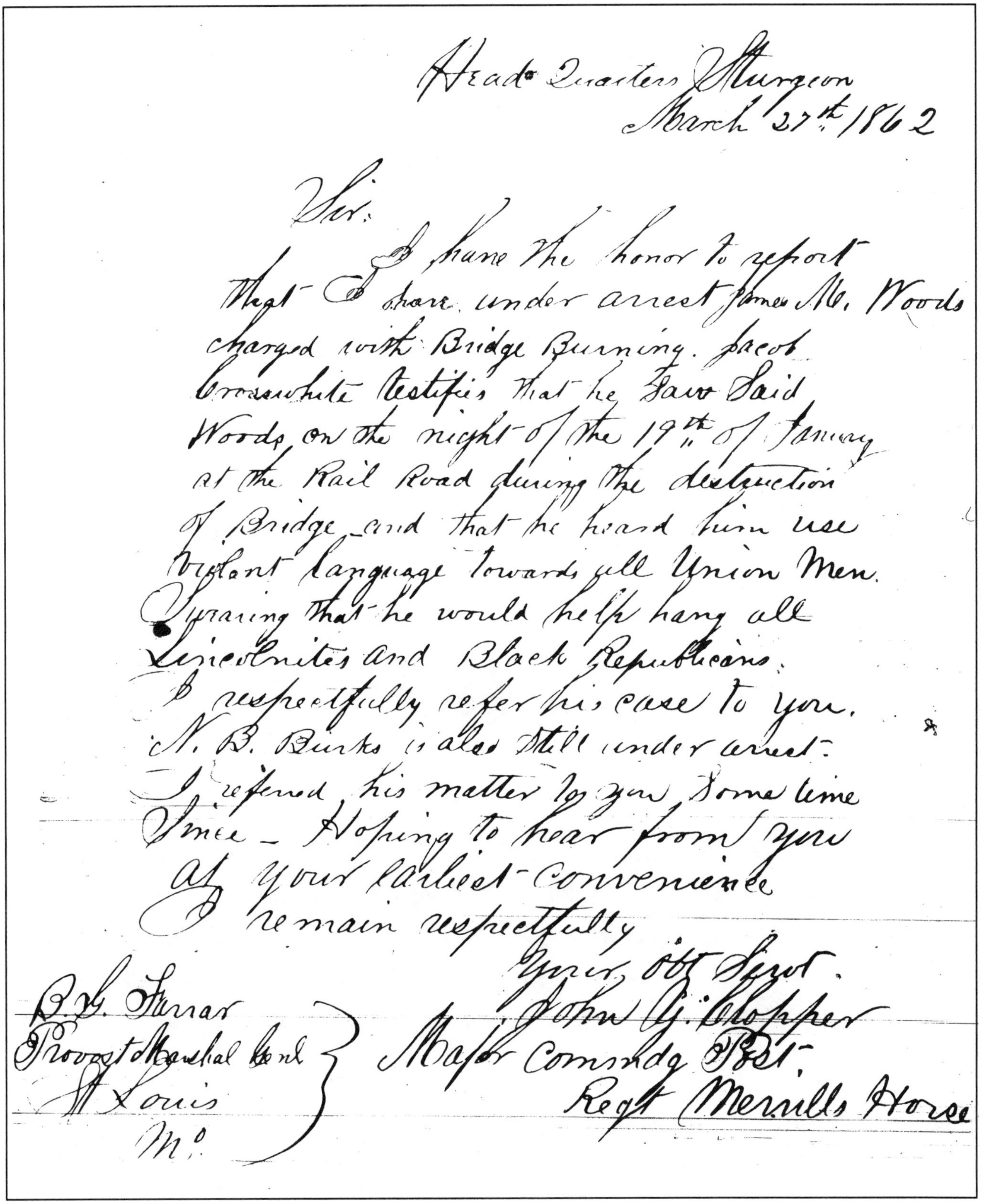

Head Quarters Sturgeon
March 27th 1862

Sir:

I have the honor to report that I have under arrest James M. Woods charged with Bridge Burning. Jacob Crosswhite testifies that he saw said Woods on the night of the 19th of January at the Rail Road during the destruction of Bridge — and that he heard him use violent language towards all Union Men. Swearing that he would help hang all Lincolnites and Black Republicans.

I respectfully refer his case to you. N. B. Burks is also still under arrest — I referred his matter to you some time since — Hoping to hear from you at your earliest convenience

I remain respectfully
Your obt Servt.
John G. Clopper
Major Comndg Post.
Regt Merrills Horse

P. G. Fanar
Provost Marshal Genl
St Louis
Mo.

REPRODUCED AT THE NATIONAL ARCHIVES

Record of persons taking the Amnesty Oath
at Columbia from September first to sep
Thirtieth 1865.

Date	No	Names	Residence
Sep 5th	209	William F Davis	Matagorda Co Texas
" "	210	Henry Bryan	Brazoria co Texas
" 6th	211	Samuel C. West	Brazoria Co Texas
" "	212	Orange Swan	Matagorda Co Texas
" "	213	Henry R Hardy	Wharton Co Texas
" "	214	John Spencer Dance	Brazoria Co Texas
" 7th	215	James Campbell	Brazoria Co Texas
" "	216	William Demison	Brazoria Co Texas

Figure 47. List of Texas Residents Who Took Oaths of Allegiance as a Condition of Being Granted Amnesty, 1865. (courtesy National Archives).

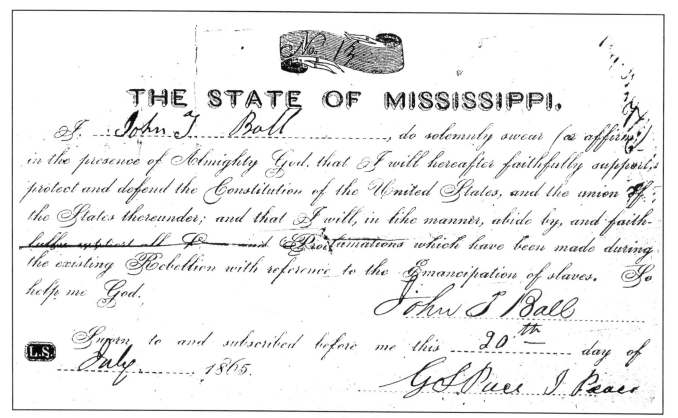

No. 14

THE STATE OF MISSISSIPPI.

I, John T Ball, do solemnly swear (or affirm) in the presence of Almighty God, that I will hereafter faithfully support, protect and defend the Constitution of the United States, and the union of the States thereunder; and that I will, in like manner, abide by, and faithfully support all ~~Laws and~~ Proclamations which have been made during the existing Rebellion with reference to the Emancipation of slaves. So help me God.

John T Ball

L.S. Sworn to and subscribed before me this 20th day of July 1865.

Gd Pue J Peace

Figure 48. Oath of Allegiance to the United States, 1865 (courtesy National Archives).

3

Resources of the National Archives Microfilm Room

3

Resources of the National Archives Microfilm Room

The National Archives, located on Pennsylvania Avenue NW (between Seventh and Ninth streets) in Washington, D.C., was established in 1934. Its mission is to store and safeguard the U.S. government's permanent records, to classify them into record groups, and to make them available to the public for scholarly research. In 1935, the National Archives instituted a comprehensive survey of federal records in Washington, D.C., and followed up with a similar survey of federal records in other parts of the country. Guidelines were established for disposition or preservation of the records, resulting in a "records administration program" to guide future policy. In 1949, the National Archives became part of the General Services Administration; it remained there until 1985, when it was granted independent status and became the National Archives and Records Administration. In 1950, congressional legislation provided for regional federal records centers (chapter 5), one of which was the National Records Center at Suitland, Maryland. The large volume of records coming into the National Archives caused the overflow of permanent records to be sent to the Suitland center as a matter of necessity; however, with the opening of National Archives II at College Park, Maryland, this will no longer be necessary.

The National Archives is the repository for original federal records, many large collections of which are available on microfilm in the Microfilm Room (room 400) of the main archives. Microfilm may also be obtained through one of the reference branches in other parts of the building, through the National Archives regional archives, at many state archives, and at major public and private libraries.

Two publications provide helpful assistance to researchers in the archives and, more specifically, the Microfilm Room:

National Archives and Records Service. *Guide to Genealogical Research in the National Archives.* Rev. ed. Washington, D.C.: 1983.

National Archives Trust Fund Board, National Archives and Service Administration. *Military Service Records: A Select Catalog of National Archives Microfilm Publications.* Washington, D.C.: 1985.

Using the National Archives

Personal Visits

On arrival at the National Archives building, researchers are required to show personal identification. A research card is not necessary to visit only the Microfilm Room, but one is required to visit other branches of the archives. The security guard in the lobby can give directions to a desk where a research card valid for two years will be issued immediately and without charge. Upon

Figure 49. National Archives Building, Washington, D.C. (courtesy National Archives).

leaving the building, briefcases and purses are inspected to insure against theft or unintentional removal of valuable documents.

A register must be signed when entering and departing the Microfilm Room. Staff members are stationed at the front desk to provide assistance as needed. The principal types of records available in this room are census enumeration schedules, ship passenger lists, military documents, and records of various government departments. Rolls of microfilm are contained in cabinets lining the wall of the main room and also in drawers in the annex room (reached through an open door near the back of the main room). Each cabinet drawer is labeled to show the name of the film stored therein. After the M or T number of a desired microfilm series is determined, the cabinet and location of the drawer (numbering from the top drawer to the bottom in each cabinet) may be determined by referring to the location register, which is located near the front desk. (The staff can point out this notebook or direct you to the desired

cabinet.) Copy machines, for which "debit cards" are now used in place of coins, are available for public use. These cards are available for purchase from machines in the Microfilm Room and the Central Reading Room.

When beginning a search for microfilmed military records, it is advisable to first check the microfilm indexes. When the name of a particular soldier or military organization is located in an index, the next step is to inspect the records themselves. Some compiled military service records and other military records are available on microfilm in the microfilm room, but others (those that have not yet been microfilmed) may be inspected in the Central Reading Room (room 203). To obtain an original record, the information found on a microfilm index must be indicated on a "Request for Military Records" form, which must then be deposited in a designated box. After a wait of approximately one hour, the record will be delivered to the Central Reading Room. A research card is necessary to enter that room, where another register must be signed.

Outer clothing, hats, fountain pens, umbrellas, briefcases, purses, personal papers, notebooks, books, and notepaper are not allowed in the Central Reading Room. Notepaper and note cards are provided near the entrance desk. Ballpoint pens are permitted, but pencils are preferred. Free lockers for storing items not allowed in the room are available in the adjacent halls. Notes necessary for research may be taken into the room if a staff member stamps them "approved." Staff members in this room will permit researchers to inspect the documents delivered there and, after approval, copy them on nearby machines. The machines will not accommodate bound volumes or oversized documents, however. In such instances, arrangements may be made in the reference branch for special copying services. Most of the military records available in the Microfilm Room are listed below by category and thereafter chronologically according to the years covered or by the name of the war. A few series (mainly primary or auxiliary correspondence or miscellaneous reports without indexes) are available but are not included in the lists on the following pages.

Mail Requests

It is possible to obtain copies of unrestricted military records by mail for a fee, although the process may take several months. Requests for records housed at the National Archives should be made on National Archives Trust Fund (NATF) form 80 (figure 50), which is available free of charge from the General Reference Branch (NNRG-P), National Archives and Records Administration, Seventh and Pennsylvania Avenue NW, Washington, D.C. 20408. (A similar form for records of service in World War I and subsequent is available from the National Personnel Records Center in St. Louis, Missouri. See chapter 5).

Instructions accompanying the form explain the procedure for payment for copies. The form should be completed according to the instructions and with as much information as possible, and it should be submitted to the above address. Required are the full name of the serviceman or -woman, the war in which served, and other known identifying information. (If the request concerns a navy enlisted person, the name of at least one vessel on which the person served, with approximate dates, is needed.) If the file for the veteran in question is located, the National Archives will supply copies of documents that provide pertinent information about the veteran and the veteran's family. Where the file consists of ten or fewer pages, the entire file will be copied; for larger files, only selected documents (the more important and non-repetitive ones) will be copied and furnished.

National Archives Microfilm Series

General (periods of years encompassing more than one war or a period of years between major wars)

Registers of Enlistments in the United States Army, 1798–1914 (M233). These indicate when, where, and by whom the soldier was enlisted; period of enlistment; place of birth; age at time of enlistment; occupation; physical description; and the unit to which assigned. The records are arranged both chronologically by time period and alphabetically by first initial of the surname. Data for these registers were gathered from enlistment papers, muster rolls, and other unit records.

Years	Roll Numbers
1796–17 May 1815	1–13
17 May 1815–30 June 1821	14–17
June 1821–1858	18–26
1859–70	27–37
1871–77	38–40
1878–84	41–43
1885–90	44–45
1891–92	46
1893–97	47–48
1898	49–50
1899	51–52
1900	53–54
1900–May 1902	55–56
June 1902–1904	57–58
July 1904–Dec 1905	59–60
1906–07	61–62
1908–June 1909	63–64
1909–13	65–68
Special and miscellaneous categories, 1816–1914:	69–81

Miscellaneous (including Mtd. Ranger, 1832–33, and Puerto Rico Prov. Inf., 1901–14)

Indian scouts, 1866–77, 1878–1914

Philippine scouts, 1866–77, 1878–1914

Ordnance, commissary, quartermaster sergeants, clerks, and messengers

Hospital stewards

Duplicates; Artillery and Infantry Regiments, 1828–52, Lists of officers, Fourth Reg't. Inf.

Prisoners

Miscellaneous indexes

Figure 50. National Archives Trust Fund Form 80 for Military Service Records Housed at the National Archives (courtesy National Archives).

ORDER FOR COPIES OF VETERANS RECORDS
(See Instructions page before completing this form)

DATE RECEIVED IN NNRG

INDICATE BELOW THE TYPE OF FILE DESIRED AND THE METHOD OF PAYMENT PREFERRED.

1. FILE TO BE SEARCHED
(Check one box only)
☐ PENSION
☐ BOUNTY-LAND WARRANT APPLICATION
(Service before 1856 only)
☐ MILITARY

2. PAYMENT METHOD (Check one box only)
☐ **CREDIT CARD** (VISA or MasterCard) for IMMEDIATE SHIPMENT of copies
Account Number: Exp. Date:
Signature: Daytime Phone:

☐
BILL ME
(No Credit Card)

REQUIRED MINIMUM IDENTIFICATION OF VETERAN - MUST BE COMPLETED OR YOUR ORDER CANNOT BE SERVICED

3. VETERAN (Give last, first, and middle names)

4. BRANCH OF SERVICE IN WHICH HE SERVED
☐ ARMY   ☐ NAVY   ☐ MARINE CORPS

5. STATE FROM WHICH HE SERVED

6. WAR IN WHICH, OR DATES BETWEEN WHICH, HE SERVED

7. IF SERVICE WAS CIVIL WAR,
☐ UNION   ☐ CONFEDERATE

PLEASE PROVIDE THE FOLLOWING ADDITIONAL INFORMATION, IF KNOWN

8. UNIT IN WHICH HE SERVED (Name of regiment or number, company, etc, name of ship)

9. IF SERVICE WAS ARMY, ARM IN WHICH HE SERVED
☐ INFANTRY   ☐ CAVALRY   ☐ ARTILLERY
If other, specify:

Rank
☐ OFFICER   ☐ ENLISTED

10. KIND OF SERVICE
☐ VOLUNTEERS   ☐ REGULARS

11. PENSION/BOUNTY-LAND FILE NO.

12. IF VETERAN LIVED IN A HOME FOR SOLDIERS, GIVE LOCATION (City and State)

13. PLACE(S) VETERAN LIVED AFTER SERVICE

14. DATE OF BIRTH

15. PLACE OF BIRTH (City, County, State, etc.)

18. NAME OF WIDOW OR OTHER CLAIMANT

16. DATE OF DEATH

17. PLACE OF DEATH (City, County, State, etc.)

NATIONAL ARCHIVES TRUST FUND BOARD   NATF Form 80 (rev. 4-92)

DO NOT WRITE BELOW - SPACE IS FOR OUR REPLY TO YOU

☐ **NO--We were unable to locate the file you requested above. No payment is required.**

DATE SEARCHED   SEARCHER

☐ **REQUIRED MINIMUM IDENTIFICATION OF VETERAN WAS NOT PROVIDED.** Please complete blocks 3 (give full name), 4, 5, 6, and 7 and resubmit your order.

☐ **A SEARCH WAS MADE BUT THE FILE YOU REQUESTED ABOVE WAS NOT FOUND.** When we do not find a record for a veteran, this does not mean that he did not serve. You may be able to obtain information about him from the archives of the State from which he served.

☐ See attached forms, leaflets, or information sheets.

☐ **YES--We located the file you requested above. We have made copies from the file for you. The cost for these copies is $10.**

DATE SEARCHED   SEARCHER

FILE DESIGNATION

Make your check or money order payable to NATIONAL ARCHIVES TRUST FUND. Do not send cash. Return this form and your payment in the enclosed envelope to:

NATIONAL ARCHIVES TRUST FUND
P.O. BOX 100221
ATLANTA, GA 30384-0221

PLEASE NOTE: We will hold these copies awaiting receipt of payment for only 45 days from the date completed, which is stamped below. After that time, you must submit another form to obtain photocopies of the file.

THIS IS YOUR MAILING LABEL.
PRESS FIRMLY.

NAME (Last, First, MI)

STREET

CITY, STATE   ZIP CODE

A806892

INVOICE/REPLY COPY - DO NOT DETACH

Name and Subject Index to the Letters Received by the Appointment, Commission, and Personnel Branch of the Adjutant General's Office, 1871–1894 (M1125). Reproduction of card indexes of correspondence. The letters contain names of individuals who may have been regular army officers.

Letters Received by the Commission Branch of the Adjutant General's Office, 1863–1870 (M1064). Letters referring to officers of the regular army. They were marked with the name of the correspondent, and a file number was assigned to each. They are arranged chronologically for the years 1863–70 and thereafter alphabetically by first initial of the surname. There is no index to these letters. See M1125 (above) for an index of similar correspondence received during the period 1871–94.

Returns From Regular Army Infantry Regiments, June 1821–December 1916 (M865). Because the forms used for these returns were amended from year to year, the data they carry varies. In general, they include names of officers and names of enlisted men if assigned to extra duty, if missing, or if a casualty. Often there is a "record of events" section describing the unit's activities.

Similar to those described above are the returns of the other regular army units cited below.

Returns From Regular Army Cavalry Regiments, 1833–1916 (M744).

Returns From Regular Army Artillery Regiments, June 1821–January 1901 (M727).

Returns From Regular Army Field Artillery Battalions and Regiments, February 1901–December 1916 (M726).

Returns From Regular Army Coast Artillery Companies, February 1901–June 1961 (M691).

Returns of the Corps of Engineers, April 1832–December 1916 (M851).

Returns From Regular Army Engineer Battalions, September 1846–June 1916 (M6790).

Index to Rendezvous Reports, Before and After the Civil War, 1846–1861; 1865–1884 (T1098). This series is a reproduction of index cards that indicate place of enlistment or vessel on which an enlistment took place; date of enlistment or the date of the "return" on which the individual's name first appeared; and his "record of service." The reports themselves have not been microfilmed but are available at the National Archives. The rendezvous reports for the Civil War period were indexed separately (see T1099). ("Rendezvous report" was the navy term for "enlistment.")

Muster Rolls of the U.S. Marine Corps, 1789–1860; 1866–1892 (T1118). Chronologically arranged copies of bound volumes that were prepared monthly, quarterly, or, in some cases, annually, by marine units aboard vessels or at land stations. They include names; dates of enlistment; term of enlistment; and dates of reassignments, promotions, discharges, or desertion.

General Registers of the United States Navy and Marine Corps, 1782–1882. (M2078). 1 roll.

Abstracts of Service Records of Naval Officers ("Records of Officers"), 1798–1893 (M330). Records containing letters pertaining to appointments or applications for appointments, commissions, admissions as cadets, and similar documents. Data is arranged chronologically in volumes labeled A to O. Some volumes list the names alphabetically; others provide an index of names for that volume.

Index to [Naval] Officers' Jackets, 1913–1925 ("Officers' Directory") and Index to Officers' Jackets, 1913–1925 ("Officers' Directory") (T1102). These refer to the Naval Bureau of Personnel's location registers for officer personnel files, or "jackets," as of March 1948. Entries are arranged by navy file number; there is no name index.

Letters Received by the Secretary of the Navy From Captains ("Captains' Letters"), 1805–1861, 1866–1885 (M125). Letters and reports from naval captains (and higher ranking officers) from both ships and shore installations. These were numbered and filed by clerks in the Office of the Secretary of the Navy. They provide much historical detail but contain few references to enlisted sailors or officers below the rank of captain. The original letters were chronologically arranged and bound in 413 volumes and were sequentially numbered, each with its own index. There is no general index.

Records of General Courts-martial and Courts of Inquiry of the Navy Department, 1799–1867 (M273). These contain the name of the sailor charged; the alleged offense; his ship or station; and data concerning his trial, including a transcript of proceedings of general court-martial or court of inquiry. Rolls 1 and 2 comprise a name index to the cases cited in the remaining rolls.

Registers of the Records of the Proceedings of the U.S. Army General Courts-Martial, 1809–1890 (M1105). Data concerning general army courts-martial. This material was labeled and registered by clerks in the War Office who placed the registers in seventeen volumes covering the period 1809–90. The eight microfilmed rolls of these volumes cover the following years:

Roll 1:	1809–27
Roll 2:	1828–63
Roll 3:	1862–65 (overlapped dates)
Roll 4:	1862–66 (overlapped dates)
Roll 5:	1862–65 (overlapped dates)
Roll 6:	1862–68 (overlapped dates)
Roll 7:	1869–83
Roll 8:	1884–90

The data relates to trials of officers and trials for serious offenses. It does not include trials resulting in regimental courts-martial, which deal with enlisted men or cadets or offenses of a less serious nature.

The Negro in the Military Service of the United States, 1639–1886 (M858). A special compilation gathered from records in the Adjutant General's Office for use in a published work and based on published and unpublished primary sources. It is arranged in five rolls of microfilm according to time period and thereafter by subject: roll 1 covers the colonial period, American Revolution, War of 1812, and Civil War (1774–1862); rolls 2–4 cover the balance of the Civil War; roll 5 covers "Treatment and Exchange of Prisoners of War" and "Regular Army" (1866–86).

Revolutionary War (1775–83)

General Index to Compiled Service Records of Revolutionary War Soldiers (M860). Name index referring to individuals who served in the regular forces of the Continental Army, militia units assigned to the Continental Army, volunteer units from the states, and naval forces organized by the Continental Congress. Excluded are militia units and state volunteer units that were not assigned to the "American Army"; i.e., those whose service was restricted to activities within the borders of a particular state. Most of the original records were destroyed by fire on 8 November 1800; thus, the records in this index primarily comprise government documents generated since that date. They also include many documents from private persons or state agencies that were subsequently sold to or turned over to the War Department, as well as records turned over to the War Department by other federal departments.

Beginning in 1894, service records were compiled by abstracting data from muster rolls, payrolls, various receipts, account entries, unit returns, correspondence, and data from 23 of the 176 numbered record books in the War Department Collection of Revolutionary War Records. A card was prepared for each abstracted entry, and these cards were arranged in jacket-envelopes—one for each individual. This index covers both M881 and M880 (revolutionary war record collections), which are described below.

Compiled Service Records of Soldiers Who Served in the American Army During the Revolutionary War (M881). Records arranged either under the designation "Continental Troops" or by the name of a state, thereafter by organization, and then alphabetically by surname of the soldier or sailor.

Compiled Service Records of American Naval Personnel and Members of the Departments of the Quartermaster General and the Commissary General of Military Forces Who Served During the Revolutionary War (M880). Unbound records consisting of muster rolls, payrolls, and lists of artillery officers of one regiment.

Revolutionary War Rolls, 1775–1783 (M246). Muster rolls, payrolls, returns, and other miscellaneous personnel records, pay records, and supply records of army units. Roll 1 is a register ("catalog of records") of the documents found in the remaining 137 rolls. These pertain to the Continental Army and to militia and state units assigned to the "American Army" during the revolutionary war.

Index to Compiled Service Records of Naval Personnel Who Served During the Revolutionary War (M879). Card index with the name of a sailor and his rank or a civilian employee and his profession. This index duplicates the names in M860 (the general index for revolutionary war soldiers).

Revolutionary War Pension and Bounty Land Warrant Application Files, 1800–1900 (M804). Between 1910 and 1912, all file jackets were consolidated into one linen envelope and arranged in alphabetical order by surname of the veteran. The previously used jackets, containing summary annotations, were flattened and placed inside the new envelope.

A pension application file might lack some documents if the veteran belonged to an organization from the state of Virginia. One collection of files contains claims by heirs who applied for "half-pay" pensions under the act of 5 July 1832 (4 Stat 563). These files were transferred to the National Archives in 1941 and were not microfilmed in this series when other claims were filmed. Abstracts of these half-pay files are cited in Gaius M. Brumbaugh's *Revolutionary War Records*, vol. 1, *Virginia* (Washington, D.C.: 1936). Another collection contains files of those whose heirs applied for half-pay pensions under the act of 5 July 1832 for Virginia State Navy officers. These files were transferred to the National Archives by the Office of Naval Records and Library in 1941 and have not been abstracted or microfilmed. Records of both groups are available at the National Archives in RG 93 (army) or RG 45 (navy).

Selected Records From Revolutionary War Pension and Bounty Land Warrant Application Files, 1800–1900 (M805). Papers in the files described in M804 (above) consisting of more than ten pages were separated into those of primary importance (selected records) and those of lesser importance or that duplicate other documents (non-selected records). Files with ten or fewer documents are marked with a star by the veteran's name and are treated as "selected." Unless otherwise requested, staff members of the National Archives will copy and mail only the "selected" documents (or the entire file if it contains ten or fewer pages) to researchers who make written requests for a revolutionary war pension/bounty-land file. Routine papers, such as attestations by witnesses to statements or endorsements by local officials, are not counted. This special microfilm series contains only the "selected" papers and files of ten or fewer pages and is used primarily by staff when they respond to written requests.

U.S. Revolutionary War Bounty Land Warrants Used in the U.S. Military District of Ohio and Related Papers (Acts of 1786, 1803, and 1807) (M829). Since a majority of the bounty land issued by the government was located in the Military District of Ohio (formerly a part of the state of Virginia), this series was prepared as a guide. It lists the warrants issued (by warrant number) pursuant to the acts of 1796, 1799, 1804, and 1806. It also contains a register of warrants presented at the treasury for locating and patenting of the claimed land, 1804–35. Roll 1 contains registers and indexes to the warrants described in the remaining fifteen rolls. Roll 15 lists the warrants issued under the acts of 1835, 1842, and 1846.

Ledgers of Payments, 1818–1872, to U.S. Pensioners Under Acts of 1818 Through 1850, From Records of the Third Auditor of the Treasury (T718). The Treasury Department recorded the semiannual payments to pensioners, primarily those who served in the revolutionary war (or their widows who qualified after 1831). This series reproduces those volumes, each covering a specific act of Congress and the specific time period during which the payments were made. To use these volumes it is necessary to determine the year of the act under which the pension was approved. These records contain the names of pensioners arranged by the year of each act and also by time periods when the pension payments were made; thereunder, they are arranged by the initial of the pensioner's surname. These volumes often reveal the date of the pensioner's death. Widow's pension payments are listed in rolls 15–23 of this series.

Numbered Record Books Concerning Military Operations and Service, Pay and Settlement of Accounts, and Supplies in the War Department Collection of Revolutionary War Records (M853). As the War Department gathered papers from many sources (muster rolls, payrolls, returns, receipts, correspondence, etc.) it separated the papers into two general categories: the first group was used to prepare abstract cards placed in jacket-envelopes (M881, *Compiled Military Service Records*); the documents in the second group were simply numbered for identification. Pages of some of the bound volumes in this second group were removed and numbered. Included are 230 orderly books, numerous letter books, receipt books, journals, ledgers, and lists of soldiers, as well as separate indexes found in some of the volumes. All loose documents and extracted pages were re-bound to form new volumes, and numbers were assigned without regard to content. A few examples of the collections found in these volumes are listed below. (Not listed are several account books, supply books, correspondence collections, and similar papers.)

- Catalog and subject index of numbered record books.
- Index to numbered orderly books.
- Index to oaths of allegiance and fidelity, oaths of office, commissions, and resignations.
- Orderly books, 1775–1783.
- Oaths of allegiance and fidelity and oaths of office, 1778, 1781.
- Commissions and resignations, 1775–1780.
- Lists of Continental and state troops and militia, 1775–1783 (by state).
- Receipt books of John Pierce, paymaster general and commissioner of army accounts. These contain an alphabetical list of officers and enlisted men due final pay certificates at the close of the war. This list was also published by the National Society of the Daughters of the American Revolution in its *Seventeenth Report.*

Miscellaneous Numbered Records (The Manuscript File) in the War Department Collection of Revolutionary War Records, 1775–1790 (M859). Papers in the *Numbered Record Books* (M853, above) were grouped into four broad categories according to content. Those papers not placed in one of the first three categories were placed in a "miscellaneous" group. This series (M859) reproduces the papers in that fourth group; they are arranged by the number placed on each paper by the National Archives. The matters discussed in these papers pertain to troops of particular states and include various records of accounts, commissions, resignations, pay, receipts, provisions, and similar subjects.

Special Index to Numbered Records in the War Department Collection of Revolutionary War Records, 1775–1783 (M847). A finding aid to the *Numbered Record Books* (M853) and *Manuscript File* (M859) described above. It reproduces the alphabetically arranged index cards that bear names of individuals mentioned in the papers of those files. The cards provide basic information about the individual and the numbers assigned to the records (often several records) to which the card pertains.

Post-Revolutionary War (1784–1811)

Compiled Service Records of Volunteer Soldiers Who Served From 1784 to 1811 (M905). Following the cessation of hostilities after the revolutionary war, Congress directed that the one remaining regiment and the one remaining artillery battalion be augmented. Four states—Connecticut, New York, New Jersey, and Pennsylvania—were required to furnish from their militia units a force of seven hundred men to serve for a period of twelve months, with annual replacements thereafter. By 1790 the authorized force numbered 1,216 individuals and by 1791 approximately 2,000, not counting those in local militia units. State and territorial militia units were authorized by Congress on 8 May 1792, setting the stage for today's state National Guard units.

The Office of the Adjutant General was responsible for keeping federal military records, including service records of volunteers who might be called upon to put down insurrections or engage in conflict with hostile Indians. In 1899 those administrative and record-keeping functions were transferred to a Record and Pension Office that brought together in one collection the original records of those who served between 1784 and 1811. Those records were re-transferred in 1904 to the Office of the Adjutant General, where, in 1912, the data therein was abstracted onto cards, placed in jacket-envelopes, and arranged alphabetically by name of the soldier to form a table of contents.

Index to Compiled Service Records of Volunteer Soldiers Who Served From 1794 to 1811 (M694). Card index to the volunteers mentioned in the title of this series.

Letters, Orders for Pay, Accounts, Receipts, and Other Supply Records Concerning Weapons and Military Stores, 1776–1801 (M1062). Reproduction of a volume containing orders for pay, letters, supply records, a receipt book, and miscellaneous unbound items pertaining to military stores.

Muster Rolls and Payrolls of Militia and Regular Army Organizations in the Battle of Tippecanoe, November 1811 (T1085). Contains names of soldiers and their units. An index refers to the names of units but not to the names of the soldiers.

War of 1812 (1812–15)

Index to Compiled Service Records of Volunteer Soldiers Who Served During the War of 1812 (M602). Alphabetically arranged index cards to the compiled service records. The cards contain the soldier's name, rank, and unit in which he served. There are separate indexes to Mississippi (M678), Louisiana (M229), North Carolina (M220), and South Carolina (M652). There are other, separate card indexes, but only the above have been microfilmed.

Index to War of 1812 Pension Application Files (M313). Each pension file for service between 1812 and 1815 was placed in a separate envelope. This index indicates the name and other information placed on the faces of those envelopes, including a file number. All pensions for service to veterans of this war or their dependents were based exclusively on service-connected disability or death. Even though the face of the envelope might not have mentioned bounty land, an inspection of the file might reveal a grant of land as well as a pension. The files themselves have not been microfilmed.

War of 1812 Military Bounty Land Warrants, 1815–1858 (M848). Reproductions of 105 bound volumes containing two series of bounty land warrants issued between 1815 and 1858 for service in the War of 1812; they are arranged chronologically by warrant number. Roll 1 indexes four volumes that refer to patentees from Missouri, Arkansas, and Illinois, and it also contains a general index of patentees under the act of 1842.

War of 1812 Papers of the Department of State, 1789–1815 (M588). The seven rolls in this series copy various documents and letters from the Department of State concerning operations during the War of 1812. They include, for example, letters of marque (which authorized owners of private vessels to operate against the enemy); lists of enemy aliens and prisoners of war; passenger lists of vessels (mostly sailing from Philadelphia); reports from U.S. marshals and secret agents of the United States; and miscellaneous correspondence.

Despatches From United States Consuls in London, 1790–1906 (T168). Roll 10 of these Department of State documents includes despatches of American consuls between 3 August 1812 and 28 November 1816 and lists of American prisoners of war returned to America on the USS *Jenny* in exchange

for British prisoners of war. Other documents list approximately one hundred Americans imprisoned in Great Britain who were proposed for exchange to be returned to America. These and similar document lists give name, rank, date of arrival in Great Britain, and name of the vessel on which the men arrived.

Computer-processed Tabulations of Data From Seamen's Protective Certificate Applications to the Collector of Customs for the Port of Philadelphia, 1812–1815 (M972). American customs officers issued certificates to American sailors for them to use to prove their citizenship when their ships were boarded or if approached in port. Chief among those issuing such certificates was the customs officer at the port of Philadelphia. He insisted upon documented proof of citizenship from American sailors before issuing the certificates to the 790 applicants cited in this series.

These papers contain much personal information about the sailors, including their physical appearance (including tattoos and scars); age; place of birth; date and place of their taking an oath that the application was correct; and degree of literacy (based on legibility of the signature or whether the applicant used his mark in lieu of his signature).

Indian Wars (1815–58)

Index to Compiled Service Records of Volunteer Soldiers Who Served During Indian Wars and Disturbances, 1815–1858 (M629). Reproduction of an alphabetical card index to the compiled service records of those who took part in the conflicts mentioned in the title of this series. See sections on Alabama, Florida, Georgia, Louisiana, North Carolina, and Tennessee in chapter 8 for records of state volunteers who served in the Creek War, the Florida War, and the Cherokee Removal. Also see the section on Louisiana for records of state volunteers who served in the second Florida Indian campaign (1837 and 1838) against the Seminoles.

Index to Indian Wars Pension Files, 1892–1926 (T318). Reproduction of an alphabetical card index to pension files for service in Indian campaigns between 1817 and 1898. In addition to other identifying information, the state from which the claim was made and a pension certificate number are given. The pension files relating to these wars have not been microfilmed.

For reference to other pension claims for service in Indian wars, also see the *Old Wars Index to Pension Files* (below). For pensions claimed for Indian war service during the War of 1812, the Civil War, or the Mexican War, see the specific pension file indexes for those wars.

"Memoir of Reconnaissances With Maps During the Florida Campaign," April 1854–February 1858 (M1090). Collection reproducing field reports filed by army officers, with accompanying maps, while serving in Florida. The maps, often hand drawn, refer to prominent rivers and lakes, military posts and roads, forts, and the locations of Indian trails and

villages. Summaries prepared at headquarters offices provide details concerning the expeditions and the names of the commanding officers.

Old Wars Index to Pension Files, 1815–1926 (T316). Reproduction of a card index to pension files created between 1815 and 1926 based on death or disability as a result of service in the regular army, navy, or marines between the close of the revolutionary war in 1783 and the beginning of the Civil War in 1861. In addition to other identifying information, the state from which the claim was filed and a certificate number are shown. The pension files have not been microfilmed.

Mexican War (1846–48)

Index to Compiled Service Records of Volunteer Soldiers Who Served During the Mexican War (M616). Reproduction of an alphabetical card index to the compiled service records mentioned in the title of this series.

Index to Mexican War Pension Files, 1887–1926 (T317). Reproduction of an alphabetical card index to pensions for service in the Mexican War during 1846–48. In addition to other identifying information, the names of any dependents, the state from which the claim was made, and a certificate number are shown. The pension files have not been microfilmed.

Compiled Service Records of Volunteer Soldiers Who Served During the Mexican War in Mormon Organizations (M351). Two organizations comprising individuals belonging to The Church of Jesus Christ of Latter-day Saints served as volunteers in the Mexican War: The first group was the Mormon Battalion Volunteers, who organized at Council Bluffs, Iowa, on 16 July 1848 and served for one year. This group was made up of Mormons who were en route to California. The second group was Captain Davis' Company A, Mormon Volunteers, who organized at Los Angeles, California, and served for six months. This series is a reproduction of the compiled service records, and it also contains "records of events" cards that provide historical data concerning the activities of the units. The names of soldiers serving in these units are included in the general index of soldiers who fought in the Mexican War.

Selected Pension Application Files Relating to the Mormon Battalion (T1196). Reproduction of an alphabetical card index of the names of volunteers who served in the Mormon Battalion. Each roll in this series contains a complete list of names.

Civil War–General (1861–65)

Official Records of the Union and Confederate Armies, 1861–1865 (M262). Reproduction of the 128 volumes bearing the above title, which are available in many large reference libraries. Each volume has an index of names for that volume; a general index (see M1036, below) that lists names and

volume numbers must be used to eliminate the need to search the separate indexes in each volume.

Military Operations of the Civil War: A Guide Index to the Official Records of the Union and Confederate Armies, 1861–1865 (M1036). General index necessary to facilitate the use of the 128-volume publication cited in the title. This index provides volume numbers, and the indexes in each volume provide page numbers.

Official Record of the Union and Confederate Navies, 1871–1865 (M275). Reproduction of the thirty-one volumes bearing the same title, available in many large reference libraries. The content is similar to that in M262 (above). The last volume is an index to all the preceding volumes.

Civil War–Union (1861–65)

A notebook titled *Compiled Service Records of Volunteer Union Soldiers* is located in the annex to the microfilm room. It contains bound pamphlets listing the military units formed in each Union state. The microfilm roll number is given for each unit and each alphabetical group sorted by the soldier's initials. After the name and unit of a Union soldier are located in the appropriate microfilmed index to compiled service records, these pamphlets must be used to ascertain the microfilm roll number that contains the service record of the soldier.

Alphabetical Card Name Index to the Compiled Service Records of Volunteer Soldiers Who Served in Union Organizations Not Raised by the States or Territories, Excepting the Veterans Reserve Corps and the U.S. Colored Troops (M1290). Reproduction of the alphabetized card indexes for the organizations listed below.

> U.S. Sharp Shooters
> U.S. Volunteers, Signal Corps
> Pioneer Brigade (Army of the Cumberland)
> U.S. Veteran Volunteers, Engineers
> U.S. Veteran Volunteers, Infantry
> U.S. Volunteer Infantry (see M1017)
> Confederate prisoners of war who enlisted in the U.S. Army
> Brigade bands
> Indian home guards
> Mississippi Marine Brigade/Marine Regiment, U.S. Volunteers
> Enlisted men transferred from the U.S. Army to the Mississippi Flotilla, 21–23 February 1862
> Departmental Corps (Department of the Monongahela)
> Varner's Battalion of Infantry
> Captain Turner's Company, Volunteer Pioneers
> Separate indexes by state or other category–Union organizations

Separate indexes of compiled service records, and the records themselves, are available on microfilm for volunteer soldiers who served in Union organizations from the states listed below.

State	Index	Records
Alabama	M263	M276
Arkansas	M383	M399
Florida	M264	M400
Georgia	M385	M403
Idaho Territory (see Washington Territory)		
Kentucky	M386	M397
Louisiana	M387	M396
Maryland	M388	M384
Mississippi	M389	M404
Missouri	M390	M405
New Mexico	M242	M427
North Carolina	M391	M401
Tennessee	M392	M395
Texas	M393	M402
Utah	M556	M692
Virginia	M394	M398
West Virginia	M507	M506

For volunteer soldiers who served in Union organizations from the states listed below, there are indexes of compiled service records on microfilm. The records themselves have not been microfilmed, but they may be requested for delivery to the Central Reading Room.

State	Index
Arizona	M532
California	M533
Colorado	M534
Connecticut	M535
Dakota Territory	M536
Delaware	M537
District of Columbia	M538
Illinois	M539
Indiana	M540
Iowa	M541
Kansas	M542
Maine	M543
Massachusetts	M544
Michigan	M545
Minnesota	M537
Nebraska Territory	M537
Nevada	M538
New Hampshire	M549
New Jersey	M550
New York	M551
Ohio	M552
Oregon	M553
Pennsylvania	M554

South Carolina	(none)
Vermont	M557
Washington Territory	M558
Wisconsin	M559
Wyoming Territory (see Washington Territory)	
U.S. Colored Troops	M589
Veterans Reserve Corps	M636

Compiled Service Records of Former Confederate Soldiers Who Served in the First Through the Sixth U.S. Volunteer Infantry Regiments, 1864–1866 (M1017). The infantry regiments described in this series were comprised of Confederate prisoners of war who gained their release by enlisting in the Union armies; they were referred to as "Galvanized Yankees." The first such regiment was formed between January and April 1864 at the prisoner-of-war camp at Point Lookout, Maryland. Between the fall of 1864 and the spring of 1865, five other such regiments were formed at prison camps in Illinois, Ohio, and Maryland. Each of these units served in the West, primarily against Indians, until mustered out of service in November 1866.

Index to Rendezvous Reports, Civil War, 1861–1865 (T1099). Series containing the names of individuals who enlisted in the navy. It is similar to the reports described in M1098 for years other than the Civil War years.

Proceedings of the U.S. Army Courts-Martial and Military Commissions of Union Soldiers Executed by U.S. Military Authorities, 1861–1866 (M1523). Proceedings of the courts-martial and military tribunals arranged in alphabetical order by name of the 267 Union soldiers who were executed during the Civil War, most of whom had been convicted of desertion or murder. The executions were commonly carried out by firing squad or by hanging.

General Index to Pension Files, 1861–1934 (T288). Pension files listed in this series refer primarily to soldiers, sailors, or marines who served in Union organizations, but also included are files of those who served in wars after the Civil War ended. In addition, some may refer to Civil War veterans with service prior to 1861.

This series reproduces alphabetized card indexes of pension applications filed by Union veterans or their dependents. Cards showing naval service are dark in color and are often difficult to read without the use of a hand lens. In addition to identifying information, application numbers and certificate numbers are shown on each card. These must be used when requesting copies of the pension files. The pension files themselves have not been microfilmed.

Organization Index to Pension Files of Veterans Who Served Between 1866 and 1900 (T289). Reproduces pension file index cards, which are arranged alphabetically by state, thereafter by unit, and thereunder by name of the soldier. This series of military unit rolls may be useful as a check against the general pension index to show Union service in the Civil

War, and it may also provide a means to discover names of unit comrades-in-arms. It may also be used when microfilm series T288 does not contain sufficient information to permit staff to locate a pension file.

Compiled Records Showing Service of Military Units in Volunteer Union Organizations (M594). As the compiled service records for individuals who served in the Civil War were being created, a complementary group of records was collected to describe the structure of the military units in which the soldiers served. Abstract cards were made from original muster rolls and the "records of events" data contained in monthly or quarterly returns filed by each unit. Records for each unit were placed in a jacket-envelope for each unit and labeled "Record of Events." Once a soldier's unit has been determined, it is possible to trace to some degree the movements and activities of his company and regiment by inspection of the records in this series.

Records are arranged alphabetically by state or territory and thereunder by organization. Units not limited to one state or one territory are arranged separately (rolls 204–225). These units include the U.S. Colored Troops, Volunteer units, and U.S. Veteran Reserve Corps.

Special Schedules of the Eleventh Census (1890) Enumerating Union Veterans and Widows of Union Veterans of the Civil War (M123). The 1890 Federal Census included a separate enumeration of names of living veterans or widows of veterans who served the United States (for the Union only) in the Civil War. However, the census enumerator sometimes inadvertently included names of Confederate veterans. Information gathered for each person included rank; name of unit; dates of enlistment and discharge; length of service; current post office and address; and disabilities incurred.

The schedules for the states of Alabama through Kansas, and approximately half of those for Kentucky, were apparently destroyed before they were transferred to the National Archives in 1943. Schedules for the remaining states are arranged by state or territory and thereafter by county and local subdivision. Counties within a state are not always arranged alphabetically, so some searching may be necessary before the correct roll is located.

Civil War–Confederate (1861–65)

The *Compiled Service Records of Confederate Soldiers* is located in the annex to the microfilm room. It contains bound pamphlets that list military units formed in each Confederate state. For each unit and each alphabetical group pertaining to the surname of the soldier, the microfilm roll number is given. After the name and unit of a Confederate soldier are located in the microfilmed index to compiled service records, these pamphlets must be used to ascertain the roll number of the microfilm that contains the soldier's service record.

There are no pension files at the National Archives for Confederate soldiers because pensions were never authorized for them by the U.S. government. See chapter 8, which describes the holdings in state repositories, for information about Confederate pensions granted by the states.

Consolidated Index to Compiled Service Records of Confederate Soldiers (M253). There are separate indexes and compiled service records of Confederate army volunteers who fought in organizations from the following states.

State	*Index*	*Records**
Alabama	M374	M311
Arizona Territory	M375	M318
Arkansas	M376	M317
Florida	M225	M251
Georgia	M226	M266
Kentucky	M377	M319
Louisiana	M378	M320
Maryland	M379	M321
Mississippi	M232	M269
Missouri	M380	M322
North Carolina	M230	M270
South Carolina	M381	M267
Tennessee	M231	M268
Texas	M277	M323
Virginia	M382	M324

*Microfilmed

Compiled Service Records of Confederate Soldiers Who Served in Organizations Raised Directly by the Confederate Government (M258). Soldiers included in this category are those whose records could not be associated with one particular state. They might have served in units formed by additions or consolidations of smaller units that were formed within a state or by more than one state. Some units were formed in the Indian Territory; some were made up of foreigners; and some were special units of the Signal Corps, Corps of Engineers, the Nitre and Mining Bureau, or a musical band.

Compiled Service Records of Confederate General and Staff Officers and Non-regimental Enlisted Men (M331). Personnel included in this category served in command units such as divisions, brigades, corps, or similar units above the regimental level. They include the general officers, certain staff officers, and enlisted men assigned to the offices of the adjutant and inspector general, the quartermaster general, the commissary general, the Medical Department, and the Ordnance Department. Also included were chaplains, physicians, drillmasters, military judges, and aides-de-camp.

Many soldiers served both in one of these types of units and also in a state volunteer unit. Both series of records should be searched to insure thoroughness.

Index to Compiled Service Records of Confederate Soldiers Who Served in Organizations Raised Directly by the Confederate Government and of Confederate General and Staff Officers and

Non-regimental Enlisted Men (M818). Index to the records described in two series above (M258 and M331). Names in this index are included in the general index of compiled service records (M253), but it is advisable to check both in the event there are omissions in one of the indexes.

Unfiled Papers and Slips Belonging to the Confederate Compiled Service Records (M347). When the service records were being compiled, many papers that mentioned soldiers who could not be identified as members of particular units were found; thus, the paper could not be filed with any jacket for a soldier with the same name. These loose papers were arranged alphabetically and microfilmed on the 442 rolls in this series. It may be possible for a researcher to identify a soldier from these papers—regardless of the fact that the clerks who attempted to do so could not.

Records Relating to Confederate Naval and Marine Personnel (M260). This series is divided into two groups: one for navy personnel and the other for marine personnel. The compiled service records in this series are similar to those for soldiers, except that the name of a ship or naval shore installation is given rather than an army unit.

Confederate States Army Casualties. Lists and Narrative Reports, 1861–1865 (M836). Lists the names of personnel who became casualties but whose names might have been omitted from inclusion in The Official Records (see chapter 9). The material was gathered from unit reports to the Confederate adjutant and inspector general pertaining to battles in which the unit participated.

Selected Records of the War Department Relating to Confederate Prisoners of War (M598). As the compiled service records for Confederate soldiers were being created, a separate group of bound volumes containing records of prisoners of war and the prisons where they were confined was placed in a separate collection. The contents of the 145 rolls in this series are shown in roll 1 as follows.

Rolls	Contents
1–6	Registers of prisoners submitted by the commissary general of prisoners (roll 4 lists deaths)
7–8	Registers of prisoners submitted by the commissary general of prisoners (roll 8 lists applications and approvals for release)
9	Registers of unclaimed money, effects of deceased soldiers, permits for furnishing of clothing to prisoners, deaths
10–12	Registers of deaths compiled by the surgeon general; arranged by state
13–139	Registers of prisons (See roll 1 for a listing of the prisons that submitted volumes of records and numbers of the rolls on which they are found.)
140–142	Division of West Mississippi
143	District of West Tennessee—provost marshal
144	Records relating to various prisons

Registers of Confederate Soldiers, Sailors, and Citizens Who Died in Federal Prisons and Military Hospitals in the North (M918). Confederate personnel who died in Union prisons dying in Union prisons were generally interred on the prison grounds—sometimes with a wooden slab marking the grave, sometimes without a marker. Pursuant to congressional legislation, a program was carried out between 1906 and 1912 to locate and mark the graves of Confederate military personnel buried in Union prisons. The graves in each of approximately sixty prisons were listed and filed in alphabetical order by prison. No general index covering all of the prisons was prepared. If it is not known in which prison an individual was buried, the alphabetical list for each prison must be searched until the name is found. If included in this register, the soldier's name, rank, unit, and precise location of the grave are given.

Muster Rolls and lists of Confederate Troops Paroled in North Carolina (M1781).

Lists of Confederates Captured at Vicksburg, Mississippi, July 4, 1863 (M2072).

Documents Relating to the Military and Naval Service of Blacks Awarded the Congressional Medal of Honor From the Civil War to the Spanish-American War (M929). In 1861 and 1862, Congress, with the approval of the president, authorized the preparation and presentation of a Medal of Honor to navy, marine, and army personnel who demonstrated "extraordinary bravery" or "gallantry in action." The first black man to receive this medal (in 1864) was an enlisted man in the navy. In 1865 the first black man serving in the army received the medal.

This series consists primarily of letters, reports, ship logs, and other papers concerning the military service of medal recipients and the basis for the awards. Descendants of blacks who married Seminole Indians and who served as scouts with the U.S. Army were included later. The records contained in this series are arranged by war or years and thereunder by name of the recipient.

Compiled Service Records Showing Service of Military Units in Confederate Organizations (M861).When the papers for compiled records of Confederate soldiers were organized, a separate abstract card labeled "Captions and Record of Events" was prepared for each mention of a Confederate military unit. The cards are arranged alphabetically by state and thereunder by name of unit. No index has been prepared.

Index to Letters Received by the Confederate Secretary of War (M409). Indexes letters described in M437. Letters received were marked by the name of the sender or other correspondent. Each letter was assigned a number and filed by year. The names of some officers, but few enlisted men, are included.

Index to Letters Received by the Confederate Adjutant and Inspector General and the Confederate Quartermaster General (M410). Indexes letters described in M474 and M469. Letters received were marked by the name of the sender or other correspondent. Each letter was assigned a number and filed by year. The names of some officers, but few enlisted men, are included.

Index and Register for Telegrams Received by the Confederate Secretary of War (M618). Telegrams were kept separate from letters. Each telegram was marked by the name of the sender or other correspondent, and each was assigned a number and logged. This series contains both the index and the registers. Each register is arranged in alphabetical order. There is no general index.

Records of the Commissioner of Claims (Southern Claims Commission), 1871–1880 (M87). Following the Civil War, citizens who had remained loyal to the Union cause often filed claims with a special commission established to consider their cases. They petitioned for redress for damages to their property growing out of the hostilities. The papers in this collection show the amount of each claim, the evidence supporting the claim, and a finding relative to the claimant's loyalty. Roll 14 is a consolidated index to the 22,298 claims considered by the commission. The records contained in this microfilm series are also available in Gary Mills' Civil War Claims in the South.

Case Files of Applications From Former Confederates for Presidential Pardons ("Amnesty Papers"), 1865–1867 (M1003). These applications were arranged in three groups: Southern states; states in the North or west; and those for which no state was identified. Papers in each group were arranged by state and thereunder alphabetically by name of the claimant. There are separate groups of papers that mention more than one claimant. There is no indication in this series as to which claims were approved or disapproved. An official document titled *Final Report of the Names of Persons Engaged in Rebellion Who Have Been Pardoned by the President, December 4, 1867* (40th Congress, 2d Sess., House Exec. Doc 16, Serial 1330) lists those that were approved. This document is available at the National Archives reading room.

Confederate Papers Relating to Citizens or Business Firms (M346). These papers consist primarily of vouchers that name individuals or firms that did business with the Confederate government or the Confederate army. The files are arranged alphabetically; no index was prepared. However, a guide that lists groups of papers alphabetically and identifies the microfilm roll where the papers may be found was created.

Papers Relating to Vessels of or Involved With the Confederate States of America ("Vessel Papers") (M909). Papers arranged in files by name of the vessel or the company that owned the vessel; each has a unique file number. The files are arranged alphabetically throughout the series. Roll 1 contains an index to the rolls in which specific files may be found.

Union Provost Marshal's File of Papers Relating to Individual Citizens (M345). After the war the provost marshals' papers were turned over to the War Department, where they were arranged alphabetically according to the individual's name. All papers referring to persons with the same name are filed in the same envelope, regardless of whether they all pertain to the same person. There is no index.

Union Provost Marshal's File of Papers Relating to Two or More Civilians (M416). As in the collection of the provost marshals' papers relating to individual citizens, other papers were arranged by criteria other than name. Some were indexed by geographical area or subject; some by names of prisoners (arranged by prison); and some by names associated with confiscation or destruction of property. Other documents (both numbered and unnumbered) were indexed chronologically. Though there is no general index to this series, the names in the series described above (M345) can serve that purpose.

Case Files of Investigation by Levi Turner and Lafayette C. Baker, 1861–1866 (M797). Turner was the U.S. Army judge advocate; Baker was a provost marshal and special agent during the Civil War. Both were involved in investigations and trials of thousands of individuals, many charged with subversion. Baker, whose jurisdiction was the District of Columbia and the adjacent Virginia counties, handled 7,748 cases. Turner dealt with fewer cases, mostly of the type tried by Baker, but he was also involved with the investigation of prospective detectives who applied for employment in the provost marshals' forces.

After the war, Turner's and Baker's papers were merged into one collection and a file number was assigned to each paper. A "B" after a file number denotes that it was one of Baker's cases. Some files contain only one paper; others contain a dozen or more. Roll 1 contains an index identifying the roll numbers according to the number assigned to each file.

Miscellaneous Pension Records, Post-Civil War

Veterans Administration Pension Payment Cards, 1907–1933 (M850). Reproduction of index cards maintained by the Veterans Administration pertaining to payments to pensioners on the pension rolls between 1907 and 1933, World War I veterans excluded. The names of Indians are indexed separately. Cards are alphabetically arranged throughout the series of 2,539 rolls of microfilm.

Index to General Correspondence of the Record and Pension Office, 1889–1920 (M686). Reproduction of a card index to general correspondence of the Records and Pension Office. Each card shows the veteran's military unit, the name of the correspondent, the subject matter, and a file number; other cards refer to names of volunteer units and to names of states. Names are alphabetically arranged throughout this series of 385 microfilm rolls.

Case Files of Approved Pension Applications for Widows and Other Dependents of Civil War and Later Navy Veterans ("Navy Widows' Certificates"), 1861–1910 (microfiche–M1279). Until 1910, applications and related correspondence were placed in jacket-envelopes. A number was assigned to each and they were numerically arranged by certificate or file number. During the 1930s the Works Progress Administration, working at the National Archives, placed each file in a large manila envelope to protect the contents from damage caused by frequent unfolding and refolding of the jacket-envelopes. The files comprise an average of sixty documents, and they are replete with military and family information. Each file was filmed on a separate microfiche (some larger files required two microfiche). These microfiche are stored in separate containers, by certificate or file number, according to whether the application was approved or disapproved. There is no separate index to this collection, but the certificate number of approved applications may be ascertained by referring to the *General Index to Pension Files, 1861–1934* (T288).

Case Files of Disapproved Pension Applications of Widows and Other Dependents of Civil War and Later Navy Veterans ("Navy Widows' Certificates"), 1861–1910 (microfiche—M1274). Collection similar to the collection of approved applications for navy pensions described in M1279 (above).

Lists of Navy Veterans for Whom There are Navy Widows' and Other Dependents' Disapproved Pension Files ("Navy Widows' Originals"), 1861–1910 (microfiche—M1291). Index, published by the National Archives, containing the disapproved applications of widows and other dependents for navy pensions. (See M1274, above.)

Spanish-American War (1898–99)

General Index to Compiled Service Records of Volunteer Soldiers Who Served During the War With Spain (M871). Reproduction of an alphabetical card index to the compiled service records of volunteer soldiers in the war with Spain. Each card lists the soldier's name, rank, and unit. Except for the records for soldiers of Florida units, these service records have not been microfilmed. See separate indexes for Florida (M1087), North Carolina (M240), and Louisiana (M13).

Philippine Insurrection (1899–1902)

Index to Compiled Service Records of Volunteer Soldiers Who Served During the Philippine Insurrection (M872). Reproduction of an alphabetical card index to the compiled service records of volunteer soldiers who participated in halting the Philippine Insurrection. Each card lists the soldier's name, rank, and unit.

World War I (1917–18)

Index to Rendezvous Reports, Armed Guard Personnel, 1917–1920 (T1101). Reproduction of alphabetical index cards that list the name, enlistment date, the name of the vessel to which the veteran was assigned, dates of service, and other miscellaneous data.

Index to Rendezvous Reports, Naval Auxiliary Service, 1917–1919 (T1100). Reproduction of alphabetical index cards that list the name, the name of the vessel to which the veteran was assigned, date of enlistment, and dates the veteran was reassigned or left the vessel.

Records of the 27th Division of the American Expeditionary Forces, 1917–1919 (M819). The New York National Guard was designated the 27th Division on 28 July 1917. After training in the United States it arrived in France between 7 May and 28 July 1917, where it underwent further training. The division participated in battles against German forces in France until it returned to the United States and was demobilized in the spring of 1919. This collection consists of unbound papers arranged according to the military decimal system based on subject matter. There is no index to these documents.

World War II (1941–45)

Mission and Combat Reports of the Fifth Fighter Command, 1942–1945 (M1065). The Fifth Fighter Command, part of the Fifth Air Force, was stationed in the Southwest Pacific area after the Philippine Islands fell to the Japanese. It participated in many air campaigns to regain the many Pacific islands. The records consist of narrative combat reports filed by squadron intelligence officers; they recount the observations of each pilot following his combat flights. Roll 1 contains a list of the fighter squadrons and groups of the Fifth Fighter Command.

Missing Air Crew Reports of the U.S. Army Air Forces, 1942–1945 (M1380). This series has not yet been transferred to the microfilm room. Check with the National Archives Military Reference Branch (chapter 4) for its present location. This series is also available at the Air Force Historical Research Agency at Maxwell Air Force Base, Montgomery, Alabama, and Bolling Air Force Base, Washington, D.C.

Military Installations and Military Academies

Historical Information Relating to Military Posts and Other Installations, ca. 1700–1900 (M661). Provides historical information for each military establishment and cites sources. Some summaries are written in longhand; others are published articles. Posts and installations are arranged alphabetically by the name of the establishment.

Lists of the Adjutant General's Office for Carded Records of Military Organizations: Revolutionary War Through Philippine Insurrection ("The Ainsworth List") (M817). Checklist used by General Ainsworth and his associates as they abstracted data from muster rolls and similar documents to create compiled service records. It is of little use to the researcher except, possibly, to learn something of the history of a given unit as it was formed or when it may have merged with another unit.

U.S. Military Academy Cadet Application Papers, 1805–1866 (M688). Reproduction of papers of cadets who applied for appointment to the U.S. Military Academy during 1805–66. These are unbound papers pertaining to the application, recommendations, and notifications of acceptance. Most are arranged by year and thereunder by file number. Papers not assigned a file number are included at the end of each year's group of papers. No papers for the year 1811 have been found. Roll 1 contains a name index by first letter of the applicant's surname. It shows the year of application, state of residence, and file number. Files containing correspondence are marked with an asterisk.

U.S. Naval Academy Registers of Delinquencies, 1846–1850; 1853–1882; and Academic and Conduct Records of Cadets, 1881–1908 (M991). Reproduction of registers of offenses or delinquencies of all naval cadets. Includes details of the misbehavior and the punishment administered, which sometimes included the imposition of demerits. Midshipmen of 1859 through 1869 were quartered on the training ships USS *Plymouth,* USS *Constitution,* and USS *Santee,* and these assignments are noted in the ledgers. Later registers also carried names and information relative to parents or guardians, previous education, and class grades. No registers for academic years 1851–53 have been found.

Selected Documents Relating to Blacks Nominated for Appointments to the U.S. Military Academy During the 19th Century, 1870– 1885 (M1002). Reproduction of documents pertaining to twenty-seven African-Americans nominated for appointment to the U.S. Military Academy between 1870 and 1887, apparently the only African-Americans nominated during that century. The papers refer to admission matters, class grades, conduct rolls, and court-martial files. The files are alphabetically arranged by name of nominee.

Military Academy Letters, 1780s–1917 (M91). Three series of letters and records as follows:

Series 1	Papers—arranged chronologically, but there is a name and subject index for each volume (1812–67)
Series 2	Academy orders—arranged chronologically with a name and subject index (1814–67)
Series 3	Miscellaneous letters and other records. There is no index to volumes 1 or 2, but there is a name and subject index to volume 3

1840 Census schedules (containing military information). Listed on each second page of the 1840 census schedules are names of revolutionary war pensioners. A few others are also included on some enumeration sheets. A government publication of 1841, *A Census of Pensioners, Revolutionary or Military Services, with Their Names, Ages, and Places of Residence,* consists of a summary of those entries. It numbers approximately 25,000 individuals arranged by state, county, and local jurisdiction. It also lists the name of the head of the household where the pensioner was living on 1 June 1840. The original census schedules may be seen on National Archives microfilm M704.

A copy of the report may also be found at the end of roll 3 of microfilm copy T498, *First Census of the United States, 1790.* An index of the report was prepared by the Genealogical Society of The Church of Jesus Christ of Latter-day Saints. The Genealogical Publishing Co. (Chicago) reprinted this index in 1965, and in 1989 it published the report and the index in one volume.

4

Resources of the National Archives Reference Branches

4

Resources of the National Archives Reference Branches

After the sources in the National Archives Microfilm Room have been exhausted, the next step is to visit one of the National Archives reference branches specializing in military records. Archivists in these branches can suggest further resources and will help the researcher examine records that may or may not have been microfilmed. The three branches comprising the generalized military reference branch are: Military Reference Branch (concerned primarily with army records); Military Reference Branch (navy); and Civil Division Reference Branch. Located in the main National Archives building in downtown Washington, D.C., these branches are located on tiers (floors) accessible only by freight elevators in the center of the building (not the passenger elevators in the main lobby). First-time users should inquire about the location of these elevators and about the appropriate tier for the desired reference branch.

Most military records pertaining to military affairs before World War II may be found at the National Archives building in Washington, D.C. In many instances, however, records of a more local nature have been transferred to an appropriate National Archives regional archives (chapter 5). In general, military records pertaining to World War II and later are housed at National Archives II in College Park, Maryland (chapter 5). Inquiries concerning the location of specific records may be directed to the Textual Reference Division (NNR), National Archives, Washington, D.C. 10408.

A research card is required when visiting reference branches, and a log must be signed when entering and leaving. Assistance is available from a specialist in these branches. He or she may suggest records or may permit the researcher to consult a *Preliminary Inventory*, prepared by the National Archives, to identify an appropriate record group, from which the researcher may select collections that appear promising. The "entry number" and title of the chosen collections must be indicated on a request form and submitted to the archivist for approval before the form is placed in a designated "pick-up" box. A searcher will then locate the desired records and deliver them to the Central Reading Room (room 203). If the records are on microfilm, they will be delivered to the Microfilm Room (room 400). There may be a wait of an hour or more. Copies can be made on nearby machines (with staff approval).

Military Reference Branch

Record collections in the Military Reference Branch are arranged in numbered record groups, each of which contains documents created by or received by a specific government office or which consists of documents relating to one particular subject. Representative record groups in this branch are listed below.

RG 15	Veterans Administration
RG 18	Textual Records of the Army Air Force
RG 49	Bureau of Land Management
RG 74	Records of the Bureau of Ordnance
RG 77	Office of the Chief of Engineers
RG 92	Office of the Quartermaster General
RG 93	War Department Collection of Revolutionary War Records
RG 94	Adjutant General's Office, 1780s–1917
RG 107	Office of the Secretary of War
RG 108	Headquarters of the Army
RG 109	War Department Collection of Confederate Records
RG 110	Provost Marshal General's Bureau (Civil War)
RG 112	Surgeon General (army)
RG 120	American Expeditionary Forces (World War I), 1917–18
RG 125	Judge Advocate General
RG 128	American Expeditionary Forces (World War I)
RG 141	Vera Cruz Occupation (1914)
RG 147	Selective Service System (1914)
RG 153	Office of the Judge Advocate General, 1808–1942
RG 156	Office of the Chief of Ordnance
RG 159	Office of the Inspector General, 1814–1949
RG 163	Selective Service System, World War I
RG 165	War Department, General and Special Staffs
RG 168	Records of the National Guard Bureau
RG 231	United States Soldiers' Home
RG 247	Office of the Chief of Chaplains
RG 249	Office of the Commissary General of Prisoners, 17 June 1862–19 August 1867
RG 391	U.S. Regular Army Mobile Units, 1821–1942
RG 392	U.S. Coast Artillery Districts and Defenses, 1901–42
RG 393	U.S. Army Continental Commands, 1821–1920 (in five parts) (formerly RG 98)
RG 394	U.S. Army Continental Commands, 1821–1920
RG 395	Operations and Commands (geographical areas)
RG 404	Records of the United States Military Academy (available at West Point, New York)
RG 407	Records of the Adjutant General's Office, 1917

Record Collections

The following are titles of selected collections, arranged by record group, that are available upon request through the Military Reference Branch. A more complete listing can be found in the appropriate *Preliminary Inventory* for each record group.

RG 15–Veterans Administration

The Veterans Administration was created by executive order on 20 July 1930 by combining these previously existing agencies: Bureau of Pensions, United States Veterans' Bureau, National Home for Disabled Volunteer Soldiers, and the functions of the Office of the Surgeon General concerned with providing artificial limbs and other appliances to veterans. The agency was given departmental status in 1989 as the Department of Veterans Affairs. (Note that World War II records have been transferred to the National Archives regional archives–see chapter 5.) Examples of records:

Unindexed Bounty Land records, 1790–1855. Includes names of men who never applied for a pension.

Registers of Appeals, 1867–70; 1880–84; 1918–20.

Indexes to Records of Civil War Military Hospitals, 1882. Most of the records refer to hospitals, 1861–66. The actual records listed in this index are now in RG 94, Office of the Adjutant General.

Register of Patients at a Convalescent Camp at Vicksburg, Mississippi, 1863.

Records of Personnel Assignments, 1881–1909. An alphabetical list of employees, apparently of the Special Examiner's Division, with related information.

Efficiency Records of Pension Bureau Employees, 1884–85. Names, dates of appointment, salaries, and related information.

Criminal and Civil Registers, 1875–1914. Summaries of proceedings and judgments in cases involving fraud in pension claims, with names and dispositions; indexed.

Lists of Dependents of Veterans Who Served in the "Old Wars," 1872–1927. Includes names of widows and minor children who applied for increases in pensions.

List of Army and Navy Officers Imprisoned in Libby Prison, Richmond, Virginia, in 1863 and 1864. Arranged by rank and alphabetically by name.

Index to General Administration Files, 1910–25.

Training Centers. Arranged alphabetically by name of school or center, 1918–25.

Card Catalog of Training Centers and Their Locations, 1918–25.

Prints and Photographs of Schools and Training Centers, 1918–25.

Department and Region Files (by name of city in which located), 1918–25.

Lists of National and State Homes for Soldiers and Sailors, 1922–27.

Register of Cases (vocational education), June 1918–July 1920.

RG 18—Textual Records of the Army Air Force

The first specific governmental unit devoted to military aircraft was the Aeronautical Division in the Office of the Signal Corps, established 1 August 1907. Subsequent aviation divisions and sections existed within the Signal Corps until 19 May 1918. The unit was reorganized on 19 March 1919 as the Bureau of Aircraft Production, Division of Military Aeronautics. On 4 June 1920, the Air Service became a component part of the army; the name was changed on 2 July 1927 to the United States Army Air Corps and eventually to the United States Army Air Force. The National Security Act of July 1947 designated the United States Air Force as a separate department, giving it equal status with the army and the navy. Examples of records:

Records of Air Service and Air Corps Units, 1917–41.

Records of Airfields, 1917–41. The name of the airfield must be specified.

RG 49—Bureau of Land Management

The land entry papers of the United States General Land Office consist of many collections of bounty land grants for military service prior to the Civil War. A series of measures authorizing bounty land to veterans of the revolutionary war were authorized by Congress. Qualifying veterans were issued warrants that permitted them to locate a plot of land in a specified territory.

This branch has the original warrants and related papers issued under the various acts of Congress, but it is necessary to identify the act under which a warrant was issued, along with the assigned number, before the record can be located. A new numbering system was instituted with the passage of each new act; thus, each series begins with number one. To ascertain the date of the act and the warrant number, the researcher may inspect the bounty land files, available in this section, or as found in one or more of the collections cited below. (Note that some Bureau of Land Management records have been transferred to the National Archives regional archives.) Examples of records:

Warrants Issued Under Act of 9 July 1788. Warrants of this series numbered 1 through 6,912 were destroyed when the British burned much of Washington in 1814.

Warrants Issued Under Acts of 3 March 1803 and 15 April 1806. These warrants could be exchanged for scrip.

Applications for Military Bounty-land Scrip (in accordance with the acts of 30 May 1830; 13 July 1832; 2 March 1833; 3 March 1835; and 31 August 1852).

Virginia Military Bounty-land Warrants Surrendered to the Federal Government. These are arranged by volume and page number of the patent record in the General Land Office.

Virginia Resolution Warrants (issued under state resolutions) and Authorizing Grants in Addition to Those Already Made.

Lists of Federal Revolutionary Bounty-land Warrants Presented for Registry (presented to claim land in the Military District of Ohio). These provide the warrant number, name of the person to whom the warrant was issued, acreage, and name of person who presented the warrant for registration.

Treasury Certificates. Statements by the secretary of the treasury to the effect that certificates under the acts of 1796 and 1799 were valid and that the holders were eligible for a land patent.

Canadian Refugee Warrants, 1802–11. Issued during the revolutionary war to individuals who fled British provinces in Canada and Nova Scotia.

Canadian Volunteer Warrants. Issued to Canadians who volunteered to serve in the military during the War of 1812.

Exchange Certificates. Issued under legislation authorizing holders of bounty-land warrants to exchange them for new locations other than where previously authorized.

Revolutionary Warrants. Issued under acts that extended the time for issuing warrants (27 January 1835; 27 July 1842; and 26 June 1848).

Papers Relating to Revolutionary Bounty-land Scrip. These relate to scrip issued under the act of 31 August 1852.

Double-bounty Warrants Issued Under Act of 6 May 1812. Authorized 320 acres rather than the previous 160 acres.

Warrants Issued Under Various Acts, as Follows:

> Sixty acres; 24 December 1811; 11 January 1812; 6 May 1812; and 27 July 1842
>
> Forty or 160 acres: 11 February 1847
>
> Forty, 80 , or 160 acres: 28 September 1850
>
> Forty, 80, or 160 acres: 22 March 1852
>
> Ten, 40, 60 , 80, 100, 120, or 160 acres: 3 March 1855

Virginia Military Warrants–Kendrick Cases. Papers chiefly relating to Virginia warrants that involved Eleazer P. Kendrick, surveyor, Virginia Military District, Chillicothe, Ohio.

Warrants Issued Under Act of 9 July 1788.

RG 74–Records of the Bureau of Ordnance

Card Index to Correspondence, 1914-26; 1926-43.

RG 77–Office of the Chief of Engineers

Before 1802 there existed a Corps of Artillerists and Engineers. An act of March 1802 divided that organization into two separate corps, directing that the Corps of Engineers was to constitute a military academy at West Point, New York. Its primary military functions are to build roads and camps and to produce and distribute maps for the army. Its civil functions are to build and maintain inland waterways, dams, and harbor facilities related to navigable waters. Examples of records:

Corres pondence, 1890-94; 1894-1923; 1917-42.

Name Index to Correspondence, 1917-42.

Card Catalog Showing Origin, Authorization, and Mobilization of Engineer Units, World War I, 1914.

Card Catalog of Designation of Posts, Buildings, and Facilities, 1922-41. Arranged alphabetically by name of establishment.

Records of Engineer Divisions and Districts, 1833-1948. The division or district must be specified.

Register of Letters Received, 1826-70. Arranged by time period and thereunder by initial of the letter writer's surname; serves as an index to the collection shown below.

Letters Received, 1826-66. Refers to name and location of military unit; consists principally of reports and correspondence.

RG 92–Office of the Quartermaster General

Congress created a Quartermaster's Department in 1818 to serve the army. The department was charged with developing efficient systems of supply, troop movement, and accountability over officers and agents charged with money and supplies. Related functions, such as those involving clothing, transportation, purchases and storage, and jurisdiction over cemeteries were added at various times, while some functions were transferred to other agencies. The National Defense Act of 4 June 1920 restored many of the department's former functions, including transportation and construction, but placed pay functions in a separate Finance Department. During World War II the transportation and construction responsibilities were removed, and responsibility for the procurement of food and clothing was transferred to the Defense Supply Agency. Other functions were later transferred to other new agencies, and the Quartermaster Department (Quartermaster Corps) was officially abolished on 23 July 1962. Examples of records:

Letter s Sent (to the secretary of war or heads of departments), 1818-70. Indexed through May 1833.

Correspondence, Claims Papers, Lists, 1890-1919. Indexes available.

Register and Reports (persons and articles hired or employed), 1834-60.

List of Officers and Their Service During the Mexican War, 1848.

Applications for Headstones for Soldiers Buried at the Soldiers' Home, 1909-23.

Applications for Headstones in Private Cemeteries, 1909-24. Arranged alphabetically by state, county, and name of cemetery.

Applications for Headstones [for soldiers] Buried Outside the United States, 1911-24.

List of Headstones for Soldiers Buried in Private Cemeteries During 1861-86. Arranged numerically.

Registers of Superintendents at National Cemeteries, 1867-83. Arranged by name and cemetery.

List of Soldiers Buried in [various states and cemeteries]. M1845, *Card Records of Headstones Provided for Deceased Union Civil War Veterans, ca 1879-ca 1903*. 22 rolls.

List of Union Soldiers Buried in Various National Cemeteries, 1861-79. Arranged by state, burial location, and name of soldier.

List of Interments of Colored Troops During the Civil War. Many lists arranged by place of burial; name of cemetery or place given.

Register of Claims Received from Civilians for Services Performed, 1848-60. Includes wagonmasters, saddlers, laborers, guides, and others.

Registers of Notaries Public, ca. 1860s and ca. 1870s.

Personal Histories of Regular Officers of the Quartermaster Department, 1846-1905. Indexes in vols. 2 and 8.

Personal Histories of Volunteer Officers in the Quartermaster Department, 1861-65; 1898-1901.

Historical Register of Clerks and Other Employees, 1861-1911. Arranged by time period and then alphabetically by name.

Personnel Records. Transfers, promotions, reductions, appointments, declinations, separations, reinstatements.

Register of Officers Reporting to Port of Embarkation, Hoboken, New York, November 1917-February 1918.

Lists of Vessels Leaving the United States to Transport Troops to Europe, 1917-19.

Alphabetical Card List of Vessels Sailing From Ports in the United States to Foreign Ports, 1917-19.

List of Vessels Sailing From Hoboken, New York, ca. 1919.

Register of Commissioned Vessels and Transports Sailing From Ports of Embarkation, 1917-18.

Outgoing Passenger Lists and Related Correspondence, 1918–19.

Incoming Passenger Lists and Related Correspondence, 1918–20.

Papers Relating to Burials of Deceased Personnel, 1915–19. Arranged alphabetically by name.

Alphabetical Card Register of Burials of Deceased American Soldiers, 1917–22.

Alphabetical Card Register of Noncombatant Deaths, 1918–19.

Alphabetical Card Register of American Soldiers Buried in Russian Cemeteries, 1918–19.

Alphabetical Card Register of German Soldiers Buried in American Cemeteries in Europe ("Allied File"), 1917–18.

Card List of Map Locations of Cemeteries. An alphabetical list of names of French communes or cities.

Alphabetical Card Register of Confirmed Disinterments and Reburials of American Soldiers, 1917–19.

Army Transport Service Records, 1918–19. Alphabetical card register of chartered vessels, 1917–19.

Lists of Chartered Vessels, 1918–19.

RG 93—War Department Collection of Revolutionary War Records

When the War Department was created on 7 August 1789, the secretary of war was given custody of all books and papers concerned with the revolutionary war. Most of those records were destroyed by fire on 8 November 1800. When several government buildings in Washington were destroyed by fires set by British soldiers in August 1814, the revolutionary war papers were in a fireproof vault and were not damaged. However, persons who entered the vault after the fire either carried the papers away or destroyed them.

In 1873 the private papers of Timothy Pickering, who held several high-level positions with the government between 1777 and 1785, were sold to the government; custody was given to the War Department. The papers were transferred to the State Department, where a planned history of the war was being prepared. When the War Department established a Record and Pension Division in 1889, Congress was asked to order that all revolutionary war papers held by other government agencies be turned over to the War Department. By legislation in 1892 and 1894, military records were transferred from the State Department to the War Department. These included the Pickering papers, some returns of the Continental Army that had once belonged to George Washington, pension files of the Department of the Interior, and the accounts of the auditor of the Treasury Department. In 1919, Henry G. Pickering, great-grandson of Timothy Pickering, donated a large

number of quartermaster records concerned with matters of supply and pay. In 1914 and 1915 the revolutionary war records held by the states of Virginia, North Carolina, and Massachusetts were copied for the War Department. Examples of records:

Index to Part of Series 5 (numbered orderly books and numbered record books) (118 volumes). Arranged by volume number and thereunder alphabetically.

Name Index to Series 5, 6, and 9 ("Special Index"). Lists names of records that were not abstracted when the military service records were compiled.

Name Index to Virginia Records in Series 9. Names of persons in Virginia military units.

Register of Army Returns. Returns of various companies and oaths of allegiance.

List of Revolutionary War Officers. Alphabetical lists of officers for each state, one list for the Continental Line, a list of officers named in the Journals of Congress, and a list of aides to General Washington. Most were prepared from the compiled service records.

List of New Hampshire Officers and Men Who Received Certificates for Depreciation of Pay.

List of Certificates Issued by the State of Pennsylvania for Depreciation of Pay.

List of Pennsylvania Officers and Men Entitled to Donation Lands.

Several miscellaneous account books, pay ledgers, receipt books and records of stores, etc. (See the *Preliminary Inventory* for this record group.)

RG 94—Adjutant General's Office, 1780s–1917

By act of the Continental Congress on 17 June 1775, an adjutant general was appointed and served until 1783. The office then remained vacant until 5 March 1792, when an adjutant, who was also to function as an inspector, was named. The Office of Adjutant and Inspector General was established on 3 March 1813. On 2 March 1821, the Office of the Adjutant General was separated from the Office of the Inspector General, and, except for the brief period between 1904 and 1907, has been in continuous existence ever since. This office has been charged with matters relating to command, discipline, and administration. It is responsible for recording, authenticating, and communicating the orders, regulations, and instructions of the secretary of war to all military units and personnel. To assure its successful operation, almost all military records were turned over to that office. In 1889, these included the papers of the Record and Pension Division of the War Department. The office was also charged with record-keeping for the military and hospital units of volunteer armies. The record collections of the Office of the

Adjutant General might well be the most helpful source of military data for the entire period of the United States' existence. Examples of records:

Index to Correspondence Relating to Officers, 1890–1917.

Personnel File, Reserve Officers. Indexed.

Muster Rolls of Regular Army Organizations, 1784–31 October 1912. In three groups: 1791–95; 1795–1821; 1821–31 October 1912. Some rolls in the second group are too fragile to handle, but the names probably were included in the "Register of Enlistments." These are generally arranged by military unit and thereunder alphabetically by name.

Muster Rolls of Volunteer Organizations: War With Northwest Indians, 1790–95 ("Wayne's War"). Generally filed according to state or special military organization.

Muster Rolls of Volunteer Organizations: War of 1812, 1812–15. Contain rolls for state militia and other volunteer organizations; arranged alphabetically by state.

Muster Rolls of Volunteer Organizations in Various Indian Wars and Other Incidents Requiring the Employment of Troops, 1811–58. Rolls for those participating in the Black Hawk War and other events.

Muster Rolls of Volunteer Organizations: Civil War, Mexican War, Creek War, Cherokee Removal, and other wars, 1836–65 (primarily for the Civil War and the Mexican War). Arranged alphabetically by state.

Muster Rolls of Volunteer Organizations: Spanish-American War, 1898. Arranged chronologically by state.

Muster Rolls of Volunteer Organizations: Philippine Insurrection, 1899–1901. Arranged by arm of service, numerically by regiment, and thereunder alphabetically by company.

The Regular Army and Indian Wars and Expeditions: Enlistment Papers, 1798–31 October 1912. Separate files for each individual; filed alphabetically by time periods.

Index to Enlistment Papers, Indian Scouts, 1866–1914. Arranged in four volumes: New Mexico; Indian Territory and Oklahoma; northern; and Arizona.

Returns of "Expeditions," 1806–1916. Pertain to miscellaneous expeditions such as those undertaken to quell the Apaches; the Fort Walla Walla and Fort Benton Wagon Road Expedition; Captain Pope's Artesian Wells Expedition; and the Pacific Railway Survey of 1855–56; arranged alphabetically by subject.

Record of Officers and Soldiers Killed in Battle and Died in Service During the Florida War. Records include names of those who died of disease.

Summaries Relating to the History of Various Regular Army Units, Date of Organization to 1902. Include organizational changes, list of engagements, and companies participating in such engagements. Except when participating in the Civil War or Mexican War, some units of the regular army were engaged during most of the nineteenth century in almost continuous offensive and defensive actions against American Indians. A

card index titled *Index to Indian Wars, 1790–1913* is available upon request in this branch. The cards in this index list the actions by location, name of the battle, and name of commanding officers. Each card cites references for historical information, both published and in National Archives holdings according to record group. See also a record kept by the U.S. adjutant generals' offices, *Chronological List of Actions, etc., With Indians From January 15, 1837 to January, 1891*, available in this branch. These entries show, among other things, the names of the military units participating in each action. In most instances, the source of the information is given (most often a regimental return).

Records Relating to Prisoners (War of 1812). These constitute original correspondence and reports chiefly concerned with American prisoners of war held by the British, and they involve negotiations for exchange of British prisoners held in America. Much of the material concerns matters of finance and supply, but it also contains some lists of prisoners as well as correspondence regarding particular prisoners. Chief among the correspondents are Reuben G. Beasley, Agent for American Prisoners of War in London; masters of American ships; United States marshals of several American cities; and officials in the Office of the Commissary General of Prisoners. The documents are arranged in ten document boxes by numbered bundles.

Indexes to Records Relating to Prisoners (War of 1812). A series of several hundred alphabetically arranged cards in three document boxes. Each card indicates the name of an individual mentioned in the collection described above, with the designation of the bundle (manuscript number). See also 2019, *Records Relating to the War of 1812 Prisoners of War*.

Register of Deceased Soldiers, Volunteers, 1861–64. Arranged by year and thereunder alphabetically by initial letter of the soldier's surname; military unit, date, cause, and place of death.

Reference Cards Relating to Courts-martial, 1861–65. Arranged by state and thereunder by regiment; names and organizations of soldiers tried.

Reports of Furloughs Granted to Sick and Wounded. Furloughs were granted pursuant to a general order issued on 9 August 1898 that authorized one month's furlough and transportation to homes when able to travel. These give name, unit, and destination; arranged numerically.

Index to Casualties (predominantly pre-Spanish-American War). Name, rank, and unit, nature of wounds, and cause of death. Some names for the Spanish-American War are included. Cards H–L are missing.

Semi-annual Rolls of Cadets, U.S. Military Academy, 1812–26; 1818–49; 1870–1915. Name, state, and district from which appointed, place of residence, date of birth, and other related information, such as the names of parents (in some instances).

Merit Rolls, U.S. Military Academy, 1818–66. Annual rolls showing names, class standing, and grades in each subject; arranged chronologically. See also similar lists of monthly reports and records of examination list in the *Preliminary Inventory*.

Register of Cadets, U.S. Military Academy, 1803-65. Arranged by initial letter of surname and thereunder by date of application. (Also see Index to Cadet Applications, 1814-66.)

Record of "Admissions to the Insane Asylum," 1862-1917. Lists soldiers committed to St. Elizabeth's Hospital for the Insane, Washington, D.C. (See also Register of Insane Soldiers, 1855-1919.)

Lists of Commissions of Officers. These are of many types. (See the *Preliminary Inventory* for specific titles of collections.)

Registers of Post Traders, 1821-89. Arranged by military post. An index is included in one of the four volumes.

Registers of Claims, U.S. Colored Troops, 1864-67. Claims by slave owners in Kentucky, Maryland, and Tennessee for use of their slaves in the military. The name of the claimant and the name of the slave are included.

List of "Minority" Cases. Contains names of minors who refunded bounty money.

Applications for Appointment (Colored Troops), 1863-65. Applications to appear before an examining board for positions of officer in the "colored troops."

Roster of Officers of U.S. Colored Troops, 1863-66.

Descriptive Lists of Colored Volunteers, 1864. Name, place of birth, occupation, enlistment data, and physical description. If the soldier was a former slave, his owner's name is included. Each of the fifty-four volumes has an index.

Index to Letters Received (Deserters' Division), 1875-89.

Registers of Prisoners, 1872-89. Names of prisoners confined in military prisons, nature of crime and sentence, and related information.

Index to Registers of Prisoners. Lists the names in the two-volume collection described above.

Field Records of Hospitals, 1821-1912. (See the *Preliminary Inventory* for this record group (entry no. 544) for specific indexes to the 11,000 volumes available.)

List of Medical Officers Serving at Permanent Posts, 1860-93.

Record of Medical Officers: Mexican War, 1846-48.

Service Record Cards of Volunteer Surgeons, 1861-65.

Reports of Sick and Wounded, 1820-60. These reports provide numbers of patients and numbers of deaths, along with names of those who died, usually listed on the reverse of the reports; arranged by state and also by stations in Mexico during the Mexican War; includes reports from Gen. Winfield Scott's army.

Reports of Sick and Wounded, 1887-1904.

Registers of the Physical Examinations of Recruits, 1864-1912.

Indexes to Casualty Lists: Civil War, 1861-65. Two lists: one is a collection of ten bound volumes; the other is a card file. Numbers on the lists refer to specific collections of casualty lists.

Death Register, 1864-65. Indexed.

RG 107—Office of the Secretary of War

The Department of War was created on 7 August 1789. It was assigned responsibility for recruiting, provisioning, and regulating all military and naval forces, administering pensions and bounty lands, and overseeing Indian affairs. The responsibility for naval matters was removed from the secretary of war when the Department of the Navy was established on 30 April 1798. Responsibility for Indian affairs was transferred to the Department of the Interior in 1849. Eventually, the pension duties were transferred to the Veterans Administration. In more modern times bureaus were added to the Department of War, and its emphasis gravitated toward policy and general administration, leaving more specific administration to various military commands. Example of records:

Letters Sent and Received, 1871-89. Index in each volume.

RG 108—Headquarters of the Army

The Office of the Headquarters of the Army existed between 1798 and 1903, with the commanding general of the army responsible for distribution of military forces and discipline of the troops. His duties were turned over to the chief of staff on 15 August 1903. Examples of records:

Name and Subject Index to Letters Received, January-August 1862; August-December 1815; 1873-1903.

Letters Received Relating to Military Discipline and Control, 1827-46; 1849-1969; 1873-1903.

Name Index to Special Orders, 1873-74.

Special Orders, 1849-1950; 1853-61; 1873-76.

Register of Discharges of Enlisted Personnel, 1853-61. Alphabetized by first letter of surname; provide name, rank, unit, commanding officer, cause of disability, and remarks.

Register of Military Personnel Applying for a Furlough, January 1902-August 1903 (refers only to those applying through the Headquarters of the Army).

Register of Officers and Enlisted Personnel Applying to Headquarters for Leaves of Absence, Resignations, and Discharges, May 1863-April 1865 (concerns only those pertaining to General Halleck).

Rosters of Troops, 1866-79. Arranged by military district, division, or department and thereunder chronologically. The name of the unit and time period must be ascertained before this collection is searched.

Registers of Letters Received, August 1863-September 1865. Indexed.

List of Officers Mustered, April-May 1863.

Register of Applications Received for Appointment as Veterinarian Surgeons, 1863-65. Name index available.

List of Buyers of Horses at Auction Sales at Giesboro Depot, 1864-66.

Letters Sent by General Grant, March 1864–December 1865. Indexed. Also available are letters sent from Washington, D.C., to General Grant.

Letters Received by General Grant, March 1864–August 1865. Indexed.

Spanish-American War Correspondence: Letters Sent From Florida, Cuba, and Puerto Rico, May–September 1896. Name and subject index in each volume.

RG 109–War Department Collection of Confederate Records

On July 21, 1865, for historical purposes, the secretary of war established a unit in the adjutant general's office that was charged with the collection, safekeeping, and publication of "Confederate Records," then referred to as the "Rebel Archives." (Note that some Confederate records have been transferred to the various National Archives regional archives.) Examples of records:

Compiled Service Records (described earlier).

Index to Appointments of Officers, 1861–65.

Casualty Lists, 1861–65.

Several Record Books for Hospitals and Patients' Registers for Hospitals in the South. The city in which the hospital was located during the Civil War must be specified.

Register of Prisoners, Office of the Commissary General of Prisoners.

Death Register of Prisoners, Surgeons, General Officers.

Parole Rolls of Confederates, 1862–65.

Lists of Civilians Taking the Oath of Allegiance or Giving Bond, 1862–64.

Reference File Relating to Signatures of Confederate Officers, 1861–65.

M1791–*Muster Rolls and Lists of Confederate Troops Paroled in North Carolina.*

RG 110–Provost Marshal General's Bureau (Civil War)

The Provost Marshal General's Bureau was established on 3 March 1863. It was charged with the responsibility of enrolling and drafting men into military service for the Union Army and of detecting and apprehending deserters. Branch offices and agents were set up in each state. Following the war, on 20 August 1866, this bureau was abolished and its records were transferred to the Office of the Adjutant General. Examples of records:

List of Deserters, Aliens, Recruits, Employees, Special Agents, Letters, etc. Arranged by state. The state and type of information desired must be specified.

Part I   Central office

Part II   Maine, New Hampshire, Vermont, Massachusetts, Connecticut, Rhode Island

Part III   New York

Part IV   New Jersey, Pennsylvania

Part V   Delaware, Maryland, District of Columbia, West Virginia, Kentucky, Missouri

Part VI   Ohio, Indiana

Part VII   Illinois, Michigan, Wisconsin, Iowa

Part VIII   Kansas, Nebraska, Colorado, Dakota, Minnesota, California, Nevada, Oregon, Washington, Arkansas, Tennessee

List of Deserters Sought Within the Military Department.

Register of Drafted Men, Recruits, and Substitutes, December 1863–April 1865.

RG 112–Surgeon General (army)

On 14 April 1818, an Office of the Surgeon General was established, and all surgeons and surgeon's mates were ordered to submit to that office reports, returns, and communications relating to medical matters. The office includes the Medical Corps, Dental Corps, Veterinary Corps, Medical Service Corps, Army Nurse Corps, and the Army Medical Specialist Corps. Examples of records:

Name Index of Civilian Doctors Volunteering Services During the Spanish-American War.

Name Index to Contract Surgeons, 1839, 1874.

Reports Relating to Living Conditions at Army Posts in North Carolina, South Carolina, Georgia, Florida, and Alabama, 1868–69.

List of Applicants for Appointment to the Medical Department, 1816–1954. A name index is in vol. 1.

Report of Examinations of Candidates for Appointment of Regular Army Surgeons ("Merit Rolls"), 1860 and 1888.

Case Files of Candidates for Appointment to the Medical Corps Who Were Examined by Army Medical Examiner Boards, 1890–1917.

Personal Histories of Candidates Seeking Appointment to the Medical Corps, 1894–1917.

Register of Applicants Seeking Appointment as Assistant Surgeons, 1898–1901.

Professional Qualification Cards of Candidates Seeking Appointment as Army Medical Surgeons, 1916–1918.

List of Officers in the Medical Department, 1775–1892.

Military Service Cards of Retired or Deceased Medical Officers, 1813–1914.

Military Service Cards of Regular Army Officers of the Medical Corps, 1894–1917.

Station Books of Medical Officers, 1857–1902. Arranged alphabetically by name of post or camp.

Register of Deaths of Regular Army Officers, 1861–96.

Case Files of Candidates Seeking Appointment as Army Nurses, 1898–1917.

Registers of Military Service of Hospital Stewards, 1856–87 (eight volumes). A name index is in each volume.

Descriptive Book of Hospital Stewards, 1863–67. Indexed.

List of Volunteer Medical Officers Who Served With the Civil War Army Corps, 1861–65.

Registers of Deaths of Civil War Voluntary Medical Officers, 1863–96.

Rosters of Regimental Medical Officers, U.S. Volunteers, Spanish-American War, 1898–1901. Alphabetically arranged by home state of the military unit.

Register of Volunteer Medical Officers Who Served in the Philippine Islands, 1898–1902.

Rosters of Contract Surgeons on Duty With Regular Army Units, 1898–1903.

Personal Data Cards of Spanish-American War Contract Nurses, 1898–1939.

Register of Civilian Employees of the Surgeon-General's Office, and of the Medical Supply Depots, 1891–97.

List of Female Nurses, Cooks, and Laundresses Employed in Army Hospitals During the Civil War. Arranged by place, name of hospital, and thereunder alphabetically by name.

Muster rolls, Walter Reed General Hospital, 1911.

Walter Reed General Hospital, Washington, D.C., 1909–19. Muster rolls.

Walter Reed General Hospital, Washington, D.C., 1911–12. Returns of hospital corps detachments.

Walter Reed General Hospital, Washington, D.C., 1909–12. Medical case files and detachments.

RG 120—American Expeditionary Forces (World War I), 1917–18

Examples of records:

General Correspondence, Office of the Commander in Chief, 1917–20. Indexed by subject: assignments and transfers, self-inflicted wounds, and personnel.

War Diaries, 1917–18. Arranged by military unit.

Name Card File of Casualties in the AEF (American Expeditionary Force), 1917–19. Compiled by the American Red Cross.

Monthly Rosters of German Prisoners of War Labor Companies Numbered 1–226, 1918–19.

Miscellaneous Correspondence, Reports, Orders, and Other Records of Various Branches and Offices of the AEF. Branches and offices and the nature of the material desired must be specified.

RG 125—Judge Advocate General

Examples of records:

Records Relating to General Courts-martial, Courts of Inquiry, Boards of Investigation, and Boards of Inquest, 1841–1943 (156 volumes). (Registers are found in vols. 28 and 44; index in vol. 33. See below.)

Register of General Courts-martial, 1861–1904. Included are case number, date and place of trial, charges, substance of specification, plea, findings, sentences, and remarks as to approval of sentence.

Records of Proceedings of Courts of Inquiry, Boards of Investigation, and Boards of Inquest, 1866–1940 (ninety-seven volumes).

Register of Prisoners Under Sentence of General Courts-martial, 1877–92.

List of Officers Tried by General Court-martial, 1879–1920. Arranged alphabetically by name of defendant.

Register of General Courts-martial, 1909–43. Arranged by naval district and thereunder chronologically.

Record of Proceedings of General Courts-martial for Personnel of the Coast Guard, 1917–19.

Rough Register of General Courts-martial ("Records"), 1924–35. Arranged numerically.

Index to Summary Courts-martial, 1855–80; 1886–95. Arranged by volume and thereunder by initial of name of defendant; name and rating, date and number of trial, and yard or vessel where the trial took place.

Register of Summary Courts-martial, 1880–87.

Index to Summary Courts-martial, 1893–1904.

Slip Record of Summary Courts-martial, 1904–30. Slips of paper arranged by year and thereunder by name of defendant. These slips are the only form in which this information has been preserved.

Slip Record of Deck Courts, 1909–30. (See above.)

Register of Examination of Regular Engineers, 1836–94. Name of candidate, rank, grade for which examined, age, experience, subjects in which examined, grade received, and date and place of examination.

Register of Retiring Boards, 1880–1911. Name, date and place of examination, rank of examining officer, date, and finding.

Register of Examining Boards, 1880–1904 (same data as above).

Index to Correspondence Relating to Desertion and Discharge, 1892–1908.

Register of Probationers, 1906–09.

Record of War Prisoners, 1917–18. Name and number, place and date captured, rank or occupation, sex, nationality, age, physical description, place of birth, home address, name and address of person to be notified, and medical record.

RG 141–Vera Cruz Occupation (1914)

Examples of records:

Card Index to Correspondence of the Officer in Charge of Civil Affairs, April–November 1914.

Card Index to Correspondence of the Administrator of Customs and Captain of the Ports, April–November 1914.

Lighthouse Service Payrolls, May–November 1914.

Index to Correspondence (various types), entries 121–131.

Photographs of prisoners, May–September 1914 (prisoners committed to the municipal jail).

Orders for Release of Prisoners, May–November 1914 (orders of the chief of police).

RG 153–Office of the Judge Advocate General (1808-1942)

With the Articles of War constituting the laws of the military establishment since the establishment of the Continental Army in 1775, attorneys were deemed necessary. The first army judge advocate was named in 1797, and in 1849 an Office of the Judge Advocate of the Army was established. That office holder was subsequently designated judge advocate general on 17 July 1862. This office was charged with keeping the records and proceedings of courts-martial, military commissions, and courts of inquiry. In 1884, the judge advocate general's office became a department and was empowered to supervise the system of military justice, perform appellate reviews of trials by court-martial, and furnish legal services to the army. Examples of records:

Index to Letters Sent, 1842–76 (four volumes). Vol. 1 is a subject index; vols. 2, 3, and 4 are name indexes.

Index to Letters Sent, 1882–95 (four volumes).

Index to Letters Received, 1871–76; 1885–88.

Court-martial Case Files, 1808–15; 1809–1938.

Civil War Courts-martial, some with Abraham Lincoln's signature. –MM761. A published index is currently being prepared by Thomas P. Lowry.

Index to Court-martial Cases, 1891–1917.

Court-martial Orders, 1810–24.

Clemency Orders, 1894–97.

Records Relating to Lincoln Assassination Suspects, April 1865. Available on microfilm M599.

Registers and Index of Court-martial Case Files, 1865–67; Index to Courts-martial Cases, 1891–1917. Included are name, rank, unit, and sentence; arranged alphabetically by name of defendant.

Court-martial Case Files, 1891–38.

Registers of Court-martial cases, 1809–90. Name and number, rank, unit, and when and where tried; arranged alphabetically by name of defendant.

Briefs of AEF (American Expeditionary Force) Court-martial Cases, 1918–20. Arranged alphabetically.

Mexican Claims Case Files, 1916. Claims by Mexicans for damages deriving from the Vera Cruz landing in 1914 and from General Pershing's "Punitive Expedition."

RG 156–Office of the Chief of Ordnance

The first Office of the Chief of Ordnance was established on 14 May 1812. In 1862 it was abolished and its functions transferred to the United States Army Materiel Command. It was responsible for procurement, distribution, maintenance and repairs, and development of new types of ordnance. Examples of records:

Military Histories of Ordnance Officers, 1832–1922.

Military Histories of Ordnance Officers Serving at Field Establishments, 1838–82.

Register of Enlisted Men's Enlistments in and Discharges From the Ordnance Corps, 1832–1907.

Register of Enlisted Men and Clerks in the Ordnance Office, 1862–99.

Various Records of Ordnance Boards. These give name of board and time period.

Various Subjects (inventions, experiments, mineral lands, inspections, claims, etc.) The subject in which the researcher is interested must be specified.

Unidentified Card Index of Names Relating to Personnel, ca. 1917–20. These cards refer to enlisted men on industrial furlough, 1918–19.

RG 159–Office of the Inspector General, 1814-1939

An inspector general was first authorized for the Continental Army in July 1777, but a separate department was not established until 3 March 1813. That office received reports from inspectors assigned to various commands, and it inspected and investigated matters of efficiency, discipline, and welfare of the army. Later this department became a part of the Department of the Army Special Staff. Examples of records:

Index to Letters Sent, 1863–69.

Index to Letters Received, 1892–94.

Index to General Correspondence, 1894–1934.

Photographs of Various Officers Who Served in the Office of the Inspector General.

List of Names of Disbursing Officers Where Accounts Were Inspected at Various Army Posts, 1874–75.

RG 163–Selective Service System, World War I

The Selective Service System for World War I was directed by the Office of the Provost Marshal General under provisions of an act of Congress of 18 May 1917. Its mission was to register, classify, and induct men into military service, and local boards were established for that purpose. Following World War I, the organization ceased to exist and the Office of the Provost Marshal General was abolished on 15 July 1919. Records of the system were transferred to the National Archives regional archives (southeast region) at Atlanta, Georgia. Other regional archives are also processing these records.

RG 165–War Department, General and Special Staffs

This record group contains several collections of correspondence and card indexes to correspondence. The name of the district (Atlanta, Chicago, etc.) must be specified to obtain appropriate collections.

RG 168–Records of the National Guard Bureau

The National Guard Bureau, established in 1933, acts as the National Guard's communications channel with the army chief of staff, the air force chief of staff, and individual states. As a part of the Office of the Adjutant General, this bureau was an outgrowth of a Militia Division created in 1903 to handle matters relating to the National Guard units not in the service of the United States. The bureau became a joint bureau of the Department of the Army and the Department of the Air Force in 1948, with direct responsibility to the chiefs of staff of those departments. An indexed collection, General Correspondence, 1916–23, is available.

RG 231–United States Soldiers' Home

The home in Washington, D.C., continues in operation, although earlier ones were closed soon after they opened in 1851. Since 1947, the home has received members of the U.S. Air Force (formerly the U.S. Army Air Corps and then the U.S. Army Air Force), and it now receives former members of all branches of the armed forces. Funds for the present home are provided by money withheld from army and air force personnel, unclaimed money from deceased servicemen's estates, forfeiture of pay because of desertion, and stoppages of pay following conviction by courts-martial. Examples of records:

Descriptive Book of Inmates Admitted May 1851–78. Indexed.

Register of Men Admitted as Inmates at the Military Asylum, Harrodsburg, Kentucky, at the Southern U.S. Military Asylum, and at the Soldiers' Home in Washington, D.C., May 1851–February 1881.

Register of Inmates, 1852–1908.

Register of Inmates Showing Dates Admitted and Discharged, 1852–80.

Daily Registers of Patients Admitted and Discharged at the Hospital, September 1939–November 1940; February–November 1943. Arranged chronologically by date of admission.

List of Men Admitted at East Pascagoula, Mississippi, July 1853–March–August 1855 (chronological listing).

Monthly Registers of Men Admitted at Harrodsburg, Kentucky, 1853–1955 (chronological listing).

Muster Rolls of Inmates, February 1870–November 1879.

Registers of Applicants for Readmission, November 1888–February 1900.

Register of Persons Admitted to the Hospital, 1872–1927.

Register of Deaths, 1852–1942.

Certificates of Deaths, 1876–89; 1913–29.

Discharges, Warrants, and Other Personnel Papers of Inmates, 1869–1922. Arranged alphabetically.

Register of Employees, Showing Transfers, Discharges, Absences, and Resignations, July 1938–June 1941. Arranged chronologically.

Reports of Civilian and Inmate Employees, 1851–62; 1938–43.

Register of Persons Confined in the Guardhouse and of Sentences Imposed, 1897–1922. Arranged chronologically by date of confinement but indexed in each of the three volumes.

RG 247–Office of the Chief of Chaplains

The Office of the Chief of Chaplains was established in July 1920. It became an independent administrative service for the army in 1950 and later became an agency of the Army Special Staff. The office is responsible for the moral training and religious administration of the army, including the recruitment and training of chaplains, and for maintaining liaison with civilian religious groups. Examples of records:

Chapel Register, 1902–03; 1939–April 1951. Arranged alphabetically by name of installation; lists baptisms, marriages, funerals. Each of the twenty-nine volumes has an index.

Chaplains' Monthly Report Files, 1917–50. Arranged alphabetically by name of chaplain.

RG 249–Commissary General of Prisoners, 17 June 1862–19 August 1867

This office was established on 17 June 1862 for the purpose of supervising the imprisonment of Confederate and political prisoners confined in federal prisons. It set up camps for paroled federal prisoners and was later made responsible for administration of claims from all prisoners of war. The office was abolished on 19 August 1867, and its records were transferred to the Office of the Adjutant General. Examples of records:

See microfilm in the Microfilm Room (room 400) for several lists of Confederate prisoners of war.

Register of Troops Captured by the Enemy.

Register of Federal Prisoners of War Confined in Confederate Prisons, 1861-64.

Register of Federal Prisoners of War Who Enlisted in the Confederate Army, 1863-64.

Register of Federal Prisoners of War From Confederate Authorities.

Register of Federal Prisoners Who Died [various states and cemeteries].

Register of Federal Paroled Prisoners of War at Parole Camps and Stations, 1862-65. Names some of the camps or stations.

Register of Rolls (Confederate prisoners) in Various Northern Prisons. (See microfilm in the Microfilm Room. Also see RG 109, above.)

Register of Settled Claims for Money Taken From Federal Prisoners in Confederate Prisons, 1866-67.

List of Funds Claimed by Federal Prisoners of War at [various Confederate prisons].

Records Relating to the *Sultana* Disaster, 1865. Lists of survivors and dead from the *Sultana*, which blew up while carrying 2,300 federal troops, resulting in the deaths of 1,500.

Name Index to Records of Paroles, Exchanges, and Deaths of Federal Prisoners of War. Undated; arranged alphabetically by state, unit, and initial of surname.

Register of Deserters, June–December 1863. Many lists providing names of prisoner of war camps or places, or unit.

RG 391–Records of United States Regular Army Mobile Units (1821-1942)

The army has always had artillery units to support the infantry, with the number of such units increasing or decreasing according to the level of wartime activity. In addition to field artillery, the army also had coast artillery and cavalry batteries or regiments, all of them mobile units. The records of these units make up this set of collections.

Collections are arranged by type of unit and by year: artillery, field artillery, coast artillery, cavalry, and infantry. The material includes letters, name indexes by a range of years, descriptions of military units, courts-martial, deceased, etc. The type of unit and a range of years must be specified.

RG 392–United States Coast Artillery Districts and Defenses, 1901-42

In 1901, the artillery was divided into field artillery batteries and coast artillery companies. Coast artillery companies were assigned to various regions and geographical defense commands and districts within the continental United States and in Hawaii, the Philippines, and Panama.

There are various types of correspondence, reports, and orders. The name of the district or defense command and nature of the material desired must be specified. (Note that some of these records have been transferred to the National Archives regional archives.)

RG 393–U.S. Army Continental Commands, 1821-1920

Before the present administrative command system of army corps was established in 1920, the nation was divided into geographical commands: eastern and western. As the country grew, new commands were established; they were sometimes later divided into departments and sometimes into divisions.

This record group comprises five parts. Name or place of military camp or post and a range of years must be specified. Data provided in these collections includes letters, accounts, lists of names, prisoners, oaths, provost marshal reports, etc.

RG 394–United States Army Continental Commands, 1920-42

In August 1920 the continental United States was divided into nine army corps, each responsible for the training and administration of army units assigned to it. When the General Headquarters, United States Army, assumed the duties of tactical command, the corps were placed in the Services of Supply in 1942 and were designated as service commands.

Various correspondence, reports, and orders are available. The name of the field installation or corps headquarters, as well as the nature of the material, must be specified.

RG 407–Records of the Adjutant General's Office, 1917

Early adjutant general records (earlier than 1917) comprise RG 94. In 1916 the adjutant general was given authority to assign, promote, transfer, retire, and discharge all army officers and enlisted men. In 1947 these responsibilities were transferred to the Department of the Army's deputy chief of staff for personnel. The Office of the Adjutant General is responsible for administrative systems, maintenance of personnel records, and administration of the various branches of the Ready Reserve.

Thirteen binders serve as finding aids, listing the adjutant general's records since 1917. To obtain this material, the organizational unit and the theater of operations must be specified.

Military Reference Branch (navy)

Records available through the naval section of the Military Reference Branch pertain to navy, marine, and Coast Guard organizations. They are arranged by numbered record groups, each containing original or microfilm documents. Each collection within a record group, identified by an "entry number," is listed and described in a *Preliminary Inventory* or similar list of holdings, usually available for inspection in the branch office. Some of the collections in the record groups pertaining to the navy were formerly housed at the National Records Center, Suitland, Maryland, which served as an overflow repository because only limited space was available at the National Archives building.

Military records available in the record groups listed below may be obtained by submitting a request slip in this branch. Specialized archivists can advise concerning the collections listed below and suggest others that might be helpful. The collections listed below serve as examples or illustrations of material that may be especially beneficial to historians or genealogists who desire to obtain facts concerning a veteran or the unit in which he served. For additional collections, refer to the appropriate *Preliminary Inventory*.

RG 19	Records of the Bureau of Ships
RG 24	Records of the Bureau of Naval Personnel
RG 26	Records of the United States Coast Guard
RG 38	Records of the Office of Naval Operations (Office of Naval Intelligence)

RG 45	Office of the Naval Records and Library: Naval Records Collection, 1775–1910
RG 52	Records of the Bureau of Medicine and Surgery (navy)
RG 71	Records of the Bureau of Yards and Docks
RG 74	Records of the Bureau of Ordnance (navy)
RG 78	Records of the U.S. Naval Observatory
RG 80	General Records of the Navy Department, 1798–1947
RG 124–125	Records of the Office of the Judge Advocate General—Navy, 1799–1943
RG 127	Records of the United States Marine Corps
RG 181	Records of the Naval Districts and Shore Establishments (available at National Archives regional archives)
RG 298	Records of the Office of Naval Research
RG 313	Records of Naval Operating Forces
RG 428	General Records of the Department of the Navy, 1947

Record Collections

The following are titles of selected collections, arranged by record group, that are available upon request through the Military Reference Branch (navy). A more complete listing can be found in the appropriate *Preliminary Inventory* for each record group.

RG 19—Records of the Bureau of Ships

The Bureau of Ships was formed on 20 June 1940 by consolidation of the Bureau of Engineering and the Bureau of Construction and Repair. The new bureau was given responsibility for the design, construction, conversion, procurement, maintenance, and repair of ships and other craft. This responsibility also included management of salvage and repair bases and shipyards and other shore facilities. The bureau continued until 9 March 1966, when it was abolished and most of its functions transferred to the Naval Ship Systems Command, operating under the chief of naval operations. To obtain records the researcher must first ascertain the name of the ship or shore station. Many records of this bureau are in the National Archives field branches. Examples of records:

Indexes to Correspondence, 1888–1910; 1904–10; 1911–22; 1922–40. Each volume is indexed.

Index to Contracts, 1914–26.

Steam Logs of Naval Vessels (by name of vessel), 1845–1906. Deck logs of daily operations.

Index Cards to Reference Data, 1887–1935.

RG 24–Records of the Bureau of Naval Personnel

On 5 July 1862, the Bureau of Navigation was given responsibility for personnel functions relating to officers. All non-personnel functions were transferred from that bureau before 1942, when its name was changed to the Bureau of Naval Personnel. This bureau is responsible for the training and education of officers and enlisted personnel. It is also responsible for supervision of the United States Naval Academy and other navy schools and for establishing personnel complements for navy ships and for the recruitment, assignment, and separation of naval personnel.

CORRESPONDENCE COVERING VARIOUS TIME PERIODS.

Registers are available as listed in the *Preliminary Inventory* for this record group. Some are alphabetical, some chronological, and some a combination of both.

LOGBOOKS

Logs of Ships and Stations, 1801–1946. Commonly called "deck logs," or "rough logs," these were kept on ships or at shore stations. The early documents were handwritten, but beginning in the early 1900s they were typewritten copies of rough logs. Logs were submitted monthly to the Bureau of Naval Personnel. Officers' names were usually included. Daily entries usually gave prevailing meteorological conditions, descriptions of battles or other activities, names of those killed or wounded, disciplinary actions taken, lists of enlisted men transferring in or transferring out, and lists of men on special duty.

There are 72,500 volumes of deck logs spanning the years 1801 through 1946. They are arranged by name of ship, group of ships, special craft (smaller than a named ship), and shore installations.

Available in this section and at some libraries is the National Archives publication *Special List 44. List of Logbooks of United States Navy Ships, Stations, and Miscellaneous Units, 1801–1948* (Washington, D.C.: 1978). Also see *List of Log Books of the United States Vessels, 1861–65, on File in the Navy Department, 1891* and *Catalog of Log Books in the Navy Commissioner's Office, 13 July 1827 and Received Thereafter Till January 1863.* The earliest log mentioned in the latter publication is that of the USS *Constitution.*

Card Index to Ships' Logs, 1801–1940. Name and type of vessel, name changes, tonnage, armament, dates built or purchased, and date decommissioned or sold; arranged alphabetically.

"List of Log Books of United States Vessels, 1861–65, on File in the Navy Department, 1891."

MUSTER ROLLS

Muster rolls have been prepared and submitted by ship captains since July 1798 and by shore installations since 1800. Muster rolls of ships are arranged in three groups, each arranged alphabetically by name of ship: group 1 (1860–79); group 2 (1880–91); and group 3 (1892–1900). For each person listed, there is enlistment data, physical description, military history, and indication of discharge, desertion, or death. Examples of records:

Muster Rolls of Ships, Stations, Together With Shipping Articles, 1891–1900. Group 1: naval vessels (alphabetical); group 2: stations, torpedo boats, signal service, coast and geodetic survey.

Microfilm Copies of Muster Rolls of Ships, Stations, and Other Naval Districts, 1939–49. These rolls are for those units that have been decommissioned. They consist of: a) quarterly rolls of enlisted men, b) reports of changes (promotions and transfers), c) passengers other than enlisted persons, and d) recapitulation sheets.

Microfilm Copies of Muster Rolls of Ships, Stations, and Other Naval Districts, 1949–56. Similar to above.

Indexes to Microfilm Copies of Muster Rolls, 1941–56. Cards or typescript lists of vessels and stations for which microfilm copies are available.

Civil War Muster Rolls, 1841–63. These rolls were prepared when foreign ships were captured by American ships. They list officers and enlisted men on board at the time of capture and were probably used as a basis for distribution of prize money paid to the officers and crew of the capturing ship.

Registers of Applications, 1897–1917. Applications for assistant paymasters, boatswains, carpenters, chaplains, civil engineers, professors of mathematics, gunners, machinists, and pharmacists; arranged alphabetically. Separate series are available for each occupation listed above.

Confirmations of Appointment of Officers, 1843–1909.

Congressional Confirmation of Officer Applicants to the Navy and Marine Corps (ten volumes). Arranged alphabetically.

Acceptances and Appointments, 1873–89. Includes oaths of allegiance.

Record of Promotions of Officers, 1909–20.

Commissions Issued to Officers, 1844–1936 (124 volumes). Consists of printed forms. Vols. 1–68 are alphabetical (A through Z) within each volume; vols. 69–124 are alphabetical (A through Z) as one volume (beginning with vol. 69 and ending with vol. 124).

Warrants Issued to Officers, 1846–1923 (eight volumes). Similar to above.

Commissions and Discharges, Resignations—Spanish-American War, 1898-99. Arranged alphabetically.

Commissions of Officers of the Naval Militia of the District of Columbia, 1898-1917.

Identification Photographs of Officers, 1889-1939 (3,300 prints). Not all officers are included.

Portraits of Officers, Passport Negatives, and Copy of Negatives of Charts, Medals, Trophies, and Vessels, 1917-32. This collection includes 1,143 prints of vessels. Photographs are arranged alphabetically by name of person or vessel.

Register of Officers of the Navy, 1799-1823. Arranged alphabetically.

"Ship Books" Containing Personnel Complements and Rosters of Officers on Vessels, 1834-65. Class of vessel, dates of sailings and arrivals, rosters of officers, and data on passengers carried. Some include names of enlisted men; arranged alphabetically by name of ship.

Register of Officers of the Engineers Corps—Navy, 1859-1901.

Letters From Officers Transmitting Statements of Their Service, June 1842-December 1844.

List of Officers Assigned to the Naval Observatory and the Naval Academy, 1865-77.

Register of Assistant Surgeons, 1876-96.

List of Officers, 1878-1909: a) on ships (1878-1905); b) on shore duty (1895-1909); c) on shore stations (1907-09).

Gunners' Registers, 1890-98.

Register of Petty Officers Holding Permanent Appointments, 1893-1902.

Register of Commissioned Officers of the Auxiliary Naval Force, 1898. Personnel records or record cards are also available for any individual listed in this register.

Microfilm Copies of an Index to Officers' Jackets ("Officers' Directory"), 1913-25. Personnel records are not available for these individuals. The index gives name, rank, location of file, cross-reference to related correspondence, and jacket number.

Abstracts of Service Records of Naval Officers, 1798-1924 (sixty volumes). Arranged in various ways, chronologically and alphabetically.

Index to Abstracts of Service of Naval Officers, 1829-1924.

Lists of Naval Officers and Records of their Service, 1884-91. Primarily of officers at navy yards and other installations; arranged alphabetically.

Records of Service of Temporary Officers in the Spanish-American War, 1898-99.

Records Summarizing Service of Officers and Men of the Naval Auxiliary Service, 1900-17.

Records Relating to Enlisted Men Who Served in the Navy Between 1842-85. There is one jacket for each man, containing documents relating to pensions, claims, and correspondence concerning military service or benefits (including possible admission to the Naval Home at Philadelphia); arranged alphabetically.

Correspondence Jackets on Enlisted Men, 1904-13. Pertain to Naval Home beneficiaries and marines.

Record Cards for Enlisted Men Who Served During the First World War ("State Cards"), 1917-19. Name, service number, place and date of enrollment or enlistment, age, rating at enlistment, home address (including county and state), place and dates of service and ratings for each period, and rating at time of discharge; arranged by state and then alphabetically by name.

Record Cards for Recipients of Medals, Badges, Bars and Pins Issued by the Navy Department, 1899-1910. Arranged alphabetically; indicate date received from various recruitment locations and receiving vessels. The names of such units must be specified.

Indexes and Records of Discharges, 1890-1920.

Descriptive Lists of Deserters, 1902-10. Contain physical descriptions and information regarding rewards offered to police units.

Record of Apprentices by Ship and Time Period. (See list in the *Preliminary Inventory* for this record group.)

Photographs, World War I. Prints of personnel, vessels, and shore units.

Photographs of Navy Personnel, 1917-19. Approximately four thousand prints of personnel who died in World War I or who received medals for wartime service.

Maps Relating to the Spanish-American War, 1898.

Index to Letters Sent, 1885-90.

Index to Letters Received, 1885-90.

Reports of Conduct of Enlisted Men . . . 1867-1910. Quarterly reports showing awards, punishments, and miscellaneous data; arranged by name of ship.

Indexes to Honorable Discharges, 1856-75.

Records of Deserters, 1867-89.

Shipping Articles (enrollments), 1867-84. Contains lists of names and signatures of those who enrolled; arranged by name of ship.

Records Relating to Biographical, Service, and Other Data About Chaplains, 1804-1923. Arranged alphabetically.

Jackets of Naval Cadets, 1862-1910; arranged chronologically by date of admission for examination.

Letters of Appointment Issued to Naval Cadets and Midshipmen, 1894-1940.

Register of Midshipmen, 1869-76. Arranged alphabetically.

RG 26—Records of the United States Coast Guard

The U.S. Coast Guard was established on 28 January 1915 by consolidation of the Department of Treasury's Revenue-Cutter Service and Life-Saving Service. The Coast Guard also took over lighthouse administration in 1939. The Coast Guard operates as part of the navy in time of war or when the president directs. (Note that all Coast Guard records have been transferred to the National Archives regional archives.) Examples of records:

Logs of Light Vessels, Buoy Tenders, Lighthouses, Vessels, Stations, Depots, and Miscellaneous Correspondence, 1873–1980.

Life-saving Stations, 1873–1945.

Vessels, Stations, Depots, 1915–41.

Components (various vessels and establishments), 1942–59. The name of vessel or station must be specified.

Summary Court-martial Case Files, 1906–51.

Records of Deck Courts, 1920–41.

General Courts-martial Case Files, 1906–63.

Special Courts-martial Case Files, 1951–73.

Record of Minor Courts, 1906–18.

RG 38—Records of the Office of Naval Operations (Office of Naval Intelligence)

The Office of Naval Intelligence was established on 3 March 1915 as a part of the Office of Naval Operations. (Note that some of these records have been transferred to the National Archives regional archives.) Examples of records:

Captured Japanese Documents and Transactions, 1942–45.

Interviews With Naval Aviation Personnel, 1942–45.

Register of Personnel of the Office of Naval Intelligence, 1882–1918. Officers only.

Secret List of Agents, 1917–20.

Lists of Office of Naval Intelligence Agents and Informants Residing in Foreign Countries, 1917–25. Arranged by country and then alphabetically.

Lists of Office of Naval Intelligence, 1917–20. Personnel of naval districts.

RG 45—Naval Records Collection of the Office of Naval Records and Library, 1775–1910

This preliminary checklist of material was turned over to the National Archives on 19 November 1942 by the Office of Naval Records and Library. That office, originally established as a library in 1882, published many manuscript naval records. It ultimately became an archival agency authorized to collect naval records from the Navy Department and navy units outside the Navy Department. Examples of records:

Index to Letters Sent, 1823–61.

Index to Letters Received, 1823–66.

Letters From Officers Commanding Squadrons, 1841–86. Indexed.

Index to Letters Received Relating to Squadrons, 1848–58. (See the *Preliminary Inventory* for this record group for an appendix that lists by squadron commanding officers and names of flagships or by time periods.)

Letters From Officers Acknowledging Receipt of Commissions and Warrants, Including Oaths of Allegiance, 1804–64.

Letters From Officers Accepting, Declining, and Resigning Appointments, 1804–26. Place of birth and residence.

Muster Rolls and Payrolls of Vessels, 1779–1885 (138 volumes). (See the *Preliminary Inventory* for this record group for an appendix that lists names of vessels.)

Muster Rolls and Payrolls of Shore Establishments of the United States Navy, 1800–42 (forty-eight volumes). (See the *Preliminary Inventory* for this record group for an appendix that lists names of shore establishments.

Lists of Naval, Marine, and Civil Officers, by Shore Establishments, 1835–89 (twenty-six volumes).

Lists of Officers of Vessels of the United States Navy, 1861–77 (thirty-four volumes).

Muster Rolls and Payrolls of Vessels of the Confederate States Navy, 1861–63. (See the *Preliminary Inventory* for this record group for a list of the names of the seventy-four vessels.)

Payrolls of Civil Personnel in Shore Establishments of the Confederate States Navy, 1861–64. (See the *Preliminary Inventory* for this record group for a list of the thirty establishments.)

Muster Rolls and Payrolls of Marine Detachments of the Confederate States Navy, 1861–64.

Register and Payments Made to Officers and Enlisted Men of the Confederate States Navy, 1861–64.

Logs and Journals of Vessels of the Confederate States Navy, 1861–65. (See the *Preliminary Inventory* for this record group for a list of the names of vessels.)

Register of United States Prisoners of War at Quebec, 1813–15. Contains considerable military history and personal information about each prisoner.

List of American Vessels Captured During the American Revolution, 1775–83.

Register of Vessels of the United States and Confederate States Navy During the Civil War, 1861–65. Arranged alphabetically by name of ship. (See appendix C of the *Preliminary Inventory* for this record group, which indicates the vessels for which lists are available.)

Logs and Journals of American Privateers and Merchant Vessels, 1776–1867. (See the *Preliminary Inventory* for this record group, which lists names of vessels.)

Logs and Journals of Vessels of the United States Navy. Listed by authors of journals and by names of vessels. These lists refer to logs, journals, and diaries of officers of the U.S. Navy at sea, 1776–1908. Some are official logs and some are personal accounts.

Register of British Prisoners of War in the United States, 1812–15.

RG 52–Records of the Bureau of Medicine and Surgery (navy)

The Bureau of Medicine and Surgery was established on 31 August 1842. It was given responsibility for administering navy dispensaries and hospitals, medical examinations, inspection of health facilities and conditions on ships and stations, research and instruction to naval medical and dental personnel, and general care of sick and wounded naval personnel. Examples of records:

Register and Index to Correspondence, 1882–83.

General Correspondence, 1912–25.

Index to General Correspondence, 1896–1925. Card index arranged by subject and facility and then alphabetically.

Index to General Correspondence, 1926–41. Card index arranged by subject and facility and then alphabetically.

Medical Journal, Shore Stations, 1812–89 (321 volumes arranged chronologically). Some volumes contain indexes. Various stations, beginning in 1867, listed name of person on sick list, rate or rank, nativity, ship or station, diagnosis, treatment, and name and rank of medical officer.

Medical Journals of Ships, 1813–89 (11,400 volumes). Arranged alphabetically by name of ship and thereunder chronologically. Some volumes contain indexes. The data given is similar to above.

Medical Journals of Expeditions, 1872–85 (three volumes). Lists names of patients, Greeley Relief Expedition, 1884; Nicaragua Survey Expedition, 1872–73; Panama Survey Expedition, 1884–85.

"Abstracts and Patients," 1830–89 (ninety-six volumes). Arranged by name of ship or shore installation and year and thereunder alphabetically); lists of those on sick call, arranged by name of ship, naval hospitals, and dispensaries at shore stations. These give name, rate or rank, age, place of birth, date of admission, disease or injury, date and name of discharge, origin of disability in terms of type of duty status, and remarks by medical officers.

Lists of Persons Invalided From the Service, 1918–19. These are copies of the slips described above, forming lists of those released from military service because of disability; arranged by year and thereunder by name.

"Hospital Tickets and Case Papers," 1825–89 (274 volumes). Letters to medical officers in charge of naval hospitals requesting admission of patients to the hospitals; name, rate or rank, age, nativity, dates of medical history, diagnosis, and list of clothing; arranged by name of the deceased.

Certificates of Death, Disability, Pension, and Medical Survey, 1861–89 (fifty-four volumes). Arranged by name of naval or marine recruiting centers at various cities; arranged alphabetically by city.

Death Lists, 1829–43; 1858–65; 1868–80. Name, rate or rank, date and cause of death, and duty status at time of disease or injury; arranged by name of ship or station; lists for 1858–65 arranged by name of the deceased.

Casualty lists, 1861–70, 1917. Vol. 1 (1861–65) arranged chronologically; (1862–70) arranged alphabetically; vol. 2 (July–December 1917–Fifth Regiment, Marine Corps in France) arranged chronologically.

List of Medical Officers, 1824–73. Arranged by name of ship or station and thereunder chronologically.

Statements of Service of Medical Officers, 1842–73. Name, dates of appointment, promotions, reassignments, and discharge or death; arranged chronologically.

Case Files for Hospital Personnel ("Personnel Papers"), 1884–1910. Arranged alphabetically.

Case Files for Patients, 1914–39 ("Patients' Jackets"). Medical charts and related papers concerning patients in naval hospitals; arranged by name of hospital and case number.

Registers of Patients, 1813–1942 (109 volumes). Lists from various naval hospitals, arranged by name of ship or station. Some volumes contain indexes.

Index to General Correspondence, 1926–51.

Registers Showing Individual Service Records of the U.S. Navy and of the Naval Reserve Force, 1820–1930 (fifteen volumes). Each volume contains an index.

Register of Patients, 1812–29 (eighty-eight volumes).

Photographs, 1900–44: Washington Naval Hospital, 1900; Norfolk Naval Hospital, 1918–19; Utah Beach, Normandy, 1944; England, 1944.

RG 71–Records of the Bureau of Yards and Docks

In 1862 the Bureau of Yards and Docks replaced the former Bureau of Naval Yards and Docks, which had been established on 31 August 1842. It was responsible for design, construction, and maintenance of all naval public works and utilities, such as drydocks, harbor and port buildings, and facilities. The bureau was abolished on 9 March 1966, and its functions were transferred to the Naval Facilities Engineering Command. Examples of records follow (many records of this bureau are also found in RG 45):

Indexes to Correspondence, 1886–99; 1899–1916; 1917–23; 1925–42.

Index to Personal Correspondence, 1917–25. Cards arranged alphabetically by name, giving data relating to appointments, resignations, and changes of status.

Payrolls, 1844–99. Arranged by name of navy yard and then by year.

"Naval Asylum" Muster Roll of Pensioners and Beneficiaries, 1850–86; 1894–97; arranged chronologically.

Records of Inmates, United States Naval Asylum, 1831–65, 1870. These give military history and personal information; arranged chronologically.

Photographs. Construction Projects, 1897–1944. (The *Preliminary Inventory* for this record group contains an appendix listing the project sites. There is also an appendix arranged by name of navy yards or stations, giving date, number, and title of photograph.)

RG 72–Bureau of Naval Aeronautics

Established on 12 July 1921, the Bureau of Naval Aeronautics was responsible for testing, making contracts, and outfitting shore establishments related to navy air operations. The bureau was abolished in 1959 and its functions transferred to the Bureau of Naval Weapons. Examples of records:

Index to General Correspondence of the Division of Aviation, 1917–19. Arranged alphabetically by subject

Index to Correspondence Concerning Officers and Enlisted Men, 1925–44. Arranged alphabetically.

Photographs, 1928–46. Prints of navy planes, supplied by contractors.

RG 74–Records of the Bureau of Ordnance (navy)

Established on 31 August 1842 as the Bureau of Ordnance and Hydrography, the bureau's name was changed to the Bureau of Ordnance on 5 July 1862 when its duties relating to hydrography were transferred to the Bureau of Navigation. The Bureau of Ordnance was responsible for procurement, maintenance, and issuance of all armament used by the navy. It was also responsible for naval gun factories and related weapons facilities. It was abolished on 18 August 1959, and its functions were transferred to the Bureau of Naval Weapons. Examples of records:

Index to Correspondence, 1885–1913; 1914–26; 1926–43. Arranged by year and then alphabetically by name or subject.

RG 78–Records of the United States Naval Observatory

An observatory was built in 1844 and subsequently placed under the general supervision of a variety of naval offices over the years. The observatory sets the national time, maintains continuous astronomical observations, and develops and services astronomical instruments.

In addition to the collections at the National Archives, several collections of letters dated prior to 1895 were transferred by the Naval Historical Foundation to the Manuscript Division of the Library of Congress. Examples of records:

Index to Letters Received, 1885–92; 1885–99.

Card Index to General Correspondence, 1909–25.

Copies of Orders and Appointments, 1889–1912. Include civil employees and naval officers; arranged chronologically.

RG 124–125–Records of the Judge Advocate General (navy), 1799–1943

The first solicitor and naval judge advocate general was appointed in 1865. The Office of Judge Advocate General was created on 8 June 1880 and merged with the Office of the Solicitor in 1921. The office has jurisdiction over military law concerned with the navy. It administers criminal justice and assists court-martial tribunals and advises about matters relative to international admiralty laws. (Note that some of these records have been transferred to the National Archives regional archives.) Examples of records:

Lists of Officers and Crews Entitled to Share in Proceeds of Prizes, 1861–63. Concerns ships captured by U.S. naval forces.

Registers of Prisoners Captured on Blockade-runners, 1862–65.

Index to Letters Received, 1880–83; 1883–89; 1890–1904.

Records of Proceedings of General Courts-martial, 1866–1940 (459 volumes). Partially indexed as shown in the collections below.

Indexes to Correspondence Relating to Courts-martial, Deck Courts, and Provost Courts, 1908–26.

Registers of General Courts-martial, 1861–1904. Case number, date and place of trial, charges, findings, sentences, and related data; indexed.

Register of Prisoners Under Service of General Court-martial, 1877–92. Arranged by place of imprisonment: Boston, Portsmouth, New York, Connecticut, Norfolk, Mare Island, and foreign ships and stations; indexed.

Register of General Courts-martial, 1909–43. Arranged chronologically.

Rough Register of General Courts-martial, 1924–35 (three volumes). The entries are almost illegible.

Index to Summary Courts-martial, 1855–80; 1866–95; 1895–1904.

Slip Records of Deck Courts, 1909–30. Arranged by year and thereunder alphabetically.

Personnel Records, 1841–1943. Several series, each indexed.

RG 127–Records of the United States Marine Corps

When the Marine Corps was created on 11 July 1798, it was subject to both army and navy regulations. Except for units detached for army service, it was placed under exclusive control of the navy in June 1834. An act of 1952 recognized the Marine Corps as a separate service. The primary duty of the Marine Corps is to provide amphibious combat forces. Marine detachments also serve on navy ships and protect the property of naval units. (Note that some Marine Corps records have been transferred to the National Archives regional archives.) Examples of records:

Orders Issued and Received, 1798-1886. Covers appointments and courts-martial; arranged chronologically.

Proceedings of General Courts-martial for Officers and Enlisted Men of the Marine Corps, 1816-52. Arranged chronologically.

Letters and Telegrams Sent to Officers Conveying Orders ("Order Books"), 1871-79; 1882-95; 1876-84. Each series is indexed.

Alphabetical Card List of Enlisted Men of the Marine Corps, 1798-1941. Name, case number, and date and place of enlistment.

Service Records of Enlisted Men, 1793-95 (a few as late as 1900). Arranged chronologically by year of enlistment; conduct records, enlistment papers, notice of discharge, medical data, service reports, and military history.

Descriptive Lists, 1878-1903; 1889-1906; 1899-1900. These give name, rank, place of birth, date and place of enlistment, age, physical description, residence, occupation, and military history; arranged alphabetically.

Registers of Appointments and Promotions for Noncommissioned Officers, 1877-99; 1914-20. Arranged chronologically.

Registers of Enlisted Men Tried by General Court-martial, 1887-1906; 1919-33. Name, rank, ship or station, kind of court-martial, date of trial, offense, and sentence; indexed.

Registers of Deserters, 1809-1907; 1910-41; name, place of desertion, and where and when apprehended or surrendered (if applicable).

Registers of Discharges, 1829-45; 1869-1906; 1838-1927. Volumes covering years to 1870 give name, rank, date of enlistment, date and place of discharge, and reason for discharge; arranged chronologically except for the last volume, which is arranged alphabetically.

Certificates of Discharge From the Marine Corps, 1838-51. Arranged alphabetically.

List of Discharges, Enlisted Men, 1921-23. Arranged chronologically.

List of Retired Enlisted Men, 1885-1906.

Original Death Registers, Enlisted Men, 1838-1906; 1908-18; 1868-1942. Name, rank, date of enlistment, cause of death, and location of death; arranged chronologically by year and thereunder alphabetically. Regiment is given for those who died during World War I.

Certificates of Indenture, 1814-56. Forms (signed by parents) of boys bound until age twenty-one as apprentices to fife and drum majors.

Muster Rolls, 1795-1945 (1,285 volumes). Arranged chronologically by name of ship or shore station.

Certificate Book of Officers and Enlisted Men (various dates between 1857 and 1911). Name, military history, personal data, wounds, and miscellaneous data. Information was gained from several sources such as size rolls, courts-martial, payrolls, etc.; name indexes for 1839-42 and beginning February 1870.

Surgeons' Certificates of Disability, 1838-68. Name, rank, date and location, reason for disability, and date of discharge; arranged alphabetically for period 1865-68; otherwise, chronologically.

Register of Badges, Medals, Bars Issued 1908-11. Arranged alphabetically.

Register of Deaths of Marine Corps Personnel During World War I, 1918-19. Name, rank, unit, cause of death, place of death, and name and address of next of kin; arranged alphabetically.

Various Miscellaneous Records for Field Units and Geographical Areas Where Marines Were Stationed. The name of the unit or the geographical area and the time period must be specified.

RG 298—Records of the Office of Naval Research

Currently there is no preliminary inventory available for this record group, but the staff may provide information concerning material available and time periods covered. Material includes data concerning officers and enlisted men, reserve officers, officer personnel, and officer candidates.

RG 313—Records of Naval Operating Forces

At various times since 1959 the navy has organized its fighting units into fleets and squadrons based on geographical location. In 1941 these comprised the Pacific, Atlantic, and Asiatic fleets. In 1967 they were reorganized into the Pacific Fleet; the Atlantic Fleet; the Naval Forces, Europe; and the Military Sea Transportation Service. The records consist of correspondence from various operating forces, arranged by geographical area.

Civil Division Reference Branch

The Civil Division Reference Branch has custody of Treasury Department records, many of which relate to military matters.

Record Collections

The following are titles of selected collections, arranged by record group, that are available upon request through the Civil Division Reference Branch. A more complete listing can be found in the appropriate Preliminary Inventory for each record group.

RG 56—General Records of the Department of the Treasury (records of the Southern Claims Commission)

By legislation of 3 March 1871, the Southern Claims Commission was appointed as a unit of the Department of the Treasury to receive, examine, and consider Civil War claims of loyal citizens who wished to file for monetary reimbursements for property confiscated by the U.S. Army. On 16 June 1880, after the last claim had been filed, the commission was disbanded. Actions taken on these claims are described in National Archives microfilm M87, *Records of the Commissioner of Claims, Southern Claims Commission*, and also in a publication by Gary Mills, *Civil War Claims in the South: An Index of claims Filed Before the Southern Claims Commission, 1871-1880* (Laguna Hills, Calif.: Aegean Park Press, 1980).

RG 217—Records of the General Accounting Office

From a huge volume of accounts records compiled by the nation's first two comptrollers and the first five auditors, the following sample collections are listed to show their diversity:

Register of Proceeds From Sale of Effects of Deceased Soldiers, 16 July 1863-10 March 1865. Arranged alphabetically.

Indexes to Registers of Warrants, 1800-13. Names of officers and others; arranged alphabetically.

Register of Payments to Indian Scouts and Indian Home Guards, 1862-82. Arranged alphabetically.

Roster of Officers and Regular Army Units Serving in the Mexican War, 1845-January 1850.

Register of Payments to Regular and Volunteer Units, 1861-70. Arranged by unit and then chronologically.

Register of Payments to Miscellaneous Units (Post Book), 1861-67. Arranged by name of unit and then geographically.

Register of Payments to Colored Troops, May 1863-June 1866.

Index to Registers of Payments to Officers, 1862-65. Arranged by rank and thereunder alphabetically.

Record of Payments to Prisoners of War, September 1863-April 1865.

Claims of Volunteer Units in the Mexican War for Three Months' Extra Pay, 1846-48.

Register of Bounty Claims, November 1865-December 1870.

Record of Actions Taken on Claims, September 1866-February 1869.

Disallowed Claims of Sutlers, 1864-94.

Vouchers for Payments of Revolutionary War Claims, September 1829-March 1831. Arranged alphabetically.

Settled Accounts for Revolutionary War Claims, July 1828-March 1871.

Muster Rolls and Payrolls, 1815-66. Arranged by name of unit.

Roster of Fremont's Battalion of California Volunteers in the Mexican War, 1846-48.

Roster of Members of Texas Volunteers in the Mexican War, 1846-48.

Register of Payments to Officers and Enlisted Men From Volunteer Units, June 1836-December 1861.

Index to Officers of Volunteer Units, 1861-65.

Card Index to Muster Rolls and Payrolls for Navy Ships and Shore Units, 1828-9 July 1903.

Muster Rolls and Pay and Receipt Rolls for Ships and Shore Units, 1820-98.

Indexes to Ships and Stations, 8 May 1878-31 December 1907.

Service Records of Navy Enlisted Men and Warrant Officers, 1825-92.

RG 366—Records of Civil War Special Agencies of the Treasury Department

Through its agents, the Treasury Department exercised authority over trade establishments created in the Confederate states, and for the collection, care of, and disposal of abandoned or captured property. The agents worked closely with military authorities after the war to coordinate the use of such properties. Entrepreneurs were required to obtain permits from the Treasury Department to operate businesses and were required to report to the department concerning their activities. RG 366 contains documents created or processed by the agents or their offices. They are arranged by location and include names of towns, counties, and states, and the name of the citizen. Records apply only to Confederate states and for the years 1864-65. In a few instances, names of treasury agents are given. When requesting material from this record group, the locality must be specified; staff archivists will then assist in obtaining records for that locality.

5

Resources of the National Archives Repositories Outside Washington, D.C.

5

Resources of the National Archives
Repositories Outside Washington, D.C.

I n addition to the records held at the main National Archives building in Washington, D.C., the National Archives and Records Administration maintains records in a nationwide network of repositories, making them more easily accessible to researchers from across the nation. The records available at these facilities are described in this chapter.

A major new repository is National Archives II in College Park, Maryland. With the recent construction and opening of National Archives II, overcrowded conditions at the main National Archives building are being relieved.

Fifteen federal records centers receive records transferred from federal courts and federal agencies when the records are no longer needed for current business. One of the centers, the National Personnel Records Center in St. Louis, Missouri, exists to provide proof of service and related military data to servicemen and -women.

The National Archives regional archives system was established to make historically important federal records more accessible to the public without the necessity of traveling to Washington, D.C. There are thirteen regional archives, each of which holds records that originate in the federal agencies and federal courts within its region.

National Archives II

University of Maryland
8601 Adelphi Road
College Park, Maryland 10740-6001
(410) 713-6800

National Archives II was established in 1993 in a new building at the University of Maryland in College Park, Maryland. It has received in transfer several record groups from the National Archives building in downtown Washington, D.C. and also from the National Records Center in Suitland, Maryland. During 1995 and 1996, all U.S. Army and Navy records dating roughly from the start of World War II were transferred, one record group at a time, to National Archives II.

Military records prior to World War II continue to be housed at the National Archives building in downtown Washington, D.C. For current information about recent transfers or location of certain record groups, telephone the National Archives (202)501-5395 or National Archives II (301)713-7250. Archival records for World War II and later which were originally housed at the National Records Center at Suitland, Maryland, have been transferred to National Archives II. The Suitland facility now operates exclusively as a federal records center and houses only those agency records not classified as archival material; thus, those

Figure 51. National Archives II, College Park, Maryland (courtesy National Archives).

records remain under the control of the federal agencies that created them. As part of the general transfer, the Center for Electronic Records and the Still Pictures Branch have moved from the National Archives building in Washington, D.C. to National Archives II.

The central portion of the new National Archives II building consists of six levels:

Level one	Reception and consultation
Level two	Textual records, including a research room that seats 175
Level three	Non-textual records, including carto-graphic records
Level four	Microfilm records
Level five	Still pictures
Level six	Electronic and classified records

The building has a cafeteria, an auditorium, conference rooms, and a parking garage.

Record Groups

Record groups of military material at National Archives II are the following. (Some of them are partial and include only the more recent records.)

RG 24–Records of the Bureau of Naval Personnel

RG 38–Records of the Office of the Chief of Naval Operations

RG 92–Quartermaster General, Office of

RG 107–Records of the Secretary of War

RG 112–Surgeon General (army), 1941–

RG 117–American Battle Monuments Commission

RG 147–Selective Service System, 1941

RG 153–Records of the Judge Advocate General (army)

RG 165–Records of the War Department General and Special Staffs

RG 247–Records of the Office of the Chief of Chaplains

RG 319–Records of the Army Staff, 1939–

RG 332–Records of U.S. Theaters of War, World War II

RG 337–Records of Headquarters Army Ground Forces

RG 338–Records of United States Army Commands

RG 389–Office of the Provost Marshal General, 1941–

RG 407–Records of the Adjutant General's Office, 1917–

The following are selected examples of record collections available at this facility; they are listed by record group. For complete listings, see the National Archives *Preliminary Inventory* for the appropriate record group, or call the telephone number for National Archives II shown above.

RG 38–RECORDS OF THE OFFICE OF THE CHIEF OF NAVAL OPERATIONS

Formerly available at the Operations Branch, Navy Historical Center, but now transferred to National Archives II, or at the National Archives in downtown Washington, D.C., the following types of Navy records pertaining to World War II are available at National Archives II: action reports, war diaries, operations plans, submarine war patrol reports, anti-submarine warfare records of the Tenth Fleet, convoy reports, armed guard reports and logs, deck logs, muster rolls, casualty reports, and others.

RG 112–RECORDS OF THE SURGEON GENERAL (ARMY)

Records Relating to Repatriated Prisoners of War, 1942–47.

RG117–A MERICAN BATTLE MONUMENTS COMMISSION

Registers of Americans interred on foreign soil.

RG 147–SELECTIVE SERVICE SYSTEM, 1941

The Selective Service System for World War II was established by executive order on 23 September 1940. Local draft boards were formed to register, classify, and select for induction male citizens and aliens subject to service. The system expired by law on 31 March 1947, but it was reinstituted on 24 June 1948. Examples of records:

Index to Diplomatic Correspondence, 1940–45 (relative to foreign diplomatic personnel).

Master List of the Lottery Drawing for Alaska, 1941.

Master List of the Lottery Drawing for Hawaii, 1941.

Master Index of Conscientious Objectors Sent to Camps, 1941–47.

Locator Cards for Conscientious Objectors Sent to Camps, 1941–47.

Individual Record Cards Showing Payments Made to Conscientious Objectors Assigned to Agricultural Projects, 1942–46.

Lists of Occupationally Deferred Federal Employees, 1943–45.

"Cover Sheets" for Conscientious Objectors Who Served in Work Camps, 1941–45. Arranged alphabetically by state and name.

RG 319–RECORDS OF THE ARMY STAFF, 1939-

Since 1947, the Army Staff has prepared plans relating to the army's role in national security and to various aspects of army administration. It is presided over by the chief of staff. Its records are those of its various military components, and they include some records of its predecessor offices. Examples of records:

Records of the Judge Advocate General. Records of investigations of atrocities committed by North Korean and communist forces against civilians and prisoners of war in Korea.

Investigation Reports Documenting the Korean War Crimes Program, 1952–54.

Interrogation Reports and Americans Hospitalized as Prisoners of War, 1943–46.

Records Relating to Atrocities in the Philippines, 1942–45.

Approved or Disapproved Applications for Decorations and Awards, 1905–51.

Index to Chaplains' Reports Relating to Funerals for Military and Authorized Civilian Personnel, 1923–55.

RG 389–OFFICE OF THE PROVOST MARSHAL GENERAL, 1941-

Before World War II, a provost marshal general was appointed only during times of active military operations, after which the post was abandoned. In 1941 the office was reinstituted, and in 1946 a corps of military police was created to consolidate personnel who perform police functions; it then become a permanent part of the army. Examples of records:

Cables From the American Red Cross Relating to Americans Captured or Interred by Germany and Japan, 1943–45.

Records Relating to the Collection and Dissemination of Information Concerning American Civilians and Military Personnel Captured or Interred in Enemy Countries, 1942–45.

Correspondence, Camp Reports, Diaries, Rosters, and Other Records Relating to American Internees by Germany and Japan During World War II, 1942–46.

Japanese-American Prisoners-of-war List.

RG 407–RECORDS OF THE ADJUTANT GENERAL'S OFFICE, 1917-

Thirteen binders list the adjutant general's records since 1917, including descriptions of combat interviews conducted by army personnel during World War II. To obtain this material, it is necessary to specify the military unit and the theater of operations. Combat interviews conducted primarily between June 1944 and May 1945 relate to actions of the Normandy landings and breakthrough; Operations Cobra, Neptune, and Market Garden; the battles of Aachen, the Bulge, and the Hurtgen Forest; the siege of Bastogne; the Rhine and Moselle river crossings; the Remagen bridgehead; the Siegfried line; Brest; the Ardennes; Ruhr to the Rhine; Rhine-Ruhr-Elba operations; and the Colmar and Ruhr pockets. Also included are interviews relating to the first contacts between the Russian and American forces and the entry of American forces into concentration camps. In addition to the interviews, there are aerial maps and photographs and several other reports, sketches, and charts.

There are also narrative reports relating to operations and activities in Belgium, Holland, France, and Germany; and records pertaining to France, Italy, Austria, and the United Kingdom. Also included are interrogations, reports, narratives, orders, bulletins, lists, maps, photographs, and other miscellaneous material. To gain access to these records it is necessary to specify the theater of operations and the organizational unit. Records are arranged first by theater of operation, then by armies, then by corps, followed by infantry divisions, armored divisions, or cavalry divisions.

For research into World War II prisoners of war and war crimes in both the European and Pacific Theaters, several record groups and collections available at National Archives II are helpful. The search should begin with examination of the finding aid *American Prisoners of War and Civilian Internees* (National Archives and Records Administration Reference Information Paper 80. Washington, D.C.: NARA, 1992).

Center for Electronic Records

The Center for Electronic Records stores and makes available data supplied by the Department of Veterans Affairs, the National Personnel Records Center, the Department of Defense, the Office of the Provost Marshal General, and the Office of the Adjutant General. The records encompass World War II, the Korean War, and the Vietnam War. The data pertains to military personnel who became casualties, were missing in action, or were prisoners of war.

All records accessioned by this center are stored on magnetic tape. Copies of these tapes are available for a fee; photocopies are also available. Lists of names pertaining to only one state, either on tape or on a tape printout, are available for a nominal fee. State archives, historical societies, and genealogical societies may wish to avail themselves of this service. Letters of inquiry should be directed to the Reference Service, Center for Electronic Records, National Archives and Records Administration, Washington, D.C. 20408.

Also available at this center is a three-volume computer printout compiled by the American Battle Monuments Commission titled *Register, World War II Dead Interred in American Military Cemeteries on Foreign Soil and World War II and Korea Missing or Lost or Buried at Sea.*

Center staff members will assist in locating individual persons named in the printouts. These printout collections are in binders and are arranged and indexed in several ways to simplify the task of locating an individual. The categories of information available are described below.

World War II–Prisoners of War
RECORDS OF THE OFFICE OF THE PROVOST MARSHAL GENERAL

United States Military Personnel Returned Alive, World War II, European Theater (85,541 names).

United States Military Personnel Returned Alive, World War II, Pacific Theater (19,202 names).

These records were compiled from a 1980 study by the Veterans Administration, based on War Department documents. A few names are missing because they were never transferred from the punch cards to an electronic medium. A few other names are missing because the individuals died in prisoner-of-war camps or were returned to the United States after being reported missing or captured. Also, the names of individuals whose surnames begin with V, W, X, Y, or Z (and perhaps a few others) were not successfully transferred to electronic tape.

Korean War
PRISONER-OF-WAR RECORDS OF THE VETERANS ADMINISTRATION

These consist of 4,447 entries created by the Veterans Administration (now the Department of Veterans Affairs) as part of its 1980 study of former prisoners of war. The original data consisted of printed lists compiled by each branch of the military. Included are name, service number, social security number, dates of capture and release, and name of prisoner-of-war camp. Since it is presumed that many of these individuals are still living, some of the data is masked to insure privacy. The Department of Veterans Affairs has a supplemental collection titled "Repatriated American Prisoners of War," but it has not been transferred to the National Archives and thus is not yet available for public research. Veterans or families of veterans may inquire of the Department of Veterans Affairs.

DEATHS BY HOSTILITIES OR WHILE IN MISSING OR CAPTURED STATUS–RECORDS OF THE OFFICE OF THE SECRETARY OF DEFENSE

These records pertain to U.S. military personnel whose deaths were reported as having been caused by hostilities or while in a missing or captured status. In the vast majority of these cases the cause of death was coded "unknown, not reported." Information in this collection was submitted by the military branches of the Department of Defense on the basis of data recorded several years ago on a Report of Casualty form. Included on the card were name, military branch, country of casualty (which, in this collection, is always "Korea"), service number, grade or rank, date of death or declared dead, home of record, year of birth, cause of casualty, and citizenship.

CASUALTIES–RECORDS OF THE ADJUTANT GENERAL'S OFFICE

These records pertain to 109,975 original notations made by the Department of the Army before they were transferred to the National Archives in September 1989. Included are names and information about individuals who died or who suffered non-fatal injuries during the Korean War. Included are name, branch of service (army), place of casualty, date of casualty, state and county of residence, type of casualty (coded), place and date of disposition, year of birth (given only for those deceased), military specialty, military unit, and race. Because the individuals in the "non-fatal" category are presumed to be alive, some data is masked to insure personal privacy. Veterans who suffered wounds during the Korean War may obtain a copy of their casualty records, available in printout form.

STATE-LEVEL CASUALTY LISTS FROM THE KOREAN WAR

Separate printouts have been prepared for each state according to the serviceman's "home of record" at the time the serviceman last entered military service. The records for army and air force veterans list county and state; records for navy and marine veterans list city/town and state. Included are name, rank or grade, branch of service, home of record, date of casualty, date of birth, and category of casualty (coded). A copy of a list for any state may be purchased by check, to be sent in advance to the National Archives Trust Fund. Lists are available either alphabetically by name or alphabetically by home of record. Also available are printouts or tape copies for every state. Price information can be provided by the center.

Vietnam War

RECORDS OF THE OFFICE OF THE SECRETARY OF DEFENSE

These records comprise three separate collections of names of those who became casualties during the Vietnam War: the current file, the casualty history file, and the casualties-returned file. Because names have been transferred from one collection to another, all files should be searched. Names included in these collections refer to those who died as a result of hostilities (killed in action, died from wounds, died while missing, or died while captured) or who died from other causes (non-hostile injuries or illness). Also included are the names of those still listed as captured. The three collections included 58,152 names, with deaths recorded during the years 1957 to 1989.

Included in the collections are names of individuals who became casualties in Cambodia, Communist China, Laos, North Vietnam, South Vietnam, and Thailand. The data included are name, branch of military service, country of casualty, type of casualty, service number or social security number, grade or rank, date of birth, cause of casualty, race, religion, length of service, marital status, citizenship, and various other miscellaneous information.

STATE-LEVEL CASUALTY LISTS FROM THE VIETNAM WAR

Separate printouts are available for each state based on an individual's "home of record" at the time the individual last entered the service. The data includes name, rank or grade, branch of service, home of record, date of casualty, date of birth, and category of casualty (coded). A copy of a state list may be purchased, as may a copy of a printout or a tape covering all states in the nation. Price information can be furnished by the center.

ACTIVE-DUTY ARMY PERSONNEL WHO DIED, 1961–81

This collection is an abstract of a more extensive database created by the Office of the Adjutant General that contains names of dead and wounded, worldwide, between 1961 and 1981. Since the data for the "wounded" category cannot be released due to Privacy Act restrictions, only the "death" category is currently available. There are two separate collections: worldwide and Southeast Asia. There are also separate lists arranged by military organization, date of casualty, and name.

Lists Available—Korean War and Vietnam War

This center has copies of the data described above, arranged by various categories, each bound in folders. A copy of one page from any of the folders cited below will be sent free of charge upon request if sufficient identifying information is provided.

KOREAN WAR

Department of Defense lists (all branches of service):

> Deaths, by name, 1950–59
>
> Deaths, by name, 1961–81
>
> Deaths, by date and name, 1950–57
>
> Casualties, by state, place, and name

Army lists:

> Deaths, by name; also gives place of casualty, state, and other identifying information.

Not recovered or missing:

> The names of 8,182 who lost their lives but whose remains were not recovered. These names are inscribed on a marble Court of Honor at the National Cemetery in the Punchbowl at Honolulu, Hawaii.

VIETNAM WAR

Department of Defense lists (all branches of service):

> Deaths, by name
>
> Deaths, by date of casualty and name
>
> Deaths, by home state and name

There are separate lists for each state, arranged by home of record and name, service occupation and name, or by name only.

Army lists:

> Deaths, by major organization and name
>
> Deaths, by date of casualty and name
>
> Deaths, by state, town, and name; gives major organization, date of casualty, date of death, and type of casualty
>
> Deaths, by state and name, of those who became casualties in places *other than* North Vietnam or South Vietnam
>
> Officers, by name

Still Pictures Branch

The Still Pictures Branch contains extensive collections of photographs (negative and positive images) and reproductions of early graphic illustrations relating to U.S. military units and activities, ships, airplanes, and other items of a military nature.

Finding Aids

Burger, Barbara Lewis, comp. *Guide to the Holdings of the Still Pictures Branch of the National Archives.* Washington, D.C.: National Archives, 1991.

Pictures of the Revolutionary War; Pictures of the Civil War; Pictures of World War I; Pictures of United States Navy Ships. These booklets list selected original photographs or copies of paintings and engravings. They are far from complete but provide examples of the holdings available in this branch.

Heller, Jonathan, ed. *War and Conflict: Selected Images From the National Archives, 1765–1970.* Washington, D.C.: National Archives, 1991. The photographs chosen for inclusion in this book may be found in a notebook available in this branch, and they may be copied.

Index Card Files

Photographs available in this branch have titles and entry numbers for identification. Each is indexed on a three- by five-inch card and is filed in a cabinet. The cards for military photographs are arranged into two groups: U.S. Navy and Signal Corps. One section of the navy index consists of cards that list naval vessels by name (arranged by type of vessel). Other cards are arranged by subject (such as a geographical location or other). The navy index is divided into two parts: 1941–45 and 1946–58.

Army Signal Corps photographs are indexed by subject. References to photographs depicting activities in all American wars dating from the American Revolution to World War II are included. The files are arranged by war.

Copies of Photographs

Any photograph located in an index may be seen upon submission of a request form showing the entry number. Pencils and note paper are provided, as no pens or personal papers may be brought into the room. Copies of any photograph may be made on copy machines available in the branch. For researchers' convenience, previously copied photographs are arranged in file folders and placed in cabinets according to subject. Typical titles of these folders are: World War I, Europe, World War II, Asia, Civil War, United States, Marines, etc. Each folder contains examples of photographs of personnel in military units, military posts and stations, and campaign and battle scenes. Professionally printed copies of any picture (black and white) may be ordered for delivery in eight to ten weeks. Order forms and price lists for prints and negatives are available at the branch.

National Personnel Records Center

9700 Page Boulevard
St. Louis, Missouri 63132-5100
Air Force Records: (314) 538-4243
Army Records: (314) 538-4261
Navy, Marine Corps, Coast Guard Records: (314) 538-4141

The National Personnel Records Center is one of fifteen federal records centers that receive records transferred from federal courts and federal agencies when they are no longer needed for current business. These records are retained in the centers pending future transfer to one of the National Archives repositories when and if they are classified as archival material; otherwise, they are scheduled for destruction. While at a records center, the records are controlled by the court or agency that placed them there. The records may be inspected and reproduced at the center only with the written approval of the appropriate court or agency.

Federal records centers are located in Boston, New York, Philadelphia, Atlanta, Chicago, Dayton, Kansas City, Fort Worth, Denver, Seattle, San Francisco, Los Angeles, St. Louis (National Personnel Records Center), and Suitland, Maryland (National Records Center). For many years, the National Records Center in Suitland served in a dual role as a federal records center and as an overflow facility for the main National Archives building in downtown Washington, D.C.

The principal service of the National Personnel Records Center is to provide proof of service and related military data to servicemen and -women and to their next of kin if deceased or if the next of kin has the veteran's written consent. Military service material is normally provided to facilitate admission to a veterans' hospital, approval of a loan from the Veterans Administration, approval of veterans' education benefit programs, and for other official purposes. Requests for data to be used for genealogical purposes are given a lower priority, and a response may take several months. Most requests are received and replied to by correspondence. There is no research room available to the public, but a personal visit can be arranged by writing or telephoning in advance. No Selective Service records or bonus records are available at this branch.

In 1973, a fire destroyed a large portion of the army and air force records for personnel who served in World War I, World War II, and the Korean War. Many files were reconstructed, however, using data collected from other agencies, such as the Veterans Administration. Veterans who wish to obtain data from their personnel files or who wish to know if their file was destroyed may submit a Request Pertaining to Military Records (standard form 180). A request may be expedited if reference is made to the Freedom of Information Act. If the center does not have the file or needs further information, it will send the inquirer a Questionnaire About Military Service (standard form 13075). At that point a reconstructed file may be developed.

Descriptive Publications

Military Service Records in the National Archives of the United States—a pamphlet prepared by this center.

General Information Leaflet No. 7. Revised in 1985. Prepared by this center.

General Records

The National Personnel Records Center has personnel records for the following U.S. military personnel:

U.S. Army: officers separated after 30 June 1917; enlisted personnel separated after 31 October 1912.

U.S. Air Force: officers and enlisted personnel separated after September 1947 (when the Department of the Air Force was established).

U.S. Navy and Marine Corps: navy officers separated after 1902; navy enlisted personnel separated after 1885; marine officers separated after 1895; marine enlisted personnel separated after 1904.

U.S. Coast Guard: officers separated after 1928; enlisted personnel separated after 1914; civilian personnel of predecessor agencies of the Coast Guard (Revenue Cutter Service, Life-Saving Service, and Light-House Service), 1864–1919.

Merchant Marine Records

Congress recently enacted legislation granting veteran status to merchant seamen who served on ships that made ocean or coastwise voyages between 7 December 1941 and 15 August 1945. To assist former merchant seamen in obtaining evidence of their wartime service, which is required to qualify for certain veterans' benefits, the U.S.

Coast Guard has set up a special administrative unit. Applicants should submit copies (not the originals) of any documents in their possession that could help verify their service, along with an official application (form DD 2168), which is available from any office of the U.S. Department of Veterans Affairs. Requests should be addressed to the Commandant (G-MVP:1/12), United States Coast Guard, 2100 Second Street SW, Washington, D.C. 10593-0001.

DATABASE OF MERCHANT MARINE SEAMEN

A computer database of names of approximately 200,000 Merchant Marine seamen who served during World War II, the Korean War, and the Vietnam War is available from the Office of Labor and Training, United States Maritime Administration, Washington, D.C. 20590; telephone: (202) 366-2646.

MERCHANT MARINE LOGBOOKS

In lieu of other documentation, Merchant Marine veterans may wish to locate logbooks of the vessels on which they served. Many logbooks are available at the National Archives' regional archives. Applicants should request logbook information in writing—including the *full* name of the vessel on which served, the name of the port where the voyage *ended*, and approximate dates of the voyage (month and year). If the requested logbook is located, the veteran will be provided one copy of the logbook pages needed to verify his presence. Since information relating to disciplinary or medical matters is restricted under the federal Privacy Act, such material may be divulged only to the veteran who requests it. Additional copies, or copies of supplementary pages, will be provided for a fee.

The contents of Merchant Marine logbooks usually include information pertaining to offenses and desertions punishable by forfeiture of wages; they also include injuries or illnesses of crew members. Some logs provide descriptions of the circumstances surrounding any collisions in which the vessel was involved, as well as entries noting deaths, births, or marriage of passengers aboard the ship. They usually do not include descriptions of wartime actions in which the vessel was involved.

Since gun crews for merchant ships were provided by the U.S. Navy, the "armed guard reports" created by the navy detachments are a better source for wartime action data. These reports are available at the National Archives' Military Reference Branch (navy) (chapter 4).

Vessels registered in foreign countries (including Panama) were not required to turn in logbooks despite the fact that they may have been owned by an American company. The whereabouts of some logbooks of vessels registered in the United States is presently unknown, but those now available are housed at some of the National Archives' regional archives and are listed according to the name of the port and the years.

Supplementary information pertaining to Merchant Marine service may be obtained by writing to the following offices:

Army Transport Service
U.S. Army Reserve Personnel Center
9700 Page Boulevard
St. Louis, Mo. 63132-5200

Naval Transportation Service
Naval Military Personnel Command
Navy Department, Washington, D.C. 20370-5300

Operational Archives, U.S. Naval Historical Center
Building 57, Washington Navy Yard
Washington, D.C. 20374-0571

(This center has vessel movement cards of the Tenth Fleet, which was in charge of convoys and routing.)

Public Health Service Data Center
GWL Hansen's Disease Center
Carville, La. 70721

(For medical ailments treated at a Public Health Service Hospital—formerly the Marine Hospital.)

U.S. Merchant Marine Academy
Attn: Director of External Affairs
Kings Point, N.Y. 11024-1699

(For records of individuals who were academy cadets; alternative source: National Archives regional archives, New York, New York—see below.)

National Personnel Records Center
9700 Page Boulevard,
St. Louis, Mo. 63132-5100

Public Records Office
Ruskin Avenue, Kew, Richmond
Surrey TW9 4DU, England

(For operations in the waters off northern Russia and the Mediterranean Sea under Royal Navy control, which were often crewed by American Merchant Marine seamen.)

National Archives Regional Archives

In 1969, the National Archives established a regional archives system to make historically important federal records more easily accessible to the public without the necessity of traveling to Washington, D.C. There are thirteen regional archives, each of which holds records that originate in the federal agencies and federal courts within its region. Exceptions occur when two or more regional archives share material that pertains to the nation as a whole or if the boundaries of a former agency changed, causing its records to be placed in a regional archives outside the area of its present location.

In 1997, the National Archives and Records Service (NARA) began a reorganization of the holdings at the regional archives, which involves, in some cases, consolidation with a federal records center, where both archival and non-archival records may become available at the same location. Also, some of the existing Regional Archives may be relocated into smaller facilities. Ask the National Archives for information concerning recent changes, or ask for an updated version of its publication, *Special List 45*.

An ongoing project to make duplicates of National Archives microfilm for use in the regional archives means that many of the more commonly used microfilm series (such as those for census records) are available at the regional archives as well as at the National Archives in Washington, D.C. A core group of microfilm collections is to be available at all twelve regional archives; additional microfilm collections available only in selected facilities are listed below. Reference staff assigned to each regional archives can assist researchers, but they cannot conduct the research. Responses may be made to written or telephone requests for one item of information at a time, but a personal visit to the center is encouraged. Visitors will receive assistance from the staff, who will locate the records and make suggestions for other sources available at that branch or elsewhere. A telephone call or an advance letter is strongly suggested to enable staff members to secure the desired records prior to arrival, or to learn if they are available at that location.

Because additional microfilm is frequently transferred to the various regional archives, it is impossible to publish a current list here. Therefore, it is important to inquire about recent additions that may be pertinent.

The regional archives are located in Boston, New York City, Philadelphia, Chicago, Atlanta, Kansas City, Fort Worth, Denver, Anchorage, Seattle, and San Bruno (near San Francisco) and Laguna Niguel (near Los Angeles), California.

Finding Aids

Szucs, Loretto D., and Sandra H. Luebking. *The Archives: A Guide to the National Archives Field Branches.* Salt Lake City: Ancestry, 1988.

Guide to Records in the National Archives–[name of region]. Washington, D.C.: National Archives and Records Administration, 1989. These booklets, one for each regional archives, list the holdings of original documents (not the microfilm) by record group. A 1991 survey of each of the regional archives ascertained changes or additions to the collections since the guides were published; such modifications are reflected below.

National Archives and Records Administration. *National Archives Microfilm Publications in the Regional Archives System.* Archives Special List 45. Washington, D.C.: 1990.

Microfilm Publications in the National Archives–[name of region]. Washington, D.C.: NARA, 1990. Special List 54. These publications have two listings: one is for each region's individual holdings, and the other is a consolidation of all individual lists in one volume.

National Archives Microfilm Available at All Regional Archives

The following is a list of National Archives microfilm titles pertaining to military records that are currently available at all of the regional archives. Additional titles will undoubtedly be added to this list.

The Negro in the Military Service of the United States, 1639–1886 (M858).

Historical Information Relating to Military Posts and Other Installations, ca. 1700–1900 (M661).

General Index to Compiled Service Records of Revolutionary War Soldiers (M860).

Index to Compiled Service Records of American Naval Personnel Who Served During the Revolutionary War (M879).

Compiled Service Records of American Naval Personnel and Members of the Commissary General of Military Stores Who Served During the Revolutionary War (M880).

Compiled Service Records of Soldiers Who Served in the American Army During the Revolutionary War (M881).

List of North Carolina Land Grants in Tennessee, 1778–1791 (M68).

Gen. James Wilkinson's Order Book, 31 December 1796 to 8 March 1803 (M654).

Registers of Letters Received, Main Series, 1800–1870 (M22).

Revolutionary War Pensions and Bounty Land Warrant Application Files, 1800–1900 (M804).

Records Relating to the United States Military Academy, 1812–1867 (M91).

Orders of Gen. Zachary Taylor to the Army of Occupation in the Mexican War, 1845–1847 (M29).

General Orders and Circulares of the Confederate War Department, 1861–1865 (M901).

Registers of Letters Received, Irregular Series, 1861–1866 (M491).

Index to Letters Received, 1861–1870 (M495).

Registers of Letters Received From the President, Executive Departments, and War Department Bureaus, 1862–1970 (M494).

The Mathew B. Brady Collection of Civil War Photographs (T252).

List of Photographs and Photographic Negatives Relating to the War for the Union (T251).

Records of the Commissioners of Claims (Southern Claims Commission), 1871–1880 (M87).

Index to Letters Sent Relating to Military Affairs, 1871–1889 (M420).

Several other registers of letters received and sent during the nineteenth century (M6, M7, M127, M221, M222, M370, M421, M492, M494). Not indexed.

NEW ENGLAND REGION–BOSTON, MASSACHUSETTS

380 Trapelo Road
Waltham, Massachusetts 02154
(617) 647-8100

Serves Connecticut, Maine, Massachusetts, New Hampshire, Rhode Island, and Vermont.

Record Groups

RG 15–RECORDS OF THE VETERANS ADMINISTRATION (12 cu. ft.)

Death and burial records, case files, lists and rosters, and miscellaneous financial records of the National Home for Disabled Volunteer Soldiers in Togus, Maine, 1866–1938; also correspondence of the Rehabilitation Division relating to the Boston and other local or regional offices, 1918–25.

RG 18–RECORDS OF THE ARMY AIR FORCES (11 CU. FT.)

Correspondence and issuances of the School of Military Aeronautics at the Massachusetts Institute of Technology, Cambridge, Massachusetts, 1917–18.

RG 24–RECORDS OF THE BUREAU OF NAVAL PERSONNEL (16 cu. ft.)

Includes correspondence and miscellaneous records, biographical sketches, lists of students, muster rolls of the V-12 unit at Dartmouth College and the Naval ROTC at Yale University, 1926–70; also correspondence and orders of the First District Office of the Coast Signal Service, Boston, 1898.

RG 26—RECORDS OF THE UNITED STATES COAST GUARD (391 cu. ft.)

Includes:

Unit logs, 1969–83.

Aids to navigation case files, 1900–65.

Correspondence, region I, 1952–65.

Coast Guard Academy records, 1894–1960.

Records of the collector of customs, Newport, Rhode Island, relating to lighthouses and revenue cutters, 1790–1902.

Logs of lifesaving stations in Rhode Island, Massachusetts, New Hampshire, and Maine, 1873–1941.

Merchant Marine logbooks (indexed by name of vessel):

>   Port of Boston, Massachusetts, 1942–53.
>
>   Port of Portsmouth, New Hampshire, 1942–55.
>
>   Port of Portland, Maine, 1941–55.
>
>   Port of Providence, Rhode Island, 1941–53.

RG 38—RECORDS OF THE OFFICE OF THE CHIEF OF NAVAL OPERATIONS (less than 1 cu. ft.)

Reports and correspondence of the aide for information, New London, Conn., office, relating to reported enemy espionage and submarine activity, 1918–19.

RG 52—RECORDS OF THE BUREAU OF MEDICINE AND SURGERY (3 cu. ft.)

Correspondence of the surgeon and medical inspector, U.S. Naval Hospital, Portsmouth, New Hampshire, 1865–95.

RG 71—RECORDS OF THE BUREAU OF YARDS AND DOCKS (5 cu. ft.)

"Journals of daily transactions" (logs) for the Boston Navy Yard, 1833–50; Portsmouth Navy Yard, 1836–51; New London Experimental Station, 1919; and New London Submarine Base, 1920–21.

RG 77—RECORDS OF THE OFFICE OF THE CHIEF OF ENGINEERS (426 cu. ft.)

Miscellaneous records relating to civil engineering projects, including the Passamaquoddy (Maine) Tidal Engineering Project, 1904–64.

Records of Providence Engineer District Office, 1824–1937.

Records of Boston Engineer District Office, 1906–35.

RG 112—RECORDS OF THE OFFICE OF THE SURGEON GENERAL, ARMY (1 cu. ft.)

General Orders, reports, issuances, and organizational planning files for the U.S. Army Hospital, Fort Devens, Massachusetts, 1950–62, and the Murphy Army Hospital, Waltham, Massachusetts, 1951–57.

RG 147—RECORDS OF THE SELECTIVE SERVICE SYSTEM, WORLD WAR II (78 cu. ft.)

Registration cards, April 1942, concerning men born between April 1877 and February 1897 for the states of Connecticut, New Hampshire, Rhode Island, and Vermont; also miscellaneous records pertaining to registration of aliens in each New England state except Massachusetts, 1942–46.

RG 156—RECORDS OF THE OFFICE OF CHIEF OF ORDNANCE (196 cu. ft.)

Miscellaneous records relating to research, production, testing, and administrative matters, primarily at the Champlain, Kennebec, and Watertown arsenals and the Springfield Armory, 1820–1942.

RG 163—RECORDS OF THE SELECTIVE SERVICE SYSTEM (WORLD WAR I) (84 cu. ft.)

Docket sheets for district and local boards, including lists of men ordered to report for induction, indexes to deserters, and lists of delinquents and deserters, 1917–19.

RG 165—RECORDS OF THE WAR DEPARTMENT GENERAL AND SPECIAL STAFFS (2,079 cu. ft.)

Correspondence of the Boston and New Haven district offices of the Plant Protection Section, Military Intelligence Division, 1918–19.

RG 181—RECORDS OF NAVAL DISTRICTS AND SHORE ESTABLISHMENTS (2,079 cu. ft.)

Miscellaneous administrative records relating to the First Naval District and to shipyards and naval air stations in New England, 1815–1973.

RG 336—RECORDS OF THE OFFICE OF THE CHIEF OF TRANSPORTATION (8 cu. ft.)

Issuances and publications, conference and committee minutes, reports and histories of the First Transportation Zone, the Boston Port Agency, and the Boston Port of Embarkation, 1942–46.

RG 338—RECORDS OF UNITED STATES ARMY COMMANDS (2 cu. ft.)

Miscellaneous administrative records for several New England military organizations, 1951–64, and technical reports of the Cold Regions Research and Engineering Laboratories, Hanover, New Hampshire, 1968–70.

RG 392—RECORDS OF THE U.S. ARMY COAST ARTILLERY DISTRICTS AND DEFENSES (44 cu. ft.)

Correspondence and issuances of the coast and harbor defenses of Boston, Narragansett Bay, New Bedford, Portland, and Portsmouth, 1901–35.

National Archives Microfilm

See page 133 for a list of National Archives microfilm available at all regional archives; also available at this archives are the following:

Special Schedules of the Eleventh Census (1890) Enumerating Union Veterans and Widows of Union Veterans of the Civil War (M123).

Records of the Fifty-fourth Massachusetts Infantry Regiment (colored), 1863-65 (M1659).

Abstracts of Service Records of Naval Officers, 1798-1893 (M330).

General Index to Pension Files, 1861-1934 (T288).

NORTHEAST REGION—NEW YORK, NEW YORK

201 Varick Street
New York, New York 10014-4811
(formerly located at Bayonne, New Jersey)
(212) 337-1300

Serves New Jersey, New York, Puerto Rico, and the Virgin Islands.

Record Groups

RG 24—RECORDS OF THE BUREAU OF NAVAL PERSONNEL (26 cu. ft.)

Logs, orders, and muster cards for enlisted men, student officers, and midshipmen; correspondence, 1941-46.

RG 26—RECORDS OF THE UNITED STATES COAST GUARD (960 cu. ft.)

Logs of various Coast Guard units including vessels, lifeboat stations, and shore units in New York, New Jersey, and overseas.

Merchant Marine logbooks, 1942-62 (indexed by name of vessel).

Logbooks for the New York area are located at this facility, but the indexes are maintained by the Coast Guard office. The year and log number must be obtained from those indexes before the regional archives can search for the logbook. Write the U.S. Coast Guard, Marine Inspection Office, Investigative Section, Room 312, Battery Park Building, New York, NY 10004-1466.

RG 77—RECORDS OF THE OFFICE OF THE CHIEF OF ENGINEERS (338 cu. ft.)

Administrative and technical records from districts in the northeast region, 1831-1943.

RG 92—RECORDS OF THE OFFICE OF THE QUARTERMASTER GENERAL (1 cu ft.)

Correspondence of the Red Bank, New Jersey, subdepot, 1918-19.

RG 163—RECORDS OF THE SELECTIVE SERVICE SYSTEM (WORLD WAR I) (133 cu. ft.)

Docket books of local boards, lists of men ordered to report to local boards for induction, lists and indexes of delinquents and deserters for New York, New Jersey, and Puerto Rico.

RG 181—RECORDS OF THE NAVAL DISTRICTS AND SHORE ESTABLISHMENTS (4,182 cu. ft.)

Correspondence and miscellaneous records from districts and establishments in New York, New Jersey, and Puerto Rico.

National Archives Microfilm

See page 133 for a list of National Archives microfilm available at all regional archives. Also available at this branch are the following:

Index to Compiled Service Records of Volunteer Union Soldiers Who Served in Organizations From the State of New Jersey (M550).

Index to Compiled Service Records of Volunteer Union Soldiers Who Served in Organizations From the State of New York (M551).

Schedule Enumerating Union Veterans and Widows of Union Veterans of the Civil War (M123).

MID-ATLANTIC REGION— PHILADELPHIA, PENNSYLVANIA

Room 1350
Ninth and Market Streets
Philadelphia, Pennsylvania 19107
(215) 597-3000

Serves Delaware, Pennsylvania, Maryland, Virginia, and West Virginia.

Record Groups

RG 24—RECORDS OF THE BUREAU OF NAVAL PERSONNEL (74 cu. ft.)

Records of the United States Naval Home, Philadelphia, 1838-1942; United States Naval Hospital, Philadelphia, 1855-71; Enlisted Naval Training School (radio) Bedford Springs, Pennsylvania, 1942-45.

RG 26—RECORDS OF THE UNITED STATES COAST GUARD (1,356 cu. ft.)

Logs of daily activities of various Coast Guard cutters and support vessels operating from ports in Pennsylvania,

Delaware, Maryland, and Virginia, 1875–82; also logbooks for light stations, merchant vessels, and other units.

Merchant Marine logbooks (indexed by name of vessel):

Port of Philadelphia, Pennsylvania, 1919–21; 1942–59; 1958–59.

Port of Baltimore, Maryland, 1942–57; 1964–67.

Port of Norfolk, Virginia (including Wilmington, North Carolina, 1940–49), 1940–55.

Port of Portsmouth, Virginia, 1956–57; 1963–64.

RG 77—RECORDS OF THE OFFICE OF THE CHIEF OF ENGINEERS (1,676 cu. ft.)

Administrative and technical records pertaining to district and other offices of the Corps of Engineers.

RG 92—RECORDS OF THE QUARTERMASTER GENERAL (970 cu. ft.)

Correspondence and administrative records pertaining to the Philadelphia Depot, Office of the Quartermaster General, Schuykill Arsenal, and Pittsburgh Storage and Supply Depot.

RG 156—RECORDS OF THE CHIEF OF ORDNANCE (1,062 cu. ft.)

Administrative and technical records pertaining to the Allegheny Arsenal, Pittsburgh, Pennsylvania; Frankfort Arsenal, Pennsylvania; and Fort Monroe Arsenal, Virginia. Includes documents from 1813; administrative and technical records pertaining to several other ordnance depots and plants in the mid-Atlantic states, 1901–41.

RG 163—RECORDS OF THE SELECTIVE SERVICE SYSTEM (WORLD WAR I) (128 cu. ft.)

Includes records of district and local draft boards, with lists of men ordered to report for induction, an index to deserters' files, lists of delinquents and deserters, and district board docket sheets.

RG 181—RECORDS OF THE NAVAL DISTRICTS AND SHORE ESTABLISHMENTS (2,559 cu. ft., with some recent additional material)

Correspondence and issuances from several naval installations in the mid-Atlantic states. Records from the Philadelphia Navy Yard date from 1794; records from Norfolk Naval Air Station from 1922; records from the Norfolk Navy Yard from 1863; records from the U.S. naval base, Philadelphia, 1838–1942. Others date from the 1940s.

RG 313—RECORDS OF THE NAVAL OPERATING FORCES

Records of Airship Squadron One, 1962; Airship Squadron Three, 1959–60.

RG 338—RECORDS OF UNITED STATES ARMY COMMANDS, 1942– (202 cu. ft.).

Administrative records of several installations and advisory groups in the mid-Atlantic states.

National Archives Microfilm

See page 133 for a list of National Archives microfilm available at all regional archives. Also available at this archives are the following:

Index to Compiled Service Records of Volunteer Union Soldiers Who Served in Organizations From the State of Delaware (M537).

Index to Compiled Service Records of Volunteer Union Soldiers Who Served in Organizations From the State of Maryland (M388).

Index to Compiled Service Records of Volunteer Union Soldiers Who Served in Organizations From the State of Pennsylvania (M554).

Index to Compiled Service Records of Volunteer Union Soldiers Who Served in Organizations From the State of West Virginia (M587).

Index to Compiled Service Records of Confederate Soldiers Who Served in Organizations From the State of Maryland (M379).

Index to Compiled Service Records of Confederate Soldiers Who Served in Organizations From the State of Virginia (M382).

Compiled Service Records of Volunteer Soldiers Who Served During the Mexican War in Organizations From the State of Pennsylvania (M1028).

GREAT LAKES REGION—CHICAGO, ILLINOIS

7358 South Pulaski Road
Chicago, Illinois 60629
(312) 581-7816

Serves Illinois, Indiana, Michigan, Minnesota, Ohio, and Wisconsin.

Record Groups

RG 15—RECORDS OF THE VETERANS ADMINISTRATION (25 cu. ft.)

Records relating to the Chicago, Cincinnati, Cleveland, and Minneapolis regional offices, 1918–26.

RG 18—RECORDS OF THE ARMY AIR FORCES (114 cu. ft.)

Records relating to facilities in Illinois, Indiana, Michigan, Minnesota, and Ohio, 1917–39.

RG 24—RECORDS OF THE BUREAU OF NAVAL PERSONNEL (45 cu. ft.)

Correspondence and administrative records of the Naval Reserve Midshipmen's School, Northwestern University, Evanston, Illinois, 1941–45.

RG 26—RECORDS OF THE U.S. COAST GUARD (600 cu. ft.)

Logs of vessels and shore facilities in the Great Lakes area; logs of lifesaving stations in the Cleveland and Chicago districts, 1876–1983.

RG 74–RECORDS OF THE BUREAU OF ORDNANCE (1,440 cu. ft.)

Drawings and revisions of naval ordnance developed or manufactured at the Louisville, Kentucky, plant.

RG 77–RECORDS OF THE OFFICE OF THE CHIEF OF ENGINEERS (1,954 cu. ft.)

Technical records from various division and district offices in the Great Lakes area.

RG 92–RECORDS OF THE OFFICE OF THE QUARTERMASTER GENERAL (77 cu. ft.)

Correspondence from depots in Illinois, Indiana, and Ohio.

RG 111–RECORDS OF THE OFFICE OF THE CHIEF SIGNAL OFFICER (5 cu. ft.)

Records relating to the Decatur Signal Depot, Decatur, Illinois, 1918-62.

RG 112–RECORDS OF THE OFFICE OF THE SURGEON GENERAL, ARMY (less than 1 cu. ft.)

Records relating to the U.S. Army Hospital, Fort Benjamin Harrison, Indiana, 1954-63.

RG 147–RECORDS OF THE SELECTIVE SERVICE SYSTEM

Registration cards for men born between 28 April 1877 and 16 February 1897 for Illinois, Indiana, Michigan, Ohio, and Wisconsin, 1942.

RG 156–RECORDS OF THE OFFICE OF THE CHIEF OF ORDNANCE (149 cu. ft.)

Correspondence and technical reports relating to arsenals, depots, ordnance districts, and ordnance plants and works in Illinois, Indiana, Michigan, Minnesota, and Wisconsin, 1926-55.

RG 163–RECORDS OF THE SELECTIVE SERVICE SYSTEM, WORLD WAR I (258 cu. ft.)

Docket books from local boards in the six states of the Great Lakes region, organized by county; lists of men ordered to report for induction; also delinquents and deserters. Genealogical information varies.

RG 165–RECORDS OF THE WAR DEPARTMENT GENERAL AND SPECIAL STAFFS (9 cu. ft.)

Records relating to correspondence of the Chicago District Office, 1918-19.

RG 181–RECORDS OF NAVAL DISTRICTS AND SHORE ESTABLISHMENTS (1,351 cu. ft.)

Correspondence from the Office of Commandments and naval training stations in Illinois, 1914-57.

RG 338–RECORDS OF U.S. ARMY COMMANDS (8 cu. ft.)

General orders, historical data, and administrative documents pertaining to signal depots, ordnance depots, storage facilities, and army administrative offices in Illinois, Indiana, Michigan, Ohio, and Wisconsin, 1946-69.

National Archives Microfilm

See page 133 for a list of National Archives microfilm available at all regional archives. Also available at this archives are the following:

Register of Army Land Warrants Issued Under the Act of 1788, for Service in the Revolutionary War: Military District of Ohio (T1008).

Selected Records From Revolutionary War Pension and Bounty-land Warrant Application Files (M805, rolls 49 and 83 only).

U.S. Revolutionary War Bounty Land Warrants Used in the United States Military District of Ohio and Related Papers (acts of 1788, 1803, and 1806) (M829).

Letters Sent by the Secretary of the Navy to Officers, 1798-1868 (M149).

Letters Received by the Secretary of the Navy: Captains' Letters, 1805-1861, 1866-1885 (M125–rolls 64 and 68 only).

War of 1812 Military Bounty-land Warrants, 1815-1858 (M848).

Index to Compiled Service Records of Volunteer Union Soldiers Who Served in Organizations From the State of Illinois (M359).

Index to Compiled Service Records of Volunteer Union Soldiers Who Served in Organizations From the State of Indiana (M540).

Index to Compiled Service Records of Volunteer Union Soldiers Who Served in Organizations From the State of Michigan (M545).

Index to Compiled Service Records of Volunteer Union Soldiers Who Served in Organizations From the State of Minnesota (M546).

Index to Compiled Service Records of Volunteer Union Soldiers Who Served in Organizations From the State of Ohio (M552).

Index to Compiled Service Records of Volunteer Union Soldiers Who Served in Organizations From the State of Wisconsin (M559).

Index to Compiled Service Records of Volunteer Soldiers Who Served From the State of Michigan During the Patriot War, 1838-39 (M630).

Index to Compiled Service Records of Volunteer Soldiers Who Served From the State of New York During the Patriot War, 1838 (M631).

Index to Compiled Service Records of Volunteer Soldiers Who Served During the Mexican War (M616).

Schedules Enumerating Union Veterans and Widows of Union Veterans of the Civil War, 1890 (M123).

SOUTHEAST REGION—ATLANTA, GEORGIA

1557 St. Joseph Avenue
East Point, Georgia 30344
(404) 763-7477

Serves Alabama, Georgia, Florida, Kentucky, Mississippi, North Carolina, South Carolina, and Tennessee.

Record Groups

RG 26—RECORDS OF THE UNITED STATES COAST GUARD

Logbooks, master's oath and licensing documents, and miscellaneous records pertaining to Merchant Marine and Coast Guard units in various southeastern states, 1954-83; logs of lifesaving stations in the Jacksonville District, 1873-1941

Merchant Marine logbooks (indexed by name of vessel):

> Port of Savannah, Georgia, 1941-53.
>
> Port of Jacksonville, Florida, 1943-51.
>
> Port of Miami, Florida, 1943-56.
>
> Port of Tampa, Florida, 1942-51.
>
> Port of Charleston, South Carolina, 1919-58 (indexed for World War II period).
>
> Port of Mobile, Alabama, 1942-58.

RG 77—RECORDS OF THE OFFICE OF THE CHIEF OF ENGINEERS (1,019 cu. ft.)

Administrative, construction, and technical material pertaining to the division of the Gulf of Mexico, 1934-35, and districts in the southeastern states, 1830-1973.

RG 92—RECORDS OF THE OFFICE OF THE QUARTERMASTER GENERAL (11 cu. ft.)

Correspondence and supply forms pertaining to depots at Savannah, Georgia, 1898-1899; Tampa, Florida, 1898-99; and Atlanta, Georgia, 1918-22.

RG 112—RECORDS OF THE OFFICE OF THE SURGEON GENERAL (ARMY) (1 cu. ft.)

Miscellaneous records of the medical supply depots at Atlanta and Savannah, Georgia, 1898-99.

RG 156—RECORDS OF THE OFFICE OF THE CHIEF OF ORDNANCE

Correspondence, morning reports, monthly returns, and administrative records for arsenals at Augusta, Georgia; Tampa, Florida; Louisville, Kentucky; Columbia, Tennessee; and Nashville, Tennessee, 1825-40; 1861-1920; 1925-39.

RG 163—RECORDS OF THE SELECTIVE SERVICE SYSTEM, WORLD WAR I (7,478 cu. ft.)

Draft registration cards and docket books from local draft boards throughout the United States. The docket books are available only on microfilm. Most male residents of the United States born between 1873 and 1900 were required to register. The registration cards list date of birth, race, citizenship, occupation, employer, nearest relative, and marital status; arranged by state and then by draft board. A standard request form has been devised for the use of researchers who wish a copy of a registration card. The individual's complete name and address at the time of the draft must be included in the request, for which there is a copy fee. An inventory of the records is available on microfilm.

RG 181—RECORDS OF NAVAL DISTRICTS AND SHORE ESTABLISHMENTS (1,780 cu. ft.)

Correspondence and other records pertaining to shipyards, naval stations, and various naval offices in South Carolina, Georgia, Florida, and Tennessee, 1845-1955; 1903-58.

National Archives Microfilm

See page 133 for a list of National Archives microfilm available at all regional archives. Also available at this archives are the following:

Index to Volunteers (M616).

Correspondence of the War Department Relating to Indian Affairs, Military Pensions, and Fortifications (M1062).

Brief Histories of United States Army Commands (army posts) and Descriptions of the Records (T912).

Revolutionary War Rolls, 1775-1783 (M246).

Special Index to Numbered Records in the War Department Collection of Revolutionary War Records, 1775-1783 (M847).

Miscellaneous Numbered Records (the manuscript file) in the War Department Collection of Revolutionary War Records, 1775-1790s (M859).

Index to Volunteer Soldiers Who Served From 1784-1811 (M694).

Index to Compiled Service Records of American Naval Personnel Who Served During the Revolutionary War (M879).

Index to Compiled Service Records of Revolutionary War Soldiers Who Served With the American Army in Georgia Military Organizations (M1051).

War Department Collection of Post-Revolutionary War Manuscripts (M904).

Register of Army Land Warrants Issued Under the Act of 1788, for Service in the Revolutionary War: Military District of Ohio (T1008)

Index to Compiled Service Records of Volunteer Soldiers Who Served During the Cherokee Disturbances and Removal in Organizations From the State of Georgia (M907).

Index to Compiled Service Records of Volunteer Soldiers Who Served During the Cherokee Disturbances and Removal in Organizations From the State of North Carolina (M256).

Indexes to Compiled Service Records of Volunteer Soldiers Who Served During the Cherokee Disturbances and Removal in Organizations From the State of Tennessee and the Field and Staff of the Army of the Cherokee Nation (M908).

Index to Compiled Service Records of Volunteer Soldiers Who Served During the Cherokee Disturbances and Removal in Organizations From the State of Alabama (M243).

Index to Compiled Service Records of Volunteer Soldiers Who Served During the War of 1812 in Organizations From the State of North Carolina (M250).

Index to Compiled Service Records of Volunteer Soldiers Who Served During the War of 1812 in Organizations From the State of South Carolina (M652).

Index to Compiled Service Records of Volunteer Soldiers Who Served During the Creek War in Organizations From the State of Alabama (M244).

Index to Volunteer Soldiers Who Served During Indian Wars and Disturbances, 1815–1858 (M629).

War of 1812 Military Bounty Land Warrants, 1815–1858 (M848).

Old War Index to Pension Files, 1815–1926 (T316).

Letters Received by the Office of the Adjutant General (main series): 1822–1860 (rolls 483, 586, and 618 only); *1861–1870* (scattered rolls); *1871–1889* (scattered rolls); *1881–1889* (scattered rolls) (M567, M619, M666, M689).

Compiled Service Records of Volunteer Soldiers Who Served During the Mexican War in Organizations From the State of Mississippi (M863).

Memoir of Reconnaissances With Maps During the Florida Campaign, 1854–1858 (M1090).

Letters Sent, Registers of Letters Received, and Letters Received by Headquarters Troops in Florida, 1850–1858 (M1084).

Index to Compiled Service Records of Volunteer Soldiers Who Served During the Florida War in Organizations From the State of Alabama (M245).

Official Battle Lists of the Civil War, 1861–1865 (M823).

Index to Compiled Service Records of Volunteer Union Soldiers Who Served in Organizations From the . . .

. . . *State of Alabama* (M263).

. . . *State of Arkansas* (M383).

. . . *Territory of Dakota* (M536).

. . . *State of Delaware* (M537).

. . . *District of Columbia* (M538)

. . . *State of Florida* (M264).

. . . *State of Georgia* (M385).

. . . *State of Kentucky* (M386).

. . . *State of Louisiana* (M387).

. . . *State of Mississippi* (M389).

. . . *State of North Carolina* (M391).

. . . *State of Oregon* (M553).

. . . *State of Tennessee* (M392).

. . . *Territory of Utah* (M556).

. . . *State of Virginia* (M394).

. . . *Territory of Washington* (M558).

Special Schedules of the Eleventh Census (1890) Enumerating Union Veterans and Widows of Union Veterans of the Civil War (M123).

Register of Confederate Soldiers, Sailors, and Citizens Who Died in Federal Prisons and Military Hospitals in the North, 1861–1865 (M918).

Letters Sent by the Confederate Secretary of War, 1861–1865 (M522).

Letters Sent by the Confederate Secretary of War to the President, 1861–1865 (M523).

Telegrams Sent by the Confederate Secretary of War, 1861–1865 (M524).

Letters and Telegrams Sent by the Confederate Adjutant and Inspector General, 1861–1865. (M627).

Confederate States Army Casualties: Lists and Narrative Reports, 1861–1865 (M836).

General Orders of the Confederate Adjutant General and Inspector General's Office, 1861–1865 (T782).

Index to Compiled Service Records of Confederate Soldiers Who Served in Organizations From the. . .

. . . *State of Alabama* (M374).

. . . *Territory of Arizona* (M375).

. . . *State of Arkansas* (M376).

. . . *State of Florida* (M225).

. . . *State of Georgia* (M226).

. . . *State of Kentucky* (M377).

. . . *State of Louisiana* (M378).

. . . *State of Maryland* (M379).

. . . *State of Mississippi* (M232).

. . . *State of Missouri* (M380).

. . . *State of North Carolina* (M230).

. . . *State of South Carolina* (M381).

. . . *State of Tennessee* (M231).

. . . *State of Texas* (M227).

. . . *State of Virginia* (M382).

Compiled Service Records of Confederate Soldiers Who Served in Organizations From the State of Kentucky (M319).

Index to Compiled Service Records of Confederate Soldiers Who Served in Organizations Raised Directly by the Confederate Government and Non-regimental Enlisted Men (M818).

Compiled Records Showing Service of Military Units in Confederate Organizations (M861).

Reference File Relating to Confederate Organizations From Georgia (T455).

Records Relating to Confederate Naval and Marine Personnel (M260).

Inspection Reports and Related Records Received by the Inspection Branch in the Confederate Adjutant and Inspector General's Office (M935)

Pardon Petitions and Related Papers Submitted in Response to President Johnson's Amnesty Proclamation, 1865 (M1003–73 rolls).

Letters Sent by Department of Florida and Successor Commands, 1861–1869 (M1096).

Records of the Southern Claims Commission, 1871–1880 (M87).

Index to Mexican War Pension Files, 1887–1926 (T317).

Index to Compiled Service Records of Volunteer Soldiers Who Served During the War With Spain in Organizations From the State of North Carolina (M413).

Compiled Service Records of Volunteer Soldiers Who Served in the Florida Infantry During the War With Spain (M1087).

CENTRAL PLAINS REGION— KANSAS CITY, MISSOURI

2312 East Bannister Road
Kansas City, Missouri 64131
(816) 926-6272

Serves Iowa, Kansas, Missouri, and Nebraska.

Record Groups

RG 15—VETERANS ADMINISTRATION (10 cu.ft.)

Correspondence and memoranda of the Rehabilitation Division, 1918–21.

RG 18—RECORDS OF THE ARMY AIR FORCES (15 cu. ft.)

Correspondence and orders, Fort Crook, Nebraska, 1936–39; Balloon School, Fort Crook, Nebraska, 1918–19; Balloon School, Omaha, Nebraska, 1917–21. Student records of David Ranken School of Mechanical Arts, St. Louis, Missouri, 1910. Correspondence of the Aviation Examining Board, Kansas City, Missouri, 1917–18.

RG 24—RECORDS OF THE BUREAU OF NAVAL PERSONNEL (1 cu. ft.)

Reports on Naval Reserve training activities in Indiana and Missouri, 1923–25.

RG 26—RECORDS OF THE UNITED STATES COAST GUARD (12 cu. ft.)

Logs of various Coast Guard cutters and support vessels operating on the Mississippi and Missouri rivers and their tributaries; also a few logs of supply depots and stations.

RG 77—RECORDS OF THE OFFICE OF THE CHIEF OF ENGINEERS (673 cu. ft.)

Administrative and technical records pertaining to construction of dams and other projects on the Mississippi River; also a few records pertaining to supply for the Panama Canal Project, 1917–32.

RG 92—RECORDS OF THE OFFICE OF THE QUARTERMASTER GENERAL (1 cu. ft.)

Administrative records pertaining to the National Cemetery at Fort McPherson, the quartermaster depot at Fort Robinson, and from the post engineer at Fort Leavenworth, 1874–1985.

RG 147—RECORDS OF THE SELECTIVE SERVICE SYSTEM, 1940- (313 cu. ft.)

Registration cards for Iowa, Kansas, Minnesota, Missouri, Nebraska, North Dakota, and South Dakota, ca. 1940; applications by aliens for relief from military service; alien personal history statements.

RG 163—RECORDS OF THE SELECTIVE SERVICE SYSTEM, WORLD WAR I (50 cu. ft.)

Docket books of local boards in Iowa, Kansas, Missouri, and Nebraska; lists of men ordered to report for induction and indexes to lists of delinquents and deserters.

RG 181—RECORDS OF NAVAL DISTRICTS AND SHORE ESTABLISHMENTS (7 cu. ft.)

Administrative records pertaining to naval air stations in Minnesota and Nebraska.

RG 338—RECORDS OF THE UNITED STATES ARMY COMMANDS

General orders and unit history files for states in the central plains region.

RG 342—RECORDS OF AIR FORCE COMMANDS (1 cu. ft.)

Committee and board records for Whiteman Air Force Base, Missouri.

National Archives Microfilm

See page 133 for a list of National Archives microfilm available at all regional archives. Also available at this archives are the following:

Special Index to Numbered Records in the War Department Collection of Revolutionary War Records, 1775–1783 (M847).

Index to Compiled Service Records of Volunteer Soldiers Who Served From 1784 to 1811 (M694).

Register of Enlistments in the United States Army, 1798–1914 (M233).

Index to Compiled Service Records of Volunteer Soldiers Who Served During the Revolutionary War in Organizations From the State of North Carolina (M257).

Revolutionary War Pension and Bounty Land Warrant Application Files, 1800–1900 (M804).

Returns From United States Military Posts, 1800–1916 (M617, scattered rolls).

Index to War of 1812 Pension Application Files (M313).

Index to Compiled Service Records of Volunteer Soldiers Who Served During The War of 1812 (M602).

War of 1812 Military Bounty Land Warrants, 1815–1858 (M848).

Index to Compiled Service Records of Volunteer Soldiers Who Served During the Cherokee Disturbances and Removal in Organizations From the State of Tennessee and the Field and Staff of the Army of the Cherokee Nation (M908).

Index to Compiled Service Records of Volunteer Union Soldiers Who Served in Organizations From the Territory of Dakota (M536).

Register of Confederate Soldiers, Sailors, and Citizens Who Died in Federal Prisons and Military Hospitals in the North, 1861–1865 (M918).

Index to Compiled Service Records of Volunteer Union Soldiers Who Served in Organizations From the . . .

. . . State of Arkansas (M383).
. . . State of California (M533).
. . . State of Colorado (M534).
. . . State of Florida (M264).
. . . State of Illinois (M539).
. . . State of Indiana (M540).
. . . State of Iowa (M541).
. . . State of Kansas (M542).
. . . State of Kentucky (M386).
. . . State of Minnesota (M546).
. . . State of Missouri (M390).
. . . State of Nebraska (M547).
. . . State of North Carolina (M391).
. . . State of Ohio (M552).
. . . State of Tennessee (M392).
. . . State of Texas (M393).
. . . State of Virginia (M394).

Index to Compiled Service Records of Confederate Soldiers Who Served in Organizations From the . . .

. . . State of Arizona (M385).
. . . State of Arkansas (M376).
. . . State of Florida (M225).
. . . State of Georgia (M226).
. . . State of Kentucky (M377).
. . . State of Missouri (M380).
. . . State of North Carolina (M230).
. . . State of South Carolina (M381).
. . . State of Tennessee (M231).
. . . State of Texas (M227).
. . . State of Virginia (M382).

Organization Index to Pension Files of Veterans Who Served Between 1861 and 1900 (T289).

Headquarters Records of Fort Dodge, Kansas, 1866–1892 (M989).

General Court-martial of Gen. George Armstrong Custer, 1867 (T1003).

Old War Index to Pension Files, 1815–1926 (T316).

Index to Mexican War Pension Files, 1887–1926 (T317).

Index to Indian Wars Pension Files, 1892–1926 (T318).

SOUTHWEST REGION—FORT WORTH, TEXAS

P. O. Box 6216
501 West Felix Street
(building 1 of the Federal Center)
Fort Worth, Texas 76115
(817) 334-5525

Serves Arkansas, Louisiana, Oklahoma, and Texas.

Record Groups

RG 26—RECORDS OF THE UNITED STATES COAST GUARD (1,174 cu. ft.)

Logs of various Coast Guard cutters and support vessels operating from Gulf Coast ports, 1868–1981, and a few logs of light stations, supply depots, and air stations; also of merchant vessels from 1942.

Merchant Marine logbooks:

Port of Brownsville, Texas, 1946–59 (not indexed).
Port of Corpus Christi, Texas, 1943–72 (indexed for World War II period).
Port of Galveston, Texas, 1941–74 (indexed for World War II period).
Port of Houston, Texas, 1942–73 (indexed for World War II period).
Port of Mobile, Alabama, 1942–56 (indexed for World War II period).
Port of New Orleans, Louisiana, 1942–76 (indexed for World War II period).
Port of Port Arthur, Texas, 1939–70 (indexed for World War II period).

RG 77—RECORDS OF THE OFFICE OF THE CHIEF OF ENGINEERS (3,440 cu. ft.)

Administrative and technical records pertaining to construction of dams and other projects in the southwest region.

RG 92—RECORDS OF THE OFFICE OF THE QUARTERMASTER GENERAL (67 cu. ft.)

Administrative records of the National Cemetery at Fort Gibson, Oklahoma, and supply depots at San Antonio, Texas, and Fort Reno, Oklahoma.

RG 112—RECORDS OF THE OFFICE OF THE SURGEON GENERAL (ARMY) (89 cu. ft.)

Administrative records of the army general hospitals at Fort Bayard, New Mexico, and Hot Springs, Arkansas, and the

Medical Supply Depot at El Paso, Texas; also a few patient registers for the hospital at Fort Bayard.

RG 156—RECORDS OF THE OFFICE OF THE CHIEF OF ORDNANCE (5 cu. ft.)

Administrative records and a few indexes and registers of correspondence concerning the San Antonio Arsenal.

RG 181—RECORDS OF NAVAL DISTRICTS AND SHORE ESTABLISHMENTS (873 cu. ft.)

Correspondence and administrative records of various districts and establishments in the southwest region.

RG 338—RECORDS OF THE UNITED STATES ARMY COMMANDS (3 cu. ft.)

Correspondence, general orders, and related records pertaining to commands in the southwest region.

National Archives Microfilm

See page 133 for a list of National Archives microfilm available at all regional archives. Also available at this archives are the following:

Register of Enlistments in the United States Army, 1798–1914 (M233).

Returns from United States Military Posts, 1800–1916 (M617). (This branch has rolls pertaining only to those posts in the Southwest.)

Letters Received by the Office of the Adjutant General (Main Series), 1822–1960 (M567—three rolls only).

Index to Compiled Service Records of Volunteer Soldiers Who Served During the Cherokee Removal in Organizations From the State of Alabama (M243).

Index to Compiled Service Records of Volunteer Soldiers Who Served During the Creek War in Organizations From the State of Alabama (M244).

Index to Compiled Service Records of Volunteer Soldiers Who Served During the Cherokee Disturbances and Removal in Organizations From the State of North Carolina (M256).

Index to Compiled Service Records of Volunteer Soldiers Who Served During the Florida War in Organizations From the State of Alabama (M245).

Index to Compiled Service Records of Volunteer Soldiers Who Served During the Florida War in Organizations From the State of Louisiana (M239).

Compiled Service Records of Confederate Soldiers Who Served in Organizations From the State of Arkansas (M317).

Index to Compiled Service Records of Confederate Soldiers Who Served in Organizations From the State of Georgia (M226—sixteen rolls only).

Records of the Military Post at San Antonio, Texas, 1866–1911 (T789).

ROCKY MOUNTAIN REGION—DENVER, COLORADO

P.O. Box 25307
Building 48, Federal Center
West Sixth Avenue and Kipling Street
Denver, Colorado 80225
(303) 236-0817

Serves Colorado, Montana, New Mexico, North Dakota, South Dakota, Utah, and Wyoming.

Records

RG 77—RECORDS OF THE OFFICE OF THE CHIEF OF ENGINEERS (75 cu. ft.)

Administrative and technical records concerning dams and other projects; records from the Fort Peck Dam project.

RG 92—RECORDS OF THE OFFICE OF THE QUARTERMASTER GENERAL (8 cu. ft.)

Correspondence relating to the Santa Fe National Cemetery; orders, memorandums, and circulars for the Ogden, Utah, General Depot, 1943–50.

RG 147—RECORDS OF THE SELECTIVE SERVICE SYSTEM, 1940–46 (53 cu. ft.)

Registration cards for men born 1877–97 for Arizona, Colorado, and Wyoming state headquarters; applications of aliens for relief from military service for Denver, Phoenix, Salt Lake City, and Cheyenne, 1940–46; alien registration forms, New Mexico, 1940–48; correspondence and reports, 1940–71.

RG 156—RECORDS OF THE OFFICE OF THE CHIEF OF ORDNANCE (24 cu. ft.)

These records are primarily administrative in nature. They include very little pertaining to military service of individuals. They consist of correspondence, orders, reports, and planning files for the following ordnance depots and arsenals: Denver and Pueblo, Colo. (1940–54); Ft. Wingate, New Mexico (1953–63); Black Hills, South Dakota (1942–53); and Deseret, Ogden, and Tooele, Utah (1944–54).

RG 163—RECORDS OF THE SELECTIVE SERVICE SYSTEM, WORLD WAR I (33 cu. ft.)

Docket books of local draft board. Lists of men ordered to report for induction and lists of delinquents and deserters for each of the states in the Rocky Mountain region, 1917–19.

RG 338—RECORDS OF THE UNITED STATES ARMY COMMANDS (3 cu. ft.)

Administrative records for depots and advisor groups in Colorado, Montana, North Dakota, Utah, and Wyoming.

National Archives Microfilm

See page 133 for a list of National Archives microfilm available at all regional archives. Also available at this archives are the following:

Registers of Enlistments in the U.S. Army, 1798–1914 (M233).

Returns from United States Military Posts, 1800–1916 (M617— scattered rolls for posts in the Rocky Mountain region and for Fort Scott, Kans.).

Letters Received by the Office of the Adjutant General (Main Series), 1871–1880 (M666—rolls 20, 120, 362, and 397–398 only).

Compiled Service Records of Volunteer Soldiers Who Served During the Mexican War in Mormon Organizations (M351).

Index to Compiled Service Records of Volunteer Union Soldiers Who Served in Organizations From the. . .

. . . Territory of Colorado (M534).

. . . Territory of Dakota (M536).

. . . State of Nebraska (M547).

. . . Territory of Utah (M556).

Compiled Service Records of Volunteer Union Soldiers Who Served in Organizations From the Territory of Utah (M692).

Proceedings of a Court of Inquiry Concerning the Conduct of Maj. Marcus A. Reno at the Battle of the Little Big Horn River on 25 and 26 June 1876 (M592).

General Court-martial of Gen. George Armstrong Custer, 1867 (T1103).

Special Schedules of the Eleventh Census (1890) Enumerating Union Veterans and Widows of Union Veterans of the Civil War (M123).

Log of the USS Nautilus, *August 1958* (T319).

ALASKA REGION—ANCHORAGE, ALASKA

654 West Third Avenue
Anchorage, Alaska 99501
(907) 271-2441

Serves Alaska.

Record Groups

RG 26—RECORDS OF THE UNITED STATES COAST GUARD (168 cu. ft.)

Unit histories compiled at the end of World War II document-ing wartime activities of district Coast Guard units; logs of Coast Guard vessels and shore installations in the Alaska Coast Guard District.

Unit logs documenting activities of Coast Guard vessels and shore installations in the Seventeenth Coast Guard District, 1969–83; records of the Nome Lifesaving Station; and Bureau of Customs records received through the Seventeenth Coast Guard District successors' offices, ca. 1903–1950.

Records of the Bering Sea Patrol, 1926–40 (transferred from the National Archives, Washington, D.C.). These are arranged numerically by vessel number and thereunder chronologi-cal-ly. Also transferred were logs, 1973–74, for the cutter *Sweetbrier* (WLB-405).

RG 41—RECORDS OF THE BUREAU OF MARINE INSPECTION AND NAVIGATION.

Applications for seamen's protection certificates, Juneau, 1932–35.

RG 77—RECORDS OF THE OFFICE OF THE CHIEF OF ENGINEERS (193 cu. ft.)

Administrative and technical records concerning river and harbor projects created from the Anchorage district office, 1915–68.

RG 80—GENERAL RECORDS OF THE DEPARTMENT OF THE NAVY (3 cu. ft.)

Records of the Navy Alaska Coal Commission at the Chick-aloon office, January 1920–June 1922 (transferred from the National Archives, Washington, D.C.).

RG 92—RECORDS OF THE QUARTERMASTER GENERAL (3 cu. ft.)

Records of the Alaska General Depot, Fort Richardson, Alaska, 1948–57 (transferred from the National Personnel Records Center, St. Louis, Missouri). These records consist of general orders, conference files, correspondence, facilities control files, photographs, manuals, operating procedures files, operating program progress report files, organization plan-ning files, standard operating procedures, training operations files, and unit history files.

RG 163—RECORDS OF THE SELECTIVE SERVICE SYSTEM, WORLD WAR I (3 cu. ft.)

Lists of men ordered to report to local boards in Alaska for induction; indexes to lists of delinquents and deserters.

RG 181—RECORDS OF NAVAL DISTRICTS AND SHORE ESTAB-LISHMENTS (486 cu. ft.)

Correspondence from the Seventeenth Naval District (including Alaska), 1941–56.

RG 336—RECORDS OF THE OFFICE OF THE CHIEF OF TRANSPORTA-TION (3.4 cu. ft.)

Records of the Excursion Inlet Port of Embarkation and the Juneau Port of Embarkation, 1942–46, and the Whittier Port, 1948–60. Included are general orders, management improve-ment files, organization planning files, standard operating procedures, unit history files, regulations, organization manuals, newspapers, and memoranda. The newspapers consist of daily issues of the Glacier News, published by the Troop I&E Section, Department of the Army, Port of Whit-tier, Alaska, 1948–55.

RG 342–RECORDS OF UNITED STATES AIR FORCE COMMANDS, AC-
TIVITIES, AND ORGANIZATIONS (17 cu. ft.)

Photographs and historical information pertaining to the Alaska
Communication System, 1929th Communications Group,
U.S. Air Force, 1900–61.

National Archives Microfilm

Eventually, this region will have the complete basic set of
military microfilm found in all other regional archives
(listed on page 133). At the time of writing, it has the
following military-related microfilm:

Revolutionary War Rolls, 1775–1783 (M246).

Miscellaneous Numbered Records (the manuscript file) in the War
Department Collection of Revolutionary War Records, 1775–
1790s (M859).

Area File of the Naval Records Collection, 1775–1910 (M625–
rolls 282–403 and 410–414).

List of North Carolina Land Grants in Tennessee, 1776–1791
(M68).

Register of Army Land Warrants Issued Under the Act of 1788, for
Service in the Revolutionary War: Military District of Ohio
(T1008).

War of 1812 Papers of the Department of State, 1789–1815
(M588).

Correspondence of the War Department Relating to Indian Affairs,
Military Pensions, and Fortifications, 1791–1797 (M1062).

Letters of Tench Coxe, Commissioner of the Revenue, Relating to the
Procurement of Military, Naval, and Indian Supplies, 1794–
1796 (M74).

General James Wilkinson's Order Book, December 31, 1796 to
March 8, 1808 (M654).

Register of Enlistments in the U.S. Army, 1798–1914 (M233).

Miscellaneous Letters Sent by the Secretary of War, 1800–1809
(M370).

Returns From U.S. Military Posts, 1800–1916 (M617–selected
rolls).

Office of the Secretary of War, Confidential and Unofficial Letters
Sent, 1814–1847 (M7).

Old War Index to Pension Files, 1815–1926 (T316).

Index to Compiled Service Records of Volunteer Soldiers Who Served
From the State of Michigan During the Patriot War, 1838–1839
(M630).

Orders of General Zachary Taylor to the Army of Occupation in the
Mexican War, 1845–1847 (M29).

Letters Received by the Secretary of War, Unregistered Series, 1789–
1861 (M222).

Registers of Letters Received by the Office of the Secretary of War,
Main Series, 1800–1870 (M22).

Letters Received by the Secretary of War, Registered Series, 1801–
1870 (M221).

War of 1812 Military Bounty Land Warrants, 1815–1858
(M848).

Letters Received by the Secretary of the Navy From Commanding
Officers of Squadrons, 1841–1886 (M89).

Index to Mexican War Files (T317).

Index to Compiled Service Records of Volunteer Union Soldiers Who
Served in Organizations From the State of Oregon (M553).

Index to Compiled Service Records of Volunteer Union Soldiers Who
Served in Organizations From the Territory of Washington
(M558).

General Orders and Circulares of the Confederate War Department,
1861–1865 (M901).

Register of Confederate Soldiers, Sailors, and Citizens Who Died in
Federal Prisons and Military Hospitals in the North, 1861–1865
(M918).

Index to Compiled Service Records of Confederate Soldiers Who
Served in Organizations From the State of Tennessee (M231).

Consolidated Index to Compiled Service Records of Confederate
Soldiers (M253).

Papers Pertaining to Vessels of or Involved With the Confederate
States of America: "Vessel Papers" (M909).

Registers of Letters Received by the Secretary of War, Irregular Series,
1861–1866 (M491).

Index to Letters Received by the Secretary of War, 1861–1870
(M420).

Indexes to Letters Received by the Secretary of War, 1861–1870
(M495).

Letters Received by the Secretary of War, Irregular Series, 1861–
1886 (M492).

Organization Index to Pension Files of Veterans Who Served
Between 1861–1900 (T289).

General Index to Pension Files, 1861–1934 (T288).

Registers of Letters Received by the Secretary of War From the
President, Executive Departments, and War Department
Bureaus, 1862–1870 (M494).

Letters Sent by the Secretary of War to the President of Executive
Departments, 1863–1870 (M421).

Pardon Petitions and Related Papers Submitted in Response to
President Andrew Johnson's Amnesty Proclamation of May 22,
1865 (M1003).

Records of the Commissioner of Claims, Southern Claims Commission, 1871–1906 (M87).

Proceedings of a Court of Inquiry Concerning the Conduct of Major
Marcus A. Reno at the Battle of the Little Big Horn River on
June 25 and 26, 1876 (M592).

Letters Sent to the President by the Secretary of War, 1880–1863
(M127).

Letters Sent by Secretary of War Relating to Military Affairs,
1880–1889 (M6).

Letters Received by the Office of the Adjutant General (main series),
1881–1889 (M666).

Special Schedules of the 11th Census (1890) Enumerating Union Veterans and Widows of Union Veterans of the Civil War (M123).

Records of the American Section of the Supreme War Council, 1917–1919 (M923).

Subject Index to Naval Intelligence Reports, 1940–1946 (M1332).

PACIFIC NORTHWEST REGION—
SEATTLE, WASHINGTON

6125 Sand Point Way, NE
Seattle, Washington 98115
(206) 526-6507

Serves Idaho, Oregon, and Washington

Records

RG 26—RECORDS OF THE UNITED STATES COAST GUARD (966 cu. ft.)

Administrative records for the districts encompassing Washington and Oregon; unit histories compiled at the end of World War II documenting wartime activities of Coast Guard units; unit histories of Coast Guard vessels and shore installations in Washington and Oregon; logs of lifesaving stations in the Seattle district, 1873-1941.

Merchant Marine logbooks (indexed by name of vessel or list):

Port of Seattle, Washington, 1890-1911; 1910-37; 1940-58.

Port of Portland, Oregon, 1942-58.

Port of Coos Bay, Oregon, 1914-27.

Port of Astoria, Oregon, 1915-40.

RG 77—RECORDS OF THE OFFICE OF THE CHIEF OF ENGINEERS (1,586 cu. ft.)

Administrative and technical records concerning river and harbor projects created in the Portland, Seattle, and Walla Walla districts.

RG 92—RECORDS OF THE OFFICE OF THE QUARTERMASTER GENERAL (13 cu. ft.)

Administrative records pertaining to the depot at Seattle, 1907-22, including supply shipments to the Philippines, 1908-11, and leasing of warehouses and docks during World War I. There are a few personnel records for 1924-39.

RG 163—RECORDS OF THE SELECTIVE SERVICE SYSTEM, WORLD WAR I (27 cu. ft.)

Docket sheets of local boards. Lists of men ordered to report for induction. Indexes and lists of delinquents and deserters for Idaho, Oregon, and Washington.

RG 181—RECORDS OF NAVAL DISTRICTS AND SHORE ESTABLISHMENTS (1,839 cu. ft.)

Correspondence and administrative records, 1901-64, for the following establishments:

Thirteenth Naval District
Puget Sound Naval Shipyard
Puget Sound Navy Base
Puget Sound Naval Station
Naval Station, Seattle
Tongue Point Naval Station (Astoria, Oregon)
Naval Communications Station, Seattle
Naval Air Station, Seattle
Naval Air Base, Seattle
Naval Air Base, Spokane
Bangor Ammunition Depot (Bremerton, Washington)
Military Sea Transport Service, North Pacific Sub-area

National Archives Microfilm

See page 133 for a list of National Archives microfilm available at all regional archives. Also available at this archives are the following:

Revolutionary War Rolls, 1775–1783 (M246).

Special Index to Numbered Records in the War Department Collection of Revolutionary War Records, 1775–1783 (M847).

Miscellaneous Numbered Records (the manuscript file) in the War Department Collection of Revolutionary War Records, 1775–1790's (M859).

Index to Compiled Service Records of Revolutionary War Soldiers Who Served with the American Army in Georgia Military Operations (M1051).

War Department Collection of Post-Revolutionary War Manuscripts (M904).

Register of Army Land Warrants Issued Under the Act of 1788, for Service in the Revolutionary War: Military District of Ohio (T1008).

U.S. Revolutionary War Bounty Land Warrants Used in the U.S. Military District of Ohio and Related Papers (acts of 1788, 1803, and 1806) (M829).

Index to U.S. Army Enlistments, 1798–1914 (M233).

Index to Compiled Service Records of Volunteer Soldiers Who Served During the War of 1812 in Organizations From the State of North Carolina (M250).

Index to War of 1812 Pension Application Files (M313).

Index to Compiled Service Records of Volunteer Soldiers Who Served During the War of 1812 (M602).

War of 1812 Military Bounty Land Warrants, 1815–1858 (M848).

Index to Compiled Service Records of Volunteer Soldiers Who Served During Indian Wars and Disturbances, 1815–1858 (M629).

Index to Compiled Service Records of Volunteer Soldiers Who Served From the State of Michigan During the Patriot War, 1838–1839 (M630)

Index to Compiled Service Records of Volunteer Soldiers Who Served During the Cherokee Disturbances and Removal in Organizations From the State of Georgia (M907).

Index to Compiled Service Records of Volunteer Soldiers Who Served During the Cherokee Disturbances and Removal in Organizations From the State of North Carolina (M256).

Letters Received by the Office of the Adjutant General (Main Series), 1822–1860 (M567—rolls 483 and 586 only).

Letters Received by the Office of the Adjutant General (Main Series), 1861–1870 (M619—roll 574 only).

Letters Received by the Office of the Adjutant General (Main Series), 1871–1880 (M666—scattered rolls).

Adjutant's Log of the Regiment of Mounted Riflemen, 1846–1861 (P8).

General Index to Pension Files, 1861–1934 (T288).

Organization Index to Pension Files of Veterans Who Served Between 1861–1900 (T289).

Old War Index to Pension Files, 1815–1926 (T316).

Index to Mexican War Pension Files, 1887–1926 (T317).

Index to Indian War Pension Files, 1892–1926 (T318).

Index to Compiled Service Records of Volunteer Soldiers Who Served During the Florida War in Organizations From the State of Louisiana (M239).

Index to Compiled Service Records of Volunteer Soldiers Who Served During the Mexican War in Mormon Organizations (M351).

Index to Compiled Service Records of Volunteer Union Soldiers Who Served in Organizations From the . . .

. . . State of Arkansas (M383).

. . . State of North Carolina (M391).

. . . State of Oregon (M553).

. . . State of Virginia (M394).

. . . State of Washington (M558).

Confederate States Army Casualties: Lists and Narrative Reports, 1861–64 (M836).

Register of Confederate Soldiers, Sailors, and Citizens Who Died in Federal Prisons and Military Hospitals in the North, 1861–1865 (M918).

Index to Compiled Service Records of Confederate Soldiers Who Served in Organizations From the State of Mississippi (M232).

Index to Compiled Service Records of Confederate soldiers Who Served in Organizations From the State of Tennessee (M231).

Pardon Petitions and Related papers Submitted in Response to President Andrew Johnson's Amnesty Proclamation of May 29, 1865 ("Amnesty Papers") (M1003).

Proceedings of a Court of Inquiry Concerning the Conduct of Major Marcus A. Reno at the Battle of the Little Big Horn River on June 25 and 26, 1876 (M592).

Reports and Correspondence Relating to the Army Investigations of the Battle of Wounded Knee and to the Sioux Campaign, 1890–91 (M983).

Papers and Minutes of Meetings of Principal WWII Allied Military Conference, 1941–45 (M995).

Pubic Hearings of the Commission on Wartime Relocation and Internment of Civilians (M1293).

PACIFIC SIERRA REGION— SAN BRUNO, CALIFORNIA

1000 Commodore Drive
San Bruno, California 94066
(415) 876-9009

Serves northern California, Hawaii, Nevada (except Clark County), American Samoa, and the Pacific Ocean area.

Record Groups

RG 26—RECORDS OF THE UNITED STATES COAST GUARD (520 cu. ft.)

Logs of lifesaving stations, 1878–1942.

Merchant Marine logbooks, 1942–61.

Merchant Marine logbooks, Port of San Francisco, 1927–57.

Merchant Marine logbooks for the San Francisco District, 1873–1941.

RG 112—RECORDS OF THE OFFICE OF THE SURGEON GENERAL (ARMY) (158 cu. ft.)

Records of the Letterman General Hospital at the Presidio of San Francisco. Includes correspondence, 1898–1908; registers of patients, 1898–1907; medical case files of patients, 1898–1908; registers of deaths and interments of patients, 1898–1910; also contains correspondence pertaining to the 1906 San Francisco earthquake.

RG 147—RECORDS OF THE SELECTIVE SERVICE SYSTEM (WORLD WAR II)

Registration cards for California—for men born between 1887 and 1897 (not indexed); also for Hawaii (indexed).

RG 156—RECORDS OF THE BENICIA ARSENAL

Monthly returns of civilian employees, ca. 1860–70.

Morning reports, 1856–72.

Bimonthly muster rolls, 1860–71.

Enlistment papers, 1873–95.

Payrolls of civilian employees, 1878–99.

Registers of deaths and burials, 1883–1911.

RG 163—RECORDS OF THE SELECTIVE SERVICE SYSTEM (WORLD WAR I) (28 cu. ft.)

Lists of men ordered to report for induction to draft boards in northern California and Nevada, 1917–19.

Index to deserters for Arizona, California, and Hawaii, 1917–18.

RG 181—RECORDS OF NAVAL DISTRICTS AND SHORE ESTABLISHMENTS (5,657 cu. ft.)

Correspondence and administrative records, 1851–1961, for the following establishments: Twelfth Naval District, Mare Island, Mare Island Shipyard; San Francisco Naval Shipyard (Hunter's Point); Fourteenth Naval District, Pearl Harbor, Hawaii, Pearl Harbor Naval Shipyard; and subordinate units such as the naval station at American Samoa.

RG 313—RECORDS OF THE NAVAL OPERATING FORCES (1,360 cu. ft.)

Administrative records pertaining to units and bases operating in formal U.S. territories and Pacific island groups under the direct administration of the United States, 1940–61.

National Archives Microfilm

See page 133 for a list of National Archives microfilm available at all regional archives. Also available at this archives are the following.

Revolutionary War Rolls, 1775–1783 (M246).

Revolutionary War Pension and Bounty-land Warrant Application Files (M804).

Special Index to Numbered Records in the War Department Collection of Revolutionary War Records, 1775–1783 (M847).

Miscellaneous Numbered Records (the manuscript file) in the War Department Collection of Revolutionary War Records, 1775–1790s (M859).

Index to Compiled Service Records of Volunteer Soldiers Who Served From 1784–1811 (M694).

Letters Sent by the Secretary of the Navy to Officers, 1798–1868 (M149).

Register of Enlistments in the United States Army, 1798–1914 (M233).

Index to Compiled Service Records of Volunteer Soldiers Who Served During the War of 1812 (M602).

War of 1812 Military Bounty Land Warrants, 1815–1858 (M848).

Compiled Military Service Records of Michigan and Illinois Volunteers Who Served During the Winnebago Indian Disturbances of 1827 (M1505).

Index to Compiled Service Records of Volunteer Soldiers Who Served During the Creek War in Organizations From the State of Alabama (M244).

Index to Compiled Service Records of Volunteer Soldiers Who Served During the Florida War in Organizations From the State of Alabama (M245).

Records of the Tenth Military Department, 1846–1851 (M210).

Returns From Regular Army Engineer Battalions, 1846–1917 (M690).

General Index to Pension Files, 1861–1934 (T288).

Alphabetical Card Name Indexes to Compiled Service Records of Volunteer Soldiers Who Served in Union Organizations Not Raised by States or Territories, Excepting the Veterans Reserve Corps and the U.S. Colored Troops (M1290).

Index to Compiled Service Records of Volunteer Union Soldiers Who Served in Organizations From the . . .

. . . State of California (M533).

. . . Territory of Colorado (M534).

. . . Territory of Dakota (M536).

. . . State of Delaware (M537).

. . . State of Florida (M264).

. . . State of Nevada (M548).

Index to Compiled Service Records of Confederate Soldiers Who Served in Organizations From the State of Florida (M255).

Index to Mexican War Pension Files, 1887–1926 (T317).

Index to Indian Wars Pension Files, 1892–1926 (T318).

Returns From Regular Army Coast Artillery Corps Companies, 1901–1916 (M691).

Brief Histories of United States Army Commands (Army Posts) and Descriptions of Their Records (T912).

PACIFIC SOUTHWEST REGION—LAGUNA NIGUEL, CALIFORNIA

P.O. Box 6719
24000 Avila Road
Laguna Niguel, California 92677-6719
(714) 643-4241

Serves Arizona, the southern California counties of Imperial, Inyo, Kern, Los Angeles, Orange, Riverside, San Bernardino, San Diego, San Luis Obispo, Santa Barbara, and Ventura; and Clark County, Nevada

Records

RG 26—RECORDS OF THE UNITED STATES COAST GUARD (202 cu. ft.)

Logs of various Coast Guard cutters and support vessels operating from southern California ports, 1970–82.

Logs for lighthouses, depots, stations, and merchant vessels, 1942–82.

Merchant Marine logbooks:

Port of Los Angeles, California, 1916–42 (indexed by name of vessel).

Port of Los Angeles, California (includes Wilmington, Long Beach, and San Pedro), 1942–60 (indexed by name of vessel).

Port of San Luis, California, 1941–54 (shipping articles and crew lists only).

Port of Port Hueneme, California, 1945 (shipping articles only).

RG 77–RECORDS OF THE OFFICE OF THE CHIEF OF ENGINEERS (1,297 cu. ft.)

Administrative and technical records pertaining to inland waterways and harbors from various district offices in the southern California area, 1899–1963.

RG 163–RECORDS OF THE SELECTIVE SERVICE SYSTEM (WORLD WAR I) (26 cu. ft.)

Docket books of local draft books. Lists of men ordered to report for induction.

List of delinquents and deserters for Arizona, southern California, and Clark County, Nevada.

RG 181–RECORDS OF NAVAL DISTRICTS AND SHORE ESTABLISHMENTS (1,712 cu. ft.)

Historical and administrative records of the Eleventh Naval District (southern California) and various bases under its command, 1941–56; also records pertaining to the "zoot suit" riots of 1943 in Los Angeles between military personnel and civilian Hispanic youths.

RG 338–RECORDS OF UNITED STATES ARMY COMMANDS (12 cu. ft.)

General orders and administrative records of the United States Army Advisory Group, Arizona, 1955–63.

RG 342–RECORDS OF UNITED STATES AIR FORCE COMMANDS, ACTIVITIES, AND ORGANIZATIONS (less than 1 cu. ft.)

Administrative records of the 6594th Aerospace Test Wing Headquarters, 1961–65.

National Archives Microfilm

See page 133 for a list of National Archives microfilm available at all regional archives. This archives has only that microfilm common to all regional archives.

6

Resources of the History and Research Centers in Washington, D.C.

6

Resources of the History and Research Centers in Washington, D.C.

Each branch of the U.S. armed forces maintains a historical center where material pertaining to its activities is available to researchers. In general, these documents and records tend to be unique to the service and usually are not available on National Archives microfilm. The material in these centers includes detailed accounts of military actions, personnel data, photographs, post-combat interviews or summaries, medical case files, unpublished unit histories, indexes and registers, muster rolls, war diaries, burial lists, etc.

In addition to the armed forces history and research centers in Washington, D.C., three other repositories in that city have significant collections of documents pertaining to military personnel. These are the Department of Veterans Affairs, the Library of Congress, and the headquarters of the National Society Daughters of the American Revolution (DAR). The holdings of each of these repositories are described in the following pages.

U.S. Army Center of Military History

Room 200
Franklin Court Building
1099 Fourteenth Street, NW
Washington, D.C. 20005-3402
(202) 761-5373

The primary mission of the U.S. Army Center of Military History is to gather historical data about units of the U.S. Army and to be responsible for their appropriate use. Unclassified material on file at this center is available to U.S. citizens and to foreign citizens who have special permission arranged through embassies located in Washington, D.C.

The center does not have official documents or lists of personnel other than those that might be reproduced in publications, but it does possess several special collections pertaining to army units, campaigns, and battles. It also has substantial holdings of reports published by state adjutants general in which the names of military personnel may be found. Finding aids and indexes are available to researchers who visit the center. The indexes are based on author, title, and origin of the office where the data was collected. One index is arranged by name or number of military organization (army, division, brigade, regiment, battalion, company, battery, wing, medical unit, or other special unit).

The center's Organizational History Branch maintains historical data on the organization, lineage, and honors of army units. The Historical Resources Branch maintains archival and library collections. These consist of unit histories, published and unpublished; personal narratives; diaries; transcripts of interviews and debriefing sessions (usually of commanding officers); miscellaneous written articles; and correspondence and reports. Also available are several biographical works pertaining to general officers and after-action interviews of participants in the Korean and Vietnam wars. Access to unclassified folders containing the above types of information is permitted. Published material is cataloged according to the Library of Congress system.

Office of Air Force History

Building 5681
170 Luke Avenue
Bolling Air Force Base
Washington, D.C. 20332-5113
(202) 767-4548

The records of this facility are almost entirely on microfilm, so extensive research is impossible without access to a microfilm reader. Since the number of microfilm reader-printers is limited, it is advisable to reserve one for a specific time. (This may also speed the process of obtaining a pass at the base entrance.)

Finding Aids

This center has not compiled its own finding aids or collections; it uses those prepared at the Air Force Historical Research Agency, Maxwell Air Force Base, Montgomery, Alabama, which in turn has furnished microfilm copies of its collections to this center as well as to the National Archives. The principal finding aids are noted below.

A *Guide to the Resources of the USAF Historical Research Center.* Montgomery, Ala.: Maxwell Air Force Base, 1983.

This guide indexes material by subject, name or number of military unit, or the military decimal classification system. Under the latter system, material is grouped by number in increments of one hundred; for example, the 100s refer to headquarters documents, the 500s refer to the European Theater, the 600s refer to the Mediterranean area, and so forth.

An alphabetical system is used to locate the names of organizations such as squadrons, groups, wings (named), wings (numbered), and other divisions or special units. Subjects include: Sixth Air Force, Chemical Warfare Section, Graves Registration Reports, Engineering Personnel, Medical Services, Narrative Mission Reports, Negro Troops, Paratroops, Provost Marshal, Strike Photos, and Submarines. The classification systems are described in the Document Classification Guide (available at this office).

USAF Oral History Catalog. Montgomery, Ala.: Maxwell Air Force Base, 1982. This catalog lists interviews (transcribed and on tape) conducted after World War II and made available at this center in January 1982. Most of the interviewees were high-ranking army and marine officers. The interviews are listed in this catalog in two modes: a) by name of the interviewee and b) by subject. The catalog provides the name of the interviewee, date and place of interview, the period and subject (including specific topics), and number of pages or minutes of tape. Also available are copies of Columbia University's "Flying Tigers" interviews and two volumes pertaining to the Korean War.

Catalog of the USAF Oral History Collection (1989). This catalog is similar to the one of 1982, but it is easier to use because it is arranged alphabetically by name of interviewee and lists the topics discussed. These include air room interviews, air intelligence contact units, escape and evasion interviews, World War II, the Korean War, and Southeast Asia. Although few of these have been published and bound, the majority have been transcribed and microfilmed.

Using the Resources

To locate the relevant microfilm material concerning a particular individual, it is necessary to know the time period and the unit in which he or she served. Staff members can provide limited instruction in the use of the catalogs and guides, but they cannot conduct research for patrons.

In addition to the microfilm collection, this office has a small library with published works pertaining to units of the U.S. Air Force and the U.S. Army Air Corps (through World War II), as well as to other branches of the armed forces. There are no lists of personnel except for microfilm copies of the *Official Army Register* for 1908–1948 and the

Official U.S. Air Force Register for 1949–1975. More complete holdings of these and similar official registers may be consulted at other repositories, particularly the National Guard library (see page 158).

Naval Historical Center

Building 57
Washington Navy Yard
Ninth and M Streets, SE
Washington, D.C. 20374-0571
(202) 433-2210

Finding Aids

Operational Archives, Naval History Division. World War II Histories and Historical Reports in the United States Naval History Division. 3rd printing. Washington, D.C.: Naval History Division, 1977. This annotated checklist of the division's holdings pertains primarily to the navy's participation in World War II; a few of the reports pertain to periods before and after the war. Most of the holdings have been transferred to National Archives II, and comprise RG 38 Records of the Office of the Chief of Naval Operations.

U.S. Naval History Division. U.S. Naval History Sources in the United States. Washington, D.C.: Department of the Navy, 1979. This is a guide to manuscript, archival, and other special collections concerning naval history deposited in more than 250 archives and libraries (including the Naval History Division). Titles of the collections are arranged by state in which the repositories are located.

Branches of the Naval Historical Center

In addition to the navy museum and the extensive library (located on the ground floor, where staff members are on duty to assist patrons), there are four branches of this division where a researcher may locate material pertaining to a specific navy unit or vessel.

Operational Archives Branch

From the beginning of World War II, reports, plans, and war diaries of naval combat commands throughout the world were forwarded to Washington, D.C.; they comprise the core of the documents at the Operational Archives Branch. The collection has been expanded to include materials relative to the wars in Korea and Vietnam, other post-war operations, data from foreign navies, and papers of some officers and other officials with ties to the navy.

SHIP'S RECORDS

War diaries and other actions reports formerly at this Center have been transferred to National Archives II.

MANUSCRIPTS

The Operational Archives Branch has extensive manuscript collections, principally the private papers of high-ranking naval officers, which are found in the *List of Unclassified/Declassified Records Collections*. It also has naval officer biography files (1775 to 1918; 1941 to present); ship historical files (1775 to 1945); places, yards, bases (1775 to 1945); and wars, operations, expeditions (1775 to 1945).

SUBMARINE RECORDS

Records of submarine operation formerly at this Center have been transferred to National Archives II.

MEDICAL RECORDS

A large collection of documents from the navy's Bureau of Medicine and Surgery for the period 1824 through 1970 was transferred to the National Archives in 1991; these supplement the collections in RG 52. Certain historical publications and medical records are also available at the bureau's archives, which are located at the old Naval

Observatory in Washington, D.C. This facility is open only by special appointment. Write to: 2300 E Street NW, Washington, D.C. 20372-5120; or telephone (202) 653-1297. (In 1982 this bureau became the Naval Medical Command; in 1989 it reverted to its former name: the U.S. Navy Bureau of Medicine and Surgery.)

Ships Histories Branch

The Ships Histories Branch compiles and maintains files on every U.S. Navy vessel existing from the establishment of the navy to the present. It collects the annual command histories from active ships and writes histories of ships for publication. It also performs staff duties in connection with the naming of new ships by the secretary of the navy.

Histories of U.S. Navy vessels are contained in the nine-volume *Dictionary of American Naval Fighting Ships* (Office of the Chief of Naval Operations, Navy Department. Washington, D.C.: Government Printing Office, 1959–91).

This branch also holds deck logs of navy ships from mid- to late 1945 to the present. Most of these logs are unclassified and are available for research. For access, write to the Naval Historical Center at the address given above. (Logs for earlier periods are held by the Military Reference Branch of the National Archives—see chapter 4.)

Many ships' crews create and publish "cruise books." Replete with photographs, they are produced as mementos for crew members. These are not official government publications, and the navy does not keep them. Some may be found in bookshops that specialize in nautical or military publications. The New York Public Library, Fifth Avenue and Forty-second Street, New York, New York 10018, has a large collection of them.

Photographic Section, Curator Branch

This branch holds collections of more than 250,000 photographs, including photographs of artifacts and art works. These collections represent the best sources of U.S. Navy photographs for the years before 1920, and they supplement the collections of other agencies covering the years since 1920. The collections also contain some photographs of foreign ships and other maritime subjects not related to the U.S. Navy. Research can be done in person in building 57 at the Washington Navy Yard. Staff members can assist in the use of the index to the photograph collections.

Researchers who wish to obtain photographs of specific ships, weapons, persons, facilities, events, or other subjects may write or call the branch for advice and for instructions on obtaining copies.

Other large official collections of navy photographs exist at the prints and photographs reading room of the Library of Congress and at the following agencies:

Still Pictures Branch, National Archives II, College Park, Maryland (especially for the 1920 through 1981 period). (See chapter 5.)

Still Media Records Center, Department of Defense (especially for the years 1981 to the present). Call (202) 433-2166 for an appointment.

Early History Branch

Presently, the Early History Branch is concerned mainly with U.S. naval history from the American Revolution through the War of 1812 in preparation for a pending publication. It also has historical material pertaining to the Barbary Wars, the Quasi-War With France, and other conflicts through World War I. The branch is insufficiently staffed to provide research or assistance except in a very limited way, but it may be helpful if other sources have not been productive. A chronological card file of military events is available. To inquire or to make an appointment for research, write to the Branch Head, Early History Branch, Naval Historical Center, Washington Navy Yard, at the above address; or telephone (202) 433-2364 or 433-3459.

Naval Historical Foundation

This foundation's collection of private papers comprises the country's largest single group of manuscripts pertaining to U.S. naval history. Most of the manuscripts are on deposit in the Manuscript Division, Library of Congress, but some are still available at the foundation. *Naval Historical Foundation Manuscript Collections: A Catalog* (Washington, D.C.: Library of Congress, 1974) lists each collection, the period covered, and the number of items (or the number of linear feet).

Those papers still at the foundation are arranged by name of navy officer or seaman or by name of vessel. Some of these collections include logs and journals.

Locating Former Naval (and other) Personnel

The Military Reunion Database Registry Service, Marie Rutledge, director, may be able to furnish a contact person who can help in arranging reunions for units of all branches of service. This data base includes names of units that have registered their reunions and provides names and addresses of persons to contact. Inquiries may be made in writing to the Military Reunion Database Registry Service, 3686 King Street, Alexandria, Virginia 23023-3023; or by telephone: (703) 998-7035.

The Veterans Electronic Telecommunications Service (VETS), based in Columbia, Missouri, is a computerized clearinghouse for veteran reunions. It currently has files for more than 11,000 veterans' groups, and it furnishes listings to the American Legion and Veterans of Foreign Wars and to individuals. Information is available by telephone for a fee; call (900) 737-8387 between noon and 8:00 p.m. central standard time.

Advertisements in various military journals and magazines may also be useful. In addition, the Naval History Institute has a data base of navy units that conduct reunions and makes it available to anyone who is interested.

Individuals attempting to locate persons who served in the navy (for reunions, for example) may be able to obtain assistance from the Naval Personnel Command (formerly the Naval Bureau of Personnel), although results are not assured. Researchers should enclose their personal letter to the person sought in a self-addressed, stamped envelope and mail it in a sealed envelope to the Assistant for Liaison and Correspondence, Naval Military Personnel Command, Washington, D.C. 20370; telephone: (202) 694-2801. A separate cover letter should provide as much information as possible concerning the individual in question. If an address is found (even though it may not be current), the command will forward the personal letter.

Some published registers list the names of former navy servicemen and -women, along with cities of enlistment and discharge; occasionally a last known address is given. Although the individual may have moved, he or she may still reside in the same city. A search of current telephone or city directories can be helpful in finding the individual or a member of the family.

The navy's Office of Public Information has a card file of navy personnel who were casualties of World War II. To confirm whether an individual is on the list, write to the Office of Public Information, Casualty Assistance Branch, Department of the Navy, Washington, D.C. 20320; telephone: (800) 368-3202 or (703) 614-2926. The National Personnel Records Center, St. Louis, Missouri (chapter 5), also has a microfilm copy of this index. The information is also available in *Combat Connected Naval Casualties, World War II, By State, United States Navy, Marine, Coast*

Guard (2 vols. Department of the Navy. Washington, D.C.). The Department of Veterans Affairs can provide information about deceased veterans.

The *Social Security Death Index* lists everyone with a social security number (including those who may have qualified for death benefits only) who has died since 1962. This index is available on compact disk (CD-ROM) at the family history centers of The Church of Jesus Christ of Latter-day Saints and in the United States Local History and Genealogy reading room, Library of Congress, Washington, D.C.

Another useful aid is *PhoneDisc, U.S.A.*, a compact disk (CD-ROM) list by Digital Directory Assistance, Inc. It purports to list the names, addresses, and some telephone numbers (unlisted numbers are omitted) of adults in the United States who have registered at one or more selected state or local agencies or are listed in a telephone directory. These disks are available in the Machine Readable Reading Room, Library of Congress, and at some other large libraries throughout the nation.

Marine Corps Historical Center

Building 58
Washington Navy Yard
Ninth and M Streets, SE
Washington, D.C. 20374-0580
(202) 433-3439

Finding Aids

Guide to the Marine Corps Historical Center. The center, n.d.

Marine Corps Personal Papers Collection Catalog. Headquarters, U.S. Marine Corps. Washington, D.C.: 1980.

Marine Corps Oral History Collection Catalog. Headquarters, U.S. Marine Corps. Washington, D.C.: 1989.

In addition to a library and a museum, the Marine Corps Historical Center has an archive and reference section where researchers may consult material pertaining to the Marine Corps since its inception in 1798. In contrast to the historical centers of other branches of the armed forces, which have a number of facilities, each specializing in particular time periods or types of records, this center collects documents and publications concerning the entire history of the Marine Corps.

Archives Section

The center's archives is a repository for five thousand cubic feet of historical material consisting mainly of reports of combat operations, plans, command diaries, chronologies, after-action reports, and related records dating generally from the World War II era to the present. Records for the period prior to 1940 are available at the National Archives, but records for 1940 through approximately 1960 are located at the National Records Center, Suitland, Maryland, and are accessible only with a letter of authorization from the Marine Corps Historical Center.

Index of Books 1–6A, an index of the holdings of records for the period ca. 1940 through 1960, is available at this center. Subject headings include: aviation, 1936–70; exercises and operations; ground units; histories; inspection reports; monograph studies (by geographical area); prisoners of war (World War II); and post and station newspapers.

Under the general heading "records" are found: World War I casualties; citations and decorations; diaries; muster rolls; journals; Vietnam histories; and woman's reserve. Under the general heading "World War II" are found: casualties and campaigns; monographs; citations and decorations; and prisoners of war.

Reference Section

Material in the reference room is divided into several files, many of which include lists of marines' names. These files are stored in cabinets and are generally arranged alphabetically by subject. Below is a brief description of these files.

Geographical File

Folders in this file are arranged alphabetically under international geographic names. They generally consist of reports, photographs, newspaper clippings, maps, personal accounts, miscellaneous documents, papers, and publications.

Subject File

This file is arranged alphabetically by subject; for example: aircraft, amphibious, bands, boats, casualties, chronology, female marines, insignia, marksmanship photos, marksmanship general, memorials, oldest marines, schools, ships (by name of ship), uniforms, war (by name of war through Vietnam), weapons, etc.

Of particular interest is a collection of folders under the heading "chronology." One folder is designated for each year beginning with 1797, and each contains correspondence and related papers pertaining to the events of the particular year. Folders labeled "marksmanship photos" include many group photographs of marines (identified) who participated in annual marksmanship tournaments.

Unit File

The unit file occupies fifteen drawers and has a folder for each marine unit. Any pertinent material, including newspaper clippings, is placed in the appropriate folder.

Biographical File

There is one folder for each person for whom there is biographical material, both officers and enlisted men. Included are biographical summaries, newspaper clippings, photographs, and miscellaneous material. The folders are arranged alphabetically by name and encompass sixty-six drawers in fourteen cabinets.

Muster Rolls (microfilm)

This collection consists of microfilmed copies of muster rolls for marine units beginning with 1798. In some instances the film is designated "bound diaries" (covering 1949 through 1958) and "unit diaries" (covering 1959 through 1966). An index for each year is on a separate reel.

Casualties (microfilm)

The names of marines who became casualties during the Korean and Vietnam wars are on microfilm. This microfilm is not available to the public because some data may still be restricted under the federal Privacy Act. Staff members will examine any requested record and provide information from it (unless the information is restricted).

Registers of Personnel

Beginning with the year 1800 and continuing to the present, these are official registers that list marine officers by name, arranged in order of rank. Navy registers for some years are intermingled on the shelves among the marine registers. Early registers are contained in boxes near the bound volumes. Those for more recent years are titled *USMC Lineal List*. Each volume is indexed. Listed in addition to the names are months in grade, social security number (last four digits only to comply with the federal Privacy Act), date of rank, and date of birth.

Coast Guard Historian's Office

2100 Second Street (at V Street), SW
Washington, D.C. 20593
(near Fort McNair)
(202) 267-0948

Most records created by the Coast Guard and by its predecessors, the Light-House Service, the Revenue-Cutter Service, and the Life-Saving Service, are at the National Archives or its regional archives (chapter 5). The Coast Guard Historian's Office, however, has some records that may be helpful to the military researcher.

Finding Aid

Special List 44 (Logbooks, U.S. Navy). This is a National Archives publication that lists official logs of navy and Coast Guard vessels and shore installations. These may, in some instances, mention the names of individuals.

The National Archives has many muster rolls for crews and personnel of Coast Guard vessels and installations during the World War II period (RG 26). At present, most of these are available either at the National Archives or one of its regional archives. A partial list of vessels and stations for which muster rolls exist is available at the Coast Guard Historian's Office. Inquiries may be made by telephone or in person.

Records

Public Affairs File of Senior Coast Guard Officers.

Some years ago, a special collection of information about Coast Guard officers was prepared. Since the information was made public at the time, it is available for examination by researchers. In general, it encompasses most officers and a few "noted" enlisted men who served after World War II.

Officers' Assignment Cards

Officers' assignment cards are records of military service for Coast Guard officers; they include promotion and transfer information. Since these cards include home addresses they are not available to the public, but staff members can provide certain other data to researchers.

Indexes of Personnel

Persons seeking to learn the addresses of retired Coast Guard personnel (officer or enlisted) may write to the individuals. Researchers should enclose their personal letter to the person sought in a self-addressed, stamped envelope and mail it in a sealed envelope to the Coast Guard Retired Affairs Office, G-PS-5, 2100 Second Street (at V Street) SW, Washington, D.C. 20593. A separate cover letter should provide as much information as possible concerning the individual in question. The letter will be forwarded to the individual's address of record at the time he or she retired from service. Note that those who left the service other than by retirement are not included in this index.

There is a supplemental card file of Coast Guard personnel (officer and enlisted). It lists individuals who served from 1915 to 1989. Records created since 1989 are available only in the form of computer-generated lists. Eventually, all of the personnel index cards will be in the data base. These records are not available to the public because they may include home addresses, telephone numbers, social security numbers, and other personal data (place and date of birth, withholdings, allotments, etc.), all of which information is restricted by the federal Privacy Act. Certain information on the cards, however, can be provided to researchers, including name, rank or rate, date of rank or rate, base salary, duty status and duty stations, military and civilian education level, information about the units in which the person served, and promotions received. Telephone the historian's office at (202) 267-1340 to obtain this information.

Photograph Collection

The Coast Guard has an impressive collection of photographs—numbering approximately 1.5 million—

primarily of vessels, shore stations, and other installations and a few of individuals. Copies are available for a fee.

Published Lists of Officers

The historian's office has a collection of the annual *Register of Officers (Coast Guard)*, some dating to 1833, although volumes for several years prior to 1915 are missing. In addition to commissioned officers, the most recent volumes include warrant officers and cadets enrolled at the U.S. Coast Guard Academy.

Also useful is the *Historical Register, U.S. Revenue-Cutter Service Officers, 1790–1914* (1990), compiled by Dennis L. Noble from the original, often handwritten, records of officers and cadets. The names of officers are arranged alphabetically followed by promotions, with dates of rank and discharge, dates of resignation, and death dates where known. Published by the Coast Guard Historian's Office, the Register has been distributed to major libraries in the United States.

Library, National Guard Association of the United States

One Massachusetts Avenue, NW
Washington, D. C. 20001
(202) 789-0031

The National Guard library, in conjunction with the Museum of the National Guard, is part of the Historical Society of the Militia and National Guard. Researchers seeking specific and detailed information about National Guard personnel should contact the headquarters of state units, the offices of state adjutants general, or state archives. This library, however, has considerable material pertaining to state organizations as well as material pertaining to other branches of the armed forces. Some material found in this library may not be available among the records of individual state units.

The library is placing its holdings in an electronic data base that eventually will replace the current card catalogs. At the same time, additional research sources will be made available. Archival material at the library is stored in boxes that are arranged principally by state. The main finding aid is a loose-leaf binder that indicates the location of the material, augmented by personal assistance from staff librarians. Material available includes scrapbooks, biographies, private papers, files of military organizations, and a few original rosters of personnel who served in the Spanish-American War and World War I.

There is a card index of past and present members of the National Guard Association (all of whom served in a National Guard unit). All issues of the *National Guard Magazine*, dating from 1907, are being indexed and will be added to the computer data base. There is also a collection of photographs of key National Guard officers, Air National Guard airplanes, and miscellaneous subjects.

The library has open shelves where a few regimental histories may be found, but the most important publications for those seeking names of particular individuals are those listed below.

State Adjutant General's Reports. These contain lists of the names of state military personnel.

Army Register, 1779–1974.

Air Force Register, 1949–1979.

Air National Guard Register, 1952–1984.

National Guard Register, 1924–1952.

National Guard Register (army), 1952–1990.

American Battle Monuments Commission

Pulaski Building (room 5119-5120)
Twenty Massachusetts Avenue, NW
Washington, D.C. 20314-0300
(202) 475-1329

Finding Aid

The booklet *American Memorials and Overseas Military Cemeteries* (The American Battle Monuments Commission. Washington, D.C.: 1989) lists and describes burial grounds in foreign countries where American veterans of the Mexican War, World War I, and World War II are buried; and the Tablets of the Missing, Honolulu Memorial, where those listed as missing in action, lost, or buried at sea during the Korean and Vietnam wars are commemorated individually by name. Maps indicate the locations of the burial grounds.

Services Performed by the Commission

The American Battle Monuments Commission was established by Congress in March 1923 as an independent agency of the executive branch of the U.S. government. It has jurisdiction over the overseas burial grounds of American military personnel. Among them are twenty-four permanent burial grounds, fifteen monuments, and two commemorative tablets. Personnel employed by the commission maintain the cemeteries and monuments under the direction of local cemetery superintendents. Marble headstones mark each grave.

The overseas burial of American veterans was done in accordance with the decisions of their next of kin. Decisions for interment in foreign cemeteries were final, and the remains may not now be moved to the United States.

Upon request, relatives of veterans buried in overseas cemeteries may receive the following information or services: time of death, military unit, and place of interment; general information about the cemetery or memorial; letters authorizing passport offices to issue "non-fee" passports to members of the immediate family who travel overseas primarily to visit the grave site; photographs of headstones or section of the tablet of the missing on which the veteran's name is engraved; large color lithographs of the cemetery or memorial where the headstone or tablet of the missing is located; assistance in placing floral arrangements on graves and memorial sites, including a photograph (for which there is a fee).

Locations of Overseas Military Cemeteries and Monuments

World War I

Aisne-Marne (France)

Audenarde Monument (Belgium)

Bellicourt Monument (France)

Brookwood (England)

Chateau-Thierry Monument (France)

Flanders Field (Belgium)

Meuse-Argonne (France)

Montfaucon Monument (France)

Montsec Monument (France)

Naval Monument at Gibraltar

Naval Monument at Brest (France)

Oise-Aisne (France)

Saint-Mihiel (France)

Somme (France)

Sommepy Monument (France)

Suresnes (France)

Tours Monument (France)

World War II

Ardennes (Belgium)

Brittany (France)

Cambridge (England)

Epinal (France)

Florence (Italy)

Henri-Chapelle (Belgium)

Honolulu Memorial (National Memorial Cemetery of the Pacific—Hawaii). The Department of Veterans Affairs can provide names of those buried in this cemetery. In addition to grave sites, this cemetery contains tablets with the names of military personnel listed as missing in the Pacific area in World War II and also those war dead listed as missing in the Korean and Vietnam wars.

Lorraine (France)

Luxembourg City (Luxembourg)

Manila (Philippines)

Netherlands (near Maastricht)

Normandy (France)

North Africa (Tunisia)

Pointe du Hoc Ranger Monument (France)

Rhone (France)

Saipan (Island of Saipan)

Sicily-Rome (Nettuno, Italy)

Utah Beach Monument (France)

Other Wars

Corozal American (Panama)

Mexico City (Mexico)

National Museum of Health and Medicine

Building 54
Armed Forces Institute of Pathology
Walter Reed Army Medical Center
(Georgia Avenue, NW)
Washington, D.C. 20306-6000
(202) 576-2334

The National Museum of Health and Medicine, originally the Army Medical Museum, has been in existence since its establishment during the Civil War. Since that time, physicians have submitted anatomical specimens and case histories of those who fell victim to a variety of diseases and injuries and whose condition would warrant study and research by medical practitioners. This museum retains historical artifacts, anatomical specimens, documentation, descriptions, photographs, and notations by attending physicians. This material helps enhance the institute's mission "to further public and professional understanding of human health and progress against disease."

The museum is part of the Department of Defense. (It is not part of the U.S. Army, although it is currently located at the Walter Reed Army Medical Center.) The medical center's grounds and museum are open to the public without appointment. However, those who wish to study particular documents should write or call the archivist in advance.

Archival Files

The museum's archival files include 17,000 patient files that are available for study. These are not hospital case files; they are reports, letters, etc., submitted by physicians and others, that pertain to patients. The files of a few civilians are included among the files of military personnel since the Civil War. A few World War I and World War II cases are also included. For the most part, the files concern Union soldiers because the physicians were officers of the Union Army and were treating their own soldiers. There are a few files for Confederate soldiers who died in Northern hospitals.

The files are arranged by number rather than chronologically or alphabetically; therefore, it is difficult to locate a file for a particular individual. Until recently, the chief finding aid was the six-volume *Medical and Surgical History*

of the War of the Rebellion (Surgeon General, U.S. Army. Washington, D.C.: Government Printing Office, 1866-88). Three volumes discuss medical cases and three discuss surgical cases. Prepared under the direction of the surgeon general of the U.S. Army, these works describe cases submitted to the museum, each identified by a "specimen number." Once an individual's name is found in one of these volumes, the museum archivist can retrieve the file and make it available for examination or can copy it for a nominal fee. The only names indexed are those of the physicians who contributed the case files. A reprint of these six volumes, titled *The Medical and Surgical History of the Civil War* (Wilmington, N.C.: Tom Broadfoot Publishing, 1991), is now available in twelve volumes, along with a two-volume index with more than 200,000 entries.

Photographs

This museum has approximately 200,000 photographs of museum subjects—patients and body specimens. These were made by various photographers and donated to the museum or made by museum staff photographers to provide pictorial records of significant medical cases. Under the auspices of the Office of the Surgeon General, four hundred photographs from the period 1862 to 1881 were published as a special collection and are available at this museum. An electronic catalog of this collection, which is predominantly of the Civil War period, is available: *Photographs of Surgical Cases and Specimens: Taken at the Army Medical Museum* (8 vols. Washington, D.C.: Surgeon General's Office, 1865–81.) Each volume contains fifty photographs (four by six inches or larger); the history of each is found on a printed slip mounted on the verso (figure 52).

Another catalog is Alfred A. Woodhull's *Catalogue of the Surgical Section of the United States Army Museum* (Washington, D.C.: Government Printing Office, 1866). This catalog describes 4,719 surgical specimens from Civil War casualties and names the physicians. Many of these cases are included in the six-volume *Medical and Surgical History of the War of the Rebellion* cited above.

In addition to official photographs, many citizens donated medical and surgical photographs to the museum between 1862 and 1916; these are cataloged as "Contributed Photographs." They have not been published as a separate collection, but the museum has an electronic data base for identification and retrieval by title (nature of the wound or disease), name of the subject photographed, rank and military unit, battle in which the wound was received, date, name of physician, and name of contributing photographer. The photographs in this archives are eight- by ten-inch black-and-white glossy prints. Copies are available for a fee.

Manuscript Collection

This archives also contains a sizeable collection of personal papers, primarily those of military physicians. These holdings are not yet indexed, but a computer data base is currently being prepared.

Another source for manuscript material relating to military medical and surgical matters is the National Library of Medicine, 9000 Rockville Pike, Bethesda, Maryland 20894; telephone (301) 496-5963. Ask for the finding aid *Manuscript Collections in the National Library of Medicine: A Provisional Guide* (History of Medicine Division, National Library of Medicine, 1988).

Department of Veterans Affairs

(formerly the Veterans Administration)

Monument Services Office
810 Vermont Avenue, NW
 Washington, D.C. 20420
(202) 233-4000

District of Columbia Regional Office
941 North Capitol Street, NE
Washington, D.C. 20421
(202) 273-5400

Guides

Department of Veterans Affairs. *Federal Benefits for Veterans and Dependents.* Washington, D.C.: Government Printing Office,

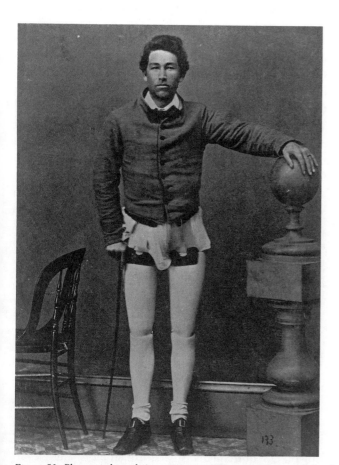

Figure 52. Photograph and Accompanying History of Private Columbus G. Rush (courtesy National Museum of Health and Medicine).

1990. This guide is available for inspection at any Department of Veterans Affairs office, or it may be purchased from the Government Printing Office, Washington, D.C. 20402.

Department of Veterans Affairs. *A Summary of Department of Veterans Affairs Benefits.* Washington, D.C.: Government Printing Office, 1989. This booklet is available free of charge from any Department of Veterans Affairs office.

Regional Offices

Regional Department of Veterans Affairs offices are located in one or more cities of every state. For addresses and telephone numbers consult a telephone directory or the pamphlet *Federal Benefits for Veterans and Dependents* (cited above under Guides).

A file (called a "C" file) is created by this office when a veteran or a member of a veteran's immediate family applies for federal veterans' benefits. Any such file may be examined by authorized persons or by a researcher, provided the records are not protected under the federal Privacy Act. In addition to a review of the file, it is also possible to learn if the department has awarded a cemetery headstone or other marker for a veteran's grave.

Administration of Federal Veterans' Programs

The Department of Veterans Affairs is the result of the most recent of many governmental reorganizations and assignments of responsibility for veterans' affairs dating from the American Revolution. These responsibilities have involved many departments, beginning with the War Department and then the Department of the Interior. A Veterans Bureau was created in 1921 to consolidate the many related governmental offices responsible for veterans' insurance, veterans' vocational rehabilitation and education, and other veterans' programs. An executive order of 20 July 1930 created the Veterans Administration, merging the Veterans Bureau with the Bureau of Pensions, the National Home for Disabled Volunteer Soldiers, and the division of the Office of the Surgeon General that was concerned almost exclusively with artificial limbs and other appliances needed by veterans. On 15 March 1989, the Veterans Administration became the Department of Veterans Affairs, but it will doubtless be commonly referred to for many years hence as the Veterans Administration.

Benefits administered by this department include the following: disability compensation, pension payments, education and training, the G.I. Bill educational assistance program, job training, "the Montgomery G.I. Bill" (for military personnel entering the service after 30 June 1985), vocational rehabilitation, special programs for unemployable veterans, special programs for those who receive pensions, home loans, benefits for the disabled (specially adapted homes, automobiles and other conveyances, clothing allowances, etc.), insurance programs, death benefits, burial in national cemeteries, headstones or grave markers (or optional money allowances), burial flags, compensation to dependents, issuance of medals, commissary and exchange privileges, review of discharges (for copies or for corrections as needed), death gratuities to spouses and dependents, and health care—including hospitalization, nursing home care, domiciliary care, outpatient medical treatment, beneficiary travel, outpatient dental treatment, Agent Orange and nuclear radiation exposure treatment, alcohol and drug dependence treatment, prosthetic appliances, aids and services for the blind, and readjustment counseling services. Eligibility requirements for the above benefits programs are explained in *A Summary of Department of Veterans Affairs Benefits* (cited above).

A veteran, surviving widow, or other close family member may examine a veteran's file at any Department of Veterans Affairs office after submitting a written request and receiving the appropriate response. If the file is not located at the office where the request was made, it will be located and transferred to the most convenient office. The letter of request must include sufficient identifying information: the veteran's full name, branch of service, service number (if known), and social security number. In many instances a member of the office staff will then provide written answers to specific questions, obviating the need for a personal visit to examine the file. Federal Privacy Act laws apply only if the veteran is still living. Next of kin or family members of deceased veterans must be able to prove their relationships.

Burials

Burial in a national cemetery administered by the Department of Veterans Affairs is reserved for any eligible veteran, spouse, unremarried widow or widower, minor children, and, under certain conditions, unmarried adult children. Eligibility requirements can be explained at any Department of Veterans Affairs office and are also described in *Interments in National Cemeteries*, a booklet also available at any of the department's offices. Application for interment in a national cemetery should be made at the time of death by contacting the director of the particular national cemetery. (Often, this is done by the funeral director.) Additionally, the graves of individuals interred in national cemeteries can be located upon request.

Some national cemeteries possess U.S. Army Quartermaster Corps forms that were once used to authorize burials. For instance, a cache of these forms was found recently in a box at the Beaufort, South Carolina, National Cemetery (formerly Hilton Head Military Cemetery). It contained 661 forms pertaining to Union soldiers, a fraction of the 9,003 or more Union soldiers who are presumed to be interred there.

For information concerning any of the approximately 2 million veterans interred in the 113 national cemeteries, contact the Director of Public Affairs, National Cemetery System, Department of Veterans Affairs, 810 Vermont Avenue NW, Washington, D.C. 20451.

Interments and burial records for Arlington National Cemetery are managed by the Superintendent, Arlington National Cemetery, Arlington, Virginia 22211; telephone: (202) 695-3253 or 695-3250. This cemetery is operated by the U.S. Army—not by the Department of Veterans Affairs.

Current rules for this cemetery limit burial to members of the Armed Forces who die on active duty, military retirees, recipients of the Medal of Honor and other top awards, former prisoners of war, the president, and former presidents. Spouses and immediate family members may also be buried together with an eligible veteran.

Members of Congress, the vice president, Supreme Court justices, Cabinet secretaries, and ranking diplomats may no longer be buried in this cemetery solely because they had previously served in the military.

Collateral death benefits to dependents, or optional monetary allowances in lieu of a burial plot in a cemetery, are awarded under certain conditions, as explained in the booklet cited above. Headstones for graves in state-owned veterans' cemeteries or private cemeteries will be provided without charge and will be shipped at government expense to the responsible party. Applications must be made on Department of Veterans Affairs form 40-1330, which is available at any department office. The cost of placing the headstone in these cemeteries must be borne by the applicant. Headstones are also available for the graves of veterans' family members who have been interred in a national cemetery or in a state-owned veterans' cemetery. Although the Department of Veterans Affairs usually cannot provide the locations of veterans' graves other than those in a national cemetery, it will provide information relative to any applications submitted to obtain a headstone or marker.

State-owned veterans' cemeteries often permit spouses of veterans to be buried in the same cemetery. A marker may be placed at the expense of the deceased spouse's family. Unfortunately, many veterans' widows are barred from interment in a state cemetery because of a form of gender discrimination. For example, the state of Maryland prohibits burial of a veteran's widow if she remarried after the veteran's death—regardless of the length of her marriage to the veteran and regardless of whether she subsequently became a widow once more or was divorced. This policy can make it difficult to obtain information about a veteran's spouse who chose to remarry.

Locations of National Cemeteries

The director of a national cemetery can determine whether or not a veteran has been interred in a national cemetery and can provide the location of the grave. National cemeteries are located in the cities listed below. Their addresses may be obtained from local telephone directories or from the booklet Interments in National Cemeteries.

Alabama	Mobile, Phoenix City
Alaska	Fort Richardson, Sitka
Arizona	Phoenix, Prescott
Arkansas	Fayetteville, Fort Smith, Little Rock
California	San Diego, San Bruno, Los Angeles, Riverside, San Francisco
Colorado	Denver, Fort Lyon
Florida	Pensacola, Bay Pines, Bushnell, St. Augustine
Georgia	Marietta
Hawaii	Honolulu
Illinois	Alton, Springfield, Danville, Mound City, Quincy, Rock Island
Indiana	Indianapolis, Marion, New Albany
Iowa	Keokuk
Kansas	Fort Leavenworth, Leavenworth, Fort Scott
Kentucky	Nicholasville, Louisville (Cave Hill Cemetery; Zachary Taylor Cemetery), Danville, Lebanon, Lexington, Mill Springs
Louisiana	Pineville, Baton Rouge, Zachary
Maine	Togus
Maryland	Annapolis, Baltimore (Baltimore Cemetery; Loudon Park Cemetery)
Massachusetts	Bourne
Michigan	Augusta
Minnesota	Minneapolis
Mississippi	Biloxi, Corinth, Natchez
Missouri	St. Louis (Jefferson Barracks), Jefferson City, Springfield
Nebraska	Maxwell
New Jersey	Beverly, Salem
New Mexico	Bayard, Santa Fe

New York	Bath, Calverton, Brooklyn, Farmingdale, Elmira
North Carolina	New Bern, Raleigh, Salisbury, Wilmington
Ohio	Dayton
Oklahoma	Fort Gibson
Oregon	Eagle Point, Roseburg, Portland
Pennsylvania	Annville, Philadelphia
Puerto Rico	Bayamon
South Carolina	Beaufort, Florence
South Dakota	Sturgis, Fort Meade, Hot Springs
Tennessee	Chattanooga, Knoxville, Memphis, Mountain Home, Nashville
Texas	Fort Bliss, San Antonio (Fort Sam Houston Cemetery; San Antonio Cemetery), Houston, Kerrville
Virginia	Alexandria (Arlington National Cemetery), Leesburg, Hopewell, Mechanicsville, Culpepper, Danville, Richmond (Fort Harrison Cemetery; Glendale Cemetery; Richmond Cemetery; Seven Pine Cemetery), Hampton, Quantico, Staunton, Winchester
West Virginia	Grafton, Pruntytown
Wisconsin	Milwaukee

Pension Files

Files of veterans' pensions granted by the federal government are generally available at the National Archives in Washington, D.C. However, when the Department of Veterans Affairs receives a claim or an inquiry from a family member of a deceased veteran or otherwise needs the file for some purpose, the file is temporarily transferred from the National Archives to the department. Such a transfer may not be apparent until a researcher requests the file from the National Archives and the request form is returned with the notation "VA." In these instances the Department of Veterans Affairs office will make the file available. If the file is not in the office where the request was submitted, arrangements will be made to have it mailed to the office most convenient for the requestor.

Other Files

Information about a veteran's hospitalization at a Department of Veterans Affairs hospital or other health care facility is not available at the department's offices but may be available at the hospital or other facility. Information concerning veterans' insurance, home mortgage loan guarantees, educational loans, and other miscellaneous matters is not made available without special authorization from the veteran (unless the veteran is deceased).

Military service files are not kept by the Department of Veterans Affairs. Requests for most of these files (generally, those created during the twentieth century) must be made to the National Personnel Records Center, 9700 Page Boulevard, St. Louis, Missouri 63132 (see chapter 5 for specific branches of the service and applicable dates).

The addresses of living veterans are not furnished by the Department of Veterans Affairs, but a written communication will be forwarded to the veteran's last known address.

Library of Congress

Thomas Jefferson Building, First Street, SE
John Adams Building, Second Street, SE
James Madison Building, Independence Avenue, SE
Washington, D.C. 20540

Main Reading Room and Local History and Genealogy Reading Room: (202) 707-5537
Manuscript Division Reading Room: (202) 707-5387
Prints and Photographs Reading Room: (202) 707-6394
Microform Reading Room: (202) 707-5471
Geography and Map Division Reading Room: (202) 707-6277

Publications

The nation's most extensive collection of publications pertaining to the United States' involvement in wars and other armed conflicts is found in the Library of Congress. The main card catalog, computer catalog, and bibliographies are available to assist researchers in locating books and periodicals germane to their studies. Requests for specific publications in the closed stacks may be submitted in the Local History And Genealogy Reading Room and in the Main Reading Room. Both reading rooms have a number of books on military affairs in their reference collections (on open shelves). Although the Library of Congress does not have original military documents, many published works concerning U.S. military involvement can be found in the Library of Congress and in other major research libraries.

On-line Access

The Library of Congress Information System (LOCIS) can be searched through Internet, a worldwide computer network. Many of the library's files, such as its card catalog and other information sources, are available through this service. Among these files are some that contain records for materials cataloged and held by the library and by other research institutions and agencies.

Internet can be accessed through a variety of sources. Local libraries and office computer centers can provide information. The Information Services Referral Desk at InterNIC will supply a list of Internet providers; telephone: (800) 444-4345. The Internet address to LOCIS is locis.loc.gov; the numeric address is 140.147.254.3.

Manuscript Division Reading Room

The Manuscript Division has personal papers and records of private and public organizations consisting of more than 50 million items organized into approximately 10,000 collections. Many of these have finding aids or guides; a number have been microfilmed.

After submission of a request slip, the manuscripts are delivered to the researcher's table. Copy machines are located in the reading room. Although bound volumes may not be copied with these machines, arrangements can be made for reproduction by the library's photoduplication service. Staff members in the reading room can provide information about costs and explain procedures.

Finding Aids

Neagles, James C. "Records Showing Military Service and Pioneer History." Chap. 6 in *The Library of Congress: A Guide to Genealogical and Historical Research.* Salt Lake City: Ancestry, 1990.

Nelville, Annette, comp. *Special Collections in the Library of Congress.* Washington, D.C.: Library of Congress, 1980.

Both of these works are available at the reference desk of the Local History and Genealogy Reading Room, the Manuscript Division Reading Room, and the Main Read-

ing Room. They may also be purchased at the Library of Congress gift shop.

Catalogs and Indexes to Collections

Library of Congress. *Manuscript Division–Dictionary Catalog of Collections.* These bound volumes describe the collections of the Manuscript Division. Some refer to inventory folders or guides to collections in the reading room; they also provide location numbers. The following are examples of some inventories or guides pertaining to military matters that are referred to in this catalog.

> Confederate States of America (personnel rolls, oaths, etc.)
>
> Foreign Copying Project—Great Britain (rosters of the American Revolution—Hessians). See below for Hessian records.
>
> Foreign Copying Project—Great Britain (microfilm—series 1: 30 reels; series 2: 141 reels).
>
> Great Britain—Commission on Loyalists (claims for losses).
>
> Great Britain, War Office—Amherst Papers, volume 76, page 138 (contains muster roll of Stockbridge Indians, 14 June 1758).
>
> Horatio Gates' Papers, 1726-1828 (orderly books of the American Revolution) (microfilm reels 18 and 19).
>
> Patton, George J., General, U.S. Army.
>
> New Hampshire Collection of Revolutionary War Materials.
>
> United States Treasury Department, Office of the Third Auditor (accounts and journal, 1775-1812, and pension claimants, 1828-32).
>
> Virginia militia, 1782-1817.

Library of Congress. *Manuscript Division–Reference Index for the Dictionary Catalog of Collections.* These bound indexes describe the division's collections in some detail. Entries are arranged by name of individual, place, and subject. Examples of entries that pertain to military matters: Civil War; Confederate(s);States of America; Indian Wars (listed by state); French and Indian War; Korean War;Mexican Punitive Expeditions; Mexican War; Revolution; Spanish-American War; U.S. Army-Navy-Air Force-Marine Corps; Vietnam War, World War I, and World War II.

Sellers, John R., et al. *Manuscript Sources in the Library of Congress for Research on the American Revolution.* Washington, D.C.: Library of Congress, 1975. Entry numbers in this volume refer to lists of personnel, payments and claims, receipts, and accounts and ledgers for various military units that served in the revolutionary war, such as the following:

> Account books, military and public: pages 55-104.
>
> Orderly books—American (includes data about courts-martial): pages 861-948. See also James C. Neagles'

Summer Soldiers: A Survey and Index of Revolutionary War Courts-martial (Salt Lake City: Ancestry, 1986).
Orderly books–British: pages 949-54.

Sellers, John R. *Civil War Manuscripts*. Washington, D.C.: Library of Congress, 1986. This volume describes 1,064 collections in the Library of Congress—diaries, correspondence, private and public papers, biographies, descriptions of battles, campaigns, etc. Few, if any, of these contain lists of military personnel.

Naval Historical Foundation Manuscript Collections–A Catalog. Washington, D.C.: Library of Congress, 1974. The Naval Historical Foundation was established in 1926 as a non-profit organization to gather documents and related historical material relative to U.S. naval forces for the period from the American Revolution to 1942. Included are diaries, journals, correspondence, recollections, and notebooks. Although most of the collection is on deposit in the Manuscript Division, some is located in the foundation's headquarters at the Washington Navy Yard (see page 154).

Index to the George Washington Papers, Seven Series, 1741-98. Washington, D.C.: Library of Congress, 1964. Both the original documents and a microfilm copy of the documents mentioned in this index are available in the Manuscript Division. Other major libraries may also have them on microfilm. The Virginia State Library at Richmond has photostats of a few of these documents, but they are poorly indexed and very difficult to read.

Series 4 of this collection concerns the French and Indian War and consists of personnel rolls, returns, and other lists. (No such rolls in this collection concern the American Revolution.) Except for comments in the "remarks" column, all data from the personnel rolls in this series were transcribed by Murtie June Clark in her *Colonial Soldiers of the South, 1732-1774* (Baltimore: Genealogical Publishing Co., 1983).

Library of Congress. *National Union Catalog of Manuscript Collections.* Published annually, this multi-volume work is available in many reading rooms at the Library of Congress and in other major libraries. It provides a brief description of manuscript collections in major repositories throughout the United States and Canada.

Hessian Records

Recently transferred from the Microform Reading Room to the Manuscript Division are 364 microfiche that comprise a copy of the Lidgerwood Collection of German records concerning Hessian soldiers in the British army during the American Revolution. The documents have been translated into English. The original collection is at the Morristown (New Jersey) National Historical Park library. (For a full description of the scope and content of this collection, see chapter 7, which describes resources available at National Park Service sites.)

John Paul Jones Papers, 1747-92

This collection, on ten reels of microfilm, includes correspondence, ships' papers, financial accounts, judicial proceedings, and miscellaneous documents at various repositories in the United States, Great Britain, and Europe. For a full description see the guide by James C. Bradford, which is available in this reading room.

Prints and Photographs Reading Room

Among the millions of photographs in the Prints and Photographs Collection, there is a special collection of Civil War portraits. Many are filed in cabinets labeled "Civil War File," for which a card catalog is available. Many units (principally of the Union Army) and many individuals are identified. The main card catalog identifies Civil War photographs available in other collections. Unfortunately, the latter are too fragile to permit copying on the coin-operated machines, but reproductions may be obtained through the library's photoduplication service. The reference staff can provide information about costs.

A selection of the photographs housed in this reading room have been recorded on compact discs that are available in the Machine Readable Reading Room. These are a part of the American Memory Project. Primarily, they are copies of photographs previously placed on microfilm. (The microfilm is also available.) The images in the collection are arranged according to the time periods of the war in three different areas of the United States, each subdivided by specific campaigns. Additional sections feature Washington, D.C., during the war and also portraits.

For assistance in using this collection, ask the staff of the Machine Readable Reading Room for a copy of Joanne B. Freeman's *Selected Civil War Photographs From the Library of Congress, 1861-1865. An American Memory Collection From the Library of Congress. User's Guide* (Washington, D.C.: 1992). A prearranged appointment is advisable.

Supplementing the photographs are publications available in the reference collection of the Prints and Photographs Reading Room that may be searched for Civil War photographs, primarily those from the Mathew B. Brady collections; copies may be made. These include:

Library of Congress. *Best Photos of the Civil War.*

National Gallery of Art. *The Civil War: A Centennial Exhibition of Eyewitness Drawings.*

Warner, Ezra. *Generals in Blue.*

Warner, Ezra. *Generals in Gray.*

Wiley, Bell. *Embattled Confederates.*

1989. This volume provides descriptions of 2,240 maps and charts and 76 atlases and sketchbooks made during the Civil War and later.

Microform Reading Room

Korean War and Vietnam War

Congress has required that all Department of Defense documents relating to American prisoners of war and those missing in action in Southeast Asia be declassified and made available to the public in an accessible format. To comply with that requirement, the Library of Congress made available in 1993 a POW-MIA data base that is now available on microfilm. One of the collections in this data base is titled Correlated and Uncorrelated Information Related to Missing Americans in Southeast Asia.

Approximately twenty percent of the documents are indexed by name. Next of kin of missing military personnel have been entitled to view this information, so they will find little, if any, new information in this collection. However, if a researcher has some indication of a specific location or a specific event surrounding the disappearance of a person, some success is possible by matching known facts (a plane crash at a certain location, imprisonment at a certain location, etc.) with a particular individual.

Eventually, this data base will contain approximately 175,000 documents. This data base is not to be confused with an unindexed 1992 collection of POW-MIA documents that relate primarily to the Korean War and were previously available to the public in the Microform Reading Room.

Geography and Map Reading Room

The Geography and Map Reading Room's collections include maps and atlases relating to military conflicts worldwide, including material for the Korean and Vietnam wars.

Finding Aids

Sellers, John, and Patricia Van Ee. *Maps and Charts of North America and the West Indies, 1750–1789.* Washington, D.C.: Library of Congress, 1981. Describes the library's maps from the American Revolution time period.

Stephenson, Richard W., comp. *Civil War Maps: An Annotated List of Maps and Atlases in Map Collections of the Library of Congress.* 2nd ed. Washington, D.C.: Library of Congress,

Headquarters and Library, National Society Daughters of the American Revolution

1776 D Street, NW
Washington, D.C. 20006-5392
(202) 879-3229

For two weeks in mid-April (inquire for specific dates), the headquarters is open only to National Society Daughters of the American Revolution (DAR) members for the society's annual Continental Congress. A daily user fee is charged to those who are not members of the DAR, the National Society Children of the American Revolution, the General Society Sons of the Revolution, or the National Society Sons of the American Revolution (SAR).

Finding Aids

A pamphlet, DAR Library, and other information sheets describing use of the facilities are available at the information desk or may be requested by mail. Multiple copies may also be requested for groups.

Publications

The society has an open-shelf library of 125,000 published and unpublished volumes of genealogical and local history materials arranged by subject or state. A general card catalog of the library's holdings, a 400-drawer analytical index to many books, and several smaller indexes are available.

A unique part of the collection is the Genealogical Records Committee Reports. These reports, available in their entirety only at the DAR library, number more than 11,000 volumes and contain local records, Bible transcriptions, cemetery records, probate records abstracts, etc. Various printed and card indexes provide access to this information. Among the most well-known and most frequently used of the society's publications are the following:

DAR Library Catalog. 3 vols., 1982, 1986, 1992. The *Catalog* contains 2,433 pages detailing family histories, record abstracts, and state and local histories. The indexes to each volume provide multiple access points for locating publications in the DAR library. The *Catalog* is also useful as a general guide to genealogical publications that might be available in other libraries across the country.

Daughters of American Revolution Patriot Index. Revised edition. 3 vols., 1994. The *Patriot Index* provides an alphabetical list of many military and civilian patriots of the American Revolution from whom members of the society have traced their lineages. Data includes names of spouses, dates of birth and death, military rank, type of service, state from which served, and whether a pension was granted to the veteran or veteran's widow. Vol. 3 of the original edition (1986) is an index to the spouses of established patriots and will not be incorporated into the new edition as a separate index.

Daughters of the American Revolution Lineage Books. These 166 volumes contain the names and "national numbers" of all the women who became members of the society between 1890 and 1921. The national number is assigned to each member's application paper. The *Lineage Books* are indexed by *Index to the Rolls of Honor in the Lineage Books of the National Society of the Daughters of the American Revolution, Volumes 1–160* (4 vols. in 2, 1916–1940. Reprint. Baltimore: Genealogical Publishing Co., 1988). A smaller index provides access to vols. 161–166. The DAR recommends that these volumes be used with the utmost caution, because there have been at least seventy years of corrections and alterations to these early records. For the most recent information on record at the DAR, contact the Office of the Registrar General. For national numbers of members, contact the Office of the Organizing Secretary General.

Applications for Membership

One way to find genealogical data about a patriot of the American Revolution is to study the membership application papers submitted by women who are or were members of the society. Under guidelines established by the society, applications may be examined by certain researchers and members of the Daughters of the American Revolution, Sons of the American Revolution, or Children of the American Revolution, as well as by those who wish to apply for membership. The application is a four-part document on which the applicant must trace her direct lineage to the patriot. The qualifying service of the patriot is stated and sources cited. In addition, spouse(s) (where known) and their dates of birth are given. A direct line of descent to the applicant is also given, with dates and places of birth, marriage, and death. Regulations require that primary sources be used to substantiate claims. In many cases, several members have qualified for membership based on the service of one particular patriot, and those applications may also be studied and compared.

The Office of the Registrar General keeps the records relating to application papers and the appropriate indexes to these. On-site researchers must complete and submit a request slip to obtain national numbers. Once they have the national number, researchers may view the application paper on microfilm in the Seimes Microfilm Center. Copies of applications must be ordered in the Office of the Registrar General. Researchers seeking copies by mail should send their requests to that office.

If there is doubt as to whether an individual is, or has been, a member of the DAR, inquiries may be made in the Office of the Organizing Secretary General. Staff members there will consult microfiche and electronic records and provide the address of a current member or the location of the chapter to which a former deceased member belonged.

Documentation Files

Sources given on membership applications often refer to vital statistics or other official documents or publications that were submitted or cited to support the application. Some references are to courthouse or state records that were copied and added to the application file; others are to family Bible pages, narrative statements by family members, wills and estate papers, and other miscellaneous records.

The surviving files of application documentation are available for the use of researchers in the DAR Library and are arranged by name of the patriot ancestor. Many applications either never had or no longer have additional supporting material on file. For organizational and space reasons there are two separate alphabets of these files, each maintained on a different floor in the library; therefore, researchers should alert the staff to the date of the application paper to insure that the proper section of the files is checked. The library's staff will also check on the availability of a file upon receipt of a mailed request. A limited number of copies may be requested.

The Grandparent Project

Membership applications are indexed only by the name of the member herself and by the name of the revolutionary war ancestor. From 1959 to 1981, the DAR conducted a voluntary project whereby a member could submit a form beginning with one of her grandparents and tracing the lineage back to the Revolutionary ancestor. The purpose was to assist potential new members by providing access to information on two generations preceding the member and, therefore, closer to the revolutionary ancestor. Cousins of members would therefore have a place to start.

The resulting "Grandparent Papers" comprise a set of 875 volumes housed in the Genealogical Records Committee office near the library. Two indexes provide access to these papers: 1) an index of the patriot ancestors, and 2) an incomplete index to the names of the grandparents themselves. Because this project was voluntary, not all members submitted forms for their grandparents' lineages; therefore, a form does not exist for every ancestor listed in the DAR Patriot Index.

Manuscript Collection

The society's library has a growing collection of research notes, personal letters, and other unpublished genealogical material. An ongoing indexing project may be used to locate this material, and staff members in the library reading room can assist in its use.

Graves of American Revolution Veterans

The office of the Historian General maintains an Americana Collection of early American manuscripts and imprints. This office also maintains a catalog of American revolutionary war veterans' graves that have been located and reported by DAR members to the national headquarters since the 1890s. A second catalog of American Revolution veterans' graves marked by the DAR is maintained. Information in these catalogs may be useful as a research lead, but much of it has not been verified and must be independently confirmed.

Archdiocese for the Military Services

924 Wayne Avenue
Silver Spring, Maryland 20910
(301) 495-4100

This office maintains a card file of Catholic priests who have served as military chaplains. The file covers World War II and also includes the names of some priests who served in World War I and the Mexican War. The priest's current address or date of death may be obtained by writing to the above address or by telephoning. Little, if any, other information is available from the Archdiocese for the Military Services.

7

Resources of the History and Research Centers Outside Washington, D.C.

7

Resources of the History and Research Centers Outside Washington, D.C.

In addition to the military history centers located in Washington, D.C., there are similar centers at Carlisle, Pennsylvania (U.S. Army), and at Montgomery, Alabama (U.S. Air Force). Archival records and special collections may also be found at the U.S. Military Academy at West Point, New York, and at the U.S. Naval Academy at Annapolis, Maryland. Records pertaining to the U.S. Coast Guard Academy, the U.S. Merchant Marine Academy, and the U.S. Air Force Academy are less extensive, but some helpful documents are available. A major non-government research facility is the LDS church Family History Library in Salt Lake City, Utah.

United States Army Military History Institute

Carlisle Barracks, Pennsylvania 17013-5008
(Upton Hall)
(717) 245-3611

The Military History Institute collects, preserves, and makes available to researchers, both civilian and military, source material pertaining to American military history. This material can include names of military personnel, but primarily it comprises documents, manuscripts, historical publications, and photographs concerning American military units in wartime and peacetime, emphasizing the role played by the U.S. Army. As such, these materials are valuable to the genealogist who has identified an ancestor who served in a particular military organization.

The nucleus of the institute library's holdings consists of documents provided by the United States Army War College, the National War College, and the United States Army Command and General Staff College. Collectively, these three schools transferred more than 120,000 volumes, the oldest of which dates to the fifteenth century. The institute has also received materials donated by libraries, organizations, and individuals. The facility has three principal branches: reference, manuscripts, and photographs.

This facility is open to researchers without appointment or admission fee. Visitors must register in the foyer, where an identification badge is issued. The staff cannot conduct research for individuals but can advise and provide assistance with bibliographies for those who visit, write, or telephone requesting help. Printed material can be copied for a fee but may not exceed one hundred pages per year.

Finding Aid

A Guide to the United States Army Military History Institute. U.S. Army Military History Institute. Carlisle Barracks, Pa.: n.d. This pamphlet provides a general description of the institute's holdings.

Reference Branch

Published Volumes and Periodicals

Organized according to the Library of Congress classification system, the institute's published material may be located through the computer catalog (by author, title, or key words of a subject) and the reference bibliography files. After finding a particular call number, the researcher may enter the stack areas to retrieve the item. Reshelving is done by staff members. In lieu of the card catalog, complete lists may be found by consulting the computer terminals available for public use in the reading room.

Those who want to learn of available publications according to subject, war, or time period should consult various bibliographies in the Reference Branch. A fairly up-to-date typescript list of bibliographies may be furnished by staff members in the office of the chief of this branch.

Subject headings of bibliographies, which number approximately three thousand, include: airborne, amphibious, armor, artillery, awards, burials, biographies (listed by name), civilians, Civil War, colonial wars, Gettysburg, engineers, forts and installations (listed by name), Indians, Korean War, marines, medical, Mexican War, military police, music, mutinies, National Guard, officers, prisoners of war, Rangers, Red Cross, revolutionary war, Signal Corps, ships (army), Spanish-American War, uniforms, units (listed by type), veterans, Vietnam War, women, World War I, World War II (by theater of operation), and many others. All bibliographies are available in an electronic data base and in printed form.

Two file drawers are devoted to bibliographic material pertaining to specific military units that participated in various wars. The first major classification is the regular army, with units listed by division, brigade, regiment, and battalion. The second major classification is the Civil War, with units listed by state (both Union and Confederate). For each unit there is a list of titles of unit histories or other publications pertaining to that unit. This information can be mailed to researchers or received by them personally .

One file drawer contains bibliographic material pertaining to historical accounts of American wars, arranged as follows: American colonial; revolutionary war (units, Hessians, battles and campaigns, casualties); War of 1812; Mexican War; Civil War (battles, units, naval); Spanish-American War; World War I; World War II (Europe, Mediterranean, Pacific); Korean War; Vietnam War.

Two drawers contain folders that summarize the contents of available biographies of army leaders; they are arranged alphabetically by surname. Another drawer has summaries of available material about army posts, arranged by name of the fort, camp, or station. A particularly helpful publication is *Special Bibliographic Series 4, United States Army Unit Histories. A Military History Institute Bibliography* (2 vols. Revised November 1981). Many unit histories have been received since publication of this guide, and reference is made to the file listings shown above for recent acquisitions. This institute probably has the most complete collection of army unit histories in the United States.

University Publications of America (UPA) and University Microfilms International (UMI) have processed microfilm collections of regimental histories of the Civil War that reproduce all of the regimental histories housed at this institute and will add others later. Included is an extremely wide range of subjects and supporting documents pertaining to the Civil War. All titles published and unpublished before 1915 and based on inclusion in Charles E. Dornbusch's *Military Bibliography of the Civil War* (3 vols. New York: New York Public Library, 1971) will become a part of the filmed material.

Other helpful bibliographies published by the Military History Institute are listed below. Some are now out of print.

The United States Army and Domestic Disturbances (with one supplement).

The United States Army and the Negro (with two supplements).

The Volunteer Army.

The Mexican War.

Pennsylvania Military History.

Colonial America and the War for Independence.

The United States Army and the Indian Wars in the Trans-Mississippi West.

Master List of Periodicals and Newspaper Holdings as of August 1984.

American Combat Divisions (various twentieth-century periods).

Microfilm Collections

The reading room has several finding aids for microfilm collections that are available on a self-serve basis.

The World War I Survey. (See below under Manuscript Branch.)

World War II Combat Interviews (Armed Forces Oral Histories).

The History of the Vietnam War.

United States Armed Forces in Vietnam, 1954–1975.

Senior Officer Debriefing Reports, Vietnam War, 1962–1972.

Korean War Studies and After-action Reports (Armed Forces Oral Histories).

United States Army Senior Officers Oral Histories (Army Forces Oral Histories, 1989).

The Cox Library Catalogue. Compiled by Virginia E. Laughlin and Linda J. Pixley. A large collection of local and county histories, biographies, and city directories; arranged alphabetically by state.

Microfilm Guide and Index to the Library of Congress Collection of German Prisoners of War Camp Papers Published in the United States of North America From 1943 to 1946. Prepared by Karl J.R. Arndt; arranged by American prisoner-of-war camps.

The Sol Feinstone Collection of the American Revolution; Guide to the Microfilm Collection (with a 1975 supplement). A collection of manuscripts, indexed by name of contributor.

Civil War Letters, 1861–1865. A collection available on fourteen microfiche.

NATIONAL ARCHIVES MICROFILM

In addition to the microfilm collections referred to above, the institute has many microfilm collections from the National Archives. These include correspondence among officials of the U.S. government, especially of the War Department. They are designated M22, M65, M66, M220, M221, M491 through M494, M621, and M624. Others are listed below:

General James Wilkinson's Order Book, December 3, 1796–March 8, 1806 (M654).

Returns From United States Military Posts, 1800–1916 (M617).

Col. Gorrell's History of the United States Air Force (M611).

Historical Information Relating to Military Posts and Other Installations, 1700–1900 (M661).

The Negro in the Military Service of the United States, 1639–1881 (T823).

Returns From Regular Army Cavalry Regiments, 1883–1916 (M744).

Documents Relating to the Military and Naval Service of Blacks Awarded the Congressional Medal of Honor from the Civil War to the Spanish-American War (M929).

Returns From Regular Army Artillery Regiments, June 1821–January 1901 (M727).

Compiled Service Records of Volunteer Soldiers Who Served From 1784 to 1811 (M905).

History of the Philippine Insurrection Against the United States, 1899–1903 (M719).

Historical Files of the American Expeditionary Forces; Forces in Siberia, 1918–1920 (M917).

Index to Compiled Service Records of Volunteer Union Soldiers Who Served With the United States Colored Troops (M589).

Index to Compiled Service Records of Volunteer Soldiers Who Served in Organizations From the State of Illinois (M539).

Index to Compiled Service Records of Volunteer Union Soldiers who Served in Organizations From the State of New York (M551).

The American Historical Association and the General Services Administration (T311—selected reels).

Indexes to Records of the War College Division and Related General Staff Offices, 1903–1919 (M912).

Selected Documents Relating to Blacks Nominated for Appointment to the U.S. Military Academy During the 19th Century, 1870–1885 (M1002).

MISCELLANEOUS MICROFILM COLLECTIONS

Frontier Wars Papers, the Draper Manuscripts, volumes 1–24.

Draper's Biographical Sketches, the Draper Manuscripts, volumes 1–3.

Pittsburgh and Northwest Virginia Papers, The Draper Manuscripts.

Discrimination in the Armed Forces, Papers of the NAACP.

Early American Orderly Books, 1748–1817.

Confederate Imprints.

Manuscript Branch

Finding Aids

Special Bibliographic Series Number 6, Manuscript Holdings of the Military History Research Collection. 2 vols. U.S. Army Military History Institute, 1972–75.

Supplementing this publication is a card catalog divided into four major categories: names of individuals; wars and time periods; military units (name or number, with Confederate units filed separately); and subject. An additional guide is a computer data base that describes the manuscript holdings. This catalog, so far, refers to more than 1,200 collections.

Several publications of this institute that describe major manuscript collections should be noted:

American Combat Division; a Bibliography of the 1st Infantry Division, 1917–1939. Special Bibliographic Series 23.

Oral History (interviews with senior officers). 2 vols. Special Bibliographic Series No. 13. 1977. See also microfilm finding aid.

A Bibliography of the Military History Institute's Company Command in Vietnam and Battalion Command in Vietnam–Oral History Collection. Special Bibliographic Series No. 26. Arranged by topic and name of interviewee.

A Suggested Guide to the Curricular Archives of the U.S. Army War College, 1907–1940. Special Bibliographic Series No. 8.

The United States Army and the Indian Wars in the Trans-Mississippi West, 1860–1898. Special Bibliographic Series No. 17.

Manuscript holdings consist primarily of personal letters, personal diaries, and personal memoirs (including transcribed oral histories and veterans' questionnaires). Other material includes the curricular archives of the U.S. Army War College and retained copies of official papers. No special request form is required for retrieval of manuscripts. The staff will offer assistance as needed.

The institute holds 6 million manuscripts grouped into 1,600 boxes, and it receives 500 boxes of new papers annually. Holdings range from King George's War through Operation Desert Storm. The Civil War, the Spanish-American War, both world wars, and the army's high command from 1940 to the present are exceptionally well represented.

Veterans' Survey Projects

In 1970, the Military History Institute conducted a five-year survey of Spanish-American War and Philippine Insurrection veterans and veterans' widows, sending an eleven-page questionnaire to all who could be located. Beginning in 1975, a similar survey was conducted among World War I veterans using a comparable questionnaire. A similar survey is currently being conducted among World War II and Korean War veterans. This questionnaire comprises eighteen pages.

Locating the veterans is expedited by the use of membership lists from veterans' organizations and addresses furnished by the Department of Veterans Affairs. As of 1993, more than 2,800 donations for the Spanish-American War survey and more than 8,000 questionnaires for the World War I survey have been received, and others for more recent wars are arriving by the thousands.

The questionnaires ask recipients to provide detailed information about their military service, both in the United States and abroad, whether or not they were in combat and whether they served with occupation or demobilization units. Many questions concern recollections and opinions about training received and the quality of leadership; relationships with comrades and civilians; and misconduct (theft, drinking, gambling, etc.). Related to overseas duty are questions about the behavior of soldiers in foreign countries and evaluations of allied and enemy soldiers. Finally, veterans are invited to donate to the institute any personal historical material they might have (diaries, photographs, insignia, etc.)

Some of the responses from the World War I survey have been microfilmed and are available in the reading room. Detailed descriptions of the Spanish-American War and World War I veterans' survey material are arranged by military unit or branch of the armed forces in Special Bibliography Number 9, *The U.S. Army and the Spanish-American War Era, 1985–1910* (1974) and Special Bibliography Number 20, *World War I Manuscripts* (1986), both published by the institute.

Some of the 5,500 questionnaires returned by World War I veterans are on thirty-nine reels of microfilm arranged as follows:

Boot camp (by name of camp) (rolls 1–4).

War in France (rolls 4–35).

Troopships, Marine Corps (roll 35).

Marine Corps, field artillery (roll 36).

Medical Corps (roll 37).

Medical Corps; Chaplains Corps (roll 38).

American Red Cross; Salvation Army, YMCA (roll 38).

YMCA; Mexican Border Service; China expedition; American expeditionary forces in north Russia; American expeditionary forces in Siberia (roll 39).

Many of the questionnaires and other papers have not yet been microfilmed and must be examined at the institute.

Photography Branch

The institute's Photography Branch has more than 950,000 photographs of U.S. Army personnel and places associated with the army. Approximately 40,000 of these comprise 168 volumes of Civil War photographs collected by the Massachusetts Commandery of the Military Order of the Loyal Legion of the United States (MOLLUS).

An additional 30,000 photographs of Civil War personnel and scenes were donated by other organizations and by individuals. The remainder of the collection concerns the Indian Wars, the Spanish-American War, and wars of the twentieth century. Also included are several dozen photographs (including two daguerreotypes) from the Mexican War.

The collection is only partially indexed (on cards and on a computer data base), but knowledgeable staff members can usually locate a photograph if supplied with sufficient identifying information, particularly the name of a military unit.

If a requested photograph is located, the curator will mail up to ten photocopied reproductions and enclose a price list for finished reproductions. Staff shortages require that limited numbers of items or individuals can be searched. A list of local professional photographers is available from the institute, and researchers may deal directly with them. Researchers may also use their own photographic equipment at the branch.

The institute accepts donated photographs of any military personnel or military scenes, especially of individuals in uniform who can be identified by unit. Donors may send original photographs (using postage-paid mailing labels provided by the institute); negatives will be made from them and the originals returned. Otherwise, the donor may send a negative directly to the institute, attention of the curator.

Air Force Historical Research Agency

(formerly the U.S. Air Force Research Center)

600 Chennault Circle
Maxwell Air Force Base
Montgomery, Alabama 36112-6424
(205) 953-5834

Finding Aids

A Guide to the Resources of the Air Force Historical Research Agency. Maxwell Air Force Base, Montgomery, Ala., 1983. This publication is an index to names of military organizations represented in the collections at this agency.

Two card catalogs cover most of the facility's holdings: one is arranged by subject, alphabetically listing organizations and names of individuals; the other is arranged by U.S. Air Force organizations and according to the military classification file system. Material may be retrieved by submitting a request slip at the reference desk.

Microfilm readers are available for material on film, but there are no microfilm printers. Original documents may be copied on a coin-operated machine.

IRIS (Inferential Retrieval Index System) is an electronic data base that lists the agency's cataloged holdings by key subject words and also by names, dates, unit designations, or military equipment.

Records

Virtually all of this facility's holdings (primarily unit histories and data concerning specific aircraft) are available for sale on microfilm by roll. Partial rolls are not available. To order microfilm, contact the Archives Branch (AFHRA/ISR). Microfilm copies are also available to researchers at the Center for Air Force History at Bolling Air Force Base, Washington, D.C., and at the National Archives.

Anyone attempting to locate air force personnel, either active duty or retired, may write to the individual by sealing a personal letter in a self-addressed, stamped envelope and enclosing it in an envelope addressed to HQ KAFMPC/MPCDOO3, Randolph Air Force Base, Texas 78150. A cover letter should request the locator to add the current address of the individual and mail your letter.

Examples of records found at this facility include:

Unit Histories

Thousands of such histories, some dating to World War I, are available as published or unpublished works or on microfilm. The researcher must identify the name or number of the unit. If a microfilm copy is desired (some records are on microfilm only), the archivist can supply the roll numbers.

Aircraft Record Cards

Assignments of aircraft that served in the air force (and its predecessors) are by military serial number and are available on microfilm for the period ca. 1926 to 1980. An index of specific serial numbers is available.

Missing Air Crew Reports

During World War II, the U.S. Army Air Force (the predecessor of the U.S. Air Force) required its air groups to report within two days the names of any members of an aircraft crew who failed to return from a combat mission and to provide details of the mission, number of aircraft, and geographic area of loss. Considerable tactical information is contained in these eyewitness accounts, and often there is much personal information about missing crew members, including name and address of next of kin. Although these reports are at National Archives II, College

Park, Maryland, this agency has microfilm indexes to these reports by aircraft serial number, date of loss, and numerically by machine gun serial number (European and Mediterranean theaters of operation only). These indexes include the geographic area of loss, date of loss, organizational group number, Missing Air Crew Report (MACR) number, aircraft type, aircraft serial number, and number of crew members.

Oral History Transcripts

After World War II, the U.S. Air Force began a formal series of oral interviews of key air force officers that continues to this day. Most of these interviews have been transcribed. They cover aviation from early flight to the present. The *Catalog of the United States Air Force Oral History Collection* (Maxwell Air Force Base, Montgomery, Ala.: n.d.) is available at this facility and at the Center for Air Force History at Bolling Air Force Base. The National Archives also has a guide. Transcripts are available in RG 407 (entry 427, boxes 2411–24123).

Personal Papers

These private papers, predominately of air force officers, are listed in *Personal Papers in the United States Air Force Historical Research Agency* (Maxwell Air Force Base, Montgomery, Ala.) These collections and the guide are available at this agency and at the Center for Air Force History at Bolling Air Force Base in Washington, D.C.

Although a great majority of the materials at this agency are unclassified and open to the public, some material is still classified. Other material is closed to the public because it contains information protected by the federal Privacy Act or by air force regulations. Check with the Archives Branch before planning to conduct research that may deal with classified material.

United States Naval Institute

118 Maryland Avenue
Annapolis, Maryland 21402-5035
(located on the campus of the U.S. Naval Academy)
(410) 268-6110

This institute, established in 1873, is a private, non-profit membership organization located on the campus of the U.S. Naval Academy. It is supported by more than 100,000 members worldwide; the Chief of Naval Operations, United States Navy, traditionally serves as the institute's president.

The primary mission of this organization is to advance professional, literary, and scientific knowledge in the maritime services. This is done through its publication of a monthly magazine, *Proceedings*, the now-bimonthly *Naval History*, the annual *Naval Review*, and more than four hundred books (through the Naval Institute Press). Other activities include seminars and an oral history program.

There is a cumulative index for *Proceedings: United States Naval Institute Proceedings*, 1874–1977, as well as individual indexes for each year since 1977. *Naval History*, a quarterly magazine from 1987 until 1993, is now a bimonthly magazine. It showcases all aspects of international naval and maritime heritage with academic analyses, popular historical narrative, and personal reminiscences.

The institute sells its publications to libraries and to individuals from its own bookstore, also located in the Preble Hall museum building. The magazines and books cover a wide range of subjects, including biographies of high-ranking officers, studies of naval campaigns and battles, individuals, vessels, political issues, international affairs, military fiction, and much more.

The institute has one of the largest private collections of naval and maritime photographs in the world—estimated at 450,000. These include U.S. Navy ships and aircraft, as well as images of foreign and other U.S. military branches, and other subjects. This collection is available for in-house examination by researchers without charge, and staff members will assist in locating prints of certain ships or aircraft. Copies, mostly black and white, are available for a fee.

As a free-of-charge service to groups seeking to locate former shipmates or planning reunions, the institute maintains a reunion data base. Those who wish to include a notice of their reunion in the data base may submit a prescribed form available from the institute's headquarters. A list is available to libraries and other institutions for a nominal fee. Questions concerning membership in the institute, free catalogs, or biographical and historical research should be directed to the Membership and Communications Department at the above address.

United States Military Academy Archives

Building 2107
Pershing Center
West Point, New York 10996-2099
(lower level of the visitors' center)
(914) 938-7052

Archival records of the United States Military Academy (USMA) have been designated National Archives RG 404. A National Archives *Preliminary Inventory* of this record group was compiled in 1976 by the chief of the academy. It pertains to activities of that institution, which is a training school for officers of the U.S. Army (including officers of the U.S. Army Air Corps and U.S. Army Air Force up to the end of World War II).

The records created through 1976 are fully described in the *Preliminary Inventory*. Of course, documents have been added to the collection since publication of the inventory.

Finding Aid

Preliminary Inventory of the Records of the United States Military Academy (RG 404). National Archives and Records Service, 1976.

Records

Examples of some groups of documents described in the above finding aid are cited below. (Some of these are also available on microfilm at the National Archives.)

Letters Sent (Office of the Superintendent), 1838-40; 1845-1902 (with an index for 1849-1902).

Cadet Grade Cards (see the Preliminary Inventory for scholastic departments and years covered).

Register of Cadet Delinquencies, 1818-29; 1838-1913.

Registers of Punishments, 1837-1900; 1933-46.

Consolidated Morning Reports, 1838-51; 1871-1946.

Annual Descriptive Lists of Cadet Candidates, 1828; 1838-1909.

Personal and School History Sheets of Cadet Candidates, 1899-1947.

Registers of Cadet Admissions (Cadets Admitted Book), 1800-1953.

List of Cadets Admitted to the United States Military Academy, 1870-1937.

Annual Rolls of Cadets, 1831-37; 1840-1915.

Oaths of Allegiance, 1838-74; 1910-47.

Consolidated Monthly Merit and Conduct Rolls, 1851-1907 (incomplete).

Register of Cadet Absences, 1880-1910.

Register of Cadet Casualties, 1802-1953.

Register of Graduates, 1802-1962.

Register of Enlistments, 1895-1905.

Cadet Portrait Negative Collection, 1955-65; 1962-71.

Post Cemeterial Records, 1816-1908 (interments). See Burials in the Academy Cemetery After 1908 (referred to below) for later burials.

Reports of Examinations of Cadet Candidates, 1901-70.

Official Register of Officers and Cadets, 1818-1966.

Registers of Patients at the Soldiers' Hospital, 1884-1907.

Register of Patients at the Cadet Hospital, 1916-20.

Register of Graduates and Former Cadets, 1946-75.

White Studio Negative Collection, 1925-66. Separate index.

Other records are as follows:

Records of the Office of the Chaplain, USMA. In five volumes: record of baptisms, births, marriages, and burials, 1857-1937; confirmation records, 1906-37; marriages, 1906-37; marriages, June 1953-August 1971; service record book (records of services performed on Sundays, holy days, and other occasions), 1955-65.

Burials in the Academy Cemetery After 1908. Arranged alphabetically by name of the deceased. In most instances, names of dependents are included. Additional information is included in some files.

Members of the USMA Band, 1953-74.

United States Naval Academy Archives

Room 320
Nimitz Library
589 McNair Road
Annapolis, Maryland 21402-5029
(410) 293-6922

Most of the records of the United States Naval Academy are in National Archives RG 405, and the records dating from 1845 to 1929 are described in a *Preliminary Inventory* compiled in 1975. For the convenience of researchers, the records are retained at the academy. The documents pertain to the institution as a training school for officers of the U.S. Navy, some of whom transfer to the Marine Corps upon earning their commissions as ensigns. In addition to records described in the *Preliminary Inventory*, this archives has several other collections, as noted below.

Finding Aid

Records of the United States Naval Academy–Inventory of Record Group 405. National Archives and Records Service, 1975. This is the preliminary inventory referred to above.

Records

Among the collections described in this publication are the following, some of which have been added to as new documents were created.

Reports of Academic and Medical Examination of Candidates for Admission and Related Correspondence, 1846-76; 1848-53.

Registers of Candidates for Admission to the Academy, October 1849-October 1860; September 1861-September 1871; June 1876-September 1930. Not indexed.

Register of Birth Dates of Candidates for Admission, 1864-84.

Register of Marks (grades) Received by Candidates for Appointment at Entrance Examinations, 1874-90.

Register of Candidates Who Failed to Pass the Required Examination for Admission to the Academy, 1857-87.

Register of Names and Addresses of Parents and Guardians of Cadets, 1871-76.

Registers of Delinquencies ("Conduct Roll of Cadets"), 1846-50; 1853-82.

Academic and Conduct Records of Cadets ("Record and Conduct Roll"), 1881-1908.

Monthly Reports of the Academic Record of Cadets, October 1850-November 1860.

Register of Officers on Duty at the Academy, 1897-1907.

Reserve Training Groups, World War I and World War II. Classes for reserve officers were held at the academy to prepare them for duty in these wars. See the *Preliminary Inventory* for documents pertaining to these individuals.

Collections in RG 405 that are not included in the *Preliminary Inventory* are described below.

Alumni Records

The U.S. Naval Academy Alumni Association publishes an annual *Register of Alumni* that lists all midshipmen who have attended the academy since its inception in 1845.

If known, the following data are included: name, graduation number, rank, last known address, date of retirement from active duty, date of death, and next of kin (if deceased). Each class is listed separately, and there is a general index for all years. Additional biographical data may be requested from the office of the U.S. Naval Academy Alumni Association, 247 King George Street, Annapolis, Maryland 21402; telephone: (410) 263-4448. For those who wish to locate former midshipmen, the association will forward a letter of inquiry (sealed in a self-addressed, stamped envelope) to the last known address of the individual.

Alumni Jackets

The alumni jackets are individual folders prepared for most persons who attended the academy. They contain biographical data, details of military career, newspaper clippings, etc.

Personnel Jackets

This collection of microfilmed documents, which dates from 1905 to 1991, is generated in the registrar's office. It contains information relating to each person attending the academy and includes admission records, personal history, and correspondence relating to the individual while attending the academy. Many of the records are restricted under the federal Privacy Act.

Photograph Collections

There are group photographs of some graduating classes, often with those depicted identified; there are also some early photographs of individual midshipmen. The group photographs were used in the academy's yearbook, *The Lucky Bag.* Copies of these photographs are available. There is also a small collection of images of academy buildings and activities of the midshipmen.

Medical Examination Files

Midshipmen receive annual physical examinations; the results for the period 1863 through 1915 were entered on large, individual sheets. These are bound in volumes, each covering four to six years. The data includes date and place of birth, residence, dates of examination, measurements of strength, physical attributes, vision and hearing scores, comments about illnesses or injuries, and, occasionally, notations about hereditary diseases.

Cemetery Records

Burial in the academy's cemetery is limited to the following individuals: a) officers, midshipmen, and enlisted men of the navy or marines who die while on active duty at the academy or at the naval station at Annapolis, or members of the Naval Medical Clinic staff at Annapolis; b) graduates of the academy who served on active duty with the rank of rear admiral, brigadier general, or in other senior positions; c) un-remarried spouses of individuals buried in the cemetery (remarriage automatically terminates eligibility); d) officers, ex-officers, and enlisted men of the navy or marines whose spouses are buried in the cemetery; e) stillborn infants and infants under age seven whose parents are eligible for burial in the cemetery. (These children are buried in a special plot). The academy security office has a list of burials and lot numbers.

United States Naval Academy Special Collections Division

Room 323-325
Nimitz Library
589 McNair Road
Annapolis, Maryland 21402-5029
(410) 293-2220

Finding Aids

U.S. Naval History Division, Department of the Navy. *U.S. Naval History Sources in the United States*. Washington, D.C.: 1979. This publication is a compilation of major naval manuscript collections found in more than 250 archives and libraries throughout the United States. Included are lists of manuscript collections at the Nimitz Library and the Naval Academy Museum.

An Annotated List of the American Naval Historical Manuscripts Collection. This is a partial list of ships' logs, letter books, and journals in the Nimitz Library's Special Collections Division. The manuscripts are organized by personal name and name of vessel and are arranged chronologically.

Collections

The reading room (room 325) contains a card catalog listing books, vertical files, and periodicals held by this department. The catalog is arranged by personal name, title, and subject. The oral history collection issued by the United States Naval Institute (see above) is also listed in this catalog.

The Special Collections Division was established in 1969 to bring together and preserve the rare books, manuscripts, and other valuable material in the academy's library. Although adjacent to the academy archives, this division operates independently from it. Its holdings comprise approximately 28,500 published works, including the original 1845 library of the Naval School at Annapolis (approximately 300 volumes). The division includes periodicals and books emphasizing naval history and sea power, as well as Naval Academy materials such as class albums, yearbooks, student publications, etc. Its collections also include 250 oral histories acquired from the Naval Institute (see above) and the navy Chaplain Corps program.

Manuscripts

Finding aids are available for all processed manuscript collections. These aids include descriptions and inventories of the collections. Subject access is through a card index.

Obituary Files

This division maintains an obituary file for navy and marine officers, with special emphasis on Naval Academy graduates.

Army and Navy Journals

This division has a complete set of the *Army and Navy Journal*, 1863-1950. Some other older publications are especially valuable for genealogical research: *Air Force Journal*, 1959-61; *Army, Navy, Air Force Journal and Register*, 1962-63; *Journal of the Armed Forces*, 1964-67; and *Armed Forces Journal International*, 1968 to date. Supplementing these publications, the Nimitz Library (located in the same building) has the *Army and Navy Register*, 1879-1948, and the *Air Force Register* covering the years prior to 1962. The Naval Academy alumni magazine *Shipmate*, 1938 to date, is also accessible through a card index.

Photograph Collections

A "general pictures" collection consists of photographs of individuals, vessels, and other subjects, most of which are listed in a card file. Many early Naval Academy photographs and pictures of Naval Academy graduates are included in the files.

The Edward J. Steichen Collection is especially noteworthy. It includes approximately 20,000 photographs depicting World War II scenes. It also includes approximately five thousand non-combat photographs by such well-known photographers as Ansel Adams, Edward and Brett Weston, and Margaret Bourke-White.

World War II Battle Reports

This is an incomplete set of action reports covering the period 1942 through 1945.

United States Coast Guard Academy

Fifteen Mohegan Avenue
New London, Connecticut 06320-4195
(203) 444-8501

The United States Coast Guard Academy was established in 1876 as the Revenue-Cutter School of Instruction, and early classes were held aboard the schooner Dobbin and the barque Chase. The Chase was retired in 1907 and replaced by the cutter Itasca. In 1910 the academy moved to Fort Trumbull, an army coastal defense installation at New London, Connecticut. The cutter Hamilton replaced the Itaska in 1914. Construction at the present site at New London was completed in 1932, and the campus now has several impressive buildings, a field house, and a visitors' pavilion. The training ship Eagle was acquired in 1946.

Inquiries concerning graduates of the academy may be addressed to the Executive Director, Office of the Alumni Association, at the above address.

United States Merchant Marine Academy

Kings Point, New York 11024-1699
(516) 773-5000

The library of the United States Merchant Marine Academy at Kings Point has a complete collection of the class yearbook,

titled Midships, which began publication in 1944. These books contain some information about cadets in each class.

Since 1944, all student records have been transferred to the Federal Records Center, New York City, following graduation. Since these records have not been classified as "archival," they are not among the collections of the National Archives regional archives. Researchers who wish to use documents of the Merchant Marine Academy must have written authorization from the academy.

United States Air Force Academy

Near Colorado Springs, Colorado

Mailing address:
U.S. Air Force Academy, Colorado 80840

The United States Air Force Academy was established in 1955, but it did not become operative until 1958. The records of this academy are located at the Federal Records Center, Denver, Colorado. They may be examined only with written authorization from the academy.

National Park Service Battle Sites

Located in twenty-one states and in the District of Columbia, the twenty-eight battle sites of the American Revolution and the Civil War are operated by the U.S. National Park Service, Department of the Interior. Many of the sites have research libraries and bookshops, and each has at least one trained historian to conduct research for the National Park Service and to assist researchers and other visitors. From the historians, it is frequently possible to learn new facts about the military units and personnel that participated in particular battles.

Finding Aid

Directory of Archives and Manuscript Repositories in the United States. Phoenix: National Historical Publications and Records Commission, 1988. This aid describes collections of military records available at some National Park Service battle sites.

Morristown National Historical Park, Morristown, New Jersey

Hours:

Research Library

9:00 A.M.–4:00 P.M., Tuesday-Saturday (By appointment.) No charge.

Museum

9:00 A.M. –5:00 P.M., daily, including weekends.
(No appointment necessary.)

The research library and museum is located in a mansion where the Jacob Ford family formerly resided, and which served as George Washington's winter headquarters during the extremely bitter winter of 1779–80. After Washington moved from this site in June 1780, smaller units of the Continental Army continued to encamp there during the winters of 1780–81 and 1781–82. Previously, Washington and his army had bivouacked at Morristown during 1775, at a time when Washington struggled to rebuild his impoverished and untrained army following its Christmas season victories at Trenton and Princetown late in 1776.

The building, turned over to the National Park Service in 1933, houses a library of more than 45,000 volumes and 125 linear feet of manuscripts. Shortly after 1955, a library wing was added to the structure after the death of Lloyd W. Smith, an avid collector of antiquarian items, predominantly of the Revolutionary War and colonial eras. Smith had willed his extensive collection of some 12,000 printed works and more than 30,000 manuscripts to the Park Service on condition that a library be constructed to house them. The records pertain both to the Continental and British armed forces and include inspection returns, muster lists, and orderly books.

The Park Collection

A collection of more than 1400 manuscripts and thousands of rare books primarily pertains to the Continental Army and the roles played by Washington and several of his generals. It also contains military records and civilian journals, diaries, and account books. Printed works include contemporary Bibles and prayer books, histories, journals and personal narratives, political monographs, and religious tracts. There are 1,300 documents concerning the Continental Army encampments at Morristown during 1777 and the winter of 1779–80. Also available are 1,000 rolls of microfilm of records of the Continental Congress and various Revolutionary War generals. Some of these records were obtained from the National Archives, the Library of Congress, and the Pennsylvania State Archives, as well as other repositories. Included are papers of George Wahington, General Anthony Wayne, and other officers. The complete *Writings of George Washington* and *The George Washington Papers* are also available in the library.

Especially valuable is a collection of orderly books. A helpful guide to this collection is a booklet compiled in 1994 by Alan Stein, Archivist, *Orderly Books of the American Revolution in the Morristown National Historical Park Library.*

The Lidgerwood Hessian Transcripts

The term "Hessian" refers to German soldiers who fought with the British Army during the American Revolution. Among other localities in Germany, these soldiers were from several principalities, including Hesse-Cassel and Hesse-Hanau, thus accounting for the term "Hessians." The German principalities were parties to a treaty with Great Britain, and the soldiers were sent to assist the British in America, with the principalities receiving remuneration for their services from Great Britain. Approximately 30,000 German soldiers, approximately matching the number of British regulars, were sent to America. It is estimated that up to fifty percent of those German soldiers might have remained in America after the war. Others returned home, but some of their descendants doubtless came to America later. Thus, Americans with German ancestry may well benefit from a study of those Hessian troops.

William Van Vleck Lidgerwood, a resident of Morristown, while living in London between 1906 and 1914, amassed a collection of records of German military units that served in the Revolutionary War. His collection includes official reports, journals, orderly books, troop returns, and correspondence. These have now been translated into the English language, microfilmed, and are available at the Morristown National Historical Park library. The collection, on 364 microfiche, is also available in the Manuscript Division, Library of Congress, Washington, D.C. An invaluable reference tool to the use of this collection is *The Guide to Hessian Documents of the American Revolution, 1776-1783* by Leon G. Miles and James L. Kochan (Morristown, N.J.: 1989).

Many other works housed in this facility's collections have also been microfilmed, and a reader and microfilm printer are available for public use. A photocopier is also available. Staff include a librarian, a National Park Service historian, and other library and research staff.

The David Library of the American Revolution

An excellent library and research center in this area that complements the Morristown facility is the David Library of the American Revolution, Washington's Crossing, Pennsylvania, located on the Delaware River, north of Philadelphia. It contains 2,500 manuscripts, mostly on microfilm, collected by Sol Feinstone. In addition, it includes some 10,000 rolls of microfilm (including copies of all the National Archives microfilm relating to the Revolutionary War), and comprises approximately seven million documents from around the world. A guide to the manuscripts collection is available.

This library is open without charge Tuesday through Saturday from 10:00 A.M. to 5:00 P.M. It is closed Sunday, Monday, and holidays. An appointment is suggested to ensure the availability of a microfilm reader.

Civil War Records Project

A three-year project was undertaken in 1991 to create a computerized directory of all those who fought with Union and Confederate forces in the Civil War. When the project is complete, computer terminals at the battle sites will enable visitors to search for particular names. Additional information, if known, will include the soldier's home state, rank, and unit; whether or not he participated in the action at that site; and place of burial if it was in one of the eleven Civil War cemeteries.

As its contribution, the Genealogical Society of Utah intends to enter into electronic data bases the names of approximately 3.5 million soldiers now in the National Park Service data base in exchange for a copy of the data for itself. Pilot programs are currently under way at the Antietam National Battlefield in Sharpsburg, Maryland, and the Shiloh National Military Park on the Tennessee-Mississippi border.

Family History Library, Genealogical Society of Utah

Thirty-five North West Temple Street
Salt Lake City, Utah 84150
(801) 240-2331

Operated by The Church of Jesus Christ of Latter-day Saints (LDS church), the Family History Library welcomes all interested genealogists of any denomination or nationality to make use of its vast genealogical resources, free of charge. Four of the building's five floors are open for public research, and modern, easy-to-use computer terminals simplify access to its huge collections. Staff members are also available for assistance.

Most of the records consist of microfilm and microfiche copies of local, state, and foreign records that have been filmed and processed by representatives of the society. The library also possesses a large amount of National Archives microfilm obtained by purchase. Copies of material (books, microfilm, and microfiche) can be made for the researcher at a nominal price. Also available are more than 650,000 books, none of which circulate or go out on interlibrary loan.

For researchers who cannot visit this facility in Salt Lake City, family history centers are available at LDS meeting houses throughout America and worldwide. Microfilm may be obtained on loan from the Family History Library and viewed on microfilm readers at these centers. There is a nominal fee to cover the cost of postage for shipping the microfilm. The locations of family history centers may be obtained by writing to the Family History Library or by consulting a local telephone directory under Church of Jesus Christ of Latter-day Saints. A helpful pamphlet titled *A Guide to Research: Using an LDS Branch Library* is available from the library.

Finding Aids

Cerny, Johni, and Wendy Elliott, eds. *The Library: A Guide to the LDS Family History Library.* Salt Lake City: Ancestry, 1988. This 763-page volume is a comprehensive guide to the largest genealogical collection in the world. It describes sources in the United States and foreign countries which have been copied by the library and made available to genealogical researchers.

A Guide to Research: Using the LDS Library in Salt Lake City. Published by the library.

National Archives Microfilm

The Family History Library has purchased a large collection of military records microfilm from the National Archives.

Finding Aids

Register of Federal United States Military Records. A Guide to Manuscript Sources Available at the Genealogical Library in Salt Lake City and the National Archives in Washington, D.C. 3 vols. Compiled by Marilyn Duputy, et al. The Church of Jesus Christ of Latter-day Saints. Bowie, Md.: Heritage Books, 1986. This publication lists, by reel number, National Archives microfilm and other state-level microfilm available at the Family History Library.

Family History Library. *Research Outline: U.S. Military Records.* Edited by Ken Nelson. Salt Lake City: the library, 1993. This thirty-nine-page pamphlet states "This outline describes the content, use, and availability of major sets of records created by the federal government . . . This paper discusses only sources that identify personal information about individual soldiers and sailors. It does not emphasize historical sources about military institutions, weapons, battles, or tactics." This finding aid lists the microfilm by title, the National Archives M number (or T number) and the Family History Library computer number.

Microfilm available at the library is listed below by category. Not included here are titles of books containing names of military personnel that have been microfilmed by the Family History Library. See this finding aid for such titles. (Also see chapter 9 of this volume for those and other such publications.)

General

Registers of Enlistments in the U.S. Army, 1798–1914 (M233; FHL 210761).

Old Wars Index to Pension Files, 1815–1926 (T316; FHL 326186).

Registers of Veterans at National Homes for Disabled Volunteer Soldiers, 1866–1937 (FHL 508537).

Soldiers' Home of Louisiana Register Books, 1884–1934 (FHL 673398).

Abstracts of Service Records of Naval Officers ("Records of Officers") 1798–1893 (M330; FHL 432711).

Abstracts of Service Records of Naval Officers ("Records of Officers") and Related Name Index, 1899–1924 (M1328; FHL 467317).

Case Files of Disapproved Pension Applications of Widows and Other Dependents of Civil War and Later Navy Veterans (Navy Widows' Originals), 1861–1910 (M1274; FHL 423822).

Lists of Navy Veterans for Whom There Are Navy Widows and Other Dependents Disapproved Pension Files (Navy Widows' Originals), 1861–1910 (M1391; FHL 423823).

Muster Rolls of the United States Marine Corps, 1798–1892 (T1118; FHL 110864).

Colonial Wars

The following are not National Archives microfilm, but they are included here as helpful sources.

The General Society of Colonial Wars. Index to Ancestors (FHL 528, 690–92; 533, 971–74).

Index to Lineage Papers (FHL 528, 677–89).

Lineage Papers, numbers 1–14, 199 (FHL 119 films).

Supplemental Papers, numbers 1–13, 850 (FHL 54 films).

Revolutionary War

General Index to Compiled Service Records of Revolutionary War Soldiers, Sailors, and Members of Army Staff Departments (M860; FHL 280117).

Compiled Service Records of Soldiers Who Served in the American Army During the Revolutionary War (M881; FHL 432762)

Revolutionary War Rolls (M246; FHL 70811).

Compiled Service Records of American Naval Personnel and Members of the Departments of the Quartermaster General and the Commissary General of Military Stores Who Served During the Revolutionary War (M880; FHL 323504).

Revolutionary War Pension and Bounty Land Warrant Applications Files, 1800–1900 (M804; FHL 178932).

Ledgers of Payments, 1818–1872, to U.S. Pensioners Under Acts of 1818 Through 1858, From Records of the Third Auditor of the Treasury (T718; FHL 210398).

U.S. Revolutionary War Bounty Land Warrants Used in the U.S. Military District of Ohio and Related Papers (Acts of 1788, 1803, 1806) (M829; FHL 68938).

Virginia Half Pay and Other Related Revolutionary War Pension Application Files (M910; FHL 211911).

War of 1812

Index to Compiled Service Records of Volunteer Soldiers Who Served During the War of 1812 (M602; FHL 375084).

Additional state indexes for Louisiana: M229; FHL 278533; North Carolina: M250; FHL 479165; South Carolina: M652; FHL 278993.

Compiled service records for Mississippi (M678; FHL 325956).

Index to War of 1812 Pension Application Files (M313; FHL 113898).

War of 1812 Military Bounty Land Warrants, 1815–1858 (M848; FHL 174912).

Mexican War

Index to Compiled Service Records of Volunteer Soldiers Who Served During the Mexican War (M616; FHL 328750).

Additional service records for Mississippi: M863; FHL 328757; Pennsylvania: M1028; FHL 110857; Tennessee: M638; FHL 279225; Texas: M278; FHL 279718.

Compiled Service Records of Volunteer Soldiers Who Served during the Mexican War in Mormon Organizations (M351; FHL 279699).

Selected Pension Application Files for Members of the Mormon Battalion, Mexican War, 1846–48 (T1196; FHL 110863).

Index to Mexican War Pension Files, 1887–1926 (T317; FHL 345826).

Civil War—Union

There is no national index to Union soldiers, but the National Archives has prepared indexes for each of the Union states and has compiled service records of Union soldiers from the southern and border states. (For a complete list of these films, including National Archives numbers and Family History Library computer numbers, see pages 18–19 of the finding aid *Research Outline: U.S. Military Records*, cited above).

Index to Compiled Service Records of Volunteer Union Soldiers Who Served in the Veterans Reserve Corps (M636; FHL 328746).

Index to Compiled Service Records of Volunteer Union Soldiers Who Served With United States Colored Troops (M589; FHL 34182).

Index to Compiled Service Records of Volunteer Union Soldiers Who Served in Organizations Not Raised by States and Territories (M1290; FHL 467348).

Compiled Service Records of Former Confederate Soldiers Who Served in the First Through Sixth U.S. Volunteer Infantry Regiments, 1864–66 (M1017; FHL 122843).

Index to Rendezvous Reports, Civil War, 1861–65 (T1099; FHL 462166).

General Index to Pension Files, 1861–1934 (T288; FHL 245945).

Veterans Administration Pension Payment Cards, 1907–1933 (M850; FHL 500541).

Organization Index to Pension Files of Veterans Who Served Between 1861 and 1900 (T289; FHL 462116).

Schedules Enumerating Union Veterans and Widows of Union Veterans of the Civil War, 1890 (M123; FHL 59376).

Civil War–Confederate

Compiled service records and indexes to compiled service records have been microfilmed by the National Archives, and copies are available at the Family History Library. Records and indexes are available for the following states: Alabama, Arizona, Arkansas, Florida, Georgia, Kentucky, Louisiana, Maryland, Mississippi, Missouri, North Carolina, South Carolina, Tennessee, Texas, and Virginia. (For National Archives M numbers and Family History Library computer numbers, see pages 23–24 of the finding aid *Research Outline: U.S. Military Records*, cited above).

Consolidated Index to Compiled Service Records of Confederate Soldiers (M253; FHL 323922).

Index to Compiled Service Records of Confederate Soldiers Who Served in Organizations Raised Directly by the Confederate Government and of Confederate General and Staff Officers and Nonregimental Enlisted Men (M818; FHL 328740).

Compiled Service Records of Soldiers Who Served in Organizations Raised Directly by the Confederate Government (M258; FHL 278791).

Compiled Service Records of Confederate General and Staff Officers and Nonregimental Enlisted Men (M331; FHL 375792).

Unfiled Papers and Slips Belonging to Confederate Compiled Service Records (M347; FHL 210198).

Records Relating to Confederate Naval and Marine Personnel (M260; FHL 327273).

Selected Records of the War Department Relating To Confederate Prisoners of War, 1861–1865 (M598; FHL 110849).

Compiled Records Showing Service of Military Units in Confederate Organizations (M861; FHL 437582).

Register of Confederate Soldiers, Sailors, and Citizens Who Died in Federal Prisons and Military Hospitals in the North, 1861–1865 (M918; FHL film 1,024,456 (not in computer listing).

PENSION RECORDS

The Family History Library has microfilm copies of pension records created by the Confederate states and border states. Many of these records have been indexed in published works; they are named in the finding aid *Research Outline: U.S. Military Records* (cited above). The microfilm may be accessed by Family History Library computer number, as shown below.

Alabama	FHL 482000
Arkansas	FHL 588054
Florida	FHL 377657
Georgia	FHL 374852
Kentucky	FHL 569186
Louisiana	FHL 248616
Mississippi	FHL 277157
Missouri	FHL 193357

North Carolina	FHL 494409
Oklahoma	FHL 197031
Tennessee	FHL 250899
Texas	FHL 318535
Virginia	FHL 534241

Indian Wars

Index to Compiled Military Service Records of Volunteer Soldiers Who Served During Indian Wars and Disturbances, 1815–58 (M629; FHL 325963).

Compiled Service Records of Volunteer Soldiers Who Served from 1784 to 1811 (M905; FHL 325325). These records are indexed by *Index to Compiled Service Records . . .* (M694; FHL 555931).

Compiled Service Records of Volunteer Soldiers Who Served in Organizations From the State of Florida During the Florida Indian Wars, 1835–1858 (M1086; FHL 110859).

Compiled Service Records of Michigan and Illinois Volunteers Who Served During the Winnebago Indian Disturbances, 1827 (M1505; FHL 511959).

Historical Information Relating to Military Posts and Other Installations, ca. 1700–1900 (M661; FHL 437595).

Returns From U.S. Military Posts, 1800–1916 (M617; FHL 467703).

Cherokee Disturbances and Removal, 1836 to 1839. Individual state indexes are available for Alabama: M243; FHL film 368685; Georgia: M907; FHL film 1,205402; North Carolina: M256; FHL film 368,686; Tennessee: M908; FHL film 1,205,384.

Index to Compiled Service Records of Volunteer Soldiers Who Served During the Creek War in Organizations From the State of Alabama (M244; FHL 278523).

Second Seminole War, 1836 to 1843. Indexes are available for Alabama: M245; FHL film 880,847; Louisiana: M239; FHL film 880,843.

Index to Compiled Service Records of Volunteer Soldiers Who Served During the War of 1837–1838 in Organizations from the State of Louisiana (M241; FHL 278508).

Index to Indian Wars Pension Files, 1892, 1926 (T318; FHL 326152).

Spanish-American War

General Index to Compiled Service Records of Volunteer Soldiers Who Served During the War With Spain (M871; FHL 288680). Individual state indexes are also available for Louisiana: M420; FHL film 880,013; and North Carolina: M413; FHL 279844.

Compiled Service Records of Volunteer Soldiers Who Served in the Florida Infantry During the War With Spain (M1087; FHL 110861).

Philippine Insurrection

Index to Compiled Service Records of Volunteer Soldiers Who Served During the Philippine Insurrection (872; FHL 290106.d).

World War I

Index to Rendezvous Reports, Naval Auxiliary Service, 1917–1918 (T1100; FHL 432725).

Index to Rendezvous Reports, Armed Guard Personnel, 1917–1920 (T1101; FHL 432736).

World War I Selective Service System Draft Registration Cards, 1917–1918 (M1509; FHL 504818). The Family History Library is currently filming this series of cards, which were previously available only at the National Archives regional archives (southeast region), Atlanta, Georgia.

Index to Officers' Jackets, 1913–1925 (officers' directory) (T1102; FHL 462253).

State Records

Separate pamphlets titled *Research Outline [name of state]* describing the genealogical resources (including a section on military records) for each state (Alabama through Wyoming) are available from the library at a nominal price. For each state, the pamphlet lists the material at the Family History Library copied from state repositories and selected National Archives microfilm. Titles of National Archives microfilm listed above and in the *Research Outline: United States* are not repeated below. Also not included below are titles of publications available at the Family History Library. These titles can be found in chapter 9 of this volume.

The above-described pamphlets ("state guides") frequently refer the researcher to the finding aid *Research Outline: United States* for more information. Titles of collections contained in that finding aid are not repeated here, but additional military records unique to the state are listed below. For more details and titles of publications, consult the appropriate state guide pamphlet.

Alabama	Indexes to the Creek War, Florida War, Cherokee Removal; Alabama Confederate pension records; state censuses of Confederate veterans, 1907 and 1921.
Alaska	Military burials at the Sitka National Cemetery since 1867.
Arizona	(See finding aid *Research Outline: U.S. Military Records.*)
Arkansas	Bounty land warrants, War of 1812; Arkansas Confederate pension records; state census of Confederate veterans, 1911.
California	State Adjutant General's records from 1849 to 1945. These cover militia and volunteer organizations, National Guard, and enlistments and records for World War I and World War II.
Colorado	(See finding aid *Research Outline: U.S. Military Records.*)
Connecticut	Selected papers of the wars between 1675 and 1775; rolls of Connecticut men in the French and Indian War; service personnel in the Spanish-American War.
Delaware	(See finding aid *Research Outline: U.S. Military Records.*)
District of Columbia	Register of officers of the militia of the District of Columbia, 1813–1830; cemetery lists of Civil War soldiers.
Florida	Publications, indexes and service records for Indian wars that took place in Florida.
Georgia	State Adjutant General's records; Georgia Confederate pension records; military discharge papers, 1917–60; photographs and service records of World War I personnel.
Hawaii	Service records of Hawaiian royal guards, navy and militia, pre-1895; members of citizen guards of the Republic of Hawaii; records of Japanese evacuees during World War II (also available at the National Archives).
Idaho	(See finding aid *Research Outline: U.S. Military Records.*)
Illinois	Muster rolls for the Black Hawk War; Index to State Adjutant General's Reports for the periods of Indian Wars through the Spanish-American War; bounty-land warrants for the War of 1812; Illinois militia rolls, 1862–63; soldiers buried in various Illinois cemeteries, 1774–1898; some county courthouse records of discharges from military service.
Indiana	Civil War substitutes; Indiana state militia; Grand Army of the Republic (GAR) records; World War I deaths.
Iowa	State adjutant general's records: Civil War, Spanish-American War, World War I, and National Guard; lists of men eligible for military duty, arranged by county; Iowa members of the Grand Army of the Republic.

Kansas	State adjutant general's records, 1861–World War II.
Kentucky	Kentucky Confederate pension records.
Louisiana	Spanish military records; state census of Confederate veterans and their widows, 1911. (Note: The Family History Library does not have copies of Louisiana Confederate pensions; they are available at the Utah State Archives.)
Maine	Soldiers who died in World War II; *Veterans' Cemetery Records Collection* (from King Philip's War through World War I).
Maryland	Muster rolls for Fort Cumberland, 1757–1758; card index to muster rolls and payrolls, 1732–72.
Massachusetts	(See finding aid *Research Outline: U.S. Military Records*.)
Michigan	Index to Patriot War; descriptive muster roll of Mexican War volunteers; alphabetical list of more than 85,000 names listed in the state adjutant general's report, 1861–65; records of the Grand Army of the Republic, 1876–1945; card index of World War I soldiers; state militia rosters, 1838–61; card index of National Guard and state troops, 1858–1905; applications to the soldiers' home at Grand Rapids, 1885–1960.
Minnesota	State census of Union veterans, 1890; state bonus recipients, primarily World War I to present.
Mississippi	Records of soldiers under French, Spanish, and English governments (in various languages), 1612–1794; service records of soldiers in Mississippi units, War of 1812; state census of Union veterans, 1890; Mississippi Confederate pension files; index to World War I army veterans.
Missouri	Bounty land warrants in Arkansas, Illinois and Missouri, with Missouri patentees indexed; Missouri Confederate pension files; applications for admission to state soldiers' home; records of state militia and volunteers; muster rolls of volunteers in Spanish-American War; service files and bonus applications for World War I; State Adjutant General's records of Black Hawk War, Seminole War, Mormon War, Heatherly War, Iowa War, Mexican War, and Civil War.
Montana	Historical sketches of army posts.
Nebraska	Burial records, Nebraska Grand Army of the Republic; card index of soldiers in Spanish-American War, World War I; Selective Service cards, World War I
Nevada	Muster rolls, 1860–1902; records of Nevada State Militia from 1865; records of Nevada National Guards; Selective Service cards, World War I through Vietnam War; biographical sketches of soldiers who lost their lives in World War I.
New Hampshire	Service record card index for the Civil War from the New Hampshire Historical Society (includes records of substitute soldiers); New Hampshire pension records from the DAR Library, 1776–1850.
New Jersey	Revolutionary war index (summaries of service records); Revolutionary War Slips . . . Department of Defense Materials (a card index); revolutionary war records of New Jersey; pension claims of New Jersey revolutionary war soldiers; muster rolls and card index to petitions, records of confiscated estates; Loyalists, 1776–1783; state adjutant general's records, War of 1812; soldiers who fought in the Mexican War; New Jersey volunteers in the Civil War; Civil War pension claims, New Jersey soldiers, Civil War; record books, Civil War (various pension and other records); card index to Civil War soldiers' graves in New Jersey; index to State Archives collections of records, Spanish-American War and Philippine Insurrection; World War I draft registration cards.
New Mexico	Records of military service in New Spain, 1786–1800 (originals are in General Archives in Simancas, Spain; muster rolls and other records for Indian wars, 1861–98.
New York	Copies of the first eight of ten volumes of *New York Military Patents and Abstracts, 1764–1846*; card index of patents and military tracts, 1775–1900; grave indexes of revolutionary war soldiers; Loyalist records from the Public Record Office in London; New York census of Civil War soldiers, 1865; draft registration cards for World War I.
North Carolina	Index to state Confederate pension records, from 1885; copies of discharge records from some North Carolina counties, 1918–60.

North Dakota	(See finding aid *Research Outline: U.S. Military Records.*)
Ohio	Bounty-land warrants for the military district in Ohio; muster rolls, Civil War; muster rolls, Spanish-American War; service cards, regular, out of state, and Marines, World War I; list of dead and missing soldiers, World War II; graves registration of soldiers buried in Ohio, all wars before 1945; Rosters, Ohio National Guard, 1874–1917; copies of discharges entered into county records (for approximately half of the counties).
Oklahoma	State Confederate pensions records and index; Confederate army casualty lists.
Oregon	(See finding aid *Research Outline: U.S. Military Records.*)
Pennsylvania	Revolutionary war abstract card file; revolutionary war pension accounts, 1807–83; revolutionary war auditor general pensions collections, soldiers lists; War of 1812 auditor's lists of soldiers; Mexican War service records and muster rolls of Pennsylvania units; Civil War manuscript sources; register of Pennsylvania Volunteers; veterans' name listings; Spanish-American War veterans' compensation files; draft, muster and some pension files of World War I and World War II.
Rhode Island	Military records of soldiers who served from 1731 to 1774; military papers for the period 1774–92; War of 1812 enlistment and other papers; card index for service between 1774 and 1805.
South Carolina	Revolutionary war stub entries to claims; claims of South Carolina Loyalists; index to service records of soldiers in South Carolina units, War of 1812 and Civil War; state Confederate pension records, muster rolls, and payrolls of South Carolina units, Civil War and Spanish-American War; copies of military records from county courthouses.
South Dakota	(See finding aid *Research Outline: U.S. Military Records.*)
Tennessee	Tennessee Confederate pension files and index; Civil War veterans questionnaire survey; Confederate soldiers' applications to the soldiers' home in Nashville.
Texas	Service records of Texas soldiers in the Mexican War; Confederate pension records and index; index of Texas Confederate soldiers; records and muster-out rolls of Texans discharged from service in the Spanish-American War.
Utah	Return lists of the Mormon Battalion, including biographical data for volunteers in companies A and B; Utah state militia records; returns of federal troops sent to Utah, 1857; Utah participants in the above-named in state militia records; card index and related papers for Utah soldiers in Indian wars; index and records of Utah soldiers who served in Utah during the Civil War; index to Utah units and muster rolls for the Spanish-American War and the Philippine Insurrection; Mexican Border Campaign muster rolls of Utah participants; Questionnaire survey replies of World War I veterans; draft records and service records of Utah participants in World War I and World War II; lists of Utah military personnel buried in Utah cemeteries.
Vermont	Roster of Vermont soldiers in the Spanish-American War.
Virginia	Revolutionary war bounty land warrants for land in Kentucky and the Virginia Military District of Ohio; military land certificates, 1782–76; lists of land warrants issued by Virginia and registered in Kentucky; papers relating to Virginians in the revolutionary war; claims by private citizens, revolutionary war; card index of Virginia in the War of 1812; index and records of state Confederate soldiers; lists of Confederate dead at the Hollywood Cemetery, Richmond.
Washington	(See finding aid *Research Outline: U.S. Military Records.*)
West Virginia	(See finding aid *Research Outline: U.S. Military Records.*)
Wisconsin	Muster and descriptive rolls, Civil War; state census of veterans, 1885 and 1895.
Wyoming	Index of returns, Civil War; copies of a few military records in county courthouses.

8

State Resources

8

State Resources

Many researchers need not leave their own states to obtain documentation of an individual's military service or to learn something about a military unit in which the individual served. The primary state organizations that hold military records are state archives, the offices of state adjutants general, historical and genealogical societies, and major research libraries. Generally, there is no charge for access to these records, except for the user fees required by some societies. Reference staff at state archives usually respond to written or telephoned inquiries if they refer to only one or two specific matters that can be answered with a minimum of effort and time. Usually, limited staffing makes staff research impossible, and researchers are urged to visit in person or to employ a professional local researcher. Names and addresses of local researchers are often available from the archives or society.

Procedures

Although procedures vary, it is possible to make some generalizations that may ease the way for first-time visitors to a state archives or historical society. Registration is universally required, accompanied by the furnishing of a set of rules and a descriptive pamphlet or leaflet describing the services of the facility. To protect against the accidental removal or theft of valuable papers, visitors usually are required to place briefcases, notebooks, purses, and coats in lockers outside the reference areas, although material necessary to the search may be taken inside. Usually, all papers are inspected when leaving the reference areas. The use of ink or ballpoint pens is normally forbidden.

To procure material from the stacks or storage spaces, a request slip is generally employed. One slip is submitted for each document or collection of documents desired. A staff member will retrieve the material and deliver it to the researcher's table or to a designated "pick-up" table. Microfilm usually may be taken directly from storage cabinets, but at some facilities staff members retrieve it. Microfilm readers may be used as they become available, or they may be assigned. Often available is a coin-operated microfilm reader-printer. Microfilm normally is refiled by staff members.

Guides to Material

Upon arrival, researchers should acquaint themselves with any available finding aids, which are usually contained in notebooks or folders. Inquiries to staff members concerning specific types of material may also result in a descriptive inventory or container list showing the records that are available. Card or computer catalogs or other indexes should also be examined. Using published microfilm holdings or merely scanning the labels on microfilm cabinets will also serve to acquaint the researcher generally with such material.

Federal Records

Most state archives and libraries have purchased copies of some National Archives microfilm of military records. For each state facility described in this chapter, there is a list of such microfilm titles. Publications by federal agencies pertaining to units and personnel of armed forces are also often available in state libraries or archives. For wars since 1917, the U.S. War Department generated lists of military personnel who served in various branches of service or who were killed, wounded, or listed as missing. Many of these lists have been acquired by state repositories.

As discussed earlier (chapter 5), the National Archives operates thirteen regional archives, each specializing in historical material relating principally to the region where it is located. Combining a visit to a state repository and a visit to a nearby regional archives may eliminate the need for a trip to the National Archives in Washington, D.C.

State Records

State military organizations usually prepare written reports about their activities and personnel. Sometimes such units are transferred to the national armed forces, and in such cases material may be found in both state and federal repositories. The prime source for data concerning local militias (later the National Guard) may be found either at state archives or in the offices of state adjutants general. Muster rolls, payrolls, and "returns" submitted by local military units are frequently found in state repositories. Most Southern states loaned Civil War muster rolls and related documents to the U.S. War Department to make possible the compilation of service records, after which the documents were returned to the states. In some cases, such state material did not reach the War Department, so the states may now have the only surviving such records.

Although records of military pensions for federal service are among federal holdings, records of pensions or bonus payments granted by the states are usually found only in state archives. These pertain not only to Confederate service but also to bonuses and pensions granted for service in other wars or armed conflicts. Some states conducted special postwar censuses or enumerations of living veterans. Questionnaires used for this purpose contain helpful genealogical

and historical information. Military land grants by the states are recorded in state repositories, many of which are not mentioned in federal records. Registers and related information concerning state homes for soldiers and sailors are also available, either at state archives or at the homes themselves.

Records furnished to state archives or historical societies by county or town governments often consist of lists of names of local citizens who served in the military, who were mentioned in local draft registration books, or whose dependents received state or local financial assistance.

Some state historical societies operate jointly with or in lieu of a state archives. If they operate independently, these societies seldom possess official military documents and usually do not have National Archives microfilm. However, they operate excellent reference libraries and maintain useful manuscript collections. Many manuscript collections contain personal diaries, journals, letters, and other material bearing upon military involvement. Generally there is a card catalog or similar index to such holdings, in which the researcher may search under the heading of a particular war or other armed conflict. In conjunction with manuscript collections, there may be photograph albums of local military establishments or units. Also, scrapbooks of newspaper clippings pertaining to military service of local residents are often maintained.

State libraries and other major reference libraries in cities may have published works that contain lists of military personnel, chiefly the annual reports prepared by the state adjutant general. Some libraries have published histories of military units and other historical works not available at other large libraries. The record collections and publications pertaining to state military service available in each state facility are named in this chapter. Researchers should be alert to other publications that supplement the titles cited here.

Alabama

1519   Spanish explorer Alonso Alvarez de Pineda sailed into Mobile Bay.

1701–02   Fort Louis was established by the French on the present site of Mobile.

1763	France ceded the area to England by the Treaty of Paris which ended the French and Indian War. (See French and Indian War in the appendix.)
1783	The Treaty of Paris which ended the American Revolution ceded British holdings in the Mobile area to the Spanish. (See American Revolution in the appendix.)
1795	The Treaty of San Lorenzo between the United States and Spain awarded all Alabama territory south of the thirty-first parallel to Spain.
1813	Spain relinquished claims to southern Alabama.
1817	Alabama became a territory.
1819	Alabama became a state.
1861	Alabama seceded from the Union but experienced little military activity except at Mobile Bay. Montgomery was briefly the first capital of the Confederate States of America. (See American Civil War in the appendix.)
1868	Alabama was readmitted to statehood.
1917-18	During World War I, Alabama's agricultural prosperity increased dramatically, as did shipbuilding in Mobile. (See World War I in the appendix.)
1941-45	During World War II, Alabama's agricultural and industrial production increased, and several military training centers were established in Alabama.

. . . .

ALABAMA DEPARTMENT OF ARCHIVES AND HISTORY

P.O. Box 300100
624 Washington Avenue
Montgomery, Alabama 36130-0100
(205) 242-4435

Finding Aids

State Agency Records. This aid consists of several notebooks that include lists of holdings of documents from the state adjutant general, who is responsible for administration of the state militia, including the National Guard, Naval Militia, State Guard, the retired lists, and the Unorganized Militia. In addition, the notebooks list documents of the state Confederate Soldiers' Home, the state Pension Commission, and the military papers of various governors.

Archives and History. This notebook includes descriptions of the 1907 and 1921 Alabama state census of Confederate veterans, listing the contents and container numbers. The questionnaires are arranged by county or military branch of service. The notebook also describes information found in the Public Information Files: Civil War Reconstruction, formerly known as the "W" files.

The collection titled Public Information Files: Alabamians at War includes information concerning Alabamians who served in the American Revolution, the War of 1812, the First Creek War, the Seminole Wars (1817-18), the Second Creek War, the Texas Revolution, the Mexican War, and the Spanish-American War.

Private Records. This aid is a series of notebooks which are the key to the manuscript collections. Some entries of possible interest to those searching for military material are:

> Civil War Soldiers' Letters, 1858-1909.
>
> Confederate Officers' Photograph Album.
>
> Confederate States of America: Furlough Requests and Passes, 1863-64.
>
> United States Infantry Division, 9th Division, 1918.
>
> Wight, Sgt., Journal, 1771.

All other entries refer to collections of named individuals, a few of which may incidentally refer to military matters.

Records

Staff members at the archives cannot search National Archives microfilm in response to written or telephoned inquiries. They prefer that inquiries for this microfilm be directed to the National Archives. The staff will respond, however, to requests to search microfilm created by Alabama agencies. Researchers who visit this archives may conduct their own searches in any of the microfilm (National Archives microfilm or Alabama microfilm) as listed below.

General

Alabama Department of Military and Naval Affairs: Rosters and Directories of Military Personnel, 1892-1941, Collected by the State Adjutant General. These name officers and enlisted men of the Alabama State Troops, Organized Militia, National Guard, and the First Cavalry of the Guard, including the Naval Militia. Rosters and directories are available for 1892, 1898, 1906-12, 1914, 1915-18, 1930, 1932, 1935-39, and 1941. Among these is a muster roll showing names and residences of Alabama volunteers in the Spanish-American War (1898-99).

State Militia Rolls on Microfilm: 1818 (M870634); 1873-98 (M870629-870654).

American Revolution (1775-83)

NATIONAL ARCHIVES MICROFILM

General Index to Compiled Service Records of Revolutionary War Soldiers (M860—one roll only).

ALABAMA MICROFILM

Revolutionary War Service, 1776-83 (M870633).

OTHER RECORDS

Register of Military Pensions Paid by the Alabama Bank, Mobile, 1833-38. This register is located in the reference room.

War of 1812 (1812-14)

NATIONAL ARCHIVES MICROFILM

Index to Compiled Service Records of Volunteer Soldiers Who Served During the War of 1812 (M602—two rolls only).

Indian Wars (1813-14; 1836-37)

NATIONAL ARCHIVES MICROFILM

Index to Compiled Service Records of Volunteer Soldiers Who Served During the Creek War in Organizations From the State of Alabama (M244).

Index to Compiled Service Records of Volunteer Soldiers Who Served During the Florida War in Organizations From the State of Alabama (M245).

ALABAMA MICROFILM

Indian War Service, 1812-14 (M870633).
Indian War Service, 1836 (A to L) (M870634).
Indian War Service, 1836 (M to Z) (M870635).

Mexican War (1846-48)

NATIONAL ARCHIVES MICROFILM

Index to Compiled Service Records of Volunteer Soldiers Who Served During the Mexican War (M616—one roll only).

ALABAMA MICROFILM

Texas War With Mexico, 1835-36 (M870635).
Mexican War Service, 1846-47 (A to L) (M870635).
Mexican War Service, 1846-47 (M to Z) (M870636).

Civil War—Union (1861-65)

NATIONAL ARCHIVES MICROFILM

Compiled Service Records of Volunteer Union Soldiers Who Served in Organizations From the State of Alabama (M2768).

Civil War—Confederate (1861-65)

NATIONAL ARCHIVES MICROFILM

Consolidated Index to Compiled Service Records of Confederate Soldiers (M253).

Index to Compiled Service Records of Confederate Soldiers Who Served in Organizations From the State of Alabama (M374).

ALABAMA MICROFILM

Confederate Pension Applications, 1868-1955 (M870891-889981). Arranged alphabetically by last name.

Confederate Service Records, 1861-65 (M1000-1066). Compiled in the 1930s, this collection consists of a card for each veteran. The data was taken from muster rolls, pension papers, and miscellaneous papers. The original records cited on the cards are also available.

OTHER RECORDS

Alabama Confederate Soldiers and Sailors Who Died in the North While Prisoners of War. This is a computer-generated list compiled by Cecil Norman and Floyd Weatherbee, Jr., using data from National Archives microfilm. It provides the soldiers' name, rank, age, military unit, date of death, location of grave, and place of death (either a prison camp or a town).

Muster Rolls and Rosters. These provide name, rank, age, and enlistment dates. The name of the military unit must be specified.

Regimental History Files: Alabama Commands (CSA). These are unit histories and other miscellaneous data. The name of the military unit must be specified.

Alabama Pension Commission: Census or Enumeration of Confederate Veterans, 1907. Arranged by county, this census names Confederate soldiers, sailors, and officers from all branches of the military who served in a unit from any state but who resided in Alabama when the census was taken. The form used in the census requested name; place of residence; date and place of birth; place and date of enlistment; military unit; whether captured, discharged, or paroled; and related information. See the "container listing" for this collection for container numbers for each county. This enumeration is also available in printed form (see Published Sources—Alabama) and is available on microfilm M443 (four rolls).

Alabama Pension Commission: Census or Enumeration of Veterans or Widows on the Pension Rolls in 1921. Arranged by military branch, this census excludes deserters and pensioners who owned real or personal property valued at more than $5,000 or whose income exceeded $1,200 per year. The information is similar to that obtained for the 1907 census but includes data concerning widows and children. See the "container listing" for this collection for container numbers.

Alabama Pension Commission: Census or Enumeration of Confederate Widows Aged Eighty Years or Older in 1927. The information includes the widow's first name; name of the veteran; and the widow's age, date of birth, and date of marriage. All records of this census are in container SG4350.

Selected Collections in the Public Information Files: Civil War and Reconstruction Files. Refer to the finding aid cited above, which contains a list of container and folder numbers. Although subject to change, the following collections, among others, are available:

Cemeteries (arranged by name of cemetery)
Confederate Army Chaplains
Deaths, Bowling Green, Kentucky
Deserters and Traitors
Furloughs and Passes
Homes for Disabled Soldiers
Hospitals (arranged by name of hospital)
Indigent Families Relief
Killed and Died of Wounds
Medals and Badges (Cross of Honor; Roll of Honor)
Medical Care
Miscellaneous Casualty Lists
Paroles
Patriotic Organizations
Pensions, Florida and other states
Personal Narratives (by name of individual)
Prisons and Prisoners (by name of prison, Confederate or Union)
Soldiers' Relief
Spies
University of Alabama Corps of Cadets
Veterans' Reunions (by year and place)
Wounded

Spanish-American War (1898-99)

ALABAMA MICROFILM

Spanish-American War Service, 1898 (A to L) (M870637).
Spanish-American War Service, 1898 (M to Z) (M870638).

OTHER RECORDS

Alabama Adjutant General Office Administrative Files: Spanish-American War Back Pay Receipts, 1908. These consist of canceled warrants and affidavits of veterans used by Alabama when it claimed reimbursement from the federal government for state services during the war.

Alabama Department of Military Affairs: Muster Rolls, Spanish-American War (RG 197).

World War I (1917-18)

World War I Soldiers' Service Records. These are card rosters for the army, Marine Corps, and Coast Guard, as well as induction records. Arranged by county.

World War I Honor List of Dead or Missing. State of Alabama. This is a publication of the U.S. War Department; it is located in the reference room. Arranged by county and then alphabetically by name, it provides name, serial number, rank, and type of casualty.

List of Casualties Incurred by United States Military Personnel in World War I. This list, arranged by home state of record (Alabama only in this case), was published by the United States secretary of defense. Included are name, rank, place of residence, date of death, and cause of death.

World War II (1941-45)

World War II Honor List of Dead and Missing. State of Alabama. This publication of the U.S. War Department is arranged by county and then alphabetically. Included are name, serial number, rank, and type of casualty.

Korean War (1950-53)

For names of casualties refer to James B. Sellers' "Alabama's Losses in the Korean Conflict." *Alabama Review* (July 1960).

Vietnam War (1961-75)

List of Casualties Incurred by United States Military Personnel in Connection With the Conflict in Vietnam. Alabama. This computer-generated list prepared by the U.S. Secretary of Defense lists deaths between 1 January 1961 and 30 September 1975. Included are name, service number, date of birth, date of casualty, and home of record.

PUBLISHED SOURCES—ALABAMA

1776-83 (American Revolution)

Alabama. Department of Archives and History. *Revolutionary Soldiers in Alabama: Being a List of Names, Compiled From Authentic Sources, of Soldiers of the American Revolution, Who Resided in the State of Alabama.* Montgomery: Brown Printing Co., 1911. Reprint. Baltimore: Genealogical Publishing Co., 1967. Includes biographical sketches of approximately five hundred veterans.

Brewer, Willis. *Alabama: Her History, Resources, War Record, and Public Men, From 1540 to 1872.* Montgomery: Barrett & Brown, Printers, 1872. Reprint. Spartanburg, S.C.: The Reprint Co., 1975.

Gandrud, Pauline J., comp., and Bobbie J. Mclane, ed. *Alabama Soldiers: Revolutionary War, War of 1812, and Indian Wars.* 15 vols. Hot Springs: the compiler, 1987.

Julich, Louise M. *Roster of Revolutionary Soldiers and Patriots in Alabama.* National Society of the Daughters of the American Revolution, Alabama Chapter. Montgomery: Parchment Press, 1979. A list of those who died in Alabama and some who died in other states.

Owen, Thomas M. *Revolutionary Soldiers in Alabama*. . . . Vol. 1. Montgomery: Brown Printing Co., 1911. Reprint. 1967, 1975.

Revolutionary War Soldiers Who Lived in Both Virginia and Alabama. Edited by Thomas H. Wood. Tuscaloosa: Wood Pub., 1988.

Thomas, Elizabeth W., ed. *Revolutionary Soldiers in Alabama*. Tuscaloosa: Willo Publishing Co., 1960-80.

1784-1860 (War of 1812, Indian Wars)

Alabama Volunteer, Cherokee Disturbances and Removals, 1836–1839. Cullman: Gregath Co., 1982.

Horn, Robert C. *Creek Indian War Index to Records of Volunteer Soldiers From Alabama*. Dadeville: The Genealogical Society of East Alabama, 1983.

_____. *Index to Compiled Service Records for Alabama Soldiers in the Florida Indian War, 1836–1838*. Auburn: The Genealogical Society of East Alabama, 1987.

Jones, Kathleen P. , and Pauline J. Gandrud, comps. *Alabama Records*. Easley, S.C.: Southern Historical Press, 1981-.

War of 1812 Pensioners Living in Alabama During the 1880's. Cullman: Gregath Co., 1982.

1861-65 (Civil War)

1907 Alabama Census of Confederate Soldiers, Autauga, Baldwin, and Barbour Counties. Indexed and compiled from Alabama State Archives microfilm. Cullman: Gregath Co., 1982.

1907 Alabama Census of Confederate Soldiers, Russell and St. Clair Counties. Indexed and compiled from Alabama State Archives microfilm. Cullman: Gregath Co., 1982.

Brewer, Willis. "Brief Historical Sketches of Military Organizations Raised in Alabama During the Civil War." In *Alabama: Her History, Resources, War Record, and Public Men, From 1540 to 1872*. Montgomery: Barrett & Brown, Printers, 1872. Reprint. Spartanburg, S.C.: The Reprint Co., 1975. Includes names of officers.

Hoole, William S. *Alabama Tories: The First Alabama Cavalry, U.S.A. 1862–1865*. Tuscaloosa: Confederate Publishing Co., 1960.

Lancaster, Dallas M., comp. *Sons of Confederate Veterans, Alabama Division, 1896–1986*. Florence: the compiler, 1987. Includes names of officers and members.

Pompey, Sherman L. *Muster Lists of the Alabama Confederate Troops*. . . . 3 vols. Independence, Calif.: Historical and Genealogical Publishing Co., 1965.

United Confederate Veterans. Alabama. Raphiel Semmes Camp, No. 11. *Confederate Gray Book, 1912*. Mobile (?): 1912 (?). Contains names of living and deceased veterans, 1912.

U.S. Adjutant General's Office. *Official Army Register of the Volunteer Force of the United States Army for the Years 1861, '62, '63, '64, '65*. Washington, D.C.: Government Printing Office, 1865. Reprint. Gaithersburg, Md.: Olde Soldier Books, 1987. Alabama is included in vol. 4.

1866-1900 (Spanish-American War)

Alabama. Adjutant General's Office. *Muster Rolls of Alabama Volunteers in the Spanish-American War of 1898*. Montgomery: 1899.

Koenigsberg, Moses. *Southern Martyrs. A History of Alabama's White Regulars During the Spanish American War*. Montgomery: Brown Printing Co., 1898. Contains rosters of every command.

1901-22 (World War I)

Alabama. Department of Archives and History. *Deaths From Alabama in the European War as Reported in the Official U.S. Bulletin January 1, 1918*. Montgomery: 1919.

Alabama. *Adjutant General's Quadrennial Report, 1914-1922*. Montgomery: 1922.

Alaska

1741	Vitus Bering, a Danish sailor working for Russia, first sighted the Alaskan coast.
1799	The Russian-American Company established headquarters at Arcangel and began exploiting the Alaskan fur trade.
1867	An impoverished Russian government sold Alaska to the United States.
1897-98	Various gold discoveries created the Alaskan Gold Rush, bringing the first significant population into the area.
1912	Alaska became a territory.
1941-45	World War II brought large numbers of American military personnel into Alaska. (See World War II in the appendix.)
1959	Alaska became a state.

ALASKA STATE ARCHIVES

141 Willoughby
Pouch C, 0207
Juneau, Alaska 99801

U.S. servicemen, almost exclusively from the lower forty-eight states, have been in Alaska since it was purchased from Russia in 1867 and placed under the jurisdiction of the War Department.

The Sitka National Cemetery has more than five hundred graves of military personnel and their families and dates from 1867. A list of these burials can be found in the *Illinois State Genealogical Society Quarterly* (Spring 1975): 17-19.

Arizona

1539	Franciscan missionary Marcos de Niza explored Arizona.
1690-1711	Jesuit missionary Eusebio Francisco Kino established missions in Arizona.
1821	The Mexican Revolution transferred Arizona from Spanish to Mexican rule.
1848	The Treaty of Guadalupe-Hidalgo, which ended the Mexican War, transferred Arizona from Mexico to the United States. (See Mexican War in the appendix.)
1854	The Gadsden Purchase added to the United States the area south of the Gila River to the present Mexican border.
1850	As part of the Compromise of 1850, Arizona became a part of the Territory of New Mexico.
1863	Arizona became a territory.
1864	Federal troops under Kit Carson defeated the Navajos. (See Navajo Wars in the appendix.)
1866	Pah-Ute County ceded to Nevada.
1886	Surrender of Geronimo ended decades of conflict between Apache Indians and white settlers. (See Apache Wars in the appendix.)
1912	Arizona became a state.

DEPARTMENT OF LIBRARY, ARCHIVES AND PUBLIC RECORDS

Room 300
State Capitol
1700 West Washington
Phoenix, Arizona 85007
(602) 542-3701

Records

General

Military Burials at Fort Huachucaa, Arizona.

Veterans' Graves in Evergreen Cemetery, Tucson, Arizona.

Fort Grant Cemetery Records, 1873-92, Graham County, Arizona.

1917-18 (World War I)

World War I List of Prisoners of War Who Entered Service From the State of Arizona.

1941-45 (World War II)

World War II Honor List of Dead and Missing. State of Arizona. This U.S. War Department publication, arranged by county and then alphabetically, provides name, serial number, rank, and type of casualty.

1951-57 (Korean War)

List of Casualties from the Korean Conflict, 1951-57. State of Arizona. This is a list obtained from the Center for Electronic Records, National Archives, Washington, D.C. It includes name, rank or grade, branch of service, home of record, date of casualty, date of birth, and category of casualty including deaths, captured, and missing.

ARIZONA HISTORICAL SOCIETY

949 East Second Street
Tucson, Arizona 85719
(602) 628-5774

This society has records of each frontier military post in Arizona as well as quartermaster records pertaining to each. The records are indexed and are available on microfilm.

Records

Civil War—Union and Confederate (1861-65)
NATIONAL ARCHIVES MICROFILM

Index to Compiled Service Records of Volunteer Union Soldiers Who Served in Organizations From the Territory of Arizona (M532).

Index to Compiled Service Records of Confederate Soldiers Who Served in Organizations From the Territory of Arizona (M375).

PUBLISHED SOURCES—ARIZONA

General

Akey, Elizabeth J. *Military Burials in Arizona.* Tucson: Arizona Genealogical Society, 1987.

Civil War (1861-65)

Pompey, Sherman L. *A Brief History of the Independent Arizona Territory Confederate States Battalions in Arizona Territory, 1861-1862.* Kingsburg, Calif.: Pacific Specialties, 1971. Provides names of officers and enlisted men.

_____. *Civil War Veteran Burial Listings.* 12 vols. Long Beach, Calif.: Southern California Genealogical Society, 1965.

Spanish-American War (1898-1899)

Herner, Charles. *Arizona Rough Riders.* Tucson: The University of Arizona Press, 1970. Appendix 3, "Muster-in Roll," pages 234-44.

Arkansas

1541   Spanish explorer Hernando de Soto entered Arkansas.

1673   French explorers Jacques Marquette and Louis Joliet reached Arkansas on the Mississippi River.

1682   The French explorer Rene-Robert Cavelier LaSalle claimed Arkansas for France.

1686   Arkansas Post, the first French settlement, was established by Henri de Tonty.

1762   France ceded Arkansas to Spain during the French and Indian War. (See French and Indian War in the appendix.)

1800   France again acquired Arkansas (from Spain).

1803   The United States acquired Arkansas from France as part of the Louisiana Purchase.

1812   Arkansas became part of Missouri Territory.

1819   Arkansas became a territory.

1836   Arkansas became a state.

1861   Arkansas seceded from the Union.

1862-63   Several Civil War battles were fought in Arkansas, most notably the Battle of Pea Ridge in 1862, before the state came under Union control in 1863. (See American Civil War in the appendix.)

1868   Arkansas was readmitted to statehood.

ARKANSAS HISTORY COMMISSION

One Capitol Mall
Little Rock, Arkansas 72201

(501) 682-6900

The history commission does not conduct research for patrons.

Finding Aids

Historical and Genealogical Source Materials at the Arkansas History Commission.

Guides to the Manuscript Collections. Twenty-nine bound volumes. (See below under Manuscript Collections.) No indexes are available.

Records

General
NATIONAL ARCHIVES MICROFILM

Register of Enlistments in United States Army, 1798-1884 (M233) (regular army, Arkansas). No index is available.

Records of Headquarters, Army of the Southwestern Frontier and Headquarters, Second and Seventh Military Departments, 1935-

1853 (M1302) (consists primarily of correspondence). No index is available.

OTHER RECORDS

Returns of Various Military Organizations in Posts and Bases in Arkansas, 1800-1916 (various collections—inquire). No indexes are available.

American Revolution (1775-83)
NATIONAL ARCHIVES MICROFILM

General Index to Compiled Service Records of Revolutionary War Soldiers (M860) (includes Continental forces, some militia units, and naval personnel).

War of 1812 (1812-14)
NATIONAL ARCHIVES MICROFILM

Index to Compiled Service Records of Volunteer Soldiers Who Served During the War of 1812 (M602).

Index to War of 1812 Pension Application Files (M313).

War of 1812 Military Bounty Land Warrants, 1815-1858 (M848—roll one: Arkansas, Missouri, Illinois). No indexes are available.

OTHER RECORDS

Military Bounty Land Grants, Arkansas, War of 1812. (See records of the state land office.)

Indian Wars (1815-58)
NATIONAL ARCHIVES MICROFILM

Index to Compiled Service Records of Volunteer Soldiers Who Served During Indian Wars and Disturbances, 1815-1858 (M629).

Mexican War (1846-48)
NATIONAL ARCHIVES MICROFILM

Index to Compiled Service Records of Volunteer Soldiers Who Served During the Mexican War (M616).

OTHER RECORDS

Selected Compiled Service Records of Volunteer Soldiers in Organizations From Arkansas Who Served During the Mexican War.

Civil War—Union (1861-65)
NATIONAL ARCHIVES MICROFILM

Index to Compiled Service Records of Volunteer Union Soldiers in Organizations From Arkansas (M399).

Civil War—Confederate (1861-65)
NATIONAL ARCHIVES MICROFILM

Consolidated Index to Compiled Service Records of Confederate Soldiers (M253).

Index to Compiled Service Records of Confederate Soldiers Who Served in Organizations Raised Directly by the Confederate Government and of Confederate General and Staff Officers and Non-regimental Enlisted Men (M818).

Index to Compiled Service Records of Confederate Soldiers Who Served in Organizations From the State of Arkansas (M376).

Compiled Service Records of Confederate Soldiers Who Served in Organizations Raised Directly by the Confederate Government (M258).

Compiled Service Records of Confederate General and Staff Officers and Non-regimental Enlisted Men (M331).

Compiled Service Records of Confederate Soldiers Who Served in Organizations From the State of Arkansas (M317).

Records Relating to Confederate Naval and Marine Personnel (M260).

Registers of Confederate Soldiers Who Died in Federal Prisons and Military Hospitals in the North (M918). (No index available.)

Confederate States Army Casualties. Lists and Narrative Reports, 1861-1865 (M836). (No index available.)

Case Files of Applications From Former Confederates for Presidential Pardons ("Amnesty Papers"), 1865-1867 (M1003) (selected papers from citizens from Arkansas).

OTHER RECORDS

Arkansas Confederate Service Records. This card catalog, begun in 1911, contains data from various official sources. It was discontinued when the National Archives published a similar list. The cards give name, rank, military unit, commanding officer, and enlistment date.

Confederate Pension Files. The original pension files, 1891-1939, are available; copies will be made for a fee. There is a card catalog: Confederate Veterans' and Widows' Pensions Paid by the State of Arkansas. The cards provide name, application number, name of widow, military unit and service record, date application was approved, county of residence, and death date of veteran or widow. Two indexes to these records are currently available for purchase.

Supplemental indexes are available at the reference desk. These may contain names not found in other indexes.

Confederate Pensions. Arranged by county and name. The microfilm roll number is shown.

Confederate Deceased Pensioners. Arranged by county and name. County of residence and identifying number are provided.

Miscellaneous Confederate Pension Records. Contains names of pensioners not found elsewhere and pensioners who had not been positively identified when previous lists were prepared.

Confederate Home. A supplemental index for the Confederate Home is available at the reference desk. It contains the names of all applicants for admission to the Confederate Home, 1907-57, regardless of whether they actually were admitted. County of residence is shown. Names in this index probably do not appear in pension lists since residents of the home did not qualify for pensions.

Census of Pensioners. A file folder available at the reference desk contains the names of 1,750 pensioners who returned questionnaires in a survey conducted in 1911 and 1912. Their names represent only a small fraction of the total number of pensioners actually on the rolls at the time. Data found in the questionnaires includes a considerable amount of personal and genealogical data, as well as dates of birth of parents. These have been published in three volumes by Bobbie J. McLane and Capitola Glazner (cited below under Published Sources—Arkansas), and they are available at this archives.

World War I (1917-18)

Arkansas World War I Nurses. This card catalog was compiled from a list prepared by the Office of the United States Adjutant General, 11 July 1919. Each card provides name, residence, hospital to which assigned, place and date of birth, military organization, discharge date, overseas duty, engagement in which participated, and wounds.

Arkansas World War I Discharge Records. This card catalog contains the names of each Arkansas soldier or sailor discharged from service. Each card provides name, rank, residence, place and date of enlistment, military units, engagements in which participated, overseas duty, discharge date, and percent of disability, if any.

World War I Draft Registration Cards. These cards from selective service boards are available on microfilm for all counties. Most counties had only one board; Jefferson County and Little Rock each had two boards. Each card provides name, address, age, date of birth, race, citizenship, occupation, name of employer, place of employment, and next of kin. The back of the card gives a "description of registrant," including any physical disabilities. The original cards are available at the National Archives—Southeast Region, Atlanta, Georgia.

County Records—Soldiers' and Sailors' Discharge Records, World War I. Available on microfilm are copies of volumes kept in county courthouses to record military discharges of any Arkansas soldiers or sailors who chose to file their discharges. The discharges were microfilmed and are indexed by county.

Manuscript Collections

Twenty-nine volumes of guides to the manuscript collections contain descriptions of several collections that in-

clude various kinds of military information. The following are selected examples.

Arkansas Adjutant General's Office Papers, 1867-1803; 1969 (book 4).

Arkansas Selective Service Material (book 6).

Little Rock Arsenal and Barracks Records (book 8).

Counsel of Defense File. Contains names of deserters and those absent without leave; also contains registers of home guards (book 13).

936th and 939th Artillery Battalion Command Reports, 1951-54 (book 19).

Raymond W. Watkins Collection of Death and Burials of Arkansas Confederate Soldiers and Veterans. Provides burial information from twenty states (book 20).

Records of State Auditors: Ex-Confederate Pension Records, 1893-1939 (book 21).

PUBLISHED SOURCES—ARKANSAS

1775-83 (American Revolution)

Dhonau, R.W. *A Roster of the Arkansas Society, Sons of the American Revolution, 1890-1985 and Register of Ancestors.* Little Rock: the author, 1985.

Payne, Dorothy E. *Arkansas Pensioners, 1818-1900: Records of Some Arkansas Residents Who Applied to the Federal Government for Benefits Arising From Service in Federal Military Organizations (Revolutionary War, War of 1812, Indian and Mexican Wars).* Easley, S.C.: Southern Historical Press, 1985. Lists nearly one thousand individuals with some miscellaneous data.

1784-1815 (War of 1812)

Christensen, Katheren, comp. *Arkansas Military Bounty Grants (War of 1812).* Hot Springs: Arkansas Ancestors, 1971. Contains some 6,600 entries. Data includes to whom patented, warrant number, patent date, and comments (if any).

War of 1812 Pensioners Living in Arkansas During the 1880s: Abstracted From the Executive Documents. Cullman, Ala.: Gregath Co., 1980.

1816-60 (Indian wars, Mexican War)

Allen, Desmond W. *Arkansas' Mexican War Soldiers.* Conway: Arkansas Research, 1988.

Morgan, James Logan. *Arkansas Volunteers of 1836-37: History and Roster of the First and Second Regiments of Arkansas Mounted Gunmen, 1836-1837, and a Roster of Captain Jesse Bean's Company of Mounted Rangers.* Newport: Morgan Books, 1984.

1861–65 (Civil War)

Allen, Desmond W., comp. *Arkansas Union Cavaliers*. Conway: Arkansas Research, 1987.

_____, comp. *Arkansas Union Infantry*. Conway: Arkansas Research, 1987.

_____, comp. *Arkansas Union Records*. 2 vols. Conway: the compiler, 1987.

_____, comp. *Arkansas Union Soldiers Pension Application Index*. Conway: the author, 1987.

_____, comp. *Arkansas' Damned Yankees: An Index to Union Soldiers in Arkansas Regiments*. Conway: the author, 1987.

_____,comp. *Index to Arkansas Confederate Pension Applications*. Conway: Arkansas Research, 1991.

_____. *Index to Arkansas Confederate Soldiers*. 3 vols. Conway: Arkansas Research, 1990.

Arkansas. Adjutant General's Office. *Report of the Adjutant General of Arkansas, for the Period of the Late Rebellion, and to November 1, 1866*. Washington, D.C.: Government Printing Office, 1866. Appendix A is a "Roster of Volunteers"; Appendix C is a "Roster of Arkansas Militia. . . ."

Collier, Calvin L. *First-in–First-out: The Capitol Guards, Arkansas Brigade*. Little Rock: Pioneer Press, 1961.

Confederate Women of Arkansas in the Civil War, 1861–65. Little Rock: United Confederate Veterans of Arkansas, 1907.

Ingmire, Frances T., comp. *Arkansas Confederate Veterans and Widows Pension Applications*. St. Louis, Mo.: the compiler, 1985. Contains name of veteran and widow (if any) with number and date of pension application; military service (company, regiment, division); state in which served if other than Arkansas; dates of service; county of residence; date of death.

McLane, Bobbie J., and Capitola Glazner, trans. and eds. *Arkansas 1911 Census of Confederate Veterans*. 3 vols. Hot Springs: Arkansas Ancestors, 1977–81.

Pickett, Connie. *Old Soldiers Home: Arkansas Confederate Soldiers and Widows*. St. Louis: Frances T. Ingmire, 1985.

Pompey, Sherman L. *Muster Lists of the Arkansas Confederate Troops*. . . . 2 vols. Independence, Calif.: Historical and Genealogical Pub., 1965.

_____. *Some Civil War Veterans Buried in Arkansas*. Fresno, Calif. (?): 1969.

Roberts, Bobby L., and Carl H. Moneyhon. *Portraits in Conflict: A Photographic History of Arkansas in the Civil War*. Fayetteville: University of Arkansas Press, 1987. Contains many photographs of officers.

Wright, Marcus J. *Arkansas in the War, 1861–1865*. Batesville: Independence County Historical Society, 1963. Lists officers by unit.

1866–1900 (Spanish-American War)

Allen, Desmond W., comp. *Arkansas' Spanish-American War Soldiers*. Conway: Arkansas Research, 1988.

Arkansas. Adjutant General's Office. *Report of the Adjutant General of the Arkansas State Guard, 1897–1900*. Little Rock: Thompson Printing Co., 1900.

California

1542	Juan Rodriguez Cabrillo, a Spanish explorer, sailed along the California coast.
1769	The first of many Spanish missions along the coast was established at San Diego.
1821	California was transferred from Spanish to Mexican rule in the Mexican Revolution.
1848	The Treaty of Guadalupe-Hidalgo, which ended the Mexican War, transferred California to the United States. (See Mexican War in the appendix.)
1848	American veterans of the Mexican War discovered gold, leading to the Gold Rush of 1849 and a massive influx of Americans.
1850	As part of the Compromise of 1850, California became a state without passing through the territorial phase.
1941–45	During World War II, major military installations were created in California from San Diego to San Francisco. (See World War II in the appendix.)

CALIFORNIA STATE ARCHIVES

1020 "O" Street
Sacramento, California 75814
(916) 653-7715

Finding Aids

Master Finding Aids, A–Z. Under the heading "Military Department" are listings of records of California militia units and elements of the California National Guard, 1849–1941. A portion of this finding aid relates to the "Indian War Papers" (see below), a calendar of all records as compiled by staff.

In the main subject card catalog under "Military" and "Militia" are references to documentation on military matters found in agency collections other than those of the State Military Department.

Militia Companies, 1849–1990. A listing of militia units arranged alphabetically by unit name. A separate worksheet contains a brief history and description of available documentation for each company.

Civil War Volunteers, 1861–1867. A listing of volunteer companies and description of available documentation for each.

Records

General

The California State Archives has no National Archives microfilm. The archives has one manuscript collection (unprocessed) relating to organization, operations, and post-war activities of the U.S. 322nd Field Signal Battalion, ca. 1917 to 1980. The California State Library, a separate organization, has the following National Archives microfilm.

Index to Compiled Service Records of Volunteer Union Soldiers Who Served in Organizations From the State of California (M553).

The library also has a collection of donated World War I papers on microfilm: *World War I Records of California Servicemen.*

Indian Wars (1851–1880)

Indian War Papers (1850–1880). This collection consists of militia muster rolls, field reports, correspondence, claims, miscellaneous other records, and two volumes of *Expenditures for Military Expeditions Against Indians During the Years 1851–1959.* The collection is arranged chronologically by date of campaign and includes, but is not limited to, the following:

> First and Second Carson Valley Expeditions (Paiute War)
>
> Catalina Island Indian Reservation
>
> First and Second El Dorado Expeditions
>
> Humbolt and Klamath Expeditions
>
> Indian War Claims
>
> Los Angeles and San Diego Expedition
>
> Mariposa Battalion

> Moduc War
>
> "Mormon Rebellion" Correspondence
>
> Owens River Expedition
>
> Tulare Expedition

Civil War–Union (1861–65)

The finding aid pertaining to Civil War volunteer units (cited above) includes the following:

> First and Second Cavalry
>
> First Veterans Infantry
>
> First Battalion Mountaineers
>
> First Through Ninth Infantry Regiments
>
> First Battalion, Native Cavalry

Most worksheets provide unit history information and documentation on dates of organization and disbanding, places each unit served, muster rolls, payrolls, monthly returns, ordnance reports, correspondence, and others. Also available are records relating to the "Capture of the Showalter Party" and names of Alameda County men of military age in 1863.

Spanish-American War (1898–99); World War I (1917–18); World War II (1941–45)

Modern Military Department records are organizational in description and content. Most such records pertain to specific units, names of which are established by U.S. military command for national uniformity. Many Californians in the National Guard were in federalized units, but few actually participated in the overseas theaters. Those units that were federalized disappear from the California records as they come under U.S. jurisdiction. Records of Californians in World War II, for example, end in 1941, when all California National Guard units were federalized. Records of post-war guard activities have not been deposited in the state archives.

By far the largest portion of the records of the Military Department document the history and activities of the National Guard in the "between war" periods. These records document all individuals who served, their terms and places of service, ranks attained, duties, operations of armories, equipment used, and other information pertinent to the history of individual units. One of the functions of the National Guard is to assist civil authorities in maintaining the peace or to provide aid in times of state and local emergencies. In this regard, special subject files exist for National Guard activities in the 1856 Vigilance Committee disturbances in San Francisco; 1871 Amador War; 1906 San Francisco earthquake and fire; 1913 Mill Valley fire; 1914 operations along the Mexican border during the Mexican Revolution; and Operation Hayfork over Nevada in 1949 (Governor Earl Warren Papers). Included in the above records can be found signed letters of such personages as Abraham Lincoln and generals George Armstrong Custer, Joe Hooker, and William Tecumseh Sherman.

A folder labeled "Military Government–California" is available from the staff. In addition to historical articles relating to various military units of the state, this folder contains a list titled "United States Personnel From the Sacramento Area Who Died in the Spanish-American War." Under the heading "Military" in the *Master Finding Aids* cited above are listed a very few documents that refer to specific military units that took part in this war.

PUBLISHED SOURCES–CALIFORNIA

Pre-1861 (Indian Wars)

Font, Pedro. *The Anza Expedition of 1775–1776.* Berkeley: University of California Press, 1913.

1861-65 (Civil War)

California. Adjutant General's Office. *Records of California Men in the War of the Rebellion, 1861 to 1867.* Compiled by Richard H. Orton. Sacramento: State Printing Office, 1890. Reprint. Detroit: Gale Research Co., 1979.

Parker, J. Carlyle, comp. *A Personal Name Index to Orton's "Records of California Men in the War of the Rebellion, 1861 to 1867."* Detroit: Gale Research Co., 1978.

Pompey, Sherman L. *Civil War Veteran Burials From California, Nevada, Oregon, and Washington Regiments Buried in Colorado.* Independence: Historical and Genealogical Publishing Co., 1965.

1866-1899 (Spanish-American War)

Bachelder, Horace W., comp. *Illustrated Roster of California Volunteer Soldiers in the War With Spain: Enlisted Under the President's Proclamations of April 23rd and May 25th, 1898.* San Francisco: Bonestell, 1898.

Colorado

1803	Though unexplored, eastern Colorado became United States territory through the Louisiana Purchase.
1806	American explorer Zebulon Pike entered Colorado and discovered the peak that bears his name.
1821	Nominally a part of the Spanish Empire, though not actually controlled by it, western Colorado became Mexican territory through the Mexican Revolution.
1848	The Treaty of Guadalupe-Hidalgo, which ended the Mexican War, transferred western Colorado to the United States. (See Mexican War in the appendix.)
1851	The first permanent non-hispanic settlers moved into the San Luis Valley.
1858–59	Pike's Peak Gold Rush brought the first significant population to Colorado.
1861	Colorado became a territory.
1862	Colorado soldiers participated on the Union side in the Battle of Glorieta Pass in New Mexico. (See American Civil War in the appendix.)
1876	Colorado became a state.
1954	The Air Force Academy was established at Colorado Springs.

COLORADO STATE ARCHIVES

Room 1-B20
1313 Sherman Street
Denver, Colorado 80203
(303) 866-2358

Finding Aids

Military Records of the State and Territory of Colorado (a leaflet).

Public Records Register: Military Affairs, National Guard. This register lists names of personnel who served in National Guard infantry and cavalry units from 1887 to 1921; indicates locations of rosters, muster-out rolls, and lists of commissioned officers for the Civil War period and between 1883 and 1915.

Records

General

NATIONAL ARCHIVES MICROFILM

Records of the 10th Military Department (California and Oregon territories) (M210).

Returns From United States Military Posts, 1800–1916 (M617— returns from active Colorado posts; 1,491 rolls: Abercrombie-Zarah).

Register of Enlistments in the United States Army, 1798–1914 (M233); roll 70: Indian Scouts, 1866–77; roll 71: Indian Scouts, 1878–1914; roll 81: Miscellaneous Indexes, 1865– 1914.

Letters Received by the Office of the Adjutant General (Main Series), 1871–80. RG 94 (M619).

Office of the Adjutant General; Doniphan's Report (RG 94).

OTHER RECORDS

Index to Muster Rolls, 1861–1930.

National Guard Roster Index, 1887–1921. (See the finding aid Public Records Register—cited above.)

National Guard Muster Rolls, 1887–1915. (See the finding aid Public Records Register—cited above.)

National Guard Service Records, 1862–1946.

Grave Registration Index, 1862–1949.

Civil War—Union (1861–65)

NATIONAL ARCHIVES MICROFILM

Index to Compiled Service Records of Volunteer Union Soldiers Who Served in Organizations From the Territory of Colorado (M534).

Compiled Records Showing Service of Military Units in Volunteer Union Organizations (M594—roll 4: Colorado).

Telegrams Sent by President Lincoln, 1864–65 (RG 94)

Letters Received by the Office of the Adjutant General (Main Series), 1861–70 (RG 94—M619).

Reports and Decisions of the Provost Marshal General, 1863–66 (M621).

OTHER RECORDS

Card File, Civil War Military Personnel.

Service Records, Third Colorado Cavalry.

Muster-out Rolls.

Discharge Certificates.

National Guard—Index to Rosters, 1861–65. Name, place of birth, age, occupation, date and place of employment, employer, years employed, physical description, dates of transfer, and date of discharge.

National Guardsmen Deceased.

National Guardsmen Killed in Action.

Governor's Guard: First Militia, Colorado Territory.

Morning Reports.

Clothing Books.

Miscellaneous Records Contained in National Archives RG 94. (See a list of holdings at the reference desk.)

Civil War Veterans Deceased.

Indian Wars (post-Civil War)

NATIONAL ARCHIVES MICROFILM

Index to Indian Wars Pension Files, 1892–1926 (T318).

Letters, Reports, Orders Relating to the Kearney Expedition, 1845 (T1115).

Spanish-American War (1898–99)

OTHER RECORDS

Card File, Spanish-American War Military Personnel.

Muster Rolls, Spanish-American War.

Records of Gen. Sherman Bell, 1897–1927.

Miscellaneous Records of the Office of the Adjutant General, 1882–1904.

Claims by Soldiers and the State of Colorado, Spanish-American War, 1900–04.

Spanish-American War Veterans Deceased.

World War I (1917–18)

World War I Veterans Deceased.

World War II (1941–45)

World War II Veterans Deceased. Some records of personnel who fought in twentieth-century wars may be restricted under the federal Privacy Act. For permission to access these records, contact the Colorado Department of Military Affairs Administration, 6848 Revere Parkway, Englewood, Colorado 80112.

PUBLISHED SOURCES—COLORADO

1861–65 (Civil War)

Colorado. Adjutant General's Office. Biennial Report. Denver: 1861–65. Contains rosters of troops.

Grand Army of the Republic. Department of Colorado and Wyoming. Official Roster, Department of Colorado and Wyoming. Grand Army of the Republic; Embracing a Digest of the

History, Organization and Growth of the Grand Army of the Republic, Ladies of the Grand Army, Women's Relief Corps and Loyal Legion. Edited by Col. William Edwin Moses. Denver (?): 1910.

Pompey, Sherman L. *Confederate Soldiers Buried in Colorado.* Independence, Calif.: Historical and Genealogical Publishing Co., 1965

_____. *Civil War Veteran Burials From California, Nevada, Oregon, and Washington Regiments Buried in Colorado.* Independence, Calif.: Historical and Genealogical Publishing Co., 1965.

Smith, George B., comp. *Official Army List of the Volunteers of Illinois, Indiana, Wisconsin, Minnesota, Michigan, Iowa, Missouri, Kansas, Nebraska, and Colorado.* Chicago: Tribune Book and Job Printing Establishment, 1862.

Whitford, William C. *Colorado Volunteers in the Civil War; the New Mexico Campaign in 1862.* Glorieta, N.M.: Rio Grande Press, 1971.

Connecticut

1614   Dutch explorer Adriaen Block entered Connecticut.

1633   Puritan settlers from Massachusetts began moving into Connecticut.

1637   English settlers vanquished the Pequot Indians. (See Pequot War in the appendix.)

1775-83   Connecticut soldiers fought on both sides in the American Revolution. (See American Revolution in the appendix.)

1788   Connecticut became one of the original thirteen states.

CONNECTICUT STATE LIBRARY

231 Capitol Avenue
Hartford, Connecticut 06106
(203) 566-3690 or 566-3692

Finding Aids

The *Connecticut Archives* collection comprises the records of the General Assembly to approximately 1820 and is grouped into broad topics. The series pertaining to military records include:

Militia:	1st series, 1678–1757
	2nd series, 1747–1786
	3rd series, 1728–1820
Revolutionary war:	1st series, 1763–1789
	2nd series, 1756–1856 (index slips only)
	3rd series, 1765–1820
War, colonial:	1st series, 1675–1775
	2nd series, 1689–1806
War of 1812:	1812–1819

A collection of bound index volumes to the Connecticut Archives is available for use in the History and Genealogy Reading Room. Documents are indexed by subject and by names of individuals, providing volume, document numbers, and page numbers. Although there is no bound index volume for revolutionary war, 2nd series, researchers may ask for the slip index covering this series. Researchers may retrieve microfilm copies of the documents from a cabinet adjacent to the bound indexes. The microfilm is arranged alphabetically by series title. The state library staff does not search or provide copies from microfilm records.

Record Groups

Finding aids for more recent archival records consist of a series of looseleaf notebooks housed near the History and Genealogy Unit's information desk. The most useful record groups for the military historian are RG 12, Records of the State Library's War Records Department; and RG 13, Records of the Military Department.

Most of the records in RG 13 refer to the period since 1820, with an emphasis on the Civil War. They are arranged (roughly) in chronological order. Records for the following military organizations are available. (The amounts held vary from unit to unit).

First through the Twenty-seventh Regiments, Infantry. (Records for some units are unprocessed or have been lost.)

First and Second Regiments, Heavy Artillery.

First Regiment, Cavalry.

Second Brigade.

Third Brigade, Signal Corps.

Independent Battalion ("Black Battalion").

Governor's Foot Guard, First Company (available only with permission of the Foot Guard).

RG 12 pertains primarily to twentieth century military activities, but it includes some lists of Connecticut military personnel for the period 1776 through 1946.

This repository has no National Archives microfilm.

Records

General

Discharges and Disapproved Applications for Admission, Fitch's Home (soldiers' home), 1891-95 (RG 13:79).

Miscellaneous Deceased Veterans' File Folders, 1887-1935 (RG 13:79).

List of Dishonorable Discharges, Soldiers' Home, Noroton, Connecticut, 1887-93 (RG 13:72).

List of Connecticut Soldiers at Dayton, Ohio, National Home for Disabled Volunteer Soldiers, 1867-80 (RG 13:66).

Petitions (militia), 1815-58 (RG 13:4). These pertain to establishment of militia units.

Returns and Reports (militia), 1810-61 (RG 13:8).

Lists of Connecticut Members of the Armed Forces, 1776-1946 (RG 12:9). Compiled from various sources, with extracts from the 1840 census of revolutionary war and military service pensioners. Itemized descriptions of the lists are available.

Discharge Certificates, 1898-1956 (RG 13:44). Photostatic copies of discharge certificates or related documents for Connecticut residents. These are grouped by war and then alphabetically by name of individual: World War I (1911-40); army, navy (except World War I); Connecticut National Guard, 1913; Home Guard, 1917-18; Spanish-American War, 1898-99; World War II; post-World War II (1947-55); post-Korean War (1952-56).

Veterans' Deaths Index. A card index prepared by the "Veterans' Grave Survey" project. Although not complete, it includes the names of many deceased veterans from the American Revolution through the Vietnam era. The cards are arranged into two groups: those for veterans buried in Connecticut and those buried elsewhere. They provide the following information: name, war, date of death, place of death, place of burial, age, branch of service, and, in some cases, the name of the unit.

Colonial Wars (pre-1775)

The index volumes to *Connecticut Archives: War, Colonial*, provide access by name of person, place, and subject. Selected topics include:

French and Indian Wars, 1753-64 (by campaign). Militia muster rolls, accounts, and reports

King Philip's War, 1675-76

King Williams' War, 1689-97

Mohawk Indians

Pensions and Relief for Disabled

Prisoners: American, French, Indian

Private Claims and Petitions

Surgeons

Sutlers

War With Spain, 1749-42 (War of Jenkins' Ear)

American Revolution (1775-83)

The index volumes to *Connecticut Archives: Revolutionary War*, series I and series III, and the slip index to series II provide access by name of person, place, and subject. Note that, because the slips on which series II is indexed are fragile, they may be used only with the permission and assistance of the History and Genealogy Unit's librarians. Selected topics include:

Commissions

Confiscated Estates (by name of those who owned the estates)

Continental Army (arranged by unit and year)

Investigations of Conduct

Militia (by name of unit and years)

Prisoners: American, British

Private Claims and Petitions

State Regiments (by name of unit)

Taxation (pertaining to relief for those who suffered damages)

War of 1812 (1812-15)

The index volumes to *Connecticut Archives: War of 1812* provide access by person, place, and subject. Selected topics include:

> Militia, National Service
>
> Private Claims and Petitions

Post-War of 1812 (1816-1860)

RG 13 includes the following selected materials:

U.S. Army Muster Rolls and Inspection Reports, 1807-08 (RG 13:7).

Lists of Men Exempt From Military Service, March-May 1815 (RG 13:2).

Resignations and Discharges, 1818-39 (RG 13:5).

Returns and Reports, 1810-61 (RG 13:8).

Town Clerks' Enrollment Reports, Listing Those Eligible for Service or Exempt, 1850-63 (RG 13:11).

List of Resignations and Appointments of General and Field Officers, 1825 (RG 13:17).

Resignations of Field Officers, 1831 (RG 13:18).

Proceedings of Courts-martial and Related Papers, 1810-60 (RG 13:22).

Civil War–Union (1861-65)

Incoming Letters and Orders, 1861-65 (RG 13:24).

Reports of Deaths, Discharges, and Desertion in the Connecticut Volunteer Force, 1862-66 (RG 13:28).

Reports of Operations, Engagements, and Casualties, July 1861-March 1866 (RG 13:29).

List of Deceased Connecticut Volunteers During the War, 1861-66 (RG 13:30).

Records of the Connecticut Volunteer Regiments, 1861-65 (RG 13:31). A twenty-seven-volume collection containing unit histories and numerical lists of men in each regiment. Vol. 28 is an index.

Muster Rolls, Descriptive Lists, Payrolls, and Related Papers, 1861-65 (RG 13:32).

Selectmen's Returns of Volunteers and Men Drafted, by Town, 1862-64 (RG 13:33).

Returns of Enrolled Militia, by Town, 1861-63 (RG 13:35).

Connecticut Men in Regiments of Other States (RG 13:36).

Nominations of Officers, 1861-62 (RG 13:37).

Notices of Discharge or Resignation, Acceptances of Appointment, 1861-63 (RG 13:42).

Contracts Between Substitutes and Drafted Men, 1862 (RG 13:43).

Stidham's List of Officers and Men in the U.S. Navy, 1861-65 (RG 13:44).

Claims for "additional bounty," 1867-77 (RG 13:50).

Record of "additional wounds," 1861-65 (RG 13:54).

Descriptive Papers, 1886-88. Requests for information on Civil War service (RG 13:56).

List of Enlisted Soldiers, 1863-65 (RG 13:67). Includes name, unit, date of enlistment, and town of residence; arranged alphabetically.

Grand Army of the Republic Records: Lists of Members, Courts-martial (RG 113).

National Guard, Colored Volunteer Regiments: Enlistment Papers, Muster Rolls, Recruits of the Twenty-ninth, Thirtieth, and Thirty-first Regiments, Various Companies, 1863-64 (RG 13:169a). Alphabetical lists of soldiers, recruits and muster rolls by regiment and company

Chronological List of Documents Pertaining to the Civil War. Miscellaneous information, 1861-March 1866 (RG 13:29).

The following materials may also be of interest to researchers:

Charles R. Hale Collection of Connecticut Cemetery Inscriptions (RG 72:1). The original slip index and volumes comprising the Hale Collection are at the state library, but these have been microfilmed by the Genealogical Society of Utah and are available through LDS Family History Centers.

Civil War Collection (PG 80). Includes 450 photographs, prints, and glass negatives of battle sites at Antietam and Gettysburg, campsites and forts, monuments, the South, Connecticut soldiers, Andersonville and Libby Prisons, and portraits of military officers and noted people of the period.

Brady Collection of Civil War Photographs, 1861-65 (PG 85). Includes approximately 7,500 photographs and 134 lantern slides by noted Civil War photographer Mathew B. Brady.

Godard Collection (PG 385). Includes lantern slides of the Civil War.

Connecticut Military Portraits, ca. 1860-1945 (PG 570). Includes individual portraits of Civil War officers, group portraits of Civil War soldiers, and other Civil War portraits.

Daguerreotypes, Tintypes, and Ambrotypes, ca. 1850-1882 (PG 860). Includes some portraits of Civil War soldiers.

Post-Civil War Period (1866-97)

Record of Pension Vouchers. List of those to whom payments were made for U.S. pensions, 1877-1923 (RG 13:58).

Photographs of National Guardsmen at Camp Cooke, Niantic, 1897 (RG 13:65).

Record of Commissions Issued, 1861-73 (RG 13:69).

Records of Naval Provisions and Stores, 1864-74 (RG 13:80). Includes some personnel lists; no index.

Spanish-American War (1898-99)

Lists of Spanish-American War Dead, 1898-1902 (RG 12:21). Two card files arranged alphabetically by town.

Also see the collections described above under Records–General for information on military discharge certificates.

World War I (1917-18)

Father Dinan's Papers on Deaths in Field and Base Hospitals, 1917-19 (RG 12:10).

Record of Service Certificates Issued, 1919-44, to Connecticut Men Who Served in World War I (RG 12:17). Five volumes with name, rank, town (by code number), nationality, dates of service, whether died of disease or killed in action, and overseas service (if applicable); indexed.

Card File of Recipients of World War I Distinguished Service Cross, 1918 (RG 12:21a).

Records of Memorial Certificates Issued to Next of Kin of Connecticut Men Who Died in Service During World War I (RG 12:22).

World War I Roll of Honor, 1917-ca. 1940 (RG 12:23). Compiled by town officials with photographs of town plaques or monuments that contain lists of those who died in service; arranged alphabetically by town, followed by names of American Red Cross workers.

Files of Selective Service Department, Office of the Governor, 1917-19 (RG 12:25). Composed mostly of correspondence and reports.

Signature Slips, Lists of Inductees, Draft Registration Cards, and Senatorial District Lists of Men Subject to Draft Calls (RG 12:27). Arranged by selected Connecticut towns.

Casualty Lists, 1917-19 (RG 12:31). A card file of Connecticut men who were killed, injured, died of disease, or classified as missing.

Papers Concerning the Memorial to Hartford Men Who Died in World War I (RG 12:36).

Army Records of the Twenty-sixth Division, 1917-19 (RG 12:40). With lists of names and historical documents.

Military Census, 1919-20 (RG 29). Includes a manpower survey of all male inhabitants over the age of sixteen (taken in 1917-18). Approximately 502,540 sheets were completed and arranged in numerical order. An index card was prepared for each sheet and arranged under each town alphabetically by surname. Each card includes the name, address, and form number. The census was microfilmed by the Genealogical Society of Utah. The Connecticut State Library regards its copy of the microfilm as the official record; therefore, microfilm is retrieved following the same procedures as other archival materials. The library's copies are not available through inter-library loan, but microfilm may be obtained through LDS Family History Centers.

Also see the collections described above under Records—General for information on military discharge certificates.

World War II (1941-45)

Lists of World War II and Korean War Dead Returned on Funeral Ships (RG 12:8).

Gold Star Lists, 1940-45 (RG 12:45). Connecticut men who died in World War II. These records consist of two groups, each alphabetically listed by town: three binders showing name, place and date of death, and name and address of next of kin; and cards showing miscellaneous data.

Card File of West Haven Servicemen, World War II (RG 12:46). Arranged alphabetically.

Service Record Summaries for Citizens of Some Connecticut Towns, World War II (RG 12:60).

World War II Honor Roll, 1945-46 (RG 12:62). Lists of those who died, with photographs of town plaques and tablets.

List of State Employees in Military Service, 1940-45 (RG 12:63).

List of Nurses, 1940-45 (?) (RG 12:64).

Also see the collections described above under Records—General for information on military discharge certificates.

Korean War (1950-53)

Card Lists of Korean War Casualties, 1950-53 (RG 12:48). Includes dead, wounded, injured, prisoners of war, etc., alphabetically by name and town.

Lists of World War II and Korean War Dead Returned on Funeral Ships (RG 12:8).

Also see the collections described above under Records—General for information on military discharge certificates.

Manuscript Collections

A card file in the History and Genealogy Reading Room provides access to the library's manuscript collections, some of which pertain to military matters. Selected subject headings include:

Andersonville, Georgia, Military Prison (Civil War)

Armstrong, H.A. (collection of French and Indian War material)

Canadian Expedition, 1746

Cemeteries

Commissions (military), various time periods

Connecticut artillery, infantry, militia, National Guard

Continental Army

DAR, Connecticut

European War (1914-18), registers, lists

Grand Army of the Republic, Connecticut Department (lists of members, obituaries, burials in Willimantic Cemetery)

Judd, Edwin D. Collection (Civil War rolls and papers, etc.)

List of persons killed in the Wyoming Battle and Massacre, 3 July 1778

Military (various subjects)

Patriotic societies

Pensions, military, Connecticut and United States

Preston, Edward V. Collection (Civil War rolls and papers)

Soldiers, Connecticut

United States Army

U.S. Army, Continental

U.S. Bureau of Pensions

U.S. History—Civil War (adjutant general, Connecticut cavalry, Connecticut infantry (Sixteenth Regiment), letters/diaries, regimental histories, registers and lists, societies).

U.S. History–French and Indian War, 1755–1763

U.S. History–King Philip's War, 1675–1676

U.S. History–Queen Anne's War, 1702–1713

U.S. History–Revolution (rolls and lists, letters/diaries, journals, regimental histories, registers, and lists)

U.S. History–War of 1812

U.S. History–War of 1898 (Spanish-American War)

U.S. History–War of 1845 (War with Mexico)

United States Navy

Veterans, Connecticut–societies

Veterans, Connecticut–portraits, 1865–1945

War with Spain, 1739–41 (list of colonists sent to Havana)

Whitney, George Q., Collection (Sixteenth Connecticut Volunteers)

Women's naval service

World War II, 1939–45

CONNECTICUT HISTORICAL SOCIETY

One Elizabeth Street (at Asylum Avenue)
Hartford, Connecticut 06105
(203) 236-5621

Records

Colonial Wars (pre-American Revolution)

Letters and Documents on Two Reels of Microfilm:

Reel 1:   Letters, 1744–62.
Reel 2:   Documents, 1709–63.

American Revolution (1775–83)

NATIONAL ARCHIVES MICROFILM

Index to Compiled Service Records of Revolutionary War Soldiers Who Served With the American Army in Connecticut Military Organizations (M920).

CONNECTICUT MICROFILM

American Revolution Collection. Includes letters, journals, orderly books, accounts, and muster rolls, 1765–1844. The seven reels in this microfilmed collection are as follows:

Reel 1:   Documents; commissary and quartermaster records.

Reel 2:   Lexington alarm list; muster rolls and payrolls; maps and miscellaneous.

Reels 3–6: Orderly books.

Reel 7:   Connecticut regiments, accounts, clothing accounts, muster rolls and payrolls, naval officers.

Manuscript Collections

A card index to the manuscript collections includes the following subject headings that may be helpful to the military records researcher.

American Revolution (account books, letters, journals, etc.)

Bounties. Military.

Bounty lands.

Civil War (diaries, letters)

Connecticut. Council of Safety.

Connecticut. Infantry (various regiments).

Connecticut. National Guard.

French and Indian Wars.

Logbooks.

Military land grants (Illinois, Iowa, and Wisconsin), 1838–58.

Militia.

Orderly books, 1757–1861.

Orderly books, British

Prisoners of war.

U.S. History–colonial period. Ca. 1600–1775.

U.S. History–French and Indian War, 1755–63

U.S. History–Revolution, 1775–83.

U.S. History–War of 1812

U.S. History–1815–1861. Connecticut Infantry, Twenty-second Regiment. Orderly book, 1833–37.

U.S. History–War with Mexico, 1845–48.

U.S. History–Civil War, 1861–65.

War of 1812.

PUBLISHED SOURCES–CONNECTICUT

Pre-1775 (colonial wars)

Andrews, Frank DeWette. *Connecticut Soldiers in the French and Indian War.* Vineland, N.J.: the author, 1923.

Buckingham, Thomas, ed. *Roll and Journal of Connecticut Service in Queen Anne's War, 1710–1711.* New Haven: Tuttle, Morehouse & Taylor Press, 1916. Reprint of The Private Journals Kept by John Birmingham of the Expedition Against Canada in the Years 1710 & 1711. New York: Wilder & Campbell, 1825. Contains muster rolls and payrolls.

Connecticut. Adjutant General's Office. *Report.* New Haven: 1939. "List of Connecticut Men Who Served in the Pequot War . . ." Includes name, town from which enlisted, and date and place of death.

Connecticut Historical Society, Hartford. *Rolls of Connecticut Men in the French and Indian Wars, 1755–1762. . . .* 2 vols. Connecticut Historical Society Collections, vols. 9–10. Hartford: the society, 1903–05.

Hedden, James S., comp. *Colonial Wars of America: A Synopsis of Military and Civil Records of Some of the New Haven Men Originally Buried on New Haven Green, Whose Grave Stones Were Later Either Installed in the Crypt of Center Church, or Removed to Grove Street Cemetery.* New Haven: 1944.

_____ . *Roster of Graves of or Monuments to Patriots of 1775–1783, and of Soldiers of Colonial Wars in and Adjacent to New Haven County, Connecticut.* 4 vols. New Haven: Gen. David Humphreys Branch, No. 1, Connecticut Society, Sons of the American Revolution, 1931–34.

Jacobus, Donald L. *List of Officials, Civil, Military and Ecclesiastical of Connecticut Colony: From March 1636 Through 11 October 1677, and of New Haven Colony Throughout its Separate Existence, Also Soldiers in the Pequot War Who Then or Subsequently Resided Within the Present Bounds of Connecticut.* New Haven: R.M. Hooker, 1935.

Pepperrell, William, Sir. *Connecticut Officers at Louisbourg . . . .* Hartford: 1860.

Shepard, James. *Connecticut Soldiers in the Pequot War of 1637, With Proof of Service, a Brief Record for Identification, and References to Various Publications in Which Further Data May Be Found.* Meriden: Journal Publishing Co., 1913. Includes name, rank, place from which enlisted, place of residence, date of death and source, number of children.

1775–83 (American Revolution)

Callahan, North. *Connecticut's Revolutionary War Leaders.* Connecticut Bicentennial Series, vol. 3. Chester: Pequot Press, 1973.

Collier, Thomas S. *Revolutionary Privateers of Connecticut, With an Account of the State Cruisers, and a Short History of the Continental Naval Vessels Built in the State, and Lists of Officers and Crews.* Records and Papers of the New London County Historical Society, vol. 1, pt. 4. New London: the society, 1892.

Connecticut. Adjutant General's Office. *Record of Service of Connecticut Men in the . . . I. War of the Revolution. II. War of 1812. III. Mexican War.* 3 vols. Hartford: Case, Lockwood & Brainard, 1889.

Connecticut Historical Society. *Lists and Returns of Connecticut Men in the Revolution, 1775–1783.* Edited by Albert C. Bates. Collections of the Connecticut Historical Society, vols. 8, 12. Hartford: the society, 1901–09.

_____ . *Orderly Book and Journals Kept by Connecticut Men While Taking Part in the American Revolution, 1775–1779.* Hartford: the society, 1899.

_____ . *Rolls and Lists of Connecticut Men in the Revolution, 1775–1783.* Hartford: the society, 1901.

Connecticut. Militia. Governor's Horse Guards, First Company. *Two Hundred Years: the First Company Governor's Horse Guards, 1778–1978.* Compiled by Clyde H. Bassett. Avon: the guards, 1978. A souvenir book.

Connecticut Revolutionary Pensioners. NSDAR 21st Annual Report, 1917–18. Reprint. Baltimore: Genealogical Publishing Co., 1982. Some ten thousand names of pensioners from documents in the old Pension Office, Washington, D.C.; place of residence, age, some data regarding service and dates of death.

Johnston, Henry P. *Yale and Her Honor-roll in the American Revolution, 1775–1783: Including Original Letters, Record of Service, and Biographical Sketches.* New York: G.P. Putnam, 1888.

Mather, Frederic G. *The Refugees of 1776 From Long Island to Connecticut.* Albany, N.Y.: J.B. Lyon Co., 1913. Reprint. Baltimore: Genealogical Publishing Co., 1972. Approximately 1,300 biographical sketches; also lists Long Island refugees who served with the military in Connecticut.

Middlebrook, Louis F. *History of Maritime Connecticut During the American Revolution, 1775–1783.* 2 vols. Salem, Mass.: Essex Institute, 1925. Ships of the Connecticut Navy and crew lists. Privateers are listed in vol. 2.

Minority Military Service, Connecticut, 1775–1783. Washington, D.C.: NSDAR, 1988.

Nell, William C. *Services of Colored Americans in the Wars of 1776 and 1812.* Boston: 1851. Reprint. New York: AMS Press, 1976.

New London County Historical Society. *Records and Papers of the New London County Historical Society. . . .* 4 vols. in 3. New London: the society, 1894–1912.

Revolutionary Characters of New Haven . . . Also, List of Men So Far as They Are Known From the Territory Embraced in the Town of New Haven . . . Who Served in the Continental Army and Militia and on Continental and State Vessels and Privateers, and Those Who Rendered Other Patriotic Services During the War of the Revolution, and a Record of Known Casualties; Together With the Location of Known Graves in and About New Haven of Patriots of 1775–1783 and Catalogue of the Officers and Members of Gen. David Humphreys Branch Since Its Organization. New Haven: Gen. David Humphreys Branch No. 1, Connecticut Society, SAR, 1911. Contains approximately one thousand names.

Rogers, John E. *Intercity Bicentennial Booklet, 1776–1976.* West Hartford: University of Hartford, 1976. Contains names of black soldiers who served in the Fourth Regiment, Connecticut Line, as well as black soldiers from other states.

U.S. Pension Bureau. *Pension Records of the Revolutionary Soldiers From Connecticut.* Washington, D.C.: 1919.

Weed, Clara L. *List of Connecticut Revolutionary Soldiers Mentioned in Beckwith's Almanac, New Haven, 1850 to 1870 Inclusive: Also War of 1812; 1856 to 1889 Inclusive.* New Haven: 1927.

White, David O. *Connecticut's Black Soldiers, 1775–1783.* Connecticut Bicentennial Series, No. 4. Chester: Pequot Press, 1973. Lists 289 soldiers, towns from which enlisted, and dates of service; pensioners noted.

1784–1815 (War of 1812)

Connecticut. Adjutant General's Office. *Record of Service of Connecticut Men in the ... I. War of the Revolution. II. War of 1812. III. Mexican War.* Hartford: Case, Lockwood & Brainard, 1889.

_____. *Report.* New Haven: State Printers, 1819. State militia.

Connecticut. Quartermaster General's Office. *Report.* Norwich, Conn.: 1819. Militia.

Daughters of the American Revolution and Mildred R. Crankshaw. *Index to Connecticut Veterans War of 1812, by Towns and Cemeteries.* The society, 1964.

1816-60 (Indian Wars)

Connecticut. Adjutant General's Office. *Report.* New Haven: state printers, 1819. State militia.

1861-65 (Civil War)

Connecticut. Adjutant General's Office. *Catalogue of Connecticut Volunteer Organizations (Infantry, Cavalry and Artillery) in the Service of the United States 1861-65, With Additional Enlistments, Casualties, &c. &c.* Hartford: Brown & Gross, 1869.

_____. *Catalogue of the 14th, 15th, 16th, 17th, 18th, 19th, 20th, and 21st Regiments, and the Second Light Battery, Connecticut Volunteers for Three Years: and the 22d, 23d, 24th, 25th, 26th, 27th, and 28th Regiments, Connecticut Volunteers for Nine Months.* Hartford: Case, Lockwood & Co., 1862. Compiled from records in the Adjutant General's Office, 1862.

_____. *Record of Service of Connecticut Men in the Army and Navy of the United States During the War of the Rebellion.* Hartford: Case, Lockwood & Brainard Co., 1889.

_____. *Report Ending March 1870. Roll of Honor.* New Haven: 1870. Contains name, rank, regiment, company, and date of death of Civil War casualties.

Connecticut. Andersonville Monument Commission. *Dedication of the Monument at Andersonville, Georgia, October 23, 1907: in Memory of the Men of Connecticut Who Suffered in Southern Military Prisons, 1861-1865.* Hartford: the state, 1908. Includes name, unit, and date of death of Connecticut soldiers buried in Andersonville National Cemetery.

Croffut, William A., and John M. Morris. *The Military and Civil History of Connecticut During the War of 1861-65.* New York: Ledyard Bill, 1868. Includes Roll of Honor of Connecticut soldiers and names of those buried at Andersonville.

Pompey, Sherman L. *Civil War Veterans Buried in the Mid-West.* Clovis, Calif. (?): 1970- (?). 4 vols. (?). Vol. 1 lists Connecticut soldiers.

Weld, Stanley B. *Connecticut Physicians in the Civil War.* Hartford (?): Civil War Centennial Commission, 1963.

1866-1904 (Spanish-American War)

Connecticut. Adjutant General's Office. *Roster of Connecticut Volunteers Who Served in the War Between the United States and Spain, 1898-1899.* Hartford: Case, Lockwood & Brainard Co., 1899.

_____. *Record of Service of Connecticut Men in the Army, Navy and Marine Corps of the United States in the Spanish-American War, Philippine Insurrection and China Relief Expedition From April 21, 1898 to July 4, 1904.* Hartford: Case, Lockwood & Brainard Co., 1919.

1917-18 (World War I)

Connecticut. Adjutant General's Office. *Service Records: Connecticut Men and Women in the Armed Forces of the United States During World War I, 1917-1918.* Hartford: 1961 (?).

Delaware

1609	Dutch explorer Henry Hudson discovered Delaware Bay.
1631	Dutch settlers established a community near Lewes but were driven out by Indians.
1638	Swedish settlers governed Delaware as New Sweden from a capital at Wilmington.
1655	Dutch regained control of Delaware from the Swedes.
1664-82	Delaware became the property of the English Duke of York, with the exception of a brief return to Dutch control in 1673-74.
1682	Delaware became the "Three Lower Counties" of Pennsylvania.

1775	Delaware became independent from Pennsylvania.
1787	Delaware became the first state to ratify the new constitution.
1861-65	Although a slave state, Delaware remained loyal to the Union because of strong economic ties to the North.

. . . .

STATE ARCHIVES

Hall of Records
Dover, Delaware 19901
(302) 739-5318

Finding Aids

Guide to the Delaware State Archives. A notebook containing listings of state records arranged by record groups; includes titles and descriptions of records from state offices and categories, including the following:

> Veterans Military Pay Commission
> National Guard
> National Guard, Mexican Border Service
> National Guard, Spanish
> National Guard, World War I
> Military
> Adjutant General
> Selective Service Division
> Department of the Interior, Bureau of Pensions
> World War II

General Photo Collection. This finding aid is contained in a notebook. Under the category "Military" are listed photographs arranged by war and by military unit. Most of the photographs from World War II are in the Delaware in World War II photo collection.

Records

General

Governor's Papers. Militia lists of the 1820s.

Miscellaneous Records (rosters, muster rolls, correspondence, cash books, personal accounts, etc.), 1862-1923. Miscellaneous records not used in the publication *Delaware Archives, 1807-29*; includes returns of fines and fines remitted,

appointments and resignations of officers, payment vouchers, expense accounts, oaths of allegiance, certificates of service, and similar papers.

Records of Retired Officers, Delaware National Guard, 1879-1907. These give name, a brief history of past military duties, and date of resignation.

Descriptive Book, Delaware National Guard, 1847-48. Name; rank; age; physical description; place of birth; occupation; when, where, and by whom enlisted; length of enlistment; and amount of pay to National Guard members.

Enlistment and Descriptive Books, Delaware National Guard, 1894-1917. Include name, company, age, physical description, dates of enlistment and discharge, and station.

Muster Rolls, Delaware National Guard, 1887-92. Include name, rank, company, and date mustered in.

Records of Commissioned Officers, Delaware National Guard, 1876-1914. Include name, rank, appointments, resignations, and place and date of birth.

Roster of Commissioned Officers, Delaware National Guard, 1895-1901. Include name, rank, date of commission, residence, appointments, and date of resignation.

Records of Examinations By Examining Surgeons, 1905-30. Certificates for pensioners claiming an increase in pensions due to health problems. These contain the history of pension processing and physical descriptions of claimants.

Colonial Wars (pre-American Revolution)

See vol. 1 of *Delaware Archives* for the following and other documents relating to colonial wars.

King George's War, 1739-48. Militia rolls and other papers.

French and Indian War, 1754-63. Various regimental papers.

American Revolution (1775-83)

NATIONAL ARCHIVES MICROFILM

Compiled Service Records of Soldiers Who Served in the American Army During the Revolutionary War (M8819—reels 380-395 pertain to Delaware).

OTHER RECORDS

See vols. 1-3 of *Delaware Archives* for the following and other documents relating to the American Revolution.

Card Index of Those Who Signed an Oath of Allegiance. Name, date, and source reference.

Pension Rolls and Correspondence. This large, bound, indexed volume was discovered in 1915 in the basement of the Farmer's State Bank in Wilmington, Delaware. It contains pension records and related papers.

Miscellaneous Records. These pertain primarily to the American Revolution through the time of the War of 1812; include payrolls, payment certificates, petitions for pensions, commissions of officers, and similar papers. A few papers refer to the period ending 1921.

Manuscripts: Lists of Riflemen, Pension Requests and Correspondence, and Persons Accused Of Treason. These are either original papers or photostats of papers held by the Delaware Historical Society, other historical societies, or the National Archives.

Unpublished Revolutionary War Papers, Vol. 6. A microfilm copy.

War of 1812 (1812-15)

See vols. 4-5 of *Delaware Archives* for the following and other documents relating to the War of 1812. See above for miscellaneous records and manuscripts pertaining to both the American Revolution and the War of 1812.

Miscellaneous Militia Records, 1798-1915. These are on microfilm.

Civil War—Union (1861-65)

NATIONAL ARCHIVES MICROFILM

Provost Marshal's File of Papers—Two or More Citizens (M416—Delaware counties only).

OTHER RECORDS

Delaware Soldiers in the Civil War. A card index: name, enlistment date and place, term of service, rank, muster-in date and place, by whom mustered in, wounds received, and place and date of discharge; also available on microfilm.

Delaware National Guard Personnel in the Civil War. Microfilm.

Register of Furloughs, 1864-65. Includes name, length of leave, dates, company, and regiment.

Regimental Book. Descriptive book (records of the state adjutant general); microfilm.

Lists of Confederate Prisoners at Fort Delaware (published pamphlet).

Spanish-American War (1898-99)

Delaware Soldiers in the Spanish-American War. A card index: name, residence, enlistment date and place, term of service, muster-in date and place, by whom mustered in, unit, and rank.

Muster-in Rolls, 1898. Enlistees in Delaware infantry; includes name, rank, age, physical description, marital status, name of parent or guardian if not married, regiment, dates of muster, and length of term; contains signatures of enlistees.

Muster-out Rolls, With Pay Account. Includes name, rank, enlistment place and date, place of residence at discharge, date discharged, and pay records; contains signature of person discharged.

Mexican Border Service (1916)

Delaware Soldiers in the Mexican Border Service. A card index: name, residence, enlistment date, unit, date and place of birth (or age), rank, muster-in date and place, and muster-out date and place.

Muster-in Roll, 1916. Includes name, date of muster-in, age, physical description, marital status, residence, name of spouse or next of kin, and address.

Muster-out Roll, 1916-17. Includes name and rank, company, term of service, and date of enlistment.

World War I (1917-18)

Delaware Soldiers and Sailors in World War I. A card index: name, rank, company, term of service, and dates of enlistment and muster.

Muster-in Roll, First Delaware Infantry. Includes name, rank, company, term of service, and dates of enlistment and muster.

Delaware Regiment Drafted Into Federal Service, 1917. Includes name of inductee, rank, date of enlistment, date of drafting, company, and date of discharge.

Inductees, 1917-19. Four volumes showing draft lottery order number; includes name of inductee, reporting date, date sent to camp, occupation, and draft classification.

Inductions for Military Service. Records of inductions showing local draft board, date of enlistment, and camp.

War Records, World War I. Four volumes containing military history of Delaware soldiers; name and address, identification number, date and place of birth, parents' names and addresses, engagements and battles, citations or decorations, particulars of death (if applicable), overseas service, discharge place and date, and vital statistics concerning wife and children (if any); arranged alphabetically by name.

Naval Service Records, 1917-19. Statements of service of personnel in naval service; name, age, rank, place and date of enlistment, home address, dates of service, date and place of discharge. Date of death and place of burial appear on most of the cards.

Miscellaneous Records, World War I Military Personnel. Included are an induction list; tombstone information; and lists of deceased, wounded, prisoners of war, and those missing in action; name, age, rank, residence, date of birth, names and residence of parents, and date of enlistment; order of arrangement not apparent; not indexed.

Passenger Lists of Soldiers Returning From Overseas, 1919. Names of Fifty-ninth Pioneer Infantry (formerly the First Delaware Infantry) personnel returning from overseas duty. Name and rank, regiment, name and address of spouse (or next of kin), name of vessel, port of sailing, date of sailing, port of arrival, and date of arrival.

Deceased Delaware Servicemen, 1918-21. Service records of personnel killed in action or as a result of wounds sustained in World War I; name; race; residence; place and date of birth; date entered service; military history; date, place and cause of death; and name and address of next of kin.

World War II (1941-45)

Delaware Soldiers and Sailors in World War II. A card index of military personnel, 1944-46; name, identification number, rank, date of birth, date of enlistment, and camp.

Enlistment Cards, 1941-46. Registration cards for those who enlisted at the Selective Service Board; name, rank, race, date entered service, branch of service, identification number, local board, and signature of enlistee.

Memorial Volumes, 1942-45. Records of Delaware military personnel killed during World War II; name; rank; branch of service; address; names of parents or spouse; date, place and cause of death; years of service; and medals and decorations; arranged alphabetically.

News Releases, 1946-47. Biographical press releases pertaining to ware citizens who served during World War II, as published in the *News Journal*. In some instances the items are accompanied by photographs. The photographs are available in this archives' World War II photograph collection.

World War II Photograph Collection, 1940-46. Primarily photographs used in the publication *Delaware's Role in World War II*, a book compiled by the archives.

Cash Bonus Claims Paid, 1949-51. Approved applications of Delaware veterans of World War II and their beneficiaries. The papers also include a copy of the separation/discharge papers. Much family and military history information is included; arranged by file number. A separate card file is arranged alphabetically by name of veteran. Access is restricted.

Delaware in World War II Photograph Collection, 1938-1945. Documents Delaware's National Guard servicemen, bases, and civilian war efforts.

Check Disbursal Sheets, 1949-51. Record of cash bonuses paid to Delaware veterans of World War II and their beneficiaries. These give name and address of veteran, amount paid, and related information.

Index to Paid and Rejected Claims for Bonuses for World War II Veterans, 1955-58. Includes papers pertaining to those who failed to apply on time in 1951 and who were again granted an opportunity in 1955. The files cited in the index provide much family and military history, but are restricted.

Applications for World War II Bonus Payments Denied by the Veterans Military Pay Commission, 1949-51. Contains the original application, copy of separation/discharge papers, and related information. A card catalog index is available. Access is restricted.

Korean War (1950-53)

Records of Cash Bonuses Paid to Delaware Veterans of World War II and the Korean War and Their Beneficiaries, 1961-62. Includes name and address of veteran, amount paid, and related information.

Cash Bonus Claims Paid, Delaware Veterans Who Served in the Korean War or Their Beneficiaries, 1955-58. Also contains applications for bonuses and copies of separation/discharge papers. These provide much family and military history. This is a separate card file, showing names of those paid or rejected; arranged alphabetically by name of veteran. Access is restricted.

Cash Bonus Claims Rejected, 1955-58. Applications for disapproved Korean War service bonuses. They contain the bonus application and a copy of the separation papers; also much family and military information. This is a separate card index arranged alphabetically by name of veteran. Access is restricted.

Vietnam War (1963-75)

Cash Bonus Claims Paid, 1968-76. Includes application for bonus and copy of separation/discharge papers. These give considerable family and military information. This is a separate card file arranged alphabetically by name of veteran. The cards show name and address of claimant and related information. Access is restricted.

HISTORICAL SOCIETY OF DELAWARE

505 Market Street Mall
Wilmington, Delaware 19801
(302) 655-7161

Finding Aid

Civil War Resources at the Historical Society of Delaware. This booklet lists books, microfilm, serials, newspapers, maps, photographs and prints, manuscripts, and museum objects pertaining to the Civil War.

Records

Civil War–Union (1861-65)

Photograph Collection. Includes photos and prints of various battle sites, Fort Delaware and other forts, members of various Delaware regiments, and miscellaneous officers and soldiers in the Civil War.

List of Able-bodied White Male Citizens of Lewes and Rehoboth, 1862.

Bounties and Pensions Papers, 1866-1918.

Records Pertaining to the First, Second, Fourth, Eighth, and Ninth regiments, Delaware Volunteer Infantry, and the National Guard of Delaware. Enrollment lists, bounty and pension lists, muster rolls, and miscellaneous documents.

Records Pertaining to the U.S. Army (some Delawareunits only) and the Medical Department.

Wilmington City Guard Muster Roll.

Commissions to Officers, 1861–66. Arranged alphabetically by surname.

Miscellaneous Manuscript And Personal Papers. (See the finding aid *Civil War Resources at the Historical Society of Delaware* for the names of donors.)

Civil War Casualties Lists. An incomplete list of names and locations of graves of Delaware casualties of the Civil War.

Delaware State Association for the Relief of Sick and Wounded Soldiers, 1862–65.

Grand Army of the Republic, 1880–1930.

Pension Board. Names of applicants from Delaware for Civil War pensions; list regiment and result of application.

Manuscript Collections

A card index indicates the presence of papers relating to the following subjects.

Revolutionary War (part of the Thomas Rodney Collection). This collection consists primarily of correspondence.

War of 1812 (correspondence, reports, and a few lists of persons).

PUBLISHED SOURCES—DELAWARE

General

Delaware. Public Archives Commission. *Delaware Archives.* 5 vols. Wilmington: Delaware Public Archives Commission, 1911–19. Reprint. New York: AMS Press, 1974. Includes rolls for King George's War, French and Indian War, War of 1812, etc.

Pre-1775 (colonial wars)

De Valinger, Leon. *Colonial Military Organization in Delaware, 1638–1776.* Wilmington: Delaware Tercentenary Committee, 1938. Payroll of 1746–47; officers, 1758.

1775-83 (American Revolution)

Bellas, Henry H. *A History of the Delaware State Society of the Cincinnati From its Organization to the Present Time; to Which is Appended a Brief Account of the Delaware Regiments in the*

War of the Revolution, Also Personal Memoirs of the officers, Rolls of Same. Wilmington: Historical Society of Delaware, 1895.

Clark, Raymond B. *Index to Delawareans in the Index of Revolutionary War Pension Application.* Arlington, Va.: R. B. Clark, 1982. Includes more than 430 names.

Gooch, Eleanor B. "Delaware Signers of the Oaths of Allegiance." *National Historical Magazine* 75 (1941) and 76 (1942).

Whiteley, William Gustavus. *The Revolutionary Soldiers of Delaware.* Wilmington: Historical Society of Delaware, 1896.

1861-66 (Civil War)

Pompey, Sherman L. *Civil War Veterans Buried in the Mid-West.* Clovis, Calif. (?): 1970– (?). 4 vols. (?). Vol. 2 covers Delaware.

Scharf, John Thomas. *History of Delaware, 1609–1888.* Port Washington, N.Y.: Kennikat Press, 1972. Appendix "Roster of Delaware Volunteers in the War of the Rebellion" appears in vol. 1, pages 1–33.

District of Columbia

1790   Congress combined territory from Maryland and Virginia to create the District of Columbia as the designated seat of the federal government.

1800   The federal government moved to the District of Columbia from Philadelphia.

1814   British troops entered the nation's capital during the War of 1812, destroying the capitol building and the White House. (See War of 1812 in the appendix.)

1846   The territory taken from Virginia for the District of Columbia was returned to that state.

1861   The nation's capital was imperiled by Confederate forces after they routed Union troops at the nearby Battle of Bull Run. (See American Civil War in the appendix.)

1871   The city of Washington was incorporated as a municipal entity within the District of Columbia.

1894   During the depression that followed the Panic of 1893, seventeen separate "armies" of men marched on the nation's capital seeking relief;

approximately 1,200 actually arrived, but they were dispersed with little violence.

1932   A "Bonus Army" of disgruntled World War I veterans seeking relief from the ravages of the Great Depression marched on the capital; they were dispersed by federal troops under Gen. Douglas MacArthur.

. . . .

PUBLISHED SOURCES—DISTRICT OF COLUMBIA

1775-83 (American Revolution)

Ely, Selden M. "The District of Columbia in the American Revolution and Patriots of the Revolutionary Period Who are Interred in the District or in Arlington." *Records of the Columbia Historical Society*, vol. 21. Washington, D.C.: the society, 1918.

Proctor, John Clagett. *Washington, Past and Present: A History.* New York: Lewis Historical Publishing Co., 1930.

1861-66 (Civil War)

Military Order of the Loyal Legion of the United States (MOL-LUS), District of Columbia Commandery. *Register of the Commandery of the District of Columbia From February 1, 1882. . . .* Washington, D.C. (?): 1910 (?).

_____. *Register . . . From February 1, 1882 (Date of Institution)* to May 31, 1891. Washington, D.C. (?): 1891 (?). Lists name and rank of active and retired members (U.S. Army, U.S. Navy, and U.S. Volunteers).

_____. *Register . . . From February 1, 1882 to June 30, 1889.* Washington, D.C. (?): 1889 (?).

Sluby, Paul E., comp. *Civil War Cemeteries of the District of Columbia Metropolitan Area.* Washington, D.C.: Columbian Harmony Society, 1982.

Florida

1513   Spanish explorer Juan Ponce de Leon discovered Florida.

1564   French Huguenots established a colony on the St. Johns River; the colonists were later massacred by the Spanish.

1565   The Spanish established a community at St. Augustine, the first permanent European colony in the present-day United States.

1702   A force of Carolinians attacked the Spanish in Florida during Queen Anne's War. (See Queen Anne's War in the appendix.)

1740   An attack from Georgia on the Spanish fort at St. Augustine failed during the War of Jenkins's Ear. (See War of Jenkins's Ear in the appendix.)

1763   By the Treaty of Paris which ended the French and Indian War, Spain ceded Florida to the English. (See French and Indian War in the appendix.)

1783   Great Britain ceded Florida to Spain in exchange for the Bahamas.

1821   The United States acquired Florida through the Adams-Onis Transcontinental Treaty with Spain; Florida became a territory.

1835-42   The Seminole Wars occurred between the U.S. Army and the Seminole Indians, resulting in removal of the Indians. (See Seminole Wars in the appendix.)

1845   Florida became a state.

1861   Florida seceded from the Union.

1864   Confederate forces defeated federal troops at the Battle of Olustee, one of the few significant Civil War battles in Florida. (See American Civil War in the appendix.)

1868   Florida was readmitted to statehood.

FLORIDA STATE ARCHIVES

R. A. Gray Building
500 South Bronough Street
Tallahassee, Florida 32399-0250
(904) 487-2073

Finding Aids

The Florida State Archives is currently in the process of placing lists of its holdings in an electronic data base. When this project is complete, a terminal will be available in the reference room for public use. Meanwhile, the following finding aids are available.

Guide to the Records of the Florida State Archives, 1988. This guide includes lists under the following headings: State Government Records, Local Government Records, and Manuscript Collections. An automated system is also available for record searches.

Five separate volumes, with more being prepared, list titles and descriptions of the manuscript collection, including the following examples.

> Blanding, Albert H.–Civil War diary
> Frier, Joshua H.–Civil War diary
> Jesup, Thomas S.–Second Seminole War diary
> Matthews Family–Civil War letters
> McGriff, Patrick–Civil War letters
> Peck, Albert W.–Civil War journal
> Scott, George W.–Civil War journal
> Stockton, William–Civil War letters

Finding Aids for Record Groups

RG 101–Territorial and State Governors, 1820–1929. Describes material relating to appointments of military officers and information pertaining to military affairs.

RG 197–Department of Military Affairs. The holdings in this group are listed by series number, with descriptive inventories for each series.

Special Archives Publications. A series of approximately one hundred fascicles of newly discovered original documents transferred to the state archives from the Florida Department of Military Affairs, Historical Services Division, State Arsenal, P.O. Box 1008, St. Augustine, Florida 32085. A complete list of titles published by that division is available at the St. Augustine address. The state archives has only a portion of this series, but the Documents Section of the state library (located in the same building) has the complete series.

Microfilm Publications. This is a notebook that lists microfilm copies of documents pertaining to Florida's territorial period and to some of the wars in which Florida participated. Microfilm originating at the National Archives is not included. The film is designated by serial number, and a descriptive inventory of each reel is included. Subjects include Indian Wars, Mexican War, Civil War, Spanish-American War, and World War I. These microfilmed records may also be searched through the automated system.

Records

General

Muster Rolls and Supporting Documents, 1870–1918–Militia. In 1885 the term "militia" was changed to "Florida state troops," which in 1918 became "National Guard." Arranged by unit, these muster rolls list personnel assigned to the units. Unit rosters are also available.

Annual Militia Returns, 1875–1912. These include names of officers, and some are "statistical strength reports" arranged by unit.

Florida Naval Militia Administrative Files, 1897–1941. These documents, some of which are muster rolls, cover three distinct periods: 1897 through 1903, 1911 through 1917, and 1934 through 1941. Personnel in these naval units were not part of the U.S. Navy but were part of the Florida state units stationed at Jacksonville or Tampa, where their mission was to defend the state's coastline. Many, however, served under federal control during the Spanish-American War.

Florida National Guard Administrative Files, 1912–63. These documents are primarily historical in nature and contain few names. However, there are payrolls for 1921–1933 (series 1145) which do provide names of national guardsmen. A descriptive inventory lists the unit designations. See also Unit Location Historical Card Files, 1890s–1960s.

Militia Photographs, 1900–50. Group photographs of militia units, predominantly of the 1920s and 1930s. Several depict the Second Florida Regiment in the 1916 Mexican Punitive Expedition.

Veterans' Graves Registration Cards. Cards prepared by the Work Projects Administration (WPA). They contain data from the gravestones of military personnel. See also a separate folder that contains submissions by Mr. Raymond D. Watkins that list Confederate graves.

Territorial and State Military Expenditures, 1839–69. Vouchers for payrolls (by unit), aid to families of veterans, and civilians. These are described under the section pertaining to RG 350.

Florida Colonial Period (pre-1812)

Spanish Archives, 1791–1821 (RG 599). Many of these documents are written in Spanish since Florida was a possession of Spain during this period. They are arranged in two sections: "new settlers," beginning in 1791; and "services," for the period 1815–21. The documents list lands granted to those who defended the province during the "Patriot War" (1811-12), to all soldiers of the militia, and to married officers and soldiers of the Third Battalion of Cuba. The number of acres granted was proportional to the size of their families.

Florida Territorial Period (1812-45)

Muster Rolls, 1826-1849. These list personnel in the Enrolled Militia (ages 18 through 45) and the Independent Volunteer companies. The companies are listed in a descriptive inventory.

Attorney General's Annual Reports, 1915-1972. Included are lists of military personnel which indicate those discharged, transferred, promoted, and retired. Most Civil War muster rolls have not survived, and this archives has only a few such rolls.

Seminole Indian Wars (1817-18, 1836-41, 1856-57)

NATIONAL ARCHIVES MICROFILM

Index to Compiled Service Records of Volunteer Soldiers Who Served During the Indian Wars and Disturbances, 1815-1858 (M629).

Compiled Service Records of Volunteer Soldiers Who Served in Organizations From the State of Florida During the Florida Indian Wars, 1835-1856 (M1086).

OTHER RECORDS

Although there were three major periods of war with native Florida Seminole tribes, this archives does not have documents pertaining to the first of these (1817-18). For the two later periods, there are muster rolls of Florida militia units that give name, age, rank, date and place of enlistment, and pay information. The rolls are arranged by unit and thereunder chronologically.

Mexican War (1846-48)

Five Florida military companies became part of the armed forces organized to fight in this war; three of them served in Mexico. Muster rolls are available for the Florida independent companies led by Allen G. Johnson, William W.J. Kelly, Robert G. Livingston, and William Fisher. The rolls give name, rank, age, date and place of enrollment, date and place where mustered in, and remarks.

Civil War-Union (1861-65)

NATIONAL ARCHIVES MICROFILM

Index to Compiled Military Service Records of Volunteer Union Soldiers Who Served in Organizations From the State of Florida (M264).

Organization Index to Pension Files of Veterans Who Served Between 1861 and 1900 (T289).

Compiled Service Records of Volunteer Union Soldiers Who Served in Organizations From the State of Florida (M400).

These records indicate that 1,290 white Floridians fought with Union forces during the Civil War. Some were deserters from Confederate units, and some were officers who resided in states other than Florida. Records for those who served in the two Union units (First Florida Cavalry and Second Florida Cavalry) are available.

Civil War-Confederate (1861-65)

NATIONAL ARCHIVES MICROFILM

Consolidated Index to Compiled Service Records of Confederate Soldiers (M253).

Compiled Service Records of Confederate Soldiers Who Served in Organizations From the State of Florida (M251).

Compiled Service Records of Confederate General and Staff Officers and Non-regimental Enlisted Men (M331).

Records Relating to Confederate Naval and Marine Personnel (M260).

Case Files of Applications From Former Confederates for Presidential Pardons ("Amnesty Papers"), 1865-1867 (M1003).

OTHER RECORDS

Muster Rolls, Confederate, 1861-65. A descriptive inventory in the finding aid for the Department of Military Affairs (RG 197) lists the units for which muster rolls are available. Some of the rolls are original documents and some are photostatic copies of rolls found in the National Archives.

Confederate Marine Corps and Navy Personnel. These are alphabetically listed in a card file of personnel who served in units from Florida. Each card indicates name, date of birth, date of appointment, rank, promotions, and military record.

Pay Vouchers, Eighth Florida Infantry, Confederate. These give place of birth, occupation, age, and physical description.

Confederate Pension Index. Names of Confederate veterans and widows. These were formerly available on computer printouts, but they are now available in two notebooks. The names are in two groups: those whose applications were approved and those whose applications were disapproved. Names are arranged a) alphabetically, with a file number; b) alphabetically by county; and c) by file number. Included are name, unit (or service in a state other than Florida), widow's name, county of residence, and number of pages in the pension file (typically four to twenty).

Confederate pension files, 1885-1954. These files have been microfilmed, and most contain considerable military and genealogical information.

The following files are available in cabinets, filed by number. They are part of RG 137, series 157 (107 reels).

Biennial Reports of the Florida Pension Board. Names of individuals receiving pensions at the time of publication.

Correspondence of the Florida Pension Board, 7 July 1887-8 November 1905. This material is arranged in nine volumes, with an index to the names of the correspondents; available on microfilm.

Miscellaneous Documents, 1885–ca. 1950. This material relates primarily to the Civil War; arranged by box number and folder number. Box six, folder sixteen, contains names of Florida military units, widows granted pensions by special acts of the Florida legislature, lists of soldiers killed at the Battle of Olustee, and a muster roll of the Thirty-third Alabama Regiment.

Confederate Soldiers' Home. Records for this home are available only at the Jacksonville Public Library, 122 North Ocean Street, Jacksonville, Florida 32202; telephone: (904) 630-2409.

Spanish-American War (1898–99)

NATIONAL ARCHIVES MICROFILM

Compiled Service Records of Volunteer Soldiers Who Served in the Florida Infantry During the War With Spain (M1087).

OTHER RECORDS

Muster Rolls, Spanish-American War. Twenty Florida companies served in this war. The muster rolls, arranged by unit, give name, rank, date and place enrolled, date and place mustered in, and remarks.

Order book, Florida Militia, 1895–1901. Contains names of Florida troops enlisted in and discharged from the militia.

World War I (1917–18)

World War I Army Card Roster, 1917–19. One or two cards were filed for each Floridian who served in World War I. The cards comprise two catalogs, one arranged by county of residence and the other alphabetically by name. They are available on microfilm. A separate reel lists those who died or were wounded, as well as those who were not recommended for promotion or reenlistment. The other reels provide name, serial number, military service, residence, place of birth, military organizations in which served, engagements, wounds or injuries, dates served overseas, discharge date, and percent of disability. The cards are separated by race (black or white).

World War I U.S. Coast Guard Roster; Marine Corps, 1917–19. Cards were completed for each Floridian who served in the coast guard or Marine Corps during World War I; name, date and place of enlistment; age; address; place or ship in which served; rate or assignment; and date and place of discharge.

World War I Induction Records. Lists of personnel called into service; name, race, address, date of induction, and, in some cases, occupation.

Graves Registration Cards, 1940–41. These cards provide lists of burial locations for many Florida veterans, but not all Florida counties were included in the survey. Prepared by the WPA, these cards provide name, address, next of kin and address, date and place of birth, race, date and place of death, date of burial and location of grave, date of enlistment and discharge, foreign service and unit, and location of cemetery plot. They also indicate whether a marker or headstone was provided.

PUBLISHED SOURCES—FLORIDA

General

Biographical Souvenir of the States of Georgia and Florida. . . . Chicago: F.A. Battey & Co., 1889.

Gaske, Frederick P. *Florida in the Civil War, 1860–1865. A Bibliography of Sources.* Tallahassee: Florida State University, 1981.

Hawk, Robert. *Florida's Air Force, Air National Guard, 1946–1990.* Florida National Guard Historical Foundation. St. Augustine: 1990.

Pre-1861 (Indian Wars)

Brown, G.M. *Ponce de Leon Land and Florida War Record.* 4th ed. St. Augustine: Record Printing Co. (?), 1902. Includes U.S. Army casualties during the Second Seminole War, listed by regiment with rank and date and place of death, pages 199–80).

Fritot, Jessie R. *Pension Records of Soldiers of the Revolution Who Removed to Florida, With Record of Service.* Jacksonville: DAR, 1946.

Record of Officers and Soldiers Killed in Battle and Died in Service During the Florida War. Washington, D.C.: Government Printing Office, 1882. Covers the period 1835–42.

Soldiers of Florida in the Seminole Indian, Civil and Spanish-American Wars. Tallahassee: Board of State Institutions, 1903. Reprint. Macclenny: R.J. Ferry, 1983. Lists officers and enlisted men by unit, date mustered in and out, and remarks (including rank).

Sprague, John T. *The Origin, Progress, and Conclusion of the Florida War.* New York: 1848. Reprint. "A Facsimile Reproduction of the 1848 Edition." Gainesville: University of Florida Press, 1964. Appendix lists U.S. Army casualties by regiment with name, rank, place and date of death, and remarks.

Watson, Larry S., ed. *Creek Soldier Casualty Lists, Seminole War, 1836.* Laguna Hills, Calif.: Histree, 1987.

1861-65 (Civil War)

Florida. Board of State Institutions. *Soldiers of Florida in the Seminole Indian, Civil and Spanish-American Wars.* Macclenny: R.J. Ferry, 1983. Lists officers and enlisted men by unit, date mustered in and out, and remarks (including rank).

Hawk, Robert. *Florida's Army: Militia, State Troops, National Guard, 1865–1985.* Englewood: Pineapple Press, 1986. Appendix 4: "Fatal War Casualties 1861–1971 Florida Militia (State Troops) National Guard." Includes name, rank, and date and place of death.

Pompey, Sherman L. *Civil War Burials From Florida.* Fresco, Calif.: 1968.

_____. *Genealogical Notes on Florida Military Units, C.S.A. (?)* 11 vols. Albany, Oreg.: the author, 1984–. Contains name and place of burial only.

_____. *Genealogical Notes on Florida Military Units, Union.* Albany, Oreg.: the author, 1984.

_____. *Genealogical Notes on Miscellaneous Florida Confederate Troops.* Albany, Oreg.: the author, 1984.

_____. *Genealogical Notes on the Florida Confederate Artillery, Engineers, and Rangers.* Albany, Oreg.: the author, 1984.

_____. *Genealogical Notes on the Florida Confederate Cavalry.* Albany, Oreg.: the author, 1984.

_____. *Muster Lists of the Florida Confederate Troops.* Albany, Oreg.: the author, 1984.

White, Virgil D., trans. *Register of Florida CSA Pension Applications.* Waynesboro, Tenn.: National Historical Publishing Co., 1989.

1866–1900 (Spanish-American War)

Florida. *Adjutant General's Report, 1902.* Tallahassee: state printer, 1902.

Florida. Board of State Institutions. *Soldiers of Florida in the Seminole Indian, Civil and Spanish-American Wars.* Macclenny: R.J. Ferry, 1983. Lists officers and enlisted men by unit, date mustered in and out, and remarks (including rank).

1901–75 (World War I through Vietnam War)

Florida. Adjutant General's Office. *Directory of Commissioned Officers of Florida National Guard.* St. Augustine: Record Press Registers of Florida Militia. The 1911, 1924, and 1950 editions include names.

Register of Deceased Veterans of Florida. 67 vols. St. Augustine: Veterans Graves Registration Project (WPA), 1941. Veterans Graves Registration Project (WPA), Sponsored by Military Department, State of Florida and American Legion, Florida. Arranged by county and thereunder alphabetically by cemetery.

Georgia

1733	James Oglethorpe established Georgia as a haven for poor Englishmen and those persecuted for their religions.
1753	Georgia became a royal colony.
1775	Georgians captured the armory at Savannah and sent the arms to the Continental Army.
1782	After several battles with British troops under Lord Cornwallis, Georgians drove the British out. (See American Revolution in the appendix.)
1788	Georgia became one of the original thirteen states.
1861	Georgia seceded from the Union.
1864	General W. T. Sherman's famous march across Georgia produced economic devastation and culminated in the burning of Atlanta. (See American Civil War in the appendix.)
1868	Georgia was readmitted to statehood.

GEORGIA DEPARTMENT OF ARCHIVES AND HISTORY

330 Capitol Avenue, SE
Atlanta, Georgia 30334
(404) 656-2350

Finding Aids

Ray, Charlotte, comp. *Civil War Sources at the Georgia Department of Archives and History.*

Index to microfilm. Index cards describe this repository's microfilm collection. The cards list the titles of the collections and show file cabinet and drawer where the film may be found.

Records

General

NATIONAL ARCHIVES MICROFILM

This archives has renumbered microfilm acquired from the National Archives, thus making it necessary to consult the card indexes to locate microfilm records. In the microfilm room, see the file box "U.S. Records" for National Archives records; see the file box "Georgia Official Records" for Georgia records.

Ledger of Payments, 1818–1872, to U.S. Pensioners Under Acts of 1818 Through 1886 (T718).

The Negro in the Military Service of the United States, 1639–1886 (M858).

OTHER RECORDS

Militia Records, 1779–1878. Records of the Office of the State Adjutant General.

Returns From Various Military Units for the Years Prior to the Civil War Until 1916.

Commissions Issued to Members of the Georgia Militia, 1775–1861 (microfilm).

Military Commissions, 1798–1865. State adjutant general records, series 3 (microfilm).

American Revolution (1775–83)

NATIONAL ARCHIVES MICROFILM

Index to Compiled Service Records of Volunteer Soldiers Who Served With the American Army in Georgia Military Organizations (M1051).

Miscellaneous Numbered Records (the manuscript file) in the War Department Collection of Revolutionary War Records, 1775–1790 (M859). The finding aid to this collection is in the Special Index in National Archives microfilm M847.

Selected Records From the Revolutionary War Pension and Bounty Land Warrant Applications Files, 1800–1900 (M805).

Indian Wars (1783–95)

NATIONAL ARCHIVES MICROFILM

Index to Compiled Service Records of Volunteer Soldiers Who Served During the Cherokee Disturbances and Removal in Organizations From the State of Georgia (M907).

Index to Compiled Service Records of Volunteer Soldiers Who Served During the Cherokee Disturbances and Removal in Organizations From the State of Tennessee and the Field and Staff of the Army of the Cherokee Nation (M908).

OTHER RECORDS

List of Muster and Payrolls of Militia, 1795.

Civil War–Union (1861–65)

NATIONAL ARCHIVES MICROFILM

Records of Volunteer Soldiers Who Served in Union Organizations From the State of Georgia (M403–First Battalion, Georgia Volunteer Infantry, U.S. Army). An index to these records is on National Archives microfilm M385, which is on the same reel that contains the records.

Civil War–Confederate (1861–65)

NATIONAL ARCHIVES MICROFILM

Compiled Service Records of Confederate Soldiers Who Served in Organizations From the State of Georgia (M319). The index to these records is in National Archives microfilm M226.

Compiled Service Records of Confederate Soldiers Who Served in Organizations Raised Directly By the Confederate Government (M258).

Compiled Service Records of Confederate General and Staff Officers and Non-regimental Enlisted Men (M331).

A combined index to the latter two collections is on National Archives microfilm M818.

Records Relating to Confederate Naval and Marine Personnel (M260).

Case Files of Applications From Former Confederates for Presidential Pardons ("Amnesty Papers"), 1865–1867 (M1003).

Confederate Papers Relative to Citizens or Business Firms (M436).

OTHER RECORDS

Index Cards of the Georgia Soldier Roster Commission (created in 1903). Using existing records, the commission compiled rosters of Georgia soldiers, sailors, and marines. These cards are arranged alphabetically and are available on microfilm.

Index Cards of Georgia Pension Applications Filed by Veterans, Widows, Or Witnesses (microfilm). Located in drawer 261, rolls 131 through 150; arranged by county and alphabetically thereunder.

Pension Files (microfilm). Located in drawers 271 through 276. A few supplemental files are in drawer 277.

Records of the Office of the State Adjutant General. (For location, see card index file Georgia Official Records.) Among others, these records include the following selected collections:

Lists of Men Subject to Military Duty, Compiled 4 March 1862. Arranged by county of residence; names of able-bodied white males between the ages of eighteen and forty-five who were not already in military service or who were exempt. Not indexed.

Militia Enrollment Lists Compiled as Required by the Act of December 4, 1863, for Reorganizing the Militia of the State of Georgia. Names of white males between the ages of sixteen and sixty who were not in military service as of January 1864; also county of residence;

age; place of birth; occupation; reason for any exemption; and whether the individual owned a gun, horse, saddle, or bridle; and the condition of each.

Muster Rolls of the Georgia State Troops and the Georgia State Line. Names of men who served in state organizations rather than the Confederate Army—although many state companies were later transferred to the Confederate Army. Soldiers who served only in these units may not be listed in the National Archives microfilm of Confederate compiled service records.

Roster of Commissioned Officers in the Georgia Militia under the Reorganization Act of 1864.

Families Supplied With Salt, 1864. A microfilm copy of a volume that contains names of soldiers' widows, families, or parents who had lost a son in service; no index.

Register of Inmates, 1901-1941. Confederate Soldiers' Home of Georgia. Contains name, military unit, battles, discharge date, next of kin, date of death (if died in the home's hospital), and place of burial. Widows who were residents of the home are not included, but their applications for admission are available. Application registers for both veterans and widows were arranged alphabetically and microfilmed.

Burial Lists. A small number of burial locations of Confederate veterans is available on microfilm or in a vertical file. Submissions by Raymond W. Watkins are included. The name is usually given, and the military unit is occasionally indicated.

MISCELLANEOUS COLLECTIONS

Some photographs of Georgia military units are available. They may be located by consulting the prints and photographs finding aids in the search room.

Under the heading Georgia Official Records is a file titled "Civil War Miscellany Subject File and Unit File." This file contains the titles of several collections. The following are selected collections that may interest the military records researcher.

Andersonville Prison

Battles

Camps; Forts

Sherman's march to the sea

United Confederate Veterans

United Daughters of the Confederacy

There are also references to cavalry, artillery, and infantry units, with citations to rosters and other documents.

SUBJECT FILES

An index to "subject files" contains the heading Civil War, under which are listed several collections:

Account books

Amnesty papers

Battles; Campaigns

Cemeteries

Diaries

Hospitals

Letters

Narratives

Medical service

Newspapers

Prisons and prisoners

Records (miscellaneous)

Regimental histories

Rosters

Union Army

Veterans

A card index to other collections—under the heading Civil War—includes the following:

CSA Army Medical Register, 1864-65.

Cemeteries, Georgia Confederate Burial Lists.

Register of Medical Examining Board. Lists names of patients in the hospital at Madison, Georgia.

Wayside Home Register, 1863-64. Contains names of soldiers who visited this home, which dispensed meals and other comforts to soldiers passing through the area.

CSA Muster Rolls: Fifth Regiment, Georgia State Guards; Ninth Regiment, Georgia Volunteers; First Georgia Regiment.

Spanish-American War (1898-99)

Enlistments, Discharges, Payrolls, Unit Returns, Oath Books, 1873-1917. State Adjutant General Records, series 13.

Muster-out Rolls, 1898 (indexed). State Adjutant General Records, series 36.

Muster-in Rolls, 1898 (indexed). State Adjutant General Records, series 38.

War Service Summary-card Files: First, Second, and Third Georgia.

Mexican Border Service (1916)

Muster-in Rolls, Mexican Border War. Records of the Office of the State Adjutant General, subgroup 3, series 45 (microfilm).

Georgia men in the National Guard in the Mexican Border War (indexed). Records of the State Adjutant General, 2 vols.

World War I (1917-18)

Register of Officers of Georgia State Troops, 1900-36.

Register of Service Medals and Service Bars Issued 1905-33.

World War I Applications for Victory Medal. Records of the Office of the State Adjutant General, subgroup 3, series 32.

Muster-in Rolls for Regiments in the Georgia National Guard Called Into Service, 1916.

National Guard Official Register. Includes officers of all Georgia National Guard units, 1915-17.

Casualties. Georgia State Memorial Book, 1921.

Statement of Service Summary-card Files. Records of the Office of the State Adjutant General, subgroup 1, series 33. These cards give name, serial number, race (army only), address, place of induction or enlistment, place of birth, age, military units, engagements in which participated, overseas service, wounds, discharge date, and disabilities.

Abstracts From World War I Service Records. Records of the Office of the State Adjutant General, subgroup 3, series 2.

World War II (1941-45)

Correspondence, Rosters, And Orders, Georgia State Guard (Home Guard), 1940-46. Records of the Office of the State Adjutant General, subgroup 1, series 11.

World War II Honor List of Dead or Missing—State of Georgia. Names of Georgia veterans in lists issued by the U.S. War Department; includes those killed in battle as well as those killed or missing in non-battle incidents. Names are arranged by county and alphabetically thereunder. Given are name, serial number, rank, and category of the casualty—KIA (killed in action), M (missing), DNB (died, not in battle), DOW (died of wounds), etc. This list is contained in a folder labeled "Georgia War Casualties, Vietnam, Korea, World War II," which is located in the reading room in a cabinet labeled "Georgia Miscellany."

Korean War (1950-53)

Korean Conflict Honor List of Dead or Missing. (See list described above under World War II heading.)

Vietnam War (1963-75)

Vietnam War Honor List of Dead or Missing. (See list described above under World War II heading.)

Manuscripts

Confederate States of America Army Papers (No. 169). This collection consists mainly of Confederate Army financial records—primarily pay vouchers. The papers in this collection were arranged and indexed by WPA workers, who bundled them by category into numbered "packages," which were then placed in numbered boxes at this archives. The index covers boxes six through twelve. It consists of an alphabetical list of names, commands, and army organizational units. The material is available as follows (though it may be difficult for staff to locate):

Boxes 1-5	Pay vouchers, 1862-63
Box 6	Miscellaneous muster rolls, payrolls, and bounty rolls, 1862
Box 7	Muster rolls and payrolls, returns for Company A, First Georgia Regiment, Volunteer Infantry, 1861-64 (Irish Jasper Greens)
Box 8	Muster rolls and payrolls of soldiers in hospitals, November 1862
Box 9	Miscellaneous muster rolls and payrolls, 1862-63
Box 10	Miscellaneous muster rolls and payrolls; petition for removal of Gen. Braxton Bragg; reports on battles of Chickamauga and Missionary Ridge
Box 11	Miscellaneous muster rolls and payrolls, 1862-63
Box 12	Descriptive lists and pay accounts, 1863; list of officers not reappointed in First, Fifty-seventh, and Sixty-third Regiments, 11 April 1865; miscellaneous papers pertaining to General Hospital No. 4, Richmond, Virginia, 1864.

PUBLISHED SOURCES—GEORGIA

General

Dictionary of Georgia Biography. 2 vols. Edited by Kenneth Coleman and Charles Stephen Gurr. Athens: University of Georgia Press, 1983.

Northen, William J. *Men of Mark in Georgia. A Complete and Elaborate History of the State . . . Chiefly Told in Biographies. . . . 7 vols*. Atlanta: A.B. Caldwell, 1907-12. Reprinted with consolidated index in vol. 7. Spartanburg, S.C.: The Reprint Co., 1974.

Payne, Dorothy E. *Georgia Pensioners*. 2 vols. McLean, Va.: Sunbelt Publishing Co., 1985. Based on National Archives pension files for the American Revolution, War of 1812, Mexican War, and some "invalid pension applications."

1775-83 (American Revolution)

Candler, Allen D., comp. *The Revolutionary Records of the State of Georgia*. 3 vols. Atlanta: Franklin-Turner Co., 1908. Reprint. New York: AMS Press, 1972.

Davis, Robert S. *Georgia Citizens and Soldiers of the American Revolution*. Easley, S.C.: Southern Historical Press, 1979.

Georgia. Secretary of State. *Authentic List of All Land Lottery Grants Made to Veterans of the Revolutionary War by the State of Georgia: Taken From Official State Records in the Surveyor-*

General Department. . . . Compiled by Alex M. Hitz. Atlanta: 1955. 2nd ed. Atlanta: secretary of state, 1966.

Hemperley, Marion R. *Military Certificates of Georgia, 1776–1800, on File in the Surveyor General Department.* Semiquincentenary ed. Atlanta: State Printing Office, 1983. Approximately two thousand names of men who received certificates for bounty land in Georgia based on service in the American Revolution, with rank and unit (if given). The appendix is an essay by military historian Gordon Smith covering the Georgia Continental Establishment, 1775–1783, with a list of 330 officers of the "Georgia Continental Line, Navy, Military and civil Staffs" (including dates and places of death, if known); also the organization of the Georgia State Line, 1776–1784; a list of eighty-seven "Officers of the American Continental and French Regular Services Who Came to Georgia After the War" (includes date and place of death if known); the "Georgia State Line, 1776–1784"; Georgia Militia, 1775–83; battalions and regiments of the Georgia Militia, 1757–83, with names of field grade officers; a discussion of "Volunteers During the Revolution" (militia); and the "Georgia State Line (1787–1790)," with names of officers.

Houston, Martha Lou, comp. *Reprint of Official Register of Land Lottery of Georgia 1827.* Milledgeville: Grantland and Orme, 1827. Columbus: 1929. Reprint. Easley, S.C.: SHP, 1986. Approximately 1,500 of the lottery winners were veterans of the American Revolution and are so designated here.

_____. *600 Revolutionary Soldiers and Widows of Revolutionary Soldiers Living in Georgia in 1827–28.* Ann Arbor, Mich.: Edwards Brothers, 1946.

Knight, Lucian Lamar. *Georgia's Roster of the Revolution: Containing a List of the State's Defenders, Officers and Men, Soldiers and Sailors, Partisans and Regulars, Whether Enlisted From Georgia or Settled in Georgia after the Close of Hostilities, Compiled . . . From Various Sources Including Official Documents, Both State and Federal, Certificates of Service, Land Grants, Pension Rolls and Other Records.* Atlanta: Index Printing Co., 1920. Reprint. Baltimore: Genealogical Publishing Co., 1967. Some names reproduced from printed material; some from source documents. Apparently a number of original certificates used for this book have been lost.

McCall, Ettie T. *Roster of Revolutionary Soldiers in Georgia.* 3 vols. Atlanta: Georgia Society DAR, 1941. Genealogical Publishing Co., 1968.

McIntosh, Lachlan. *Lachlan McIntosh Papers in the University of Georgia Libraries.* Edited by Lilla Mills Hawes. Athens: University of Georgia Press, 1960. Includes lists of officers, pages 43 through 47 and 59; indicates where from, when appointed brigadier, when promoted, and occurrences. Also see the index.

Richardson, Marian M., and Jessie J. Mize. *1832 Cherokee Land Lottery: Index to Revolutionary Soldiers, Their Widows and Orphans Who Were Fortunate Drawers.* Taken From Cherokee Land Lottery, by James F. Smith . . . 1838. Danielsville: Heritage Papers, 1969.

Smith, James F. *The Cherokee Land Lottery, Containing a Numerical List of the Names of the Fortunate Drawers in Said Lottery.* . . . New York: Harper, 1838. Reprint. Vidalia: Georgia Genealogical Reprints, 1968.

The Third and Fourth, or 1820 and 1821 Land Lotteries of Georgia. Easley, S.C.: Georgia Genealogical Reprints; Southern Historical Press, 1973. Revolutionary War veterans are so designated.

Wilson, Caroline P. *Annals of Georgia: Important Early Records of the State.* 3 vols. Vol. 1, Liberty County Records and a State Revolutionary Payroll. New York: Grafton Press, 1928–33. Reprint. Easley, S.C.: Southern Historical Press, 1968. Includes amounts paid for services, merchandise sold to the military, and soldiers' pay from auditor's account books.

1784–1860 (War of 1812)

Kratovil, Judy Swaim. *Index to War of 1812 Service Records for Volunteer Soldiers From Georgia.* Atlanta: the author, 1986. Includes name, unit, and rank of veteran.

Miller, Stephen Franks. *The Bench and Bar of Georgia: Memoirs and Sketches.* . . . 2 vols. Philadelphia: J.B. Lippincott, 1858. Biographical sketches and correspondence of some military officers.

War of 1812 Pensioners Living in Georgia During the 1880's. Cullman, Ala.: Gregath Co., 1982. Pensioners listed by county.

1861–65 (Civil War–Confederate)

Buzzett, Isabell S., comp. *Confederate Monuments of Georgia.* Atlanta (?): I.S. Bussett, 1984.

Folsom, James M. *Heroes and Martyrs of Georgia: Georgia's Record in the Revolution of 1861.* Macon: Burke, Boykin & Co., 1864.

Georgia. State Division of Confederate Pensions and Records. *Roster of the Confederate Soldiers of Georgia, 1861–1865.* 6 vols. Edited by Lillian Henderson. Hapeville: Longino & Porter, 1959–64. Contains rosters of infantry regiments.

_____ . *Roster of the Confederate Soldiers of Georgia, 1861–1865: Index.* Compiled by Juanita S. Brightwell, Eunice S. Lee, and Elsie C. Fulghum for the Lake Blackshear Regional Library. Spartanburg, S.C.: The Reprint Co., 1982.

Herbert, Sidney. *A Complete Roster of the Volunteer Military Organizations of the State of Georgia.* Atlanta: J.P. Harrison, 1879.

Huxford, Folks. *Pioneers of Wiregrass Georgia.* . . . 7 vols. Adel: Patten Publishers, 1951–.

Jones, Charles Edgeworth. *Georgia in the War, 1861–1865: A Compendium of Georgia Participants.* Atlanta (?): 1909 (?). Reprint. Georgia Military History Series. Jonesboro: Freedom Hill Press, 1988. Includes lists of field officers.

Myers, Robert M. *The Children of Pride: A True Story of Georgia and the Civil War.* New Haven: Yale University Press, 1972. "Who's Who," pages 1,450-1,738.

Pompey, Sherman L. *Civil War Veteran Burials, Georgia Confederate Regiments.* N.p., 1970 (?).

Stegman, John F. *These Men She Gave. . . .* Athens: University of Georgia Press, 1964.

1866-1900 (Spanish-American War)

Thaxton, Carlton J., et. al., eds. *A Roster of Spanish American War Soldiers From Georgia.* Americus: Thaxton Co., 1984.

Hawaii

1778	Captain James Cook, a British explorer, discovered Hawaii and named the islands after the Earl of Sandwich.
1790-1810	Kamehameha I united the islands politically and created the Hawaiian monarchy.
1820	Missionaries began bringing Christianity to the islands.
1835	Sugar plantations run by Americans were established.
1876	Reciprocity Treaty created close economic ties with the United States.
1893	Queen Liliuokalani was deposed by U.S. troops and the Republic of Hawaii created.
1898	Hawaii was annexed by the United States.
1900	Hawaii became a territory.
1941	Japan's attack on the American naval base at Pearl Harbor led to the United States' entry into World War II. (See World War II in the appendix.)
1959	Hawaii became a state.

HAWAII STATE ARCHIVES

Iolani Palace Grounds
Honolulu, Hawaii 96813
(808) 586-0329

This archives has military records of the Kingdom of Hawaii for the period just prior to the twentieth century, before it became a U.S. territory. Military records for U.S. personnel are described below.

Records

General

Bonus Applications, 1936-1939. Copies of applications made by Hawaii veterans to the Veterans Administration for adjusted-service compensation. Gives applicant name, place of birth, date of birth, service number, date of enlistment and discharge, address, and fingerprints.

HAWAII NATIONAL GUARD

Personnel Rosters, 1893-1914. Name, rank, date of appointment, date of enlistment, date of discharge, unit assignment, previous service, drill attendance, and previous service information. Cataloged as series no. 156 at the Hawaii State Archives.

Personnel Rolls, 1893-1906 (indexed). Name (arranged chronologically), rank, age, physical description, place of birth, occupation, date of enlistment, enlistment officer, length of service, and date of discharge. Cataloged as series no. 157 at the Hawaii State Archives.

Civil War–Union (1861-65)

Card File of Deceased Veterans. Name, address, date of death, and name and location of cemetery. Some cards include additional information.

Spanish-American War (1898-99)

Card File of Deceased Veterans. Name, address, date of death, and name and location of cemetery. Some cards include additional information.

World War I (1917-18)

Card File of Deceased Veterans. Name, date of death, and name and location of cemetery. Some cards include additional information.

Muster Rolls, 1918. Initial muster rolls of the Second Hawaiian Infantry Regiment of the Hawaii National Guard at Fort Armstrong, Honolulu; name, rank, enlistment date, and attendance at drills. Cataloged as series no. 155 at the Hawaii State Archives.

Hawaiian War Records, ca. 1917-1920. Volumes compiled from the records of the First National Guard Hawaii list veterans who enlisted between 1914 and 1918. Records contain name, address, service record, etc.

World War I Army Service Records, ca. 1919-1926. Card file of residents of the Territory of Hawaii who served in the U.S. Army; information for those inducted into the army dating from 1915 to discharge in 1921; name, serial number, race, residence, place of birth, age, and service record. Some cards give additional information.

Word War I Navy Service Records, ca. 1919-1927. Card file detailing the service history of residents of the Territory of Hawaii enlisted in the navy between 1912 and 1921. Gives name, address, age, service number, and service history. Some cards give additional information.

World War II (1941-45)

Card File of Servicemen Wounded in World War II. Name, rank, and a summary newspaper account of the injury (including newspaper citation).

PUBLISHED SOURCES—HAWAII

1928-39 (post-World War I)

Hawaii. Adjutant General. *Annual Reports of the Military Department, Territory of Hawaii, 1928-1939.* Honolulu: Printshop Co., 1939.

Idaho

1803   Previously an unexplored possession of Spain and France, Idaho became United States property through the Louisiana Purchase.

1805-06   American explorers Lewis and Clark traveled through Idaho.

1860   Mormon colonists at Franklin established the first permanent white community in Idaho.

1860   Discovery of gold led to the first large influx of white settlers.

1863   Idaho became a territory.

1877   Chief Joseph and the Nez Perce Indians were defeated by federal troops. (See Nez Perce War in the appendix.)

1890   Idaho became a state.

• •

IDAHO STATE HISTORICAL SOCIETY

450 North Fourth Street
Boise, Idaho 83702-6027
Historical Library: (208) 334-3356
Genealogical Library: (208) 334-2305

Records

General

Applications for Admission to the Idaho Soldiers' Home, 1894-1983 (indexed). Name, age, nativity, date of admission, military history, pensions, disabilities, occupation, social condition, literacy, and county of residence.

Collection of Official Correspondence, Records, and Documents, 1877-1927. Concerns Indian wars of 1877 and 1878, including requests for arms and ammunition and for discharges and pensions; includes a few actual discharges from the Nez Perce and Bannock Indian wars.

Spanish-American War (1898-99)

A collection of payroll vouchers and discharge statements from the First Regiment, Idaho U.S. Volunteer Infantry, between 1898 and 1899, relating to their service in the Spanish-American War. They contain:

File 1: Payroll vouchers, November and December 1898.
Field Staff and Band
Companies A–H

File 2: Payroll vouchers, July 1899
Field Staff and Band
Capt. Frank W. Hunt, Company A
Companies B–H

File 3: Discharge statements, July 1899 (with the exception of Stainton—April 1899)
Robert D. Stainton, 1st Sergeant, Company B (no. 212)
Mark A. Graham, Private, Company E (no. 566)
Frank Ray, Private, Company G (no. 567)
Burton O. Compton, Private, Company E (no. 593)
Alfred Allard, Private, Company G (no. 721)
John D. Clark, Private, Company G (no. 722)
John C. Gaunt, Private, Company A (no. 744)

Horace D. Van Alstine, Private, Company B (no. 745)
John W. Luitjens, Private, Company B (no. 746)
Martin Sterling, Private, Company B (no. 747)
Thomas E. Griffin, Private, Company D (no. 748)
Nicholas F. Tigne, Private, Company G (no. 749)
Robert Mills, Private, Company C (no. 771)
James Patterson, Private, Company F (no. 772)

Mexican Border Service (1916)

Rosters of National Guard units that served during the Mexican Border Campaign.

World War I (1917-18)

Miscellaneous papers relating to the military draft.

PUBLISHED SOURCES—IDAHO

1917-75 (World War I through Vietnam War)

Idaho. Adjutant General. *Biennial Report, 1917–1918.* Boise: ca. 1918.

Idaho. Veterans Welfare Commission. *Report.* Boise: n.d.

Illinois

1673   Jacques Marquette and Louis Joliet explored Illinois along the Mississippi River.

1680   French explorer La Salle established the first permanent French settlement at Fort Crevecoeur (modern Peoria).

1717   Illinois was placed under the control of the French government of Louisiana.

1763   Illinois was ceded to the British as part of the Treaty of Paris which ended the French and Indian War. (See French and Indian War in the appendix.)

1778   George Rogers Clark captured British forts in Illinois during the American Revolution. (See American Revolution in the appendix.)

1783   The Treaty of Paris which ended the American Revolution transferred Illinois to the United States. (See American Revolution in the appendix.)

1800   Illinois became part of Indiana Territory.

1809   Illinois became a territory.

1818   Illinois became a state.

1832   The Black Hawk War occurred in Illinois. (See Black Hawk War in the appendix.)

1861–65   During the Civil War, Illinois contributed 259,092 soldiers to the Northern cause, second in the Midwest only to Ohio. (See American Civil War in the appendix.)

• •

Illinois State Archives

Archives Building
(near the state capitol)
Springfield, Illinois 62756
(217) 782-4682

Finding Aids

Descriptive Inventory of the Archives of the State of Illinois. A copy of this guide may be purchased from the archives. It is also available for use in the reading room, and it can be found in many Illinois public libraries.

A Summary Guide to Local Governmental Records in the Illinois Regional Archives.

Records

As a service to researchers, the state archives will transfer microfilm records to any of the seven state universities that cooperate to form the Illinois Regional Archives Depository System (IRAD). The universities in this system are: Eastern Illinois University, Illinois State University, Northeastern Illinois University, Northern Illinois University, Sangamon State University, Southern Illinois University, and Western Illinois University.

Indexes of names of soldiers and sailors, arranged by war in which served, including the War of 1812, Black Hawk War, Mexican War, Civil War, and Spanish-American War, are available at the Illinois State Library, 300 South Second Street, Springfield, Illinois 62756. Any request to use these indexes through the interlibrary loan system must specify the name being searched, war served in, and military unit name or number.

In most cases, the collections of Illinois records cited below include the record group numbers, which, if listed, must be used when requesting the described material.

General

Illinois Veterans Commission's *Honor Roll of Veterans Buried in Illinois*. Lists places of all veteran burials prior to 1 July 1955; arranged by county and cemetery within county and alphabetically by name thereunder; gives name, war, rank, branch of service, unit, date of death, and location of grave.

Illinois Veterans Commission. Burial Places in Illinois, 1774-1898. Index cards that give name, unit, war, next of kin, and location of grave.

American Revolution (1775-83)

NATIONAL ARCHIVES MICROFILM

Selected Records From Revolutionary War Pension and County Land Warrant Application Files, 1800-1900 (M805).

Post-American Revolution (1783-1809)

Donation Lists for Head Grants and Militia Claims, September 21, 1805 (RG 952.7. See also RG 952.8).

Militia Claims Confirmed by the Governors, ca. 1804-09 (RG 952.29. See also RG 952.30; RG 952.31; and RG 952.32).

War of 1812 (1812-15)

NATIONAL ARCHIVES MICROFILM

Index to War of 1812 Pension Application Files. (M313)

OTHER RECORDS

Militia Muster Roll, 27 February 1813-17 March 1813. Lists only field and staff officers of the Third Infantry Regiment, Illinois militia (RG 100.13).

Militia Claims for Which Certificates of Confirmation Issued, July 1814-October 1814 (RG 952.33).

Winnebago War (1827)

See RG 301.4 (militia files, 1826-1859). Includes numerous muster rolls of men called into service in the 1827 Winnebago War (Fever River Expedition).

Black Hawk War (1831-32)

Militia Returns and Arms Issues, 1832-33 (RG 301.6). Lists officers of militia units as well as records of arms issued for use in the Black Hawk War.

Black Hawk War Records, ca. 1832-91 (RG 301.7). Contains both original muster rolls of Illinois men and copies of muster rolls filed with the federal government pursuant to Illinois legislation providing for their transcription. Original rolls are

arranged by brigade; federal rolls are arranged by county. They include name, rank, date and length of enrollment, county of residence, amount of pay due, and number of rations drawn; other data relating to mounted soldiers is included. The names of soldiers who fought in this war can be found in Ellen M. Whitney's *The Black Hawk War, 1831-32* (cited below under Published Sources—Illinois).

Military Bounty Land (1831-55)

Register of Forfeited Land Stock and Military Bounty Land Scrip Received:

> 5 January 1831-30 June 1846. Kaskasia District (RG 952.48).
>
> 6 April 1831-26 October 1846. Shawneetown District (RG 952.95).
>
> 1 January 1831-31 October 1836. Edwardsville District (RG 952.149).
>
> February 1831-November 1837. Vandalia District (RG 952.186).
>
> 1 June 1831-1 February 1851. Palestine District (RG 952.217).
>
> 1 September 1838-10 November 1838. Danville District (RG 952.291).

Register of Suspended Military Land Warrants, 23 May 1851-11 December 1855. Vandalia District (RG 952.197. See also RG 952.1961).

Record of Notices of Suspended and Canceled Locations on Military Land Warrants, ca. October 1855. Springfield District (RG 952. 245.4).

Register of Military Exchange Location Certificates Issued, 15 November 1832-5 May 1845. Quincy District (RG 952.271).

Register of Military Land Warrants Received in Payment for Land, 7 June 1843-3 February 1850. Northeastern District (RG 952.325).

Register of Military Land Scrip or U.S. Treasurer's Receipts Received, 1 January 1840-December 31, 1844 (RG 952.344).

Register of Military Land Warrants Received, 1 July 1848-29 November 1848. Northwestern District (RG 952.354).

List of Military Land Warrants on Which Patents Issued: 1817-1819. Kaskasia District (RG 952.73).

Mexican War (1846-48)

Militia Files, 1826-59 (RG 301.4). A substantial portion of these records pertain to the Mexican War.

Mexican War Records, ca. 1846-90 (RG 301.8). This file contains both original muster rolls and copies of muster rolls filed with the federal government pursuant to Illinois legislation providing for their transcription. Original rolls are arranged by brigade; federal rolls are arranged by county. The rolls include name, rank, age, date, place and term of enrollment, and other data. The file also includes a list of Illinois soldiers of the Fourteenth and Sixteenth Infantry Regiments of the U.S. regulars and soldiers from the Second Illinois Infantry Regiment who were killed, wounded, or missing in action at the battle of Buena Vista. Names of Illinois soldiers who fought in this war may be found in pages 194-316 of Isaac H. Elliott's *Record of the Services of Illinois Soldiers in the Black Hawk War, 1831-32 and in the Mexican War, 1846-48. . . .* (Springfield: 1902).

Register of Ex-soldiers of the Black Hawk, Mexican, and Civil Wars Attending Reunion of 1878 (RG 301.10; also see RG 301.11, a register of visitors to Memorial Hall, 4 September 1884-25 August 1887).

Civil War–Union (1861-65)

The following are selected collections of particular interest to military records researchers. See the finding aid *Descriptive Inventory . . .* (cited above) for other collections.

Administrative Files on Civil War Companies and Regiments (RG 301.18). Contain muster rolls, enlistment certificates, soldiers taken prisoner, discharges, battle accounts, and similar data concerning all infantry, cavalry, and artillery units. These files often give name, rank, birthplace, age, occupation, marital status, physical description, enlistment and discharge data, injuries, and other facts (not indexed).

Company Muster Rolls, 1862-65 (RG 301.19) (not indexed).

Muster and Descriptive Rolls, 1861-65 (RG 301.20). Data in these volumes forms the basis for the *Report of the Adjutant General of the State of Illinois for the Years 1861-66* (cited below under Published Sources–Illinois).

Company Descriptive Books (RG 301.50). Rolls of officers and enlisted men arranged by military unit. These give personal and military service data. Books are for eight selected infantry regiments. (See descriptive pamphlet for lists of companies.) See also RG 301.51; RG 301.52; RG 301.53; RG 301.54; RG 301.55; RG 301.56; RG 301.57.

Band Muster Rolls (RG 301.21). Seven folders (not indexed).

Roster of Illinois Men in the U.S. Navy During the Civil War (RG 301.22). Indexed; gives name; place of birth; rank; enlistment data; names of vessels on which served; and discharge, desertion, or death. Names and birthplaces of sailors listed in this collection appear in Marion D. Pratt, ed., "Illinois Men in the Union Navy During the Civil War." *Illinois Libraries* 44 (6) (June 1962): 435-59.

Roster of Officers (RG 301.24). Arranged by military unit (not indexed). See also RG 301.25; RG 301.26; RG 301.27; RG 301.28 for officers of other regiments (no indexes).

Military Census, 1861-1862 (RG 301.29). Arranged by county. Gives information concerning Illinois men serving in militia units including personal and military data (not indexed).

Militia Payrolls, 24 June 1861-19 August 1861 (RG 301.32). Payrolls for various Illinois militia units (not indexed).

Certificates of Enlistment, 7 November 1863-14 September 1865 (RG 301.34). Contains stubs of certificates issued to verify a soldier's enlistment; name, date, unit, and place of muster (not indexed).

Register of Recruits (RG 301.38). Lists arranged by county, giving name and residence of each recruit; contain some recruits not from Illinois–Indiana, Kentucky, Michigan, Mississippi, New York, and Ohio. See also RG 301.39.

Sick-list of Recruits at Camp Yates (Springfield), 20 January 1865-April 1864 (not indexed). See also Register of Illinois Soldiers in Nashville Hospitals (RG 301.59)

List of Illinois Soldiers Buried at Andersonville, Georgia, 19 March 1964-18 March 1865 (RG 301.60) This list can also be found in *Report of the Adjutant General . . . 1861-66* (cited below under Published Sources–Illinois).

List of Union and Confederate Soldiers Buried at Camp Butler, Oak Ridge, Hutchinson (Springfield), Woodland (Quincy), and Alton City Cemeteries, April 1861-August 1866 (RG 301.61). Separate lists for Union and Confederate soldiers; name, unit, state of residence, and grave location (not indexed).

Record of Requests for Discharge Certificates, ca. July 1865-1868 (RG 301.65). Veterans' names arranged alphabetically.

Civil War Scrapbook (RG 301.67). Contains official circulars, orders, proclamations, and the official report of the Battle of Pea Ridge in Arkansas (not indexed).

Record of Illinois Soldiers' Claims (RG 502.3). Records of claims filed by Illinois soldiers for compensation for service in the Civil War, including bounty, pension, back pay, and bounty payments, and rations while a prisoner of war. Refers to claims processed 1 December 1865-26 February 1875. Index for 1 December 1865-29 September 1866 only. See also RG 502.4 for records of disallowed claims.

Civil War–Confederate (1861-65)

See above for lists of Confederate burials (RG 301.61).

Soldiers' and Sailors' Home

In 1885 the Soldiers' and Sailors' Home was established at Quincy, Illinois, to care for honorably discharged and disabled veterans of the Mexican War and Civil War. Beginning in 1904, wives of veterans were also admitted if they met certain age and marriage requirements. In some cases, daughters and mothers were also admitted. Those unable to meet the requirements for admission to the home at Quincy were sometimes admitted to the Soldiers' Widows' Home at Wilmington, Illinois. In 1963 the Wilmington home was closed, and its residents were transferred to the Quincy home. The Quincy home was renamed the Illinois Veterans' Home in 1973. The following collections refer to records kept by those homes.

ILLINOIS SOLDIERS' AND SAILORS' HOME (ILLINOIS VETERANS' HOME)

Veterans' Admission Record, ca. 1887–1967 (RG 259.1). Fifty volumes (not indexed); name, register number, residence, military unit, amount of pension, date of discharge, and date of death.

Veterans' Case Files, ca. 1887–1963 (RG 259.2). Applications for admission give name, age, place of birth, residence, physical description, military service, and disability (if any); includes other personal papers. Beginning in 1919, the files also include medical information, dependents, and other documents. Index available for 1887 and 1898 only.

Women's Admission Record (RG 259.3) and Women's Case Files (RG 259.4) are similar to the collections pertaining to veterans, but neither is indexed.

Veterans' Case Records, March 1877–16 January 1950 (RG 259.5). Contains much data concerning the veterans' military, domestic, and institutional history (not indexed). See also RG 259.6 (First Admissions); RG 259.7 (Readmissions); RG 259.8 (Hospital Admissions); RG 259.9 (Furlough Register); and RG 259.10 (Journal). None of these is indexed, and they pertain to various periods of years. See the finding aid *Descriptive Inventory*, cited above, for details.

ILLINOIS SOLDIERS' WIDOWS' HOME

Admission Files, ca. 1896–1960 (RG 260.1). These contain evidence for meeting admission requirements, marriage and family information, pension information, and other personal data (not indexed).

Resident Card File, 1895–1961 (RG 260.2). A card for each resident shows information similar to the case files cited above. Beginning around 1920, the cards also include race, religion, and war in which the veteran served. See also RG 260.3 (Death Record); RG 260.4 (Journal); RG 260.5 (Record Book); and RG 260.6 (Photograph File), all of which pertain roughly to the years 1902 through 1963. (None of these is indexed.) See the *Descriptive Inventory* for details. The photographs in the photograph file are of Illinois governors and matrons of the home; no photographs of residents are included.

Illinois Soldiers' Orphans' Home (Soldiers' and Sailors' Children's Home)

RG 255 describes records of the Illinois Soldiers' Orphans' Home, established in 1865 to care for orphaned or indigent children of Illinois veterans of the Civil War. In later years such children were often placed in foster homes, and the program is now the responsibility of the Illinois Department of Children and Family Services. Registers of children placed in the program contain military data concerning their fathers.

Federal Soldiers' Home, Danville, Illinois

The National Archives has the complete records pertaining to this federal institution, which was created in 1897. In 1985 the Illinois State Archives microfilmed the historical registers of this home for the years 1898 through 1934. There are thirty-two reels of registers and a two-reel index.

Data contained in the registers includes military history, domestic history, home history (including admission data, pensions, and burials), and general remarks (including official documentation of military and pension matters).

In addition to those in the Illinois State Archives, copies of these registers may be seen at the Illinois State Library in Springfield or at the Illiana Genealogical and Historical Society, P.O. Box 207, Danville, Illinois 61832. The microfilm is available from the Illinois State Archives for a fee. Partial reports for a particular veteran are also available. Name and "home number" must be included with the request.

Index Cards Listing the Names of Residents of This Home. Name, unit, war in which served, next of kin, and grave location.

World War I (1917–18)

Selective Service Draft Registration Cards for Illinois (microfilm). These records consist of cards, arranged by county and draft board within county, for men between the ages of eighteen and forty-five inclusive who were eligible for the draft (National Archives RG 163).

A state Service Recognition Board was created in the 1920s to provide compensation to World War I veterans or their survivors, including dependents of those who had died while in military service. This board was abolished in 1927, and its records were transferred to the adjutant general. The following collections are available on microfilm. (Access to bonus records is restricted to bonus recipients in accordance with Illinois statutes.)

World War I Bonus Applications From Veterans and Beneficiaries, 1923–1927 (RG 503.1). Arranged alphabetically, these applications contain considerable information concerning the veteran's personal history; residences; draft records; military history; voting place; and names of spouse, parents, and previous employer. Reasons for denial of any application are also given. Material supplied by dependents is also very helpful. Many of these records were destroyed or damaged by a fire at the State Arsenal in 1934.

Abstract of World War I Bonus Applications, 1923–1927 (RG 503.2). An index card for each application (veteran or beneficiary) lists name, claim number, length of active military service, amount and date of bonus payment, and name of deceased veteran (in beneficiary applications). These cards include data from all bonus applications, including those destroyed in the 1934 fire. See also RG 503.3, Schedules of

Vouchers for World War I Bonus Payments, ca. 1923-1924 (not indexed).

World War II (1941-45)

A new Service Recognition Board was created in 1948 to provide compensation to World War II veterans or their survivors. The board was abolished in 1953, and the adjutant general deposited all of the board's records in the state archives. In 1973 the bonus payment program was reinstituted, and responsibility for its administration was assigned to the state Department of Veterans Affairs (created in 1975). The following collections are available on microfilm. (Access to bonus records is restricted to bonus recipients in accordance with Illinois statutes.)

World War II Bonus Applications From Veterans, 1947-1953 (RG 504.3). Applications are filed by claim number, but there is an alphabetical index of names. Each application includes name, claim number, service number, address at time of application, address when entered service, military history (including place enrolled), and amount of bonus paid. Early applications include proof of service. See also RG 504.4, World War II Bonus Applications From Beneficiaries of Deceased Veterans, 1947-1953.

Abstract of World War II Bonus Applications, 1947-1953. An index card was prepared for each application. The card gives the essential information contained in the application. These abstracts are arranged alphabetically by name and are available on microfilm.

See also RG 504.5 and RG 504.7 through RG 504.22 for other related collections, which are described in the finding aid *Descriptive Inventory* . . . (cited above).

Korean War (1950-53)

Access to bonus records is restricted to bonus recipients in accordance with Illinois statutes.

Bonus Payments. Index cards list bonus payments to veterans of the Korean War.

ILLINOIS STATE HISTORICAL LIBRARY

Old State Capitol
Springfield, Illinois 62701
(217) 782-4836

The Illinois State Historical Library holds a significant number of manuscript collections that pertain to military service. Most of these collections consist of letters and diaries written by soldiers while in military service. The Black Hawk War, Mexican War, Civil War, Spanish-American War, World War I, and World War II are represented in the collections. Much of the material for the Black Hawk War can be found in Whitney's *The Black Hawk War, 1831-32* (cited below under Published Sources—Illinois). The greatest number of collections pertain to the Civil War. Some of these are mentioned in William L. Burton's *Descriptive Bibliography of Civil War Manuscripts in Illinois* (Springfield: Northwestern University Press, 1966) and Victor Hicken's *Illinois in the Civil War* (Urbana: University of Illinois Press, 1966. 2nd ed. 1991). An appendix in Hicken's book lists the manuscript collections by regiment. Also see Donald J. Berthrong, *The Civil War Collection of the Illinois State Historical Library* (Springfield: the library, 1949).

In addition, the library holds the records of the Grand Army of the Republic, Department of Illinois, 1880-1930; and the records of the Military Order of the Loyal Legion, Commandery of the State of Illinois, 1868-1988, which consist of minutes, correspondence, annual reports, membership records, and published material relating to commemorative ceremonies for President Lincoln. The records of the United Spanish War Veterans, Department of Illinois, 1904-1970, are incomplete.

There is a card file index, arranged by regiment, to many soldiers' letters that appeared in Illinois newspapers during the Civil War. Civil War holdings include photographs of battle scenes, camps and forts, regiments, officers, and ordnance and supplies.

The World War I collection covers such topics as training activities at Fort Sheridan, Camp Grant, and the Great Lakes Naval Station, and R.O.T.C. training at the University of Illinois. The role played by industry in the war effort is documented, and photographs of soldiers stationed in Germany and France are also included in this collection.

UNIVERSITY OF ILLINOIS ARCHIVES

Main Library, Room 19
University of Illinois
1408 West Gregory Drive
Urbana-Champaign, Illinois 61801
(217) 333-0798

The University of Illinois library has a large number of manuscript collections, many of which include documents pertaining to military service. The University of Illinois Archives holds material pertaining to military service, including information on alumni who served in World War I and World War II, and the archives of the Third Armored Division Association from World War II. See Maynard J. Brichford, Robert M. Sutton, and Dennis F. Walle, *Manuscripts Guide to Collections at the University of Illinois at Urbana-Champaign* (2 vols. Urbana: University of Illinois Press, 1976).

PUBLISHED SOURCES—ILLINOIS

General

Coulter, O.H., comp. *Roster of Illinois Soldiers Residing in Kansas.* . . . 2 vols. Topeka, Kans.: Western Veteran, 1889 (?).

Illinois. Adjutant General's Office. *Roll of Honor: Record of Burial Places of Soldiers, Sailors, Marines, and Army Nurses of All Wars of the United States Buried in Illinois.* 2 vols. Springfield: 1929. Reprint. Springfield: Illinois State Historical Society, 1976. Biographical sketches, including military service, with sources cited.

Illinois Soldiers' and Sailors' Home at Quincy: Admission of Mexican War and Civil War Veterans. 2 vols. Indexed by Lowell M. Volkell. Thomson: Heritage House, 1975-80. Includes veterans of the Mexican, Civil, and Spanish-American wars.

Walker, Homer A. *Illinois Pensioners List of the Revolution, 1812, & Indian Wars.* Washington, D.C.: 1955. Biographical sketches of approximately seven hundred soldiers; also includes widows and orphans.

1775-83 (American Revolution)

Clift, Garrett G. *A List of Officers of the Illinois Regiment, and of Crockett's Regiment Who Have Received Lands for Their Service: A List of Officers of the Illinois Regiment, Who Have Not Received Lands for Revolutionary Services, a List of Non-commissioned Officers and Soldiers of the Illinois Regiment, and the Western Army, Under the Command of General George Rogers Clarke [sic] Who are Entitled to Bounty Land, A List of Captain Francis Charloville's Volunteers Entitled to Two Hundred Acres of Land Each.* Richmond, Va.: 1883. Reprint. Anchorage, Ky: Borderland Books, 1952.

Illinois State Genealogical Society. *Soldiers of the American Revolution Buried in Illinois.* . . . Compiled by Mrs. John S. Devanny. Springfield: the society, 1976.

Walker, Harriet J. *Revolutionary Soldiers Buried in Illinois.* Los Angeles: The Standard Printing Co., 1917. Reprint. Baltimore: Genealogical Publishing Co., 1967. Biographical sketches of approximately seven hundred soldiers.

1784-1860 (Indian Wars; War of 1812; Black Hawk War; Mexican War)

Coltrin, Gerald E., comp. *Black Hawk War Veterans Buried in the State of Illinois.* Peoria: Coltrin, 1879.

Crim, Ruth. *1812 Soldiers From Illinois Territory.* Peoria: 1957. Also in: Illinois Adjutant General. *Report.* Vol. 9, pages 318-43. Springfield: 1902

Elliott, Isaac H. *Record of the Services of Illinois Soldiers in the Black Hawk War, 1831-32, and in the Mexican War, 1846-48 . . . With an Appendix Giving a Record of the Services of the Illinois Militia, Rangers and Riflemen, in Protecting the Frontier From the Ravages of the Indians From 1810 to 1813.* Springfield: H.W. Rokker, 1902.

Herberger, Margaret. *Soldiers of the War of 1812 Buried in Illinois.* Peoria: 1957.

Illinois. Adjutant General's Office. *Record of the Services of Illinois Soldiers in the Black Hawk War, 1831-32, and in the Mexican War. . . .* Springfield: H.W. Rokker, 1882.

Myers, Lee. *Illinois Volunteers in New Mexico, 1847-1848.* Santa Fe, New Mexico: 1972.

U.S. General Land Office. *Index of the Illinois Patent Book.* Compiled by George C. Camp. Peoria: 1853.

———. *War of 1812 Bounty Lands in Illinois.* Originally published as *Lands in Illinois to Soldiers of Late War.* House Doc. 262, 26th Cong., 1st sess. Washington, D.C.: 1840. Reprint. Thomson: Heritage House, 1977. Listed by date of patent with number of warrant; name of patentee and military rank; corps or regiment; description of tract (quarter section, township, range); and to whom and date delivered.

Whitney, Ellen M., comp. *The Black Hawk War, 1831-32.* 3 vols. Vol. 1, *Illinois Volunteers.* Collections of the Illinois State Historical Society, vols. 25-27. Springfield: Illinois State Historical Library, 1970-78.

1861-65 (Civil War)

Beveridge, John L., David B. Vaughan, and Joseph B. Greenhut. *Illinois Monuments at Gettysburg.* Springfield: state printer, 1892.

Illinois. Adjutant General's Office. *Report of the Adjutant General of the State of Illinois, 1861-1866.* 8 vols. Springfield: H.W. Rokker, 1886.

Illinois. Adjutant General's Office. *Report of the Adjutant General of the State of Illinois. . . .* 8 vols. Springfield: Baker, Bailhache, 1867. Reprint. Springfield: state printer, 1886. Vols. 1-3: Civil War officers; vols. 3-8: Civil War enlisted men.

———. *Report of the Adjutant General of the State of Illinois.* 9 vols. Springfield: Phillips Bros., 1900-02. Vols. 1-8: roster of officers and enlisted men, with unit, name and rank, date of enlistment, and when mustered out (or discharged, deserted, or died); vol. 9: index.

Illinois Military Units in the Civil War. Springfield: Civil War Centennial Commission of Illinois, 1962.

Illinois. Vicksburg Military Park Commission. *Illinois at Vicksburg.* Chicago (?): Blakely Printing Co. (?), 1907.

Pompey, Sherman L. *Confederates Buried in Illinois.* 2 vols. Clovis, Calif. (?): 1970 (?).

Pratt, Marion D., ed. "Illinois Men in the Union Navy During the Civil War." *Illinois Libraries* 44 (6) (June 1962): 435-59.

Report of the Adjutant General of the State of Illinois for the Years 1861-66. 8 vols. Rev. ed. Springfield: 1900-1901.

Wilson, James Grant. *Biographical Sketches of Illinois Officers Engaged in the War Against the Rebellion of 1861.* Chicago: James Barnet, 1862.

1898-1971 (Spanish-American War through Vietnam War)

Illinois. Adjutant General's Office. *Report Containing the Complete Muster Out Rolls of Illinois Volunteers. . . .* 5 vols. Springfield: 1904.

_____ . *Roster of Officers of the Illinois National Guard and the Illinois Naval Militia.* Springfield: Schnepp & Barnes, 1923.

Indiana

1731-32	French fur traders established a fort at Vincennes.
1763	The Treaty of Paris which ended the French and Indian War transferred Indiana to the British. (See French and Indian War in the appendix.)
1778	George Rogers Clark captured British forts in Indiana during the American Revolution. (See American Revolution in the appendix.)
1783	The Treaty of Paris which ended the American Revolution transferred Indiana to the United States. (See American Revolution in the appendix.)
1787	Indiana became part of the Northwest Territory.
1800	Indiana became Indiana Territory, which included Michigan and Illinois.
1805	Michigan was separated from Indiana Territory.
1809	Illinois was separated from Indiana Territory.
1811	Battle of Tippecanoe between federal troops under William Henry Harrison and Indians under Tecumseh broke the Shawnee Confederation. (See Battle of Tippecanoe in the appendix.)
1816	Indiana became a state.

Indiana State Archives

Room 117
State Library Building
140 North Senate Avenue
Indianapolis, Indiana 46204-2215
(317) 232-3660

Finding aids and indexes and a few published records are available in a small reading room, but all records, original or microfilmed, must be requested from the staff. One microfilm reader is available. Except for one series containing correspondence from the office of the secretary of war for the period 1835 through 1869, this archives holds no National Archives microfilm. However, the state library in the same building (second floor) has a sizeable collection of National Archives microfilm, as described below.

Finding Aids

Descriptive Inventory–Adjutant General's Ledger Books, 1812–1920. This pamphlet contains a list of collections and records from the office of the Indiana adjutant general pertaining to records of the War of 1812, the Black Hawk War, the Civil War, and miscellaneous collections.

Guide to Indiana Civil War Manuscripts. This book, compiled in 1960 by Ann Turner on behalf of the Indiana Civil War Centennial Commission, contains summary histories of Indiana regiments that participated in the Civil War and manuscripts relating to those regiments. Symbols indicate the various state repositories at which the material may be found.

Grand Army of the Republic Post Records, 1879–1938. These are records for individual posts, including descriptive books, minute books, and post histories. Personal data is often included.

Records

General

Index to Indiana Militia, 1877-1896. Alphabetically arranged index cards, each pertaining to a militiaman. Each card includes name, unit, place, muster date, age, and occupation.

Indiana State Militia, 1812-1851. Index cards for commissioned officers in the militia; name, rank, and unit.

Indiana Legion and Indiana National Guard Service Records, 1880-1917. Arranged alphabetically; name, unit, station, rank, residence, date of enrollment and discharge, and, occasionally, physical description.

Veterans' Graves Registration File. Index cards prepared by the WPA. They cover fifty-one of the state's ninety-two counties. The cards are arranged by county and thereunder alphabetically by veteran's name. They include name, address, date and place of birth, war participated in, rank, unit, enlistment date, and discharge date. The cards have not been microfilmed.

Indiana Soldiers' Home. Four bound volumes of computer-generated lists of residents (men and women) for the periods 1890–1964 and 1964–1977; name, rank, unit, and war in which participated. Residents' records are also housed here.

Indiana Soldiers' Home. Index to Men, 1878–1967. Computer-generated list similar to above. Residents' records are also housed here.

Indiana Soldiers' Home. Additions, Men And Women, 1898–1980. Computer-generated list similar to above. Residents' records are also housed here.

Soldiers' and Sailors' Orphans' Home, 15 February 1847–26 July 1941. Three reels of microfilm.

Enrollment of Soldiers. The state of Indiana enumerated the veterans (or, if deceased, their family members) who resided in the state during the years 1886, 1890, and 1894. The archives has microfilm copies of the enumeration sheets. For each of the three enumerations the sheets give the following information: name, rank, unit, race, war participated in, address, and number of children under age sixteen. For deceased veterans the following data was collected: date and place of death, residence at time of death, place killed or wounded, nature of injuries, nature of military disease, and whether indigent. The names of widows and sons or daughters were also listed for this group. A card index to these enrollment sheets is available at the state library—see the Indiana State Library section below.

A fourth enrollment was conducted for the period 1913–1922. This data includes name, age, state from which enlisted, war participated in, unit, and branch of service.

Military Separation Records (DD 214) for All Indiana Military Personnel Separated From Service After 1979. These records are not available to the public because of federal Privacy Act restrictions.

War of 1812 (1812–15)

Indiana Territorial Militia in Federal Service, Battle of Tippecanoe, 1811, and War of 1812. Muster rolls and payrolls; Indiana adjutant general's records.

Commissioned Officers, War of 1812. Alphabetized index of paper slips; name, rank, unit, and date of commission.

Black Hawk War (1832)

Alphabetical Card File of Soldiers. Name, rank, unit, term of enlistment, and by whom enlisted.

Muster Rolls and Payrolls Arranged by Unit: U. S. Army, First Mounted Ranger Battalion.

Mexican War (1846–48)

Indiana Mexican War Volunteer Index (microfilm). Alphabetical card file for five Indiana volunteer regiments. Cards give name, rank, and muster-in and muster-out dates.

Indiana in the Mexican War. A published index to a book of the same title (see Published Sources—Indiana). The archives does not have a copy of the book—only Barbara S. Wolfe's index, published in 1985.

Civil War—Union (1861–65)

Alphabetical Card File of Indiana Civil War Volunteers (microfilm). Compiled from original muster rolls. Researchers requesting a copy of a soldier's Civil War file receive the following information: name, rank, unit, time of service, date and location mustered in (for federal service), age, physical description, nativity, occupation, and date discharged. The cards may contain other information, but it is not routinely abstracted for the researcher.

Indiana Legion (Civil War state militia) (microfilm). An alphabetical card file compiled from original muster rolls. The cards list name, unit, period of active duty, and age.

Civil War Substitutes (microfilm). An alphabetical card file listing Indiana citizens who hired substitutes for military duty. The cards provide the name of the individual hiring the substitute, name of the substitute, and unit to which assigned. There is also a separate index of those who hired substitutes.

Militia Enrollment, 1862. Large sheets listing the able-bodied men of Indiana over age eighteen and under forty-five. The data includes name, age, and occupation. Also indicated are those who were not able-bodied and the reason, and those exempt from service and the reason. The "remarks" column notes those who actually served in the military and the nature of such service. These records are stored in large boxes that are labeled by county.

Grand Army of the Republic Post Membership Register. Bound volumes giving name of member, company, post office address, and city address. There is a separate publication for each post. Additional information is written in the margins.

Register of Visitors to the National Encampment of the Grand Army of the Republic at Indianapolis, 4–9 September 1893. This register comprises thirty-three volumes, each devoted to an Indiana Civil War regiment or battery. Included are veteran's name, unit, hometown, and state of residence in 1893.

Indiana Adjutant General (1864–1914) and Grand Army of the Republic (1895–1918) Letter Books. An alphabetical card index to correspondence is available.

Union Soldiers Buried in Indiana. Index cards prepared from vol. 1 of the eight volumes by Adjutant General W. H. H. Terrel, 1865–69; includes rosters of Civil War regiments.

Indiana Adjutant General's Records (a selected list. See the finding aid *Descriptive Inventory . . .* above for other records).

Register of Commissions Issued, 1863; 1864–65.

Field Officers, by Regiment.

Register of Men in Draft of 1862.

Drafted Men and Substitutes Unaccounted for, 1862.

Descriptive Books, by Regiment, Listing Personnel.

Register of Railroad Passes Furnished to Indiana Soldiers and Dependents, 1863-64.

Camp Enrollment, Camp Sullivan, 1862.

Registers of Hospitalized Soldiers: Nashville, 1862-63; Murfreesboro, 1863-64; Vicksburg, 1862-65; Chattanooga, 1862; and Evansville, 1863.

Spanish-American War (1898-99)

Indiana Spanish-American War volunteers, 1898-1899. Registration cards from the office of the Indiana adjutant general (microfilm); name, unit, rank, age, physical description, place of birth, occupation, and muster-in and muster-out dates. See also annual reports by the adjutant general, 1895-1899.

United Spanish War Veterans. Records of the organization, Indiana department, 1903-ca. 1964; name, rank, unit, and date and place of death.

World War I (1917-18)

Indiana World War I Draft Registration File (microfilm). Lists individuals registered in the first and second drafts, 1917 and 1918; name, address, race, and place registered. For those who served in the military, the following data is also included: place and location of service, branch of service, and place and date of discharge.

Indiana Gold Star Records. The Indiana Historical Commission published several volumes containing separate sheets for each Indiana man or woman who died during World War I. A gold star is attached to each sheet. Data includes name; date and place of birth; marital status; names and addresses of widow or children; next of kin; enlistment date; occupation; branch of service; date and place of death; and whether killed in action, died of wounds, or died of disease. Some contain letters from family members, and some are accompanied by photographs. See also "Gold Star Honor Roll," based on these volumes.

Indiana World War I Service Records. Included are cards representing those who served in the army, navy, and marines.

World War II (1941-45)

Indiana World War II Casualties, Army and Navy. An alphabetical card file with a separate card file for Marion County deaths; name, rank, address of next of kin, and date and theater of military action. See also *Combat Connected Naval Casualties, World War II* (U.S. Department of Defense).

Index to World War II Bonus Applications. Records of the State Auditor (microfilm). See also *Applications for Bonus of Deceased Veterans of World War II* (microfilm).

Discharge Certificates and Separation Records for Indiana Residents, World War II. These records are not available to the public because of federal Privacy Act restrictions.

Korean War (1950-53)

Korean War Bonus Index. Records From the Indiana Adjutant General (microfilm). See also adjutant general publications, six volumes, 1950-53, listing Indiana servicemen in the Korean War, arranged by county.

Indiana Korean War Discharges. These records are not available to the public because of federal Privacy Act restrictions.

Vietnam War (1963-75)

Indiana Vietnam War Discharges. These records are not available to the public because of federal Privacy Act restrictions. However, archives staff may provide selected information to veterans or their next of kin.

INDIANA STATE LIBRARY

140 North Senate Avenue (second floor)
Indianapolis, Indiana 46204-2296
(317) 232-3675

Finding Aid

The genealogy section of the state library contains an Index to Indiana Enrollment of Soldiers, Their Widows and Orphans, 1886, 1890, 1894. The cards list name, county, and year and date of enrollment. After obtaining data from the index, researchers may go to the state archives on the library's first floor and request to see the original enrollment sheets.

NATIONAL ARCHIVES MICROFILM

General Index to Compiled Military Service Records of Revolutionary War Soldiers (M860).

Selected Records From Revolutionary War Pension and Bounty Land Warrant Application Files, 1800-1900 (M805).

U.S. Revolutionary War Bounty Land Warrants Used in the U.S. Military District of Ohio and Related Papers (Acts of 1786, 1803, and 1806) (M829).

Index to War of 1812 Pension Application Files (M313).

War of 1812 Military Bounty Land Warrants, 1815-1858 (M848—roll 1 contains an index).

General Index to Pension Files, 1861-1934 (T288).

The Negro in the Military Service of the United States, 1639–1886 (M858).

Also in this building are the Indiana Reference Section (room 210), the Indiana Historical Society (third floor), and the Indiana Pioneer Society (basement). See Eric Pumroy, with Paul Brockman, *A Guide to Manuscript Collections of the Indiana Historical Society and Indiana State Library* (Indianapolis: Indiana State Library, 1986).

PUBLISHED SOURCES—INDIANA

General

A History of the National Guard of Indiana: From the Beginning of the Militia System in 1787 to the Present Time, Including the Services of the Indiana Troops in the War With Spain. Indianapolis: W.D. Pratt, 1901. Includes rosters.

Indiana. Adjutant General. *Exhibits and Proof of the Indiana War Claims.* Indianapolis: ca. 1902.

Turner, Ann. *Guide to Indiana Civil War Manuscripts.* Indianapolis: Civil War Centennial Commission, 1965.

1775–83 (American Revolution)

Daughters of the American Revolution. Indiana. *Roster of Soldiers and Patriots of the American Revolution Buried in Indiana.* Compiled and edited by Estella A. O'Byrne. Brookville: 1938. Reprint. Baltimore: Genealogical Publishing Co., 1968. Approximately 1,400 names, alphabetically arranged, with sources.

English, William H. *Conquest of the Country Northwest of the River Ohio, 1778–1783, and Life of Gen. George Rogers Clark.* . . . Indianapolis: Bowen-Merrill, 1896. Reprint. New York: Arno Press, 1971. Lists soldiers who served with Clark and were granted land in Indiana.

Ticusan, Sarah G. H., comp. *An Index to Roster of Soldiers and Patriots of the American Revolution Buried in Indiana, Published by the Indiana Daughters of the American Revolution, 1938.* Indianapolis: Indiana State Library, 1974.

Waters, Margaret R. *Revolutionary Soldiers Buried in Indiana: 300 Names Not Listed in the "Roster of Soldiers and Patriots of the American Revolution Buried in Indiana."* Indianapolis: the author, 1949. Reprint. Baltimore: Genealogical Publishing Co., 1970.

———. *Revolutionary Soldiers Buried in Indiana: A Supplement; 485 Names Not Listed in the "Roster of Soldiers and Patriots of the American Revolution Buried in Indiana" (1939); nor in "Revolutionary Soldiers Buried in Indiana" (1949).* Indianapolis: the author, 1954. Reprint. Baltimore: Genealogical Publishing Co., 1970.

Wolfe, Barbara S. *Index to Revolutionary Soldiers of Indiana and Other Patriots.* Indianapolis: Ye Olde Genealogie Shoppe, 1983.

1784–1860 (War of 1812; Indian Wars; Mexican War)

Franklin, Charles M. *Indiana, War of 1812 Soldiers: Militia.* Indianapolis: Ye Olde Genealogie Shoppe, 1984. Regiments listed by county.

Indiana. Adjutant General's Office. *Indiana in the Mexican War.* Indianapolis: state printer, 1908.

Loftus, Carrie. *Indiana Militia in the Black Hawk War.* The author, n.d.

Wolfe, Barbara S. *Index to Mexican War Pension Applications.* Indianapolis: Heritage House, 1985. Transcribed from records held by the National Archives.

1861–65 (Civil War)

Indiana. Adjutant General. *Report of the Adjutant General of the State of Indiana.* . . . 8 vols. Indianapolis: state printer, 1867–69. Includes Civil War rosters.

Indiana. Adjutant General's Office. *Annual Reports, 1861–1865.* 5 vols. Indianapolis: state printer, 1861–65.

Indiana. Andersonville Monument Commission. *Report of the Unveiling and Dedication of Indiana Monument at Andersonville, Georgia (National Cemetery) Thursday, November 26, 1908.* . . . Indianapolis: state printer, 1909. Indiana soldiers and regiments.

Indiana. Commissioners for the Chickamauga and Chattanooga National Park. *Indiana at Chickamauga, 1863–1900.* Indianapolis: W.B. Burford, 1901. Participating units with names of officers.

Indiana. Gettysburg Anniversary Commission. *Indiana at the Fiftieth Anniversary of the Battle of Gettysburg . . . with Rosters of the Army of the Potomac and the Army of Northern Virginia, and a Brief History of Each of the Regiments From Indiana.* . . . Indianapolis (?): 1913 (?). "Names of Veterans Who Visited Gettysburg" (1913), pages 110–21.

Indiana Veteran Association of the State of Kansas. *Roster of Indiana Soldiers in the State of Kansas.* Topeka, Kans.: Indiana Veteran Association of the War of the Rebellion of the State of Kansas, 1888.

Merrill, Catharine (?). *The Soldiers of Indiana in the War for the Union.* . . . 2 vols. Indianapolis: Merrill and Co., 1866–69.

Robbins, Coy D., comp. *African American Soldiers From Indiana With the Union Army in the Civil War, 1863–1865.* Bloomington: the compiler, 1989.

Stevenson, David. *Indiana's Roll of Honor.* 2 vols. Indianapolis: A.D. Streight, 1864–66. Regimental histories with names of officers.

Trapp, Glenda K. *Index to the Report of the Adjutant General of the State of Indiana. First Volume: An Every Name Index to Volumes I, II, and III. Second Volume: An Every Name Index to Volume IV.* 2 vols. Evansville: Trapp Publishing Service, 1986–87.

1866-99 (Spanish-American War)

Indiana. Adjutant General's Office. *Record of Indiana Volunteers in the Spanish-American War, 1898-1899.* Indianapolis: W.B. Burford, 1900.

1900-71 (World War I through Vietnam War)

Indiana. *Honor List of Dead and Missing and Returning Veterans Separated Under Honorable Conditions.* U.S. Department of Defense. All branches of service, Korean War.

_____ . *Indiana Veterans, Korean Conflict.* 6 vols. U.S. Department of Defense. Lists veterans who served between 25 June 1950 and 27 July 1953. Arranged by county and alphabetically thereunder.

Indiana Historical Commission. *Gold Star Honor Rolls 1914-1918.* Indianapolis: the commission, 1921.

Indiana. Office of the Adjutant General. *Names, Addresses and Serial Numbers of Indiana Persons Serving in the World War.* Arranged by county and alphabetically thereunder.

Iowa

1673	French explorers Jacques Marquette and Louis Joliet claimed Iowa for France.
1762	France ceded Iowa and the remainder of Louisiana to Spain.
1800	Spain returned Louisiana to France.
1803	Possession of Iowa passed from France to the United States as a result of the Louisiana Purchase.
1804	American explorers Lewis and Clark passed through Iowa.
1805	Zebulon Pike entered Iowa during his exploration of the Mississippi River.
1808	Iowa was made part of Illinois Territory.
1812	Iowa was included in Missouri Territory.
1838	Iowa became a territory.
1846	Iowa became a state.

STATE HISTORICAL SOCIETY OF IOWA

Centennial Building
402 Iowa Avenue
Iowa City, Iowa 52240
(319) 335-3916

Library/Archives Bureau
State Historical Building
600 East Locust
Des Moines, Iowa 50319
(515) 281-6200

Except for the Grand Army of the Republic records, which are housed in both of the above facilities, all of the records listed below are housed in the Des Moines facility.

Records

General

Persons Subject to Military Duty, 1861-ca. 1916. Lists arranged by county and township.

Clothing Books. Records of clothing and equipment issued and amount charged to each soldier's account.

Reports of Military Units. Document when and where various units were engaged in battle and names of injured, sick, and killed. Correspondence pertaining to some units is also available.

Mexican War (1846-48)

Muster Rolls. Arranged by regiment and company; name, rank, muster dates, nativity, and remarks.

Civil War (1861-65)

NATIONAL ARCHIVES MICROFILM

Index to Compiled Military Service Records of Volunteer Union Soldiers Who Served in Organizations From the State of Iowa (M542).

OTHER RECORDS

Muster Rolls. Arranged by regiment and company; name, rank, muster dates, nativity, and remarks.

Certificates of Service. Name, nativity, residence, physical description, rank, when and where enlisted, by whom enlisted, when and where mustered into service, and date of termination of service.

Grand Army of the Republic (GAR) Post Minutes and Roster Books. These include rosters of members.

Spanish-American War (1898-99)

Muster Rolls. Arranged by regiment and company; name, rank, muster dates, nativity, and remarks.

World War I (1917-18)

Casualty File. Contains information about servicemen and some photographs.

PUBLISHED SOURCES—IOWA

General

Iowa. Adjutant General's Office. *Roster and Record of Iowa Soldiers in Miscellaneous Organizations of the Mexican War, Indian Campaigns, War of the Rebellion, Spanish-American, and Philippine Wars.* Vol. 6. Des Moines: 1914.

_____. *Persons Subject to Military Duty, ca. 1862-1910.* Available on microfilm.

1775-83 (American Revolution)

Revolutionary War Soldiers and Patriots Buried in Iowa. Marceline, Mo.: Walsworth Publishing Co., 1978. Published for the Iowa Society, DAR by the Abigail Adams Chapter, Des Moines, Iowa.

1861-65 (Civil War)

Byers, S.H.M. *Iowa in War Times.* Des Moines: W.D. Condit & Co., 1888.

Ingersoll, Lurton D. *Iowa and the Rebellion.* 3rd ed. Philadelphia: J.B. Lippincott & Co., 1867. Lists officers by unit.

Iowa. Adjutant General's Office. *List of Ex-soldiers, Sailors and Marines Living in Iowa.* Des Moines: G.E. Roberts, 1886.

_____. *Roster and Record of Iowa Soldiers in the War of the Rebellion: Together With Historical Sketches of Volunteer Organizations, 1861-1866.* 6 vols. Des Moines: E.H. English, 1908-11. Vol. 6 also includes miscellaneous units of Iowa soldiers in the Mexican War.

_____. *Reports, 1861-1867.* 9 vols. Des Moines: state printer, 1861-68.

Stuart, Addison A. *Iowa Colonels and Regiments. . . .* Des Moines: Mills & Co., 1865.

1916 (Mexican Border Campaign)

Dreyer, Richard H. *Iowa Troops in Mexican Border Service, 1916-17.* Iowa City: the author, 1917 (?).

Kansas

1541	Spanish explorer Francisco Vasquez de Coronado entered Kansas.
1803	Part of the Louisiana country, Kansas became United States property as a result of the Louisiana Purchase.
1854	The Kansas-Nebraska Act made Kansas a territory.
1856	Violence among settlers over the slavery issue caused the territory to be known as "Bleeding Kansas."
1861	Kansas became a state.
1861-65	Although a strong Union state during the Civil War, Kansas was the scene of many guerilla actions from Southern raiders on its frontier. (See American Civil War in the appendix.)

KANSAS STATE HISTORICAL SOCIETY

Library and Archives Division
120 West Tenth Street
Topeka, Kansas 66612-1291
(913) 296-4776

Finding Aids

Manuscript Sources. This aid lists record and manuscript collections, published and unpublished, that list or group names of individuals in military service in Kansas or other states. Included with the major collections are several that pertain to only one county or town (not cited below).

Kansas State Archives Sources: Civil War–World War II. This aid lists and describes record collections that pertain to the military organizations from Kansas that served in various wars and during various time periods. Included with the major collections are several that pertain to only one county or town (not cited below).

National Archives and Other Microfilm Held by the Manuscripts Division (federal records only). Many, but not all, of the microfilm series cited in this finding aid are listed below.

Library and Archives Division, Military Sources for Kansas. This is a bibliography of published works available in this library.

Many, but not all, of the works included in this bibliography are cited below.

Records

General

NATIONAL ARCHIVES MICROFILM

Returns From Regular Army Cavalry Regiments, 1833–1916 (M744–selected rolls. See the finding aid for Kansas units).

Returns From United States Military Posts, 1800–1916 (M617–selected rolls. See the finding aid for Kansas posts. Also see M661–historical information relating to military posts, etc.).

United States Army; Continental Army Commands (T837–selected rolls relating to Kansas posts).

Letters Received by the Office of the Adjutant General (Main Series), 1822–1860 (M567).

MICROFILM IDENTIFIED ONLY BY KANSAS "MS" NUMBERS

United States Army Records, 1848–1854 (MS236). These relate to Kansas posts.

Post Returns of Fort Mackay; New Post; Arkansas River; and Fort Atkinson, 1853–54 (MS80).

OTHER RECORDS

Military Collection, 1840–1973 (?). Contains many records, such as muster rolls, hospital registers, casualty lists, court-martial proceedings, etc., for many military units, both in Kansas and neighboring states. They are arranged as follows: pre-territorial period (to 1854); territorial period (1854–61); Civil War; Indian campaigns (1865–79); Spanish-American War; World War I; World War II; Vietnam conflict. Time period and name of military unit must be specified. (See folder list for this collection for lists of units.)

Forts, 1853–1902. Muster rolls and payrolls of detachments, U.S. Army Hospital Corps, Fort Riley; and interments at Fort Dodge post cemetery, 1865–79.

State Decennial Census, 1865, 1885–1915. Censuses compiled for the state Board of Agriculture. The census for 1865 lists regiment and company of those involved in the Civil War. The censuses of 1885 through 1915 include discharge status, state where enlisted, branch of service and unit, and name of prison (if a prisoner). Indexes are available for 1865 and for other years for scattered localities. They are arranged by county and city or township.

Civil War (1861–65)

NATIONAL ARCHIVES MICROFILM

Compiled Service Records of Confederate Soldiers Who Served in Organizations Raised Directly by the Confederate Government (M258).

MICROFILM IDENTIFIED ONLY BY KANSAS "MS" NUMBERS

Register of Sick and Wounded at USA General Hospital, Fort Scott, Ks, Hospital Records, Register No. 15 (MS1010).

Compiled Military Service Records, Co. F, 15th Kansas Cavalry, Relating to Orren A. Curtis. (MS735.02 or MS960.02) These records concern Curtis' court-martial.

Records of Soldiers Buried at Fort Wallace (MS85.06). Compiled when bodies where reinterred at Fort Leavenworth in 1866.

OTHER RECORDS

Descriptive Book, 1862–64. Lists of officers, deserters, discharges, descriptive rolls of companies, transfers; records of the Kansas adjutant general; one volume.

Descriptive Rolls, 1861–65. Men in various Kansas volunteer regiments and batteries; name, rank, physical description, nativity, and residence; arranged by regiment and company. Seventeen volumes.

Enlistment Papers, Kansas Volunteer Regiments, 1862–65. Forms filled out for each recruit; name, nativity, occupation, and physical description; arranged by regiment and company; seven boxes.

Enrollment of . . . Soldiers, Their Widows and Orphans, 1883 (microfilm). Rolls include name; race; rank; unit; state where served; arm of service; injuries, wounds, and diseases; post office; date and place of death; and whether widow remarried or indigent, dependent on others, or in an almshouse. They are arranged by county and thereunder alphabetically.

Enrollment of Ex-soldiers and Sailors, Their Widows and Orphans, 1889. Documents prepared in enrolling of Union veterans in Kansas, 1889; arranged by service, regiment, and company.

Hospital Reports, 1862–64. Kansas volunteers who were treated or had died in military hospitals; name, rank, unit, admission date, disease or wound, and remarks; arranged chronologically.

Index of Volunteer Officers, 1861–65. Arranged alphabetically.

Officers Commissioned, 1861–65. Name, rank, date of commission, and remarks. Final register includes Home Guard; arranged chronologically or by regiment.

Rosters of Cavalry and Infantry, 1861–65. Arranged by unit.

Roster of Enlisted Men, 1861–65. Arranged by regiment and company.

Roster of Deceased Members of the Kansas Volunteers, 1861–65. Name, rank, unit, and year and location of death; arranged by unit and thereunder by rank and alphabetically.

Volunteer Regiment Files (Correspondence), 1861–79. Miscellaneous documents pertaining to recruits in various regiments. (See folder list for this collection for names of units.)

List of Members of the Eighth Kansas Volunteers Buried at Stones River National Cemetery Murfreesboro, Tennessee. A computer printout giving name, rank, date of death, state, company, and grave number; arranged alphabetically.

Index of Volunteers, 1861-65. All servicemen in Kansas volunteer regiments.

Muster Rolls and Payrolls, 1861-65. Rolls for several Kansas military units (see folder list for this collection); name, rank, age, when and where joined, length of service, pay, age at discharge, bounty due or property unaccounted for, etc; arranged by regiment and company; some available on microfilm.

Muster-out Rolls, 1861-65. Rolls for several Kansas units; name, rank, age, date and location of enlistment, last paid, bounty paid and due, and remarks (promotions, desertions, deaths, etc.; arranged by regiment and company; available on microfilm.

KANSAS STATE MILITIA

Several collections of muster rolls, payrolls, and other records pertaining to certain Kansas counties.

Index to Militia officers, 1861-65.

Muster Rolls and Payrolls, 1861-64

Muster Rolls, 1861-75.

Officers Commissioned, 1863-83.

Post-Civil War—Volunteer Regiments, Militia and National Guard; Indian Campaigns (1866-)

NATIONAL ARCHIVES MICROFILM

Letters Received by the Office of the Adjutant General (Main Series), 1861-1870 (M619—selected rolls. See finding aid).

Letters Received by the Office of the Adjutant General (Main Series), 1871-1880 (M666—selected rolls. See finding aid).

Letters Received by the office of the Adjutant General (Main Series), 1881-1889 (M689—selected rolls. See finding aid).

OTHER RECORDS

Descriptive Rolls, Nineteenth Kansas Volunteer Cavalry, 1868. Lists of servicemen who served in a campaign against hostile Indians; name, rank, place of birth, age, occupation, enlistment date, and physical description; arranged alphabetically by company and surname.

Enlistment Papers, 1868-69. Pertain to Kansas State Militia.

Enlistment and Discharge Papers, 1880-84.

Enlistment and Discharge Papers, National Guard, 1893-1915.

Muster Rolls and Payrolls, 1867-1917.

Muster Rolls, etc., Volunteer Regiments, 1867-69. List men in the Eighteenth and Nineteenth Volunteer Cavalry Regiments in campaigns against hostile Indians.

Muster Rolls and Payrolls—Indian Scare, 1874.

Officers Commissioned, 1873-86.

Registers of Officer and Brevet Commissions, 1880-1917.

Roster, Nineteenth Volunteer Regiment, 1868.

Roster Books, National Guard, 1882-1914.

Undelivered Armory Drill Pay, National Guard, 1914-41.

Spanish-American War; Philippine Insurrection (1898-1901)

Alphabetical Roll of Officers and Men of the Twentieth-Twenty-third Kansas Volunteers, 1898-99. Name, regiment, and company.

Descriptive Lists and Accounts of Pay and Clothing, Twenty-second Kansas Volunteer Infantry, 1898.

Muster Rolls of Officers, Twentieth-Twenty-second Kansas Volunteer Infantry, 1898-99.

Returns of Casualties, Twentieth Kansas Volunteers, 1899.

Spanish-American War Files, 1898-99. A variety of documents concerning the regiments that participated in this war; contain varied information for each serviceman listed. Arrangement varies.

Roster of Company A, Thirty-second U.S. Volunteer Infantry, Philippine Insurrection, 1899-1901.

World War I (1917-18)

Applications to Enter Camp Taylor Training Camp, 1918. Letters and telegrams.

Classification Book, 1917-18. Selective Service System book for Wyandotte County, Kansas; name, race, serial number, date questionnaire mailed, date questionnaire returned, classification, and date notified, etc.; arranged by order number.

Draft Registration Cards, 1917-18. Cards for Wilson, Woodson, and Wyandotte counties only (very difficult to read).

Selective Service, Kansas, 1917-18. Lists of men inducted or rejected; name of draftee, nativity, camp sent to for training, etc; arranged alphabetically by county.

Enlistment and Discharge Records, 1917-19. Photostatic copies of enlistment and discharge papers and other documents submitted by World War I veterans or their widows or orphans when applying for a state bonus; name, rank, physical description, age, character, vocation, nativity, and battles or skirmishes; arranged alphabetically.

Index to Enlistment Papers, 1917.

Kansas Casualties in the World War (with supplements). Name, rank, residence, regiment, when enlisted or commissioned, date and cause of death, relatives and friends of the deceased; arranged alphabetically.

List of Commissions Issued to Kansas State Guard, 1917. Arranged by town.

Muster Rolls, First Kansas Cavalry, ca. 1917.

Residents of Kansas Whose Military Service . . . Terminated by Dishonorable Discharge, by Desertion, or . . . Discharged Not Honorably, 1917-18.

Roster, 117th Ammunition Train, Rainbow Division, 1917-18.

Post-World War I (1919-38)

Rosters of Station Hospital, Fort Leavenworth, Ks, 1918; Returns of Station Hospital, Fort Leavenworth, Ks, 1919. (MS386)

Index to National Guard Troops, ca. 1918-24.

National Guard Duty Reports, 1926-38. Arranged chronologically.

World War II (1941-45)

Armed Forces Personnel Who Served Between 16 September 1940 and 30 June 1946. Lists of personnel including name, order number, branch of service, date of induction or enlistment, county of residence, etc.; arranged by county and surname.

Vietnam War (1963-75)

Roster of Personnel Called to Active Service, January and May 1968.

Manuscripts

See the finding aid *Manuscript Sources* (cited above) for a complete list of titles of collections that include military material. The following are examples of the data available.

Abbott, James Burnett. Contains staff rolls of officers, etc.

Blackman, William I.R. Rolls of Kansas volunteers, 1855, and muster roll of the Scott Guards, 1861(?).

Blood, James. Includes a muster roll of officers, 1856.

Cheyenne Indians, 1879-1947. Includes list of wounded in action and claims filed by victims of Cheyenne Indian attacks.

Daughters of the American Revolution, Kansas Society. Service records of society members' descendants.

Frontier Guard. Includes names of men organized to protect Washington, D.C., in 1861.

Gilbert, David N. Includes a roster of Company E, Nineteenth Cavalry, Kansas State Militia, 1863 (?).

Goodrich, Eliza (Edwards). Rosters of the 137th Infantry Brigade, World War I.

Grand Army of the Republic, 1871-1916. Includes a list of 356 Civil War veterans.

Harvey, James Madison. Muster rolls, Fourth Kansas Infantry, Civil War.

Hommell, Seth. Medical records of the Twentieth Kansas Infantry.

United Spanish War Veterans. Membership cards, arranged alphabetically; name, address, military record, and, in some cases, date of death.

Kidder, Lyman Stockwell. Names of men of Company M, Second U.S. Cavalry, killed by Indians at Beaver Creek, Kansas ca. 1 July 1867.

Military Order of the Loyal Legion of the U.S. (MOLLUS) Kansas Commandery. Monthly membership lists, 1894-1906.

Miller, Martin G. Considerable material relating to World War I units. (See finding aid.)

Robinson, Charles, Governor. Records of commissions, 1862.

Soldiers' Reunions, 1881-1913; includes list of ex-prisoners of war, register of Ohio Brigade, and registers of those in attendance at Gettysburg, Pennsylvania, reunion, 1913.

Whitaker, James Burns. Contains a ledger book of war claims.

World War I (Kansas veterans). Card indexes to various types of documents, including biographies, Gold Star material, letters, and photographs.

PUBLISHED SOURCES—KANSAS

1861-65 (Civil War)

Coulter, Orel H., comp. *Roster of Illinois Soldiers Residing in Kansas. . . .* 2 vols. Topeka: Western Veteran, 1899 (?).

_____, comp. *Roster of Ohio Soldiers Residing in Kansas. . . .* Topeka: Western Veteran, 1899 (?).

Crawford, Samuel J. *Kansas in the Sixties.* Chicago: A.C. McClurg & Co., 1911. Roster of officers, Eighty-third Colored Infantry, U.S. Army.

Daughters of the American Revolution. John Haupt Chapter (Topeka, Kansas). *Index to the Kansas Militia in the Civil War.* Topeka: 1979.

Dunnett, D.W. *List of Michigan Soldiers Residing in Kansas, 1887.* Howard: Courant Job Print, 1887.

Grand Army of the Republic. Department of Kansas. *Roster of the Members and Posts, Grand Army of the Republic, Department of Kansas . . . Also Rosters of all Auxiliary Organizations.* Topeka: Frost Printer, 1894. See the finding aid *Manuscript Sources* for titles of other Grand Army of the Republic publications for various posts.

Indiana Veteran Association of the War of the Rebellion of the State of Kansas. *Roster of Indiana Soldiers in the State of Kansas. . . .* Topeka: Order of the Indiana Veteran Association of the War of the Rebellion of the State of Kansas, 1888.

Kansas. Adjutant General's Office. *Report of the Adjutant General of the State of Kansas . . . 1861-1865.* 2 vols. Leavenworth: 1867-70. Reprint. Topeka: Kansas State Printing Co., 1896. Rosters of Kansas regiments, including name and rank, residence, dates of enlistment and muster, and remarks.

_____. *Index to the Reprint Edition of the Report of the Adjutant General of the State of Kansas, 1861-1865: A-Z.* Topeka: Kansas Historical Society Library, n.d.

Kansas. Historical Society. Library. *Index to Lists of Pensioners on the Roll, January 1, 1883, Residing in Kansas.* Topeka: the society, 1972.

Knight, J. Lee. *Reunion Memorial, Being the Proceedings and List of Veterans Present at the Second Annual Reunion of Soldiers and Sailors Held at Topeka, Kansas, Sept. 11th to 16th, 1882.* Topeka: Daily Capital Publishing Co., 1883.

Military Order of the Loyal Legion of the United States (MOL-LUS). *Register...to August 1st, 1895.* Leavenworth (?), 1895 (?). Name, rank, and address of members.

_____. Kansas Commandery. *Register of the Commandery of the State of Kansas.* Fort Leavenworth (?): 1891 (?).

Moore, C.E. *List of Old Soldiers That Registered at the Soldiers' Reunion in Cherryvale, Kansas, August 19–24, 1901.* Cherryvale: Cherryvale Republican, 1901.

Moser, O.A. *Roster of Iowa Soldiers in Kansas.* Emporia: E. Lamborn, 1886.

Pompey, Sherman L. *An Honor Roll of Kansas Civil War Veterans.* Kingsburg, Calif.: Pacific Specialties, 1972.

_____. *Burial List of the Indian Home Guard Units of the Union Army From Kansas and Missouri.* Salt Lake City: Research Associates, 1975.

Wilder, Daniel W. *The Annals of Kansas.* Topeka: 1875. New ed. Topeka: G.W. Martin, 1886. Reprint. New York: Arno Press, 1975. The Mid-American Frontier, rosters of Civil War officers.

1866-1902 (Spanish-American War)

Fox, S.M. *Thirteenth Biennial Report of the Adjutant General of the State of Kansas, 1901–02.* Topeka: Kansas Adjutant General's Office, 1902.

Kansas. Adjutant General's Office. A *Roster of Volunteer Troops Furnished by the State of Kansas for the Spanish-American War, 1898. . . .* Topeka: state printer, 1899.

_____. *Kansas Troops in the Volunteer Service of the United States in the Spanish and Philippine Wars.* Topeka: state printer, 1900.

1917-75 (World War I through Vietnam War)

Burial in France of World War Soldiers From Kansas, Remarks of Hon. Arthur Capper of Kansas in the Senate . . . Sept. 14, 1919. Washington, D.C.: Government Printing Office, 1919.

Freemasons, Ancient, Free and Accepted. *Dedicated to the 6357 Masons of Kansas Whose Names are Recorded on the Honor Roll . . .World War of 1914–1918. . . .* N.p., n.d.

Haulsee, W.M., et al., comps. *Soldiers of the Great War.* Vol. 1, *List of Kansans Killed in the War.* Washington, D.C.: Soldiers' Record Publishing Association, 1920.

Kansas. Adjutant General. *History and Roster of the Kansas State Guard, August 6, 1917 to November 11, 1919.* Topeka: state printer, 1925. Supplements. 1921, 1922, 1925.

_____. *Kansas Casualties in the World War, 1917–1919, Regular Army, National Guard, National Army, Enlisted Reserve Corps.* Topeka: state printer, 1921.

_____. *Kansans Who Served in the World War (?).* 4 vols. N.p., n.d. Arranged by county.

_____. *Roster and Directory of the Commissioned Officers of the Kansas National Guard.* Topeka: state printer, 1919.

U.S. Department of Defense (?). *U.S. Military Personnel Who Died From Hostile Action in the Korean War, 1950–1953 (?).* Washington, D.C.: n.d.

_____. *List of Casualties Incurred by U.S. Military Personnel in Connection With the Conflict in Vietnam . . . Kansas . . . Deaths From 1 January 1961 Thru 31 March 1973.* Washington, D.C.: 1973.

U.S. Naval Air Station, Hutchinson, Kansas. *Roster of Officers, U.S. Naval Air Station, Hutchinson, Kansas. . . . Feb. 1, 1944.* N.p., n.d.

U.S. Navy Department. *State Summary of War Casualties [Kansas].* Washington, D.C.: Government Printing Office, 1946.

Kentucky

1774   American settlers created the community of Harrodsburg.

1775   Daniel Boone opened the route from Virginia through the Cumberland Gap and established Boonesborough.

1775-78   Hostile Indians, encouraged by the British during the revolution, plagued Kentucky settlers until George Rogers Clark captured British forts in Indiana and Illinois. (See American Revolution in the appendix.)

1792   Kentucky separated from Virginia and became a state.

1861-65   Although a slave state, Kentucky remained loyal to the Union during the Civil War. (See American Civil War in the appendix.)

KENTUCKY DEPARTMENT OF LIBRARIES AND ARCHIVES

300 Coffee Tree Road
(near the east-west connection of Route 676)
Frankfort, Kentucky 40602
(502) 875-7000

Most Kentucky military records have been retained by the Kentucky State Department of Military Affairs. The Kentucky Archives, however, has purchased microfilm copies of military records from the National Archives and has some Kentucky military records. The Kentucky Genealogical Society has a library that is open to the public. It is located in the archives building.

Records

American Revolution (1775-83)
NATIONAL ARCHIVES MICROFILM

General Index to Compiled Military Service Records of Revolutionary War Soldiers (M860).

General Index to Compiled Service Records of American Naval Personnel Who Served During the Revolutionary War (M879).

Revolutionary War Rolls, 1775-1783 (M246).

Indian Wars (1784-1811)
NATIONAL ARCHIVES MICROFILM

Compiled Service Records of Volunteer Soldiers Who Served From 1784 to 1811 (M905—rolls 7-15 pertain to Kentucky units).

OTHER RECORDS

Records of Kentuckians who served in U.S. military forces between the American Revolution and the War of 1812 are available on microfilm (M905-9 through M905-15). They are arranged by military unit and are not indexed. A list of units and corresponding microfilm roll numbers is available at the reference desk.

War of 1812 (1812-15)

The official papers of Kentucky governors Shelby (1812-16) and Slaughter (1816-20) include militia returns that list officers and their ranks and dates of commission, as well as muster rolls of both officers and enlisted men.

Civil War–Union (1861-65)
NATIONAL ARCHIVES MICROFILM

Index to Compiled Military Service Records of Volunteer Soldiers Who Served in Organizations From the State of Kentucky (M386).

Compiled Service Records of Volunteer Union Soldiers Who Served in Organizations From Kentucky (M397).

OTHER RECORDS

"Misc. Card Abstracts" and "Personal Papers." This material is not included in the compiled service records for the Union Army. The abstracts are arranged by unit, and the personal papers are arranged alphabetically by surname. None of this data refers to regular army personnel, U.S. Colored Troops, the navy, or the marines, but it does refer to all other Union and Kentucky army personnel.

Civil War–Confederate (1861-65)
NATIONAL ARCHIVES MICROFILM

Index to Compiled Service Records of Confederate Soldiers Who Served in Organizations From the State of Kentucky (M377).

Compiled Service Records of Confederate Soldiers Who Served in Organizations From the State of Kentucky (M319).

Register of Confederate Soldiers, Sailors, and Citizens Who Died in Federal Prisons and Military Hospitals in the North, 1861-1865 (M918).

Selected Records of the War Department Relating to Confederate Prisoners of War, 1861-1865 (M598—rolls 88 and 89 pertain to the Louisville Military Prison, which served as a major shipping point for prisoners bound for prison camps in Ohio, Indiana, and Illinois; also see Kentucky microfilm M598-88 and M598-89).

Pardon Petitions and Related Papers Submitted in Response to President Andrew Johnson's Amnesty Proclamation of May 29, 1865 ("Amnesty Papers") (M1003—rolls 25 and 26 pertain to Kentucky).

OTHER RECORDS–PENSIONS

Pensions were granted by the state of Kentucky to qualifying veterans who served with Confederate forces or to their widows. The Kentucky Historical Society, which once had custody of the pension files, turned them over to the state archives in 1951. They are too fragile to be handled, but microfilm copies may be viewed at the state archives or at the historical society. The index is on the first roll of this fifty-roll collection. A published list of names prepared in 1978 by Alicia Simpson, *Index of Confederate Pension Applications–Kentucky* (cited below under Published Sources–Kentucky) is also available.

OTHER RECORDS–MILITARY SERVICE

The Kentucky Adjutant General's Report of Confederate Soldiers may be seen at the state archives. It exists on microfilm and in printed form. The data is arranged by military unit, but a separate index of names is available.

OTHER RECORDS—PEWEE CONFEDERATE HOME

Kentucky veterans who served in Confederate units were eligible for admission to the Confederate Home at PeWee Valley, Kentucky, which was established in 1902. Residence in the home caused them to be ineligible for a state pension. A list of residents was prepared by the pension board in 1912, and a microfilm copy is available at this archives. The original handwritten list may be seen at the Military Records and Research Branch of the Kentucky Department of Military Affairs (see below).

World War I Through Vietnam War (1917-75)

The Kentucky Archives has some county records with names of military personnel who served in some of the above-mentioned wars, as well as for a few personnel dating from the Civil War who registered their discharges with the county clerks. The archives also has a few "Militia Books" compiled by county clerks. (If such records are not found at the archives, they may still exist in county courthouses.) No other records pertaining to twentieth-century wars are available at this archives; however, a *Vietnam Casualty List* is published by the U.S. Department of Defense.

KENTUCKY DEPARTMENT OF MILITARY AFFAIRS

Military Records and Research Branch
Pinehill Plaza
1121 Louisville Road
Frankfort, Kentucky 40601-6169
(502) 564-4883

Finding Aid

Military Records and Research Library (typescript).

Records

General

Personnel files (201 files) for all Kentucky National Guardsmen are available at this center, but they are not open for public inspection because of federal Privacy Act restrictions. Files for those who were discharged prior to 1940 or who were born before 1923 have been microfilmed.

Kentucky Militia Records. Hundreds of folders containing original rosters, lists, and other historical data concerning the Kentucky Militia, Kentucky Enrolled Militia, Kentucky National Legion, Kentucky State Guard units, and many others are available at this center. They are arranged by unit prior to 1860 and by county and unit thereafter. Microfilm copies are available at the Kentucky Historical Society.

Unit Returns, Kentucky National Guard, 1804-1989. Arranged by brigade, division, and county. The data refers to claims, bounties, oaths, and commissions for enrolled militia. Originals have been microfilmed through 1899.

Veterans' Graves Registration Project. In 1938 the WPA began a survey of Kentucky cemeteries to record the graves of all military veterans. The project was supervised by officials of the Kentucky Department of Military Affairs, but the survey was conducted at the county level. All counties except Bullitt, Garrard, and Hardin participated. An estimated 85,000 graves were recorded, and these have been supplemented by periodic submissions of Confederate graves located by Raymond W. Watkins, of Falls Church, Virginia, and from records at the National Archives.

The original survey sheets were handwritten, usually in pencil on mimeograph paper. Beginning in 1983 they were transcribed on typewritten sheets, arranged alphabetically, and made available at this center. The Kentucky Historical Society microfilmed the sheets and arranged them by county.

Military Unit Histories, 1880-1989. These relate to various Kentucky units; include original documents and some muster rolls.

Discharges, Korean War to Present. Privacy Act restrictions apply to these records. Inquire about possible access to the records.

War of 1812 (1812-15)

Muster Rolls, Kentucky State Guard.

Mexican War (1846-48)

Muster Rolls, Kentucky State Guard (also available on microfilm).

Officers and Soldiers in the War With Mexico, 1846-47 (indexed).

Index to Mexican War Rosters.

Civil War—Union and Confederate (1861-65)

Muster Rolls, Kentucky State Militia, 1860-65. Arranged by unit. The originals and microfilmed copies are available.

Muster Rolls, Kentucky State Guard. These were microfilmed in the same order as published in the *Report of the Adjutant General . . . 1861-65*, pages 754-903. (See Published Sources—Kentucky.)

Muster Rolls, Union and Confederate (separate). Units arranged by infantry, cavalry, artillery, and colored artillery.

Some rolls have been microfilmed, but the following are available only in original form: Invalid Corps; Engineer, Quartermaster, or Commissary Department; Colored Volunteers; Colored Substitutes; Volunteer Enlistments; White Enlistments; Unassigned Recruits; Regimental Recruiting Returns.

Discharges. Lists were upgraded during the late 1880s to add some names not published in the *Report of the Adjutant General . . . for 1861-65.*

Miscellaneous Historical Data in Original Form. On microfilm and available at the Kentucky History Society and the state archives. Examples of such collections are: coffins ordered for deceased veterans; lists of officers with dates of appointment and dates of discharge; register of colored volunteers; servants for officers; Battle of Shiloh and Kentucky battles (veterans killed, wounded, or cared for); military hospital payrolls.

Confederate Home at Pewee Valley, Kentucky. Original papers including lists of officers and employees, 31 October 1917; list of inmates, 24 May 1912. Microfilm copies are available at the Kentucky Historical Society and the state archives.

Index of Kentucky Confederate Pension Files. Microfilmed by the Kentucky Historical Society in 1952.

Spanish-American War (1898-99)

Muster Rolls, Kentucky State Guard.

Discharges and Applications for Bonuses. Kentucky awarded bonuses to qualified veterans of all wars, beginning with the Spanish-American War and continuing through the Vietnam War.

Payrolls, Kentucky State Guard. For some companies of the First and Third Regiments, Kentucky Infantry, prior to the Spanish-American War; available as originals and on microfilm.

Mexican Border Service (1916)

Muster Rolls. Kentucky State Guard members who participated in the Mexican Border Service.

World War I (1917-18)

Muster Rolls, World War I. Kentucky State Guard (First, Second, and Third Regiments).

Index Cards Listing Those Who Applied for Kentucky State Bonus for Service in World War I and Later Wars. Applications are on microfilm. Privacy Act restrictions may apply. Inquire of staff concerning possible access to these records.

World War I Casualties. Index cards for Kentucky soldiers that provide name, rank, home address, service address, name and address of nearest relative, nature of casualty, and place where casualty occurred.

Selective Service Board Records. Lists of inductees and draft evaders provided by county boards.

Lists of Prisoners of War, Courts-martial.

Statements of Service (microfilm). Cards for Kentucky veterans supplied by the U.S. War Department.

Casualty Lists Supplied by the U.S. War Department for Kentucky Veterans (microfilm). Pertain only to the thirty-eight Kentucky counties having names beginning with M through W. Other lists and index cards show casualties of all Kentucky counties.

Discharges and Bonus Applications, World War I. List gives name and claim number. The applications can be provided after the claim number is determined.

World War II (1941-45)

Active Militia Officers, 1941-45, With Enlistment Documents.

Casualty lists supplied by the U.S. War Department (all counties).

Discharges and Bonus Applications, World War II. List gives name and claim number. Applications can be provided after the claim number is determined.

Discharges as Reported by Selective Service Boards. Name, mailing address, and race; not alphabetized.

Korean War (1950-53)

Casualty Lists Supplied by the U.S. War Department (all counties). Name, rank, service number, date of birth, address, date of casualty, and name and address of next of kin.

Discharges and Bonus Applications, World War II. List gives name and claim number. Applications can be provided after the claim number is determined.

Records and Registers (1922-present)

Official Army National Guard Registers, 1922-present (except 1932-35, 1937-38, 1940, and 1942).

Official Army Registers of Officers, 1936-72 (except 1942-46, 1950, and 1967).

Air National Guard Records of Officers, 1948-present (except 1967-71 and 1973).

Official Air Force Records of Officers, 1952-61 (except 1953-55 and 1960).

Vietnam War (1963-75)

Casualty Lists Provided by the U.S. War Department, 1965-72. Lists give same data as do Korean casualty lists (see above). Also available is the "Directory of Veterans," which shows the names engraved on the Vietnam War Memorial in Washington, D.C.

Kentucky Historical Society

Old Capitol Annex
300 West Broadway
Frankfort, Kentucky 40602
(502) 564-3016

The society maintains an excellent genealogical library, with many publications concerning military records. It also has an extensive manuscript collection and microfilm copies of the Kentucky Graves Registration Project worksheets.

Finding Aid

A pamphlet: *Kentucky Historical Society. Research Library and Preservation Services.*

Manuscript Collections

A guide to the society's manuscript collections was published by Garrett G. Clift, *Guide to the Manuscripts of the Kentucky Historical Society* (Frankfort: Kentucky Historical Society, 1955. Reprint. 1968). It is available in book form and on microfilm. An updated guide is being completed by the society's current curator and archivist, Mary Margaret Bell. The following are selected prepublication samples of subjects pertaining to military records extracted from that guide.

> American Revolution (claims, land grants, veterans)
>
> Civil War (Battle of Bull Run, claims, Battle of Shiloh)
>
> Confederate States of America (various Kentucky regiments)
>
> Hessians
>
> Indian Wars (land grants)
>
> Kentucky Home Guard
>
> Kentucky Militia
>
> Kentucky State Guard
>
> Land (claims, grants)
>
> Prisoners of war
>
> United States Army (various regiments)
>
> United States War Department Pension Office
>
> War of 1812
>
> World War II

National Society Sons of the American Revolution

National Headquarters
1000 South Fourth Street
Louisville, Kentucky 40203
(502) 589-1776

This headquarters office operates an extensive genealogical and historical reference library, and it maintains a file of applications for membership in the society. A separate George Washington Room houses a valuable collection that includes The George Washington Papers and many rare publications relating to George Washington. The office also has a microfilm copy of the Morristown, New Jersey, collection pertaining to George Washington. Nonmembers may visit the museum and use the library facilities for a nominal fee. Members may do so without charge.

Records

NATIONAL ARCHIVES MICROFILM

General Index to Compiled Service Records of Revolutionary War Soldiers (M860).

Compiled Service Records of Soldiers Who Served in the American Army During the Revolutionary War (M881).

Index to Compiled Service Records of American Naval Personnel and Members of the Departments of the Quartermaster General and the Commissary General of Military Stores Who Served During the Revolutionary War (M880).

MEMBERSHIP APPLICATIONS

Membership in this society, through one of its local chapters, is open to those who can trace and document their lineage to a patriot of the American Revolution. Application for membership is made on a standard two-page form, which provides space for family lineage and reference material cited as proof (figure 53). Microfilm copies of applications are on file at this facility. Copies of applications for active and non-active members may be obtained upon request and payment of a fee.

The Filson Club Historical Society

1310 South Third Street
Louisville, Kentucky 40208
(502) 635-5083

The Filson Club was named for John Filson, Kentucky's first historian. The club, founded in 1884, has a genealogical and historical library and museum. Since 1986 it has been located in a historic mansion in old Louisville.

In addition to published sources, the library has a collection of scrapbooks containing news clippings relating to World War II. There are also 144 volumes of World War I records compiled by the Kentucky Council of Defense. The first four volumes consist of individual records of local citizens who were involved in wartime community groups. Vols. 5 through 15 are local histories of wartime activities arranged by county. Vols. 16 through 144, inclusive, contain official statements of service of the men and women from Kentucky in all branches of the service. These are arranged alphabetically by name.

Photograph Collections

Photographs of Kentucky places and persons are available from the club, but there is no separate category of military subjects. One separate collection consists principally of photographs of Camp Zachary Taylor, Louisville, but no military groups are identified. There are also prints and some photographs of Civil War officers; they are indexed by name. Copy machine duplicates of photographs are not permitted. Eight- by ten-inch copies are available for a fee.

PUBLISHED SOURCES—KENTUCKY

Pre-1775 (colonial wars)

Kentucky. Land Office. *A Calendar of the Warrants for Land in Kentucky Granted for Service in the French and Indian War.* Abstracted by Philip Fall Taylor. Society of Colonial Wars, 1917. Reprint. Baltimore: Genealogical Publishing Co., 1967.

1775-83 (American Revolution)

Blue Licks Battle Field Monument Commission. *The Battle of Blue Licks.* Louisville: Westerfield-Bonte Co., 1927.

Harding, Margery Heberling, comp. *George Rogers Clark and His Men, Military Records, 1778-1784.* Frankfort: Kentucky Historical Society, 1981. Contains names, ranks, and dates of enlistment, discharge, and payment.

Jillson, Willard Rouse. *The Kentucky Land Grants: A Systematic Index to All of the Land Grants Recorded in the State Land Office at Frankfort, Kentucky, 1782-1924.* "With a new preface...." Filson Club Publication No. 33. Louisville: 1925. Reprint. Baltimore: Genealogical Publishing Co., 1971.

_____ . *Old Kentucky Entries and Deeds.* . . . Filson Club Publication no. 35. Louisville: Standard Printing Co., 1926. Reprint. Baltimore: Genealogical Publishing Co., 1978.

Lindsay, Kenneth G. *Kentucky's Revolutionary War Pensioners, Under the Acts of 1818-1832.* Evansville: Kenma Publishing Co., 1977.

McAdams, Ednah W. *Kentucky Pioneer and Court Records, Abstracts of Early Wills, Deeds and Marriages From Court Houses and Records of Old Bibles, Churches, Grave Yards, and Cemeteries.* Lexington: Keystone Printery, 1929. Reprint. Baltimore: Genealogical Publishing Co., 1967. Includes some pensioners of the revolution.

Quisenberry, Anderson C., comp. *Revolutionary Soldiers in Kentucky: Containing a Roll of the Officers of Virginia Lines Who Received Land Bounties, a Roll of the Revolutionary Pensioners in Kentucky, a List of the Illinois Regiment Who Served under George Rogers Clark in the Northwest Campaign, Also a Roster of the Virginia Navy.* Compiled from various sources. Louisville: 1896. Reprint. Baltimore: Southern Book, 1959. Reprint. Baltimore: Genealogical Publishing Co., 1968.

Seineke, Katherine W. *The George Rogers Clark Adventure in the Illinois and Selected Documents of the American Revolution at the Frontier Posts.* New Orleans: Polyanthos, 1981.

Stone, Richard G. *A Brittle Sword: The Kentucky Militia, 1776-1912.* Lexington: University of Kentucky Press, 1977.

U.S. War Department. *Kentucky Pension Roll of 1835.* Reprinted from United States. Secretary of War. *Report.* . . . Washington, D.C.: 1835. Baltimore: Southern Book Co., 1959.

1784-1815 (War of 1812)

Clift, Garrett G. *The "Corn Stalk" Militia of Kentucky, 1792-1811: A Brief Statutory History of the Militia and Records of Commissions of Officers in the Organization From the Beginning of Statehood to the Commencement of the War of 1812.* Frankfort: Kentucky Historical Society, 1957. Officers listed with rank, unit, and date of commission.

_____ . *Notes on Kentucky Veterans in the War of 1812.* Anchorage: Borderland Books, 1964.

_____ . *Remember the Raisin! Kentucky and Kentuckians in the Battles and Massacre at Frenchtown, Michigan Territory, in the War of 1812.* Frankfort: Kentucky Historical Society, 1961. Commissioned officers listed by county with rank and date of commission.

Kentucky. Adjutant General. *Kentucky Soldiers of the War of 1812. With an Added Index Compiled by Minnie S. Wilder, 1931, and a New Introduction by G. Glenn Clift.* Originally published as *Report of the Adjutant General . . . of Kentucky.* . . . Frankfort: E.P. Johnson, 1891. Reprint. Baltimore: Genealogical Publishing Co., 1969. Organized by regiment and company, including name, rank, date of appointment or enlistment, period of service, and remarks (if any).

Kentucky Soldiers of the War of 1812. Frankfort: 1891. Reprint. Baltimore: Genealogical Publishing Co., 1969.

Quisenberry, Anderson C. *Kentucky in the War of 1812.* Frankfort: 1915. Reprint. Baltimore: Genealogical Publishing Co., 1969. Officers listed by regiment, pages 174-98.

Figure 53. Application for Membership, National Society Sons of the American Revolution (courtesy National Society Sons of the American Revolution).

**APPLICATION
FOR MEMBERSHIP**

National number... *115512*

State number... *2514*

Application submitted must be made in duplicate (or triplicate if required by local chapter) and sent to the Secretary of the State Society, who will forward the **original, typed application**, when approved, to the Registrar General of the National Society.

JOHN HANSON CHAPTER .... XXXXXXXX ... MARYLAND ... XXXXXXXX

NATIONAL SOCIETY

SONS OF THE AMERICAN REVOLUTION

.... James .... Arthur .... McCafferty ....
(First) (Middle) (Last)

Descendant of .... Isaac Sharp ....

who assisted in establishing American Independence while acting in the capacity of Patriot's Oath of Allegiance at SHEPARDSTOWN, BERKLEY, (W.VA) VIRGINIA in 1777.

The applicant resides in the County of .. Prince George's .. Town or City .. Oxon Hill ..

Street or R.D. .. 613 Rosier Road .... State of .. Maryland .... and married on

.. June 13 ,. 1948 ., to .. Jane Roush .... who was born October 2, 1925

at .. Gallipolis .... County of .. Gallia .... State of .. Ohio ..

having living children as follows:

Name and Relationship	Date of Birth	Street	Town	State

Lucinda Jane Martin-(d) April 20,1950, Rt.1, Box 161, Union, West Virginia
James Stanley Thomas McCafferty (s)
.... February 20, 1953, 2832 Rouen Ave.,Melbourne, Florida
Bridget Anne Green, (d) March 25, 1955, 410 Compton St., Laurel, Maryland

The applicant served in the armed forces of the United States of America as follows: ....
103rd Army Airways Communications System Detachment, Corporal ASN 35085771
May 6, 1944 to June 20, 1946   2 years, 1 month and 15 days

THE FOLLOWING FORM OF AFFIDAVIT IS REQUIRED

Signed by the applicant as being true and correct to the best of his knowledge and belief, on this

.. 22nd .. day of .. January ., 19.79. Signature ....

Occupation ....

Subscribed and sworn to before me at .. Washington DC ..

this .. 22nd .. day of .. January .... 19.79..

Official Signature,

NOTARY PUBLIC   My Commission Expires Mar. 14, 1981

(L.S.)

MAILING ADDRESS (Please Print or Type)

Name and Title .... James A. McCafferty ....
Street, R.D. or P.O. Box .. 613 Rosier Road ....
Post Office .. Oxon Hill .... State .. Maryland .... Zip Code .. 20022 ..

Application examined and approved .... 19.79.

State Registrar

Accepted by the State Board of Management
FEB 10 1979 .... 19..........

State Secretary

Recommended by the undersigned members
(Please Type or Print)

Name Henry A. HAMANN
Street 3707 WALTON AVE
Town Camp Springs MD 20023

Signed

Co-Sponsor   Signed

Filed with State Secy .... 19..........
Fees Paid .... 19..........
Sent to Nat. Hqts. .... 19..........
Registered by Nat. .. JUN 18 1979 .. 19..........
Transferred .... 19..........
Certificate ordered .... 19..........

Figure 53. SAR Membership Application (continued).

IMPORTANT: It is required that complete dates, month, day and year, be supplied for generations (1), parents, and (2), grandparents of applicant. Complete dates for all generations should be given if possible. Also all names should be given in full.

I, ...James Arthur McCafferty..being of the age..53....... years

hereby submit my lineage. That I was born at....Columbus..

County of..Franklin.......... State of......Ohio.............. on the.....1....day of......January..1926.

(Give all dates in numerals, month first. Include wives maiden names.)

(1) I am the son of James Arthur McCafferty, May 18, 1907, Corlos & Ohio

NSSAR #................................. died..

and his (1) wife Marjorie Gilchrist born Aug. 27, 1906, Oregon City, Oregon

NSDAR #................................. died..

(2) grandson of James Duffy McCafferty married Oct. 24, 1926, Columbus, Ohio
born Oct. 10, 1883, Vinton Twp, Vinton Co. Ohi
died March 26, 1959, Columbus, Ohio

and his (1) wife Lena Wilson born Jan. 8, 1888, Logan Co. Ol
died..

(3) great-grandson of James McCafferty married Oct. 27, 1906, Logan Co. Ohio
born March 20, 1830, Butler Co., Pa.
died March 11, 1894, Vinton Co. Ohio

and his (2) wife Melissa Sharp born March 8, 1845, Meigs Co. Ohio
died Sept. 8, 1895, Vinton Co. Ohio

(4) great-grandson of Thomas Jeff. Sharp married April 10, 1874, Vinton Co. Ohio
born Dec. 31, 1812, Meigs Co. Ohio
died Sept. 24, 1886, Meigs Co.

and his (1) wife Dysey Farley born May 22, 1813 Virginia
died_____ 1882, Ohio Meigs Co. Ohio

(5) great-grandson of Thomas Sharp married Sept. 16, 1834, Jackson Co. Ohio
born 1781 Washington Co. Pa.
died Aft. 1860, Ohio Meigs Co.

and his (1) wife Unity Merritt born Jan. 16, 1784, Pa.
died May 27, 1826, Ohio Vinton Co.

(6) great-grandson of Isaac Sharp married March 24, 1801, Wash. Co. Ohio
born April 13, 1750, New Jersey or S.C.
died Oct. 1830, Amwell Twp. Wash. Co. Pa.

and his (1) wife Mary Wolverton born April 22, 1761, New Jersey
died Aug. 26, 1822, Amwell Twp. Wash. Co. Pa

(7) great-grandson of William Sharp married 1777 ca.
born..

and his (1) wife Mary ??? died killed in Indian Wars
born..

(8) great-grandson of .... married..
born..
died..

and his ( ) wife.......................... born..
died..

(9) great-grandson of .... married..
born..
died..

and his ( ) wife.......................... born..
died..
married..

References to ancestor's Revolutionary War services (name of record, volume and page) of above (No...6..........).

Commemorative Biographical Record of Washington County, Pa. by J.H. Beers & Co. 1893. Page 170. Oath of Allegiance taken the 13th of September 1777 before Colonel John Morrow at Shepardstown, Berkley County, Virginia. (Now Jefferson County, West Virginia)

Buried in the Old Waynesburg.....................................Cemetery at Waynesburg, Greene County, Pa.

References: Please cite author and title, volume and page of publications. Quote Bible, church, court, cemetery, census and other records to establish birth, death and marriage dates and relationship.

3rd Gen. Marriage Record, Vinton County, Ohio

4th Gen. Marriage record, Jackson County, Ohio

5th Gen. Marriage record, Washington County, Ohio

6th Gen. Commemorative Biographical Record of Washington County, Pa. by J.H. Beers & Co. 1893. Page 171

7th Gen. Ibid: page 171

8th Gen. 6th & 7th. Ten mile Country (Pa) & Its Pioneer Families, by Leckey reprinted in 1977. P. 456.

9th Gen. SAR National #.186548 Pa.#.7976 for Boyd Sayer Sharp

Young, Bennett H. *The Battle of the Thames, in Which Kentuckians Defeated the British, French, and Indians, October 5, 1813. . . .* Louisville: J.P. Morton and Co., printers to the Filson Club, 1903. Appendix 2 includes "Roll of Field, Staff, Company Officers and Privates" and "Roll of . . . Kentucky Volunteers and Mounted Infantry."

1816-60 (Mexican War)

Kentucky. Adjutant General. *Report of the Adjutant General of the State of Kentucky: Mexican War Veterans (1846–1847).* Frankfort: 1889. Reprint. Frankfort: Historical Society, 1966.

Encarnacion Prisoners: Comprising an Account of the March of the Kentucky Cavalry From Louisville to the Rio Grande, Together With an Authentic History of the Captivity of the American Prisoners; Includes Incidents and Sketches of Men and Things on the Route and in Mexico. Louisville: Prentice and Weissinger, 1848.

Quisenberry, Anderson C. *History by Illustration.* Frankfort: Kentucky State Historical Society, 1911. Includes roster of Kentucky officers in the Mexican War.

1861-65 (Civil War)

Cook, Michael L. *Kentucky Confederate Veteran and Widows Pension Index. From Data Compiled by Alicia Simpson: Supplementary Index.* Hartford: Cook & McDowell Pub., 1979.

Davis, William C. *The Orphan Brigade: The Kentucky Confederates Who Couldn't Go Home.* New York, 1980. Reprint. Baton Rouge: Louisiana State University Press, 1983.

Dilts, Bryan L., comp. *1890 Kentucky Census Index of Civil War Veterans or Their Widows.* Salt Lake City: Index Pub., 1984.

Kentucky. Adjutant General. *Report of the Adjutant General of the State of Kentucky.* Frankfort: state printer, 1867. These are the Rosters of Federal regiments raised in Kentucky.

_____ . *Report of the Adjutant General of the State of Kentucky: Confederate Kentucky Volunteers, War 1861–65.* 2 vols. Frankfort (?): state printer, 1915-19 (?). Reprint. Hartford: Cook & McDowell Pub., 1979-80. Listed by regiment: name, rank, date of enlistment, when and where mustered out, and remarks.

Kentucky. Confederate Pension Board. *Civil War Pension Applications.* Frankfort: State Journal Co., 1920 (?). List of persons receiving pensions under Confederate Pension Act.

Kentucky. Division of Archives and Records Management. *Index of Confederate Pension Applications, Commonwealth of Kentucky.* Compiled by Alicia Simpson. Frankfort: 1979. Reprint. Frankfort: Archives Branch, Department of Library and Archives, 1981.

Pompey, Sherman L. *Register of the Civil War Dead: Kentucky.* Clovis, Calif., 1970.

Simpson, Alicia. *Inventory of Confederate Pension Applications, Commonwealth of Kentucky.* Frankfort: Kentucky Division of Archives and Records Management, 1981.

1866-99 (Spanish-American War)

Kentucky. Adjutant General. *Report of the Adjutant General of the State of Kentucky: Kentucky Volunteers, War With Spain, 1898–99.* Frankfort and Louisville: Globe Printing Co., 1908. Reprint. Frankfort: Historical Society, 1966.

Military History of Kentucky, Chronologically Arranged, Written by Workers of the Federal Writers Project of the WPA for the State of Kentucky. Frankfort: printed by the *State Journal,* 1939.

Kentucky. Department of Military Affairs. *Kentucky State Guard in the Spanish-American War, 1898–1899.* 2 vols. Frankfort: Kentucky Department of Military Affairs, 1988.

1900-71 (World War I through Vietnam War)

Sponsored by the Military Dept. of Kentucky. . . . Frankfort (?): printed by the state journal, 1939 (?). Appendix F: Kentucky National Guard Officers, World War I; appendix G: Roster of Kentucky National Guard as of 31 December 1938; biographical notes and portraits throughout the text.

Kentucky. Department of Military Affairs, Military Records and Research Library. Julia D. Rather and Jeffrey M. Duff, eds. *Register of Vietnam War Casualties From Kentucky.* Frankfort: Department for Libraries and Archives, Public Records Division, ca. 1988.

Louisiana

1530	Spanish explorer Cabeza de Vaca crossed Louisiana.
1699	The French colony of Louisiana was established, with boundaries extending north to Canada.
1762	France ceded Louisiana to Spain.
1800	France reacquired Louisiana.
1803	The United States acquired Louisiana from France through the Louisiana Purchase.
1804	Louisiana became a territory.
1812	Louisiana became a state.
1815	Gen. Andrew Jackson halted a major British campaign in the Battle of New Orleans. (See War of 1812 in the appendix.)
1861	Louisiana seceded from the Union.

1862	A Union naval force under David Farragut captured New Orleans and began securing the Mississippi River for the Union. (See American Civil War in the appendix.)
1868	Louisiana was readmitted to statehood.

. . . .

LOUISIANA STATE ARCHIVES

P.O. Box 94125
3851 Essen Lane
Baton Rouge, Louisiana 70804-9125
(504) 922-1200

Finding Aids

Computer Catalog. Most titles of this archives' holdings now exist in a computer catalog. One terminal is available in the reading room for use by researchers and two terminals are for use by archives staff. Instruction in use of the terminal is provided to researchers who wish to identify records and obtain accession numbers.

Index to Confederate Pension Applications. This alphabetical list of pensioners (veterans and their widows) indicates the name, parish of residence, and number of pages in the pension file. This index has many errors, but a corrected list is currently being published. The corrected index is available in the computer catalog.

Confederate Burials. This aid lists burial locations of Confederate veterans, including cemeteries in Union prisoner-of-war camps and in states other than Louisiana. Entries are based on lists of Confederate graves submitted by Raymond W. Watkins, a Falls Church, Virginia, researcher who specializes in locating Confederate graves and furnishes lists of them to state archives and libraries.

Records

General

Monthly Returns, 1821-1920. Records collected by the state adjutant general for miscellaneous Louisiana army units; arranged by name of military unit.

American Revolution (1775-83)

NATIONAL ARCHIVES MICROFILM

General Index to Compiled Military Service Records of Revolutionary War Soldiers (M860).

War of 1812 (1812-15)

NATIONAL ARCHIVES MICROFILM

Compiled Service Records of Volunteer Soldiers Who Served During the War of 1812 in Organizations From the State of Louisiana (M229).

OTHER RECORDS

Pensions for Service in the War of 1812. An alphabetical list of veterans and widows who filed claims, and accompanying court documents submitted to prove eligibility.

Florida Indian Wars—Seminoles (1837-38)

NATIONAL ARCHIVES MICROFILM

Index to Compiled Service Records of Volunteer Soldiers Who Served in Organizations From the State of Louisiana (M239).

Index to Compiled Service Records of Volunteer Soldiers Who Served During the War of 1837-1838 in Organizations From the State of Louisiana (M241).

Civil War—Union (1861-65)

NATIONAL ARCHIVES MICROFILM

Index to Compiled Military Service Records of Volunteer Union Soldiers Who Served in Organizations From the State of Louisiana (M387).

Compiled Service Records of Volunteer Union Soldiers who Served in Organizations From the State of Louisiana (M396).

Federal Census Schedules Enumerating Union Veterans and Widows of the Civil War, Louisiana, 1890. Arranged by parish; microfilm L170 (two reels).

Civil War—Confederate (1861-65)

NATIONAL ARCHIVES MICROFILM

Compiled Service Records of Confederate Soldiers Who Served in Organizations From the State of Louisiana (M320).

Compiled Service Records of Confederate General and Staff Officers and Non-regimental Enlisted Men (M331—some rolls).

Records Relating to Confederate Naval and Marine Personnel (M260).

Records of the Louisiana State Government, 1850-1888, in the War Department Collection of Confederate Records ("Rebel Archives") (M359—includes lists of military personnel).

Microfilm series M320 and M260 are available both at the state library and at the state archives. The National Archives microfilm cited below is available only at the Louisiana State Library, 760 Riverside Mall North, Baton Rouge, Louisiana.

Index to Compiled Service Records of Confederate Soldiers Who Served in Organizations From the State of Louisiana (M378).

OTHER RECORDS

In lieu of service records and muster rolls, Louisiana relies on a publication by Andrew W. Booth: *Records of Louisiana Confederate Soldiers and Louisiana Confederate Commands* (cited below under Published Sources—Louisiana), as well as the National Archives microfilm cited above. Booth's publication is available on microfilm at this archives. Reel one contains an index of companies, an index of battles, and an index of individuals (Aaron through Reese); reel two continues the index of individuals (Reese through Zylkus).

LOUISIANA ADJUTANT GENERAL RECORDS

Register of Militia Officers, 1855–1862. Name, rank, unit, date elected or appointed, and date of oath or acceptance; arranged by first letter of surname.

Register of Militia Officers, 1861–1862. Name, rank, unit, and date of commission; arranged by first letter of surname.

Register of Officers, Louisiana State Troops, 1861–1863. Name, rank, unit, and date elected or appointed; arranged by first letter of surname.

General and Field Officers, 1862. Name, rank, unit, and date; arranged by first letter of surname.

List of Officers Who Served in Louisiana Volunteer Regiments, 1861, 1863. Comprises a portion of the "Records of the Louisiana State Government, 1850–1888 (Rebel Archives)." The card file in the reading room cites all of the records included in this collection. See also National Archives microfilm M359 (cited above).

Post-war Muster Roll of Company B, Second Louisiana Infantry, 1861–1862. Part of the William Hustmyre Manuscript Collection.

Collected Records of Gen. Leroy Stafford, Camp No. 3, United Confederate Veterans, 1893–1934, in Shreve Memorial Library, Shreveport, Louisiana; microfilm L118 (two reels).

Confederate Veteran (1893–1934), a periodical. Microfilm L153 (eight reels).

Confederate Soldiers Who Died in Prison Camp at Morton, Indiana. This list gives name and unit. Also available is a similar list for those who died in the prison camp at Rock Island, Illinois, giving name, unit, and date of death.

Civil War Veterans From Louisiana Who Applied for a Pension in Florida. A computer-generated list furnished by the Florida Archives.

Confederate Pension Applications With Accompanying Documents, 1898–. Alphabetical and indexed on microfilm. The originals are not available to the public. This is a copy of the finding aid cited above. Copies are available for a fee.

Confederate Pensions Record of Payment, 1906–26.

Confederate Proofs and Land Warrants Issued Pursuant to Act 86 (1884); Act 116 (1886); Act 55 (1896). This list, compiled in 1988 by Houston C. Jenks of Baton Rouge, is available in the reading room. Section A lists applicants, including name, parish, widow, rank, regiment, date wounded or killed, battles, and number of the microfilm reel; section B lists warrants issued to successful applicants, including name, grant site, acreage, to whom sold, and number of the microfilm reel. The material cited in these lists is available at this archives.

Confederate Veteran Census, 1911. A notebook in the reading room contains an index of Confederate veterans or their widows who were residents of Louisiana in 1911 and who were receiving a pension. Data includes name, parish, regiment, whether or not a property owner, occupation, infirmities, date of widow's marriage to the veteran, and number of the microfilm reel. This index was compiled by Houston C. Jenks in 1989 (see above). The material cited in this list is available at this archives.

Louisiana veterans residing in Tennessee, 1922. Copies of questionnaires completed by Louisiana veterans during a 1922 census enumeration of pensioners residing in Tennessee.

1890 Louisiana Census Index of Civil War Veterans and Their Widows (microfiche).

Louisiana Secretary of State Records: Appointments, 1860–69; Commission Book, 1856–65

Spanish-American War (1898–99)

NATIONAL ARCHIVES MICROFILM

Index to Compiled Service Records of Volunteer Soldiers Who Served During the War With Spain in Organizations From the State of Louisiana (M248).

OTHER RECORDS

Account Books of the State Service Commission for the United States Spanish-American War Veterans. This commission served veterans of the Spanish-American War, the Philippine Insurrection, and the China Boxer Rebellion, and it helped the veterans process their claims arising from their military service. The books cover the period 1 July 1848–29 April 1857.

World War I (1917–18)

World War Soldiers, by Parish. Name, address, age, date of birth, unit, wounds, time in service, and rank. Officers in each parish are listed first.

World War I Pensioners. Registers of the Louisiana Pension Board. Lists deaths of veterans and widows who received pensions from Louisiana.

Bonuses Given to World War I Veterans. Names arranged alphabetically, with file number included. The file number is necessary to obtain the microfilm record.

World War II (1941–45)

Officers of Louisiana in Military Units, World War II. There is a card for each officer, 1943–45, and a folder for each company. This index is part of the Lt. Perry Cole Manuscript Collection.

Bonuses Given to World War II Veterans. Names arranged alphabetically with bonus number, a copy of discharge, and date bonus check was mailed. The bonus number is necessary to obtain the microfilm record.

Korean War (1950-53)

Bonuses Given to Korean War Veterans. Names arranged alphabetically followed by bonus number. The bonus number is necessary to obtain the microfilm record.

Vietnam War (1963-75)

Louisiana Soldiers Killed or Missing in Action in Vietnam. An alphabetical list.

Bonuses Given to Vietnam War Veterans. Names arranged alphabetically with bonus number, copy of discharge, and date bonus check was mailed. The bonus number is necessary to obtain the microfilm record.

Manuscripts

The computer catalog lists dozens of private papers, miscellaneous reports and correspondence, legislation, battle accounts, and similar material referring to Louisiana's role in various wars. Some of these records contain names of personnel, but they primarily contain historical information.

PUBLISHED SOURCES—LOUISIANA

Pre-1783 (colonial and territorial wars)

Beers, Henry P. *French and Spanish Records of Louisiana: A Bibliographical Guide to Archive and Manuscript Sources.* Baton Rouge: Louisiana State University Press, 1989.

Churchill, E. Robert, comp. *Soldiers of the American Revolution Under Bernardo De Galvez.* Of the five printed copies, one is in the Library of Congress.

De Ville, Winston. *Louisiana Recruits, 1752–58: Ship Lists of Troops From the Independent Companies of the Navy Destined for Service in the French Colony of Louisiana.* Cottonport: Polyanthos, 1973.

———. *Louisiana Troops, 1720–1770.* Fort Worth, Tex.: American Reference Pub., 1965.

———. *Louisiana Soldiers in the American Revolution.* Ville Platte: Smith Books, 1991. Based on lists of the Charles Robert Churchill Collection, Papeless Procedentes de Cuba, General Archives of the Indies, Spain.

Holmes, Jack D.L. *Honor and Fidelity: The Louisiana Infantry Regiment and the Louisiana Militia Companies, 1766–1812.* Birmingham, Ala.: Holmes, 1965. More than 1,500 names of commissioned and noncommissioned officers.

Kinnaird, Lawrence, ed. *Spain in the Mississippi Valley, 1765–1794.* Vol. 2 of American Historical Association Annual Report, 1945. Washington, D.C.: Government Printing Office, 1949. Contains lists of officials and militia officers.

Maduell, Charles R., comp. and trans. *The Census Tables for the French Colony of Louisiana From 1699 Through 1732.* Baltimore: Genealogical Publishing Co., 1972. Military personnel are so designated.

Mills, Elizabeth S. *Natchitoches Colonials: Censuses, Military Rolls, and Tax Lists, 1722–1803.* Cane River Creole Series. Tuscaloosa, Ala.: Mills Historical Press, 1981.

Robichaux, Albert J., comp., trans., ed. *Louisiana Census and Militia Lists, 1770–98.* 2 vols. Harvey: the author, 1973.

Sanders, Mary E. *Records of Attakapas District, Louisiana.* Reprint. 3 vols. Fort Worth, Tex.: American Reference Pub., 1969–74. Vol. 1: 1739–1811; covers Attakapas Spanish militia, Attakapas militia, and census of 1792.

Vidrine, Jacqueline O. *Marriage Contracts of the Opelousas Post, 1766–1803.* Ville Platte (?): 1960. Includes many military personnel with name, rank, names of parents, and place of birth.

1784-1815 (War of 1812)

Casey, Powell A. *Louisiana in the War of 1812.* Baton Rouge: the author, 1963. Includes a "Roster of Louisiana Troops" and a partial list of casualties.

De Grummond, Jane L. *The Baratarians and the Battle of New Orleans.* Baton Rouge: 1961. Reprint includes *Biographical Sketches of the Veterans of the Battalions of Orleans, 1814–1815* by Ronald R. Morazan. Baton Rouge: Legacy Publishing Co., 1979.

De Verges, Marie C., comp. *American Forces at Chalmette. Veterans and De[s]cendants of Battle of New Orleans, 1814–1815.* Battle of New Orleans 150th Anniversary Committee, Women's Committee: 1956 (?). Lists the soldiers of Louisiana by unit.

Morazan, Ronald R. *Biographical Sketches of the Veterans of the Battalion of Orleans, 1814–1815.* Baton Rouge: Legacy Publishing Co., 1979. (See De Grummond, above.)

Pierson, Marion J.B. *Louisiana Soldiers in the War of 1812.* Baton Rouge: Louisiana Genealogical and Historical Society, 1963. Includes name, rank, and company.

1816-60

McClure, Mary L. *Louisiana Leaders, 1830–1860.* Shreveport: Journal Printing Co., 1935.

1861-65 (Civil War)

Adams, Donna B. *Civil War Records of the "Florida Parishes" of Louisiana.* 3 vols. Baton Rouge: the author, 1985–89.

Bartlett, Napier. *Military Record of Louisiana: Including Biographical and Historical Papers Relating to the Military Organizations of the State.* Baton Rouge: Louisiana State University Press, 1964.

Bergeron, Arthur W., Jr. *Guide to Louisiana Confederate Military Units, 1861–1865.* Baton Rouge: Louisiana State University Press, 1989.

Booth, Andrew B., comp. *Records of Louisiana Confederate Soldiers and Louisiana Confederate Commands.* 3 vols. New Orleans: 1920. Reprint. Spartanburg, S.C.: The Reprint Co., 1982.

Burt, W.G. *Annual Report of the Adjutant General of the State of Louisiana for the Year Ending December 31st, 1899.* New Orleans: State Papers, 1890.

Dilts, Bryan L., comp. *1890 Louisiana Census Index of Civil War Veterans or Their Widows.* Salt Lake City: Index Pub., 1984.

Louisiana. General Assembly. *Biennial Report of the Board of Directors of Camp Nicholls, the Soldiers' Home of Louisiana....* Baton Rouge: 1908. Residents of Camp Nicholls, April 1906 through March 1910.

Louisiana Soldiers' Relief Association and Hospital in the City of Richmond, Virginia. *Louisiana Soldiers' Relief Association and Hospital in the City of Richmond, Virginia. . . .* Richmond: Enquirer Book and Job Press, 1862. Officers of Louisiana regiments in Virginia.

Marchant, Sidney A. *Forgotten Fighters, 1861–1865.* Donaldsonville (?): 1966 (?). Residents of Ascension Parish, Louisiana, who joined various military units of the Confederacy; listed by unit with name and comments.

Moneyhon, Carl H., and Bobby Roberts. *Portraits of Conflict: A Photographic History of Louisiana in the Civil War.* Fayetteville: University of Arkansas Press, 1990.

United Daughters of the Confederacy,Louisiana Division. *Index, Membership Applications, 1898–1988 and Patriot Index.* 2 vols. Covington: J. Monroe, 1985–88.

1898-99 (Spanish-American War)

Wright, Nancy Lowne. *Louisiana Volunteers in the War of 1898.* Wright Shannon Pub., 1989.

Maine

1498-99	The Maine coast was explored by John and Sebastian Cabot.
1620	Sir Ferdinando Gorges and John Mason received a grant to colonize Maine.
1647	Massachusetts claimed Maine but did not finally buy out Gorges's heirs until 1677.
1820	Maine separated from Massachusetts and became a state.
1839	The Aroostook War, a dispute over Maine's northeastern border, occurred between Maine and Canadian loggers. (See Aroostook War in the appendix.)
1842	The Webster-Ashburton Treaty established the border between Maine and Nova Scotia.

MAINE STATE ARCHIVES

Cultural Building
State House Station 84
Augusta, Maine 04333-0084
(207) 287-5790

Finding Aids

Finding Aid for the Office of the Adjutant General. This aid lists holdings created by the state adjutant general, but it does not include the holdings listed in "Adjutant General—Old Records" (see below).

Defense and Veterans Services. This aid lists various military record collections. It provides box numbers and location symbols and is used by both staff members and researchers. Holdings are listed under the following headings:

> Adjutant General—Old Records:
> Burial places of revolutionary war soldiers
> Graves registration, 1941–42
> Muster rolls of various regiments
> Post-Civil War claims, arranged by town
> Victory medal applications
> World War I bonus applications (allowed and disallowed)
> World War I draft registration
> World War I soldiers' bonus receipts

Civil War Obituaries

Cemetery Records

Pensions/State Aid

Veterans Financial Assistance Cases

World War I Discharges

World War I Selective Service Cards

World War I Relief Commission

Records

General

Executive Council Reports (showing the organization of militia units). This notebook includes an index for reports of the Maine Executive Council, 1831–35. Under the heading "Militia" are several references to petitions from citizens who desired to form militia companies. Given are the names of the town, year, and box number where the records may be found.

Legislative Resolutions for Claims for Military Service. Reference is made to the book *Archives of the Legislature of Maine, Legislative Index Series, 1831–35*. (Maine State Archives, 1987.) A name index is available.

Register of Commissions (military officers), 1820–1952. Name, rank, residence, unit, date of rank, and date of commission.

Pensions Awarded by Maine, 1845–81 (indexed). Name, date, warrant number, terms of the pension, and amount of pension; also similar information relating to the persons listed in the finding aid *Defense and Veterans Services* (see above).

Militia Rolls And Returns, 1820–1971. Seventy volumes of militia rosters, the first fifty of which contain names of militia officers; the remaining are rosters of various militia units. There is a card index for the period 1820–50.

Military Discharges, 1834–1942. Name, residence, rank, unit, date of discharge, and remarks.

Courts-martial, 1820–1921. Name of individual tried, location of the court, charges, and disposition.

Cemetery Lists. Maine veterans buried in Maine cemeteries; data (name and regiment) supplied by various persons and groups. This data also appears in the *Annual Report of the Maine Adjutant General* for 1864.

Graves Registration Cards. These cards are an inventory of grave sites of all veterans, beginning with colonial wars and ending with World War I. Collections consist of individual cards, a cemetery card index, and cemetery plots showing graves of veterans. They are generally indexed by county, town, and name of deceased.

Veterans' Financial Assistance Cases, World War I, World War II, Korean War, Vietnam War (restricted under federal Privacy Act provisions).

American Revolution (1775-83)

Maine was a part of Massachusetts during the American Revolution. Refer to the records listed in the Massachusetts section.

NATIONAL ARCHIVES MICROFILM

Miscellaneous Numbered Records (The Manuscript File) in the War Department Collection of Revolutionary War Records, 1775–1790's (M859).

Special Index to Numbered Records in the War Department Collection of Revolutionary War Records, 1775–1783 (M847).

OTHER RECORDS

Revolutionary War Pension and Bounty Land Applications. Documents necessary to obtain a federal grant are cited in Maine Land Office and Maine court records. This finding aid contains an alphabetical list of the names of applicants, indicating their towns of residence and whether they applied to a Maine court, a Massachusetts court, or a county court. It also contains the actual documents (applications and supporting papers) relative to the land grants filed in Maine or Massachusetts courts and the courts of Hancock and York counties. Those for Lincoln County are on microfilm. Maine grants were made under acts of 1835, 1836, and 1838. Massachusetts grants were made under acts of 1820, 1828, 1829, and 1831. Also see *Massachusetts Archives* (cited under Published Sources—Maine).

Henry Sewall Papers, 1781–1820. A manuscript collection devoted primarily to the Eighth Division, Maine Militia; also contains several papers from the American Revolution era; rosters of officers, returns, and muster rolls.

War of 1812 (1812-15)

Because Maine did not become a state until 1820, records for the War of 1812 can be found in the Massachusetts section. Also see various collections cited under Records— General (above) that include records for this time period.

Index to Regular Army Rolls, Maine and Massachusetts.

Descriptive Books for the Thirty-third Infantry Regiment, Thirty-fourth Infantry Regiment, and USS *Adams* (sunk 3 September 1814).

Aroostook War (1839-40)

Aroostook War Vouchers, Secretary of State

Aroostook War Records in Land Office—civil posse

Aroostook War Drafted Militia, 1839 (indexed).

Muster Rolls and Payrolls, 1839.

Also see various collections cited under Records—General (above) that include records for this time period.

Mexican War (1846-48)

Roster of Officers.

Descriptive Rolls, First Regiment, 1846, and Receipt-of-bounty Roll.

Miscellaneous Descriptive Rolls.

Also see various collections cited under Records—General (above) that include records for this time period.

Civil War (1861-65)

NATIONAL ARCHIVES MICROFILM

Index to Compiled Military Service Records of Volunteer Union Soldiers Who Served in Organizations From the State of Maine (M543).

OTHER RECORDS

Regimental Records and Index. Beginning in 1895, all extant Maine Civil War regimental rolls were mounted on transparent linen sheets, each roll becoming a separate page and consecutively numbered. A card index was created to list the pertinent information for each soldier or sailor. The card indicates the location of the original document and lists name, age, unit, branch of military service, rank, marital status, physical description, enlistment date, muster-in date, place of birth, residence, discharge date, how left the service, muster-out date, reenlistment date, and remarks. If a soldier's or sailor's military unit is known, an appropriate finding aid or index may then be consulted to discover what other information exists.

Medical Examinations, 1861-62. Arranged by military unit or by county and town.

Recruits, United States Navy (also navy substitutes), 1864. Arranged by county and then alphabetically.

State Bounty Records, 1862-64. Arranged alphabetically by name of the soldier or town of residence.

State Aid Vouchers, 1863-65. Names of individuals receiving state financial aid are listed in the finding aid *Defense and Veterans Services* (cited above).

Civil War Obituaries. Newspaper obituaries for those individuals listed in the finding aid *Defense and Veterans Services*. There are also lists arranged by name of regiment. See the finding aid for name of regiment.

Hospital Returns, 1862-63. List patients in various hospitals; name, rank, unit, date, and remarks (illness or wound); also arranged by name of regiment.

Seventh Maine Regiment. The Lt. William Cosby Collection, 1861-66, contains a list of deserters, 1864-65, and a register of discharges (officers only), 1861-66.

Photograph Collection, Officers. Names and units are given.

Post-Civil War Period (1866-)

The finding aids refer to the following types of records relating to individuals after the close of the Civil War.

Civil War Claims

Deserters, 1881-1926

Enrolled Militia, 1873-1911. Arranged alphabetically by county and town.

Gettysburg Reunion (Maine veterans of Gettysburg).

Service Records (twelve volumes), 1890-1913. Include records of Civil War service, with copies of certificates bound in leather volumes. Each volume is indexed.

Spanish-American War (1898-99)

Card index. Name, unit, term of service, age, physical description, rank, enlistment date, muster-in date, occupation, place of birth, residence, discharge date, how left the service, and remarks. This index also appears in the *Annual Report of the Maine Adjutant General, 1898*.

Certificates of Service.

Bounties Paid to Veterans of the Spanish-American War.

Roster of Officers, 1898.

Soldiers to Whom Certificates Were Sent (also service chevrons).

World War I (1917-18)

The following publication of the Maine legislature is available in the Office of Defense and Veterans Service (adjacent to the state archives building): *Roster of Maine in the Military Service of the United States and Allies in the World War, 1917-1919.* 2 vols. (2 vols. Augusta, 1929). (See also the same publication under Maine Adjutant General's Office in the Published Sources—Maine section.) This publication provides a brief summary of each veteran, giving name, place and date of birth, residence, place and date of enlistment, rank, unit, overseas service, and honorable discharge date. Includes alphabetical lists of members of the U.S. Army, Army Nurse Corps, Navy Nurse Corps, Yeomen, U.S. Navy, Marine Corps, and U.S. Coast Guard. A card index in the archives contains similar data.

Index to Draft Registrations, 1918. Included are name, age, residence, serial number, order number, place and date of birth, nationality, draft classification, occupation, physical description, name of local board, induction date, acceptance date, and remarks.

An inventory in the finding aid *Defense and Veterans Services*, under Office of the Adjutant General, contains the following entries, among others, referring to World War I veterans: citations, commissioned officers, deaths, deceased soldiers, deserters (navy), honor roll letters, lists of women (navy and marines), lists of officers, newspaper clippings, officers' roster (navy and marines), prisoners, prisoners of war, service cards for other states, U.S. Coast Guard, U.S. Marine Corps, Victory Medal applications, women.

Selective Service Cards, 1914–22. Alphabetically arranged cards give the following information, where pertinent, for individuals on the registers of draft boards: killed in action or died of disease; war bonus disallowed; war bonus allowed; war bonus for women; recruits—USNRF, USN, NG, USA; reported to provost marshal.

Discharge Papers. Collections arranged as follows:

Medical discharges, by county.

Alphabetical, 1914–22.

National Guard discharges, 1914–22.

Final county deserter lists, 1914–22.

Miscellaneous correspondence, 1914–22.

Notification of wounded in action; severity of wounds, 1925–26.

Veterans' financial assistance cases. Papers processed for those applying for or receiving aid; arranged alphabetically.

Relief Commission Papers. A 1929 act provided for relief of needy dependents of disabled veterans of World War I. Records consist primarily of correspondence; arranged alphabetically by name of veteran; additional records labeled "American Red Cross."

Cemetery Records of Deceased Veterans, 1940s and 1950s. Names can be found in the finding aid Defense and Veterans Services. Name and county are given.

World War II (1941–45)

Index of Veterans. Name, address, enlistment date, discharge date, physical description, length of service, and comments (restricted under federal Privacy Act provisions).

Casualties. Name; address; reason for casualty; whether killed in action, died of wounds, died of disease, wounded, missing, or prisoner-of-war; next of kin; decorations and citations; and military history (restricted under federal Privacy Act provisions).

Women in Service Since World War II. Name, place of birth, place and date of enlistment, marital status, place and date of discharge, and remarks (restricted under federal Privacy Act provisions).

Korean War (1950–53)

Index of Veterans—Casualties (similar to the index for World War II veterans; restricted under federal Privacy Act provisions).

MAINE HISTORICAL SOCIETY

485 Congress Street
Portland, Maine 04101
(207) 774-1822

Manuscript Collections

An index to subjects in the manuscript collections includes:

King William's War, 1689–97
King George's War, 1744–48
Revolution
Tripolitan War, 1801–03
War of 1812
War with Mexico, 1845–48
Civil War

Documents Containing Lists of Individuals Who Enlisted in a French and Indian War company. French and Indian War journal/orderly book.

Zebulon Harmon Collection. Contains revolutionary war affidavits; muster rolls for Maine, Massachusetts, and Vermont; names of units; and pension and bounty claims.

Revolutionary War Diaries and Orderly Books (miscellaneous).

Lists of Revolutionaries From Litchfield, Lisbon, Monmouth, and Bowdoin.

Men to Whom Meals Were Furnished in Colonel Frye's Regiment, Revolutionary War.

Returns From War of 1812. Payrolls of Fourth Regiment; crew lists of prize vessels.

List of Officers, Soldiers and Chaplains, Revolutionary War.

Civil War Muster-out Rolls, 1865 (miscellaneous units).

PUBLISHED SOURCES—MAINE

Pre-1775 (colonial wars)

Massachusetts. State Archives. *Massachusetts Archives.* 328 vols. A manuscript collection of the Massachusetts Archives. Vol. 98 contains a list of men who enlisted in 1760.

Society of Colonial Wars, Maine. *Register of the Officers and Members of the Society of Colonial Wars in the State of Maine; Also History, Roster and Record of Col. Jedidiah Preble's Regiment, Campaign of 1758; Together With Capt. Samuel Cobb's Journal* [1758]. Portland: Marks Printing House, 1905. Includes the period of the French and Indian War.

1775-83 (American Revolution)

Daughters of the American Revolution (Maine). *Ancestral Roll and Chapter Roster. . . .* The society, 1975.

_____ . *Maine Revolutionary Soldiers' Graves*. Augusta: the society, 1940.

_____ . *Roster and Ancestral Roll, Maine Daughters of the American Revolution, and the List of Maine Soldiers at Valley Forge, 1777–1778*. Compiled by Mrs. Percy L. Tate. Farmington (?): 1948.

Fisher, Carleton E., and Sue G. Fisher, comps. *Soldiers, Sailors, and Patriots of the Revolutionary War, Maine*. Louisville, Ky: National Society Sons of the American Revolution, 1982.

Flagg, Charles A. *An Alphabetical Index of Revolutionary Pensioners Living in Maine*. Dover: 1920. Reprint. Baltimore: Genealogical Publishing Co., 1967.

House, Charles J. *Names of Soldiers of the American Revolution, Who Applied for State Bounty Under Resolves of March 17, 1835, March 24, 1836, and March 20, 1836, as Appears of Record in the Land Office*. Augusta: Burleigh & Flynt, 1893. Reprint. Baltimore: Genealogical Publishing Co., 1967.

Kidder, Frederic. *Military Operations in Eastern Maine and Nova Scotia During the Revolution, Chiefly Compiled From the Journals and Letters of Colonel John Allen*. Albany, N.Y., 1867. Reprint. Millwood, N.Y.: Kraus Reprint, 1985 (?). Includes names of some Indians who served the patriots' cause.

Maine at Valley Forge: Proceedings at the Unveiling of the Maine Marker, October 17, 1907; Also Roll of Maine Soldiers at Valley Forge. 2nd ed. Augusta: Burleigh & Flint, 1910. Soldiers listed by regiment and company with rank and comments, pages 23–56.

Minority Military Service, 1775–1783: Maine. Washington, D.C.: National Society Daughters of the American Revolution, 1990.

1784-1860 (Aroostook War)

Aroostook War. Historical Sketch and Roster of Commissioned Officers and Enlisted Men Called Into Service for the Protection of the Northeastern Frontier of Maine, From February to May 1839. Baltimore: Clearfield Co., 1989.

1861-65 (Civil War)

Dilts, Bryan L., comp. *1890 Maine Census Index of Civil War Veterans or Their Widows*. Salt Lake City: Index Pub., 1984.

Hodson, John L. *Annual Report of the Adjutant General of the State of Maine, for the Year Ending December 31, 1863*. Augusta: 1863.

Maine. Adjutant General. *Annual Report of the Adjutant General of the State of Maine, 1861–1866*. 7 vols. Augusta: Stevens & Sayward, 1862–67. *Annual Report, 1861–1866. Supplement: Alphabetical Index of Maine Volunteers, Etc., Mustered Into the Service of the United States During the War of 1861*. Augusta: Stevens & Sayward, 1867.

_____ . *Returns of Desertions, Discharges, Deaths, etc., in Maine Regiments for the Months of August, September and October, 1864*. Augusta (?): 1864 (?).

Maine. Gettysburg Commission. *Maine at Gettysburg: Report of Maine Commissioners Prepared by the Executive Committee. . . .* Portland (?): Lakeside Press (?), 1898. List of Maine casualties at Gettysburg.

Maine. Salisbury Monument Commission. *Report of the Maine Commissioners on the Monument Erected at Salisbury, N.C., 1908*. Waterville: Sentinel Publishing Co., 1908. Includes list of Maine soldiers who died at Salisbury.

Whitman, William E.S. *Maine in the War for the Union: A History of the Part Borne by Maine Troops in the Suppression of the American Rebellion*. Lewiston: N. Dingley Jr. & Co., 1865. Lists officers by regiment.

1901-75 (World War I through Vietnam War)

Historical and Pictorial Review. National Guard of the State of Maine, 1939. State of Maine, n.d. Contains many identified photographs.

Maine. Adjutant General's Office. *Roster of Maine in the Military Service of the United States and Allies in the World War, 1917–1919. . . .* 2 vols. Augusta: 1929.

_____ . *Maine National Guard Roster of Officers*. Augusta, n.d.

_____ . *Report of the Adjutant General of the State of Maine for the Period of the World War, 1917–1919*. Augusta: 1929.

Maryland

1524	Giovanni da Verrazano, exploring for France, probably entered Maryland.
1632	Maryland was granted as a proprietary colony to the Calvert family by King James I of England.
1634	The first English settlers arrived.
1649	Passage of the Act of Toleration attracted many religious dissenters from England, including Catholics and Quakers.
1689	Maryland's proprietary government was ended and religious tolerance replaced by Anglican conformity. The capital was moved from St. Mary's to Annapolis.
1715	The proprietary government was restored when Lord Baltimore converted to Protestantism.
1767	The Mason-Dixon Line established the border between Pennsylvania and Maryland.

1788	Maryland became a state.
1791	Maryland territory was combined with territory from Virginia to form the District of Columbia.
1814	Maryland was invaded by British troops during the War of 1812. (See War of 1812 in the appendix.)
1861	Although a slave state, Maryland remained loyal to the Union.
1862	At the Battle of Antietam (Sharpsburg), Gen. George McClellan drove Gen. Robert E. Lee's Confederate forces back into Virginia. (See American Civil War in the appendix.)

. . . .

MARYLAND STATE ARCHIVES

350 Rowe Boulevard
Annapolis, Maryland 21401
(410) 974-3914

Finding Aids

Guide to the Finding Aids at the Maryland State Archives. These sheets list the indexes available in the search room by title and index number. The reading room contains several indexes, both on cards and in volumes, each with its own identification number. Strategically placed signs on the file cabinets and on various tables around the room identify these numbered indexes. Each index provides reference data that must be used when requesting records. Members of the reference staff procure the requested records and deliver them to a work desk assigned to the researcher. When the records are ready to be returned, they are taken to the reference desk and deposited.

Card indexes relating to military service are numbered 45, 47, 48, 49, 50, 51, and 52. Index 53 (Civil War Records) has been withdrawn in favor of a published version available in the search room.

A Guide to Government Records at the Maryland State Archives—Comprehensive List by Agency and Record Series. This aid lists the archival holdings of Maryland agencies. Cited below are selected holdings as examples of military material.

Microfilmed County Records.

Records

General

Available on computer terminals in the reading room is the J. Thomas Scharf Collection and its index. This is a comprehensive collection of material relating to the history of Maryland. Subjects covered, in addition to political papers, court and public officer records, and similar subjects, are matters concerned with the colonial, revolutionary, and federal periods of history.

Military Papers, 1792-1835: S926, adjutant general.

Militia Appointments, 1794-1816: SM104, adjutant general; 1794-1910: S348, adjutant general.

Pension roll, military, 1852-88: S688, comptroller of the treasury; 1867-80: SM121, comptroller of the treasury.

Muster and Payrolls, 1867-1906: S944, adjutant general.

Naval Papers, 1893-1905: S937, adjutant general.

Discharge Papers, 1979-84: T1644, Maryland Veterans Commission; 1982-90: TM461, Maryland Veterans Commission.

Military Discharges: TM461, Maryland Veterans Commission.

Military Discharges. On file at various county courts. See the finding aid *Microfilmed County Records* (twentieth-century registrations).

Colonial Wars (pre-1775)

Muster and Payroll Index, 1732-72 (index 45). Alphabetical card index. Name of the soldier, military unit, and county of residence. Source references by box, folder, and year (or similar references) are provided, and they must be used in addition to the individual's name when requesting the records.

American Revolution (1775-83)

Revolutionary War Records Index, 1775-98 (index 50). Alphabetical card index; name of the soldier and date and title of the records; includes letter books, agents' ledgers, account books, depreciation pay, etc.

Revolutionary War Papers Index, 1775-89 (index 49). Card index; also available on an electronic data base; name of the soldier, date of the record, and type of document on which the soldier's name appears. These documents include muster rolls, receipts, account books, etc. Source references (box and folder number) are provided.

Pension Records, Revolutionary War Index, 1775- (index 48). Alphabetical card index. The cards are filed by name of the veteran or name of his widow or other heir who received a pension on the basis of the veteran's military service. Given are the pensioner's name, city or county of residence (or other state), relationship to the veteran, and legislative authority for the pension. The basis for the payment of the pension (disability, etc.) is given, and original sources are provided.

Oaths of Fidelity Index, 1778 (index 47). Alphabetical card index; gives name and county of residence of persons who signed an oath of fidelity to the state of Maryland. Source references (box and folder number, liber and folio number, minute book, etc.) are provided.

Army Officers' Accounts, 1777–83: S148, auditor general.

Muster Rolls, 1776–80: S152, SM118, auditor general.

Pension Record, 1785–97: S153, auditor general.

Day Books, Journals, and Ledgers: See finding aid *A Guide to Government Records* . . .

Post-American Revolution (1784–)

Militia Records Index, 1794–1824 (index 51). Alphabetical card index; names of militiamen and suppliers of arms; includes Baltimore County Military Registration of 1794; place of appointment or registration. Source references (book number and page, appointment number, arms account number) are provided.

Armorers' Papers, 1783–1839: S928, adjutant general.

Pay Accounts, 1784–98: S144, commissioner of army accounts.

Receipt Book, 1787–91: S145, commissioner of army accounts.

War of 1812 (1812–15)

Pension Record, War of 1812 Index (index 52). Alphabetical card index; arranged by name of veteran or widow of veteran who received a pension; place of residence, period of payment, and basis for payment of pension. Source references are provided.

Depreciation Certificates Register, 1781–97: S170, Commission to Settle and Adjust Pay Due Officers and Soldiers.

Depreciation Pay, 1781–91: S169; 1781–86: SM86, Commission to Settle and Adjust Pay Due Officers and Soldiers.

Mexican War (1846–48)

Mexican War Papers, 1851–61. S934, adjutant general.

Civil War–Union (1861–65)

NATIONAL ARCHIVES MICROFILM

Index to Compiled Military Service Records of Volunteer Union Soldiers Who Served in Organizations From the State of Maryland (M388).

OTHER RECORDS

Muster Rolls, 1860–67: S936, adjutant general.

Civil War Papers, 1860–67: S935, adjutant general.

Commission Applications, 1862–65: S324, adjutant general.

Descriptive Roll, 1861–64: S325, adjutant general.

Draft Record, 1862–64: S340, adjutant general.

Muster Roll Record, 1861–67: S343, adjutant general.

Bounty Certificates, 1864–67: S624, comptroller of the treasury.

Bounty Claims, 1866–67: S625, comptroller of the treasury.

Bounty Rolls, 1864–80: S629, comptroller of the treasury.

Officers List, 1863–68: S677, comptroller of the treasury.

MARYLAND HISTORICAL SOCIETY

201 West Monument Street
Baltimore, Maryland 21201
(410) 685-3750

This society has no military records for twentieth-century wars. It transferred the U.S. War Department card file for World War II veterans to the War Memorial Building, 101 North Gay Street, Baltimore, Maryland 21202 (opposite the city hall). Insofar as federal Privacy Act provisions allow, data from those cards may be supplied to relatives or researchers.

The library of the Maryland Historical Society has two volumes of photostated revolutionary war militia rolls. Names are arranged by unit, and a separate volume contains an index to the collection.

Finding Aid

Guide to the Research Collections of the Maryland Historical Society. Baltimore: 1981 supplement to 1978 edition.

The index to the finding aid cited above reveals that the manuscript collection includes documents pertaining to the following subjects:

> Battles
> Civil War
> Fort Warren Prisoners' Record Book
> Fourth Regiment, Maryland Account Book
> Logbooks
> Maryland Cadets and Maryland National Guard
> Maryland Corps of Artillery
> Maryland Guard, Fifty-third Regiment
> Maryland Line
> Maryland National Guard
> Maryland National Guard, Air Wing
> Maryland Volunteer Infantry
> Maryland Volunteers
> Maryland World War II Collection
> Mexican War Collection
> Military Collection
> Militia, Maryland
> Militia, New Hampshire

Militia, Pennsylvania

Military Journals

Ninth Maryland Volunteers

Revolutionary War

Revolutionary War (various counties)

Revolutionary War Collection

Revolutionary War Military Life

Sons of the American Revolution, Maryland Chapter

Spanish-American War

U.S. Air Force

U.S. Army (several subheadings)

U.S. Marine Corps

U.S. Merchant Marine

U.S. Naval Academy

U.S. Naval Reserves

U.S. Navy

War of 1812 Collection

World War I Collection (several subheadings)

World War II Collection (several subheadings)

PUBLISHED SOURCES—MARYLAND

Pre-1775 (colonial wars)

Stormont, Edith F., and Betty D. Aul, comps. *Maryland Colonial Military Service Index; With Roster of Colonial Ancestors of Members of the Society. . . .* Florida (?): Daughters of Colonial Wars in the State of Florida, 1988. Covers the period 1637 through 1776.

1775-83 (American Revolution)

Brumbaugh, Gaius M. *Maryland Records: Colonial, Revolutionary, County and Church, From Original Sources.* 2 vols. Baltimore: Williams & Wilkins, 1915. Reprint. Lancaster, Pa.: Lancaster Press, 1928. Reprint. Baltimore: Genealogical Publishing Co., 1985.

_____. *Revolutionary Records of Maryland.* Washington, D.C.: Rufus H. Darby Printing Co., 1924. Reprint. Baltimore: Genealogical Publishing Co., 1967.

Calendar of Maryland State Papers: The Red Books; the Brown Books; the Executive Miscellanea. Annapolis: Hall of Records, 1950-55.

Carothers, Bettie S., comp. *Maryland Oaths of Fidelity.* 2 vols. Vol. l, 9000 Men Who Signed the Oath of Allegiance and Fidelity to Maryland During the Revolution (counties of Anne Arundel, Cecil, Charles, Frederick, Harford, Montgomery, Prince George[s], Queen Ann, Somerset, Talbot, and Washington). Vol. 2, *Signers of the Oath of Fidelity to Maryland During the Revolution* (counties of Baltimore,

Montgomery, Dorchester, Caroline, and Calvert). Lutherville: the author, 1975.

_____, comp. *Maryland Soldiers Entitled to Lands West of Fort Cumberland.* Lutherville (?): Carothers, 1973.

Clark, Raymond B. *Marylanders in the Index of Revolutionary War Pension Applications.* Arlington, Va.: R.B. Clark, 1982. Alphabetically arranged with survivor's or widow's pension or bounty-land warrant number.

Clements, S. Eugene, and F. Edward Wright. *The Maryland Militia in the Revolutionary War.* Silver Spring: Family Line Publications, 1987.

Meyer, Mary K. "Revolutionary War Soldiers Granted Pensions by the State of Maryland." *Bulletin of the Maryland Genealogical Society,* 4 (Nov. 1963) and 7 (Feb. 1966).

Muster Rolls and Other Records of Service of Maryland Troops in the American Revolution: 1775-1783. Archives of Maryland, vol. 18. Baltimore: Maryland Historical Society, 1900. Reprint. Baltimore: Genealogical Publishing Co., 1972.

Newman, Harry W., comp. *Maryland Revolutionary Records: Data Obtained From 3,050 Pension Claims and Bounty Land Applications, Including 1,000 Marriages of Maryland Soldiers and a List of 1,200 Proved Services of Soldiers and Patriots of Other States.* Washington, D.C.: 1938. Reprint. Baltimore: Genealogical Publishing Co., 1967.

Papenfuse, Edward C. *An Inventory of Maryland State Papers.* Vol. 1. *The Era of the American Revolution, 1775-1789.* Annapolis: Hall of Records Commission, 1977.

Scharf, John T. "List of Officers and Men Entitled to Lots Westward of Fort Cumberland." *History of Western Maryland* 1:145-61. Baltimore: Regional Pub. Co., 1968.

Steuart, Reiman. *A History of the Maryland Line in the Revolutionary War, 1775-1783.* Towson: Society of the Cincinnati of Maryland, 1969. Contains biographical sketches of Maryland officers.

1784-1815 (War of 1812)

The Citizen Soldiers at North Point and Fort McHenry. Baltimore: Charles Saffell, 1858. Reprint. Baltimore: C.C. Saffell, 1889.

Culver, Francis B. *Historical Sketch of the Militia of Maryland.* Baltimore (?): 1907 (?). Contains biographical sketches of the adjutants general, 1810-1908.

Huntsberry, Thomas V., and Joanne M. Huntsberry. *Maryland Privateers, War of 1812.* Baltimore: J. Mart, 1983. Includes officers and enlisted men by company.

Huntsberry, Thomas V. *North Point.* Baltimore: J. Mart, 1985. Maryland militia participating in the Battle of North Point, Maryland, 1814.

_____. *Western Maryland, Pennsylvania, Virginia Militia in Defense of Maryland, 1805 to 1815.* Baltimore (?): the author, 1983. Personnel of militia companies.

Marine, William M., ed. *The British Invasion of Maryland, 1812-1815.* With an appendix, containing eleven thousand names, by Louis Henry Dielman. Baltimore: Society of the

War of 1812 in Maryland, 1913. Reprint. Baltimore: Genealogical Publishing Co., 1977. Appendix lists soldiers by rank, their commanding officer, and regiment.

Wright, F. Edward. *Maryland Militia, War of 1812. Abstracts of Muster, Pay, and Receipt Rolls . . . By Company.* 8 vols. Silver Spring: Family Line Publications, 1979-92. Listed by county.

1816-60 (Mexican War)

Kenly, John R. *Memoirs of a Maryland Volunteer: War with Mexico in the Years 1846-7-8.* Philadelphia: J.B. Lippincott, 1873. Includes First Battalion of Baltimore and Washington Volunteers, 1846-47; First District of Columbia and Maryland Regiment, 1847-48.

Wells, Charles J. *Maryland and District of Columbia Volunteers in the Mexican War.* Westminster: Family Line Publications, 1991.

1861-65 (Civil War)

Dilts, Bryan L., comp. *1890 Maryland Census Index of Civil War Veterans or Their Widows.* Salt Lake City: Index Pub., 1985.

Goldsborough, W.W. *The Maryland Line in the Confederate Army, 1861-1865.* Baltimore: 1869. Reprint of second edition published 1900, *With an Introduction by Jean Baker and Index Prepared by Louise Q. Lewis.* Middle Atlantic States Historical Publications Series, no. 19. Port Washington, N.Y.: Kennikat Press, 1972 (?).

Hartzler, Daniel D. *Marylanders in the Confederacy.* Silver Spring: Family Line Publications, 1986.

Huntsberry, Thomas V., and Joanne M. Huntsberry. *Maryland in the Civil War.* 2 vols. Baltimore: J. Mart, 1985. Includes soldiers with rank and unit and some biographical sketches.

Maryland. Gettysburg Monument Commission. *Report of the State of Maryland Gettysburg Monument Commission to His Excellency E.E. Jackson, Governor of Maryland, June 17th, 1891.* Baltimore: William K. Boyle & Son, 1891. Maryland casualties at Gettysburg.

Pompey, Sherman L. *Civil War Veterans Buried in the Mid-West.* 4 (?) vols. Clovis, Calif. (?): 1970-(?). Vol. 4 covers Maryland.

_____. *Muster Lists of the American Rifles of Maryland, Baltimore Artillery, Dias Maryland Artillery, Maryland Guerilla Zouaves, and Captain Walter's Company, Maryland Zarvona Zouaves of the Confederacy.* N.p., 1965.

Reamy, Martha, and Bill Reamy. *History and Roster of Maryland Volunteers, War of 1861-1865: Index.* Westminster: Family Line Publications, 1990. Indexes two volumes of L. Allison Wilmer, et al., *History and Roster of Maryland Volunteers, War of 1861-1865.* Baltimore: Guggenheimer, Weil & Co., 1898-99. Reprint. 1987.

Society of the Army and Navy of the Confederate States, in the State of Maryland. *Roster of Officers and Members of the Society of the Army and Navy of the Confederate States in the State of Maryland, With Constitution and By-laws.* Baltimore: Sun Job Printing Office, 1883.

Toomey, Daniel Carroll. *Index to the Roster of the Maryland Volunteers, 1861-1865.* Harmans: Toomey Press, 1986.

Wilmer, L. Allison. *History and Roster of Maryland Volunteers, War of 1861-5.* 2 vols. Baltimore: Guggenheimer, Weil & Co., 1898-99. Reprint. Silver Spring: Family Line Publications, 1987.

1866-99 (Spanish-American War)

Maryland. Adjutant General's Office. *Annual Report, 1898-99.* Baltimore: state printer, 1900.

Payne, William C. *The Cruise of the U.S.S. Dixie; or, On Board With Maryland Boys in the Spanish-American War.* Washington, D.C.: E.C. Jones, 1899. Includes some portraits.

Riley, Hugh Ridgely. *Roster of the Soldiers and Sailors Who Served in Organizations From Maryland During the Spanish-American War.* Silver Spring: Family Line Publications, 1990.

1900-75 (World War I through Vietnam War)

Maryland. National Guard. *Official Register of the Officers Serving in the Organized Militia of Maryland.* Annapolis: Headquarters, Maryland National Guard, Adjutant General's Office, 1909.

Maryland Historical Society. *Maryland in World War I: Register of Service Personnel.* Baltimore: the society, 1965.

Maryland in World War II. 2 vols. Baltimore: War Records Division, 1950-51. Vol. 1 includes names of Marylanders in the armed forces.

Massachusetts

1620	English Puritans known as "Separatists" or "Pilgrims" established the first colony at Plymouth.
1630	The Massachusetts Bay Colony was founded at Boston by Non-separatists.
1675-76	King Philip's War ended Indian resistance to white settlement in the area. (See King Philip's War in the appendix.)
1691	Massachusetts became a royal colony.
1702-13	Queen Anne's War saw a French raid on Deerfield and three British offensives into Canada from Massachusetts. (See Queen Anne's War in the appendix.)

1740–48   King George's War included an assault from Massachusetts on the Canadian city of Louisburg. (See King George's War in the appendix.)

1775   The first shots of the American Revolution were fired at the Battles of Lexington and Concord. These were followed by the Battle of Bunker Hill in June. (See American Revolution in the appendix.)

1786–87   Shays' Rebellion pitted debt-ridden farmers against the Massachusetts government. (See Shays' Rebellion in the appendix.)

1788   Massachusetts became one of the original thirteen states.

1820   Maine separated from Massachusetts to become a separate state.

1861–65   During the Civil War, Massachusetts contributed 146,730 soldiers to the Union cause, the highest total of any New England state. (See American Civil War in the appendix.)

. . . .

MASSACHUSETTS ARCHIVES

220 Morrissey Boulevard
(at Columbia Point, south of downtown Boston)
Boston, Massachusetts 02125
(617) 727-2816

Finding Aids

Massachusetts Archives. A 328-volume collection of seventeenth- and eighteenth-century records held by the state archives. Contains records pertaining to the colonial era, revolutionary war, loyalists, and Shays' Rebellion.

Military Records at the Massachusetts Archives. This pamphlet briefly describes the available military records, including holdings from the colonial period through the Spanish-American War. This archives does not have military records for twentieth-century wars or conflicts, but it does have some card indexes listing names of those who served in World War I and World War II.

Pensions. This notebook lists individuals who claimed bounty (cash or land). The first part pertains to bounties in Maine; the second part is a list of names and Massachusetts towns, with symbols denoting where the original records may be found.

This archives has no National Archives military microfilm.

Records

Colonial Wars (pre-1775)

Lists of Men Who Served in British Military Organizations, 1710–74. Name, enlistment date, time in service, and amount of pay due; available on microfilm reels 91–99; arranged chronologically. There is an alphabetical name index on microfilm.

Government Responses to Petitions Claiming Remuneration for Military Service Rendered or for Losses as a Result of Hostile Actions Against or by Indians, 1643–74. Each set of records is accompanied by a table of contents and a name index; available on microfilm reels 67–80 of *Massachusetts Archives;* arranged chronologically.

Officers of Militia Regiments, 1767–74.

Field Officers of Massachusetts Regiments, 1767–74.

Military Records of the General Court, 1643–1775. Proposed legislation, correspondence, and petitions from individuals claiming remuneration or redress. Each volume is accompanied by a table of contents and a name index; in vols. 67–80 of *Massachusetts Archives* and available on microfilm; arranged chronologically.

Military Accounts and Billeting Accounts, 1741–63. In vols. 89, 90, 268, and 269 of *Massachusetts Archives* and available on microfilm. Vols. 89 and 90 have a table of contents; vols. 268 and 269 are indexed in the main catalog for the collection.

American Revolution (1775–83)

It is important to know from which county or town a Massachusetts officer or soldier came, and also in which military unit he served, before attempting to find documentary evidence of his service. The primary sources of this information are published volumes titled *Massachusetts Soldiers and Sailors of the Revolutionary War . . .* (cited below under Published Sources—Massachusetts). The next step can be to inspect a notebook available at the front desk, a part of which consists of several pages titled Revolutionary Rolls. These pages list record collections by county, name of regiment or company, or name of commanding officer. Each collection cited on those pages is accompanied by a location symbol, which must be used when requesting the material. The collections listed below are representative examples of the types of material available.

Many documents have come to light since *Massachusetts Soldiers and Sailors of the Revolutionary War* was published, and they now comprise a supplementary index consisting of sixteen microfilm reels as part of the manuscript collection "Massachusetts Archives." Material in these reels is indexed on alphabetically arranged cards. The drawers containing the cards for these specific materials are marked with blue labels to differentiate them from index cards for other material found nearby.

MASSACHUSETTS MICROFILM

Rhode Island Service; Muster Rolls, 1776–80.

Town Rolls (Six-Month Enlistments). Not indexed.

Bonds for Privateers, Armed Vessels, by Name of Vessel.

Charter Parties and Bonds for Vessels; Documents Relating to Prisoners.

Lists of Prisoners, British and American; Cartels and Exchanges of Prisoners, Paroles, 1776–80.

Bounty Receipts Pertaining to Prisoners of Berkshire County (also other miscellaneous documents related to Berkshire County).

Invalid Pensioners, 1779–83.

Deserters From Massachusetts Continental Regiments, 1777–80.

Rolls, Hampshire County Men, 1782.

Rolls, Lists, Certificates, Continental Regiments, 1777–82. Also a few militia regiments (1775).

Lexington Alarm: Orders, Discharges, Receipts, 1776–82. Rolls arranged alphabetically by name of captains, 1775.

OTHER RECORDS

Rolls of Army at the Siege of Boston, August 1775.

Rolls of Various Companies Arranged Alphabetically by Name of Captain, 1776–81.

Rolls, The Castle and Harbor (Hull, Rutland, Springfield, others), 1776–80.

Company Officers of Continental and Militia Regiments, 1775–82.

Rolls of Col. H. Jackson's Continental Regiment, 1780, and Colonel Dike's Militia Regiment, 1776–77. Lists of men "transferred" or "not included."

Books Containing Lists of Enlisted Men and Officers. Various Continental Army men from towns of Massachusetts; York County, Maine; and Massachusetts counties, 1778–80.

Field Officers, 1775, With Dates of Commission.

Field and Company Officers, Militia Regiments.

Officers of Reinforcements for Canada and Ticonderoga, 1776.

Officers of Sea Coast Companies, 1777–79.

Settlement of Rank at West Point, 1775–79.

Officers of the Massachusetts Navy, 1776–77.

Half Pay of Officers (deceased), 1786–89.

Books Containing Lists of Enlisted Men (militia and Continental Army). Descriptive lists, returns, enlistment lists, entitlements to $20 bounty or two hundred acres of land.

Books Containing Militia or Continental Army Payrolls and Books Containing Abstracts of Rolls and Depreciation Rolls.

Bounty Receipts, by County.

Sea Coast Defence Muster Rolls, 1775–79.

Sea Coast Defence, Penobscot Expedition Rolls, 1779–80.

Naval Service. Payrolls and papers pertaining to eight war vessels.

Naval Service, Privateers. Lists of recruits, 1780–81.

Lists of Vessels of Penobscot Expedition, 1779.

Crew of *Reprisal*—Captured by the British, 1778.

Enlistment Rolls, Bounties, Returns. Officers, various regiments and various counties, 1776–81. (See listings in the "Revolutionary Rolls" mentioned above.)

PENSIONS

The finding aid *Pensions*, cited above, contains an alphabetical list of individuals who claimed bounty ($20 or $50) or land in Maine according to Massachusetts laws of 1801, 1833, and 1835. The location of such land and the name of any widow claiming it are shown in the finding aid. A letter (I, J, H, or K) following the entry indicates that the original documents are available in this archives and can be retrieved by the staff. The lack of such a character indicates the information was extracted from the 1835 publication *200-acre Grants to Soldiers of the Massachusetts Continental Army*. This publication is available upon request.

The finding aid *Pensions* also contains a list of names and the town of residence of pensioners. Demarcations following each entry (*Maine, Mass., LCCR, HCCR, YCCR*) indicate that the original documents can be seen at the following locations:

> "Maine"—(pertains to records after 1820). See Maine archives records.
>
> "Mass."—may also include some Maine records. See the alphabetical list mentioned above.
>
> "LCCR"—may be seen at the Lincoln County courthouse.
>
> "HCCR"—may be seen at the Hancock County courthouses.
>
> "YCCR"—may be seen at the York County courthouse.

The three counties named above processed claims for federal pensions under the Act of 1818 and claims for Massachusetts land grants.

Shays' Rebellion (1786–87)

Muster Rolls and Certificates of Service, Shays' Rebellion, 1787 (microfilm).

Miscellaneous Documents—in manuscript collection *Massachusetts Archives* (reels 318, 319).

War of 1812 (1812–15)

Governor's and Executive Council Papers, War of 1812. Includes petitions for commissions (with signatures of petitioners) and petitions to form independent companies of infantry or similar units for purposes of defense (with signatures of petitioners).

Rolls of Detached Units of the Massachusetts Militia (muster rolls, payrolls, inspection rolls, company rolls). Located in the "Massachusetts Archives" manuscripts collections; indexed by regiment, brigade, and division.

Muster Rolls and Payrolls of the Massachusetts Militia, 1812–15.

Civil War–Union (1861–65)

Most of the original records pertaining to Massachusetts men in the Civil War are in the custody of the state adjutant general's office (see below). Several manuscript collections pertaining to the war are available at this archives. They are found in a collection of manuscripts titled "Massachusetts Archives." Illustrative examples of such manuscript material are presented below. For a more detailed list, see a guide to this collection that is available upon request.

To facilitate a search for documentary records pertaining to a Civil War soldier or sailor, it is advisable to first consult the published volumes *Massachusetts Soldiers and Sailors in the Civil War*. It is then feasible to inspect original documents available at this facility if either the county or name of a military organization in which an individual served is known. Illustrative examples are listed below.

List of Boston Seamen in the United States Navy, 1861–65.

Monthly Bounty Payrolls of Massachusetts Volunteers, 1865–67.

List of Soldiers Receiving Municipal Bounties, 1862–65.

Bounty Claims, 1866–70.

Additional Bounty Payments, 1867–70,

Pension Claims, 1864–70.

Discharge Register, 1863–64.

Lists of Recruits Credited to Municipalities, 1862–64.

Lists of Draft Substitutes by District, 1863–65.

Muster Rolls of Drafted Men and Substitutes, 1863–64.

Descriptive Rolls of Rejected Recruits, 1862–65.

Descriptive Rolls of Massachusetts Volunteers, 1863–65.

Naval Enlistment Rolls, 1862–65.

Descriptive rolls of Massachusetts Volunteers, 1861–65.

Enrollment Lists From Cities and Towns, 1862–64.

Naval Enlistments by Town, 1861–70.

Index to Naval Bounty Payments, 1864.

Bounty payrolls of Massachusetts Volunteers, 1863–66.

Company Rolls of the Massachusetts Volunteer Militia, 1863–65.

Muster-out Rolls, 1865.

Hospital Registers, 1864–65.

Reports of Massachusetts Soldiers in New York Hospitals, 1862–65.

Returns of Southern Recruits, 1864–65.

Index to Payrolls of Recruiting Agent, Norfolk, Virginia, 1864–65.

Card Index of Bonuses for Civil War Service.

Gardiner Tufts Collection, Civil War. As the state military agent, Tufts compiled an extensive collection of papers including, among others, the following:
Accounting records, 1862–66
Hospital cards, 1863–65
Lists of casualties and hospitalizations, 1862–66
Index to and correspondence concerning the Massachusetts volunteers, 1861–65

Post-Civil War Period (1866–)

Index to Naval Personnel From Massachusetts, 1885–89.

Index to Transfers From Army to Navy, 1861–1917.

Index to Correspondence Regarding Records of Officers, Sailors, and Marines in the United States Navy, 1893–97.

Letters Concerning Transfers to the United States Navy, 1954–90.

List of Entitlement to Prize Money, 1884–85.

Spanish-American War (1898–99)

Descriptive Rolls of Massachusetts Volunteers, 1898–99.

Reenlistment Rolls of the Massachusetts Volunteer Militia, 1898–99.

Photographs, Massachusetts Volunteer Militia, 1894–98.

Spanish-American War Pay Claims, 1898–1901.

Card Index of Bonuses for Spanish-American War Service.

Payments Made at Boston to Spanish-American War Soldiers and Sailors. Name, unit, amount paid, and period of service; arranged chronologically.

Mexican Border Service (1916)

Card Index of Bonuses for Mexican Border Service.

World War I (1917–18)

Card Index of Bonuses for World War I Service.

World War II (1941–45)

Index of Massachusetts Military Casualties in World War II.

Card Index of Bonuses for World War II Service.

MILITARY RECORDS SECTION, MILITARY DIVISION

Office of the Adjutant General
Room 1000
100 Cambridge Street
Boston, Massachusetts 02202
(617) 727-2964

This facility has information on index cards, computer printouts, and microfilm pertaining to veterans of the twentieth-century wars (Mexican Border Service, 1916, through the Vietnam War); and index cards pertaining to Massachusetts militia from 1780 through the Civil War years.

Because of lack of space, visits to this office for research are not possible. However, written replies will be made in response to telephone calls or letters requesting basic information concerning a specific veteran. For soldiers and marines, this will include name, serial number, race, place of birth, residence, place and date of enlistment, unit, rank, engagements, wounds, overseas duty, and date and place of discharge. For sailors, this will include the same general information but will also show place of enrollment, dates served at various stations, and rank held at each station. Replies are made on a "statement of service" form that contains the data found on the index cards or printouts.

The large body of records from the office of the Massachusetts adjutant general are available at a supply depot located at Natick, Massachusetts (see below), rather than at this headquarters office.

MILITARY DIVISION OF HISTORY, RESEARCH AND MUSEUM

Worcester Armory
Worcester, Massachusetts

Formerly located in Natick, Massachusetts, this facility relocated to Worcester in 1994. For the current address and telephone number, contact the Military Records Section, 100 Cambridge Road, Boston, Massachusetts 02202; telephone: (617) 727-2964.

This state facility is under the control of the Military Division, Commonwealth of Massachusetts. Available for inspection at this facility are original documents, bound and unbound, pertaining to Massachusetts militia beginning with the American Revolution, and similar documents relating to veterans of all American wars and conflicts from the Civil War through the Spanish-American War and the Philippine Insurrection. Some of the documents are on microfilm and are available at this facility as well as the Church of Jesus Christ of Latter-day Saints Family History Library, Salt Lake City, Utah.

Records

General

Resignations and Discharges of Officers, 1853–1910.

Resignations of Officers and Applications for Discharge, 1786–89. Each bound volume, arranged by military division, contains an index of names.

Officers' Notices of Acceptance, 1865–1905.

Enlistment Rolls of Boston Cadets, 1796–1841.

Camp Duty Payrolls and Inspections, by Organization and Year, 1859–97.

Records of Courts-martial, 1828–32; 1833–39; 1858.

Militia, 1778–1848

Indexes to Rosters, Rosters of Officers, Orders of the Governor and Council and General Orders, Resignations of Officers, Rolls of Companies, Index to Discharges and Special Orders, Letter Books, Records of Courts-martial, Reports of Gardiner Tufts (state military agent). These documents are arranged by time period and by military division, by Massachusetts Artillery, or by Massachusetts Voluntary Militia. Indexes are available for the various county divisions. To locate the pertinent documents, it is helpful to know in which county division or time period an individual served in the militia for local service or as part of the federal army.

Oaths of Officers, Massachusetts Volunteer Militia, 1861–85.

Shays' Rebellion (1787)

Rolls of Soldiers (five volumes).

War of 1812 (1812–15)

Maine Rolls, 1812–14.

Orderly Books, Various, 1813–15.

Assistance Given to Individuals, by Towns, 1815–22.

Civil War—Union (1861–65)

Descriptive Books, Eleventh Regiment, Massachusetts Volunteers, 1861–62.

Enlistees, by Massachusetts Town. A folder for each town. Name and regiment are shown.

Enrollment in the Military, by Town, 1862. Name, age, occupation, whether in service at time of enrollment, and remarks; arranged in folders by Massachusetts towns and cities.

Battle Casualties, by Regiment, 1861–65. Type and number of regiment must be specified.

Roster of Commissioned Officers, 1861–62.

Notices of Discharge, 1861–78. Arranged chronologically.

Character of Returned Soldiers, Civil War, 1865.

Soldiers and Sailors of Concord, Massachusetts, 1861–65; 1898.

Annual Return of Enrolled Militia, Marblehead, Massachusetts, 1863.

Bounty Payrolls, Various, 1864.

Bounty Payrolls of Massachusetts Volunteers, 1864. Name, serial number, unit, age, date of muster, residence, and amount of bounty paid; also contain the soldier's signature.

Bounty Payrolls of Braman Galloupe Island, 1864.

Bounty Payrolls of Massachusetts, 1865.

Muster Rolls, Various Infantry Regiments; Heavy Artillery Regiments; Light Artillery Regiments, 1861.

Muster Rolls, Various Regiments, 1861–64; Division Roster, 1852.

Supplementary Rolls of New Recruits for New Regiments, 1862; Thirty-second, Thirty-third, Thirty-fourth Infantry Battalions.

Enrollment and Medical Examinations. Arranged alphabetically by county; four volumes.

Descriptive Rolls and Elective Rolls, United States Artillery, 1864.

Medical Certificates for Extension of Furloughs, Civil War, 1861–65.

Index to Cases by Name of Massachusetts Individuals Described in *Medical and Surgical History of the War of the Rebellion*; six volumes.

Enlistment Papers, Various Infantry, Cavalry, Heavy Artillery Regiments, 1863–65.

Bounty Numbers, U.S. Colored Troops and Enlistments in Other States, 1864–65.

Washington Enlistments, 1864.

Naval Enlistments, by Cities and Towns, 1861–64.

Regimental Rosters and Rosters of Officers, by Name of Regiment, Massachusetts Volunteers and Massachusetts Militia, 1861, 1862, 1864.

Casualties, Various Regiments, 1861–65.

Desertions and Discharges, Massachusetts Volunteers, 1862–64.

Letter Books of Provost Marshal and Military Commander, 1862–65.

Medical Letters, 1861–64.

Muster Rolls, Various Regiments, 1861–64.

Copies of Discharges, Various Regiments, 1861–66.

Deaths of Prisoners and Certificates of Death, 1864–65.

Deaths of Prisoners in Various States, 1863–64.

Deaths in Rebel Prisons and Exchanged Prisoners, by Regiment, 1864.

Roll of Honor: Names of Soldiers Buried in Various States, 1866.

Roll of Honor No. XIV: Names of Soldiers Who Suffered in Prison Pens Throughout the South, 1868.

Deaths of Massachusetts Volunteers in Washington Hospitals and Andersonville Prison, 1864.

Massachusetts Dead in Andersonville Cemetery, 1864–65.

Provost Marshal Muster Rolls, 1863–65.

Enlisted Nurses, 1862–64.

MOLLUS PHOTOGRAPH COLLECTION

The Military Order of the Loyal Legion of the United States (MOLLUS) was formed following President Lincoln's assassination. The founding members were the president's pallbearers. Their organization accepted all officers who had served in the army, navy, or marines during the Civil War. The Massachusetts commandery is said to have been the largest state group of the organization.

Around 1900, the organization began to amass a photograph collection of the war, and by 1927 the collection had grown to more than 40,000 photographs. In 1980 the entire collection of photographs was donated to the United States Army History Research Center at Carlisle, Pennsylvania. A copy of the collection was made for Massachusetts, and it is now available for inspection in this facility. The collection is indexed by state and then by regiment (including ships). It includes photographs from the Spanish-American War, Mexican Border Service, World War I and World War II, the Korean War, and the Vietnam War. In 1985 the Commonwealth of Massachusetts accessioned the complete library holdings of MOLLUS, and they are now housed at this facility.

Spanish-American War (1898–99)

Muster Rolls, Sixth Regiment, 1898.

Card file: Statements of Service for the Spanish-American War (army, navy, marines). Arranged alphabetically.

Card File: Statements of Service for the Spanish-American War and Philippine Insurrections, 1898–1901. Arranged alphabetically.

Testimonial for Service in the Spanish-American War. Arranged alphabetically.

List of Towns and Names of Men Who Were in the Service (army and navy) in the Spanish-American War. Arranged alphabetically.

List of Men in the Spanish-American War Who Were Discharged Without Honor, or Deserted (army, navy, and marines).

Mexican Border Service (1916)

Muster Rolls, Second and Fifth Infantry; Eighth and Ninth Infantry, Massachusetts National Guard, 1916.

Muster rolls, First Regiment Field Artillery; First Squadron Cavalry; First Battalion Signal Corps, 1915.

Muster Rolls, Field Hospitals, Ambulance Companies, Headquarters Companies, 1916.

Muster Rolls of Recruiting Detachments, 1916.

Card File: Statements of Service, Mexican Border War, 1916.

List of Men and Companies That Served in Mexican Border War.

World War I (1917–18)

Official List of Officers of the Officers Reserve Corps, 1919.

List of Members, Massachusetts State Guard, various units, 1917–20.

Casualty List, Twenty-sixth Division, 1918–19.

Disability Discharges, Army, World War I.

American Red Cross Members Who Died in World War I, 1918–19.

Officers and Enlisted Men Discharged From Massachusetts, 1917.

Officers, Massachusetts Naval Militia and Marine Corps, 1917. Arranged by city and town.

List of Officers, Twelfth Division, 1920.

Casualties of Seventy-sixth Division, 1919.

List of Men From Boston Killed in Action or Dead From Injuries, 1919.

Statements of Service, World War I.

Red Cross Casualty List, Twenty-sixth Division.

Consolidated Index, Federal Muster Rolls, Massachusetts National Guard, World War I, 1917.

Enlisted Reserve Corps, Date of Reporting, 1917,

Enlisted Reserve Corps, Honorable Discharges, 1917. Arranged alphabetically.

Deserters' Records, 1917–18.

Regular Army Reserve, Dates of Furlough, 1919–20.

Army Engagements, Wounded Records, 1917. Arranged alphabetically.

Commissioned and Enlisted Personnel of the Army Who Entered Service From Massachusetts and Were Prisoners of War While Serving in the American Expeditionary Forces.

Sailing List, Twenty-sixth Division, by Name of Ship, 1917.

Massachusetts Army Deaths in Europe; Disposition of Bodies, 1917.

Draft Registration Lists, Various Massachusetts Towns, 1917–18.

Classification List, 1917.

List of Persons Who Failed to Report for Physical Examination, 1917.

List of Persons Inducted Into Military Service Who Failed to Report, 1917.

Names of Delinquents Reported to Local Police, 1917.

Local Draft Boards: Lists of Men in Service, Various Towns, 1919.

World War II (1941–45)

Reports of Physical Examinations of Enlisted Men, 1940.

List of Massachusetts Men Killed in the Navy, World War II.

Applications for Certification of Death, 1945.

List of Missing in Action and Formerly Reported as Deceased; Released Prisoners of War, 1945.

World War II Dead, Army and Air Force.

Naval Non-combat Dead, World War II, 1948.

Enlisted Records and Reports of Separation, Honorable Discharge, World War II.

MASSACHUSETTS HISTORICAL SOCIETY

1154 Boylston Street
Boston, Massachusetts 02215
(617) 536-1608

The Massachusetts Historical Society, established in 1791, has a large collection of manuscripts that chiefly concern the American Revolution era. Guides are available for approximately ten percent of the holdings, and the remainder may be found in the extensive card catalog.

Records

American Revolution (1775–83)

Among the extensive manuscript collections pertaining to military events of the revolutionary war are the following.

Benjamin Lincoln Collection. Includes muster rolls and lists as well as individual papers and correspondence pertaining to the American Revolution.

William Heath Collection. This revolutionary war general's papers have been placed on microfilm (three reels). They include orderly books and other papers pertaining to military life at the time.

Orderly Books Collection. Names of the commanding officers and units to which these books pertain have been indexed and microfilmed. The books are also on microfilm (six reels) and are arranged by name of the regiment. They include regiments for Massachusetts, New Hampshire, Connecticut, and Rhode Island; and Continental Army artillery, Continental Army headquarters, and Continental Army, miscellaneous. There are also some books for regiments of the British army and British marines.

Civil War–Union (1861–65)

This society has an extensive collection of Civil War–related manuscripts. There is a twenty-eight-reel collection of microfilm copies of these papers; reel 29 is an index. The papers consist largely of diaries, journals, and correspondence. Noteworthy are documents pertaining to Massachusetts regiments that saw service in this war.

Index to Manuscript Collection

In the card catalog of manuscript holdings, two full drawers of cards are required for the revolutionary war papers and one full drawer is required for the Civil War papers. The following subject headings, listed under U.S. History, indicate other helpful collections for military records researchers.

American forces

Army

Army orderly books

Campaigns

Claims

German mercenaries

Hospitals

Indian participation

Muster rolls (approximately sixty different collections contain muster rolls)

Naval

Personal narratives

Prisoners and prisons

Regimental histories

War with France, 1783–1825

War of 1812 (in collections, army, naval operations, prisoners and prisons)

War with Algeria, 1815

Mexican War, 1845–48

Mexican War, 1845–48, naval operations

Tripolitan War, 1801–05

Civil War (campaigns, in collections, medical and sanitary, medical correspondence, naval operations, participation by African-Americans, personal narratives, regimental histories)

War of 1898 (a small number of manuscripts)

European War, 1917–18 (a small number of manuscripts)

NEW ENGLAND HISTORIC GENEALOGICAL SOCIETY

99-101 Newbury Street
Boston, Massachusetts 02116-3087
(617) 536-5740

This society, founded in 1845, has a very large collection of manuscripts pertaining to military affairs. A notebook titled *New England Historic Genealogical Society Manuscript Index*, by James W. Flint, lists the subject-added entry headings for cataloging for collections that had been inventoried as of July 1992. Special Collection No. 7, Military Papers, contains correspondence, muster rolls, orderly books, supply records, pension abstracts, commissions, and other records of American forces, 1762 to 1867. The society also holds a microfilm copy of a typescript listing pensioners who served from New Hampshire in the revolutionary war, and a microfiche copy of the Civil War enlistment papers for New Hampshire. These and other collections are listed in the large card catalog available in the society's library. Some subject headings for collections helpful to military researchers are the following.

American loyalists

Bounties, military

Courts-martial and courts of inquiry, Rhode Island

Massachusetts history—revolution

Massachusetts history—King William's War, 1689–97

Massachusetts history—Queen Anne's War, 1702–13

Pensions, military, New England

Pensions, United States

Pensions, military, Massachusetts—Barnstable County

Pensions, military, United States, War of 1812

Prisoners of war, Massachusetts

Shays' Rebellion, 1786–87

Shays' Rebellion, 1786–87, correspondence, reminiscences

Shiloh, battle of, 1862

Sons of Liberty, Attleboro, Massachusetts

Under the general heading "United States history" are the following subheadings.

King William's War, 1689–91 (campaigns and battles, registers and lists)

Queen Anne's War, 1702–13, registers and lists

King Philip's War: John Hull's pay accounts for Massachusetts Bay soldiers

French and Indian War, 1755–63 (correspondence and reminiscences, registers and lists)

Revolution (American loyalists, campaigns and battles, claims, correspondence, naval operations, personal narratives, prisoners and prisons, recruiting and enlistment, registers and lists, Ticonderoga campaign)

War with France, 1798–1800, registers and lists

War of 1812 (correspondence, Maryland forces, pensions, prisoners and prisons)

War with Mexico, 1845, correspondence and reminiscences

Civil War (campaigns and battles, correspondence and reminiscences, personal narratives, women's work)

War of 1898, correspondence and reminiscences

Spanish-American War, medical and sanitary officers

European War, 1914–18 (correspondence and reminiscences, medical and sanitary officers)

United State Army, Continental Army (Fourth, Fifteenth, Seventeenth Massachusetts regiments)

United States Army, Corps of Engineers, Tenth Regiment, 1917–18

United States naval officers

United States Navy surgeons—biographies

United States Continental Navy, enlistment

United States Continental Navy, signalling

PUBLISHED SOURCES—MASSACHUSETTS

Pre-1775 (colonial wars)

Bodge, George M. *Soldiers in King Philip's War: Being a Critical Account of That War, With a Concise History of the Indian Wars of New England From 1620–1677, Official Lists of the Soldiers of Massachusetts Colony Serving in Philip's War and Sketches of the Principal Officers, Copies of Ancient Documents and Records . . . Lists of the Narraganset Grantees of the United Colonies, Massachusetts, Plymouth and Connecticut.* Boston: 1906. Reprint of 3rd edition. Baltimore: Genealogical Publishing Co., 1967.

Cowan, Maude R. *Members of the Ancient and Honorable Artillery Company in the Colonial Period, 1638–1774. . . .* Revised edition by Mrs. William Home Watkins. Washington, D.C.: 1958. Reprint. National Society, Women Descendants of the Ancient & Honorable Artillery Co., 1989. Contains genealogical data of members, 1638–1774.

Donahue, Mary E. *Massachusetts Officers and Soldiers, 1702–1722: Queen Anne's War to Dummer's War.* Boston: Society of Colonial Wars in the Commonwealth of Massachusetts, 1980.

Doreski, Carole, ed. *Massachusetts Officers and Soldiers in the Seventeenth Century Conflicts.* Boston: Society of Colonial Wars in the Commonwealth of Massachusetts and New England Historic Genealogical Society, 1982. Approximately 6,500 names with rank (if appropriate), date of account, probable residence, unit, and commanding officer.

Ellis, George W., and John E. Morris. *King Philip's War: Based on the Archives and Records of Massachusetts, Plymouth, Rhode Island and Connecticut. . . .* New York: Grafton Press, 1906. Reprint. New York: AMS press, 1980.

Goss, K. David, and Davis Zarowin. *Massachusetts Officers and Soldiers in the French and Indian Wars, 1755–1756.* Boston: Society of Colonial Wars in the Commonwealth of Massachusetts and New England Historic Genealogical Society, 1985.

Graham, Gerald S. *The Walker Expedition to Quebec, 1711.* Publications of the Champlain Society, No. 32. Toronto: Champlain Society, 1953. Reprint. New York: Greenwood Press, 1969. Appendix includes several lists of ships, and their commanders or masters, that transported men and supplies to Canada.

Hall, Charles W. *Regiments and Armories of Massachusetts; An Historical Narration of the Massachusetts Volunteer Militia, With Portraits and Biographies of Officers Past and Present.* 2 vols. Boston: W.W. Potter Co., ca. 1899–1901 (?).

MacKay, Robert E., ed. *Massachusetts Soldiers in the French and Indian Wars, 1744–1755.* Boston: Society of Colonial Wars in the Commonwealth of Massachusetts, 1978.

Maas, David E. *Divided Hearts: Massachusetts Loyalists, 1765–1790: A Biographical Directory.* Boston: Society of Colonial Wars in the Commonwealth of Massachusetts, 1980.

Peirce, Ebenezer W. *Civil, Military and Professional Lists of Plymouth and Rhode Island Colonies: Comprising Colonial, County and Town Officers, Clergymen, Physicians and Lawyers . . . 1621–1700.* Boston, 1881. Reprint. Baltimore: Genealogical Publishing Co., 1968. Includes militia officers.

Roberts, Oliver A. *History of the Military Company of the Massachusetts, Now Called the Ancient and Honorable Artillery Company of Massachusetts, 1637–1888.* 4 vols. Boston: Alfred Mudge & Son, 1895–1901. Vol. 1 covers 1637 through 1738.

Roll of Members of the Military Company of the Massachusetts: Now Called the Ancient and Honorable Artillery Company of Massachusetts, With a Roster of the Commissioned Officers and Preachers, 1638–1894. Boston: A. Mudge & Son, 1895.

Society of Colonial Wars, New York. *A Copy of Original Massachusetts Muster Rolls, the Property of the Society of Colonial Wars in the State of New York.* New York (?): the society, 1899. Infantry: Hanover Foot Co., 1750; Hingham 2nd Foot Co., 1755.

Stachiw, Myron O. *Massachusetts Officers and Soldiers, 1723–1743: Dummer's War to the War of Jenkins' Ear.* Massachusetts Archives, vols. 91–92. Boston: Society of Colonial Wars in the Commonwealth of Massachusetts, 1979.

Voye, Nancy S. *Massachusetts Officers in the French and Indian Wars, 1748–1763.* Boston: Society of Colonial Wars in the Commonwealth of Massachusetts, 1975.

Watkins, William K. *Soldiers in the Expedition to Canada in 1690 and Grantees of the Canada Townships.* Boston: the author, 1898.

1775-83 (American Revolution)

Allen, Gardner W. *Massachusetts Privateers of the Revolution.* Collections of the Massachusetts Historical Society, vol. 77. Boston: the society, 1927. Privateers, masters, owners, and bondsmen.

Boston City Council. *The Bunker Hill Memorial.* Boston, 1896. Names of participants at the battle of Bunker Hill; unit, residence, and names of American prisoners.

Cash, Phillip. *Medical Men at the Siege of Boston, April 1775 to April 1777.* Philadelphia: American Philosophical Society of Pennsylvania, 1973. Appendix 4 lists the physicians, place of birth, age, college (if attended), medical education, medical career after the war, and other careers after the war.

Hambrick-Stowe, Charles E., and Donna D. Smerlas, eds. *Massachusetts Militia Companies and Officers in the Lexington Alarm.* Boston: Society of Colonial Wars in the Commonwealth of Massachusetts, 1976.

Massachusetts Soldiers and Sailors of the Revolutionary War: A Compilation From the Archives. 17 vols. Boston: Wright & Potter Printing Co., 1896-1908. Alphabetically arranged. Note multiple listings for the same individual under variant spellings. This publication also includes Maine (which was part of Massachusetts until 1820).

Minority Military Service, Massachusetts, 1775-1783. Washington, D.C.: National Society Daughters of the American Revolution, 1989. Discusses African-American participants.

The Minute Men, 1775-1975. Historians of the Council of Minute Men. . . . Southborough: Yankee Colour, 1977.

Reade, Philip Hildreth. *Dedication Exercises at the Massachusetts Military Monument, Valley Forge, Pa. . . . Also, List of Officers in Massachusetts Organizations . . . Who Served at Valley Forge.* Boston: Wright & Potter Printing Co., 1912. Contains approximately one thousand names.

Society of the Cincinnati (Massachusetts). *Memorials of the Massachusetts Society of the Cincinnati.* Several editions. Boston: the society, 1964.

Sons of the American Revolution, Massachusetts Society. *Roll of Membership With Ancestral Records. . . .* Boston: the society, 1893-19–.

Sons of the American Revolution. *Soldiers and Sailors Whose Graves Have Been Designated by the Markers of the Society.* Boston, 1901.

Tucker, Charles C. *A List of Pensioners in the State of Massachusetts, Comprising Invalid Pensioners, and Revolutionary Pensioners Under the Act of Congress Passed March 18, 1818, May 15, 1828, and June 7, 1832.* Washington, D.C.: Henry Polkinhorn, 1854.

1784-1815 (War of 1812)

Records of the Massachusetts Volunteer Militia Called Out by the Governor of Massachusetts to Suppress a Threatened Invasion During the War of 1812-14. Boston: Gardner W. Pearson, 1913. Contains the names of officers and enlisted men in each company.

1861-65 (Civil War–Union)

Boston. City Council. Joint Special Committee on the Burial of Massachusetts Dead at Gettysburg. *Report of the Joint Special Committee on the Burial of Massachusetts Dead at Gettysburg; With a List of the Massachusetts Soldiers Buried in the National Cemetery, and Other Matters in Relation Thereto.* Boston: city printer, 1863.

Bowen, James L. *Massachusetts in the War, 1861-1865.* Springfield: C.W. Bryan & Co., 1889. Contains biographical sketches of officers.

Devereux, John F. *Our Roll of Honor.* N.p., 1870 (?). Biographical data of Massachusetts war casualties.

Dilts, Bryan L., comp. *1890 Massachusetts Census Index of Civil War Veterans or Their Widows.* Salt Lake City: Index Pub., 1985.

Gay, George H. (?). *Report to Wm. J. Dale, Surgeon General, Massachusetts, by John S. Blatchford, Secretary, of a Group of Physicians and Surgeons Who Left for Washington on August 31, 1862.* Boston (?): *Boston Post,* 1862 (?). List of and report on wounded Massachusetts soldiers.

Headley, Phineas Camp. *Massachusetts in the Rebellion. A Record of the Historical Position of the Commonwealth, and the Services of the Leading Statesmen, the Military, the Colleges, and the People in the Civil War of 1861-65.* Boston: Walker, Fuller and Co., 1866.

Higginson, Thomas W. *Massachusetts in the Army and Navy During the War of 1861-1865.* 2 vols. Boston: Wright & Potter Printing Co., 1895-96.

Massachusetts. Adjutant General's Office. *Massachusetts Soldiers, Sailors, and Marines in the Civil War.* 8 vols. and index vol. Norwood: Norwood Press, 1931-35. Listed by regiment.

———. *Record of the Massachusetts Volunteers, 1861-1865.* 2 vols. Boston: adjutant general, 1868-70.

Massachusetts. Commission on Andersonville Monument. *Report of the Commission on Andersonville Monument.* Boston: Wright & Potter Printing Co., 1902. Lists known Massachusetts soldiers buried at Andersonville prison.

Military Order of the Loyal Legion of the United States (MOLLUS). Massachusetts Commandery. *Register of the Commandery of the State of Massachusetts, November 1, 1912.* Cambridge: University Press, 1912. Alphabetically listed with rank, military service, date and place of death if applicable, and other comments.

Nason, George W. *History and Complete Roster of the Massachusetts Regiments: Minute Men of '61 Who responded to the First Call of President Abraham Lincoln, April 15, 1861, to defend the Flag and Constitution of the United States . . . and Biographical Sketches of Minute Men of Massachusetts.* Boston: Smith & McCance, 1910.

Souvenir Portrait Album of Members, Ancient and Honorable Artillery Company of Massachusetts. Boston: W.S. Best, 1903. Contains numerous photographs of Civil War-era personnel.

1866–99 (Spanish-American War)

Massachusetts. Adjutant General's office. *Annual Report, 1898.* Boston: state printer, ca. 1901 (?).

1900–75 (World War I through Vietnam War)

Massachusetts. Adjutant General's Office. *Annual Reports, 1900–1920.* Boston: State Printer, ca. 1920 (various years).

Michigan

1618	Michigan was first entered by French explorer Etienne Brule.
1701	Detroit became Michigan's first permanent settlement when French fur traders built a fort there.
1763	By the Treaty of Paris which ended the French and Indian War, Michigan came under British control. (See French and Indian War in the appendix.)
1763	Indian leader Pontiac led an Indian rebellion against British rule at Detroit; the rebellion spread to New York and Pennsylvania. (See Pontiac's Rebellion in the appendix.)
1783	Although the Treaty of Paris, which ended the American Revolution, ceded Michigan to the United States, the British refused to evacuate it until 1796.
1796–1800	Michigan was part of Northwest Territory.
1800–03	Michigan was part of the Northwest Territory and Indiana Territory.
1803–05	Michigan was part of Indiana Territory.
1805	Michigan became a territory.
1812–14	Michigan and other Great Lakes states became an important theater of the War of 1812. (See War of 1812 in the appendix.)
1835	The Toledo War with Ohio over disputed land produced no fatalities, and it resulted in

Ohio land being exchanged for the Upper Peninsula.

1837	Michigan became a state.

. . . .

STATE ARCHIVES OF MICHIGAN

717 West Allegan Street
Lansing, Michigan 48918
(517) 373-1408

Finding Aids

Records of the Michigan Military Establishment, 1838–1941 (archival no. 1).

Records of the Grand Army of the Republic, Michigan Department (archival no. 15).

Records of the Michigan Veterans' Facility (archival no. 17).

Circular No. 4, Military Records I.

Circular No. 7, Military Records II.

Circular No. 20, Civil War Manuscripts.

Circular No. 26, Military Commissions.

Circular No. 27, Military Records III.

Records

General

Michigan National Guard Registers, 1838–1900.

General Roster of Officers (vol. 5), 1838–48.

Record of Commissions, Officers (vol. 2), 1881–1911.

Roster of the Militia of Michigan (vol. 3.5), 1846–61.

Michigan National Guard (vol. 4), 1858–84.

Descriptive Rolls of State Troops (National Guard), 1874–98. Arranged by military unit, including First–Fifth Regiments; Michigan National Guard, 1896–1905; First–Third Infantry; First Independent Battalion; Mexican War Regiment.

Records of Officers, Soldiers and Sailors, 1838–January 1, 1901. Arranged alphabetically by name.

Roster of Officers in State Troops (National Guard), 1874–85.

Roster of Commissioned Officers, 1905–20.

Roster of Noncommissioned Officers, 1899–1916.

Roster of Michigan Naval Brigade, 1894–1912.

Roster of Soldiers Residing in Michigan, 1888. Includes soldiers from Michigan and from other states; indicates name, rank, unit, post office address, and, in some cases, date of death.

Index to Letters Received, Adjutant, 1900.

Descriptive Rolls of Units, 1838–1911.

Roster of the Militia of Michigan, 1858–60.

Descriptive Rolls, Michigan National Guard, 1838–65.

Roster of Commissioned Officers in Michigan State Troops (National Guard), 1874–85.

History of United States Officers, 1873. Consists of a form for each officer identical to those that appear in "regimental histories–history of officers."

Personal Record of Appointed or Commissioned Officers in the Michigan State Troops (National Guard), ca. 1940. Standard forms include name, place and date of birth, rank, date of appointment or commission, current military status, nature of business, marital status, number of children, and former military education or service; arranged alphabetically.

Record of Arrivals and Departures of Men From Camp Grayling, 1932–39.

Photographs, 1900–62. Arranged alphabetically by individual and numerically by unit designation.

Photographs, 1945–55. Primarily of Camp Grayling, troop training, demonstrations, and parades.

Officer Biographies, National Guard, 1947–66.

Records of Enlistments, National Guard, 1908–17. Includes enlistment rolls and muster rolls; arranged by unit designation; includes those mobilized into United States service during the Mexican Border Service and World War I.

Reports of Physical Examination of Officers, National Guard, 1911. Arranged alphabetically.

Certificate of Disability for Discharge, National Guard, 1917.

Enlistment and Muster rolls, National Guard, First Division, Second Division, Fifth Division, 1908–17.

Enlistment Papers (naval), 1917; 1921–49. Separate index.

Register of Personnel, 1947–53.

Register of Officers, 1948–59.

History of Officers, 1948–59.

Enlistments, National Guard, 1908–19.

Muster Rolls and Payrolls of State Troops (National Guard), 1905–16.

Records of the Michigan Naval Brigade, 1905–19.

Official Oaths of Staff and Officers, 1881–1901.

Black Hawk War (1832)

Miscellaneous Records Pertaining to the Black Hawk War, Including Muster Roll of Men Called Into Service 21 May 1832.

Mexican War (1846–48)

Records Relating to the Mexican War, 1847. Enlistment papers, draft of historical account, list of men, and report of the adjutant general, 1848; 1849.

Descriptive Roll of the First Regiment of Michigan Volunteers, 1847–48.

Civil War–Union (1861–65)

Descriptive Rolls of Units, 1861–65. Available for the following units: First–Thirtieth Infantry; First–Eleventh Cavalry; First Lt. Cavalry; First Engineers and Mechanics; First Sharpshooters; Stanton Guard; Provost Guard; First Lancers; Chandler Guard; Howland's Engineers; Merrill Horse; First Colored Infantry; unassigned men (by state); brigade bands, U.S. Veterans Reserve Corps; Hancock's Army Corps; Blacksmith Regiment.

Regimental Service Records (payrolls, muster rolls, lists of dead, transfer rolls) for those units listed in the above entry.

Record of Michigan Volunteers, 1861–66. Consists of eleven record books.

Index to Michigan Volunteers in United States Service, 1861–65.

Roster of Commissioned Officers in Michigan Volunteers, 1861–65.

Index of Officers and Record Books, 1861–65.

Record of Commissions, 1862–66.

Record of Bounty to Volunteers. Arranged by unit, 1863–65.

Roster of Men Furnished for Draft Quota, 1862–63. Arranged by county.

Resignations of Officers, 1862–65. Arranged by unit.

Muster and Descriptive Rolls, 1861–65.

Official Oaths of Staff and Officers, 1861–65

Lists of Patients, 1864–65.

Report of Michigan Soldiers Who Have Died in Hospitals, etc., 1866.

Soldiers' Mortuary Lists, 1861–68.

Claims of Lafayette Light Guard, 1861–63.

History of Officers in Civil War, 1873.

Muster Roll of Boys in Blue Association, 1866. Includes name, rank in the association and while in service, post office address, place of voting, signature, remarks.

Descriptive Lists of Deserters, 1864–65.

List of Dead, 1863. Prepared for a "Roll of Honor" prepared in 1872; includes name; age; rank; time and place of enlistment; time and place of mustering into service; and remarks regarding time, place, and manner in which soldier met his death; arranged by unit; also available in the Michigan State Library.

Census of Veterans, 1888. Information gathered included name, rank, unit, county of residence, and post office address.

Graves Registration, Compiled by the Civil War Centennial Observance Commission. Arranged by county (not all counties are included). The forms indicate name, enlistment service records, place and date of birth, place and date of death, name and location of cemetery, and remarks.

Muster Rolls of the Grand Army of the Republic in Michigan—to which most of the Union veterans belonged. Indexed by unit and name. (See the finding aid *Records of the Grand Army of the Republic . . .*, cited above.)

Manuscript Collections. Various Civil War collections include diaries, certificates, discharges, journals, letters, and miscellaneous military material.

Records of the Veterans' Facility (formerly known as the Soldiers' and Sailors' Home) Established for Civil War Veterans. It now serves veterans of all United States wars. (See the finding aid *Records of the Michigan Veterans' Facility*, cited above.)

Spanish-American War (1898–99)

Certificates of Service, 1898–1907.

Record of Distribution of Spanish-American War Medals, 1902.

List of Dishonorable Discharges, 1899–1905.

List of Dishonorable Discharges of Men in First, Second, and Third Infantry and First Independent Battalion, 1899–1905.

Records of Michigan and United States Infantry Units, 1897–1900.

Records of the Navy in the Spanish-American War, 1898.

Michigan Military Forces in the Spanish-American War, 1898.

Official Oaths of Recruiting Officer, 1898.

Roster of Thirtieth United States Infantry, 1900.

Index to Michigan Volunteers, 1898–99. Refers to descriptive rolls.

Muster-out Rolls of Michigan Volunteers in the Spanish-American War, 1898.

Records Relating to Camp Eaton, Island Lake, 1898. Includes lists of men and other information.

Records Relating to Thirty-first–Thirty-fifth Infantry, Navy, and Thirtieth United States Infantry, 1898–1906.

Register of Personnel Who Served in the Philippine Insurrection, 1900. A card file of those who served in the insurrection following the Spanish-American War; includes name, unit, battles, skirmishes, occasional notes about place of enlistment, and applications for medals.

Mexican Border Service (1916)

Muster Rolls of Units in Mexican Border Service, 1916–17.

World War I (1917–18)

Record of Officers and Men Comprising the 125th Infantry as Organized on Leaving Germany ca. 1919. These consist of alphabetically arranged cards containing considerable information about each individual.

Census of World War I Veterans, 1917–19. This census was taken by members of the Daughters of the American Revolution, with financial assistance from the state of Michigan. Each county was canvassed to obtain names of servicemen who had served during World War I. The forms used in this project requested the veteran's name; serial number; address; date and place of birth; nationality; "color"; occupation before and after the war; marriage date; wife's name; date and place of wife's birth; names of children and their dates of birth; parents' names and addresses; first camp entered and date; rank; unit; transfers and promotions; battles engaged in; date and reason for discharge; and additional information. The census is arranged by county.

Michigan Club Register, 1918–19. These records consist of copies of a guest register used at a canteen in New York City where servicemen visited. Given are name, residence, organization, station, next friend, and remarks; arranged chronologically.

Muster Roll and First Return of Units Mobilized Into United States Service, 1917.

Register of Deserters From Draft, 1918.

Veterans' Bonus Records, 1921–35. These papers pertain to World War I veterans who qualified under the Michigan bonus laws. Index cards include name, address, serial number, race, place and date of induction, place and date of birth, rank, training camp, assignments and transfers, engagements, overseas service, discharge date, and disability; separate collections for army, navy, and marines; arranged alphabetically.

List of Army, Navy, and Marine Dead, 1917–19. Includes name, serial number, race, residence, age, place of birth, date and place of enlistment, rank, promotions, units served with, overseas assignments, when died, and person notified.

Victory Medal Applications, 1920–24. These records consist of applications for the medals and provide name, rank, serial number, clasps for service, approving officers, signature, and rank; arranged alphabetically.

World War II (1941–45)

Veterans' Bonus Records. Same procedure as for World War I bonus applications (see above). No index exists.

Beneficiary Claims Files, 1947–85. These reflect payments of compensation up to $500 to heirs of veterans who died of service-related causes. Records include name of deceased, serial number, branch of service, names and addresses of parents, claim number, date and amount paid. Indexed.

Korean War (1950–53)

Veterans Bonus Records, 1955–58. Card files include name, serial number, branch of service, address, and claim number.

Beneficiary Claims Files, 1955–58. These records are similar to those pertaining to World War II veterans (see above).

BENTLEY HISTORICAL LIBRARY

University Of Michigan
1150 Beal Avenue
Ann Arbor, Michigan 48109-2113
(313) 764-3482

The Bentley Historical Library holds records relating specifically to Michigan units in the Civil War. The library holds the U.S. Army Adjutant General's Office records (1861–65), various quartermaster records, and several infantry and regiment records. Researchers will find an up-to-date listing of the library's holdings through the national bibliographic database known as RLIN.

The William L. Clements Library, also at the University of Michigan, has a comparable number of military collections. See Arlene P. Shy, assisted by Barbara A. Mitchell, *Guide to the Manuscript Collections of the William L. Clements Library* (Boston: 1978).

DETROIT PUBLIC LIBRARY

Burton Historical Collection
5201 Woodward Avenue
Detroit, Michigan 48202
(313) 833-1480

The Burton Historical Collection at this library contains a considerable amount of military records. A reference source is Catalog No. 13, which is arranged chronologically by war and thereunder by state and county. The wars begin with the several colonial wars and end with the Vietnam War. This repository also has copies of National Archives microfilm for some wars. See Joseph Oldenburg, *A Genealogical Guide to the Burton Historical Collection.* (Salt Lake City: Ancestry, 1988).

PUBLISHED SOURCES—MICHIGAN

1775-83 (American Revolution)

Daughters of the American Revolution. Michigan. *Historical Record of the Michigan Daughters of the American Revolution, 1893–1952.* 4 vols. Vol. 1 edited by Emily Sarah (Watkins) Clarkson; vol. 2 compiled by May (Rockwell) Howlett. Ann Arbor: Ann Arbor Press, 1930–52. Includes names of veterans buried in Michigan.

Silliman, Sue I. *Michigan Military Records, the D.A.R. of Michigan Historical Collections: Records of the Revolutionary Soldiers Buried in Michigan; the Pensioners of Territorial Michigan; and the Soldiers of Michigan Awarded the Medal of Honor.* Lansing: Michigan Historical Commission, 1920. Reprint. Baltimore: Genealogical Publishing Co., 1969.

1784-1815 (War of 1812)

Miller, Alice T., comp. *Soldiers of the War of 1812 Who Died in Michigan.* Ithaca: the compiler, 1962. Typescript.

1816-60 (Mexican War)

Welch, Richard W., comp. *Michigan in the Mexican War.* N.p., 1967. Based on records in the Michigan Historical Commission.

1861-65 (Civil War—Union)

Alphabetical General Index to Public Library Sets of 85,271 Names of Michigan Soldiers and Sailors Individual Records. Lansing: Wynkoop, Hallenbeck Crawford Co., 1915.

Belknap, Charles E. (?). *History of the Michigan Organizations at Chickamauga, Chattanooga and Missionary Ridge, 1863.* 2d ed. Lansing: R. Smith Printing Co., 1899. Includes names of those killed in the three battles.

Boies, A.H. *Roster of the Survivors of the Battle of Gettysburg Living in the State of Michigan, May, 1913.* Hudson: Gazette, 1913.

Dilts, Bryan L., comp. *1890 Michigan Census Index of Civil War Veterans or Their Widows.* Salt Lake City, Utah: Index Pub., 1985.

Genealogists of Clinton County Historical Society, St. Johns, Michigan. *United States Civil War Soldiers Living in Michigan in 1894.* St. Johns: the society, 1988.

Katz, Irving I. *The Jewish Soldier From Michigan in the Civil War.* Detroit: Wayne State University Press, 1962.

McRae, Norman. *Negroes in Michigan During the Civil War.* Lansing (?): Michigan Civil War Centennial Observance Commission, 1966 (?).

Michigan. Adjutant General's Department. *Michigan in the War.* Rev. ed. Lansing: state printers, 1882. Registers of commissioned officers, pages 753–73; regular and volunteer general officers, pages 974–93.

———. *Record of Service of Michigan Volunteers in the Civil War, 1861–1865.* 46 vols. Kalamazoo: Ihling Bros. & Everard, 19—. Also see *Alphabetical General Index to Public Library Sets of 85,271 Names of Michigan Soldiers and Sailors Individual Records.* Lansing: Wynkoop, Hallenbeck Crawford Co., 1915.

Michigan. Gettysburg Battle Field Commission. *Michigan at Gettysburg, July 1st, 2d and 3rd, 1863. June 12th 1889. Proceedings Incident to the Dedication of the Michigan Monuments Upon the Battle Field of Gettysburg June 12th, 1889.* . . . Detroit: Winn & Hammond, 1889.

Michigan. Michigan-Vicksburg Military Park Commission. *Michigan at Vicksburg.* . . . Detroit: Moore Print Co., 1917. Contains lists of Michigan regiments and officers at Vicksburg.

Robertson, John. *Annual Report of the Adjutant General of the State of Michigan for the Year 1864.* Lansing: 1865.

_____ . *Annual Report of the Adjutant General of the State of Michigan for the Years 1865–1866.* Lansing: 1866.

Williams, Frederick D. *Michigan Soldiers in the Civil War.* 2d ed. by Roger L. Rosentreter. Lansing (?): Michigan Department of State, 1988.

Minnesota

1671	France laid claim to a vast area of the Old Northwest that included Minnesota.
1762	France ceded Minnesota to Spain.
1763	The Treaty of Paris which ended the French and Indian War ceded eastern Minnesota to the British. (See French and Indian War in the appendix.)
1800	Spain returned Louisiana to France, including western Minnesota.
1803	The United States acquired western Minnesota from France through the Louisiana Purchase.
1849	After having been part of several different territories, including the Northwest, Indiana, Louisiana, Missouri, Illinois, Michigan, and Wisconsin territories, Minnesota became a territory.
1858	Minnesota became a state.
1862	A Sioux uprising ended with the Sioux being driven from the state. (See Sioux and Cheyenne Wars in the appendix.)

MINNESOTA HISTORICAL SOCIETY

Research Center
345 Kellogg Boulevard West
St. Paul, Minnesota 55102-1906
(612) 296-2143

Finding Aids

This society houses the state's archival records, and most are described in finding aids available in the reference room.

Official Records–State Agencies. This notebook contains descriptive inventories of records held by Minnesota agencies. The following agencies and organizations, among others, contain military records.

> Adjutant General
>
> Grand Army of the Republic, 1866–1954. These records include material relating to seventy local posts, descriptive books, and records of the Thirtieth National Encampment, St. Paul, 1896.
>
> Military Affairs Department
>
> Public Safety Commission, 1917–1921. These contain the Gold Star Rolls, which include biographical sketches, service records, photographs, etc., pertaining to World War I service personnel.
>
> Soldiers' Bonus Board, 1920s.
>
> Soldiers' Home, 1887–1980s.
>
> Territorial Archives, 1849–1858.
>
> Treasurer. Includes Civil War allotment rolls and bonus payments for World War I.
>
> War Records Commission. Includes some draft registration lists and service records for World War I.

Official Records–Local Agencies. This is a guide to records of the state's counties and towns held by this society. May include some draft records or service records for World War I and bounty payments for the Civil War.

Records

General

NATIONAL ARCHIVES MICROFILM

Register of Enlistments in the United States Army, 1796–1914 (M233).

Returns From United States Military Posts, 1800–1916 (M617) (selected volumes).

Adjutant General's Office Information Relating to Military Posts (M661).

Adjutant General's Office Papers, 1862–1916.

Letters Received by the Adjutant General's Office, Main Series, 1812–1821 (M466—selected rolls).

Letters Received by the Adjutant General's Office, Main Series, 1822–1842 (M567).

Letters Received by the Adjutant General's Office, Main Series, 1861–1916 (M619).

Letters Received by the Adjutant General's Office, 1872–1873 (M666).

Letters Sent by the Adjutant General's Office, Main Series, 1812–1890 (M565).

Letters Sent by the Office of the Adjutant General (Main Series), 1800–1890 (M565).

Adjutant General's Office; Surgeon's Files, 1818–1899.

Adjutant General's Office; Surgeons' Quarterly Reports of Sick and Wounded, Fort Snelling, 1823–1858.

Letters Received by the Secretary of War, Main (Registered) Series, 1801–1870 (M221).

Letters Received by the Secretary of War, Unregistered Series, 1789–1861 (M222).

Letters Sent by the Secretary of War to the President, 1800–1863 (M127).

Letters Sent by the Secretary of War to Congress, 1803–1870 (M220).

Letters Sent by the Secretary of War, Confidential and Unofficial, 1814–1847 (M7).

Letters Sent by the Secretary of War Relating to Military Affairs, 1808–1830 (M6—rolls 4–5; 9–12).

OTHER RECORDS

Minnesota Adjutant General's Office Records Pertaining to Service Personnel From Minnesota Who Served in the Civil War, Indian Wars, Spanish-American War, and World War I. Much of this material consists of correspondence, but also included are morning reports, general orders, special orders, and hospital reports. To obtain this material, the war or time period and the name or number of the military unit must be specified.

Minnesota National Guard Records, 1871–1947. These include correspondence, muster rolls, orders, inspection reports, some personnel records, and miscellaneous documents.

Service Record Cards: Civil War, Spanish-American War, Mexican Border Service, and World War I. These cards are available on microfilm (SAM 1). They refer to Minnesotans who entered federal service (all branches) through the Minnesota National Guard or its predecessor, the Minnesota Militia. Information given includes name, service number, where and when enrolled, age or date of birth, place of birth, residence, dates and places of service, military unit, rank or rate, where and when discharged, and civilian occupation (for members of the Home Guard).

Indian Wars (pre-1861)

NATIONAL ARCHIVES MICROFILM

Letters Received by the Secretary of War Relating to Indian Affairs, 1800–1823 (M222).

Letters Sent by the Secretary of War Relating to Indian Affairs, 1800–1824 (M15).

Civil War–Union (1861–65)

NATIONAL ARCHIVES MICROFILM

Compiled Records Showing Service of Military Units in Volunteer Union Organizations (M594—Minnesota units, rolls 90–91).

Letters Sent by the Secretary of War, Irregular Series, 1861–1866 (M492).

OTHER RECORDS

See service record cards, above.

Civil War Muster Rolls, 1861–1865. Muster-in and muster-out rolls for all Minnesota units and the Veterans Reserve Corps. The name or number of the military unit must be specified.

Civil War Pension Registers, ca. 1877–1949.

Bounty Payments to Families of Residents Serving in the Civil War. (See the finding aid for local agencies, above.)

Indian Wars (1862)

(See service record cards and adjutant general's records, above).

Indian War Pension Records, 1905–ca. 1950. These consist of pension papers filed by veterans or veterans' families for service in the Dakota Indian war of 1862. Included are the application, affidavits describing military service, death certificates, marriage licenses, and discharge papers. There is a supplementary index of names of pensioners for whom no files were located. Arranged alphabetically.

Indian War Pension Register, 1905–1937.

Spanish-American War (1898–99)

See service record cards and adjutant general's records, above.

Spanish-American War Soldiers Bonus Records. An alphabetical file of relief payments. Available on microfilm (SAM 3).

Spanish-American War Veterans Relief Board, 1931–42. These records consist of applications for financial relief for soldiers who took part in the Spanish-American war, the Philippine Insurrection, and the China Relief Expedition. They include affidavits of service, medical reports describing injuries sustained during service, marriage and death certificates filed by widows, discharge papers, and returned vouchers. They are arranged numerically and indexed in the microfilm roll cited above. One volume contains a register of approved applications.

Philippine Insurrection; China Relief Expedition

See above under Spanish-American War.

Mexican Border Service (1916)

See Minnesota National Guard records, 1871–1947. Includes payrolls listing individuals who served in the Mexican Border Service.

World War I (1917-18)

Also see service record cards and adjutant generals' records, above.

Soldiers' Bonus Records, World War I. Alphabetical file of bonus payments including name, address, warrant number, and amount paid. Available on microfilm (SAM 3).

Soldiers' Bonus Records, World War I, 1920–22. Service and financial records. Arranged alphabetically in two boxes.

Correspondence With Local Minnesota Draft Boards and Other Records Relating to National Guard Units Remaining in the State After Other Units Were Transferred to Federal Service.

Records of the Tuition Department. Records of authorization, abstracts of expenses, and other financial records pertaining to the administration of the Soldiers' and Sailors' Fund, which was established to support educational expenses for World War I veterans.

World War II (1941-45)

Service Record Cards for Veterans of Hennepin County and Approximately Half of Chicago County, Wyoming Township. See the finding aid for local agencies, above.

Korean War (1950-53)

Korean War Bonus Records, 1950s–1960s. Copies of applications for bonus payments to veterans and beneficiaries of veterans are available on microfilm. Indexed.

Vietnam War (1963-75)

Vietnam War Bonus Records, 1970s. Copies of applications for bonus payments to veterans and beneficiaries of veterans are available on microfilm. Arranged alphabetically.

Manuscripts

The society has approximately 1,800 manuscript collections, many of which relate to military history, especially to the Civil War, the Dakota Indian War, and the Spanish-American War. A manuscripts catalog is available in the reference room. It lists titles of a large number of manuscript collections, many of which pertain to military service. See Lydia A. Lucas' *Manuscripts Collections of the Minnesota Historical Society–Guide Number 3* (St. Paul: 1977).

PUBLISHED SOURCES—MINNESOTA

1861-65 (Civil War, Indian Wars)

Dilts, Bryan L, comp. *1890 Minnesota Index of Civil War Veterans or Their Widows*. Salt Lake City: Index Publishing, 1985.

Minnesota. Adjutant General's Office. *Annual Report . . . for the Year Ending December 1, 1866 and of the Military Forces of the State, From 1861 to 1866*. St. Paul: Pioneer Printing Co., 1862–66. Covers the Dakota Indian Wars of 1862 and 1863 and the Civil War, 1861 through 1865. Arranged by regiment and company, this report lists officers with rank, age, place of birth, dates of commission and muster, residence (town, country, and state) and remarks.

Minnesota. Adjutant General's Office. *Annual Reports, 1812–1865*. St. Paul: state printer, various years.

Minnesota. Board of Commissioners on Publication of History of Minnesota in Civil and Indian Wars. *Minnesota in the Civil and Indian Wars, 1861–1865*. 2 vols. St. Paul: Pioneer Press Co., 1890–93.

Minnesota Historical Society. *Minnesotans in the Civil and Indian Wars: An Index to the Rosters in Minnesota in the Civil and Indian Wars, 1861–1865*. St. Paul: the society, 1936.

Peterson, Clarence S. *Known Military and Civilian Dead During the Minnesota Sioux Indian Massacre in 1862. Known Dead During the Great Blizzard in Minnesota in January 1873*. Baltimore: the author, 1958.

1866-99 (Spanish-American War)

Minnesota. Adjutant General's Office. *Eleventh Biennial Report . . . 1900*. St. Paul: state printer, 1901.

1900-1975 (World War I through Vietnam War)

Minnesota. Adjutant General's Office. *Roster, Stations, Organizations and Commissioned Personnel of the Minnesota National Guard and Naval Militia. . . .* St. Paul: Adjutant General's Office, 1929–33.

Mississippi

1540	Spanish explorer Hernando de Soto crossed Mississippi.
1699	The French established the first permanent colony at Biloxi.
1763	The Treaty of Paris which ended the French and Indian War transferred Mississippi from France to Great Britain. (See French and Indian War in the appendix.)
1779	Great Britain ceded Mississippi to Spain.
1795	The Treaty of San Lorenzo (Pinckney's Treaty) transferred Mississippi to the United States.
1798	Mississippi became a territory.
1817	Mississippi became a state.
1861	Mississippi seceded from the Union.
1863	The successful siege of Vicksburg by Union forces under Gen. Ulysses S. Grant led to the opening of the Mississippi River to the Union. (See American Civil War in the appendix.)
1870	Mississippi was readmitted to statehood.

· ·

MISSISSIPPI DEPARTMENT OF ARCHIVES AND HISTORY

100 South State Street (Capitol Green)
Jackson, Mississippi 39201

Mailing Address:
P.O. Box 571
Jackson, Mississippi 39205-0571
(601) 359-6876

Except for microfilm records, researchers must submit a call slip for all records, including card indexes.

Finding Aids

Official Records–State Agencies. These aids consist of several notebooks that list records created by various state agencies, each designated as a record group. Those groups that are likely to include records pertaining to the military are listed below. Researchers should consult the lists in each of the following groups:

RG 2	Territorial Governors
RG 9	Confederate Records
RG 23	Veterans Farm and Home Board
RG 24	French Provincial Records (correspondence)
RG 25	English Provincial Records
RG 26	Spanish Provincial Records
RG 27	Governor's Records
RG 29	Auditor's Records
RG 33	Adjutant General's Records
RG 44	Veterans Affairs Board
RG 58	United States Military Records
RG 77	Jefferson Davis Beauvoir Soldiers' Home

Subject File. This aid is located in the reference area. Among the subjects included are those listed below as examples of likely sources of military information.

Confederate records. These include bibliographies, chaplains, cemeteries and grave markers, commissions, deceased personnel, discharges, medal of honor recipients, reunions, spies, widows, and designations of various military units

Civil War records. These include diaries, letters, photographs, and names of personnel

Mexican War

Spanish-American War

World War I

World War II

Korean War

Manuscript Collections. A set of twenty-seven notebooks lists manuscript collections. Two are listed below as examples of those that pertain to military matters.

United Daughters of the Confederacy (membership rolls for 1897–1933; honor roll of Mississippians in World War II; certificates of eligibility for crosses of honor; members' lineage sheets)

World War I (honor roll, by Mississippi counties; lists of Mississippi veterans)

A separate, computer-generated list of manuscripts that relate to particular Confederate personnel is available at the reference desk. It provides name, branch of service, unit, and the accession number of the collection in which the name appears.

Records

General

NATIONAL ARCHIVES MICROFILM

Historical Information Relating to Military Posts and Other Installations, ca. 1700–1900 (M661).

Letters Received by the Secretary of the Navy From Captains ("Captains' Letters"), 1805–1861; 1866–1885 (M125).

OTHER RECORDS

Graves Registration, Mississippi:

> Veterans of the Revolutionary War, War of 1812, Indian wars, Mexican War, and Confederate veterans (A–E) of the Civil War (MF 1).
>
> Civil War: Confederate (F–Z) and Union veterans (MF 2, 3, 4, 5).
>
> World War I (microfilm roll 6).
>
> Veterans of the Revolutionary War, War of 1812, Indian wars, Mexican War, Civil War, Spanish-American War, and the Philippine Insurrection (microfilm roll 191).
>
> Veterans of World War I (microfilm roll 192).
>
> Veterans of World War II and the Korean War (microfilm roll 194).

Veterans Farm and Home Board (RG 23). An act of the Mississippi legislature in 1936 provided for farm and home aid to veterans, with a board to approve loan applications. The procedure involved the state of Mississippi's purchasing land and awarding it to a veteran in exchange for a deed of trust calling for eventual payment. This program was extended through the Korean War to include all veterans. In later years, however, such loans were approved only in cases where the Veterans Administration had denied a veteran's application under federal procedures. Files containing the loan documents are available and give name, page, and volume where the deed is recorded; the date; and location of the property and its value.

American Revolution (1775–83)

NATIONAL ARCHIVES MICROFILM

General Index to Compiled Military Service Records of Revolutionary War Soldiers (M860).

Gen. James Wilkinson's Order Book, Dec. 31, 1796–March 8, 1808 (M654).

Territorial Records (territorial governors' papers—1784–1817)

NATIONAL ARCHIVES MICROFILM

Index to Compiled Service Records of Volunteer Soldiers Who Served From 1784 to 1811 (M694).

OTHER RECORDS

Register of Civil and Military Appointments by the Territorial Governors, 1797–1802; 1812–1817 (RG 2).

War of 1812 (1812–15)

NATIONAL ARCHIVES MICROFILM

Compiled Service Records of Volunteer Soldiers Who Served During the War of 1812 in Organizations From the Territory of Mississippi (M678).

Post-territorial Period (1817–70)

Resignations and Commissions, Civil and Military, 1817–1835 (RG27).

Register of Military Commissions, 1837–46; 1848–61.

Militia Rolls: 1847 (three counties); 1875 (five counties); 1870 (Chickasaw County).

Mexican War (1846–48)

NATIONAL ARCHIVES MICROFILM

Compiled Service Records of Volunteer Soldiers Who Served During the Mexican War in Organizations From the Territory of Mississippi (M863).

Civil War—Union (1861–65)

NATIONAL ARCHIVES MICROFILM

Index to Compiled Service Records of Volunteer Union Soldiers Who Served in Organizations From the State of Mississippi (M389).

Compiled Service Records of Volunteer Union Soldiers Who Served in Organizations From the State of Mississippi (M404).

Civil War—Confederate (1861–66)

NATIONAL ARCHIVES MICROFILM

Compiled Service Records of Confederate Soldiers Who Served in Organizations Raised Directly by the Confederate Government (M258—rolls 34, 35, 40–46, and 64–66 relating to Lay's Regiment Cavalry, Wood's Regiment Cavalry, and a few other regiments).

Records Relating to Confederate Naval and Marine Personnel (M260).

Selected Records of the War Department Relating to Confederate Prisoners of War, 1861–1865 (M596).

Register of Confederate Soldiers, Sailors, and Citizens Who Died in Federal Prisons and Military Hospitals in the North, 1861–1865 (M918).

Index and Register for Telegrams Received by the Confederate Secretary of War (M618).

Records of the Commissioner of Claims ("Southern Claims Commission"), 1871–1880 (M187).

Case Files of Applications From Former Confederates for Presidential Pardons ("Amnesty Papers"), 1865–1867 (M1003).

Deck Logs, USS Forest Rose, 1863; USS Petrel, 1863. Bureau of Naval Personnel records.

OTHER RECORDS

Muster Rolls and Payrolls. Arranged by regiment and subdivided by subject. The original documents are in archival boxes and are listed in a special finding aid which the staff can provide. Records must be requested by box number.

The following are examples of Confederate records, some of which may be available on microfilm.

Roll of Mississippi Confederate Soldiers, 1861–65.

Indigent and Disabled Soldiers and Dependents, 1864–65.

Paroles of Honor: Prisoners of War.

Deceased Soldiers' Claims.

Proceedings of Courts-martial.

Petitions for Exemption From Military Duty and for Furlough

Military Service Discharges, 1862–64.

Register of Commissions, Army of Mississippi, 1861–65.

Pension Files. Arranged alphabetically. Applications and supporting documents for veterans and widows are available on microfilm. The original files, arranged by year, are not generally available to researchers because of their fragile condition.

Burials. The finding aid *Subject File* noted above has a section on "Confederate graves." Entries include the reports furnished by Raymond W. Watkins, a native of Virginia who locates and reports the whereabouts of Confederate graves.

Confederate Soldiers' Home—Inmate Register. This bound volume gives the name of the veteran, date of admission, date of departure (either released or deceased), and military unit. Inmates buried at the home are listed in the Cemetery Register for the period 21 March 1907 through 10 December 1951. In addition, there is a bound volume of admissions for the period 2 December 1903 through 19 February 1957. Although all these volumes are still on file at the home, microfilm copies are available at the Mississippi archives.

Work Projects Administration (WPA) Collection. Card indexes are available for several collections (arranged by county). They include the following:

> County rosters of Civil War veterans
>
> Confederate regiments and companies
>
> Partial burial lists of Confederate veterans; headstone applications; out-of-state burials
>
> Census of veterans, 1907. Some counties conducted censuses; the results are available at the county courthouses

Spanish-American War (1898–99)

Card Index of Soldiers Who Served in the Spanish-American War. Cards show name, rank, regiment, residence, date mustered in, and date mustered out.

Military Service Records, Spanish-American War. Arranged alphabetically by name in vols. 8–11. Available on microfilm MF 2.

List of Mississippi Volunteers in the First and Second Regiments, Spanish-American War. Available on a microfilm copy of the state adjutant general's *Biennial Reports, 1898–99.*

World War I (1917–18)

Card Index of Soldiers Who Served in World War I. Cards give name, county of residence, branch of service, date of death, whether death occurred while in or out of service, and name and location of the cemetery. Arranged by county.

World War II (1941–45)

Card Index of Soldiers Who Served in World War II. (Cards give same data as the index for soldiers who served in World War I.)

Military Service Records. Available in vols. 12 and 13 and on microfilm MF 2 (combined with World War I soldiers).

Statements of Service Cards, World War II. Cards are available for personnel who served in the army, navy, marines, and coast guard. Arranged by county in vols. 61R, 62R, and 63R (RG 58).

Returns of Deceased Servicemen, World War II (RG 58). Contains the following:

> Notifications of next of kin, 1948–49 (vols. 8–9)
>
> Navy war casualties, 1947 (vol. 90)
>
> Honor list of dead and missing, June 1946; also a roster of Company B, 155th Infantry, 25 January 1940 (vol. 90)

Korean War (1950–53)

Card Index of Soldiers Who Served in the Korean War. Arranged by military unit. Name, rank, serial number, unit, and promotions. Not available on microfilm.

PUBLISHED SOURCES—MISSISSIPPI

General

Biographical and Historical Memoirs of Mississippi: Embracing an Authentic and Comprehensive Account of the Chief Events in the History of the State and a Record of the Lives of Many of the Most Worthy and Illustrious Families and Individuals. 2 vols. Chicago: Goodspeed Publishing Co., 1891. Reprint. Baton

Rouge, La. (?): 1961 (?). Reprint. Spartanburg, S.C.: The Reprint Co., 1978. Includes some portraits.

Mississippi. Department of Archives and History. *Military History of Mississippi, 1803–1898.* Taken From the Official and Statistical Register of the State of Mississippi, 1908. By Dunbar Rowland with a new index by H. Grady Howell, Jr. Nashville, Tenn.: 1908. Reprint. Spartanburg, S.C.: The Reprint Co., 1978.

King, J. Estelle S., comp. *Mississippi Court Records, 1799–1835.* Beverly Hills, Calif.: 1936. Reprint. Baltimore: Genealogical Publishing Co., 1969. Includes a few pensioners in Tennessee and Mississippi.

1775-83 (American Revolution)

Welsh, Alice T. *Family Records: Mississippi Revolutionary Soldiers.* Jackson, Miss. (?): Daughters of the American Revolution, 1956. Reprint. Baltimore: Genealogical Publishing Co., 1956. Veterans and their widows who settled in Mississippi. Includes dates of birth, marriage, and death and names of children.

1784-1815 (War of 1812)

Rowland, Eron O.M. *Mississippi Territory in the War of 1812.* Jackson: Mississippi Historical Society, 1921. Reprint. Baltimore: Genealogical Publishing Co., 1968.

1861-65 (Civil War)

Dilts, Bryan L., comp. *1890 Mississippi Census Index of Civil War Veterans or Their Widows.* Salt Lake City: Index Publishing, 1985.

Mississippi. Department of Archives and History. *Official and Statistical Register of the State of Mississippi.* Reprint. Spartanburg, S.C.: The Reprint Co., 1978.

Pompey, Sherman L. *Register of Civil War Dead: Confederate and Federal Troops, Mississippi.* Clovis, Calif.: 1970.

Rietti, John C. *Military Annals of Mississippi: Military Organizations Which Entered the Service of the Confederate States of America From the State of Mississippi.* Reprint. Spartanburg, S.C.: The Reprint Co., 1976.

Wiltshire, Betty C. *Mississippi Confederate Grave Registrations.* 2 vols. Bowie, Md.: Heritage Books, 1991. Includes name, service unit, years of birth and death, county or state of birth, and county where buried.

1900-1975 (World War I through Vietnam War)

Mississippi. Adjutant General's Office. *Annual Report.* Jackson: 1980-. Reports for 1980-83 include retired list with name and rank, awards and decorations.

Missouri

1682   French explorer La Salle claimed Missouri for France.

1803   The United States acquired Missouri from France as part of the Louisiana Purchase.

1812   Missouri became a territory.

1821   Missouri became a state as part of the Missouri Compromise.

1861-65   Although it was a slave state, Missouri remained loyal to the Union during the Civil War. Guerillas fighting in Missouri and along the Arkansas border attempted unsuccessfully to separate Missouri from the Union. Missouri contributed 109,111 soldiers to the Union effort during the Civil War, more than any other border state. (See American Civil War in the appendix.)

MISSOURI STATE ARCHIVES

P.O. Box 778
600 Main Street
(west of the capitol)
Jefferson City, Missouri 65102
(314) 751-3280

Finding Aids

Preliminary Descriptive Inventory: Adjutant General (RG 133).

Manuscripts Collection: Guide to the Mormon War Papers, 1838-41.

Military Land Warrants in Missouri, 1819 (available on microfilm S-1; also cited below under Published Sources—Missouri). This book contains an alphabetical list of those who claimed military lands in Missouri. There is an index of Missouri patentees, a list of regiments, and locations of land awarded for War of 1812 service. The list of patentees includes date, name, warrant number, regiment, and location of the land (section, township, range). Indexed.

Military Records on Microfilm. This is a list of records transferred from the Missouri Office of the Adjutant General to the archives (RG 133).

This archives has no National Archives microfilm.

Card File Index

Index cards prepared by the Work Projects Administration (WPA) show company/regiment, which refers to the service card file abstracts and original Confederate pension and Confederate Home applications.

> Ex-Confederate pension applicants
>
> Confederate Home applications index
>
> Confederate service (name, rank, unit, remarks, source data)
>
> War of 1812 (name, rank, unit, source data)
>
> Civil War–Union/Mexican War index (name and unit)

Card Files Containing All Information Available

The following index cards contain name, regiment, and dates of enlistment and discharge:

> Militia: revolutionary war (very few cards)
>
> Mormon War
>
> War of the Osage
>
> Iowa (honey) War
>
> Heatherly War
>
> Confederate service cards; arranged alphabetically by name.

Card File Abstracts

Cards prepared by the WPA contain data apparently taken from original muster rolls. Some cards cite source documents, although these documents may no longer be available. This file is arranged according to the following headings:

Confederate Records, Civil War

> Service record cards abstract arranged by regiment and then alphabetically by name.
>
> Missouri State Guard: Cavalry and Infantry, by regiment and then alphabetically by name
>
> Confederate State Army: Cavalry and Infantry, by regiment and then alphabetically by name
>
> Miscellaneous named regiments

Union Records, Civil War

> Enrolled Missouri Militia (EMM)
>
> Provisional Enrolled Missouri Militia (by regiment)
>
> Home Guard regiments
>
> Cavalry volunteers regiments
>
> Infantry volunteers regiments
>
> Artillery volunteers regiments
>
> Miscellaneous named regiments
>
> USRC (U.S. Reserve Corps), three month, three year
>
> USCT (U.S. Colored Troops) by regiment

Records

War of 1812 (1812-15)

Records of War of 1812 Soldiers Buried in Missouri (microfilm). Under the sponsorship of the National Society of the United States Daughters of 1812, students participated in a scholastic contest by preparing a sheet for each soldier. The data was taken from muster rolls at the National Archives and from Missouri Land Department microfilm. Included are name, date and place of birth, date and place of death, burial location, military history, marriage information, names of children, and whether or not a pension was granted.

Osage War (1837)

Names of Individuals Who Served in the Osage War. On index cards. Arranged alphabetically.

Mormon War (1838)

File Cards of Various Pay Accounts of Individuals and Units in the Mormon War.

Iowa War (1839)

An Alphabetical List of Individuals Who Served During the Iowa War.

Mexican War (1846-48)

See records pertaining to the Civil War (below). Most records of the Mexican War are included with the Civil War material. The card files are helpful, however, in finding names of those who served in the Mexican War and determining the units in which they served.

Civil War–Union and Confederate (1861-65)

Index cards–Mexican War, Civil War (Union and Confederate). The cards are alphabetically arranged by name, and they note the unit in which the individual served.

Miscellaneous Records–Union and Confederate (Missouri units). Several manuscript volumes which include hospital registers, lists of deserters, descriptive rolls, and orders.

List of Military Units During the Civil War and the Mexican War. (See above under Mexican War.)

Alphabetical List of Burials for Missouri Men Who Served and Died During the Civil War.

Manuscript Collection of United Daughters of the Confederacy. This is a joint collection of the Western Historical Manuscripts Collection and the State Historical Society of Missouri Manuscripts.

Civil War–Union (1861-65)

Index to Enrollment Cards of Individuals Who Served in the Mexican War or With Union or Confederate Organizations in the Civil War. (See above under Mexican War.) The cards are arranged alphabetically by the first three letters of the surname and thereunder by given name. Units in which the individual served are noted. Enrollment cards for those who served in the Civil War are arranged alphabetically under the units.

Union Army Records, Artillery. Various records pertaining to several Missouri Civil War organizations. Records include descriptive rolls, registers, orders, correspondence, account books, morning reports, and records of clothing and equipment.

Separate Collections of Records for the Following Missouri Organizations:

> Union Army, Enrolled Missouri Militia
> Union Army, cavalry
> Union Army, infantry
> Union Army, Missouri State Militia
> Union Army, Missouri Volunteers
> Union Army, engineers
> Union Army, militia
> Union Army, Adjutant General's Office

Miscellaneous Records Pertaining to Union and Confederate Military Units. Include loyalty oaths, resignations, enlistments, discharges, regimental histories, general and special orders, court-martial procedures, requests for commissions as officers, hospital registers, lists of deserters, descriptive rolls, registers, letters, account books, morning reports, clothing issue records and equipment issue records. Papers are currently being processed (sorted and microfilmed), but those for the following units have been arranged and microfilmed and are now available for examination:

> Enrolled Missouri Militia: First–Seventeenth Regiments; Nineteenth–Twenty-first Regiments; Twenty-third–Eighty-ninth Regiments
> Provisional Enrolled Missouri Militia: First–Eleventh Regiments
> United States Reserve Corps
> United States Colored Troops
> General Orders, Provisional Enrolled Missouri Militia
> Phelps' Regiment Infantry
> Van Horn's USRC

Wachman's First Battalion Missouri State Militia

> Special and general orders (Not all special and general orders are available–inquire at reference desk.)
> Missouri Volunteer Infantry: First–Fifteenth Regiments; Seventeenth–Eighteenth Regiments; Twenty-first Regiment; Twenty-third–Fifty-sixth Regiments
> Missouri Volunteer Cavalry: First–Sixteenth Regiments
> Engineers of the West
> Home Guard, 1861 (Adair County–northeast Missouri; Knox–Webster)
> Missouri Light Artillery: First–Second Regiments
> Missouri State Militia
> Missouri State Militia, cavalry: First–Ninth Regiments; Eleventh–Twelfth Regiments; Fourteenth Regiment

Index Cards Showing County Enrollment, 1861-65. Alphabetically arranged by name with county of residence

Civil War–Confederate (1861-65)

Confederate Units. An alphabetical and numerical list of Confederate units from Missouri.

Index to Enrollment Cards for Individuals Who Served in the Civil War (Union and Confederate) and the Mexican War. (See above under Mexican War.)

Alphabetical List of Approximately Half of the 40,000 Missouri Men Who Enrolled in the Confederate Army. Information on these cards was taken from original muster rolls and various books. In most cases the cards indicate what material is available.

Miscellaneous Records Pertaining to Units of the Confederate Cavalry, Confederate Infantry, and Missouri State Guard. Consists of muster rolls, final statements (1865), and one pension roll.

Ex-Confederate Pension Applications. An alphabetical list of men who applied for service during the Civil War.

Index to Confederate Home Applications. An alphabetical list of men who applied for admittance to Missouri's Confederate Home at Higginsville, Missouri, which operated between 1892 and 1951.

Confederate Home Applications. A transcript of a handwritten record kept at the home between 1891 and 1893. Entries are arranged in the order in which the applications were placed in the original register. They include name, rank, age at the time of application, date of admittance, place of residence when admitted, military history (including wounds), reason for the application, and date of death (where applicable).

Heatherly War (1876)

Names of Missouri militiamen who were ordered into service to put down depredations by members of the "Heatherly gang," a band of outlaws in northwest Missouri. See the footnotes in Willis B. Hughes' "The Heatherly Incident of 1836"

(*Missouri Historical Society Bulletin*, January 1957). These cite manuscripts at the National Archives pertaining to this affair.

Spanish-American War (1898-99)

Muster Rolls and Registers, First–Sixth Regiments of Infantry.

World War I (1917-18)

Service Record Cards of the Adjutant General's Office (microfilm). File cards containing regiment, service information, and birth information for army and navy personnel. Arranged alphabetically.

MISSOURI ARMY NATIONAL GUARD

1717 Industrial Drive
Jefferson City, Missouri 65109-1468
(314) 751-9890

This facility holds military records pertaining to Missourians who served in World War II, the Korean War, and the Vietnam War. Records include separation notices and discharge records. This facility also has books that list casualties of the above-cited wars, and it has an *Honor Roll* published by the U.S. Department of Defense (for the same wars) that includes those who were declared dead or missing in action.

STATE HISTORICAL SOCIETY OF MISSOURI

1020 Lowry Street
Columbia, Missouri 65201-7298
(East wing, Ellis Library, University of Missouri)
(314) 882-7083 or (800) 747-6366

This society was formed in 1898 by the Missouri Press Association, and it possesses the largest state (Missouri) newspaper collection in the nation. Since 1901 the society has been a trustee of the state and has been supported by state funds, augmented by dues and contributions from more than 10,000 members. It maintains a newspaper/census library, manuscript, map, and photograph collections, and a reference library on the history of Missouri and western America. This society does not have any military records, but it does have diaries, regimental histories, casualty lists, county histories, autobiographies, etc., which provide data on individual soldiers as well as on entire military units. Some National Archives microfilm for the following wars is held by the newspaper library.

War of 1812 (1812-15)

Index to War of 1812 Pension Applications Files (M313).

War of 1812 Military Bounty Land Warrants, 1815-1858 (M484).

Old War Index to Pension Files, 1815-1926 (T316).

Mexican War (1846-48)

Index to Mexican War Pension Files, 1887-1927 (T317).

Civil War–Union (1861-65)

Index to Compiled Service Records of Volunteer Union Soldiers Who Served in Organizations From the State of Missouri (M390).

WESTERN HISTORICAL MANUSCRIPT COLLECTION

Twenty-three Ellis Library
University of Missouri
Columbia, Missouri 65201
(314) 882-6028

These collections are held jointly with the State Historical Society of Missouri (see above).

Finding Aid

Collection Guide–Military. This guide is an alphabetical list of collections held either at Columbia, Missouri, or at the locations shown below. The title of each collection has a numerical prefix that denotes the repository where it may be found.

University of Missouri, Kansas City. 5100 Rockhill Road, Kansas City, Missouri 63121; (816) 276-1543.

University of Missouri, St. Louis. 8100 Natural Bridge Road, St. Louis, Missouri 63121; (314) 353-5143.

University of Missouri, Rolla. Rolla, Missouri 65401; (314) 341-4874.

In addition to the above guide, the Columbia facility has a card catalog of all the manuscript collections. These contain military material consisting largely of private papers and reports, newspaper clippings, diaries, journals, biographies, muster rolls, descriptions of battles, and miscellaneous papers pertaining to specific wars. The military-related collections are indexed by name of war, with subheadings such as battles, claims, pensions, prisons and prisoners, and unit histories.

MISSOURI HISTORICAL SOCIETY

225 South Skinker Boulevard
St. Louis, Missouri

Mailing Address:
P.O. Box 11940
St. Louis, Missouri 63112-0040
(314) 746-4500

Finding Aids

Guide to the Manuscript Collections at the Missouri Historical Society. Under the general subject heading "War" in this finding aid are the following subheadings:

> Civil–Pilot Knob [Missouri] papers, 1861–1914
>
> War of 1812, 1807-1973
>
> Mexican War, 1846–1940
>
> Revolutionary war, 1770–1957
>
> Revolutionary war–Sons of the American Revolution, 1919–1931
>
> Spanish-American War, 1898–1934
>
> World War I, 1915–1970
>
> World War II, 1941–1954

A finding aid to the Civil War collections is currently being compiled. There is a collection titled Missouri Militia Collection, 1793–1930.

Military Clubs and Societies–Holdings. This is a typescript list of clubs and societies that have records (usually bound books) pertaining to Missourians in the Civil War and some pertaining to later wars. A description of each collection is included. Examples of subjects found in this list:

> American Expeditionary Force, Thirty-third Division, 138th Infantry
>
> Confederate States Army, First Army, Fourth Cavalry Division
>
> Enrolled Missouri Militia, Fifty-fourth Regiment
>
> Grand Army of the Republic (posts thirteen, twenty-three)
>
> Hodges, W.D., Veterans Association Record Book, 1887–1913
>
> Lyon's Legion (Company I, Fourteenth Missouri Volunteers)
>
> Mesker, Frank, Collection (news clippings, payrolls)
>
> Missouri Militia paymaster
>
> National Guard of Missouri, First Regiment, St. Louis, 1873–1910
>
> Old Guard (St. Louis)
>
> St. Charles Post (provost marshal)
>
> St. Louis Grays, 1834–1860

> St. Louis Montgomery's Guard, 1842–1846
>
> Schenk, John, Captain, Seventeenth Missouri Volunteers
>
> Third Ward Union Guards (St. Louis), 1861.
>
> USS *Tennessee*, journal, 1875.
>
> U.S. Army of the Southwest (Battle at Pea Ridge)
>
> U.S. Army Reserve, 406th Infantry
>
> U.S. Navy, Mississippi Squadron
>
> Twenty-first National Encampment, GAR (St. Louis) Register, 1887

Card Catalog

An extensive card catalog of the collections pertaining to military matters includes the following examples:

American Revolution (journals, private papers).

War of 1812 (pensions granted by Congress, burials in Missouri, private papers). See also "Army Bounty Land Warrants."

Civil War (narratives, diaries, private papers, deserters, exemptions, prisons and prisoners, Pea Ridge casualties, Col. Joseph Wedemeyer Collection, names of St. Louisians).

Mexican War (diaries, private papers).

World War I (soldiers and casualties, St. Louisians, roster of First Missouri Infantry, 128th Field Artillery, medals and decorations, private papers).

World War II (journals, private papers).

Vietnam War.

Muster rolls (various Missouri units in the Civil War, Pilot Knob, home guards, St. Charles and Gasconade home guards).

Several bound volumes pertaining to:

> George Rogers Clark Collection, 1814–1884
>
> Ulysses S. Grant Collection, 1791–1961
>
> Jefferson Barracks Collection, 1826–1921

PUBLISHED SOURCES–MISSOURI

1775-1783 (American Revolution)

Daughters of the American Revolution. Missouri. *Annual State Conference. 15th Conference.* St. Louis: 1914. Includes names of veterans of the revolution buried in Missouri.

Houts, Alice K., comp. *Revolutionary Soldiers Buried in Missouri.* Kansas City: Daughters of the American Revolution, 1966. Includes more than eight hundred names (alphabetized) with biographical sketches.

Pompey, Sherman L. *A Partial Listing of Veterans of the American Revolution, the Civil War, and the Spanish-American War*

Buried in Certain Missouri Cemeteries. Warrensburg: Johnson County Historical Society, 1962.

1784-1860 (War of 1812)

Dunaway, Maxine. *Missouri Military Land Warrants, War of 1812.* Springfield: the author, 1985.

1836 (Heatherly War)

Hughes, Willis B. "The Heatherly Incident of 1836." *Missouri Historical Society Bulletin* (January 1957).

1861-65 (Civil War)

Anders, Leslie, comp. *Confederate Roll of Honor: Missouri.* Warrensburg: West Central Missouri Genealogical Society and Library, 1989. A register of some 6,519 Confederate casualties from Missouri. Name, rank, unit, cause and place of death, and source references are included.

Bailey, Elizabeth, comp. *Missouri Ex-Confederate Soldiers—Pension Lists and Deaths at the Confederate Soldiers' Home, Higginsville, Missouri.* Columbia: State Historical Society of Missouri, 1984.

Civil War Veterans. 6 vols. Jackson (?): Cape Girardeau County Genealogical Society, 1982-(?). Includes counties of Cape Girardeau, Madison, Mississippi, Perry, Scott, and St. Genevieve.

Dilts, Bryan L. *1890 Missouri Census Index of Civil War Veterans or Their Widows.* Salt Lake City: Index Publishing, 1985.

Missouri. Adjutant General's Office. *Adjutant General's Report of Missouri State Militia.* St. Louis: G. Knapp & Co., 1862.

_____ . *Annual Report, 1863-1865.* 3 vols. Jefferson City: ca. 1865.

_____ . *Official Register of Missouri Troops for 1862.* St. Louis, 1863.

Pompey, Sherman L. *Confederate Soldiers Living in Missouri in 1890, Regiment Not Stated.* Albany, Oreg.: the author, 1984.

_____ . *Genealogical Notes on Missouri Military Units in the Civil War* (?). 5 vols. Albany, Oreg.: the author, 1984-.

_____ . *Muster Lists of the Missouri Confederates.* 9 vols. Independence, Calif.: Historical and Genealogical Publishing Co., 1965.

U.S. Congress. House. Committee on Invalid Pensions. *Pensions for the Militia of Missouri and of Other States.* Washington, D.C.: Government Printing Office, 1912.

U.S. Record and Pension Office. *Organization and Status of Missouri Troops, Union and Confederate, in Service During the Civil War.* Washington, D.C.: Government Printing Office, 1902. Pages 213-36 contain a list of Union military organizations and officers; pages 329-35 list Confederate organizations and officers.

1866-99 (Spanish-American War)

Missouri. Adjutant General's Office. *Military Records, Spanish-American War, 1897-98.* Jefferson City: 1898. Rosters of Missouri Troops Mustered into U.S. service for the Spanish-American War.

_____ . *Adjutant General's Report of Missouri State Militia, 1909-10.* State of Missouri, 1910. Includes a roster of officers.

_____ . *Roster of Commissioned Officers in the United States Missouri Volunteers Who Were Mustered Into the United States Service Under the First and Second Calls of the President of the United States.* Jefferson City: 1898.

1916 (Mexican Border Service)

Missouri. Adjutant General's Office. *Service of the Missouri National Guard on the Mexican Border. . . .* Jefferson City: Hugh Stevens Co., 1919.

1917-18 (World War I)

Missouri. Adjutant General's Office. *Report of the Adjutant General of Missouri, January 1, 1917-December 31, 1920.* Jefferson City, 1921 (?).

Montana

1803	France sold Montana, an unexplored part of the Louisiana territory, to the United States in the Louisiana Purchase.
1805-06	American explorers Lewis and Clark crossed Montana on their way to the Pacific.
1862-63	Gold discoveries at Bannack and Alder Gulch brought the first significant numbers of white settlers to Montana.
1864	Montana became a territory.
1876	Sioux and Cheyenne Indians destroyed Lt. Col. George A. Custer's Seventh Cavalry at the Little Big Horn. (See Sioux and Cheyenne Wars in the appendix.)

1877   Nez Perce Indians under Chief Joseph were pursued into Montana by Col. Nelson A. Miles. (See Nez Perce War in the appendix.)

1889   Montana became a state.

. . . .

MONTANA HISTORICAL SOCIETY

Library and Archives Division
225 North Roberts (Capitol Complex)
Helena, Montana 59620-1201
(406) 444-2681 (library)
(406) 444-4774 (archives)

Records

General

(Records are requested at the library and delivered there from the archives, which is located on a separate floor.)

Muster Rolls of National Guard Units, Various Years. The military unit must be specified.

Muster Rolls of Military Personnel Stationed at Fort Asseniboine, Fort Benton, Fort Ellis, Fort Keogh, and Fort McGinnis.

Records Kept at Fort Harrison From 1895 Until the Facility Was Converted to a Veterans Administration Facility. Includes a veterans index.

Rosters and Related Data Collected by Veterans' Organizations—Grand Army of the Republic and Others.

Miscellaneous and Scattered Records on Microfilm, Pertaining Primarily to local Indian wars.

Several Transcripts of Interviews From the Oral History Collection, Mainly Pertaining to the Montana National Guard for Recent Time Periods.

Spanish American War, World War I, World War II (1898-1945)

Card Catalog of Military Personnel From Montana Who Served in the Spanish American War, World War I, or World War II. Name, service number, place and date of enlistment, age at entrance, rank or rate, home address, military history, and discharge information are included.

PUBLISHED SOURCES—MONTANA

1876 (Indian wars)

Carroll, John M., and Byron Price. *Roll Call on the Little Big Horn, 28 June 1876.* Fort Collins, Colo.: The Old Army Press, 1974.

Hammer, Kenneth. *Men With Custer: Biographies of the 7th Cavalry, 25 June 1876.* Fort Collins, Colo.: The Old Army Press, 1972.

Nebraska

1803   A largely unexplored part of the Louisiana territory, Nebraska was sold by France to the United States in the Louisiana Purchase.

1804–06   American explorers Lewis and Clark crossed Nebraska on their way to the Pacific.

1854   Nebraska became a territory as part of the Kansas-Nebraska Act, with its northern boundary the Canadian border.

1865–67   Many Civil War veterans acquired land in Nebraska under the Homestead Act of 1862.

1867   Nebraska became a state with its present boundaries.

. . . .

NEBRASKA STATE HISTORICAL SOCIETY

P.O. Box 82554
1500 R Street
Lincoln, Nebraska 68501
(402) 471-4771 (or 471-4772)

Finding Aid

A Guide to Resources in the Library/Archives Division. This booklet includes a section on military records available at this society.

Nebraska Goes to War—Selected Resources on Nebraska in World War II. This booklet describes available manuscript collections, photograph collections, and published material concerning Nebraska in World War II.

Records

General

RG 018, Nebraska Military Department, contains material concerning Nebraska militia and National Guard units since 1854. The records are classified in three subgroups: 1855-80; 1881-1970s; 1918-19.

Rosters of Soldiers, Sailors and Marines, 1887-1925—volumes listing veterans from the Mexican War and the Civil War. These rosters were furnished by Nebraska county clerks or assessors to the Nebraska secretary of state, who printed and published them. They list name, unit, and post office address.

1855-90 (Civil War—Union)

Militia Units' Muster Rolls and Correspondence, 1855-80.

Volunteer Units' Muster Rolls and Correspondence, 1861-80.

Orders and Circulars, 1861-80.

Muster Rolls, Rosters, Descriptive Books, 1861-80. Includes rolls for military units that fought in the Civil War and against the Plains Indians. This series includes many local and county militia units; also includes general historical data concerning the First Nebraska Regiment, 1861-65, and other units.

Reports and Returns, 1861-69.

Clothing and Property Records, 1861-69.

Miscellany, 1959-80

Grand Army of the Republic (GAR) membership files. Although not every Union soldier became a member of the GAR, most did. These files give name, date of military service, unit and state from which served, GAR post number, and Nebraska post office address.

Grand Army of the Republic (GAR) Burial Records. An alphabetical list of Civil War veterans buried in Nebraska. Name, unit, date of death, place of burial, and often date and place of birth are included.

Rosters of Nebraska Soldiers in the Civil War, 1861-65. See Betty Loudon, *Index-guide, Nebraska History Magazine, 1959-1979* (Vols. 40-60. Lincoln: Nebraska State Historical Society, 1984).

1890 Federal Census of Civil War Veterans and Widows.

1881 (Nebraska National Guard)

Much of the material in this group of records is arranged chronologically and thereunder by unit designation.

Correspondence and Reports, 1881-1963.

Orders and Circulars, 1881-1941.

Quartermaster's Records, 1891-1908.

Muster Rolls, Rosters, Personnel Records, Payrolls, 1881-1956.

Armory Files, 1895-1955.

Inspection and Training Records, 1912-59.

134th Infantry Regiment Records, 1927-51.

Administrative and Fiscal Records, 1888-1951.

Emergency Duty Records, 1913-62.

Fourth Army Records, 1937-38.

Morning Reports, Monthly, Quarterly, and Annual Reports, 1871-1974.

Descriptive Books and Lists, 1881-1911.

1917-19 (Nebraska Home Guard)

Home Guard Units of the National Guard in Nebraska Counties. Material consists primarily of correspondence, applications, certificates of elections of officers, rosters, and muster rolls.

Mexican War (1846-48)

See above for rosters furnished by county clerks or assessors and published by the secretary of state.

Spanish-American War (1898-99)

Service Cards of Nebraskans Who Fought in the Spanish-American War. Included are name, place of birth, date of birth, age, residence, dates of service, and unit.

See above for rosters furnished by county clerks or assessors and published by the secretary of state.

World War I (1917-19)

Service Cards of Nebraskans Who Fought in World War I. Name, serial number, residence, age or date of birth, and dates of service are included.

See above for rosters furnished by county clerks or assessors and published by the secretary of state.

World War II (1941-45)

Index of Nebraska Servicemen Who Fought in World War II. Compiled from items in Nebraska newspapers.

See the finding aid cited above, *Nebraska Goes to War*, for material pertaining to World War II.

PUBLISHED SOURCES—NEBRASKA

General

Nebraska. Secretary of State. *Roster of Soldiers, Sailors, and Marines of the War of 1812, the Mexican War, and the War of the Rebellion Residing in Nebraska, June 1, 1893. . . .* Lincoln: Jacob North & Co., 1893.

_____. *Roster of Soldiers, Sailors, and Marines of the War of 1812, the Mexican War, and the War of the Rebellion Residing in Nebraska, June 1, 1895. . . .* Lincoln: Jacob North & Co., 1895.

_____. *Roster of Soldiers, Sailors, and Marines of the War of 1812, the Mexican War, and the War of the Rebellion Residing in Nebraska, June 1, 1898. . . .* Lincoln: 1898(?).

_____ . *Roster of Veterans of the Mexican, Civil, and Spanish-American Wars Residing in Nebraska, 1915.* Lincoln: 1915 (?).

1861-65 (Civil War)

Nebraska. Adjutant General. *Roster of Nebraska Soldiers From 1861 to 1869. . . .* Compiled by Edgar S. Dudley. Hastings: Wigton & Evans, 1888.

Pompey, Sherman L. *Register of the Civil War Dead: Nebraska.* Clovis, Calif.: 1970.

Nevada

1826	American explorer and trapper Jedediah Smith crossed Nevada.
1848	Nevada was part of the area ceded to the United States by Mexico in the Treaty of Guadalupe-Hidalgo, which ended the Mexican War. (See Mexican War in the appendix.)
1850	Nevada was made part of Utah Territory, which was created by the Compromise of 1850.
1859	Discovery of gold and silver in the Comstock Lode at Virginia City brought the first significant numbers of settlers.
1861	Nevada became a territory.
1864	Nevada became a state.

NEVADA STATE LIBRARY AND ARCHIVES

Division of Archives and Records
100 Stewart Street (at Musser Street)
Carson City, Nevada 89710
(702) 687-8313

Records

Civil War—Union (1861-65)
NATIONAL ARCHIVES MICROFILM

Index to Compiled Service Records of Volunteer Union Soldiers Who Served in Organizations From the State of Nevada (M548).

OTHER RECORDS

Muster Rolls and Descriptive Lists, 1863-66. Indexed.

World War I Through Vietnam War (1917-1975)

Service Cards for Nevada Veterans Who Served in the Above-listed Wars.

Discharge Papers for Nevada Veterans of the Above-listed Wars.

PUBLISHED SOURCES—NEVADA

1861-65 (Civil War)

Nevada. Adjutant General's Office. *Annual Report, 1865.* Carson City, 1865.

_____. Annual reports and biennial reports, 1865-1947.

Pompey, Sherman L. *Civil War Veteran Burials From California, Nevada, Oregon, and Washington Regiments Buried in Colorado.* Independence, Calif.: Historical and Genealogical Publishing Co., 1965.

1917-18 (World War I)

Nevada's Golden Stars. Reno: Nevada Adjutant General's Office, 1924. Reprint. Tucson, Ariz.: W.C. Cox Co., 1974. Contains biographical sketches of soldiers who were killed during the war.

New Hampshire

1623	The first English settlers created a community on the present site of Portsmouth.
1679	New Hampshire became a Royal Colony.
1689	New Hampshire was invaded by French forces from Canada during King William's War. (See King William's War in the appendix.)
1745	New Hampshire men participated in an invasion of Canada during King George's War. (See King George's War in the appendix.)
1788	New Hampshire became one of the original thirteen states.

. . . .

NEW HAMPSHIRE STATE ARCHIVES

Seventy-one South Fruit Street
Concord, New Hampshire 03301
(603) 271-2236

Finding Aids

Checklist for Researching Family Genealogy (military records). A leaflet.

Genealogical Sources in New Hampshire (military records). A leaflet.

New Hampshire Records and Archives Microfilm. A leaflet.

Mevers, Frank C., and Harriett S. Lacy. *Early Historical Records (ca. 1620 ca. 1817) at the New Hampshire State Archives.*

Guide to Early Documents (ca. 1680-1900) at the New Hampshire Records Management and Archives Centers—Treasurer (Record Group V; Military Records (Record Group XII). A notebook.

Military Records. An archives catalog of New Hampshire military collections.

Records

The state archives has no National Archives microfilm dealing with military matters.

Colonial Wars

See Potter's *The Military History of the State of New Hampshire, 1623-1861 . . .* (cited below under Published Sources—New Hampshire). This book contains names of veterans of colonial wars as well as other wars prior to the Civil War.

Index to Indian Wars and French and Indian Wars, and Revolutionary Papers. Arranged alphabetically, giving volume and page of the source documents.

Court-martial papers, 1694-1959. Undated.

Enlistment papers. Undated.

Rolls of Military Personnel, 1690-1775. Undated.

Certificates, 1777-84.

Enlistment Papers, 1775-85.

Oaths, 1778-85.

Military Rolls, 1775-82.

Accounts (treasurer), 1692-1769; 1720-69.

American Revolution (1775-83)

See Frank C. Mevers' *Compiled Index to Volumes XIV–XVII, New Hampshire State Papers.* Available at the archives in notebook form. Contains a name index and a subject index, as well as a list of military units, rolls, accounts, receipts, etc.

Revolutionary War Rolls.

Cilley's New Hampshire Regiment. Indexed.

Capt. Farwell's Company Book, 1771-82. Microfiche.

Captain Ebenezer Frye's Company Account Book. Microfiche.

Reid's New Hampshire Regiment. Indexed. Microfiche.

Index to Scammel's Regiment papers. The original papers are not in the New Hampshire Archives.

Roster of Field Officers, 1768-1809.

Accounts (Treasurer), 1770-85.

Army Rolls. Indexed.

Invalids' Accounts. Indexed.

Pre-Civil War (1802-59)

Military Certificates, 1802-20 (lists of officers).

Returns of Various Militia Units, 1824-26.

Rosters, 1820-55.

Rosters of Officers, 1819-38.

Orderly Books of Various Regiments, 1821-50.

Non-resident Tax Lists. Eleven volumes, 1849-59.

War of 1812 (1812-15)

See Potter's *The Military History of the State of New Hampshire, 1623-1861 . . .* (cited below under Published Sources—New Hampshire).

Mexican War (1846-48)

See Potter's *Military History of the State of New Hampshire* (cited below under Published Sources—New Hampshire).

Civil War—Union (1861-65)

Registers of Soldiers and Sailors. This is a microfilm reprint of a publication by Augustus D. Ayling, state adjutant general, in which the military history of each New Hampshire soldier and sailor in the Union forces is provided. Also available on microfiche. (Also see citation below under Published Sources—New Hampshire.)

Inventory of Volumes and Pages of the Civil War Enlistment Papers Collection. This inventory lists volume number and page number of several indexes to New Hampshire regiments. Included are regiments One-Seventeen; U.S. Sharp Shooters; miscellaneous enlistments; miscellaneous three-month enlistments; miscellaneous three-year enlistments; First Cavalry; New Hampshire Cavalry; Heavy Artillery; and First New Hampshire Battery. Copies of the enlistment papers are on both microfilm and microfiche.

Recruiting Station Records, 1861-62. Miscellaneous papers arranged by town in which the recruiting station was located.

Miscellaneous Records of Various New Hampshire Regiments. Consult the finding aid *Military Records* for names of specific collections. These include documents such as rosters, muster rolls, receipts, morning reports, courts-martial, discharges for disability, certificates for substitutes, claims, reenlistments, and casualties.

Casualties; certificates of death, 1861-65.

Regimental Histories. Consult the finding aid *Military Records* for specific regiments.

Town Returns. Consult the finding aid *Military Records* for names of towns.

Service Cards, Substitute File, and Soldiers' File. These cards provide name, place of birth, age, residence, enlistment date, term of service, date mustered in, final record (rank), date mustered out, and date and place of death. The substitute file shows the names of individuals who sent a substitute in lieu of military service. The names of the substitutes are also shown. Arranged alphabetically.

Oaths of Allegiance. Eighteen bound volumes that contain oaths made by soldiers. Arranged by regiment.

Deaths and Burials, Thirteenth New Hampshire Regiment.

Surgeons' Records, 1861-65.

Honor Roll.

Registers of Discharged Soldiers and Sailors.

Allotment Rolls.

Sick and Wounded Rolls.

Muster-in and Muster-out Rolls. Arranged by regiment.

Medal of Honor Awards, Civil War. This notebook devotes a page to each individual. Name, unit, military service, and reason for the award. Arranged alphabetically. Also available on microfiche.

Petition Index. This is a set of two notebooks. Under the heading Military are alphabetically arranged names of petitioners who filed for relief for disability, back pay, expenses, etc., from the state legislature. Available upon request is a sheet that lists the names of the petitioners.

Civil War pensioners. Pension papers arranged by town. Each town folder contains records of disbursements to indigent veterans or members of their families. Given are name, unit, date of muster, name and age of each person who received assistance, relationship to the veteran, and dates and amounts of payments.

Post-Civil War; Spanish-American War (1866-99)

Commission Records: descriptive books of various regiments, 1871-80. See the finding aid *Military Records* for names of regiments.

Enlistment Books, Various Regiments and Companies, 1877-1905. See the finding aid *Military Records* for names of regiments and companies.

Enlistment Papers. Alphabetically arranged by name of soldier.

Payrolls, Receipts, Miscellaneous Documents, 1898-1915.

World War I (1917-18)

Roster of Officers, New Hampshire; New Hampshire National Guard.

Company Descriptive Book and Clothing Book, Hospital Corps Detachments (1909-11); Detachment, Signal Corps, Nashua (1908-10).

Local Draft Board Registration Lists. There is a folder for each town or county. Provided are name and address of registrant. Names are arranged in order of the individual's liability for military service. Available upon request is a sheet that lists the names of the sixteen New Hampshire draft boards.

NEW HAMPSHIRE HISTORICAL SOCIETY

Thirty Park Street
Concord, New Hampshire 03301
(603) 225-3381

This society's manuscript collections are indexed on cards arranged by name, town, and subject. Examples are:

Civil War (by name, battles, places, New Hampshire volunteers, unit, commissions)

French and Indian War

Indian conflicts

Militia (name, regiment, orderly books, appointments, detached militia)

Revolutionary war (name of collection, miscellaneous)

Spanish-American War

United States Army

United States Navy

War of 1812

Records

General

Locations of Graves of New Hampshire Revolutionary Soldiers. This is an index arranged by county and town. Provided are name, date of death, and name of cemetery. This index is a bound volume donated by the Rumford Chapter, Daughters of the American Revolution, as copied from records of the graves registration officer of the New Hampshire American Legion.

Diaries and Letters Concerned With Military Matters. Available upon request is a list of the names of the more important collections.

Orderly Books, Roll Books, and Organizations Books. There are fifty to sixty books pertaining to New Hampshire military units (mostly militia units) prior to the Civil War.

Pre-Civil War (ca. 1794-1860)

Orderly Books (1820-1850) for Infantry Companies From Various Towns. Some for light infantry, riflemen, and cavalry; roll books and muster rolls; certificates, orders, oaths, notices, and other papers.

Civil War (1861-65)

Personal Papers Such as Diaries and Correspondence. Approximately one hundred collections varying in size from a few letters to hundreds of letters.

Post-Civil War–Present

A relatively small amount of personal papers such as diaries and correspondence.

PUBLISHED SOURCES—NEW HAMPSHIRE

Pre-1775 (colonial wars)

Gilmore, George C. *Roll of New Hampshire Men at Louisburg, Cape Breton, 1745.* Concord: Edward N. Pearson, 1896. Roll includes name, place of residence, date of enlistment, rank, company, and regiment.

Hammond, Isaac W., comp. *Rolls of the Soldiers in the Revolutionary War.* 4 vols. Concord: 1885-89. Reprint. New York:

AMS Press, 1973. Appendix of vol. 3 has some colonial rolls for 1712-55 (including French and Indian War).

New Hampshire. Adjutant General's Office. *Report.* Concord: 1858-59. Annual reports for 1858-59 through 1915-16 include militia rosters.

Potter, Chandler E. *The Military History of the State of New Hampshire, 1623-1861, From Its Settlement, in 1623, to the Rebellion, in 1861 . . . Biographical Notices of Many of the Officers. . . .* Concord: 1866 [1868]. Reprint "with added indexes. . . ." Baltimore: Genealogical Publishing Co., 1972.

1775-83 (American Revolution)

Batchellor, Albert S., ed. *Miscellaneous Revolutionary Documents of New Hampshire, Including the Association Test, the Pension Rolls, and Other Important Papers. . . .* New Hampshire Provincial and State Papers, vol. 30. Manchester: J.B. Clark Co., 1910.

Draper, Mrs. Amos C., comp. *New Hampshire Pension Records.* 13 vols. Typescript.

Gilmore, George C. (?). *Roll of New Hampshire Men at Bunker Hill, June 17, 1775.* Manchester: 1899.

_____. *Roll of New Hampshire Soldiers at the Battle of Bennington, August 16, 1777.* Manchester: J.B. Clarke, 1891.

Hammond, Isaac W. *Rolls of the Soldiers in the Revolutionary War, 1775-82.* New Hampshire Provincial and State Papers, vols. 14-17. Vol. 1, *Revolutionary War Rolls, 1775-77.* Vol. 2, *New Hampshire Men in Massachusetts Regiments.* Vol. 3, *Revolutionary War Rolls, 1775-83 and 1780-82.* Vol. 4, pt. 1, *War Rolls and Documents, 1774-82.* Concord: state printer, 1885-89. Reprint. New York: AMS Press, 1973.

New Hampshire. Department of State. *Manual for the General Court. No. 6.* Concord: the department, 1889-. Reprint. Manchester: J.B. Clarke Co., 1899. Includes a roll of New Hampshire men at the Battle of Bunker Hill, 17 June 1775.

Potter, Chandler E. *The Military History of the State of New Hampshire, 1623-1861, From Its Settlement, in 1623, to the Rebellion, in 1861 . . . Biographical Notices of Many of the Officers. . . .* Concord: 1866 [1868]. Reprint "with added indexes. . . ." Baltimore: Genealogical Publishing Co., 1972.

1861-65 (Civil War)

New Hampshire. Adjutant General's Office. *Revised Register of the Soldiers and Sailors of New Hampshire in the War of the Rebellion. 1861-1865.* Concord: state printer, 1895.

Waite, Otis F.R. *New Hampshire in the Great Rebellion: Containing Histories of the Several New Hampshire Regiments, and Biographical Notices of Many of the Prominent Actors in the Civil War of 1861-65.* Claremont: Tracy, Chase & Co., 1870.

New Jersey

1638   Swedes and Finns made the first permanent settlements in New Jersey.

1660   Dutch settlers took over the area, establishing farms in northern New Jersey.

1664   The British drove the Dutch out, making New Jersey part of the royal colony of New York in 1665.

1673-74   The Dutch briefly regained control of New Jersey but lost it again to Great Britain.

1738   New Jersey became a royal colony.

1776-78   New Jersey became a major battleground of the American Revolution, with dramatic battles at Trenton, Princeton, and Monmouth. (See American Revolution in the appendix.)

1787   New Jersey became one of the original thirteen states.

. . . .

NEW JERSEY STATE ARCHIVES

185 West State Street
CN-307
Trenton, New Jersey 08625
(609) 292-6260

Finding Aids

Guide to Family History Sources in the New Jersey State Archives. This booklet contains a section titled Military Records that briefly lists certain manuscripts and other records pertaining to the colonial wars through the Spanish-American War, and also to state militia and National Guard units.

Department of Defense. This aid lists military collections at the archives. It is arranged by the following subjects, among others.

    Adjutant general's office
    Civil War
    Colonial wars
    Forfeited estates
    Mexican Border War
    Militia

    National Guard
    Pennsylvania Insurrection and Indian Campaign, 1791
    Pension claims
    Philippine Insurrection
    Spanish-American War
    Volunteers-loyalists
    War with Mexico
    War of 1812
    World War I

Military Records–Microfilm. This pamphlet lists microfilm copies of records that originated in the New Jersey Department of Defense or the New Jersey Genealogical Society. Records are grouped under the following subjects:

    Revolutionary War:
        Card files of compiled service records
        Manuscripts, numbered and unnumbered
        Manuscripts in books
        Pension claims
        Slips (index slips)
        Damages in New Jersey (arranged by county)
        Loyalists, 1776–83
        Loyalists (company notes)

    Military records:
        Indian campaigns, 1791
        Pennsylvania Insurrection, 1794
        Militia officers, colonial wars
        New Jersey records, various periods, 1780–1845

    War of 1812:
        New Jersey pensioners and claims. Indexed.

    Civil War:
        Index to Stryker's *Record of Officers and Men of New Jersey in the Civil War*
        Pension claims–annual, 1775–1824
        Regimental rosters, New Jersey Volunteers (First-Forty-first Regiments); navy; U.S. Colored Troops; New Jersey Volunteers of the Civil War and Spanish-American War
        Pension claims, Spanish-American War
        Publications, pension files, claims, volunteers, discharges pertaining to World War I
        Unofficial service records
        Pension files, claims, and inquiries (mixed)
        War Book: Militia enrollments and miscellaneous records

The New Jersey Archives has two rolls of National Archives microfilm: *The Negro in the Military Service of the United States, 1639–1886* (M858; local designation T823); the other is a roll that pertains to the Fifteenth New Jersey Infantry in the Civil War (microfilm number not shown).

Records

General

Militia, 1793–1868. Arranged by county and year, but not all counties and years are represented.

Elections of Officers.

Militia Commissions.

Militia Resignations.

Petitions, Leaves of Absence, Courts-martial, Oaths, Accounts, Returns, and Muster Rolls.

Colonial Wars (pre-1775)

Card File for Personal Names on Colonial Deeds, Many of Which Are Those of Militia Officers. The date, type of record, liber and page number for the entries are also included.

Manuscripts are described in the finding aid titled *Department of Defense.* Included are lists of casualties at Fort Ticonderoga, rosters of officers, and payrolls.

American Revolution (1775–83)

Card File With Names of New Jersey Men Who Served in the American Revolution. Although the cards are located in the closed archives stacks, a microfilm copy is available.

Index of commissioned militia officers.

Miscellaneous Bond Books. These contain lists of men who served in the militia or the Continental Line. Names are arranged by county and military unit.

Forfeited Estates, 1775–95. These records provide names of those who aided the enemy.

Pension Claims:

> Abstracts of New Jersey federal pension claims
>
> Federal pension claims for Hunterdon and Somerset counties
>
> Account book, New Jersey pensions, 1833–43

Indents, Revolutionary War, Consisting of Miscellaneous Papers.

Continental Army: Account Papers of the Quartermaster Department.

List of Revolutionary War Federal Pensions.

List of Rejected Claims for Federal Pensions.

Loyalists: Manuscripts and Muster Rolls of British Units, Officers and Enlisted Men.

Card File of Loyalists. With names, ranks in British regiments, and page number where the names appear on a master roll.

Pennsylvania Insurrection and Indian Campaigns (1784–1811)

Pennsylvania Insurrection Officers and Men: Muster Rolls.

Indian Campaigns, 1791. Description of Col. George Gibsons' Second Regiment.

"Whiskey Insurrection." New Jersey muster rolls.

War of 1812 (1812–15)

Roster of Officers, Detailed Militia.

Lists of New Jersey Militia Units.

Lists of Land Warrant Grantees.

Payrolls of Gen. Ebenezer Elmer's Brigade.

Service Records of New Jersey Men in the United States Army and Marine Corps.

Pension Claims Under the Act of 1874.

Mexican War (1846–48)

Elections of Officers; Accounts; Casualty Lists; Correspondence.

Muster Rolls and Returns, Tenth Regiment, United States Infantry, New Jersey Battalion.

Civil War–Union (1861–65)

Officers and Men Who Served in the Civil War, 1861–65. Microfilm copies of two volumes. Indexed.

Miscellaneous Rolls and Lists. Elections of officers; list of battles; resignations; burials; memorials of officers; enlistments; naval rolls; list of New Jersey men serving on vessels lost at sea; recruits; "colored" troops; muster and descriptive rolls; substitutes; reenlistments; bounty recipients.

Regimental Records, by Regiment: First–Fortieth Regiments, Infantry; New Jersey Volunteers; First Regiment, Artillery; Veterans Reserve Corps; enlistments in states other than New Jersey. Included in this category are muster rolls, lists of deserters, discharges, and payrolls.

Assessors' Returns and Militia Enrollments, by County.

Substitutes and Drafted Personnel, Including Muster Rolls and Descriptive Rolls. Arranged by Congressional districts 1–5.

New Jersey Soldiers in Hospitals.

Pension Claims, New Jersey.

Pension Claims, Mixed ("letters").

State Bounty Rolls.

Soldiers' Children's Home, Trenton, New Jersey, 1865–76. Includes admissions, minute books, accounts, and ledger.

Photographs. See the finding aid *Department of Defense* for an alphabetical list.

Lists of Volunteers by County and Military Unit. Prepared in the county clerks' offices.

List of Discharged Men and Deserters, 1812. Prepared in the county clerks' offices.

Naval Records and United States Marine Corps Service Records. Arranged alphabetically. Include enlistment papers and commissions.

Marine Corps "Size Rolls." Name, date, residence, and physical description.

Marine Enlistment Lists. See the finding aid *Department of Defense* for an alphabetical list of names.

Post-Civil War, Spanish-American War (1866–1913)

National Guard, First and Second Regiments:

> Muster rolls, 1912–13
>
> Courts-martial, 1899; 1901; 1904
>
> Elections of corporals and sergeants, 1895–1903
>
> Orders, 1879–86 (First Regiment); 1872–76 (Second Regiment)

Lists of Officers, Muster Rolls, and Correspondence for the First–Seventh Regiments, the Twenty-eighth Regiment, and the Navy.

Pension Claims. Arranged alphabetically.

Coast Signal Service. Includes enlistment papers; applications for commission; New Jersey Volunteers (by regiment); Camp Voorhees; state headquarters at Sea Girt, New Jersey. Indexed.

Mexican Border Service (1916)

Muster Rolls for the First–Fifth Regiments, First Field Artillery, and Miscellaneous Headquarters and Other Units. See the finding aid *Department of Defense* for names of the units.

National Guard Records for Miscellaneous Lists.

Card Index File for Personnel. On microfilm.

World War I (1917–18)

The bulk of the records pertaining to twentieth-century wars are at the New Jersey Department of Military and Veterans Affairs, Eggert Crossing Road, CN-340, Trenton, New Jersey 08625-0340. However, the following records may be found at the state archives:

Unofficial Service Cards. Arranged alphabetically.

National Guard Units in United States Service. Arranged by unit.

National Guard Records Including Correspondence, Muster Rolls, Returns, and Miscellaneous Lists.

State Militia in World War I.

Duplicate Bonus Case Records, 1929–38. Arranged alphabetically.

NEW JERSEY HISTORICAL COMMISSION

113 West State Street
CN-520
Trenton, New Jersey 08625
(609) 292-6062

The New Jersey Historical Commission has a large manuscript collection that includes many documents pertaining to military service. See Mary R. Murrin's *New Jersey Historical Manuscripts: A Guide to Collections in the State.* (Trenton: New Jersey Historical Commission, 1987).

NEW JERSEY HISTORICAL SOCIETY

230 Broadway
Newark, New Jersey 07104
(201) 483-3939

The New Jersey Historical Society also has a large collection of manuscripts, including many pertaining to military service. See Don C. Skemer's and Robert C. Morris' *Guide to the Manuscript Collections of the New Jersey Historical Society* (Newark: New Jersey Historical Society, 1979).

PUBLISHED SOURCES—NEW JERSEY

1775–83 (American Revolution)

Brace, Frederic R. *Brief Sketches of the New Jersey Chaplains in the Continental Army.* New Jersey Historical Society Proceedings, ser. 3, vol. 6. Reprint. Paterson: Press Printing and Publishing Co., 1909.

Campbell, James W.S. *Digest and Revision of Stryker's 'Officers and Men of New Jersey in the Revolutionary War,' for the Use of the Society of the Cincinnati in the State of New Jersey.* New York: Williams Printing Co., 1911. Supersedes Stryker's *General Maxwell's Brigade.* . . .

Detwiler, Frederic C. *War in the Countryside: The Battle and Plunder of the Short Hills, New Jersey, June 1777.* N.p., 1977. Lists troops of four units in addition to miscellaneous names.

Hayward, Elizabeth M. *Soldiers and Patriots of the American Revolution: A List Compiled From Baptist Periodicals at the Shirk Library, Franklin College.* Ridgewood: 1947.

Jackson, Ronald V., and Gary R. Teeples. *Index to Military Men of New Jersey, 1775–1815.* Bountiful, Utah: Accelerated Indexing Systems, 1977. Index to Stryker's *Official Register* and the New Jersey adjutant general's *Official Register of the Officers and Men.* . . .

Lender, Mark E. *The New Jersey Soldier.* Trenton: New Jersey Historical Commission, 1975.

New Jersey. Adjutant General's Office. *Official Register of the Officers and Men of New Jersey in the Revolutionary War.* Compiled by William S. Stryker and James W.S. Campbell. Trenton: W.T. Nicholson & Co., 1872. New edition supplemented by an index. Baltimore: Genealogical Publishing Co., 1967.

Society of the Cincinnati. New Jersey. *The Society of the Cincinnati in the State of New Jersey, With the Institution, Rules and Regulations of the Society . . . Officers of the New Jersey Society . . . Interesting Documents From the Archives of the Society, etc.,* etc. Washington, D.C.: 1981. Supersedes 1949 publication. Includes biographical notes about original members.

Stryker, William S. *General Maxwell's Brigade of the New Jersey Continental Line in the Expedition Against the Indians, in the Year 1779.* Trenton: W.S. Sharp Printing Co., 1885. Superseded by Campbell's *Digest. . . .*

Stryker, William S. *New Jersey Continental Line in the Virginia Campaign of 1781.* Trenton: L.J. Murphy, 1882.

Waldenmaier, Inez. *Revolutionary War Pensioners Living in New Jersey Before 1834.* Tulsa, Okla.: the author, 1983.

1784–1815 (War of 1812)

Jackson, Ronald V., and Gary R. Teeples. *Index to Military Men of New Jersey, 1775–1815.* Bountiful, Utah: Accelerated Indexing Systems, 1977. Index to Stryker's *Official Register* and the New Jersey adjutant general's *Official Register of the Officers and Men. . . .*

New Jersey. Adjutant General's Office. *Records of Officers and Men of New Jersey in Wars, 1791–1815.* Trenton: State Gazette Publishing Co., 1909. Reprint. Baltimore: Genealogical Publishing Co., 1970. Includes "St. Clair's Campaign, 1791; Pennsylvania Insurrection, 1794; War with Tripoli, Africa, 1801–1805; War with France, 1798–1800; War with Tripoli, Africa, 1801–1805; War of 1812; War with Algiers, Africa, March 3 to August 9, 1815."

1816–60 (Mexican War)

New Jersey. Adjutant General's Office. *Records of Officers and Men of New Jersey in the War With Mexico, 1846–1848.* Trenton: 1900.

1861–65 (Civil War)

New Jersey. Adjutant General's Office. *List of Promotions, Appointments and Casualties in the New Jersey Regiments, in the Service of the United States, Since January 1, 1865, March 1, April 1, July 1, 1883, August 1, 1864, October 1, December 1, 1864, February 1, August 1, 1865.* Trenton: 1863–66.

New Jersey. Adjutant General's Office. *Record of Officers and Men of New Jersey in the Civil War, 1861–1865.* Compiled in the Office of the Adjutant General. 2 vols. Trenton: J.L. Murphy, 1876.

New Jersey. Adjutant General's Office. *Register of Commissioned Officers of the New Jersey Volunteers, in the Service of the United States.* 4 vols. Trenton, 1882–65.

New Jersey. Department of Defense. *Roster of Personnel, New Jersey Army National Guard, New Jersey Air National Guard, Ordered Into the Active Military Service of the United States, 1961.* Compiled in the Office of the Chief of Staff, Department of Defense, N.J. Trenton (?): 1962 (?).

Princeton University. *Roll of the Alumni and Former Students of the College of New Jersey Who Served in the Army or Navy of the United States in the War for the Union.* Philadelphia: McCalla & Stavely, 1867.

Toombs, Samuel. *New Jersey Troops in the Gettysburg Campaign, From June 5 to July 31, 1863.* Orange: Evening Mail Pub., 1888. Reprint. Highstown: Longstreet House, 1988. "Biography of Officers," pages 359–406.

1866–99 (Spanish-American War)

Roster and Addresses of the Second New Jersey Volunteer Infantry in the Spanish-American War, 1898. Patterson: 1898.

1900–75 (World War I through Vietnam War)

New Jersey. Department of Defense. *Roster of Personnel, New Jersey Army National Guard, New Jersey Air National Guard, Ordered Into the Active Military Service of the United States, 1961.* Compiled in the Office of the Chief of Staff, Department of Defense, New Jersey. Trenton (?): 1962.

New Mexico

1539	Spanish Franciscan missionary Marcos de Niza and a black slave named Estevan explored into New Mexico.
1598	The first Spanish settlements were established in the Rio Grande Valley.
1680	Pueblo Indians revolted, driving the Spanish out of New Mexico.
1692	Don Diego de Vargas began the reconquest of New Mexico.
1821	As a result of the Mexican Revolution, New Mexico passed from Spanish to Mexican rule.
1848	Mexico ceded New Mexico to the United States by the Treaty of Guadalupe-Hidalgo,

which ended the Mexican War. (See Mexican War in the appendix.)

1850   The Compromise of 1850 created the Territory of New Mexico, which included Arizona.

1854   The Gadsden Purchase added some former Mexican territory to southern New Mexico.

1862   Confederate forces were defeated in the Battle of Glorieta Pass near Albuquerque. (See American Civil War in the appendix.)

1863   The Territory of Arizona was created from the western portion of the Territory of New Mexico.

1864   U.S. forces under Kit Carson defeated the Navajo Indians and sent them into exile in New Mexico until 1868. (See Navajo Wars in the appendix.)

1870-86   The Apache Wars raged across New Mexico until the surrender of Geronimo in 1886. (See Apache Wars in the appendix.)

1912   New Mexico became a state.

1916   The U.S. Army launched the Mexican Punitive Expedition into Mexico in retaliation for Pancho Villa's raids in southern New Mexico. (See Mexican Punitive Expedition in the appendix.)

1943   Testing grounds were created at Los Alamos for the development of atomic weapons.

. . . .

NEW MEXICO RECORDS CENTER AND ARCHIVES

404 Montezuma
Santa Fe, New Mexico 87503
(505) 827-7332

Records

Indian Wars (1850s)

Unindexed muster rolls and campaign records exist within a record group known as Territorial Archives of New Mexico.

Civil War—Union (1861-65)

NATIONAL ARCHIVES MICROFILM

Index to Compiled Service Records of Volunteer Union Soldiers Who Served in Organizations From the Territory of New Mexico (M242).

Compiled Service Records of Volunteer Union Soldiers Who Served in Organizations From the Territory of New Mexico (M427).

Civil War—Confederate (1861-65)

Some folders containing data pertaining to Confederate soldiers are available, but other data may be obtained at the New Mexico Sons of Confederate Veterans, 3021 Espanola NE, Albuquerque, New Mexico 87125. Such data may also be found at the Confederate Research Center at Hill Junior College, P.O. Box 619, Hillsboro, Texas 76645.

Spanish-American War (1898-99)

Cavalry and mounted riflemen from New Mexico served under Capt. Leonard Wood and Lt. Col. Theodore Roosevelt. They received notoriety as Roosevelt's "Rough Riders." This service took place between June and September 1898. A roster and information about this regiment may be obtained from the Las Vegas Rough Rider's and City Museum, P.O. Box 179, Las Vegas, New Mexico 87701.

PUBLISHED SOURCES—NEW MEXICO

General

New Mexico (Territory) Adjutant General's Office. *Report.* Santa Fe, n.d. Reports of 1886-1931 include militia rosters.

Pre-1861 (Mexican War)

Twitchell, Ralph E. *The History of the Military Occupation of the Territory of New Mexico From 1846 to 1851 by the Government of the United States. . . .* Denver: 1909. Reprint. New York: Arno Press, 1976. Biographical sketches and some portraits of officers, pages 203-394.

_____. *The Leading Facts of New Mexico History.* 5 vols. Cedar Rapids, Iowa: The Torch Press, 1911-17.

1861-65 (Civil War)

Hall, Martin H. *The Confederate Army of New Mexico.* Austin: Presidial Press, 1978.

_____. *Sibley's New Mexico Campaign.* Austin: University of Texas Press, 1960 (?). Includes muster rolls.

Pompey, Sherman L. *New Mexico Honor Roll.* Independence, Calif.: Historical and Genealogical Publishing Co., 1965.

1898-99 (Spanish-American War)

History of New Mexico: Its Resources and People. 2 vols. Los Angeles: Pacific States Publishing Co., 1907.

New York

1609	English explorer Henry Hudson discovered the Hudson River.
1624	The Dutch founded the colony of New Amsterdam on Manhattan Island.
1650	English settlers on Long Island divided that island with the Dutch by treaty.
1664	The English overthrew the Dutch and renamed the colony New York.
1673-74	The Dutch briefly recaptured the colony, but were again defeated by the English.
1690	The French invaded New York during King William's War. (See King William's War in the appendix.)
1745-46	The French burned Saratoga and Albany and fought against the English in Mohawk Valley during King George's War. (See King George's War in the appendix.)
1758	During the French and Indian War, a major battle was fought at Fort Carillon on Lake Champlain. (See French and Indian War in the appendix.)
1763	Pontiac's Rebellion against British rule in Michigan spread to New York. (See Pontiac's Rebellion in the appendix.)
1775-79	New York was the theater for several encounters during the American Revolution, especially at Fort Ticonderoga, New York City, and Saratoga. (See American Revolution in the appendix.)
1788	New York became one of the original thirteen states.
1861-65	New York contributed 448,850 Union soldiers to the Union cause during the Civil War, more than any other state. (See American Civil War in the appendix.)

NEW YORK STATE ARCHIVES

Cultural Education Center
Room 11D40
Empire State Plaza (on Madison Avenue)
Albany, New York 12230
(518) 474-8955

Finding Aid

Inventory to Civil War Records in the New York State Archives.

Records

Colonial Wars (pre-1775)

Original muster rolls are available, as described in a publication of the New York Historical Society, *Muster Rolls of New York Provincial Troops, 1755–1764* (cited below under Published Sources—New York). These pertain to the French and Indian War (Seven Years' War) and give name, enlistment date, age, place of birth, trade, militia unit, enlisting officer, and, occasionally, a physical description. The rolls for 1757 are missing.

Rosters and lists of personnel taken from muster rolls were published in the *Annual Report of the State Historian of the State of New York.* 2 vols. (New York City and Albany: 1897-98.) Names are arranged by unit, usually under the name of the commanding officer. Militia companies from the following counties and towns are included: Westchester, Orange, Kings, Queens, Flushing, Salem, Richmond, Ulster, city and county of Albany, and others. Muster rolls pertain to 1715 and a few additional years. Additional rosters from various muster rolls of militia units are available for the period 1755 to 1759. The original rosters were destroyed by fire in 1911 at the state capitol.

American Revolution (1775-83)
NATIONAL ARCHIVES MICROFILM

Miscellaneous Numbered Records (the Manuscript File) in the War Department Collection of Revolutionary War Records, 1775–1790s (M859—32 reels).

OTHER RECORDS

Muster Rolls, Bounty Records, and Pension Files (A0200). Many of these records were destroyed by fire in 1911 at the state capitol. Recently, well-trained volunteers carefully examined all surviving charred documents and transcribed the data found. The result of their work, but not the actual documents, will be available on a computer printout. The data usually includes name, rank, type of military organization, levies, name of town or county, and a symbol that denotes the source document from which the information was taken. No names of vessels are included. The publication *New York in the Revolution as Colony and State* (cited below under Published Sources—New York) includes an alphabetical roster of state troops and other details extracted from muster rolls.

The Surveyor General's Original Sales Book (B0255) refers to military bounty lands and the men of each regiment of the State Line and Artillery who were recipients of land granted by the state of New York. Records of the New York auditor and other state agencies also include some documents that refer to soldiers and state pensioners of the American Revolution. (These records are not indexed, and the archives will not search them. Researchers must visit the archives and search the records themselves.)

War of 1812 (1812-14)

Payroll Cards for Soldiers of the War of 1812 (B0810). Transcripts from the original payrolls, which were destroyed. These give name, unit, commanding officer, period for which they were paid, and the amount paid.

Claims for Awards (A0020). Claims for reimbursement for the cost of clothing, arms, and equipment furnished at soldiers' own expense. Documents are available as noted in the New York adjutant and inspector general's report for 1860, *Index of Awards on Claims of the Soldiers of the War of 1812* (cited below under Published Sources—New York). This gives name of applicant, residence, amount allowed, and case number.

Also see publications listed below for names of pensioners and survivors, as well as information concerning them in military minutes of the Council of Appointment. The New York State Archives has all records cited therein.

Civil War—Union (1861-65)

NATIONAL ARCHIVES MICROFILM

Index to Compiled Service Records of Volunteer Union Soldiers Who Served in Organizations From the State of New York (M551).

OTHER RECORDS

For a complete listing of the archives' records, see the finding aid cited above. Examples are:

Registers Kept by Town Clerks Listing the Officers, Soldiers, and Seamen Who Filled the Town or County Quotas of Troops to be Furnished to the United States (13774). The registers are available for most—but not all—towns and for a few cities (Buffalo, Oswego, and Syracuse but not Albany, Brooklyn, New York, Troy, or Utica). Both the original documents and microfilm copies are available. The registers are actually a collection of printed forms completed by town clerks and submitted to the state Bureau of Military Records.

The information includes name, residence, date and place of birth, rank, unit, dates of enlistment and muster, length of enlistment, place of enlistment, race, amount of bounty paid by a town or county, marital status, previous occupation, parents' names, and dates of promotions, resignations, discharges, and deaths. For seamen the information also includes the name of the vessel(s) on which they served. Names are arranged alphabetically by county and thereunder by city, town, or village. (Many data elements are missing.)

Registers of Officers and Enlisted Men Mustered into Federal Service or Naval Service During the Civil War (six volumes) (A0389). This information was gathered from questionnaires distributed after the war to veterans, relatives, friends, local officials, and medical officers in federal hospitals. The registers are divided into three series: those who were then in military service; those who had previously been in military service; and those who died in service. A tremendous amount of military and personal history information is included in the questionnaires. Arranged alphabetically by county, city and town. Available on microfilm. No index. Registers include lists of soldiers and sailors from cities and towns not found in series 13774 (above).

Accounts Submitted by Local Officials Detailing Monies Raised and Expended, and Men Furnished to the Service During the Civil War (A4114). Consists of voluminous correspondence, much of which lists those mustered into service, those who received financial assistance, etc. No index.

Index of Militia Volunteers and Militia Men Transferred to the Union Army. This is a typescript manuscript in two bound volumes with an index. It includes names and units of men who are found in records of the state adjutant general.

Register of Letters Received, 1862-66 (fourteen volumes) (13722). This refers to correspondence processed by the Office of the State Adjutant General.

Abstracts of Military Commissions, 1823-1909 (fifteen volumes) (13728). Vols. 12 and 13 pertain to commissions issued during the Civil War. No index.

Organization Rosters of Military Officers, 1800-99 (fourteen volumes) (13729). Vols. 7, 8, 9a, and 9b contain names of officers in New York volunteer regiments during the Civil War. A separate volume lists officers of the state militia and the National Guard who retired or were discharged. No index.

Resignations of Militia and National Guard Officers, 1861-62 (B0463). No index.

Roster of Officers of State Volunteer Regiments, 1861-62. Arranged by regiment and company.

Registers of United States "Colored Troops" Who Filed Claims Against the Federal Government, 1866-69 (A4160). Claims were made for back pay and for bounties based on service during the Civil War. Note that these claims refer to those filed against the federal government, not against the state of New York.

Descriptive Rolls: Howitzer Battery, Eleventh Brigade, National Guard, 1864–84 (13725); 193d New York Volunteer Infantry Regiment, 1865 (B0633). No indexes.

Regimental Records: First Regiment of Artillery, New York State Volunteers, 1863–65 (A0227); Twenty-second Regiment of New York State Volunteers, 1861–65 (A4166). No indexes.

Registers of Soldiers' Claims Expedited by the New York Military Agency, 1866–68 (twenty-four volumes) (A4135). These describe claims filed and processed relative to Civil War pensions and bounties for back pay and rations reimbursement. Generally arranged alphabetically for each office that processed the claim. An exception is the Washington, D.C., office of the agency, for which there is a name index.

Register of Soldiers Who Visited the Washington, D.C., Office of the New York Military Agency, 1863–65 (A4136). No index.

Register of Bounty Claims, ca. 1864–65 (A4159). Contains names of soldiers who had not been paid a bounty. Lists only those of the 106th through the 146th Volunteer Regiments.

Bounty Payment Register, 1865–67 (A4161). Includes date of payment, name, regiment, and amount paid. Arranged by first initial of the claimant's name.

Register of Bounty Applications, 1876–82 (A4164). Arranged by month and date. There is no name index.

Roster of Medical Staff on New York State Volunteer Regiments, 1861–65 (B0311). Contains names of surgeons and assistant surgeons. Indexed.

Abstracts of Muster Rolls for Men Who Served in the United States Navy, 1861–65 (ninety-six volumes) (B0383). Arranged by a) navy regular officers, b) navy volunteer officers, and c) navy enlisted men. Information includes name, place of birth, date and place appointed, rank, promotions, names of vessels, and final disposition (resigned, died, dismissed). Alphabetically arranged for each category.

Abstracts of Civil War Muster Rolls (1,363 volumes) (13775). This series is arranged by regiment or other unit, then alphabetically. A name index is available. Microfilming is in progress.

OTHER ABSTRACTS OF ROLLS

United States Marine Corps (four volumes) (B0804).

National Guard Units Mustered Into Federal Service (ninety-two units) (B0800).

Veteran Reserve Corps Troops (Invalid Corps) (B0806). Denotes the individual's military history prior to and after becoming incapacitated for full duty.

Men Not Assigned to Any State or Federal Unit (B0805).

"Colored" Enlisted Men Not Assigned to Any State or Federal Unit (B0812).

Substitutes Who Served in Lieu of Others (B0813).

Record of Claims, 1862–68 (A4141). The results of claims presented to the auditing board, April 1862 through April 1868. Indexed.

Spanish-American War; Philippine Insurrection; China Relief Expedition (1898–1904)

Card Catalog for New York Men Who Served in Volunteer Organizations During the Above Military Actions (B0809).

Abstracts of Muster Rolls Related to the Above Military Actions (B0801).

Mexican Border Service (1916)

Rosters of Military Personnel Who Were Involved in Various Border Clashes with Mexico (B0802). The name of a soldier's unit must be specified to locate records. See also the card index for veterans of World War I (including some who participated in the Mexican Border Service). No index.

World War I (1917–18)

Card Catalog of New York Men Who Served in World War I (B0808). Includes some who served in the Mexican Border Service.

World War II (1941–45)

Card Catalog of New York Men Who Served in World War II. This index is currently maintained by the Division of Military and Naval Affairs, 330 Old Niskayuna Road, Latham, New York 12110; telephone: (518) 786-4500.

NEW YORK STATE LIBRARY

Cultural Education Building (seventh floor)
Empire State Plaza (on Madison Avenue)
Albany, New York 12230
(518) 474-4461

The state library has a genealogy section and a microform section. Available in the genealogy section are the following pamphlets: *Starting Your Family Tree, Card Indexes Description, Loyalist Records, New York State Military Records* (for both pre and post-Civil War), and *DAR Records*. Each of these pamphlets cites published works available in both the library and the state archives. A card index of graves of revolutionary war dead was prepared by the Daughters of the American Revolution.

Finding Aid

The microform section furnishes a finding aid titled *A List of Microforms in the Manuscripts and Special Collections Section, New York State Library,* compiled by Kathleen Barber (1990). Included are references to several New York regimental histories, diaries, journals, and orderly books.

Also cited are several reels of film pertaining to Loyalist claims.

Records

General

George Washington Papers. A microfilm copy (124 reels) of original documents in the Manuscript Division, Library of Congress. These include considerable information concerning both the French and Indian War and the American Revolution.

Manuscript Collections

Computer terminals located in the reading room of the archives provide a means of retrieving military-type manuscripts. Instructions for use of the terminals and other assistance is provided by archives personnel. Access is available by subject, personal name, or title of the document (using key words). Manuscripts must be requested by submitting a special request slip.

A card catalog for the manuscript collection is also available. Subject headings pertaining to military matters include: French and Indian War, American Revolution, War of 1812, Mexican War, Civil War (with many subheadings), Spanish-American War, European War (World War I), United States Military Academy, United States Navy, United States Pension Bureau, and United States War Department.

NEW YORK HISTORICAL SOCIETY

170 Central Park West at Seventy-seventh Street
New York, New York 10024-5194
(212) 873-3400

Finding Aids

Breton, Arthur J. *A Guide to the Manuscript Collections of the New York Historical Society.* 2 vols. Westport, Conn.: Greenwood Press, 1975. Vol. 1: Descriptive Inventories; vol. 2: Index and Chronological Listing of Entries. Vol. 2 should be consulted first to locate manuscript collections by name or subject. A more complete description of the collections, which are either in original form or on microfilm, can then be located in vol. 1.

Card index. An extensive card catalog (continued in an electronic data base) lists published volumes and manuscripts collections held at this facility. These are available from the stacks upon submission of a request form. Available are such documents as muster rolls, orderly books, receipt books, and other material relating especially to the era of the American Revolution. Much of this material has been microfilmed and is therefore available through interlibrary loan.

Many of the collections have been reproduced in various issues of the society's *New York Historical Society Collections.*

PUBLISHED SOURCES—NEW YORK

Pre-1775 (colonial wars)

Fish, Stuyvesant. *The New York Privateers, 1756–1763: King George's Private Ships of War Which Cruised Against His Enemies.* . . . New York: George Grady Press, 1945. Appendix 1: ships taking out privateer's licenses in New York, 1756–63 (name of vessel, number of guns, captain, date of permit, and owners); appendix 2: list of ships' officers; appendix 3: ship owners.

Great Britain. Public Record Office. *Calendar of State Papers, Colonial Series.* . . . 44 vols. London: 1860–1969. Note Jacob Leister's militiamen in 1691, item 162.

Lists of Inhabitants of Colonial New York. Excerpted From The Documentary History of the State of New York. . . . Baltimore: Genealogical Publishing Co., 1979. Includes militia companies.

New York Historical Society. *Muster Rolls of New York Provincial Troops, 1755–64.* New York Historical Society Collection, vol. 24. New York: the society, 1892. Reprint. Bowie, Md.: Heritage Books, 1990.

New York (state). State Historian. *Third Annual Report of the State of New York.* . . . 3 vols. Albany: Wynkoop Hallenbeck Crawford Co., 1896–98. Vol. 2 (1896), Appendix H: "Muster Rolls of a Century, From 1664 to 1760." Vol. 3 (1897), Appendix M: "Colonial Muster Rolls . . . Up to the . . . War of the Revolution."

O'Callaghan, Edmund B. *Calendar of New York Colonial Commissions, 1680–1770.* New York: New York Historical Society, 1929.

———, and Berthold Fernow. *The Documentary History of the State of New-York.* . . . 4 vols. Albany: Weed, Parson & Co., 1849–81. Reprint. Baltimore: Genealogical Publishing Co., 1979. Includes rolls of militia companies.

Rogers, Mary C. *Rogers' Rock, Lake George, March 13, 1758. A Battle Fought on Snow Shoes.* Derry, N.H.: the author, 1917. Contains muster rolls.

1775-83 (American Revolution)

Bascom, Robert. *The Ticonderoga Expedition of 1775.* New York State Historical Association, vol. 9. Reprint. N.p., 1910.

Fernow, Berthold. *New York in the Revolution.* With an Introduction by Kenn Stryker-Rodda. Originally vol. 15 of *Documents Relating to the Colonial History of the State of New York.* Albany: 1887. Reprint. Cottonport, La.: Polyanthos, 1972. Rosters of New York troops, casualties, pensioners, Green Mountain Boys, etc.

New York. Governor. *Public Papers of George Clinton, First Governor of New York, 1777-1795, 1801-1804.* 10 vols. New York, 1899-1914. Reprint. New York (?): AMS Press, 1972 (?). Scattered tables of returns of military officers. Analytical index volume notes military rank.

New York. Secretary of State. *The Balloting Book and Other Documents Relating to Military Bounty Lands in the State of New York.* Albany: Packard & Van Benthuysen, 1825. Reprint with additions. Ovid: W.E. Morrison Co., 1983. Contains a list of persons "entitled to a gratuity of lands for their military services." Includes name with rank arranged alphabetically under regiment, under town, and under name of patentee with occasional remarks. Includes invalids and discharged men.

_____. *A List of the Names of Persons to Whom Military Patents Have Issued Out of the Secretary's Office, and to Whom Delivered.* Albany: Francis Childs & John Swaine, 1793. Lists almost two thousand veterans to whom military patents were issued.

New York. Comptroller's Office. *New York in the Revolution as Colony and State.* 2 vols. Compiled by Berthold Fernow. Albany: 1898-1901. Reprint. Albany: J.B. Lyon Co., 1901-04. Transcription of official documents including names of some 50,000 men who served in the military.

_____. *New York in the Revolution as Colony and State. Supplement.* Albany: J.B. Lyon, 1901, and reprint, 1904.

New York (state). State Historian. *Third Annual Report of the State of New York. . . .* 3 vols. Albany: Wynkoop Hallenbeck Crawford Co., 1896-98. Vol. 2 (1896), Appendix H: "Muster Rolls of a Century, From 1664 to 1760." Vol. 3 (1897), Appendix M: "Colonial Muster Rolls . . . Up to the . . . War of the Revolution."

New York Historical Society. *Muster and Pay Rolls of the War of the Revolution, 1775-1783.* 2 vols. Collections of the New York Historical Society for the Year 1914-15. New York: the society, 1916.

Thomas, William S. *The Society of the Cincinnati in the State of New York; Its History, Aims and Requirements for Membership.* New York: the society, 1921.

Whittemore, Henry. *The Heroes of the American Revolution and Their Descendants: Battle of Long Island.* New York: Heroes of the Revolution Publishing Co., 1897.

Wright, Albert H. *The Sullivan Expedition of 1779: The Losses.* New York Historical Studies. Ithaca: 1943 (?).

_____. *The Sullivan Expedition of 1779; the Regimental Rosters of Men.* Ithaca: 1943. Contains over 5,800 names with rank.

1784-1815 (War of 1812)

Council of Appointment of the State of New York. *Military Minutes of the Council of Appointment of the State of New York, 1783-1821.* Compiled and edited by Hugh Hastings, State Historian. Henry Harmon Noble, Chief Clerk. 4 vols. Albany: state printer, 1901-02.

New York (state). Adjutant General's office. *Index of Awards on Claims of the Soldiers of the War of 1812, as Audited and Allowed by the Adjutant and Inspector Generals, Pursuant to Chapter 176, of the Laws of 1859.* Albany: 1860. Reprint with added introduction by Francis J. Higgins. Baltimore: Genealogical Publishing Co., 1969. Applicants listed alphabetically with number, place of residence, and amount allowed for military clothing and equipment "which were depreciated, worn out, lost and destroyed in said service for which he had not received payment."

1816-60 (Mexican War)

Clark, Francis D. *The First Regiment of New York Volunteers.* [Mexican War]. New York: G.S. Evans & Co., 1882.

The New York Volunteers in California. "With Stevenson to California" by James Lynch. "Stevenson's Regiment in California" by Francis Clark. Glorieta, N.M.: Rio Grande Press, 1970. Reprint of works published in 1896 and 1882 respectively.

New York (State) Adjutant General's Office. *Official Register of the National Guard, S.N.Y.* Albany (?), 1853-(?). For the period 1853 to 1944, each register includes a list and directory of militia personnel.

1861-65 (Civil War)

Dilts, Bryan L., comp. *1890 New York Census Index of Civil War Veterans or Their Widows.* Salt Lake City: Index Pub., 1984.

Military Order of the Loyal Legion of the United States. New York Commandery. *Register of the Commandery of the State of New York From 17th January, 1866, to 1st January, 1888.* N.p., 1888 (?).

New York. Adjutant General. *Registers of New York Regiments in the War of the Rebellion.* 43 vols. Albany: 1894-1906. Contains annotated listings for all soldiers, including enlisted men.

New York Adjutant General's Office. *A Record of the Commissioned Officers, Non-commissioned Officers and Privates, of the Regiments Which Were Organized in the State of New York. . . .* 8 vols. Albany: Comstock & Cassidy, printers, 1864-68.

New York. Board of Managers of the Soldiers' Depot. *Report of the Board of Managers of the New York State Soldiers' Depot, and of the Fund for the Relief of Sick, Wounded, Furloughed and Discharged Soldiers.* Albany: Van Benthuysen's Steam

Printing House, 1864. A list of New York soldiers whose graves were identified at Antietam in August 1863, who were killed 17 September 1862, or who died of wounds and were subsequently buried near the battlefield. Includes name, regiment, rank, place of burial.

Phisterer, Frederick, comp. *New York in the War of the Rebellion, 1861–1865.* 6 vols. Albany, 1890. Reprint. Albany: state printers, 1912. Service records by regiment.

Townsend, Thomas S. *Heroes of the Empire State in the War of Rebellion.* New York: Lowell & Co., 1889.

1866–99 (Spanish-American War)

National Guard Association of the State of New York. *Annual Convention.* Buffalo, n.d. For the period 1885 to 1915, each annual report includes a roll of participants with name, rank, and unit.

Naval and Military Order of the Spanish-American Wars: New York Roster of Members. The order, 1904.

New York. Adjutant General's Office. *New York in the Spanish-American War, 1898. . . .* 3 vols. Albany: 1902.

_____. *Index to New York in the Spanish-American War.* Albany: J.B. Lyon Co., 1914.

Saldana, Richard H. *Index to the New York Spanish-American War Veterans, 1898.* 2 vols. North Salt Lake City: AISI Publishers, 1987. A reprint with an index of the original report of the New York Adjutant General's Office.

1917–18 (World War I)

Century Association, New York. *Record of Service Rendered in the Great War.* New York: DeVinne Press, 1920.

New York. Adjutant General's Office. *Report of the Adjutant-General's Department. . . .* Albany: 1918.

_____. *Roll of Honor. Citizens of the State of New York Who Died While in the Service of the United States During the World War.* Albany: J.B. Lyon Co., 1922.

1963–75 (Vietnam War)

Murphy, Edward F. *Vietnam Medal of Honor Heroes.* New York: Ballantine Books, 1987.

North Carolina

1497	English explorer John Cabot established the English claim to the Carolinas.
1653	The first permanent colony was established by English settlers from Virginia.
1663	Charles II awarded eight proprietary claims in the Carolinas to English lords who had helped him gain his throne during the Restoration.
1729	The Carolina proprietors sold their claims to James II, ending the proprietary period.
1729	North and South Carolina became separate royal colonies.
1760–61	Cherokee Indians resisted white encroachment. (See Cherokee Uprising in the appendix.)
1771	The Regulators protested unfair taxation practices. (See War of Regulators in the appendix.)
1775	North Carolina became the first colony to declare independence from England.
1780–81	Lord Cornwallis' army was driven out of North Carolina. (See American Revolution in the appendix.)
1789	North Carolina became one of the original thirteen states.
1861	North Carolina seceded from the Union. Though not ardently secessionist, North Carolina contributed 125,000 soldiers to the Confederate effort, more than any other state. (See American Civil War in the appendix.)
1868	North Carolina was readmitted to statehood.

NORTH CAROLINA STATE ARCHIVES

109 East Jones Street
Raleigh, North Carolina 27601-2807
(919) 733-3952

Finding Aids

A series of notebooks titled *State Agencies* is available on open shelves near the reference desk. One of the series is labeled

Military Collections, and the others are labeled according to the state agencies that provided the records. Military records are found in the offices of the adjutant general, auditor, treasurer and comptroller, secretary of state, veterans' commission, and the Gettysburg Memorial Commission. *Military Collections* cites records according to the following categories:

Spanish invasion (1742-48)

Frontier scouts and Indian wars (1758-85)

War of the Regulators (1778-79)

Troop returns (1747-1859)

War of the Revolution

Cumberland Battalion (1778-92)

War of 1812

Mexican War

War for Southern Independence (Civil War)

World War I

World War II

North Carolina's Revolutionary War Records of Primary Interest to Genealogists (a circular).

North Carolina Civil War Records: An Introduction to the Printed and Manuscript Sources. This book is available at the reference desk.

Records

General

NATIONAL ARCHIVES MICROFILM

The Negro in the Military Service of the United States, 1639-1886 (M858).

OTHER RECORDS

Troop Returns for Several Units. Arranged by county and thereunder by unit; separated into two categories: militia units and Continental Line.

North Carolina Soldiers' Home Visitors' Register, 1902-07.

Spanish Invasion (1747-48)

Muster Rolls, 1747-48.

List of Prisoners Sent on a Flag of Truce to St. Augustine, 1748.

Indian Wars (1747-98)

List of Men at Fort Moore, 1759.

Rolls of Scout Companies, 1759.

Claims for Bounty on Indian Scalps, 1764.

Payrolls of Militia Companies Protecting Fincastle Company Against Cherokee Indians, 1777.

Service Records and Final Settlements, 1766-92 (see below under American Revolution).

State Pensions to Invalids and Widows, 1766-92 (see below under American Revolution).

French and Indian War Pensions, 1766. Office of Treasurer and Comptroller.

French Prisoners, 1747. Office of Treasurer and Comptroller.

Payrolls, Vouchers, Certificates, Chickamauga Indian War, 1788-98.

War of the Regulators (1768-79)

Payrolls of the Granville Militia, Hillsborough, 1768.

Payrolls, Various Militia Units, 1771.

Enlistment Certificates, Various Militia Units.

Pay to Individuals Serving in the Expedition, 1771.

Pensions for Soldiers Disabled at Alamance; Orderly Books and Journals, 1771-79; 1785.

American Revolution (1775-83)

NATIONAL ARCHIVES MICROFILM

Compiled Service Records of Soldiers Who Served in the Military Army During the Revolutionary War (M881—rolls 781-786 pertain to North Carolina).

OTHER RECORDS

Revolutionary War Papers. A card index that contains data gathered from various sources. Cards provide individual's name, unit, and miscellaneous data.

Revolutionary War Final Settlements. A finding aid to this collection lists records in the office of the state treasurer and comptroller. Alphabetically lists names and counties of those who received final pay.

Service Records and Final Settlements, 1766-92. Boxes 13-24, Office of State Treasurer and Comptroller. An index of names is available at the reference desk.

State Pensions to Invalids and Widows, 1766-92. Boxes 25-30. A finding aid to this collection lists records in the office of the state treasurer and comptroller. Alphabetically lists names of pensioners. An index of names is available at the reference desk.

Declarations of Service to Accompany Applications for United States Pensions. Obtained from minutes of county courts. The finding aid *State Agencies (Military Collections)* alphabetically lists ninety-eight names, with county and date.

Orderly Books. These contain court-martial records.

List of North Carolina Officers and Accounts, Revolutionary War. Box 64, Office of State Treasurer and Comptroller.

North Carolina Revolutionary Army Accounts. Boxes 66.1 and 66.2.

North Carolina Muster Rolls, Revolutionary Army. Box 66.3.

North Carolina Continental Line, 1776-83. Box 66.4.

Cumberland Battalion (1786–92)

List of Troops, 1786.

Monthly Returns, 1787–89.

Payrolls (three companies), 1787–89.

Final settlements. The finding aid *State Agencies (Military Collections)* lists names alphabetically.

War of 1812 (1812–15)

MICROFILM RECORDS

(These records are contained in a drawer labeled Miscellaneous Records.)

Military Collection, War of 1812. Index to muster rolls and pay vouchers (two reels).

Military Collection, War of 1812. Military papers, pay and receipt rolls (two reels).

OTHER RECORDS

Muster Rolls, 1813–15. Detached militia units of North Carolina in the service of the United States. (See *Muster Rolls of the Soldiers of the War of 1812.*)

War of 1812 Vouchers. Boxes 75–86. Militia returns, orders of officers, 1811–13; 1813–17. Office of the Adjutant General. Alphabetically arranged.

Rosters of Generals and Field Officers of Militia, 1813–47; 1825–26; 1828. Office of the Adjutant General.

Mexican War (1846–48)

Muster Rolls, Discharges, Certificates of Service, 1847. (See *Roster of North Carolina Troops in the War with Mexico.*

List of First Volunteers, Arranged by County, 1846–47. Office of the Adjutant General.

Descriptive Roll of Regiments, 1847. Includes rosters and data concerning each soldier. Office of the Adjutant General.

Civil War—Union and Confederate (1861–65)

Guide to Military Organizations and Installations, North Carolina, 1861–65. This booklet is available at the reference desk. It lists both the named and numbered designations of Union and Confederate military units as well as camps, posts, and stations. Use of this guide enables the researcher to cross-reference a named unit to its official numbered designation.

NATIONAL ARCHIVES MICROFILM

Index to Compiled Service Records of Confederate Soldiers Who Served in Organizations From the State of North Carolina (M230).

Compiled Service Records of Confederate Soldiers Who Served in Organizations From the State of North Carolina (M270).

OTHER RECORDS

Confederate Gravestone Records. This card index (drawers 205–212) refers to volume and page numbers of books published by the United Daughters of the Confederacy. These cards provide name, location of grave and cemetery, and date.

Map of Gettysburg Battleground. This map shows locations of graves of North Carolina soldiers (published by the Gettysburg Memorial Commission).

Index to Military Units Cited in the finding aid *State Agencies (Military Collections)*. Units are grouped as follows:

> Numbered units, Confederate
>
> Named units, Confederate
>
> Other states, Confederate
>
> Union units
>
> Personal names

Regimental and Unit Records, Including Muster Rolls (boxes 47–63).

Payrolls (box 30).

Military Records in Microfilmed "Military Collection." One reel labeled Miscellaneous Records (near the microfilmed newspapers of the state) includes records of conscription, exemptions, free Negroes, and deserters. Another reel includes lists of the dead, wounded, and missing.

Bounty Payrolls, Arranged by County and Unit (boxes 9–16). Disabled veterans' claims and compensation to artificial limb companies. Includes names of those who received prostheses or cash in lieu of a prosthesis (box 41).

Claims for Bounty Pay and Allowance Due Deceased Officers and Soldiers of North Carolina (boxes 37–40).

Register of Troops of North Carolina, 1861. Office of the Adjutant General.

Register [officers] of North Carolina troops, 1861–64; 1861–65. Office of the Adjutant General.

Roster [officers] of North Carolina Militia, 1861–62; 1864. Ledger, 1861–63. Accounts indexed, 1861–65. Office of the Adjutant General.

Roll of Honor, 1861–63 (incomplete). Nine volumes. Gives name, rank, county of residence, enlistment, age, whether volunteer or conscript, and date of death or discharge. Material is also available on microfilm and in a scrapbook.

CONFEDERATE PENSIONS

Two indexes containing the names of those who applied for pensions are available at the reference desk. One notebook contains names of those who filed under the original 1885 pension law, and the other contains names of those who filed under the revised laws of 1901 or later. They contain the names of approximately 45,000 veterans and widows. After a desired name is located in one of these indexes, a staff member will procure the original application for inspection. (None have been microfilmed.)

Also available are annual reports filed by the counties. These provide names of those still on the pension rolls. (The county must be specified.) Other lists of pensions, including those filed in later years, may be found in the finding aid *North Carolina Civil War Records: An Introduction to the Printed and Manuscript Sources.*

Confederate Soldiers' Home Records. (Includes the home at Raleigh and the home for African-American veterans at Goldsboro).

Confederate Soldiers' Home Roll Book, 1890–1911. Office of the Auditor (no. 7.3).

Confederate Soldiers' Home Inmate Records, 1911–36. Questionnaires completed by the residents. Names of next of kin are often given. Office of the Auditor (no. 7.5).

Confederate Soldiers' Home Inmate Register, 1890–1917. Office of the Auditor (no. 7.4).

Petitions for a Pardon. This archives has the photostated applications of nearly two thousand North Carolinians who applied for pardons after the Civil War. This is a portion of the Amnesty Papers, which are on microfilm at the National Archives. The applications are cited CWC 1–18, and a card index is available.

Spanish-American War (1898–99)

Roster of North Carolina Volunteers in the Spanish-American War. Available on microfilm (Z 2.31) or in the original (see citation below under Published Sources—North Carolina). Not indexed.

Spanish-American War Fund, 1907–20. Box 121.B.

World War I (1917–18 and subsequent years)

Dead and Wounded, World War I. A card index (drawers 12, 13).

Certificates of Service, Enlisted Men, North Carolina National Guard. Issued 1917 and 1918. Also, similar certificates for commissioned officers.

Officers of the North Carolina National Guard, 1919–24; 1921–40.

National Guard Rosters, 1877–1940.

World War I Papers, 1903–33:

> County War Records and Private Papers
>
> North Carolina Military Organizations, With Rosters
>
> Compiled Service Records
>
> Roll of Honor
>
> World War I Loan Fund, 1927–38; 1938–42 (boxes 122, 123)

World War II (1941–45)

Family History Papers Prepared by Army Specialized Training Program (ASTP).

Enlisted Men of the National Guard Commissioned and Inducted Into Active Federal Service, 1940–44.

North Carolina Selective Service Registration Index, 1940–53. Index cards arranged alphabetically. Also contains names of "non-registrants." Microfilm (170 reels).

Naval Papers. A roster of officers and men of the USS *North Carolina*, with photographs.

Korean War (1950–53)

Korean War Veterans. State Veterans' Commission records. Names arranged by county.

Manuscripts

See Barbara T. Caine with Ellen Z. McGrew and Charles E. Morris: *Guide to Private Manuscript Collections in the North Carolina State Archives.* 3rd rev. ed. (Raleigh: North Carolina Department of Cultural Resources, Division of Archives and History, 1981).

UNIVERSITY OF NORTH CAROLINA

Wilson Library
CB No. 3926
Chapel Hill, North Carolina 27514-8890
(919) 962-1345

The Southern Historical Collection at the University of North Carolina's Wilson Library has a large manuscript collection. Many of these documents pertain to military service. See Susan Sokol Blosser and Clyde Norman Wilson, Jr., *The Southern Historical Collection: A Guide to Manuscripts.* (Chapel Hill: the library, 1970).

DUKE UNIVERSITY

P.O. Box 90185
Special Collections Library
Durham, North Carolina 27708-0185
(919) 660-5822

The Special Collections Library has a large manuscript collection. Many of these documents pertain to military service. Especially helpful may be family letters of the Civil War era. See Richard C. Davis and Linda Angle Miller, eds., *Guide to the Catalogued Collections in the Manuscript Department of the William R. Perkins Library, Duke University* (Santa Barbara, Calif.: Clio Books, 1980).

PUBLISHED SOURCES—NORTH CAROLINA

1775-83 (American Revolution)

Bailey, James D. *Commanders at King's Mountain.* Gaffney, S.C.: E.H. De Camp, 1926. Reprint. Greenville, S.C.: A. Press, 1980. Contains biographical information for officers involved in the battle.

Battey, George M. *The Tennessee Bee-Hives; or Early (1778–1791) North Carolina Land Grants in the Volunteer State, Being an Index with Some 3100 Names of Revolutionary Soldiers and Settlers Who Participated in the Distribution of More Than 5,000,000 Acres of Land.* Typescript. Washington, D.C.: 1949.

Burgner, Goldene F., comp. *North Carolina Land Grants in Tennessee, 1778–1791.* Revised edition of same title compiled by Betty Goff Cook Cartwright and Lillian Johnson Gardiner. Southern Historical Press, 1981.

Camin, Betty J. *North Carolina Revolutionary War Pension Applications.* 3 vols. Raleigh: Southern Historical Press, 1981.

Cox, William E. *Battle of King's Mountain Participants, October 7, 1780.* Eastern National Park and Monument Association, 1972. Reprint. Abingdon, Va.: Historical Society of Washington County, 1972. Approximately two thousand soldiers from North and South Carolina, Kentucky, Tennessee, and Virginia fought in this battle, which took place in western North Carolina.

Crow, Jeffrey J. *The Black Experience in Revolutionary North Carolina.* North Carolina Bicentennial Pamphlet Series, vol. 16. Raleigh: North Carolina Department of Cultural Resources, Division of Archives & History, 1977. An appendix lists fifty-six men who were in military service during the American Revolution; includes comments.

Daughters of the American Revolution. North Carolina. *Roster of Soldiers From North Carolina in the American Revolution: With an Appendix Containing a Collection of Miscellaneous Papers.* Durham: the society, 1932. Reprint. Baltimore: Genealogical Publishing Co., 1967. Roster includes name, rank, unit, date enlisted, and casualties.

Davis, Charles L. *A Brief History of the North Carolina Troops of the Continental Establishment in the War of the Revolution: With a Register of Officers of the Same; Also a Sketch of the North Carolina Society of the Cincinnati.* Philadelphia: 1896.

Fitch, William E. *Some Neglected History of North Carolina, Being an Account of the Revolution of the Regulators and of the Battle of Alamance, the First Battle of the American Revolution.* New York, 1905. Reprint. New York: Fitch, 1914.

Haun, Weynette P. *North Carolina Revolutionary Army Accounts: Secretary of State, Treasurer's and Comptroller's Papers.* 5 vols. 2nd ed. Durham: the author, 1988–90.

Lazenby, Mary E., comp. *Catawba Frontier, 1775–1781: Memories of Pensioners.* Washington, D.C.: 1950.

Moore, John W. *History of North Carolina; From the Earliest Discoveries to the Present Time.* 2 vols. Raleigh: A. Williams & Co., 1880.

North Carolina. *The State Records of North Carolina.* 26 vols. Edited by Walter Clark. Raleigh: P.M. Hale, 1886–1907. Vols. 16 and 17 include thousands of names from payrolls, lists of officers, prisoners, etc.

Rouse, J.K. *Another Revolutionary War Hero Dies.* Kannapolis: privately printed, 1978. Obituaries from North Carolina newspapers.

Russel, Phillips. *North Carolina in the Revolutionary War.* Charlotte (?): Heritage Printers, 1965 (?). Contains a register of Continental Army officers, pages 34–74.

Schenck, David. *North Carolina, 1780–81; Being a History of the Invasion of the Carolinas by the British Army Under Lord Cornwallis in 1780–81, With Particular Design of Showing the Part Borne by North Carolina in That Struggle for Liberty . . . .* North Carolina Heritage Series, no. 6. Raleigh: Edwards & Broughton, 1889. Reprint. Spartanburg, S.C.: The Reprint Co., 1967. Lists almost 1,000 officers of the Continental Line with dates of commission.

White, Katherine K. *The King's Mountain Men: The Story of the Battle, With Sketches of the American Soldiers Who Took Part.* Dayton, Va.: 1924. Reprint. Baltimore: Genealogical Publishing Co., 1966. Contains biographical sketches of approximately 350 participants.

1784-1815 (War of 1812)

North Carolina. *County Index to Muster Rolls of the Soldiers of the War of 1812.* Winston-Salem Printing Co., 1926.

North Carolina. Adjutant General's Department. *Muster Rolls of the Soldiers of the War of 1812 Detached From the Militia of North Carolina in 1812 and 1814.* Winston-Salem: Barber Printing Co., 1826. Reprint. Raleigh: C.C. Raboteau, 1851. Reprint with added index. Baltimore: Genealogical Publishing Co., 1976.

Simpson, Kenrick N. *Index to the Manuscript Rolls of the War of 1812.* The author, 1980. Based on the state adjutant general's records.

1816-60 (Post-War of 1812)

North Carolina Genealogical Society. *Abstracts of Letters of Resignations of Militia Officers in North Carolina, 1779–1840.* Compiled by Timothy Kearney. Raleigh: the society, 1992.

1861-65 (Civil War)

Almasy, Sandra Lee. *North Carolina, 1890 Civil War Veterans Census. . . .* Joliet, Ill.: Kensington Glen Publishing, 1990. Includes indexes.

Birdsong, James C. *Brief Sketches of the North Carolina State Troops.* Raleigh: Josephus Daniels, 1894.

Clark, Walter. *Histories of the Several Regiments and Battalions From North Carolina in the Great War.* 5 vols. Raleigh: state of North Carolina, 1901.

Cook, Gerald W. *The Last Tarheel Militia, 1861–1865. . . .* Winston-Salem: the author, 1987. Pages 67–147 list "Northwest North Carolina Militia Officers" with rank and date of commission; pages 148–82 list officers by county and regiment.

Manarin, Louis H., comp. *North Carolina Troops, 1861–1865: A Roster.* 12 vols. to date. Raleigh: North Carolina Department of Archives and History, 1968–.

North Carolina. State Auditor. *Applications for Confederate Soldiers' and Widows' Pensions in North Carolina, 1885–1953.* Raleigh: the department, 1958.

North Carolina. Department of Archives and History. *Applications for Confederate Pensions After 1901.* 4 vols. Raleigh: the department, 1858.

North Carolina. General Assembly. *Roster of North Carolina Troops in the War Between the States.* 4 vols. Raleigh: Edwards, Broughton & Co., 1882. Also see *Index to John W. Moore's Roster of North Carolina Troops in the War Between the States.* Microfilm; 2 reels. Compiled by WPA Historical Records Survey. Raleigh: North Carolina Department of Archives and History, 1958.

Pompey, Sherman L. *The Confederate Military Prison and the National Cemetary (sic) at Salisbury, North Carolina: A Study Into the History and Men That Were Interned at Salisbury During the Civil War With Military Data on Some of These Men.* Florence, Oreg.: the author, 1981.

United Daughters of the Confederacy. North Carolina Division. Pamlico Chapter, No. 43, Washington. *The Confederate Reveille, Memorial Edition.* Raleigh: Edwards & Broughton, 1898. Includes biographical sketches of some officers.

1866–99 (Spanish-American War)

North Carolina. Adjutant General's Department. *Roster of the North Carolina Volunteers in the Spanish-American War, 1898–1899.* Raleigh: Edwards & Broughton and E.M. Uzzell, 1900.

1900–18 (World War I)

Graham, J.R. *Tar-Heel War Record (In the Great World War.)* Charlotte: World War Publishing Co., n.d. Includes biographical statements and photographs of soldiers and sailors from North Carolina.

North Carolina. Adjutant General's Department. *Annual Reports, 1917–1918.* Raleigh: Edwards & Broughton, 1920.

North Dakota

1738	French explorer Pierre de la Verendrye established the French claim to North Dakota.
1803	North Dakota passed to the United States by the Louisiana Purchase.
1804–06	American explorers Lewis and Clark traveled through North Dakota.
1812	English and American fur traders established the first settlements in North Dakota.
1818	British claims to part of North Dakota were abandoned by treaty with the United States.
1849	The first large numbers of American settlers began arriving after the creation of Minnesota Territory.
1861	The Dakota Territory was organized.
1867–68	Treaties with the Sioux Indians ended several years of warfare and led to increased immigration. (See Sioux and Cheyenne Wars in the appendix.)
1889	North Dakota became a state.

STATE HISTORICAL SOCIETY OF NORTH DAKOTA

State Archives and Historical Research Library
612 East Boulevard Avenue
Bismarck, North Dakota 58505
(701) 224-2668

Records

Civil War–Union (1861–65)
NATIONAL ARCHIVES MICROFILM

Index to Compiled Service Records of Volunteer Union Soldiers Who Served in Organizations From the Territory of Dakota (M536).

PUBLISHED SOURCES—NORTH DAKOTA

General

Cooper, Jerry. *Citizens as Soldiers: A History of the North Dakota National Guard.* Fargo: North Dakota Institute for Regional Studies, 1986.

Cropp, Richard. *The Coyotes.* Mitchell: Educator Supply Co., 1962. A history of the North Dakota Militia and National Guard—War of 1812 through World War II. Some lists of officers.

1898-99 (Spanish-American War)

Lounsberry, Clement A. *Early History of North Dakota.* Washington, D.C.: Liberty Press, 1919.

1917-18 (World War I)

North Dakota. Adjutant General's Office. *Roster of Men and Women From the State of North Dakota in the World War, 1917–1918.* 4 vols. Bismarck: 1931.

North Dakota State Historical Society. *North Dakota Soldiers, Sailors and Marines in World War I, 1917–1918.* 4 vols. Bismarck: the society, 1931.

World War II (1941-45)

North Dakota. Adjutant General's Office. *Register of North Dakota Veterans, World War II, 1941–45, and Korean Conflict, 1950–53.* Bismarck: 1968.

Ohio

1667	The French explorer La Salle established the French claim to Ohio.
1747	British colonists from Virginia began to move into the Ohio River Valley.
1763	The Treaty of Paris which ended the French and Indian War transferred Ohio to British control. (See French and Indian War in the appendix.)
1783	The Treaty of Paris which ended the American Revolution transferred Ohio to the United States. (See American Revolution in the appendix.)

1787	Ohio became a part of the Northwest Territory.
1799	Ohio became a territory.
1803	Ohio became a state.
1812-14	Ohio was a major theater of the War of 1812, the scene of Oliver Hazard Perry's Lake Erie victories and William Henry Harrison's invasion of Canada. (See War of 1812 in the appendix.)
1861-65	Ohio contributed 313,180 soldiers to the Union, more than any other western state. (See American Civil War in the appendix.)

• •

OHIO HISTORICAL SOCIETY

Archives-Library Division
1982 Velma Avenue
Columbus, Ohio 43211
(614) 297-2510

The Ohio Historical Society, with financial assistance from the state of Ohio, serves as the state archives and is the primary repository of historical and genealogical material pertaining to the state. The society is located in the Ohio History Center building, near Interstate 71 at 17th Avenue, north of Columbus. The archives-library reading room is located on the building's first floor; the records are on the second floor. The Ohio Historical Society at Columbus serves as coordinator of the state's eight regional American History Research Centers and also serves as one of the centers. The county records at this center are available in a separate section of the archives-library reading room.

The Ohio State Library, 65 Front Street, downtown Columbus, has no military manuscripts or original military documents.

American History Research Centers

A network of American History Research Centers was established in Ohio in 1970 to aid in the collection, preservation, and accessibility of research materials related to the state's history. The network is divided into eight geographical areas, each being a repository of records for the surrounding counties. A map showing the location and counties covered by each center is available upon request from any of the centers. The scope of the military records found in the regional centers is restricted primarily to county militia rolls, discharge records, bounty records, burial records, and financial relief payments made to veterans, but a few other miscellaneous military records may be included. Some, but not all, of the regional centers have prepared guides to their holdings. The Ohio Historical Society at Columbus does not have a complete set of such regional guides, but it does have one for the Bowling Green center: *Guide to Local Government Records, Bowling Green Center No. 2, 1988*. The Columbus center plans to add similar guides for other regional centers as they become available. For further information concerning other regional holdings, contact the regional centers, which are listed below.

Archives Services, Pierce Library, University of Akron, Akron, Ohio 44325-1750.

Center for Archival Collections, Bowling Green State University, Bowling Green, Ohio 43403-0175.

Archives and Rare Book Department, Blegen Library, University of Cincinnati, Cincinnati, Ohio 45211-0113.

Archives-Library Division, Ohio Historical Society, 1982 Velma Avenue, Columbus, Ohio 43211-2497.

Archives and Special Collections, Alden Library, Ohio University, Athens, Ohio 45701-2978.

Western Reserve Historical Society, 10825 East Boulevard, Cleveland, Ohio 44106-1788.

Archives and Special Collections, Wright State University, Dayton, Ohio 45435-0001.

Youngstown Historical Center of Industry and Labor, P.O. Box 533, 151 West Wood Street, Youngstown, Ohio 44501.

National Guard Records

Military service records of all servicemen from Ohio who enlisted during World War I, World War II, the Korean War, and the Vietnam War (those who applied for an Ohio bonus for Vietnam War veterans), and all Ohio National Guard enlistment records since 1903, are located at the Division of Veterans Affairs, Room 1825, 30 East Broad Street, Columbus, Ohio 43266-0422. It is recommended that researchers telephone before visiting: (614) 446-5453. Access to recent personnel records may be restricted in order to comply with the federal Privacy Act.

Finding Aids

Adjutant General, Department of The. This aid lists military holdings. Before requesting records shown in this finding aid, researchers should consult the files that contain folders with lists and inventories of the collections' contents. One such folder is titled Adjutant General, Civil War, Ohio Military Agency. Another is titled Adjutant General, Personnel Records.

State Archives—Special Boards and Commissions. This finding aid lists records of the War History Commission and its collections (pertaining primarily to the Thirty-seventh Division in

the United States, New Zealand, and Fiji Islands ca. 1940-45).

State Archives—Institutions. This finding aid lists records from the Soldiers' and Sailors' Home in Ohio.

General Indexes

A card catalog of the library holdings, many of which contain published lists and registers in addition to historical information, contains the following entries, among others (see U.S. History with subheadings).

American Loyalists

Colonial Period

King William's War, King George's War, Queen Anne's War, French and Indian War, Revolution (1775–83)

War of 1812, War With Algeria (1815), Black Hawk War (1832), War with Mexico (1845–58)

Civil War (biography, officers, naval operations, personal narratives, pictorial works, prisoners and prisons, regimental histories)

War of 1898 (Spanish-American), regimental histories, registers

Military (bases, heroes)

Military Order of the Loyal Legion (Ohio Commandery)

Manuscript Collections

A card catalog enables a search by name of war or name of collection. Look under headings: Ohio artillery, Ohio cavalry, Ohio infantry.

A folder available at the reference desk contains lists and inventories of the Civil War Collection. This collection consists of forty-six individual collections on twenty-six reels of microfilm (MIC 17). These recount the experiences of both Union and Confederate soldiers.

Adjutant General Records

A card catalog lists the holdings gathered by this office. See also the finding aid *Adjutant General, Department of the* (cited above).

Records

The Ohio Historical Society has no National Archives microfilm or military records. Examples of its own military collections are listed below. For others, consult the above-cited finding aids and general indexes. Where folders containing inventories are available, they are so noted here.

General

Certificates of Election of Militia Officers, 1803–1857. These give name, date, unit, location of regiment.

Ohio Militia Records, 1805–48.

Soldiers' Claims (muster rolls by county). (See inventory.)

Letters From Paroled Prisoners (usually addressed to the governor) Regarding Pay and Subsistence Claims. (See inventory.)

Abstracts of Soldiers' Allotments From the Counties and Funds Issued to Soldiers for Their Families' Support. Included are name, military unit, and name of recipient of funds. (See inventory.)

Graves Registration Records (microfilm GR 1346–3252). These are alphabetically arranged cards: American Revolution to World War I, ca. 1810 through 1957. They provide name, residence, place and date of death, cause of death, place of burial, place and date of birth, name and location of cemetery, name and address of relatives, and military history.

Commissioned Officers' Rosters, by Company, 1875–1917 (eight volumes). These lists name the unit, date it was organized, location, names of officers, and related data. Arranged by company.

Record of Commissioned Officers, 1903–39 (three volumes). Provides names, rank, unit. Arranged alphabetically or indexed.

Regimental Rosters, 1863; 1870–1904 (fifty-six volumes). These contain an entry for each guardsman, with descriptive and personal data.

Ohio Soldiers' and Sailors' Home. Admission Record, 1888–1919 (microfilm GR 3397–3440); *1919–61* (microfilm GR 3862–3869).

Ohio Soldiers' and Sailors' Home. General Record, 1888–1966 (microfilm, forty-three volumes). These contain one page for each individual giving military history, personal history, history while at the home, and general remarks. Arranged chronologically by date of admission. (An index is available in series 1141.)

Ohio Soldiers' and Sailors' Home. Death Book, 1888–1963 (microfilm series 1111). Gives name, registry number, unit, age, date admitted, date and cause of death, where buried, and grave number. Arranged by date of death.

Veterans' Orphans' Home. Hospital Register, 1871–1902 (two volumes; series 1492). Provides name of patient, parents' names, and related data.

American Revolution (1775–83)

Tax Duplicates By County, 1800–35 (microfilm GR 2336). Contains names of proprietors in the Virginia Military District. Arranged alphabetically.

Official Roster of Soldiers of the American Revolution Buried in Ohio (microfilm FLM 288–289).Compiled by Daughters of the American Revolution, 1929.

Official Roster, Soldiers and Sailors of the American Revolution From Ohio (microfilm GR 6767).

War of 1812 (1812–15)

Roster of Ohio Soldiers in War of 1812 (microfilm GR 3358). (See inventory.)

Soldiers From Ohio in War of 1812. Index (microfilm GR 6769–70).

Proceedings of Courts-martial, 1807–15. Arranged chronologically. Provides names of defendants, accuser(s), court personnel.

Rank and Pay Receipt Rolls, 1807–15. Given are name, rank, date of commission or enlistment, unit, amount paid, discharge date.

Record of First Regiment, First Brigade, Third Division, Ohio Militia, 1810–1914. Arranged chronologically.

Mexican War (1846–48)

Index to Mexican War Rosters, 1845 (microfilm GR 6768).

Descriptive Book, Mexican War Veterans, ca. 1870–1900 (one volume). Given are name, rank, unit, military history, postwar employment. Refers to personnel of First–Fifth Ohio Volunteer Infantry regiments and Fifteenth U.S. Infantry.

Ohio War Records, War With Mexico, 1846–48 (one volume). Name, rank, age, enrollment data, military history.

Civil War–Union (1861–65)

Roster of Ohio Soldiers, 1861–66 (with index). (See inventory).

Record of Military Units. Name, rank, age, military history (see inventory, which contains a list of the units).

Records of Ohio Volunteer Regiments, 1861–65 (thirty-one volumes). Name, rank, age, enrollment data, and whether died, discharged, promoted, or transferred.

Ohio War Records, 1861–65 (forty-five volumes). Compiled by the Ohio adjutant general from Civil War muster rolls. Arranged numerically by regiment and thereunder alphabetically by company. Gives data for each soldier.

Muster-in Roll Books, Ohio Volunteers, 1861–65 (179 volumes). Name, enrollment data, military history. Arranged by regiment and company. See also index of officers of regiments.

Volunteer Enlistment Papers, 1861–65. Individual enlistment papers. Name, place of birth, age, occupation, enlistment data. Also see reenlistment rolls, 1861–64; 1865.

Muster-in and Muster-out Rolls, 1861–65 (microfilm GR 1678–2061—385 reels). Arranged by military unit. Name, rank, age, enrollment data, bounty due, place of birth, physical description, occupation, deserters. Includes United States Colored Troops. (See inventory.)

Record of Appointments, Commissions and Promotions in Ohio Volunteer Regiments, 1861–65 (twenty-one volumes). Given are name, rank, date, residence, remarks. Arranged by regiment (see inventory).

Officers' Certificates of Qualification and Acceptance of Commissions, 1861–62. Lists camp name, date, name of officer, unit, and post office address. Arranged by regiment.

Roster of Officers, 1862–65 (one volume). Name, county, rank, date of commission and resignation.

Report of Examination of Candidates of Officers in Colored Regiments, 1863 (microfilm GR 3987).

Roster of Ohio Militia, 1863. Arranged by county (Knox through Wyandott only).

Record of Volunteer Militia Enrollment, 1863–66. Arranged by battalion. Name, rank, age, date of enlistment, residence, discharge date (see inventory).

Squirrel Hunters' Records, 1862–64 (original and microfilm GR 3986). Name, rank, unit residence, discharges of the volunteers. An alphabetical index (by county) of personnel in these units, prepared by Gerald M. Petty, is also available (cited below under Published Sources—Ohio).

Naval Records of Ohio Personnel, 1861–65. Name, place of birth, enlistment and military data. Arranged by enlisted men, officers, volunteers, and regular navy personnel.

List of Volunteer Surgeons, 1861–65. Names of surgeons and candidates for surgeon.

Muster-in Roll of Surgeons and Nurses, ca. 1861–62.

Deaths, Resignations and Transfers of Ohio Infantry Officers, 1861–63. An index is also available.

Record of Militia Drafted in 1862. Name, place, regiment, name of substitute, remarks. Arranged by county.

Descriptive Rolls of Drafted Men at Various Camps: Camp Dennison, Cincinnati; Camp Zanesville (see inventory).

Rolls of Drafted Men and Substitutes, by County, 1862.

Descriptive Rolls, Muster Rolls, and Returns: Miscellaneous Ohio Military Units. See inventories for individual units. Specify number or name of unit.

Record of Burials at Greenwood National Cemetery and Camp Chase Cemetery, 1863–65 (microfilm GR 3475).

Dead Book of General Hospital, Columbus, Ohio, 1863 (one volume and microfilm GR 3987). Name, regiment, date of admission, death and burial, where buried, name of disease or type of injury, address, and disposition of soldier's effects. Arranged chronologically.

Index to Prisoners at Andersonville, Ga., and Salisbury, N.C., 1864–65 (one volume and microfilm GR 3674). Name, discharge, transfer or death, date captured, residence or place of capture, how released. Arranged by prisoner number.

Military Prison Record, Camp Chase and Johnson's Island, 1861–62 (one volume and microfilm GR 3674).

Book of the Confederate Dead, 1862–65 (one volume and microfilm GR 3674). Given are name, date of death, rank, unit, and remarks.

Book of the Union Dead, 1861–65 (one volume and microfilm GR 4031). Contains records for the following cemeteries: Spring Grove, Camp Dennison, Green Lawn, North Cemetery (Columbus), West Side Cemetery (Cleveland), Johnson's Island, City Cemetery (Gallipolis), Camp Thomas. Name, rank, unit, date of death, grave number, and, occasionally, cause of death and remarks. Arranged by cemetery and thereunder chronologically.

List of Union Troops Buried in the National Cemetery, 1863–65. Arranged by state.

Records of Ohio Soldiers Buried in Antietam and Andersonville Cemeteries, 1862–65.

Index to Casualties, ca. 1862 (fourteen volumes). Gives name and page number of volumes. Arranged alphabetically by name of soldier.

Roll of Deserters From Ohio Regiments, 1861–65. Includes name, unit, residence, where enlisted, where and when deserted. Alphabetical and by regiment.

Index to Record of Discharge Papers Sent to Veterans of the Civil War, 1886–88 (one volume). Name, unit, discharge date, address. Arranged alphabetically.

Record of Ohio Civil War Service Medals Sent, 1894–1912 (two volumes). Name, date medal was delivered, place medal was sent. Arranged by regiment.

Veterans' Claim Books, 1865–68 (two volumes). Name, rank, unit, date claim filed, data relative to claim processing. Arranged alphabetically.

Pension Record Book of Civil War veterans, 1866–99 (two volumes). Name, address, unit, data pertaining to claim, data concerning wife who made a claim. Not arranged.

Index to Pension Increase Applications for Civil War Veterans, 1922–26. Name, address, date of application, grant or rejection of claim. Arranged chronologically by date of claim.

Letterbook of the Adjutant General Regarding Soldiers' Claim, 1867–68. Correspondence to various persons. Indexed.

Civil War Bounty Claims Remittances, 1864–1911. Arranged alphabetically (see inventory).

Spanish-American War (1898-99)

Spanish-American War Muster Rolls, 1898 (microfilm GR 2062–2087). (See inventory. Also see a publication by the Ohio adjutant general: *The Official Roster of Ohio Soldiers in the War With Spain, 1898–1899*, cited below under Published Sources—Ohio.)

Officers' Roster of State Volunteers, 1898 (one volume). This roster lists the organizations mustered into state service as replacements for Ohio National Guard troops federalized during the Mexican War. Name, rank, place and date of discharge. See also "roster of state volunteers, 1898" for physical descriptions of the volunteers (twenty-four individuals).

Histories and Photographs of Infantry, Cavalry, and Field Artillery Troops, 1898-1967. Arranged by regiment.

Descriptive Book, Co. B., 77th Infantry, 1894-96 (one volume). Name, rank, physical descriptions, place of birth, residence, military dates. Indexed.

Spanish-American War Claims, 1898; 1901-02 (one volume and one folder). Correspondence arranged chronologically.

Abstract of the fifth installment of Spanish-American War claims, 1901 (one volume). Lists voucher data. Arranged by regiment.

Officers' Register, War With Spain, 1898 (one volume). Arranged numerically.

Payroll Roster, War With Spain, 1898 (twelve volumes). Lists names of payees. Arranged by regiment.

Squirrel Hunters' Claims, 1908. Correspondence. Arranged alphabetically by name of claimant.

Mexican Border Service (1916)

Register of Soldiers Receiving Medals for Mexican Border Service, 1918-21. Name, rank, unit, date medal issued, post office of veteran. Arranged alphabetically.

World War I (1917-18)

Compensation Fund: Record of Warrants Redeemed, 1925 (microfilm series 1059). Gives warrant number and amount.

Roster of Soldiers, Sailors and Marines of World War I (microfilm GR 6744-6765; GR 6766 contains corrections and a list of Ohioans buried in France).

Certificates of Service, 1917-20. Included are name, age, rank, unit, military history, and date certificate issued. Arranged alphabetically.

Record of World War I Claims, 1919-39 (indexed). Given are name, address, date enlisted and discharged, data pertaining to the claim.

World War I records are also available at the Division of Veterans Affairs, Thirty East Broad Street, Columbus, Ohio 43215.

World War II (1941-45)

Honor List, World War II. (microfilm GR 6767). Names of those missing—army, air force, navy, marines, coast guard.

World War II records are also available at the Division of Veterans Affairs, Columbus. (See above.)

Korean War (1950-53)

Korean War records are also available at the Division of Veterans Affairs, Columbus. (See above.)

Vietnam War (1963-75)

Vietnam Veterans' Bonus Commission Applications, 1975-80 (microfilm series 2540—101 reels).

Index to Above Applications. Microfilm series 2540 (twelve reels). Name, social security number, whether a bonus was paid in cash or as educational grant, claim number. (Reduced magnification of these cards when they were microfilmed requires use of a hand lens to read them.)

Vietnam Veterans' Bonus Commission Warrants Redeemed, 1975-80 (microfilm 2542—fourteen reels). Given are name, address, warrant number. (Use of a hand lens is required.)

Vietnam War records are also available at the Division of Veterans Affairs, Columbus (see above).

WESTERN RESERVE HISTORICAL SOCIETY

10825 East Boulevard
Cleveland, Ohio 44106
(216) 721-5722

The Western Reserve Historical Society Library has a large manuscripts collection that includes many documents pertaining to military service. See Kermit J. Pike's *A Guide to Major Manuscript Collections Accessioned and Processed by the Library of the Western Reserve Historical Society Since 1970* (Cleveland: the society, 1987).

PUBLISHED SOURCES—OHIO

1775-83 (American Revolution)

Ohio. Adjutant General's Office. *The Official Roster of the Soldiers of the American Revolution Buried in the State of Ohio.* 3 vols. Columbus: 1929-59. Reprint. Mineral Ridge: Trumbull County Chapter, Ohio Genealogical Society, 1974. 1 vol. (originally vols. 1 and 2). Contains biographical sketches.

Pabst, Anna Catherine (Smith). *Revolutionary War Records, National and Local, From Original Manuscripts.* Delaware, Ohio: the author, 1966.

Phillips, W. Louis. *Annotated Bibliography of Ohio Patriots: Revolutionary War and War of 1812.* Bowie, Md.: Heritage Books, 1985.

1784-1815 (War of 1812)

Diefenbach, Josephine C.Z., and Mr. and Mrs. C.O. Ross, comps. *Index to the Grave Records of Soldiers of the War of 1812 Buried in Ohio.* N.p., 1945.

Garner, Grace, comp. *Index to Roster of Ohio Soldiers: War of 1812*. Spokane, Wash.: Eastern Washington Genealogical Society, 1974.

Index to the Grave Records of Servicemen of the War of 1812: State of Ohio. Compiled 1988 by the Ohio Society, United States Daughters of 1812; edited by Phyllis Brown Miller. Brookville: the society, 1988. Compiled from grave location forms submitted by members of the society from 1939 through 1987. More than five hundred graves are listed.

National Society, United States Daughters of 1812. Ohio Society. *Index to the Grave Records of Servicemen of the War of 1812, State of Ohio*. Lancaster: the society, 1969.

Ohio. Adjutant General's Department. *Roster of Ohio Soldiers in the War of 1812*. Columbus: The Edward T. Miller Co., 1916. Reprint. Baltimore: Genealogical Publishing Co., 1968. Contains names listed by regiment and company.

Phillips, W. Louis. *Annotated Bibliography of Ohio Patriots. Revolutionary War and War of 1812*. Bowie, Md.: Heritage Books, 1985.

1816-60 (Mexican War)

Official Roster of the Soldiers of the State of Ohio in the War With Mexico, 1846-1848. Originally published 1897. Reprint. Columbus: 1916. Reprint. Mansfield: Ohio Genealogical Society, 1991.

1861-65 (Civil War)

Coulter, O.H., comp. *Roster of Ohio Soldiers Residing in Kansas*. Topeka, Kans.: Western Veteran, 1889 (?).

Howe, Henry. *Historical Collections of Ohio. . . .* 2 vols. Columbus: H. Howe & Son, 1890-91.

Military Order of the Loyal Legion of the United States. Ohio Commandery. *Register of the Commandery of Ohio, From July 15, 1904, to September 15, 1909*. N.p., 1909 (?). Includes other years.

Ohio. Adjutant General's Office. *Official Roster of the Soldiers of the State of Ohio in the War of the Rebellion, 1861-1866*. 10 vols. Akron and Cincinnati: The Werner Co., 1886-95. Also see *Alphabetical Index to Official Roster of the Soldiers of the State of Ohio in the War of the Rebellion*. Works Progress Administration, 1938.

Ohio Association of Union Ex-prisoners of War. *Constitution and By-laws of the Ohio Association of Union Ex-prisoners of War*. Cincinnati: T. Mason, printer, 1892. Includes names of members, regiment, date and place of capture, and period of imprisonment.

Ohio Boys in Dixie: the Adventures of Twenty-two Scouts Sent by Gen. O.M. Mitchell to Destroy a Railroad, With a Narrative of Their Barbarous Treatment by the Rebels, and Judge Holt's Report. New York: Miller & Mathews, 1863.

Petty, Gerald M. *Index of the Ohio Squirrel Hunters Roster*. Columbus: the author, 1984. The "Squirrel Hunters" were special volunteer militia called up to repel an anticipated Southern attack on Cincinnati in 1862.

Phillips, W. Louis. *Index to Ohio Pensioners of 1883*. Bowie, Md.: Heritage Books, 1987.

Poland, Charles A., comp. *Army Register of Ohio Volunteers in the Service of the United States, Comprising the General Staff of State, Staff of the Various Departments, List of Brigadiers, Roll of Field, Staff and Commissioned Officers of Each Regiment, Present Place of Service, Rank of Each Officer, Date of Commission, and a Complete List of Casualties, Compiled From Official Records in the Adjutant General's Office*. Columbus: State Journal Print Co., 1862.

Reid, Whitelaw. *Ohio in the War; Her Statesmen, Her Generals and Soldiers*. 2 vols. Cincinnatti, Ohio: Moore, Wilstach & Baldwin, 1868. Columbus: Eclectic, 1893. Contains biographical sketches and some portraits.

Stevens, A. Parsons (?). *The Military History of Ohio*. New York, 1885. Reprint. New York: H.H. Hardesty, 1887.

1866-99 (Spanish-American War)

Broglin, Jana S., comp. *Index to Official Roster of Ohio Soldiers in the War With Spain, 1898-1899*. Mansfield: Ohio Genealogical Society, 1991 (?).

Ohio. Adjutant General's Department. *Roster of Ohio Volunteers in the Service of the United States, War With Spain*. Columbus: state printer, 1898.

1900-75 (World War I through Vietnam War)

Ohio. Adjutant General's Department. *The Official Roster of Ohio Soldiers, Sailors and Marines in the World War, 1917-18. . . .* 23 vols. Columbus: F.J. Heer Printing Co., 1923-29 (?).

Ohio. Division of Solders' Claims. Veterans Affairs. *Vietnam Casualties, 1 January 1961 Thru 31 December 1970*. Columbus: 1971.

Oklahoma

1803   An unexplored part of the Louisiana territory, Oklahoma was transferred from France to the United States by the Louisiana Purchase.

1825-42   Oklahoma was set aside as the Indian Territory, where the Indians of the Southeast were sent when driven from their homeland.

1845	The Oklahoma panhandle was annexed when the Republic of Texas acquired statehood. (See War of Texas Independence in the appendix.)
1850	Congress purchased the Oklahoma panhandle but did not add it to the Indian Territory.
1866	Treaties with Indians in the Indian Territory reduced the size of their reservations, and whites began settling illegally in the Indian Territory.
1889	The first of several "runs" by white settlers into land not occupied by Indians occurred.
1890	Oklahoma was divided into Oklahoma Territory and Indian Territory.
1907	The two Oklahoma territories were admitted to statehood as the state of Oklahoma.

. . . .

DEPARTMENT OF LIBRARIES

Archives and Records Division
200 Northeast Eighteenth Street
Oklahoma City, Oklahoma 73105
(405) 521-2502

Records

Civil War—Confederate (1861-65)

Pension Files for Confederate Veterans or Widows Who Resided in Oklahoma Following the Civil War.

PUBLISHED SOURCES—OKLAHOMA

1861-65 (Civil War)

Foreman, Grant. *History of the Service and List of Individuals of the Five Civilized Tribes in the Confederate Army.* 2 vols. Oklahoma City: Oklahoma Historical Society, 1948.

Index to Applications for Pensions From the State of Oklahoma, Submitted by Confederate Soldiers, Sailors, and Their Widows. Oklahoma City: Oklahoma Genealogical Society Projects Committee, 1969. Includes 3,790 names.

Oklahoma. Board of Pension Commissioners. *Confederate Pension Applications for Soldiers and Sailors.* Oklahoma City: Archives and Records Division, 1975.

Oklahoma. *Civil War in Indian Territory, 1861–1865.* Oklahoma City: Oklahoma Historical Society, 19- (?).

Oregon

1778	British explorer Captain James Cook sailed along the Oregon coast.
1791	American explorer Captain Robert Gray sailed into the Columbia River and claimed the area for the United States.
1805-06	American explorers Lewis and Clark reached Oregon by an overland route from St. Louis and wintered at Ft. Clatsop.
1811	John Jacob Astor's Pacific Fur Company established a trading post but sold out to the British Northwest Company during the War of 1812. (See War of 1812 in the appendix.)
1818	The Anglo-American Convention agreed to temporary joint occupancy by British and Americans.
1829	Dr. John McLaughlin of the British Hudson's Bay Company founded Oregon City.
1834	The first American settlers, a group of Methodist missionaries led by Jason Lee, established a community on the site of modern Salem.
1846	The U.S.-Canadian border was established permanently at the forty-ninth parallel, placing Oregon within the United States.
1848	Oregon became a territory that included present-day Washington.
1855-58	The Yakima Wars occurred over white encroachment into Indian territory. (See Yakima Wars in the appendix.)
1859	Oregon became a state.

OREGON STATE ARCHIVES

800 Summer Street, NE
Salem, Oregon 97310
(503) 373-0701

Finding Aid

Records of the Military Department. This publication contains a history of the Military Department and describes its series of holdings, which date from 1847 to 1986. Other records are available at the Office of the Adjutant General, State of Oregon Military Department, 1776 Militia Way SE, Salem, Oregon 97309-5047; telephone: (503) 378-3980.

Records

To gain access to specific records that make up the following series, it may be necessary to provide the name or number of a military unit or to provide a pertinent time period.

General

NATIONAL ARCHIVES MICROFILM

Letters Received by the Office of the Adjutant General, 1822–1860 (M567—contains references to the Rogue River and Yakima Indian War; Oregon State Archives (OSA) film REFLIB0657).

Letters Sent by the Secretary of War Relating to Military Affairs, 1800–89 (M6; OSA film REFLIB0696).

Letters Received by the Secretary of War, Registered Series, 1801–60 (M221; OSA film REFLIB0695).

United States State Department, Appointment and Recommendation Nominating War Records and military Bounty Land Files, 1836–71; Relating to Oregon (RG 59; OSA film REFLIB0698).

United States Army, Continental Commands, Fort Oxford Morning Reports, 1853–56; Letter and Order Book, 1851–52; Orders and Letters Received, 1850–56 (RG 391, 393, 394; OSA film REFLIB0660).

Records of the Tenth Military Department, 1846–51 (M210; OSA film REFLIB0655).

United States Navy Department. *Expedition under Wilkes; Files, 1836–42* (M75; OSA film REFLIB0690).

United States Army: Fort Yamhill Morning Reports, 1858–60; Report of Guard, 1860; Record of Letters, 1865–66. Yale University Library, Coe Collection (OSA film REFLIB0661).

OREGON STATE ARCHIVES MICROFILM

Provisional and Territorial Records. Oregon Military Department (OSA film REFLIB0521).

OTHER RECORDS

Adjutant General's Correspondence, 1847–1986.
Company Officers Election Returns, 1856.
Delinquency Committee Docket, 1887–90.
Delinquency Court Docket, 1901–07.
Enlistment and Service Records, 1847–1920; 1930–77.
Governor's Correspondence, 1855–56.
Jackson, Oregon Volunteers Hospital Patient Record, 1855–56.
Military Court Case Records, 1884–1958.
Military Rolls, 1863–95.
Military Reserve Records, 1965–85.
Military Unit Records, 1917–48.
Morning Reports, 1855–1949.
Muster Rolls, 1850–1936.
Officers' Federal Service Records, 1887–1922.
Oregon Soldiers' Home Discipline Ledger, 1894–1927.
Oregon Soldiers' Home Patient Histories, 1894–1933.
Index to Oregon Soldiers' Home Patient Histories, 1894–1933.
Oregon Soldiers' Home Applications, 1894–1933.
Petitions, 1855–1906.
Service Medal Applications, 1905–16; 1929.
Surgeon General's Correspondence, 1856.
USS *Boston* Steam Log, 1912–16.
Unit Orders, 1927–68.
Unit Activity Reports, 1847–1929.
Unit Reorganization Records, 1863–1928.
Unit Rosters, 1865–1939.

Indian Wars (1847–1877)

Disallowed Indian War Claims Records, 1903–17.
Indian Discharge Certificates, 1872–75.
Indian War: Horse Use Claim Records, 1913.
Cayuse Indian War (1847–50):
    Bonds, 1847–50.
    Claim records, 1847–58.
Rogue River Indian War (1855–56):
    Enlistment rosters, 1854–58.
    Claim records, 1853–59.
    Maps, 1855–56.
    Supply records, 1853–57.
Moduc Indian War (1872–73):
    Campaign journal, 1873.
    Claims certificates, 1873–74.
    Supply records, 1870–78.

Vouchers, 1872–87.

Muster rolls, 1850–1936.

Umatilla Indian War (1878):

Claims register, 1877–79.

Umatilla Reservation peace council minutes, 1878.

Bannock Indian War (1878):

Claim records, 1878–91.

Civil War—Union (1861–65)

NATIONAL ARCHIVES MICROFILM

Index to Compiled Service Records of Volunteer Union Soldiers Who Served in Organizations From the State of Oregon (M553).

Special Schedules of the Eleventh Census (1890) Enumerating Union Veterans and Widows of Union Veterans of the Civil War (M123).

OTHER RECORDS

Bounty Certificate Register, 1865.

Bounty Claim Records, 1865–68.

Expense Claim Records, 1860–68.

Spanish-American War (1898–99)

Spanish-American War Muster Vouchers, 1902–10.

Mexican Border Service (1916)

Adjutant General's Correspondence.

World War I (1917–18)

Federal Enlistment Rosters, 1916 (indexed).

State Bonus Records.

Loan Applications From Veterans.

World War II (1941–45)

Index to the Oregon State Reserve, 1940–45.

Korean War (1950–53)

Korean War Casualty Lists, 1950–53.

Vietnam War (1961–73)

Vietnam War Casualty Lists, Oregon Servicemen, 1961-68.

Vietnam War Veterans' Correspondence, 1970–86.

PUBLISHED SOURCES—OREGON

Pre-1861 (Indian Wars)

Victor, Frances (Fuller). *The Early Indian Wars of Oregon.* Salem: F.C. Baker, 1894. Contains muster rolls of Oregon militia.

1861–65 (Civil War)

Myers, Jane, comp. *Honor Roll of Oregon Grand Army of the Republic, 1881–1935: Deaths Reported in Oregon of Members of the GAR, Extracted From Proceedings of the Annual Encampments of the Department of Oregon. . . .* Cottage Grove: Cottage Grove Genealogical Society, 1980.

Oregon. Adjutant General's Office. *The Oregon Guardsman.* Salem: 1921.

_____ . *Annual Report, 1865–1866.* Salem: state printer, 1866.

Pekar, M.A., and Edna Mingus. *Soldiers Who Served in the Oregon Volunteers; Civil War Period Infantry and Cavalry.* Portland: Genealogical Forum of Oregon, 1961.

Pompey, Sherman L. *Burial List of Oregon and Washington Territory Soldiers of the Civil War: Prepared for the Military Museum of the Oregon National Guard, Salem.* N.p., (1974).

_____ . *Confederate Indian Records.* Florence, Oreg.: Western Oregon Genealogical Research Library, 1980 (?).

_____ . *Register of the Civil War Dead: Oregon.* Clovis, Calif.: 1970.

Victor, Frances F. *The Early Indian Wars of Oregon.* Salem: F.C. Baker, 1894. Includes muster rolls. Covers the period 1847–65.

1866–99 (Spanish-American War)

Oregon. Adjutant General's Office. *The Official Records of the Oregon Volunteers in the Spanish War and the Philippine Insurrection.* Salem: state printer, 1902.

_____ . *Eighth Biennial Report, 1901–02.* Salem: 1902 (?).

Pennsylvania

1638	Swedes established the first European settlement in Pennsylvania.
1655	The Dutch added Pennsylvania to New Netherland.
1664	The English took control of Pennsylvania from the Dutch.

1673-74 The Dutch briefly regained control of Pennsylvania, but control soon returned to the English.

1681 Charles II granted Pennsylvania as a proprietorship to William Penn, who established religious toleration and attracted many settlers.

1754-63 The French and Indian War began with a British assault on Fort Duquesne (later Fort Pitt) and included other clashes in Pennsylvania. (See French and Indian War in the appendix.)

1763 Pontiac's Rebellion, which began in Michigan, spread to Pennsylvania. (See Pontiac's Rebellion in the appendix.)

1769 The Mason-Dixon Line established the border between Pennsylvania and Maryland and became the famous line of demarcation between North and South.

1774 Lord Dunmore's War against Indians occurred, in part, around Fort Pitt. (See Lord Dunmore's War in the appendix.)

1776-81 Pennsylvania was a major theater of the Revolutionary War, and Valley Forge was Washington's infamous winter headquarters. (See American Revolution in the appendix.)

1782 Boundary disputes with Connecticut were resolved.

1787 Pennsylvania became one of the original thirteen states after the Constitutional Convention was held in Philadelphia.

1790-1800 Philadelphia was the capital of the United States.

1794 The Whiskey Rebellion in western Pennsylvania tested the authority of the new national government. (See Whiskey Rebellion in the appendix.)

1861-65 Pennsylvania contributed 337,936 soldiers to the Union cause during the Civil War, a total second only to New York. (See American Civil War in the appendix.)

1863 The Battle of Gettysburg turned back the Confederacy's only offensive onto Northern soil. (See American Civil War in the appendix.)

PENNSYLVANIA STATE ARCHIVES

P.O. Box 1026
Third and Forster Streets
Harrisburg, Pennsylvania, 17108-1026
(717) 783-3281

Finding Aids

Dructor, Robert. *Guide to Genealogical Sources at the Pennsylvania State Archives.* Harrisburg: Pennsylvania Historical and Museum Commission, 1980. This book is available in the archives reading room, and it may be purchased at the bookstore of the state museum neighboring the archives. The chapter titled Military and War Records describes the military collections available at this repository and provides the record group number for each.

Guide to the Record Groups in the Pennsylvania State Archives. Compiled and edited by Frank M. Susan. Harrisburg: Pennsylvania Historical and Museum Commission, 1980. This guide lists the collections in RG 19, Department of Military Affairs, 1793 through 1950. This department is responsible for the Pennsylvania National Guard, the State Veterans Commission, the State Armory Board, the Soldiers' and Sailors' Home at Erie, and various programs relating to veterans' assistance.

Guide to the Manuscript Groups in the Pennsylvania State Archives. Compiled and edited by Harry E. Whipkey. Harrisburg: Pennsylvania Historical and Museum Commission, 1976. This guide lists collections of private papers related to the French and Indian War, American Revolution, War of 1812, Mexican War, Spanish-American War, Philippine Insurrection, and World War I; and to the Pennsylvania National Guard and peacetime military service. It also lists collections containing references to some military units, prisoner-of-war lists, courts-martial, fines, and a receipt book. These collections form Manuscript Group MG-7, Military Manuscripts Collection.

Pre-revolutionary Military Service in Pennsylvania. Information Leaflet No. 2. Division of Archives and Manuscripts, 1969 (out of print). This leaflet contains excellent descriptions of pre-revolutionary war armed conflicts and points out published records sources pertaining to such conflicts.

The Military System of Pennsylvania During the Revolutionary War. Information Leaflet No. 3 (out of print). Division of Public Records, n.d.. This leaflet is intended mainly to help the researcher understand the terms used in describing records of Pennsylvania military organizations. Serving as a brief description of the types of organizations in the state during the American Revolution, it explains the historical background under the following headings:

Duration of the Revolutionary War

The Civil Leadership of Pennsylvania During the Revolution

The Military Association

The Pennsylvania Militia

Line Troops and the Pennsylvania Line

The Pennsylvania Navy

Munger, Donna B. *Pennsylvania Land Records: A History and Guide for Research.* Wilmington, Del.: Scholarly Resources, 1991. This guide describes several record collections that concern donation lands and depreciation lands, including lists of claimants.

Archives staff will conduct record searches for a prepaid fee. An "Explanation of Services" form available at the archives also lists costs for photoduplication of certain documents.

This archives has no National Archives microfilm relating to military matters, but several of its military collections are available on locally produced microfilm, as indicated below. The Pennsylvania portion of the 1890 special census of Union veterans and their widows is available.

Records

General

Pennsylvania National Guard and Reserve Militia:

> National Guard Veteran's Card File, ca. 1867–1921
>
> Enlistment Records, 1867–1945
>
> Field Training Muster and Payrolls, 1873–1912
>
> Military Organization and Commission Books, 1866–1929
>
> Muster Rolls and Related Papers, ca. 1867–1917
>
> Undelivered Discharge Certificates, 1894–95; 1900; 1903–17
>
> Directory of the Pennsylvania National Guard and Roster of the Commissioned Officers, August 5, 1917
>
> Roster, Philadelphia City Cavalry, Second Troop, 1898–1915
>
> Pennsylvania Reserve Militia. Alphabetical list of members, undated
>
> Pennsylvania Reserve Militia. Various types of muster rolls, 1918–21

Military Pension Accounts, ca. 1790–1883. These include various pension books and lists; a pension warrant book index, 1866–80; and a census of pensioners for revolutionary and military service (from the 1840 federal census).

> Absentee returns, Philadelphia City, 1777–91
>
> Militia accounts, 1793–1809; 1809–64

Militia enrollment books, Philadelphia, 1867–68, 1870–72

Militia Enrollment Lists and Related Records, 1870–72

Roster, Fifteenth U.S. Engineer Regiment, ca. 1939–41

Military Commission Books, 1800–1944. These books include a volume titled "Commissions to Pennsylvania Volunteers in Service of U.S., 1898." Data includes military and discharge data.

Colonial Wars (1681–1774)

See the finding aid *Pre-revolutionary Military Service in Pennsylvania* (cited above) for volume numbers of the *Pennsylvania Archives* that contain provincial records. A small number of the records referred to in that publication are available at this archives, but others have been lost.

Records of the Provincial Council (RG 21)

Manuscript groups:

> Military Manuscripts Collection (MG 7)
>
> Pennsylvania Collection (MG 8)
>
> Map Collection (MG 11)
>
> Sequestered Baynton, Wharton, and Morgan Papers (MG 19)
>
> Burd-Shippen Family Collection (MG 30)
>
> Edward Shippen Thompson Collection (MG 125)
>
> Fort Pitt Museum Collection (MG 193)
>
> General Microfilm Collection (MG 262)

Pennsylvania Archives:

> *Colonial Records,* vols. 5–9
>
> 1st series, vols. 2–4
>
> 2nd series, vol. 2, pages 487–615 (name lists)
>
> 4th series, vols. 2–3
>
> 8th series, vols. 5–6

Statutes at Large of Pennsylvania, 1744–59, vol. 5.

American Revolution (1775–83)
MICROFILM

Revolutionary War Associators, Line, Militia and Navy Accounts, and Miscellaneous Records Relating to Military Service, 1775–1809. These consist of receipts, accounts, returns, payrolls, muster rolls, and lists of soldiers. The associators' records (1775–77) are arranged by county; the line accounts (1775–1809) are arranged by regiment and thereunder alphabetically by surname; the militia accounts (1777–94) are arranged by county and thereunder by company and battalion; the navy accounts (1775–94) are arranged chronologically and grouped by stations of duty.

Revolutionary War Pension File and Related Accounts, 1785–1893. Certifications relating to compensation paid to veterans or their widows under various acts. Information provided varies but may include family data. Arranged alphabetically by name of pensioner. Indexed as follows.

Pension Index, Book A, 1790-91. Contains pensioner's name, service, unit, amount of pension, and date pension was granted.

Pension Ledger, Book 1, 1785-89. An incomplete record of disabled soldiers of the Pennsylvania Line or the militia. Includes information relating to the nature and circumstances of the disability.

Pension Ledger, Book B, 1790-93. A record of payments made to veterans or dependents under the act of 11 March 1790.

Pension Ledger, Book C, 1794-1804 (indexed). Includes names of veterans or dependents, military organization, period and amount of pension received, and a statement by the veteran explaining his disability.

Revolutionary War Soldiers' Claims and Related Papers, 1786-1789. This collection consists of petitions submitted to the State Supreme Court, Eastern District. Data includes name, rank, and corps and, occasionally, occupation, age, and residence. Also included is a statement explaining the disability. Arranged alphabetically by surname of the soldier.

Appointments File (Military), 1775-90. Petitions filed by persons seeking a military commission. Arranged alphabetically by surname of the applicant.

OTHER RECORDS

Applications for Passes, ca. 1778-83. Applications for permission to pass through enemy lines. The information provided varies. Arranged alphabetically by applicant's surname. Also available on microfilm.

Depreciation Certificate Accounts, 1781-92. Name, rank, organization, and the amount of interest earned by soldiers who had been paid in Continental Bills of Credit, which rapidly became almost worthless. Grouped by military unit and thereunder alphabetically by surname. See *Pennsylvania Archives,* vol. 4.

Forfeited Estates File, 1777-90. These records describe persons whose estates were seized because they were loyal to the British cause. Usually given are name and residence and a description of the estate with an inventory of the property seized. The records are available also on microfilm, and the names are listed in *Pennsylvania Archives,* 6th ser., vols. 12 and 13.

Militia Fine Exonerations, 1777-93. Lists of names of persons seeking exemption from fines levied for not attending militia functions. The information provided varies. Arranged by county; not indexed.

Papers in Attainder, ca. 1778-91. Lists of persons deemed loyal to the British cause. Name, residence, and, in some cases, occupation are provided. Not indexed.

Revolutionary War Military Abstract Card File, ca. 1775-83. Consists of approximately 100,000 index cards compiled with information gleaned from original muster rolls, payrolls, and various other accounts papers. Approximately ninety percent of the persons named belonged to a militia unit which probably did not see active military service in the Continental Line. Information includes name and county and perhaps other data. Arranged alphabetically by surname. Also available on microfilm.

Return of Pennsylvania Line Entitled to Donation Lands (undated). Provides name, rank, corps, and number of acres awarded in the western portion of Pennsylvania as compensation for service in the revolutionary war, and possibly other data concerning the soldier. Further details concerning these lands may be obtained from the Pennsylvania Bureau of Land Records in the Department of Community Affairs (located near the archives).

Return of Officers and Soldier to Whom Patents Were Not Issued (undated). These refer to land granted to soldiers but for which patents were never issued. Given is the soldier's name, the lot number of the land, and the number of acres.

Revolutionary War Pension List, 1834-37. This volume contains records of revolutionary war veterans or their widows who applied for a pension under the act of 13 April 1834. Data includes name, date pension was due, and the amount. Arranged by county and thereafter alphabetically by surname.

Delaware River Fortification Accounts.

Commissary Accounts—Hessians at Lancaster. Also available on microfilm.

Militia Absentee Returns, Philadelphia.

Damage Claims for Goods Seized by the British.

Anthony Wayne Papers, 1777-96. An orderly book and correspondence pertaining to courts-martial and Indian campaigns.

Militia (1789-1861)

Militia Accounts (auditor general), 1809-64.

Militia Returns, Frontier Defense, 1792-94.

Office of the Register General. Selected records, 1789-1809. Records consist of militia certificates from the Pennsylvania Land Office, 1789-93; accounts-settled registers, 1792-94; 1801-09; warrant book and register, 1789-94; 1797-1802.

Register of Militia and Volunteers, 1841-44. Adjutant general, one volume.

See *Pennsylvania Archives:* 2nd ser., vol. 2; 3rd ser., vol. 23; 6th ser., vols. 3-5.

Whiskey Rebellion (1794-95)

See *Pennsylvania Archives:* 2nd ser., vol. 4; 4th ser., vol. 4; 9th ser., vol. 2.

Western Expedition Accounts, 1794-1804. Also available on microfilm.

War of 1812 (1812-15)

MICROFILM

War of 1812 Militia Accounts and Related Papers, 1812-38. Contains accounts and orders, receipts, pay vouchers, payrolls, and muster rolls for Pennsylvania militiamen who served during the War of 1812. Arranged by unit.

War of 1812 Pension File, ca. 1866-1896. Records of soldiers (or their wives) who had served at least two months or who had been wounded or otherwise disabled during the War of 1812. Files usually contain original applications with military service information. Widow's files also contain original applications, data relating to marriage and husband's death, and other family data. Files are arranged alphabetically by pensioner's surname, and a separate name list is available for quick reference.

See *Pennsylvania Archives*, 2nd ser., vol. 12 (muster rolls); 4th ser., vol. 4 (list of medalists); 6th ser., vols. 7-10 (muster rolls and payrolls).

War of 1812 Index of Soldiers. Alphabetically arranged list of names of soldiers by unit. Name, term of service, and name of commanding officer and battalion. Remarks may include other data (such as desertion).

Mexican War (1846-48)

MICROFILM

Mexican War Accounts and Related Papers, 1846-80. These papers include muster rolls for the First and Second Regiments, Pennsylvania Volunteers, arranged by company. They also include claims for pay arranged by unit and thereunder alphabetically by surname. Information about deaths or desertions and wounds is also noted along with military service dates. There is a separate alphabetical list (by company) of soldiers attached to regiments.

Mexican War Service Index, 1846-48. This is an alphabetical list of the soldiers who were attached to the First Pennsylvania Volunteers. Given are name, dates of muster and discharge, and unit. Remarks usually also include data concerning desertion, death, or discharge.

See *Pennsylvania. Archives*, 6th ser., vol. 10.

Civil War—Union (1861-65)

MICROFILM

Records of Drafted Men and Substitutes, Including County and Township Draft Lists, Muster, and Descriptive rolls, and Lists of Deserters and Conscientious Objectors, 1862. Separate lists for each county.

Civil War Veterans' Card File, 1861-66. These cards were prepared to serve as an index to Bates' *History of Pennsylvania Volunteers, 1861-65.* Later, additional information was placed on the cards: physical description, age at enrollment, military unit, residence and birthplace, date and place enrolled and mustered in, and date of discharge. Arranged alphabetically.

Conscientious Objector Depositions, 1862. These forms were completed by persons who refused to enter military service. Name and county of residence are given.

Substitutes' Depositions, 1862. These papers include the name of a substitute for military service, township and county, date, name of the person for whom he was a substitute, and his signature.

OTHER RECORDS

Civil War Service and Pension Accounts, 1861-73. Files of approximately a dozen widows or orphans of Civil War veterans.

Discharge Orders and Letters of Notice of Alien Status of Individuals Serving in the Military, 1862-63. Petitions submitted by foreigners for exemption from military service. Arranged by county. Alien's name, residence, and native country.

List of Sick and Wounded Soldiers, Pennsylvania Volunteers, 1861-64. Information includes name, unit, whether victim of disease or casualty, and place hospitalized.

Military Claims File and Claims Register With Index, 1862-1905. This file is replete with information concerning claims for pay for all Pennsylvania Volunteers and others who acted in the capacity of officer. The register is arranged by claim number and shows name, rank, unit, time claimed, pay rate per month, and dates the claim was received and paid.

Miscellaneous Discharge Certificates, 1861-66. Documents for approximately thirty persons, with physical descriptions and military history.

Miscellaneous Registers, Rosters, and Lists, 1859-72. Rolls and records of men mustered into service during 1861. Also available is a Muster Roll Book, 1863-65, which is an appended roll of officers with military history information and data concerning bounty claims. There is also a roster of commissioned officers of the Pennsylvania Volunteers, 1861-65, arranged alphabetically by surname; a register of "three month troops," 1861; and a register of men mustered in for "three years or duration of the war."

Muster Rolls and Related Records, 1861-66. There are several types of rolls (muster in, muster out, descriptive, alphabetical, and deserters) for most Pennsylvania regiments.

Record Book of Zouave Cadets of Penn Yan, 1861-65. Contains the names of the founding members, with data indicating whether the cadets enlisted into the regular service, died, or left town. Arranged by date of the group's meetings.

Record of Candidates Examined by the Pennsylvania State Medical Boards for Appointment as Surgeons and Assistant Surgeons, 1861-65. Shown are each candidate's name, address, county of residence, age, institution from which he graduated, date of examination, and miscellaneous data. Also available is a record of candidates examined by the state medical board.

Records of Applications for Military Positions, Vacancies, Appointments and Resignations, and Commissions Issued,

1861–65. Lists arranged by corps and thereunder chronologically.

Record of Claims for Arrears of Pay and Bounty, 6 June 1864–24 August 1869. Papers related to claims filed. Indexed.

Register of Sick and Wounded Soldiers, Pennsylvania Volunteers, ca. 1861–65. Shown are name, residence, unit, disease or impairment, and hospital where treated.

Registers of Pennsylvania Volunteers, 1861–65 (microfilm). Name and data concerning military history. Arranged alphabetically.

Returns of Medical Officers Connected With Pennsylvania Regiments, 1861–64. Lists surgeons and assistant surgeons and related military history. Arranged by regiment.

SOLDIERS' AND SAILORS' HOME RECORDS

Roster of Admissions, 12 April 1864–21 May 1872. Name, age, place of birth, date of admittance, disease and treatment given, date released or died, and miscellaneous data.

Descriptive List, Soldiers' Home, Philadelphia, 1 June 1866–12 March 1867. Name, age, marital status, nativity, number of children, previous occupation, military history, prior residence, nature of disability, amount of pension received, and reasons veteran was unable to support self. Other information is also frequently noted. These names are arranged by date, but the House Register (see below) can be used as an index.

House Register, Soldiers' Home, Philadelphia, 13 December 1864–28 March 1872. This list contains name, ward and bed number, dates of admission and discharge, and number of page on which name is listed on the Descriptive List (see above).

Muster Roll of Pennsylvania Soldiers Admitted to the National Home for Disabled Volunteer Soldiers, Central Branch, Dayton, Ohio, 12 November 1880. Includes those admitted since 1867. Name, unit, disability, amount of monthly pension, and date of death or discharge from the home. Arranged alphabetically by surname.

Spanish-American War (1898–99)

MICROFILM

Spanish-American War Veterans' Card File. These are cards prepared from official records of the U.S. War Department. Data usually includes name, race, age, birthplace, residence, rank, date and place of enlistment, dates and places of service, and unit. Remarks may include date and place of discharge and prior military service.

Veterans' Compensation File. This file was created in 1934 and includes various documents pertaining to persons who served in the Spanish-American War and in the occupation of the Philippines from 1898 to 1904. The documents may include applications for veterans' compensation; they all contain considerable military and personal information.

Verification of Service and Bonus Payments. Arranged alphabetically by surname.

OTHER RECORDS

Muster Rolls and Related Records, 1898. Muster-in and muster-out rolls are available for several regiments. Name or number of the regiment must be known.

Mexican Border Campaign (1916–17)

Mexican Border Campaign Veterans' Card File, 1916–17. These cards refer to those who served in response to the "emergency call" of 18 June 1916. Name, rank, unit, age, place of birth, occupation, marital status, physical description, residence, date of commission or enlistment, home station, date of rendezvous, and date of acceptance into service. Also usually given are date discharge was due and name of next of kin. Arranged alphabetically.

Muster Rolls and Related Papers, 1916–17. These are muster rolls of Pennsylvania National Guardsmen. Name, rank, occupation, marital status, place of birth, physical description, unit, date of commission or enlistment, date of muster, and name of next of kin. Guardsmen's signatures also appear.

Descriptive Lists of Companies B and C, Second Infantry, and Battery D, Second Artillery, of the Pennsylvania National Guard, 1917. Information given is similar to that on the muster rolls and related papers (see above).

World War I (1917–18)

Card Records of National Naval Volunteers, 1917. Name, rating, residence, date and place enrolled into service, unit to which assigned. Arranged alphabetically.

Draft Board Records, Consisting Primarily of Lists of Persons Whose Registration Cards Are in the Possession of Their Local Board, ca. 1917–18. Registration and induction lists arranged by region. Name, address, age, and, occasionally, occupation.

Muster Rolls, 1917. Rolls for the Pennsylvania National Guard. They show unit to which attached and other related information.

Undelivered Discharge Certificates, 1918–19. Certificates of soldiers attached to the U.S. Army. Each contains considerable military and personal history. Arranged alphabetically.

World War I Veterans Service and Compensation File. These files may contain "service statement cards," "compensation applications," and "war service record of soldiers, sailors and marines." These last are the Pennsylvania War History Commission questionnaires returned by World War I veterans. (See the section on the National History Institute, Carlisle Barracks, Pennsylvania (chapter 7), for a full description of these questionnaires.)

World War II (1941–45)

Applications for Veterans' Compensation, 1950. These records are applications for bonuses under the act of 1 June 1947 for those who served in World War II. The applications contain considerable military and personal history, including names and addresses of the veterans' beneficiaries, living parents, and dependents and their ages. Arranged alphabetically.

U.S. Army infantry regiments (by name or number)

U.S. Marine Corps

U.S. Navy

U.S. Selective Service System

U.S. War Department

THE HISTORICAL SOCIETY OF PENNSYLVANIA

1300 Locust Street
Philadelphia, Pennsylvania 19107-5699
(215) 732-6201

The society's manuscript department holds more than 15 million documents, and its library has more than 500,000 monographs, pamphlets, and serials. The society's genealogical holdings are among the largest in the nation.

Finding Aids

Colonial Muster Rolls at the Historical Society of Pennsylvania. This soft-bound volume contains several lists of holdings of the society's collection of colonial-era muster rolls. It is intended for internal use as a location guide.

Guide to the Manuscript Collections of the Historical Society of Pennsylvania. Philadelphia: 1991. The index headings to this publication indicate the many manuscript collections that contain material bearing on military matters. The following are some topics that may bear examination.

Military service:
Compulsory
Draft registers
Voluntary
Training camps

Military life

Order books

Prisons

Recruiting

U.S. Army:
Biography
Courts-martial
Enlistments
Revolutionary
Continental Army
War of 1812
Civil War
Mexican War
World War I
World War II
Medals and badges, decorations

U.S. Army Air Force

U.S. Army Corps of Engineers

PUBLISHED SOURCES—PENNSYLVANIA

General

Daughters of the American Revolution. *The Golden Book: Revolutionary Soldiers' Graves, Pennsylvania.* The society, 1982.

Trussell, John B.B. *Pennsylvania Military History.* U.S. Army Military History Research Collection, special bibliographic series no. 10. Carlisle Barracks: U.S. Army Military History Research Collection, 1974.

Wilson, Helen, comp. *A Bibliography of Sources for Civil War, Mexican War, and Spanish-American War Research in Western Pennsylvania.* Pittsburgh: Western Pennsylvania Genealogical Society, 1978.

Pre-1775 (colonial wars)

Bradshaw, Audrey E. *Pennsylvania Soldiers in the Provincial Service, 1746–1759.* From *Pennsylvania Archives,* Second Series, vol. 2. Ashland, Oreg.: the author, 1985.

Laverty, Bruce. *Colonial Muster Rolls at the Historical Society of Pennsylvania.* Philadelphia: Historical Society of Pennsylvania, 1983. Reproduces the original rolls; includes an index.

Linn, John B. (?). *List of Officers of the Colonies on the Delaware and the Province of Pennsylvania, 1614–1776.* From *Pennsylvania Archives,* 2nd ser., vol. 9, pt. 2, pages. 621–818. Harrisburg: state printer, 1890.

Richards, Henry M.M. *The Pennsylvania-German in the French and Indian War: A Historical Sketch . . . Pennsylvania German Society Proceedings and Addresses of 1905.* Vol. 15. Lancaster: the society, 1905. A "Roster of the German Regiment" appears on pages 195–307. "On the Frontiers Against the Indians" lists officers by county throughout the text, pages 329–514.

1775-83 (American Revolution)

Clarke, William P. *Official History of the Militia and the National Guard of the State of Pennsylvania, From the Earliest Period of Record to the Present Time.* 3 vols. Philadelphia (?): C.J. Hendler, 1909. Pages 88–89: revolutionary war battalions with a list of officers. Some biographical sketches and portraits are included.

Closson, Bob, and Mary Closson. *A Census of Pennsylvania Pensioners for Revolutionary or Military Services: With Their Names, Ages, and Places of Residence, as Returned by the Marshals of the Several Judicial District (sic) Under the Act for

Taking the Sixth Census. Apollo, Pa.: the authors, 1978. Pensioners alphabetically arranged with age, county, town (or other division), and with whom resided on 1 June 1840.

_____. *1840 Census of Pennsylvania Pensioners for Revolutionary or Military Services.* Evansville, Ind.: Cook Pub., 1978.

_____ . *Register of Invalid Pensions: Revolutionary Service, 1789.* Apollo: Closson Press, 1981.

Cope, Harry E., comp. *List of Soldiers and Widows of Soldiers Granted Revolutionary War Pensions by the Commonwealth of Pennsylvania.* Edited by Mrs. Daniel L. Whitehead. Greensburg: Phoebe Bayard Chapter, Daughters of the American Revolution, 1976.

Lists of Persons Pensioned by the United States, Residing in Pennsylvania, Who Served in the War of the Revolution, 1820–1825. Harrisburg: 1890.

Pennsylvania, State. *Pennsylvania Archives.* 138 vols. in 9 series. Harrisburg: Pennsylvania Historical and Museum Commission, 1852–1914. Muster rolls and other records of soldiers and sailors of the American Revolution are contained in the 2nd ser. (vols. 1, 3, 8–11); 3rd ser. (vol. 23); 5th ser. (vols. 1–8); 6th ser. (vols. 1–2; index to 5th ser. in vol. 15); and 7th ser. (vols. 1–4; index to 6th ser. in vol. 5). For a full description of this publication see Henry H. Eddy, comp.: *Guide to the Published Archives of Pennsylvania, Covering the 138 Volumes of "Colonial Records" and "Pennsylvania Archives," Series 1–9; With an Alphabetical Finding List and Two Special Indexes.* Harrisburg: Pennsylvania Historical and Museum Commission, 1949. In addition to Eddy's guide see Lois Horowitz's: *A Bibliography of Military Name Lists From Pre-1675 to 1900: A Guide to Genealogical Sources* (Metuchen, N.J.: Scarecrow Press, 1990) , pages 333–36 and specific Pennsylvania counties. The Library of Congress has an incomplete set of the published volumes but has a complete set on microfiche (microfiche 1018). A few of the major works in the Pennsylvania Archives that pertain to the American Revolution are listed below.

Pennsylvania Archives. 2nd ser., vol. 15, *Journals and Diaries of the War of the Revolution, With Lists of Officers and Soldiers, 1775–1783.* Edited by W.H. Egle. Harrisburg: 1892. Includes militia rolls, lists of pensioners, etc.

Pennsylvania Archives. 6th ser., vol. 4, *Military Abstracts from Executive Minutes.* Harrisburg: 1907.

Pennsylvania Archives. 6th ser., vol. 3, *Militia Rolls, 1783–1790.* Harrisburg: 1907. Includes Bedford to York counties.

Pennsylvania Archives. 3rd ser., vol. 23, *Muster Rolls of the Navy and Line, Militia and Rangers, 1775–1783.* With List of Pensioners, 1818–1832. Edited by W.H. Egle. Harrisburg: 1898.

Pennsylvania Archives. 2nd ser., vols. 13–14, *Pennsylvania in the War of the Revolution: Associated Battalions and Militia, 1775–1783.* Harrisburg: 1890–92.

Pennsylvania Archives. 2nd ser., vols. 10–11, *Pennsylvania in the War of the Revolution: Battalions and Line, 1775–1783.* Harrisburg: 1880.

Pennsylvania Archives. 2nd ser., vol. 15, *Rolls of Soldiers of the Revolution: Pennsylvania Line Found in the Department of State, Washington, D.C.* Harrisburg: 1890.

Pennsylvania Archives. 3rd ser., vols. 5–7, *State of the Accounts of the County Lieutenants During the War of the Revolution, 1777–1789.* 3 vols. in 2. Philadelphia: 1896. Alphabetically arranged by county with companies listed. Indicates supplies purchased, from whom, and amount paid. Military tracts granted to veterans of the Pennsylvania line appear in vol. 7.

Pennsylvania. Surveyor General's Office. *Donation of Military Tracts of Land Granted the Soldiers of the Pennsylvania Line.* Harrisburg: 1896.

Richards, Henry M.M. *The Pennsylvania-German in the Revolutionary War, 1775–1783.* Reprint of the 1908 edition. Issued as vol. 17 of the Pennsylvania German Society Proceedings and Addresses. Lancaster: Pennsylvania German Society, 1908. Baltimore: Genealogical Publishing Co., 1978.

1784–1815 (War of 1812)

Muster Rolls of the Pennsylvania Volunteers in the War of 1812–1814: With Contemporary Papers and Documents. Excerpted and reprinted from Pennsylvania Archives, 2nd ser., vol. 12. Harrisburg: 1890. Reprint. Baltimore: Genealogical Publishing Co., 1967.

National Society of United States Daughters of 1812. Pennsylvania. *Lineage Book, 1895–1929.* Scranton: Westmoreland Chapter, the society, 1812. Pages 83–175 contain "Ancestors of Members . . ."

Pennsylvania Archives. 6th ser., vol. 3, *Muster and Pay Rolls, Pennsylvania Militia, 1790–1800.* Harrisburg: 1907.

1816–60 (Mexican War)

Pennsylvania Archives. 6th ser., vol. 10, *Mexican War, 1846–47.* Includes name, unit, date and place of enrollment, and date of discharge or death.

1861–65 (Civil War)

Bates, Samuel P. *History of Pennsylvania Volunteers, 1861–65.* 5 vols. Harrisburg: state printer, 1869–71. Includes names of officers and soldiers by regiment and other biographical information.

_____. *Martial Deeds of Pennsylvania.* Philadelphia: T.H. Davis & Co., 1875. Contains biographical sketches of many officers.

Ferguson, Joseph. *Life-struggles in Rebel Prisons: A Record of the Sufferings, Escapes, Adventures and Starvation of the Union*

Prisoners; Containing an Appendix With the Names, Regiments, and Date of Death of Pennsylvania Soldiers Who Died at Andersonville. Philadelphia: the author, 1865.

Pennsylvania. Antietam Battlefield Memorial Commission. *Pennsylvania at Antietam; Report of . . . Ceremonies at the Dedication of the Monuments Erected by the Commonwealth of Pennsylvania to Mark the Position of Thirteen of the Pennsylvania Commands Engaged in the Battle . . . .* Harrisburg: state printers, 1906.

Pennsylvania. Chickamauga-Chattanooga Battlefields Commission. *Pennsylvania at Chickamauga and Chattanooga. . . .* Harrisburg: W.S. Ray, state printer, 1900.

Pennsylvania. Gettysburg Battlefield Commission. *Pennsylvania at Gettysburg. . . .* 2 vols. Harrisburg: W. S. Ray, state printer, 1904.

Pennsylvania. Salisbury Memorial Commission. *Pennsylvania at Salisbury, North Carolina: Ceremonies at the Dedication of the Memorial . . . in Memory of the Soldiers of Pennsylvania Who Perished in the Confederate Prison at Salisbury . . . .* Harrisburg: C.E. Aughinbaugh, 1910.

Pennsylvania. Surgeon General's Office. *List of Soldiers, (Prisoners of War,) Belonging to Pennsylvania Regiments, Who Died at the Military Prison, at Andersonville, Georgia, from February 26, 1864, to March 24, 1865.* Harrisburg (?): state printer, 1865 (?).

Speece, Jody Rogers, comp. *Every Name Index, Fort Ligonier and Its Times. . . .* Apollo: Closson Press, 1983.

1866-99 (Spanish-American War)

Pennsylvania. Adjutant General's Office. *Record of Pennsylvania Volunteers in the Spanish-American War, 1898.* Harrisburg: W.S. Ray, state printer, 1901.

1900-18 (World War I)

Pennsylvania State Publications Society. *Pennsylvanians in the World War; an Illustrated History of the Twenty-eighth Division. . . .* 2 vols. Pittsburgh: the society, 1921.

Rhode Island

1636	Puritan dissenter Roger Williams was banished from Massachusetts and established a haven for dissenters in Rhode Island.
1642	Rhode Island became a royal colony.
1675-76	King Philip's War between colonists and Indians involved Rhode Island. (See King Philip's War in the appendix.)
1778	General John Sullivan and a French force tried unsuccessfully to destroy a British garrison at Newport. (See American Revolution in the appendix.)
1790	Rhode Island became a state.
1841	The Dorr Rebellion broke out when voters who wanted liberalization of Rhode Island's voting requirements challenged the state. (See Dorr Rebellion in the appendix.)

· ·

RHODE ISLAND STATE ARCHIVES

337 Westminster Street
Providence, Rhode Island 02903-3302
(401) 277-2353

Finding Aid

Genealogical Sources in the Rhode Island State Archives. This booklet contains the following sections that pertain to military records: Military Records—Revolutionary War; Military Records—1730-1848; Military Records—Civil War; Military Records—World War I and II. This aid lists the collection number ("C" number) for each category, which must be indicated when requesting the papers.

Other records of military service (through World War I) may be found at the Office of the Adjutant General, 1051 Main Street, Providence, Rhode Island 02904. This archives has no National Archives military microfilm.

Records

General

Returns, 1801-67.

Lists of Officers and Soldiers (C1144). Arranged chronologically.

Returns, Chartered Companies, 1815-1857.

Lists of Companies (C1153). Includes some accounts and payrolls.

Payrolls, 1815-1857.

Payrolls of Artillery Companies, Guards, and the American Brass Band (C1154).

Colonial Wars (pre-1775)

Muster Rolls, Accounts, and Correspondence (C00248). Correspondence relating to the Crown Point Expedition. Two volumes.

Miscellaneous Documents Relating to the French and Indian War, Including Conflicts at Fort Schuyler, Fort Ontario, Fort Stanwix, and Fort George.

A List of Men in the Canadian Expedition and Some Documents From the Crown Point Expedition (C00246). An index is located in a file drawer. Also available on microfilm 00151.

American Revolution (1775-83)

Revolutionary War Names Index, 1770-85 (C1089).Card index: that shows name, unit, dates, and source of data. Also available on microfilm.

Muster Rolls for Regiments Commanded by Colonels Crary, Topham, Elliot, 1740, 1758, 1762, 1785 (C1156). These show name and regiment only.

Invalid Pensioners, 1790 (C00506). A return of invalid (wounded) pensioners in Rhode Island and also a return of officers who died (whose ancestors were thus entitled to seven years' half pay); also returns made to General Knox, secretary of war, 8 April 1790.

Revolutionary Pension Correspondence, 1850-58 (C1165). Letters from pensioners or family members.

Suspected Persons, 1775-83 (C00918). Lists, complaints, warrants, evidence, and petitions relating to suspected disloyal citizens.

Confiscated Estates (general treasurer's papers), 1779-81 (C1259). Inventories of estates of Tories whose property was confiscated and names of persons.

Miscellaneous Papers, Revolutionary War, 1770-1790.

Thirteen Volumes of Letters, Vouchers, Lists of Names, and Accounts (C00247).

Historical Cemeteries (C00955). A volume prepared by the graves registration committee, 1950-89. Lists towns where veterans from all wars were buried in designated historic cemeteries. Locations of graves shown on maps.

Returns, Revolutionary War, 1776-1781 (C00486). Six volumes of documents of returns of military units, payrolls, clothing accounts, and other records. An index for these documents is in a file drawer.

Transcripts of Military Records, 1774-1726 (C00482). Two volumes of transcripts of regimental returns and payrolls, showing the source.

Regimental Book of the Rhode Island Regiment (C00505). Lists names of officers, place of birth, dates and length of service, occupation, age, and physical description.

Revolutionary Claims of Archibald C. Crary, 1793 (C1142).

War of 1812 (1812-15)

Miscellaneous Documents, 1812-16 (C00212). Accounts Papers, Governmental Orders, Reports of Town Meetings, Commissions. Also available on microfilm.

Pension Correspondence, War of 1812, 1855-60 (C1166). Three letters only.

Dorr's Insurrection (1842)

Pay Vouchers, 1842 (C1161). Arranged alphabetically.

Militia Returns, 1842 (C1159). Rolls and returns and correspondence.

Insurrection Claims, 1842 (C1157). Lists of soldiers who fought in the insurrection and the amounts paid.

Mexican War (1846-48)

Accounts and Narratives Relative to Raising of Volunteers (C1162).

Civil War–Union (1861-65); Post-war Period

Papers of the Adjutant General (C00489). These consist of 159 boxes, including the following collections (C00792).

> Navy Name List, 1861-62
>
> Muster Rolls, various regiments, 1861-63; 1873-96
>
> Enlistment Papers, 1861-79
>
> Payrolls, 1861-79; 1861-97; 1872-92; 1899-1901
>
> Desertion Papers, 1861-63
>
> Descriptive Rolls of Deserters, 1861-65
>
> Descriptive Rolls, 1861-1908
>
> Medical Examinations, 1861-65
>
> Returns of Deceased Soldiers, 1861-91
>
> Discharge Papers, 1863-69
>
> Certificates of Exemption, 1850-80
>
> Court-martial Papers, 1859-62; 1906
>
> Appointments and Registers, 1879-83

Lists of Rhode Island Military Personnel Killed in the Civil War, 1861-69 (C00878). Two booklets listing name and rank of officers, soldiers, and seamen in Rhode Island regiments.

Draft Lists (Board of Enrollment), 1863 (C00783). Town records consisting of names, date of draft, and whether paid commutation, furnished a substitute, or served.

Exemptions and Commutations, 1863-64 (C1168). Town records of state payments to drafted men who procured substitutes.

Exemptions From Service, 1863-64 (C1169). Draft notices and receipts for payments for exemptions; also town of residence.

Releases From Service, 1864 (C1176). Board of Commissioners records of drafted men who paid commutation or procured substitutes; also town of residence.

Commutation Commission Minutes, 1864–66 (C00452). Names of individuals who served, commuted, or provided a substitute, and town of residence.

Correspondence, Commutations, and Draftees, 1864 (C1154). Some petitions and letters that relate to bounty payments.

Payrolls of the Paymaster General, 1857–63 (C1154). Lists of soldiers and pay.

Militia Papers, Pawtucket Light Guard, 1860–74 (C1163).

Commutation Commission Reports, 1864 (C1167). Names of drafted men, date, and to whom a bounty was paid.

Rolls, First Regiment of Rhode Island Volunteers, 1861–62 (C1320).

Petitions for Bounty, Fourteenth Regiment, Rhode Island Volunteers (C1170).

Spanish-American War (1898–99); Post-war Period

Muster Rolls, 1891–97; 1892–1917.

Payrolls, 1892–1917.

World War I (1917–18)

Navy Register, 1920 (adjutant general's papers) (C00489).

Liability Rolls, 1917–18 (C00085, C00077). Nine volumes. Names, addresses, "color," military liability, and serial numbers of males aged 21 to 30. Also a separate roll for Pawtucket, Rhode Island.

Rhode Island Veterans' Discharge Papers, Jamestown, Rhode Island, 1929–57 (C00534). Exemptions from military service. Also available on microfilm. Indexed.

World War II (1941–45)

Lists, Enrollments, and Inductions into the United States Military, 1943 (C00086). Lists of names and addresses of those who served in the army, navy, coast guard, marines, and Women's Auxiliary Army Corps (WAAC).

Veterans' Discharge Papers, Jamestown, Rhode Island (see above under World War I) (C00534).

Scrapbooks, World War II, 1941–45 (C00633). Newspaper articles and miscellaneous material pertaining to the war effort. Also available on microfilm.

The Library of the Rhode Island Historical Society

121 Hope Street (at Power Street)
Providence, Rhode Island 02906
(401) 331-8575

Manuscript Collections

For a complete list of the library's holdings, request a copy of the February 1993 inventory of military collections in the manuscript division.

Card Index of Manuscript Holdings. Researchers may select collections under headings for individual wars or under other headings. Some ship logs are included.

Historical Cemeteries. Four large boxes of copies of typewritten sheets list veterans of all wars and their places of burial.

Published Sources—Rhode Island

General

Pierce, Grace M., comp. *Rhode Island Pension Records.* 6 vols. Typescript, 1919.

Pre-1775 (colonial wars)

Chapin, Howard M. *Rhode Island in the Colonial Wars: A List of Rhode Island Soldiers & Sailors in the Old French & Indian War, 1755–1762.* Providence: Rhode Island Historical Society, 1918.

_____. *Rhode Island Privateers in King George's War, 1739–1748.* Providence: Rhode Island Historical Society, 1926.

_____. *Rhode Island in the Colonial Wars: A List of Rhode Island Soldiers & Sailors in King George's War, 1740–1748.* Providence: Rhode Island Historical Society, 1920.

Richards, John J. *Rhode Island's Early Defenders and Their Successors.* East Greenwich: Provisional Regiment of Chartered Command, Rhode Island Militia, 1937. Includes names of militia officers, 1638–1917.

Smith, Joseph J. *Civil and Military List of Rhode Island.* Vol. 1, *1647–1800.* 3 vols. Providence: Preston and Rounds Co., 1900–01. Includes muster rolls. Also see Smith's *New Index to the Civil and Military Lists of Rhode Island: Two Volumes in One. . . .* Providence: the author, 1907.

Society of Colonial Wars. Rhode Island. *The Muster Rolls of Three Companies Enlisted by the Colony of Rhode Island in May, 1746, for an Expedition Against Canada Proposed by Great Britain.* Providence: the society, 1915.

_____. *Nine Muster Rolls of Rhode Island Troops Enlisted During the Old French War: to Which is Added the Journal of Captain William Rice in the Expedition of 1746.* Providence: the society, 1915.

1775-83 (American Revolution)

Chamberlain, Mildred M. *The Rhode Island 1777 Military Census.* Published under direction of the Rhode Island Genealogical Society. Baltimore: Genealogical Publishing Co., 1985. Lists more than eight thousand men aged sixteen to sixty, naming place of residence and those in service. Not available for Exeter, Little Compton, and New Shoreham. Because Middletown, Newport, and Portsmouth were then occupied by the British, no census was enumerated in those towns.

Cowell, Benjamin. *Spirit of '76 in Rhode Island: or, Sketches of the Efforts of the Government and People in the War of the Revolution; Together with the Names of Those who Belonged to Rhode Island Regiments in the Army. With Biographical Notices, Reminiscences, &c., &c.* Boston: A.J. Wright, 1850. Reprint. With James N. Arnold's *Cowell's 'Spirit of '76'; An Analytical and Explanatory Index.* Baltimore: Genealogical Publishing Co., 1973.

Field, Edward. *Revolutionary Defenses in Rhode Island; an Historical Account of the Fortification and Beacons Erected During the American Revolution; With Muster Rolls of the Companies Stationed Along the Shores of Narragansett Bay.* Providence: Preston and Rounds, 1896.

Minority Military Service, Rhode Island, 1775-1783. Washington, D.C.: National Society of the Daughters of the American Revolution, 1988. Participation of African-Americans in the American Revolution. Includes name, year, and source.

Murray, Thomas H. *Irish Rhode Islanders in the American Revolution.* . . . Providence: American-Irish Historical Society, 1903.

Rhode Island. Adjutant General's Office. *Names of Officers, Soldiers and Seamen in Rhode Island Regiments, or Belonging to the State of Rhode Island, and Serving in the Regiments of Other States and in the Regular Army and Navy of the United States, Who Lost Their Lives in the Defence of Their Country in the Suppression of the Late Rebellion.* Providence: Providence Press, 1869.

Rider, Sidney S. *An Historical Inquiry Concerning the Attempt to Raise a Regiment of Slaves by Rhode Island During the War of the Revolution.* Rhode Island Historical Tracts, 1st ser., no. 10. Providence: the author, 1880. Slaves enlisted in regiments of the Rhode Island Continental Line.

Smith, Joseph J. *Civil and Military List of Rhode Island. Vol. 1, 1647-1800.* 3 vols. Providence: Preston and Rounds Co., 1900-01. Includes muster rolls. Also see Smith's *New Index to the Civil and Military Lists of Rhode Island: Two Volumes in One.* . . . Providence: the author, 1907.

Walker, Anthony. *So Few the Brave: Rhode Island Continentals, 1775-1783.* Newport: Seafield Press. East Greenwich:

Rhode Island Society, Sons of the American Revolution, 1981.

1861-65 (Civil War)

Bartlett, John R. *Memoirs of Rhode Island Officers Who Were Engaged in the Service of Their Country During the Great Rebellion of the South. Illustrated With Thirty-four Portraits.* Providence: S.S. Rider & Bro., 1867.

Rhode Island. Adjutant General's Office. *Annual Report . . . Official Register of Rhode Island Officers and Men Who Served in the U.S. Army and Navy, From 1861-66.* 2 vols. Providence: state printers, 1893-95.

_____. *Names of Officers, Soldiers and Seamen in Rhode Island Regiments, or Belonging to the State of Rhode Island, and Serving in the Regiments of Other States and in the Regular Army and Navy of the United States, Who Lost Their Lives in the Defence of Their Country in the Suppression of the Late Rebellion.* Providence: Providence Press, 1869.

_____. *Report Upon the Disabled Rhode Island Soldiers; Their Names, Condition, and in What Hospital They Are . . . Presented to the General Assembly, January Session, 1863, by Mrs. Charlotte F. Dailey, Commissioned by the Governor to Visit the Hospitals, etc.* Providence: state printer, 1863.

1914-18 (World War I)

Freemasons, Rhode Island Grand Lodge. *Honor Roll: Rhode Island Masons Who Served in the World War, 1914-1918.* Central Falls: E.L. Freeman Co., 1921.

South Carolina

1497	English explorer John Cabot established an English claim to South Carolina.
1663	Charles II granted a proprietorship to eight English lords during the Restoration.
1670	The first permanent English settlement was established at "Old Town" on the Ashley River.
1702-06	During Queen Anne's War, forces from South Carolina mounted two expeditions against the Spanish in Florida and drove off a French invasion. (See Queen Anne's War in the appendix.)
1715-16	During the bloody Yamasee War, Indians attempted to drive out the white settlers in

South Carolina. (See Yamasee War in the appendix.)

1729   South Carolina became a royal colony.

1760   White settlers in South Carolina retaliated against Cherokee attacks. (See Cherokee Uprising in the appendix.)

1780-81   Invaded by British Generals Tarleton and Cornwallis, South Carolina was the scene of several major battles, notably the Battle of Camden, in the later years of the American Revolution. (See American Revolution in the appendix.)

1788   South Carolina became a state.

1860   South Carolina was the first state to secede from the Union. (See American Civil War in the appendix.)

1861   The siege of Fort Sumter in Charleston Harbor was the first battle of the Civil War.

1864   Gen. William T. Sherman invaded South Carolina and inflicted much damage.

1868   South Carolina was readmitted to statehood.

. . . .

SOUTH CAROLINA DEPARTMENT OF ARCHIVES AND HISTORY

1430 Senate Street
Columbia, South Carolina

Mailing Address:
P.O. Box 11669
Columbia, South Carolina 29211
(803) 734-8577

Finding Aids

Adjutant General of South Carolina. *Records Of The Military Department*. A notebook.

McCawley, Patrick. *Confederate Records*. A booklet.

Records

Cherokee Expedition (1759-60)

Index to Militia Payrolls, Expedition to Fort Prince George, October 1759-January 1760. A card index (in two drawers near the reference desk) alphabetically lists names of commissioned officers. Original documents are available.

American Revolution (1775-83)

NATIONAL ARCHIVES MICROFILM

Revolutionary War Rolls, 1775-1783 (M246—roll 1: Index to Organizations; roll 89: South Carolina; roll 106: Virginia Regiment)

Numbered Record Books Concerning Military Operations and Service, Pay and Settlement of Accounts, and Supplies in the War Department Collection of Revolutionary War Records (M853—roll 1, comprehensive index). Includes records of North Carolina and South Carolina officers and troops.

War Department Collection of Post-Revolutionary War Manuscripts (M904).

OTHER RECORDS

Accounts Audited of Claims Growing Out of the Revolution. For a complete description of this collection, see a comprehensive descriptive pamphlet bearing the same title, prepared by Judith M. Brimlow, South Carolina Department of Archives and History. Also see publications by Alexander S. Salley and Bobby Moss (cited below under Published Sources).

Card Index. Contains thousands of cards citing revolutionary war veterans and civilians who filed pay claims after the war, with supporting papers, against the state of South Carolina. Claims were made on the basis of vouchers (indents) previously issued by the state government after Charleston capitulated to the British in 1780.

The above records are on 165 reels of microfilm, the last roll being a finding aid consisting of three separate indexes: the first by name, the second by file number; the third is a reproduction of the card index. The cards include name, grade, unit, and account number (underlined in red). Cross-references refer to other account files. Using this information, archives staff can furnish the original files.

Card Index—Loyalists. These cards list persons whose names appeared on a list of actual or suspected Loyalists submitted by militia officers (also named). Cards are arranged alphabetically by name of the alleged Loyalist.

War of 1812 (1812–14)

NATIONAL ARCHIVES MICROFILM

Index to Compiled Service Records of Volunteer Soldiers Who Served During the War of 1812 in Organizations From the State of South Carolina (M652).

OTHER RECORDS

War of 1812. A card index (in cabinets near the reference desk). Comprises two drawers of cards prepared by the state comptroller general, giving name, rank, and unit for War of 1812 veterans. Arranged alphabetically.

Seminole War (1836)

Journal of the Volunteer Troops From Columbia in the Seminole War, 1836. Office of the Adjutant and Inspector General.

Civil War–Confederate (1861–65)

NATIONAL ARCHIVES MICROFILM

Consolidated Index to Compiled Service Records of Confederate Soldiers (M253).

Compiled Service Records of Confederate Soldiers Who Served in Organizations From the State of South Carolina (M267).

Records Relating to Confederate Naval and Marine Personnel (M260).

Compiled Service Records of Confederate General and Staff Officers, and Non-regimental Enlisted Men (M331).

Register of Confederate Soldiers, Sailors, and Citizens Who Died in Federal Prisons and Military Hospitals in the North, 1861–1865 (M918).

Records of the Commissioner of Claims ("Southern Claims Commission), 1871–80 (M187).

Prison Roll of the "Immortal 600" on Morris Island (RG 109).

Muster Rolls of Volunteer Organizations, Civil War. Adjutant General's Records (RG 94—one roll comprises South Carolina organizations).

Adjutant General's Records; List of South Carolina Organizations (sic) *Records (RG 94—one roll).*

OTHER RECORDS

South Carolina Personnel of the Civil War. A card index comprising a very incomplete list. Gives name, rank, unit, branch of service (artillery, cavalry, infantry).

List of Draft Substitutes, 1862. Adjutant general's records. Included are name of draftee and name of substitute. British subjects and other aliens are also noted.

Overseers Exempted From the Draft, 1862. Adjutant general's records. Names of persons who employed the overseers are provided, but the overseers' names are not. These also give place of residence.

Militia Enrollments, 1869. Adjutant general's records.

Confederate Graves. Three folders labeled "Civil War–Cemeteries" contain lists of Confederate graves, many submitted by Raymond W. Watkins of Falls Church, Virginia, or by the Sons of Confederate Veterans. Lists are arranged alphabetically by state. Folder one lists graves in cemeteries in Arkansas through Pennsylvania (except those found separately in folder three); folder two lists graves in South Carolina; folder three lists graves in Louisiana, Mississippi, Oklahoma, Texas, and Washington state.

Confederate Home. Applications for admission and related papers pertaining to the Confederate Home are available but have not been microfilmed. Many are not indexed. For a list of these records see Marion C. Chandler and Earl W. Wadee, *South Carolina Archives: A Temporary Summary Guide.* (Columbia: South Carolina Department of Archives and History, 1976.)

CONFEDERATE PENSIONS

Original Applications (one page each) for State Pensions Based on Confederate Service, Arranged by County. If the county is specified, a staff member will obtain the pension file. Even if the veteran's file cannot be located, his name may be found in the computer printout Applications Index, 1919-1925, where the names are listed alphabetically. Given are town and county of residence, unit, date of application, and cross-references to other applications that contain the veteran's name. In addition to identifying personal and military history information, the pension applications contain names of comrades-in-arms, information concerning income, and value of any property owned.

For other material concerning pensions not cited above, consult the section on Office of the Confederate Historian in the finding aid *Records of the Military Department*. Miscellaneous collections in that section include the following examples:

> Roster of Officers
>
> Roll of Troops
>
> Memory Roll of the Gist Rifles
>
> Gettysburg Soldiers
>
> Deceased Soldiers

Mexican War (1846–48)

The Palmetto Regiment. A card index referring to South Carolina veterans who served in the Mexican War. The cards were prepared from information found in two bound volumes: vol. 1 is available at this archives and provides name, unit, rank, and notations such as "killed," "died," or "promoted." These cards have not been microfilmed.

Muster Roll (and payroll) of Company H, 15 May 1846–30 June 1848. Adjutant general's records.

Spanish-American War (1898–99)

Personnel who served in the Spanish-American War are listed in a two-drawer card index.

Spanish-American War Muster Rolls, 1898–99. Adjutant general's records.

Duty Roster, Training Camp, 1904–11. Adjutant general's records.

Roll of National Guard officers, 1905–1921. Adjutant general's records.

Sick-calls, 1903–12. Adjutant general's records.

Punitive Expedition into Mexico (Mexican Border Service) (1916).

Muster Rolls, 1916–17. Adjutant general's records.

World War I (1917–18)

Enlistment Contracts: 1916 (cavalry, coast artillery); 1904–21 (infantry); 1907–18 (Naval Battalion and Engineer Company). Adjutant general's records.

Enlistment Contracts: 1917–18 (reserve militia). Adjutant general's records.

Muster Rolls and Enlistment Records, 1907–22. Adjutant general's records.

"History of Service" Cards for Soldiers and Sailors Serving in World War I, 1923. Arranged by white soldiers, "Negro" soldiers, and sailors. Adjutant general's records.

Individual Records of Decorations and Citations, 1899–1929. Adjutant general's records.

Applications for World War I Victory Medals, 1920–21; 1925–26. Adjutant general's records.

Officers' Oaths, 1919–27. Adjutant general's records.

Officers' Record Cards, 1878–1921. Adjutant general's records.

Casualty Lists for South Carolina Troops in the AEF (American Expeditionary Force), 1917–19. Adjutant general's records.

World War II (1941–45)

State Guard Enlistment Records, 1941–47. Adjutant general's records.

Manuscript Collections

The state archives emphasizes the public records and refers researchers who desire to see manuscript material to the South Caroliniana Library at the University of South Carolina, located a few blocks away. The library has a card index of its manuscript holdings. See *A Guide to the Manuscript Collections of the South Caroliniana Library* (Columbia: University of South Carolina, 1982).

Sample subject headings for manuscript material in this library pertaining to military actions:

> Cherokee War
> Civil War
> War of 1812
> French and Indian War
> King George's War
> Mexican War
> Philippine Insurrection
> Revolutionary War
> Seminole War
> Spanish-American War
> Vietnam Conflict
> World War I
> World War II

SOUTH CAROLINA HISTORICAL SOCIETY

100 Meeting Street
Charleston, South Carolina 29401
(803) 723-3225

The South Carolina Historical Society has a large collection of manuscripts, many of them pertaining to military service. See David Moltke-Hansen and Sallie Doscher, *South Carolina Historical Society Manuscript Guide* (Charleston: the society, 1979).

PUBLISHED SOURCES—SOUTH CAROLINA

General

South Carolina. Adjutant General's office. *Annual Reports, 1876–1989* (some years missing). Columbia: various years.

Pre-1775 (colonial wars)

Andrea, Leonardo. *South Carolina Colonial Soldiers and Patriots.* Columbia: R.L. Bryan, 1952.

Draine, Tony, and John Skinner, comps. *South Carolina Soldiers and Indian Traders, 1725–1730.* Columbia: Congaree Publications, 1986. Abstracts of payrolls of Fort Moore, Pallachoucular Fort, Johnson's Fort, scouts, rangers—including participants in the Yamasee Expedition.

Salley, Alexander S. *The Independent Company From South Carolina at Great Meadows.* Columbia: printed for the commission by the State Co., 1932. Battle of Fort Necessity, 1754.

1775-83 (American Revolution)

Bailey, James D. *Some Heroes of the American Revolution.* Spartanburg: Band and White, Printers, 1924. Includes biographical sketches of some high-ranking officers.

Bearss, Edwin C. *The Battle of Sullivan's Island.* Washington, D.C.: National Park Service, Department of the Interior, 1968. Lists those killed and wounded during an engagement with naval vessels on 28 June 1776.

Boddie, William W. *Marion's Men: A List of Twenty-five Hundred.* Charleston: Heiser Printing Co. (?), 1938.

DeSaussure, Wilmot G. *The Names as Far as Can be Ascertained of the Officers Who Served in the South Carolina Regiments, on the Continental Establishment; of the Officers Who Served in the Militia; of What Troops Were Upon the Continental Establishment and of What Militia Organizations Served.* Charleston: South Carolina Yearbook, 1893.

Ervin, Sara S., ed. *South Carolinians in the Revolution: With Service Records and Miscellaneous Data . . . 1775-1855.* Ypsilanti, Mich., 1949. Reprint. Baltimore: Genealogical Publishing Co., 1965. Contains names gleaned from a variety of sources.

Garden, Alexander. *Anecdotes of the Revolutionary War in America, With Sketches of Character of Persons the Most Distinguished, in the Southern States, for Civil and Military Services.* Charleston: 1822. Reprint. Spartanburg: The Reprint Co., 1972.

Maddox, Joseph T., and Mary Carter, comps. *South Carolina Revolutionary Soldiers, Sailors, Patriots, and Descendants.* Albany, Ga.: Georgia Pioneers Publications, ca. 1976.

Moss, Bobby G. *The Patriots of the Cowpens.* Greenville: A. Press, 1985. Contains biographical sketches of those who fought in the Battle of Cowpens, 17 January 1781.

_____. *The Patriots at Kings Mountain.* Blacksburg: Scotia-Hibernia, 1990.

_____. *Roster of South Carolina Patriots in the American Revolution.* Baltimore: Genealogical Publishing Co., 1983.

Pruitt, Jayne C.G. *Revolutionary War Pension Applicants Who Served From South Carolina.* Fairfax County, Va.: the author, 1946.

Revill, Janie. *Revolutionary Claims Filed in South Carolina.* Reprint. Baltimore: Genealogical Publishing Co., 1969.

Salley, Alexander S., Jr. *Documents Relating to the History of South Carolina During the Revolutionary War.* Columbia: State Co., 1908. A miscellaneous collection of correspondence, petitions, receipts, claims, muster rolls, and payroll rosters.

_____. *Records of the Regiments of the South Carolina Line in the Revolutionary War.* Reprinted with an index by Alida Moe. Baltimore: Genealogical Publishing Co., 1977.

_____. *South Carolina Provincial Troops: Named in Papers of the First Council of Safety of the Revolutionary Party in South Carolina, June-November, 1775.* Compiled and published by Alexander S. Salley in the *South Carolina Historical and Genealogical Magazine,* vols. 1-3 (1900-02). Reprinted with

an index by Alida Moe. Baltimore: Genealogical Publishing Co., 1977.

South Carolina. *Stub Entries to Indents Issued in Payment of Claims Against South Carolina Growing Out of the Revolution.* 12 vols. Edited by Alexander S. Salley. Excerpted from the *South Carolina Historical and Genealogical Magazine,* vols. 1-3 (1900-02). Columbia: University of South Carolina Press, 1910-27 (?). Reprint. Columbia: Printed for the South Carolina Historical Society, 1939.

South Carolina. Commissioners of the Navy Board. *Journal of the Commissioners of the Navy of South Carolina: October 19, 1776-March 1, 1779, July 22, 1779-March 23, 1780.* 2 vols. Columbia: Historical Commission of South Carolina, 1912-13.

South Carolina. State Auditor. *Copy of the Original Index Book Showing the Revolutionary Claims Filed in South Carolina Between August 20, 1783 and August 31, 1786. Kept by James McCall, Auditor General.* Copied by Janie Revill. Columbia (?): Janie Revill, 1941 (?). Reprint. Baltimore: Genealogical Publishing Co., 1969.

South Carolina. Treasury. *Accounts Audited of Revolutionary Claims Against South Carolina.* 3 vols. Edited by Alexander S. Salley. Columbia: Historical Commission of South Carolina, 1935.

1861-65 (Civil War—Confederate)

Flynn, Jean M. *The Militia in Antebellum South Carolina Society.* Spartanburg: The Reprint Co., 1991.

Ladies' Memorial Association, Charleston, South Carolina. *Confederate Memorial Day at Charleston, S.C.* Charleston: W.G. Mazyck, printer, 1871. Lists Gettysburg casualties buried at Magnolia Cemetery, Charleston.

South Carolina. Archives Department. *South Carolina Troops in Confederate Service.* 3 vols. Columbia: R.L. Bryan Co., 1913-30.

South Carolina. Commissioner of Confederate Rolls. *Report of M.P. Tribble, Commissioner of Confederate Rolls, to the General Assembly.* Columbia: state printer, 1904.

United Confederate Veterans. South Carolina Division. Camp Maj. A. Burnett Rhett, no. 767. *Confederate Gray Book.* Charleston, n.d.

United Daughters of the Confederacy. South Carolina Division. *South Carolina Women in the Confederacy.* 2 vols. Columbia: state printer, 1903-07.

1917-46 (World War I; World War II)

South Carolina. Adjutant General. *The Official Roster of South Carolina Soldiers, Sailors, and Marines in the World War, 1917-18.* 2 vols. Columbia: 1929. Columbia: 1932 (?) Vol. 1 contains an alphabetical list of names arranged by county. Vol. 2 contains biographical summaries arranged alphabetically. Included are name, address, summary of service, rank, and discharge date.

_____ . *The Official Roster of South Carolina Servicemen and Servicewomen in World War II, 1941–46.* 5 vols. Columbia: 1967. Vol. 1 contains names of those who were awarded the Medal of Honor and those on the Honor Roll. All volumes contain names of South Carolinians who served. Included are name, serial number, address, summary of service, rank, and discharge date.

South Dakota

1742–43	French explorer La Verendrye entered South Dakota.
1803	The French sold South Dakota to the United States in the Louisiana Purchase.
1804–06	American explorers Lewis and Clark crossed South Dakota.
1854	South Dakota became a part of Nebraska Territory.
1861	Dakota Territory was created, consisting of North and South Dakota.
1862	The Homestead Act increased the flow of settlers into South Dakota.
1874	Gold discovered in the Black Hills brought prospectors into South Dakota and created friction with the Indians, leading to war. (See Sioux and Cheyenne Wars in the appendix.)
1889	South Dakota became a state.
1890	Conflict between whites and Sioux Indians led to the massacre at Wounded Knee. (See Sioux and Cheyenne Wars in the appendix.)

SOUTH DAKOTA STATE HISTORICAL SOCIETY

900 Governors Drive
Pierre, South Dakota 57501-2217
(605) 773-3458

Records

General

NATIONAL ARCHIVES MICROFILM

Returns From Regular Army Infantry Regiments, June 1821–December 1916 (M665—only those rolls pertaining to military posts in Dakota Territory or South Dakota).

Letters Received by the Office of the Adjutant General (Main Series), 1861–1870 (M619—only those rolls pertaining to Dakota Territory or South Dakota).

Letters Received by the Office of the Adjutant General (Main Series), 1871–1880 (M666—only those rolls pertaining to Dakota Territory or South Dakota).

OTHER RECORDS

Veterans' Grave Registrations. Completed in 1941 by the Work Projects Administration (WPA). Arranged by county and veteran's name.

Indian Wars (1856–)

Muster Roll and Payroll for Company H, Sixth Infantry, 1856.

Monthly Returns of the Seventh Cavalry, January–December 1874.

Names of some Dakota Territory militiamen may be found in *Memorandum and Official Records Concerning Dakota Militia, Organized in 1862 for the Protection of the Frontier Settlements From the Hostile Sioux Indians,* compiled by R.C. McDowell in connection with Senate Bill No. 5353, Doc. 241, 58th Cong., 2nd sess., Washington, D.C., 1904.

Spanish-American War (1898–99)

No records pertaining to this war are available at this facility, but a roster of soldiers from the First Infantry Regiment, South Dakota Volunteers, in the Spanish-American War may be found in Doane Robinson's *History of South Dakota.* (2 vols. Chicago: B.F. Bowen & Co., 1904.)

World War I (1917–18)

World War I Veterans' Bonus Records, 1925. List of veterans and index to microfilm.

World War I Veterans' Bonus Records. Original list of paid bonuses.

Mothers' Pension (emergency relief) Benefits. Although some restrictions may apply, records are available for the following counties: Deuel (1913-40), Hughes (1923-40), Kingsbury (1922-40), Lawrence (1918-40), McCook (1917-31), Mellette (1914-40), Minnehaha (1913-40), Union (1922-40), and Walworth (1926-40).

World War II (1941-45)

World War II Veterans' Bonus Records, 1949-53.

World War II Veterans' Roster, 1950.

Bonus Miscellaneous File, 1949-82. (See the finding aid for this file.)

Korean War (1950-53)

Korean Conflict Veterans' Bonus Records, 1955-57.

Bonus Miscellaneous File, 1949-82. (See the finding aid for this file.)

Manuscripts

The South Dakota Historical Society has several collections of manuscripts, some of which contain material relating to military matters. There is a computer-generated printout of the available titles. Many consist of correspondence, reminiscences, diaries, and miscellaneous papers. The following appear to contain important data relative to names of military personnel.

South Dakota National Guard.

Roster of the Northwest Association of Veterans Philippine Service (First South Dakota Volunteer Infantry).

List of Officers, Muster Roll, Dead, Desertions, etc., Dakota Cavalry, Co. B., 1862-65.

Biographical Sketches of War Dead Who Served in World War I. Arranged alphabetically by town. Prepared by the American Legion Auxiliary of South Dakota.

Register Book for South Dakota Servicemen at the USO Club in Saigon, Vietnam, 1969-72.

PUBLISHED SOURCES—SOUTH DAKOTA

General

McDowell, R.E., comp. *Memorandum and Official Records Concerning Dakota Militia, Organized in 1862 for the Protection of the Frontier Settlements From the Hostile Sioux Indians.* Based on Senate Bill No. 5353, Doc. 241, 58th Cong., 2d sess. Washington, D.C.: 1904.

Tarbell, Wright. *History of the South Dakota National Guard: Including the Territorial Guard From the Year 1862 to the*

Present Time. Vol. 6, *South Dakota History Commission*, pages 361-490. Contains names and cause of death of servicemen from South Dakota who were killed or died during the Spanish-American War, 1898-99.

1866-99 (Spanish-American War)

Robinson, Doane. *History of South Dakota.* 2 vols. Chicago: B.F. Bowen & Co., 1904. Contains a roster of soldiers from the First Infantry Regiment, South Dakota Volunteers, who served in the Spanish-American War, 1898-99.

South Dakota. Adjutant General's Office. *Annual Report, 1898.* Pierre: State Publishing Co., 1898.

Tennessee

1672	French explorers Jacques Marquette and Louis Joliet explored the Mississippi River past Tennessee.
1756	The British built Fort Loudon in east Tennessee.
1763	By the Treaty of Paris which ended the French and Indian War, Tennessee was transferred from France to Great Britain. (See French and Indian War in the appendix.)
1771	Americans formed the Watauga Association and began settling in Tennessee.
1784	Frustrated by lack of representation in the legislature of North Carolina, which claimed Tennessee, settlers in east Tennessee seceded and formed the independent State of Franklin.
1788	The State of Franklin failed, and North Carolina again assumed government of Tennessee.
1790	Part of Tennessee became the "Territory South of the River Ohio."
1796	Tennessee became a state.
1861	Tennessee seceded from the Union.
1862-64	Tennessee became the main theater of the Civil War in the West and was the scene of more than four hundred battles, among them Shiloh, Murfreesboro, and Chattanooga. (See American Civil War in the appendix.)
1866	Tennessee was readmitted to the Union.

Tennessee State Library and Archives

403 Seventh Avenue, North
(south of the capitol)
Nashville, Tennessee 37243-0312
(615) 741-2764

Finding Aids

Microfilm catalogs to manuscripts: *Register No. 10–Civil War Collection* and *Record Group Numbers* (in folders). Both of these aids are located in the manuscript room.

Bamman, Gale. *Research in Tennessee*. NGS special publication no. 72. Arlington, Va.: 1993. This aid discusses much of Tennessee's military record collections.

Guide to the Processed Manuscripts of the Tennessee Historical Society. This book describes a variety of collections, including a Civil War collection and correspondence pertaining to the Civil War and the Mexican War.

Guide to the Microfilmed Manuscript Holdings of the TSLA (1983).

Records

General

NATIONAL ARCHIVES MICROFILM

The Negro in the Military Service of the United States, 1639–1886 (T823; Tennessee accession no. 862).

Records Relating to the U. S. Military Academy, 1812–1867 (M91).

Compiled Service Records of Volunteer Soldiers Who Served From 1784 to 1811 (M905—rolls 26–32, territory south of the Ohio River; Tennessee accession no. 877).

American Revolution (1775-83)

NATIONAL ARCHIVES MICROFILM

Index to Compiled Service Records of Volunteer Soldiers Who Served During the Revolutionary War in Organizations From the State of North Carolina (M257; Tennessee accession no. 861).

OTHER RECORDS

Revolutionary Soldiers in Tennessee. An alphabetical card index. Name, county, rank, unit, and source of information.

Microfilm Copies of Warrants Issued From 1783 to 1799 for Land in the Military Reservation of North Carolina (now middle Tennessee). Arranged by the names of North Carolina secretaries of state (Glasgow, White, and Hill) who issued the warrants. The last roll of this sixteen-roll collection lists names of those soldiers who protected the land surveyors while engaged in their duties.

North Carolina Land Grants (in Tennessee). A twenty-two-roll collection of grants. Also exists in published form (see below under Published Sources–Tennessee).

Manuscripts (see card index for manuscript collections). Headings include Pensions, Registers and Lists, etc.

War of 1812 (1812-15)

NATIONAL ARCHIVES MICROFILM

Index to Compiled Service Records of Volunteer Soldiers who Served During the War of 1812 (M602; Tennessee accession no. 976).

Index to War of 1812 Pensions Applications (M313; Tennessee accession no. 938).

OTHER RECORDS

Manuscripts (see card index for manuscript collections): "pensions," "prisoners," "registers and lists," "registers of dead," "spies and spying."

Indian Wars (pre-Civil War)

NATIONAL ARCHIVES MICROFILM

Index to Compiled Service Records of Volunteer Soldiers Who Served During the Cherokee Disturbances and Removal in Organizations From the State of North Carolina (M908; Tennessee accession no. 865).

TENNESSEE MICROFILM

Cherokee Removal of 1836. Name index to Tennesseeans. Microfilm (Tennessee accession no. 866, reel 2).

Tennesseans in Seminole Wars, 1818–1836. Index of names. Microfilm (Tennessee accession no. 867).

Officers of the Cherokee War. Muster rolls, 1836–46. Microfilm (Tennessee accession no. 866, reel 1)

OTHER RECORDS

Militia Commissions, 1796–1903 (Tennessee). A card index to some commissions. Name, rank, unit, county, and date.

Manuscripts (see card index to manuscript collections): look under name of Indian tribe (Cherokee, Creek, Seminole); also "muster rolls" and "payrolls."

Mexican War (1846-48)

NATIONAL ARCHIVES MICROFILM

Index to Compiled Service Records of Volunteer Soldiers Who Served During the Mexican War (M616).

Compiled Service Records of Volunteer Soldiers Who Served During the Mexican War in Organizations From the State of Tennessee (M638).

MANUSCRIPTS

See card index to manuscript collections. Subjects include "muster rolls" and "pensions."

Civil War–Union (1861–65)

NATIONAL ARCHIVES MICROFILM

Index to Compiled Service Records of Volunteer Union Soldiers Who Served in Organizations From the State of Tennessee (M392).

Compiled Service Records of Volunteer Union Soldiers Who Served in Organizations From the State of Tennessee (M395).

Compiled Records Showing Service of Military Units in Volunteer Union Organizations (M594–roll 206, U.S. Colored Troops). This is a "record of events" pertaining to the history of Tennessee units.

OTHER RECORDS

Civil War Collection, Confederate and Federal Documents. See finding aid *Register No. 10–Civil War Collection* in the manuscript reading room. Twelve boxes of material relating to federal troops contain mainly diaries and letters but also rosters and other military records. The inventory to this collection is indexed by name, subject, and unit.

Executive Documents, U.S. Senate, 1882–82. Five volumes. A pamphlet titled *Vol. 5, Part 5*, available in the archives reading room, lists Tennessee pensioners. Included are name, certificate number, address, cause for which pensioned, monthly rate, date of original allowance, and type of disability. Also includes names of widows receiving pensions. Arranged alphabetically under each county. For details, see below under Confederate Pension Records. Also see the publications *The Tennessee Civil War Veterans Questionnaires* and *Index to Questionnaires of Civil War Veterans* (see below under Published Sources–Tennessee).

Record of Interments in the National Cemetery, Murfreesboro (at the Stone's River National Battlefield) (microfilm). Alphabetically lists names. Rank, unit, date of death, grave marker, army serial number in the "remarks" column.

Civil War–Confederate (1861–65)

NATIONAL ARCHIVES MICROFILM

Consolidated Index to Compiled Service Records of Confederate Soldiers (M253).

Index to Compiled Service Records of Confederate Soldiers who Served in Organizations From the State of Tennessee (M231).

Compiled Service Records of Confederate Soldiers Who Served in Organizations From Tennessee (M268).

OTHER RECORDS

Tennessee Confederates. Microfilm copy (ten reels) of a card index prepared from various sources during the 1920s and 1930s.

Cites several collections pertaining to the Civil War. In some instances names, units, and source of information are given.

Register No. 10–Civil War Collection, Confederate and Federal–Microfilm. (See the finding aid in a folder located in the manuscript reading room.) Consists of a directory and inventory of 150 boxes of material relating to the Civil War gathered by the Tennessee Archives between ca. 1819 and 1865. The table of contents lists names of the collections and box numbers or microfilm numbers. Contains name and subject indexes; some collections have their own index. Sources from which the material was gathered include casualty lists, cemetery records, newspaper clippings, diaries, scrapbooks, photographs, rosters, and many others. Microfilmed collections are located in the microfilm room in cabinets labeled "Manuscript Collection." There are thirty-three drawers labeled "Microfilmed Manuscripts."

"Commission Books" list names of officers of militia units for various time periods. Vol. 7 includes the Civil War years. Names are alphabetically listed for the years 1862–65, but not for 1861–62. A microfilm series labeled "state militia" provides copies; Civil War militia is located on reel three.

"Record Group Numbers." Located in the manuscript reading room. Lists Civil War collections according to record group numbers (assigned to various state agencies). Below are some sample headings.

> Civil War Centennial Commission (RG 22)
> Confederate Soldiers' Home (RG 2)
> Army of the Tennessee–Correspondence (RG 4)

A publication by the Civil War Centennial Commission, *Tennesseans in the Civil War: A Military History of Confederate and Union Units, With Available Rosters of Personnel* (see below under Published Sources–Tennessee) is divided into two sections: "Confederate Rosters" and "Federal Rosters." These alphabetized lists were prepared chiefly from National Archives records, but they also contain names gleaned from other sources.

Confederate Muster Rolls. Three reels of microfilm contain copies of muster rolls loaned to the War Department when it created the compiled service records. The original muster rolls are too fragile to be handled (Tennessee accession no. 872).

CONFEDERATE PENSION RECORDS

Index to Tennessee Confederate Pension Applications. (Nashville: Tennessee State Library and Archives, 1964). This book, available in the archives reading room, provides name, certificate number, and unit. Using this information, a microfilm copy of a pension application may be located. The original application papers are too fragile to be handled. The film consists of 113 reels in drawers labeled "Soldiers–Pension Applications"; 60 rolls labeled "Widows' Pension Applications"; and 5 rolls labeled "Colored Soldiers' Pensions." Rolls are arranged by certificate number.

Four-page questionnaires were distributed to Union and Confederate pensioners in 1914–15 and again in 1920. The questionnaires that were returned were microfilmed and are available on nine rolls containing approximately 1,700 questionnaires, most of them Confederate. Available in the archives reading room is an *Index to Questionnaires of Civil War Veterans.* The original documents may be obtained upon request in the manuscript room. Index cards used to facilitate the distribution of the 1920 questionnaires are available (RG 133). These give name, county, unit, and date questionnaire was sent. These cards are available on one roll of microfilm.

Confederate Cemetery, Franklin, Tennessee. A list prepared in 1910 gives names according to location of the graves in the cemetery (which is divided into a sections for each state represented). Name, unit, grave number, and state section.

Locations of other Confederate graves may be found in a vertical file labeled "Confederate Burials–State." This file is located in the library reading room. This information includes submissions by Raymond W. Watkins of Falls Church, Virginia.

Confederate Prisoners Held at Clarksville, Tennessee, 1862–64. One roll of microfilm lists name, residence, charges, and date and place of arrest. Data was provided by the provost marshal records, Montgomery County, Tennessee.

United Daughters of the Confederacy. Tennessee Division–Membership. A folder in the manuscript reading room cites microfilm copies of membership lists, 1896–1986 (rolls 39, 42–56). Lists of veterans awarded metal crosses signifying military service are found in rolls 7–11, 40, and 41 of this series.

United Confederate Veterans, Tennessee Division. A folder in the manuscript room labeled "Bivouac records, 1887–1922" includes membership lists. This folder also contains a scrapbook collection of the United Daughters of the Confederacy (assembled 1927–53) that includes some names of Confederate veterans.

Manuscripts (see card index to manuscript collections): name of state; atrocities; campaigns and battles; claims; hospitals; muster rolls; Negroes; officers; physicians, prisoners, regimental histories, registers, lists, etc.; registers of dead; spies and spying; women.

Confederate Home. The manuscript room has an indexed register of residents of the home, which was established at Hermitage in 1889. It also has the applications for admission and related documents (originals and microfilm).

Spanish-American War (1898–99)

Personnel Rosters of Units Raised in Tennessee for Service in the Spanish-American War, April and May 1898. These name soldiers mustered in at Nashville and upon arrival at Manila in the Philippines, December 1898. Includes rolls for the First, Second, Third, and Fourth Regiments.

Spanish-American War Veterans' Roster, prepared 1942. Names of veterans contacted; name, address, service history, and date of death of those deceased. Deaths that occurred after 1942 have been noted. Available on microfilm (Tennessee accession no. 69).

World War I (1917–18)

World War I veterans and ex-servicemen are listed in a folder and also in a microfilmed copy. Arranged alphabetically for each county. Name, serial number, hometown, place of enlistment, age, organizations in which served, and date of discharge. Includes biographical sketches. Another folder contains a scrapbook, 1919–20, with a handwritten index.

See county records for discharges of some veterans; also for names of men who died in service (Gold Star records).

World War II (1941–45)

A folder labeled "World War II Collection" contains newspaper clippings, lists, and photographs. Pertains to soldiers as well as naval personnel and Women Accepted for Volunteer Emergency Service (WAVES).

Armed Forces Absentee Ballots, 1944–62. Arranged by county in volumes, with an index for each volume. Microfilmed copies have an alphabetical index (by first initial only) arranged by county. Name, military serial number, service address, home address, and date the ballot was sent.

PUBLISHED SOURCES–TENNESSEE

1775–83 (American Revolution)

Allen, Penelope J. *Tennessee Soldiers in the Revolution.* Baltimore: Genealogical Publishing Co., 1975. References to accounts in the North Carolina State Archives.

Bates, Lucy W. *Roster of Soldiers and Patriots of the American Revolution Buried in Tennessee.* Brentwood: Tennessee Society, Daughters of the American Revolution, 1974. Rev. ed. 1979.

Burgner, Goldene F. *North Carolina Land Grants in Tennessee, 1778–1791.* Easley, S.C.: Southern Historical Press, 1981. Revised edition of the same title by Betty G.C. Cartwright and Lillian J. Gardner. Memphis: 1958.

Crutchfield, James A. *Tennesseans at War: Volunteers and Patriots in Defense of Liberty.* Nashville: Rutledge Hill Press, 1987. Includes some lists of names and some biographical sketches with portraits for the American Revolution through the Vietnam War, with those awarded the Medal of Honor.

Daughters of the American Revolution. Tennessee Society. General Francis Nash Chapter. *Index: Roster and Soldiers, the Tennessee Society of the DAR.* 2 vols. Nashville: 1976.

Haywood, John. "List of North Carolina Revolutionary Soldiers Given Land in Tennessee, by the Act of 1782–83" in *The Civil and Political History of the State of Tennessee. . . . ,* pages 218–20. Knoxville: 1823. Reprint. New York: Arno Press, 1971.

Whitely, Edythe. *Revolutionary Soldiers Who Were Granted Land in Tennessee for Their Services in That War.* Nashville: 1939 (?).

1784-1815 (War of 1812)

Allen, Penelope J. *Tennessee Soldiers in the War of 1812; Regiments of Colonel Allcorn and Colonel Allison.* Chattanooga: Tennessee Society, United States Daughters of the War of 1812, 1947.

Armstrong, Zella. *Twenty-four Hundred Tennessee Pensioners: Revolution, War of 1812.* Chattanooga: Lookout Publishing Co., 1937. Reprint. Baltimore: Genealogical Publishing Co., 1975. Includes an alphabetical list of names, date of pension list, age, where served, and in what county drew pension.

McCown, Mary H. *Soldiers of the War of 1812 Buried in Tennessee: Names Abstracted From Colonel David Henley's "Wastebook," Regular and Militia Personnel for Period 1793–1798, in Southwest Territory (Tennessee). . . .* Johnson City: Tennessee Society, United States Daughters of the War of 1812, 1959. Reprint. Johnson City (?): McCown, 1977. Contains biographical notes on veterans; arranged alphabetically.

Moore, Mary B. D., comp. *Record of Commissions of Officers in the Tennessee Militia, 1796–1815 . . . With a New Introduction by Robert M. McBride and an Index for the Years 1812–1815 by Anite Comtois.* Baltimore: Genealogical Publishing Co., 1977. Contains names listed by county with rank and date of commission. Pt. I: 1786-1801, 1807-1811 (indexed); pt. II: 1812-1815 (indexed).

1816-60 (Mexican War)

Brock, Reid, et al. *Volunteers: Tennesseans in the War with Mexico.* 2 vols. Nashville (?): Kitchen Table Press, 1986. Contains name, rank, unit, date and place of enlistment, age, and some comments.

1861-65 (Civil War)

Humes, Thomas W. *The Loyal Mountaineers of Tennessee.* Knoxville: 1888. Reprint. Spartanburg, S.C.: The Reprint Co., 1974.

Lindsley, John B., ed. *The Military Annals of Tennessee. Confederate. First Series: Embracing a Review of Military Operations, With Regimental Histories and Memorial Rolls, Compiled From Original and Official Sources.* Nashville: the editor, 1886. Reprint. Spartanburg, S.C.: The Reprint Co., 1974. "Two additional parts ('series') were planned, but never published."

Pompey, Sherman L. *Tennessee Confederates Buried in Illinois.* Clovis, Calif. (?): 1970 (?).

Sistler, Byron. *1890 Civil War Veterans Census, Tennesseans in Texas.* Nashville: B. Sistler & Associates, 1978. Alphabetically arranged with county of residence, enumeration district, and page number; name of widow (if any); veteran's alias (if any); rank and unit; dates of enlistment and discharge; post office address; disability incurred; and remarks.

Tennessee. Adjutant General's Office. *Report of the Adjutant General of the State of Tennessee, of the Military Forces of the State, From 1861 to 1866.* Nashville, S.C.: state printer, 1866.

Tennessee. Civil War Centennial Commission. *Tennesseans in the Civil War: A Military History of Confederate and Union Units, With Available Rosters of Personnel.* 2 vols. Nashville: the commission, 1964. Reprint. Knoxville: University of Tennessee Press, 1981. Index by Tennessee State Library. Pt. II: Confederate and Union rosters with name, rank, company and regiment.

Tennessee. State Library and Archives, Nashville. Manuscript Division. *Index to Questionnaires of Civil War Veterans.* Nashville: the archives, 1962. A three-part index: white veterans, widows, and "colored" veterans.

The Tennessee Civil War Veterans Questionnaires. Compiled by Gustavus W. Dyer and John Trotwood Moore. 5 vols. Easley, S.C.: Southern Historical Press, 1985. The result of approximately 1,600 questionnaires completed by Union and Confederate Tennessee Civil War veterans, 1915 to 1922; alphabetically arranged. Includes personal and family data, military service, and opinions regarding specific matters.

United Confederate Veterans. Tennessee Division. Confederate Historical Association, Camp No. 28, Memphis. *Confederate Gray Book, 1909.* Memphis: the association, 1909. Includes some portraits.

Wiefering, Edna. *Tennessee Confederate Widows and Their Families: Abstracts of 11,190 Confederate Widows' Applications.* Cleveland, Tenn.: Cleveland Public Library, 1992.

Wright, Marcus J. *Tennessee in the War, 1861–1865.* New York: A. Lee Publishing Co., 1908. Tennessee Union and Confederate regiments and names of officers.

Texas

1682	The Spanish established a settlement at Isleta, the first of a series of missions across Texas.
1803-06	A boundary dispute arose between Texas and Louisiana after the Louisiana Purchase.
1819	The Adams-Onis Transcontinental Treaty with Spain permanently fixed the Texas-Louisiana border.
1821	Mexico achieved independence from Spain, and Texas became Mexican territory.
1821	Moses Austin and other Americans received permission from Mexico to settle in Texas.
1836	American settlers in Texas won their independence from Mexico. (See War for Texas Independence in the appendix.)

1845	The independent Republic of Texas was annexed by the United States as the State of Texas.
1846–48	Boundary disputes and conflicts between Texas and Mexico led to the Mexican War. (See Mexican War in the appendix.)
1861	Texas seceded from the Union. (See American Civil War in the appendix.)
1866	Texas was readmitted to the Union.

. . . .

TEXAS STATE LIBRARY AND ARCHIVES

1201 Brazos Street
Austin, Texas

Mailing Address:
P.O. Box 12927
Capitol Station
Austin, Texas 78711-2927
(512) 463-5480

Finding Aids

Index to Applications for Texas Confederate Pensions, With Supplemental Indexes. This finding aid is in three parts: "Approved Applications," "Confederate Home Inmates," and "Rejected Applications for Pensions." This guide updates and corrects errors found in a previous publication: *Index to Applications for Confederate Pensions*; this guide can be found in many libraries.

Index to Rejected Pension Applications. This notebook supplements part three of the above finding aid.

Confederate Homes. This notebook is in three parts: "The Men's Home," "The Women's Home," and "Roster Index."

A Guide to Genealogical Resources in the Texas State Archives. Austin: Texas State Library, Archives Division, 1984. Included are titles of manuscript collections, some of which contain references to military personnel.

Official Records–State Agencies. This finding aid lists and describes collections of records by name and record group. Collections with genealogical or military information are the following:

> Governor's Office (RG 301)
> Secretary of States (RG 307)
> Comptroller of Public Accounts (RG 304)
> General Land Office (RG 305)
> Legislature (RG 100)

> Adjutant General (RG 401)
> Convention of 1836 (RG 008)
> State Board of Control (RG 303)
> Texas Historical Survey Committee (RG 808)
> Texas Military Board (RG 014)
> Nacogdoches Archives (RG 004)
> Secession Convention (RG 010)
> Records Relating to Indian Affairs (RG 005)
> Laredo Archives (RG 025)

Records

General

General Service Records, 1836–1902.

Muster Rolls, 1836–1917.

Claim Records, 1836–46.

Adjutant General's Records: Muster Rolls, 1836–1911.

Adjutant General's Records: General Service Records, 1836–1902.

Legislature Records: Memorials and Petitions.

Secession Convention Records: Memorials and Petitions.

State Board of Control Records: State Cemetery List.

Republic of Texas (1835–45)

Donation Lands Granted to Widows and Surviving Veterans (as of 1881). See Thomas Lloyd Miller, *Bounty and Donation Land Grants of Texas, 1835–1888.* (Austin: University of Texas Press, 1967.)

Comptroller of Public Accounts Records: Pensions, Republic.

Comptroller of Public Accounts Records: Unpaid Claims, Republic.

Comptroller of Public Accounts records: Audited Military claims, Republic.

General Land Office Records: Muster Roll Book, Texas Revolution.

Civil War–Confederate (1861–65)

NATIONAL ARCHIVES MICROFILM

Index to Compiled Service Records of Confederate Soldiers Who Served in Organizations From the State of Texas (M227).

TEXAS MICROFILM

Confederate Military Service Records. These are copies of muster rolls for Texas military units.

OTHER RECORDS

Confederate Pension Files for Disabled Veterans and Widows, if Classified Indigent. These files are not on microfilm, but the original applications and supporting papers are available for inspection. The files are arranged in numerical order and must be requested by number (or by name if the application was rejected). The file numbers may be obtained by consulting the finding aids cited above.

Pensions were paid either in cash or as scrip that entitled the veteran or his widow to 1,280 acres of land. A 1925 amendment to the pension laws extended pension privileges to those who saw military service relative to hostilities against Indians and Mexican raiders. In 1917, another amendment provided for payment of burial expenses. This obligation generated documents titled "Confederate Mortuary Warrants"; copies were placed in the pension file.

Lists of Confederate Indigent Families, 1863-65. County courts compiled lists of needy families of Confederate soldiers who received financial relief. These names are arranged by county; it is necessary to search the names of each county list to determine the exact location of the record.

Comptroller of Public Accounts Records: Audited Military Claims, Civil War.

Confederate Soldiers' Home Files. Files for inmates of the men's home cover the periods 1836-91, during which the home was supported by private donations; 1891-63, during which it was under state jurisdiction; and 1963 to the present, during which it was administered by the state hospital at Kerrville.

The women's home was established in 1908 by the United Daughters of the Confederacy. It was taken over by the state in 1911, and the state continued to support the home until it was closed in 1964.

Before allowing inspection of men's or women's home records, staff members will examine files to determine if there is any medical information of a confidential nature.

Graves of Civil War Veterans. The Texas Historical Survey Committee located and cataloged many graves of Civil War veterans. Considerable biographical information is included, as are the gravestone inscriptions.

Raymond W. Watkins Collection of Confederate Graves. This archives maintains a card catalog of submissions by Mr. Watkins, a native of Falls Church, Virginia, who regularly submits to southern state archives and libraries data pertaining to Confederate graves that he locates.

Manuscripts available at this archives are cataloged in a card index. The following are examples of some collections that contain references to military matters:

Confederate Regiments From Texas—"administrative control documents" for records held by the U.S. War Department.

Declarations for Survivors' Pensions, Indian Wars. These are claims by veterans or widows of veterans for military service in the Indian Wars. Eligibility was extended also to Texas Rangers who assisted the army in suppression of Indian hostility.

Harbert Davenport Collection—biographical studies of Col. James W. Fannin's command at Goliad.

Houston Wade Papers—biographical sketches of participants in the Mier Expedition, the Somervell Expedition, and the Dawson Massacre.

Louis Wiltz Kemp Papers—biographical sketches of participants of the Battle of San Jacinto.

DESCENDANTS OF MEXICAN WAR VETERANS

P.O. Box 830482
Richardson, Texas 75083-0482

This organization is a private, nonprofit national lineage society that assists researchers who seek ancestors who participated in the Mexican War (1846-48). Most pensions for military service in this war were awarded from 1887 until as late as 1926, but invalid pensions (due to war wounds) and widows' pensions for women whose husbands were killed in the war were awarded as early as 1848. The organization will check the printed index to Mexican War Pension Files as well as the printed index to Old Wars Pension Files. The organization will also check the printed index of *Known Military Dead of the Mexican War*.

The organization is compiling a collection of Mexican War regimental rosters and currently has complete or partial holdings for the following states and organizations: Texas, Arkansas, Maryland and the District of Columbia, Mississippi, Georgia, and Massachusetts, the Mormon Battalion and Doniphan's Missouri Mounted Volunteers. Acquisition of National Archives microfilm records pertaining to Mexican War military service is under way.

All requests are researched by volunteers. Requests should be limited to no more than three specific individuals per request. No lengthy surname searches can be accommodated. A self-addressed, stamped envelope should be included with each request.

PUBLISHED SOURCES—TEXAS

General

Devereaux, Linda E. *The Texas Navy*. Nacogdoches: the author, 1983. Distributed, St. Louis: Ingmire, 1983. Lists commissioned officers and muster rolls, 1835-1938.

Miller, Thomas L. *Bounty and Donation Land Grants of Texas, 1835-1888*. Austin: University of Texas Press, 1967. Approximately 15,000 names arranged alphabetically with bounty warrant or donation certificate number (or both);

number of acres; dates of military service; and location of land assigned. Sources cited.

Pre-1860 (Indian Wars; War of 1812; Texas Revolution)

Barron, John C., et al. *Republic of Texas Pension Application Abstracts.* Austin: Austin Genealogical Society, 1987.

Brown, John H. *Indian Wars and Pioneers of Texas.* Austin: L.E. Daniell, 1880. Reprint. Austin: State House Press, 1988. Covers the period 1815–76; includes some portraits.

Daughters of the Republic of Texas. *Roster of Texas Daughters of Revolutionary Ancestors.* The society, 1976.

_____. *Defenders of the Republic of Texas.* Vol. 1. Austin: Laurel House Press, 1989. Contains Texas Army muster rolls, receipt rolls, and other rolls, 1836–41.

_____. *Muster Rolls of the Texas Revolution.* Lubbock: the society, 1986.

Everyname Index of 7,000 Entries Extracted From the Indian Wars and Pioneers of Texas by John Henry Brown. Compiled by William H. McLean. Edited by Mrs. Harry J. Morris. Dallas: Texas State Genealogical Society, 1976.

Dixon, Samuel H., and Louis W. Kemp. *The Heroes of San Jacinto.* Houston: Anson Jones Press, 1932. Contains biographical sketches from official documents.

Fay, Mary S. *War of 1812 Veterans in Texas.* From notes compiled by Mae W. McFarland. New Orleans: Polyanthos, 1979. Contains biographical data for each veteran.

Ingmire, Frances T., comp. *Texas Frontiersmen, 1839–1860: Minute Men, Militia, Home Guard, Indian Fighters.* St. Louis: Ingmire Publications, 1982.

Kemp, Louis W. *The Honor Roll of the Battle.* San Jacinto Monument, Texas (?): San Jacinto Museum of History Association (?), 1951 (?). A roster of officers and men who participated in the skirmish of 20–21 April 1836, pages 37–43.

Pohl, James W. *The Battle of San Jacinto.* Austin: Texas State Historical Association, 1989.

Reid, Samuel C. *The Scouting Expeditions of McCulloch's Texas Rangers; or, the Summer and Fall Campaign of the Army of the United States in Mexico, 1846. . . .* Philadelphia: 1847. Reprint. Freeport, N.Y.: Books for Libraries Press, 1970 (?).

Rosenthal, Phil, and Bill Groneman. *Roll Call at the Alamo.* Fort Collins, Colo.: The Old Army Press, 1985.

Spurlin, Charles D., comp. *Texas Veterans in the Mexican War: Muster Rolls of Texas Military Units.* Nacogdoches: Ericson Books, 1984. Veterans listed by regiment and company.

Stapp, William Preston. *The Prisoners of Perote: Containing a Journal Kept by the Author, Who was Captured by the Mexicans, at Mier, December 25, 1842, and Released From Perote, May 16, 1844.* Philadelphia: G.B. Zieber and Co., 1845. Reprint. Barker Texas History Center Series, no. 1. Austin: University of Texas press, 1977.

1861–65 (Civil War)

Dilts, Bryan L., comp. *1890 Texas Census Index of Civil War Veterans or Their Widows.* Salt Lake City: Index Publishing, 1984.

Fitzhugh, Lester N., comp. *Texas Batteries, Battalions, Regiments, Commanders, and Field Officers, Confederate States Army, 1861–1865.* Midlothian (?): Mirror Press (?), 1959 (?).

Johnson, Sidney S. *Texans Who Wore the Gray.* Tyler (?): 1907 (?). Includes rosters and biographical sketches.

Kinney, John M., comp. *Index to Applications for Texas Confederate Pensions.* Austin: Archives Division, Texas State Library, 1975. Revised edition by Peggy Oakley. Austin: Archives Division, Texas State Library, 1977.

Miller, Thomas L. *Texas Confederate Scrip Grantees.* Austin: the author, 1985.

Pompey, Sherman L. *Genealogical Notes on Texas Military Units, C.S.A.* (?). 12 vols. Albany, Oreg.: the author, 1984.

_____. *Muster Lists of the Texas Confederate Rangers.* Albany, Oreg.: the author, 1984.

_____. *Muster Lists of the Texas Confederate Troops.* 8 vols. in 1. Independence, Calif.: Historical and Genealogical Publishing Co., 1966.

Sistler, Byron. *1890 Civil War Veterans Census, Tennesseans in Texas.* Nashville, Tenn.: Sistler & Associates, 1978.

Thompson, Jerry D. *Mexican Texans in the Union Army.* Southwestern Studies, no. 78. El Paso: Texas Western Press, 1986. Includes name, rank, age, occupation, date of death, and place of birth (if known), pages 45–75.

White, Virgil D., trans. *Index to Texas CSA Pension Files.* Waynesboro, Tenn.: National Historical Publishing Co., 1989.

Wright, Marcus J. *Texas in the War, 1861–1865.* Hillsboro: Hill Junior College Press, 1965 (?). Revised 1984.

Yeary, Mamie, comp. *Reminiscences of the Boys in Gray, 1861–1865.* Dallas: Smith & Lamar Publishing House, 1912.

Utah

1765	Spanish explorer Juan Maria de Rivera made two expeditions into southern Utah.
1776	Spanish missionaries Dominguez and Escalante crossed Utah, proceeding as far north as Utah Lake.
1841	The Bidwell-Bartleson party of California emigrants took the first wagons across Utah.
1847	Mormons led by Brigham Young established Salt Lake City.
1850	As part of the Compromise of 1850, Utah became a territory.
1857–58	Motivated by reports of despotic government, United States troops established Camp Floyd west of Utah Lake. (See Utah War in the appendix.)
1890	The "Manifesto" issued by Mormon President Wilford Woodruff ended Mormon sanction of polygamy, paving the way for statehood.
1896	Utah became a state.

. . . .

UTAH STATE ARCHIVES AND RECORDS SERVICE

Research Center
Archives Building, State Capitol
Salt Lake City, Utah 84114
(801) 538-3013

This repository's archival records are stored offsite. Therefore, it is recommended that requests (by mail, telephone, or in person) be made at least twenty-four hours in advance.

Records

General

Military Service Cards, 1898–1975. This card catalog contains basic information concerning the military service of Utah residents who served in the armed forces. Most of the cards pertain to World War I and World War II, but there are also some pertaining to the Spanish-American War and the Mexican Border Service. A few others pertain to the Korean War and the Vietnam War.

Military separation forms and benefit records, 1917–79. These consist of various forms showing separation from the military service; they pertain primarily to World War II and post-World War II. The cards provide personal data about the veteran and data relating to transfer and discharge, selective service, military service, and various other related matters. Consult the inventory of holdings in this collection.

Also included among these papers are some that pertain to educational benefits and exemption from property taxes. Some newspaper clippings, muster rolls from the Mormon Battalion, and lists of military personnel from Utah killed during World War II can also be found.

Military Discharge Records, 1905–47; 1925–59. These are certificates of discharge from the army or navy. Name, age, physical description, civilian occupation, and date of discharge. Indexed.

Military Discharge Records Recorded With County Recorders. These cover various dates, generally between 1919 and 1973, and represent the following counties: Box Elder, Duchesne, Emery, Juab, Millard, Sevier, and Wayne.

Territorial Period (1850–95)

Militia Records, 1849–77. These refer to the territorial militia known as the Nauvoo Legion, and consist of correspondence, receipts and bills, diaries and journals, muster rolls, payrolls, rosters, reports, and returns. Also available on microfilm.

Militia Service Cards, 1850–80. Microfilm. This card file lists the personnel of the Nauvoo Legion. Name, rank, name of company captain, and dates of service.

Indian Wars (1850–95)

Affidavits by Soldiers Who Participated in Indian War Service During the State's Territorial Period. Affidavits include name, residence, length of residence, age, date of enrollment, type of company (infantry, cavalry, etc.), company captain, length of service, date of release, and other miscellaneous data. A space was also provided for a description of duties and engagements in which participated. Also shown are witnesses named and an oath taken concerning the accuracy of the data (which often was supplied by the widow or child of a deceased veteran).

Indian War Veteran Medal Records. Applications by a veteran or next of kin for a medal for Indian war service during the state's territorial period. Such service might have been as a soldier in the Black Hawk War, the Walker War, Navajo raids, Shoshone War, Paiute raids, and Tintic skirmishes. The applications give name, enrollment age, place of birth, current residence, company commander's name, place, years and type of military service, and the applicant's signature. The statements of two witnesses are also included.

Mexican Border Service (1916)

Military Service Cards. Microfilm. This is part of the card catalog cited above. Name; rank; enlistment date, place, and troop; and discharge date or muster-out date and place.

World War I (1917-18)

World War I Service Records. Microfilm. Statements of service for army and marine personnel in World War I. Typical information provided includes name, service number, race, residence, whether enlisted or inducted, place and date of entry into service, place and date of birth, military history, and discharge data. Consult the inventory of holdings in this collection.

Service Questionnaires, 1914-18. Questionnaires, often with photographs appended, submitted by Utah veterans for the purpose of compiling a state history of World War I participation. The questionnaires contain data pertaining to induction, overseas service, promotions, and casualties; also remarks. Also given are personal and family history and training camp data.

World War II (1941-45)

Selective Service Cards, 1940-57. Name, address, rank, branch of service, local draft board number and location. Includes World War II veterans and others who entered the service following that war.

Veterans' Educational Benefits. Microfilm. This collection consists of Veterans Administration forms used by veterans who applied for educational or training benefits. It also includes forms required by the University of Utah for veterans who enrolled at that institution. Consult the inventory of holdings in this collection.

Vietnam War (1963-75)

Veterans' Case Files, 1973-79. Microfilm. These are records used to assist veterans in establishing their rights to compensation or privileges as a result of their military service. These documents are restricted under the federal Privacy Act and are available to the veteran or his family only under certain conditions.

FAMILY HISTORY LIBRARY, GENEALOGICAL SOCIETY OF UTAH

Thirty-five North West Temple
Salt Lake City, Utah 84150
(801) 240-2331

This library is operated under the auspices of the Church of Jesus Christ of Latter-day Saints (LDS) and is not part of the state or local government. It operates as a service not only to the members of the society but also to any researcher without regard to religious denomination. See chapter 7 for a full description of the resources available at this library.

PUBLISHED SOURCES—UTAH

General

Utah State Archives. *Veterans With Federal Service Buried in the State of Utah, Territorial Period to 1965.* Salt Lake City: the archives, 1965.

_____. *Veterans Buried in Utah.* Salt Lake City: the archives, 1983. Microfiche.

Vermont

1609	French explorer Samuel de Champlain discovered the lake that bears his name.
1724	English settlers established Fort Dummer.
1764	A long-standing boundary dispute between New York and New Hampshire over ownership of Vermont ended with the area going to New York.
1775-77	During the American Revolution, the Battles of Ft. Ticonderoga and Bennington took place in Vermont. (See American Revolution in the appendix.)
1777	Vermont declared itself independent of both New York and New Hampshire.
1791	Vermont became a state.
1814	Thomas MacDonough defeated a British fleet on Lake Champlain in the War of 1812. (See War of 1812 in the appendix.)
1861-65	Vermont contributed a greater percentage of money and men to the Union effort than any other state during the Civil War. (See American Civil War in the appendix.)

The Vermont State Archives, a division of the Office of the Secretary of State, has no military record holdings. Such records may be obtained at the state facilities described below.

GENERAL SERVICES CENTER

Located in Middlesex, Vermont, five miles west of Montpelier on Route 2W.

Mailing address:
Vermont Agency of Administration
General Services Center
133 State Street
Montpelier, Vermont 05633-7601

Records

The holdings of this center consist entirely of microfilmed records. Although there are no finding aids, there is a card index that lists microfilm titles.

A fire in 1945 at the Office of the State Adjutant General destroyed virtually all of the state's military records for the years prior to 1920. Fortunately, each town had created records relating to its soldiers and sailors, including summaries of their military service and records of bounties received, especially for the Civil War era. Those summaries were loaned to the center, where they were microfilmed and then returned. These are possibly the most useful military records in this center. They provide name, unit, date enlisted, and dates mustered in and mustered out. A separate column notes the amount of any bounty paid by the town, state, or the United States.

General

NATIONAL ARCHIVES MICROFILM

Register of Enlistments in the United States Army, 1796–1914 (M233). This center has only the rolls that cover the period prior to 17 May 1815.

OTHER RECORDS

Graves Registration Cards. The original cards may be examined in the Office of the State Adjutant General (see below under Records—General).

Vermont Militia: Second Brigade, Third Division, 1839–44.

Civil War–Union (1861–65)

Manuscripts (letters, diaries, and memoirs submitted by various donors).

Atwater, Dorance. *Union Soldiers Buried at Andersonville, 1864– 65.* A microfilm copy.

DEPARTMENT OF VETERANS AFFAIRS, OFFICE OF THE ADJUTANT GENERAL

120 State Street
Montpelier, Vermont 05620-4401
(802) 828-3379

This organization maintains records of discharges, separation papers, and statements of service for Vermont residents who served during World War I, World War II, the Korean War, and the Vietnam War. Most of these records are restricted under federal Privacy Act provisions.

Records

General

National Guard Rosters, Payrolls, Muster Rolls, and Morning Reports for Several Units After 1916. An index is available for National Guard and militia personnel, primarily beginning with the World War I period. Except for the very early records, federal Privacy Act restrictions apply. However, staff members can furnish most of the information contained on the cards.

Graves Registration Cards. A project undertaken by the Work Projects Administration (WPA) during the 1940s involved taking inventories of cemeteries to record the graves of veterans of all wars. Cards are available for those who served in the American Revolution, War of 1812, Spanish-American War, Mexican War, Civil War, World War I, World War II, and Korea.

Spanish-American War (1898-99)

Card Index of Vermont Soldiers Who Served in the Spanish-American War.

VERMONT HISTORICAL SOCIETY LIBRARY

109 State Street
Montpelier, Vermont 05609
(802) 828-2291

Although this society has no original military documents, it does have some publications of the state adjutant general that contain names of military personnel (cited below under Published Sources—Vermont). These include:

Roster of Soldiers in the War of 1812–1814.

Revised Roster of Vermont Volunteers and Lists of Vermonters Who Served in the Army and Navy of the United States During the War of the Rebellion, 1861–1866.

Roster of Vermont Men and Women in the . . . World War, 1917–1919.

Roster of Vermonters in Uniformed Service of the United States During the Second World War, 1941–45.

Also available in this library and in the Office of the Department of Veterans Affairs (see above) is a copy of *Roster of Vermonters Who Served in the Vietnam War Era, 1964–1975.*

PUBLISHED SOURCES—VERMONT

1775-83 (American Revolution)

Bascom, Robert O. *The Ticonderoga Expedition of 1775; List of Men With Ethan Allen.* N.p., 1910.

Crockett, Walter H. *Revolutionary Soldiers Interred in Vermont.* Burlington: 1905. Reprinted as *Soldiers of the Revolutionary War Buried in Vermont and Anecdotes and Incidents Relating to Some of Them.* Baltimore: Genealogical Publishing Co., 1973. Rutland: Tuttle Antiquarian Books, 198- (?). Originally published in *Proceedings of the Utah Historical Society 1903-04, 1907.* Alphabetically arranged by locale, the list includes pensioners under the acts of 1812 and 1832 as well as invalid pensioners.

Goodrich, John E. *Rolls of the Soldiers in the Revolutionary War, 1775 to 1783.* Rutland: Tuttle Co., 1904.

The Green Mountain Boys; and Men With Ethan Allen at Ticonderoga. Burlington: 1905-05.

Vermont. *Rolls of Soldiers in the Revolutionary War, 1775–1782.* Compiled and edited by John E. Goodrich. Rutland: Tuttle Co., 1904.

1784-1815 (War of 1812)

Clark, Byron N., ed. *A List of Pensioners of the War of 1812: With an Appendix Containing Names of Volunteers for the Defence of Plattsburgh From Vermont Towns, a Description of the Battle From Contemporary Sources, the Official Statement of Losses, and Names of United States Officers and Soldiers at Burlington, Vermont, as Shown on Army Pay and Muster Rolls Recently Brought to Light.* Burlington: 1904. Reprint. Baltimore: Genealogical Publishing Co., 1969. Pensioners and widows with service record, date and place of death, and other data.

Vermont. Adjutant General's Office. *Roster of Soldiers in the War of 1812-14.* St. Albans: Messenger Press, 1933. Alphabetically arranged with service data and sources.

_____. *Muster Rolls of the Virginia Militia in the War of 1812, Being a Supplement to the Pay Rolls Printed and Distributed in 1851.* Richmond: state printer, 1852.

The Vermont Historical Gazetteer. . . . Edited by Abby M. Hemenway. 6 vols. Burlington: the editor, 1868-1923. Includes muster rolls of various military units, some guarding "the northern frontier," some in the Mexican War—vols. 2, 3, and 4. Also see *Index to the Contents of The Vermont Historical Gazetteer.* Edited by Abbie M. Hemenway. Rutland: Tuttle, 1923.

1861-65 (Civil War)

Benedict, George G. *Vermont in the Civil War . . . 1861-5.* 2 vols. Burlington: Free Press Association, 1886-88. Includes some portraits.

Muster Rolls of the Vermont Regiments Mustered Into the Service of the United States Since the Commencement of the Rebellion. Rutland: G.A. Tuttle, 1862.

Pompey, Sherman L. *Civil War Veterans Buried in the Mid-West.* 4 (?) vols. Clovis, Calif. (?): 1970-(?) Vol. 4: Vermont.

Vermont. Adjutant and Inspector General's Office. *Register of Commissioned Officers of the Vermont Volunteers, in the Service of the United States.* Montpelier (?): Walton's Steam Press (?), 1983.

_____. *Revised Roster of Vermont Volunteers and Lists of Vermonters Who Served in the Army and Navy of the United States During the War of the Rebellion, 1861-66.* Montpelier: Press of the Watchman Publishing Co., 1892.

Waite, Otis F. R. *Vermont in the Great Rebellion: Containing Historical and Biographical Sketches, etc.* Claremont, N.H.: Tracy, Chase and Co., 1869.

1866-99 (Spanish-American War)

Vermont. Adjutant and Inspector General's Office. *Vermont in the Spanish-American War. . . .* Montpelier: Capital City Press, 1929.

1900-45 (World War I; World War II)

Vermont. Adjutant General's Office. *Roster of Vermont Men and Women in the Military and Naval Service of the United States and Allies in the World War, 1917-1919.* Montpelier: Rutland, Tuttle Co. (?), 1927.

_____. *Roster of Vermonters in Uniformed Service of the United States During the Second World War, 1941-1945. . . .* 2 vols. Montpelier: 1972-1974. Alphabetically arranged with name, date and place of birth, place of residence, date of enlistment, dates of active duty, place of foreign service, and other data.

1964-1975 (Vietnam War)

Vermont. Adjutant General's Office. *Roster of Vermonters Who Served in the Vietnam War Era, 1964-1975.* Montpelier: 1986.

Virginia

1607   The first permanent English colony in America was established at Jamestown.

1612   John Rolfe began growing tobacco, which became Virginia's first cash crop.

1618   The House of Burgesses became America's first representative governmental body.

1622-44   Conflicts with Indians led to virtual extermination of them by the white settlers. (See Jamestown Conflicts in the appendix.)

1625   Virginia became a royal colony after James I revoked the Virginia Company's charter the previous year.

1676   Dissatisfaction with the royal governor and colonists' desire for Indian lands led to Bacon's Rebellion. (See Bacon's Rebellion in the appendix.)

1754-55   Virginia militiamen participated in two assaults on the French Fort Duquesne in the French and Indian War. (See French and Indian War in the appendix.)

1774   Lord Dunmore's War was a conflict between white settlers and Indians on the Ohio River frontier of Virginia. (See Lord Dunmore's War in the appendix.)

1781   The Revolutionary War moved into the South and culminated with the defeat of Lord Cornwallis' army at Yorktown by combined American and French forces under Washington and Lafayette. (See American Revolution in the appendix.)

1788   Virginia became a state.

1792   Kentucky was separated from Virginia and became a state.

1814   A British fleet sailed up the Potomac River to attack Washington, D.C. (See War of 1812 in the appendix.)

1861   Virginia seceded from the Union.

1861-65   Richmond became the capital of the Confederate States of America, and Virginia was the main eastern theater of the Civil War. Many battles and campaigns were played out on Virginia soil. (See American Civil War in the appendix.)

1863   West Virginia separated from Virginia, establishing Virginia's present borders.

1870   Virginia was readmitted to the Union.

VIRGINIA STATE LIBRARY AND ARCHIVES

Eleventh Street at Capitol Square
Richmond, Virginia 23219
(804) 786-8929

Finding Aids

Military Records Guide. This notebook lists the military collections in the archives.

Guide to State Records in the Archives Branch, Virginia State Library. Compiled by John S. Salmon, these notebooks list selected records. See this finding aid for the precise location of each record.

Office of the Second Auditor Inventory. Compiled by Emily J. Salmon and John S. Salmon.

Guide to Miscellaneous Microfilm. A list of titles of film available in the microfilm reading room.

Records

General

War Office Collection. Returns, Army Lists, Certificates of Birth, etc., 1755-1908. These records are cited in *A Key to Survey Reports and Microfilm of the Virginia Colonial Records Project* (2 vols. Richmond: Virginia State Library and Archives, 1900). Militia fines collected, 1789; 1797-1856; 1859-1861; 1865; returns of fines collected and supporting record books; returns arranged alphabetically by locality. These give name of person fined and amounts assessed, including delinquents and insolvents, and those who paid their fines. Records of the adjutant general.

Rejected Claims, 1779-1860 (microfilm). Records of the adjutant general.

Rosters of Virginia Volunteers, 1866-1920. Records of the adjutant general.

Colonial Wars

Dunmore's War. A card index; name, county, unit, source reference.

French and Indian War Certificates. A typed list of these is contained in a binder labeled "Veterans of wars between 1754-83." Gives name, rank, county, and certificate number.

Military Accounts Ledger, 1762-84 (microfilm). Accounts of expenses of the French and Indian War—principally of pensions to disabled soldiers and their widows. Records of the adjutant general.

Washington Manuscripts. Photostats of some of the enlistment rolls, rosters, and payrolls of the French and Indian War. A complete, much more legible set of these papers is available in the Manuscript Division, Library of Congress.

American Revolution (1775-83)

NATIONAL ARCHIVES MICROFILM

General Index to Compiled Military Service Records of Revolutionary War Soldiers (M860).

Index to Compiled Service Records of American Naval Personnel Who Served During the Revolutionary War (M879).

OTHER RECORDS

Bounty warrants were issued to veterans who served three or more years in a state or Continental Line unit or to heirs of those who died while in service. A card index lists those who received military bounty land warrants. The cards give name, rank, and warrant number. Index cards giving name, rank, and source reference (cross-referenced to pension records) are available. The bounty land was located in the military districts of Ohio and Kentucky. An index of those who were awarded land in the Virginia Military District of Ohio can be found in Gaius Brumbaugh's *Revolutionary War Records. . . .* (cited below under Published Sources—Virginia). Kentucky grants may be listed in Willard Rouse Jillson's *The Kentucky Land Grants. . . .* (cited below under Published Sources—Virginia). The Virginia archives can supply names and certificate numbers. The actual land office records must be obtained at the Ohio or Kentucky archives.

Virginia Revolutionary War Pension Applications. This collection consists of applications for state pensions—not pensions from the federal government. Since there was no general Virginia pension legislation, each of the approximately six hundred applications was considered individually by the state legislature. The decisions were published in *Acts of Assembly*.

Public Service Claims by Citizens Who Helped Support the Fighting Forces by Supplying Goods or Services. A card catalog lists the claimants. The cards give name, county, and source reference.

RECORDS OF THE STATE ADJUTANT GENERAL

Impressed Property Claims, 1779-85 (microfilm).

Pensions, 1784-1835 (microfilm). Includes a few French and Indian War pensions. For published abstracts, see Virginia Genealogical Society, *Virginia Revolutionary War State Pensions* (Richmond: Virginia Genealogical Society, 1980).

Journal, Commissioners of Military Accounts, 20 January-30 September 1776. This is an alphabetical list of payments. Given are name of person paid and date and amount of payment.

Half-pay Claims, 1783; 1791-1851. Records of payments to officers and their widows and orphans. Names of claimants are indexed in a card file in the archives reading room.

Miscellaneous Accounts of Payments to Officers and Soldiers. See the finding aid *Military Records Guide*, items 211-17.

List of Officers and Soldiers of Virginia Continental Line, 1782-87 (microfilm). An alphabetical list of those who received certificates for pay due.

List of Officers and Soldiers of the State Line (microfilm). An alphabetical list of those who received certificates for pay due.

Militia Lists, 1779-82. Lists of pay for militia duty; arranged by county.

Recruitment of State Troops for the United States Army, 1778; 1780-85; 1789. Accounts of money disbursed by recruiting officers. (Also found in auditor's records.)

Militia Recruits to Serve in the Continental Army, Culpeper County, 1781. (There is a similar list that pertains to Lancaster County.)

Accounts With Pensioners; Ledger, 1778-88. Gives name, disabilities, dates, and amount of warrants issued. Indexed. (Also found in auditor's records. See the finding aid *Office of the Second Auditor Inventory*.)

RECORDS OF THE STATE AUDITOR

Military and Contingent Account Book, 1776-78.

Militia Lists, 1779-82.

Illinois Department: George Rogers Clark Papers. These pertain to the conquest of the Northwest Territory.

Muster Rolls, Payrolls, Kentucky Militia, 1779-84.

Military Service Pay, 1775-76; 1782-83.

Tobacco Certificates (as bounties) for Continental Service.

Militia Certificates and Lists of Claimants, 1781-82; 1784; 1782-89.

Officers and Soldiers of Virginia Continental Line, 1782-87. "Martin Papers." This is a card index to a collection of papers created by Mr. Martin, a Richmond attorney who prepared claim papers for veterans of the American Revolution, War of 1812, and other military service. Cards give name of claimant and a source reference to Martin's original papers.

See the finding aid Guide to Miscellaneous Microfilm. This aid lists a large number of microfilm records pertaining to the American Revolution, many of which contain information not included in other collections. Examples:

American Loyalist Transcripts.

Lists of Officers and Men Who Served in Revolution, in Continental Line, Pay, Time of Service, Etc.

Minute Book Showing a List of Certificates of Those Entitled to Bounty Lands, Dated 1 May 1784–31 May 1785.

Officers, NCOs, Soldiers and Sailors Who Have Received Bounty Lands From Virginia for Revolutionary Service.

Officers, Seamen, and Vessels, U.S. Navy, 1776–90.

Ohio Land Office. Records Relating to Virginia Military land, 1787–1851.

Pension Roll of Virginia 1786 to 1816.

War of 1812 (1812–15)

Index to Virginia Soldiers in the War of 1812 (microfilm).

RECORDS OF THE STATE ADJUTANT GENERAL

Muster Rolls and Payrolls, 1812–15. Indexed by name of the captains; names of officers and soldiers and dates paid.

List of Certificates Issued for Militia and War of 1812 Expenses, 1807–08; 1812–17; also List of Certificates Issued for War of 1812 Expenses, 1812–17.

Register of Claims, 1813–14.

Register of Furloughs, 1814.

Federal Pensions, 1814–42. Pensions for the War of 1812 were authorized by Congress, but the states were responsible for paying them. Virginia did not award bounty lands for service in the War of 1812. This collection consists largely of letters from agents requesting payments.

War of 1812 Payrolls and Vouchers, 1811–20.

RECORDS OF THE STATE AUDITOR

War of 1812 Payrolls of Militia; Muster Rolls of Militia.

Payrolls of Militia Entitled to Land Bounty Under Act of Congress, 28 September 1858.

Muster Rolls of the Virginia militia in the War of 1812–supplement to the payrolls. Available in published form as *Muster Rolls of the Virginia Militia in the War of 1812, Being a Supplement to the Pay Rolls Printed and Distributed in 1851 by the Virginia Auditor of Public Accounts* (Richmond: W.F. Ritchie, 1852).

See the finding aid *Guide to Miscellaneous Microfilm.* Examples:
 Pay accounts of soldiers of the War of 1812.
 Muster rolls of officers and men of certain regiments in Virginia, 1814–15.

Mexican War (1846–48)

RECORDS OF THE STATE ADJUTANT GENERAL

Mexican War Volunteers. Correspondence, Payrolls and Muster Rolls, Vouchers, 1846–48; 1850–53; 1860.

Expenses of Volunteers–a list, April 1849–7 March 1855.

Book of Allowances for Entering Militia claims, 1847–49. Contains names of clerks, musicians, adjutants, and other militia staff, and dates of claims and amounts paid.

Civil War–Confederate (1861–65)

NATIONAL ARCHIVES MICROFILM

Compiled Service Records of Confederate Soldiers Who Served in Organizations From the State of Virginia (M324).

Index to Compiled Service Records of Confederate Soldiers Who Served in Organizations From the State of Virginia (M382).

Selected Records of the War Department Relating to Confederate Prisoners of War (M596–roll 4 is a register submitted by the commissary general–deaths; rolls 10 and 11 are registers of deaths compiled by the surgeon general).

OTHER RECORDS

Confederate Veterans. A card catalog that provides name, volume, and page number of a collection of "simulated" muster rolls available in the reading room. These rolls were compiled from names found in newspaper clippings, journals, and other sources. They are bound in twenty volumes. Staff assistance may be needed to locate the records of a particular county.

The finding aid *Military Records Guide* lists various Civil War records, each with a code number that must be placed on a request slip to obtain the record. Examples of records are:

> Men Killed in Battle (by name and battle).
> Prisoners of War.
> Unit Lists (various types of lists, by unit).
> Vouchers.

Confederate Pension Index (microfilm). After a name is located in this index, the veteran must be identified by county (or independent city) and the Virginia legislative act under which the pension was authorized. The staff can then obtain the original pension file.

RECORDS OF THE STATE ADJUTANT GENERAL

Pension Applications, Acts of 1888, 1900, 1902 (see above).

Confederate Pensions. Journals and Registers, 1888–1928.

Payments to Disabled Soldiers, 1883–84.

RECORDS OF THE STATE AUDITOR

Payments Made to General Officers; and Virginia Forces, 1861–63.

General Register of Pensioners, 22 March–3 April 1888.

Register of Disabled Civil War Pension Applications, 1902–06.

Pension Registers, 1915–37.

Payment Registers, Veterans and Widows, 1933–58.

Roll of Needy Confederate Women, 1915–24.

Register of Confederate Veterans, 1922.

Floyd's Army (Confederate). Vouchers for provisions.

Secretary of Virginia Military Records. Confederate rosters, 1861–1922.

Rolls, Confederate Daughters, 1925–58.

Robert E. Lee Camp Confederate Soldiers' Home, Richmond. Opened 1885; closed 1941. Records available:
> Applications for Admission, 1884–1941
> Registers of Residents, 1885–1941
> Applications for Leaves of Absence and Honorable Discharges, 1913–20

Spanish-American War (1898–99)

Muster Rolls: Second, Third, Fourth, and Sixth Virginia Regiments, United States Volunteers.

Virginia Veterans' Pay and Ration Claims, 1906–13.

World War I (1917–18)

Adjutant General: Induction Records, 1917–18; Officers' Registers, 1899–1915.

Research and Data Files of the World War I History Commission, 1919–20; Also Scrapbooks of Newspaper Clippings, 1915–20.

World War II (1941–45)

Personal War Service Records of Virginia's War Dead, 1942–45.

Separation Notices, 1942–45.

VIRGINIA HISTORICAL SOCIETY

428 North Boulevard
Richmond Virginia

Mailing Address:
P.O. Box 7311
Richmond, Virginia 23221-0311
(804) 358-4901

The Virginia Historical Society has a large manuscript collection that includes many documents pertaining to military service. Also available are a large number of Confederate regimental histories. See Waverly Winfree, comp., Nelson D. Lankford, ed., and Sara B. Bearss, indexer, *Guide to the Manuscript Collections of the Virginia Historical Society*. Richmond: the society, 1985.

PUBLISHED SOURCES—VIRGINIA

General

Virginia Military Records: From the Virginia Magazine of History and Biography, the William and Mary College Quarterly, and Tyler's Quarterly. Baltimore: Genealogical Publishing Co., 1983. Includes data from muster rolls, pension records, and other documents.

Pre-1775 (colonial wars)

Brookes-Smith, Joan E., comp. *Master Index Virginia Surveys and Grants, 1774–1791*. Frankfort, Ky.: Kentucky Historical Society, 1976. A list of recipients of bounty lands in Kentucky granted to those with military service under the British, including militia, during the Colonial era. Data includes original survey number and date, name, acreage, county, watercourse, grantee, and date of grant.

Bockstruck, Lloyd D. *Virginia's Colonial Soldiers*. Baltimore: Genealogical Publishing Co., 1988. Militia rosters, muster rolls, petitions, bounty-land applications and warrants, court-martial records, etc.

Crozier, William A. *Virginia Colonial Militia, 1651–1776*. New York: Genealogical Association, 1905. Reprint. Washington, D.C. (?): 1938 (?). Reprint. Baltimore: Genealogical Publishing Co., 1973. Includes more than three thousand names from a variety of sources.

Neville, John D., comp. *Bacon's Rebellion: Abstracts of Materials in the Colonial Records Project*. Jamestown (?): Jamestown Foundation, 1976 (?).

Taylor, Philip F. *A Calendar of the Warrants for Land in Kentucky, Granted for Service in the French and Indian War*. 1917. Reprint. Baltimore: Genealogical Publishing Co., 1967.

Virginia Military Records: From Virginia Magazine of History and Biography, the William and Mary College Quarterly, and Tyler's Quarterly. Indexed by Elizabeth P. Bentley. Baltimore: Genealogical Publishing Co., 1983. Includes data from muster rolls, pension records, and other documents.

Virginia State Library. Department of Archives and History. *List of the Colonial Soldiers of Virginia. . . .* Originally published as " Special Report of the Department of Archives and History for 1913" in the thirteenth annual report of the Library Board of the Virginia State Library, 1915–16. Richmond: 1917. Reprint. Baltimore: Genealogical Publishing Co., 1961. Contains approximately 6,700 names.

1775-83 (American Revolution)

Brumbaugh, Gaius M. *Revolutionary War Records: Virginia Army and Navy Forces With Bounty Land Warrants for Virginia*

Military District of Ohio and Virginia Script, From Federal and State Archives. Washington, D.C.: 1936. Reprint. Baltimore: Genealogical Publishing Co., 1967. Includes more than seven thousand names.

Brown, Margie G. *Genealogical Abstracts: Revolutionary War Scrip Act ,1852.* Abstracted from the Bureau of Land Management, Record Group 49, National Archives Branch, Suitland, Maryland. Oakton: M.G. Brown, 1990.

Burgess, Louis A., comp. and ed. *Virginia Soldiers of 1776: Compiled From Documents on File in the Virginia Land Office; Together With Material Found in the Archives Department of the Virginia State Library, and Other Reliable Sources.* 3 vols. Richmond: Richmond Press, 1927-29. Reprint. Baltimore: Genealogical Publishing Co., 1973.

Couper, William. *The V.M.I. New Market Cadets: Biographical Sketches.* . . . Charlottesville: Michie Co., 1933.

Dorman, John F., comp. *Virginia's Revolutionary Pension Applications Abstracted.* 44 vols. to date (alphabetically arranged). Washington, D.C.: J.F. Dorman, 1958-.

Eckenrode, H.J., comp. *Virginia Soldiers of the American Revolution.* 2 vols. Richmond: Virginia State Library and Archives, 1989.

Egle, William H. *Old Rights, Proprietary Rights, Virginia Entries, and Soldiers Entitled to Donation Lands.* . . . Pennsylvania Archives, ser. 3, vol. 3. Harrisburg, Penn.: C.M. Busch, 1896. A number of Virginia claims to land in western Pennsylvania.

Gardner, Malcolm, and Louise Gardner. *Virginia Revolutionary War State Pensions.* Virginia Genealogical Society special publication no. 7. Richmond: 1980. Reprint. Easley, S.C.: 1982. From records in the Virginia State Library.

Gwathmey, John H. *Historical Register of Virginians in the Revolution: Soldiers, Sailors, Marines: 1775-1783.* Richmond: Dietz Press, 1938. Reprint. Baltimore: Genealogical Publishing Co., 1973.

Hopkins, William L. *Virginia Revolutionary War Land Grant Claims, 1783-1850 (rejected).* Richmond: the author, 1988. Abstracted from records at the Virginia State Library.

Jillson, Williard R. *The Kentucky Land Grants; a Systematic Index to All of the Land Grants Recorded in the State Land Office at Frankfort, Kentucky, 1782-1924.* Filson Club Publications, no. 33. Louisville, Ky.: 1925. Reprint. Baltimore: Genealogical Publishing Co., 1967.

Latham, Allen, and Benjamin Leonard. *A Roll of the Officers in the Virginia Line of the Revolutionary Army Who Have Received Land Bounty in the States of Ohio and Kentucky: To Which is Added a List of Non-commissioned Officers and Privates* . . . . Chillicothe, Ohio: 1822. Reprint. Washington, D.C. (?): 1941 (?). Reprint. Chillicothe, Ohio: Ohio Valley Folk Research Project, 1962. Reprint. Louisville, Ky.: Lost Cause Press, 1969.

A List of Non-commissioned Officers and Soldiers of the Virginia Line on Continental Establishment: Whose Names Appear on the Army Register, and Who Have Not Received Bounty Land, and a List of Non-commissioned Officers and Soldiers of the Virginia State Line, and Non-commissioned Officers and Seamen and Marines of the State Navy, Whose Names Are on the Army Register, and Who Have Not Received Bounty Land for Revolutionary Services.* Doc. no. 44, 43. Compiled by Virginia commissioners of revolutionary claims. Richmond: Samuel Shepherd,1835. Reprint. Indianapolis: Ye Olde Genealogie Shoppe, 197- (?).

McAllister, Joseph T. *Index to Saffell's List of Virginia Soldiers in the Revolution.* Hot Springs: McAllister Pub., 1913. Reprint. Baltimore: Genealogical Publishing Co., 1969. Also see McAllister's *Partial Index to Saffell.* Vol. 1 includes officers in *Calendar of Virginia State Papers.*

_____. *Virginia Militia in the Revolutionary War.* Hot Springs: McAllister Publishing Co., 1913.

Revolutionary War Soldiers Who Live in Both Virginia and Alabama. Edited by Thomas H. Wood. Tuscaloosa, Ala.: Wood Pub., 1988.

Society of the Cincinnati. Virginia. *Officers of the Virginia Forces in the Revolutionary War at Present Represented in the Society of the Cincinnati in the State of Virginia, With Names of Their Representatives October 19, 1912.* Richmond (?): 1913.

Sons of the Revolution. Kentucky Chapter. *Year Book of the Society. Sons of the Revolution, in the Commonwealth of Kentucky, 1894-1913: and Catalogue of Military Land Warrants Granted by the Commonwealth of Virginia to Soldiers and Sailors of the Revolution.* Lexington, Ky.: the society, 1913.

Stewart, Robert A. *The History of Virginia's Navy of the Revolution.* Richmond: Mitchell and Hotchkiss, 1934. Contains approximately two thousand names.

Summers, Lewis P. *Annals of Southwest Virginia, 1769-1800.* 1 vol. in 2. Abingdon: the author, 1929.

Tazewell, Littleton W. *A List of Claims for Bounty Land for Revolutionary Services Acted Upon by the Governor Since April, 1884.* Richmond: Virginia State Library, 1835.

U.S. Congress. House of Representatives. *Committee on Revolutionary Claims–Bounty Land and Commutation Pay, April 24, 1840. To Which is Added, "Views of the Minority of Said Committee."* 26th Cong., 1st sess., House of Representatives report no. 4361. Washington, D.C., 1840. Appendices 8 and 11 list names.

U.S. General Land Office. *Report From the Secretary of the Treasury . . . Show in the Amount of Land Script Issued . . . to the Officers and Soldiers of the Virginia Line and Navy, and of the Continental Army, During the Revolutionary War.* Senate Doc. 4, 23rd Cong., 2nd sess., SS 266. Washington, D.C.: 1834.

Virginia. *Calendar of Virginia State Papers and Other Manuscripts . . . Preserved in the Capitol at Richmond.* 11 vols. Richmond: 1875-93. Reprint. New York: Kraus Reprint, 1968. Volumes 1-3 cover 1782-31 December 1784.

Virginia Genealogical Society. *Virginia Revolutionary War State Pensions.* Virginia Genealogical Society special publication no. 7. Richmond: the society, 1980. Reprint. Easley, S.C.:

Southern Historical Press, 1982. Abstracts from 465 files of veterans including name of veteran and widow, date of death, and other data.

Virginia. State Library, Archives Division. *List of the Revolutionary Soldiers of Virginia; Special Report . . . for 1911*. Richmond: state printer, 1912. Also see *Supplement* to above publication. Richmond: state printer, 1913.

Virginia Military Records: From Virginia Magazine of History and Biography, the William and Mary College Quarterly, and Tyler's Quarterly. Indexed by Elizabeth P. Bentley. Baltimore: Genealogical Publishing Co., 1983. Includes data from muster rolls, pension records, and other documents.

Wardell, Patrick G., comp. *Virginia/West Virginia Genealogical Data From Revolutionary War Pension and Bounty Land Warrant Records*. Bowie, Md.: Heritage Books, 1988.

Wilson, Samuel M., comp. *Catalogue of Revolutionary Soldiers and Sailors of the Commonwealth of Virginia to Whom Land Bounty Warrants Were Granted by Virginia for Military Service in the War for Independence*. Lexington, Ky.: 1913. Reprint. Baltimore: Genealogical Publishing Co., 1967.

_____. *Virginia Revolutionary Land Bounty Warrants*. Baltimore: Genealogical Publishing Co., 1953.

Worrell, Anne L. *Revolutionary Records Gathered From County Court Records in Southwest Virginia*. Roanoke: 1936.

1784-1815 (War of 1812)

Butler, Stuart L. *A Guide to Virginia Militia Units in the War of 1812*. Athens, Ga.: Iberian Publishing Co., 1988. Includes names and ranks of officers.

_____. *Virginia Soldiers in the United States Army, 1800-1815*. Athens, Ga.: Iberian Publishing Co., 1986.

Virginia. Auditor of Public Accounts. *Militia Rolls of the Virginia Militia in the War of 1812 . . . Copied From Rolls in the Auditor's Office at Richmond*. Richmond: state printer, 1851.

_____. *Muster Rolls of the Virginia Militia in the War of 1812, Being a Supplement to the Pay Rolls Printed and Distributed in 1851*. Richmond: W.F. Ritchie, 1852.

_____. *Pay Rolls of Militia Entitled to Land Bounty Under the Act of Congress of Sept. 28, 1850*. Richmond: state printer, 1851.

Virginia. *Calendar of Virginia State Papers and Other Manuscripts . . . Preserved in the Capitol at Richmond*. 11 vols. Richmond: 1875-93. Reprint. New York: Kraus Reprint, 1968. Volumes 5-7 include some names of those who served in the military.

Wardell, Patrick G. *War of 1812: Virginia Bounty Land & Pension Applicants: A Quick Reference Guide to Ancestors Having War of 1812 Service Who Served, Lived, Died, or Married in Virginia or West Virginia*. Bowie, Md.: Heritage Books, 1987. Data from pension and bounty-land warrant application files at the National Archives.

1861-65 (Civil War)

Blanton, Wyndham B. *Medicine in Virginia in the Nineteenth Century*. Richmond: Garrett & Massie, 1933. Covers 1800 to 1900; "Virginia Surgeons in the Civil War," pages 393-420.

Confederate States of America. War Department. *Report of the Adjutant and Inspector General in Regard to Findings of the General Court Martial Held at Headquarters, Richmond, for the Month of January, in the Cases of Persons Charged With Desertion and Absence Without Leave (?)*. Richmond (?): 1863 (?).

Dickinson, Jack L. *Confederate Soldiers of Western Virginia*. Barboursville, W.V.: J.L. Dickinson, 1986.

Dilts, Bryan L. *1890 Virginia Census Index of Civil War Veterans or Their Widows*. Salt Lake City: Index Publishing, 1986.

Hotchkiss, Jedediah. *Virginia*. Atlanta (?): Confederate Publishing Co. (?), 1899 (?). Contains biographical sketches of Confederate soldiers.

Howard, John. *R.E. Lee Camp, No. 1, Confederate Veterans, vs. W. Wythe Davis*. Richmond: Ware, Duke & Taylor, 1891 (?).

Neal, Lois S., comp. *Personal Name Index to the Expanded Edition of Jedediah Hotchkiss' Virginia, Volume 3 of Confederate Military History in 12 Volumes*. Wendell, N.C.: Broadfoot's Bookmark, 1976.

Pompey, Sherman L. *Register of the Civil War Dead: Virginia Confederate Regiments*. Clovis, Calif.: 1970.

_____. *Sailors and Marines of the United States Living in the Southern Branch, National Home for Disabled Soldiers, Elizabeth City, County, Virginia in 1890*. Albany, Oreg: the author, 1985 (?).

Virginia. *Calendar of Virginia State Papers and Other Manuscripts . . . Preserved in the Capitol at Richmond*. 11 vols. Richmond: 1875-93. Reprint. New York: Kraus Reprint, 1968. Vol. 11 includes appointments of army and navy officers, chaplains, surgeons, etc.

Virginia. Auditor of Public Accounts. *Roster of Confederate Pensioners of Virginia*. Richmond, n.d.

Virginia. Military Institute, Lexington. *Register of the Officers and Cadets, July, 1863*. Richmond: Macfarlane & Fergusson, 1863.

Wallace, Lee. A. *A Guide to Virginia Military Organizations, 1861-1865*. Rev. 2d ed. Lynchburg: H.E. Howard, 1986.

REGIMENTAL HISTORIES

Using the services of several authors, the publishing company of H.E. Howard, Lynchburg, Virginia, is producing a one-hundred-volume set of Virginia Confederate regimental histories. Several are now available. Each contains a muster roll and some photographs. Inquire at reference libraries in Virginia and other states.

1900–45 (World War I; World War II)

Virginia. Adjutant General's Office. *Report of the Adjutant General . . . Virginia.* Richmond: 1919.

Virginia Military Institute, Lexington. *Roster of Army Students Enrolled From May 7, 1943 to April 27, 1946, in the Army Specialized Training Program (ASTP).* Richmond (?): Division of Purchase and Print. (?), 1946.

_____. *Record of Service in the World War of V.M.I. Alumni and Their Alma Mater.* Richmond: Richmond Press, 1920.

Washington

1778	English explorer Captain James Cook sailed along the Washington coast.
1810	Canadian fur traders established a trading post at Spokane.
1818	As part of the Oregon country, Washington was subject to joint occupation by English and American settlers according to the Anglo-American Convention.
1846	The permanent northern border of the Oregon country was established at the forty-ninth parallel.
1848	Washington became part of the Oregon Territory.
1853	Washington became a territory.
1855–58	The Yakima Wars broke out over encroachment by white prospectors into Indian territory. (See Yakima Wars in the appendix.)
1889	Washington became a state.

WASHINGTON STATE ARCHIVES

P.O. Box 40238
1120 Washington Street, SE
Olympia, Washington 98504-0238
(206) 586-1492

Finding Aid

Field, Virgil F., and Washington State Military Department, Office of the Adjutant General. *Washington National Guard Pamphlet.* 17 vols. Tacoma: ca. 1960–70. This finding aid describes the state National Guard during the territorial period, Indian Wars, Civil War, Philippine Insurrection, World War I, World War II, and post-World War II.

Records

General

Residents of the State Soldiers' Home and State Veterans' Home Until the Mid-1930s.

Indian Wars

Service Records That Include Muster Rolls and Vouchers.

World War I, World War II (1917–45)

Service Cards for National Guardsmen Who Participated in World War I or World War II.

Applications for State Bonuses for Service in World War I or World War II. These give name, residence, occupation, relationships, place of birth, and military history.

PUBLISHED SOURCES—WASHINGTON

1850s (Indian wars)

Field, Virgil F. *Washington National Guard Pamphlet: The Official History of the Washington National Guard.* 3 vols. Tacoma: Office of the Adjutant General, 1961.

1861–65 (Civil War)

Pompey, Sherman L. *Burial List of Oregon and Washington Territory Soldiers of the Civil War, Prepared for the Military Museum of the Oregon National Guard, Salem.* N.p., 1974 (?).

_____. *Burial List of Some Civil War Veterans Buried in the State of Washington, From Washington State Library Records and*

Tombstone Inscriptions. Harrisburg, Oreg.: Pacific Specialties, 1974.

_____ . *Civil War Veteran Burials From California, Nevada, Oregon, and Washington Regiments Buried in Colorado.* Independence, Calif.: Historical and Genealogical Publishing Co., 1965.

_____ . *Register of the Civil War Dead: Washington Territory.* Clovis, Calif. (?): 19–.

Washington (state) Adjutant General's Office. *The Official History of the Washington National Guard.* 6 vols. Camp Murray: 1961–62 (?). Militia in the Civil War, pages 240–47.

West Virginia

1730s	The first white settlers established a community in Berkeley County, Virginia.
1754–63	English settlers in the western part of Virginia came into conflict with the French, leading to the French and Indian War. (See French and Indian War in the appendix.)
1774	Lord Dunmore's War was a conflict between whites and Indians on the Ohio River frontier of western Virginia. (See Lord Dunmore's War in the appendix.)
1788	Virginia became a state that included Kentucky and West Virginia.
1861	When Virginia seceded from the Union, the western counties, where slavery had never taken deep root, repudiated the act.
1863	West Virginia became a state.

· ·

ARCHIVES AND HISTORY LIBRARY

1900 Kanawha Boulevard, East
Charleston, West Virginia 25305-0300
(304) 558-0230

Since West Virginia was formerly a part of the Commonwealth of Virginia, this archives and library has considerable material concerning Virginia dating prior to 1861 as well as to West Virginia. However, access to more complete military records pertaining to individuals who lived in what is now West Virginia before 1861 requires research in Virginia, principally at the state archives and state library at Richmond.

Except for microfilm copies, this facility has few original records of military personnel who served in wars predating the Civil War. Some information may be obtained, however, from certain manuscript collections cited below.

Finding Aid

Military Record Collections of the West Virginia Adjutant General's Office. Located in the guide to the archives collections.

Records

General

WEST VIRGINIA MICROFILM

These are copies of records at the Virginia State Library:

Miscellaneous Military, Preemption, and Land Warrant Bounties, Surveys, Grants, Etc.

Virginia Military Land Certificates, 1782–1876.

OTHER RECORDS

Order books, 1861–78; 1924–50. Office of West Virginia Adjutant General. Fifteen volumes.

Records of Accounts, 1861–1908. Office of West Virginia Adjutant General. Two volumes.

Muster and Description Records, 1892–1920. Office of West Virginia Adjutant General. Four volumes.

National Guard Service Records, ca. 1898–1917.

Armed Forces of the United States Reports of Transfer or Discharge, 1950–79 (microfiche). Arranged alphabetically.

Payrolls, Army National Guard, 1926–41 (microfiche). Quarterly drill attendance and field training.

Forms 100, Army National Guard, 1926–41 (microfiche). Monthly roster of personnel showing attendance at unit assemblies, schools, and field training; also shows enlistments, discharges, promotions, etc.

Orders, Army and Air National Guard. Written directives, specific in nature, pertaining to individuals and organizations or the West Virginia National Guard (microfiche).

> Special orders (Army National Guard), 1952–79.
>
> Special orders (DAAF-Army National Guard), 1961–64.
>
> General orders, 1931–74.
>
> Special orders (Air National Guard), 1962–79.
>
> Special orders (DAAF-Air National Guard), 1965–72.

Colonial Wars (pre-1775)

WEST VIRGINIA MICROFILM

These are copies of records at the Virginia State Library:

Virginia Land Bounty Certificates, French and Indian War.

American Revolution (1775-83)

NATIONAL ARCHIVES MICROFILM

Revolutionary War Rolls, 1775-1783 (M246).

General Index to Compiled Service Records of Revolutionary War Soldiers (M860) (T515).

WEST VIRGINIA MICROFILM

These are copies of records at the Virginia State Library:

Revolutionary War Public Service Claims.

Revolutionary War Public Service Commissioners' Books.

Revolutionary War Bounty Warrants.

Virginia Revolutionary War Land Bounty: Virginia Continental Army Lands, 1822.

Revolutionary War Pensions (includes rejected claims). Reel 1 is an index.

OTHER RECORDS

Index Card File: Soldiers' Graves. Information from U.S. War Department graves registration cards. Included are name, rank, war, race, family information, and place of burial. Soldiers named are those who served either in the American Revolution or the War of 1812.

Post-American Revolution (1784-1811)

NATIONAL ARCHIVES MICROFILM

Index to Compiled Service Records of Volunteer Soldiers who Served From 1784 to 1811 (M694).

War of 1812 (1812-15)

NATIONAL ARCHIVES MICROFILM

Index to Compiled Service Records of Volunteer Soldiers Who Served During the War of 1812 (M602).

OTHER RECORDS

Card Catalog, Graves Registrations. See above under American Revolution.

Civil War—Union (1861-65)

NATIONAL ARCHIVES MICROFILM

Compiled Service Records of Volunteer Union Soldiers Who Served in Organizations From the State of Virginia (M398).

Index to Compiled Service Records of Volunteer Union Soldiers Who Served in Organizations From the State of Virginia(M394).

WEST VIRGINIA MICROFILM

West Virginia Union Soldiers. Records of the Office of the West Virginia Adjutant General. Index cards; name, rank, and unit of regular army and militia soldiers; arranged alphabetically; eight rolls.

West Virginia Union Soldiers—Cavalry. Arranged by regiment and company; one roll.

West Virginia Union Soldiers—Infantry. Arranged by regiment and company; militia arranged by county; one roll.

West Virginia Union Soldiers—Artillery, Militia. Artillery arranged by regiment and company; militia arranged by county; one roll.

West Virginia Burial and Cemetery Records. Office of the West Virginia Adjutant General; arranged alphabetically and also by county where the cemetery is located; eight rolls.

Records of the Civil War, West Virginia. Clifford Myers, state historian; one roll.

OTHER RECORDS

Card Catalog—apparently created by the Work Projects Administration (WPA); incomplete. Most cards include name, rank, and military unit. A few drawers contain the notation "Civil War Claims Paid After the War." These pertain to both military and civilian personnel, with name, military unit (where applicable), and basis for the claim.

Unclaimed Civil War Medals. Approximately five thousand bronze medals for Union service during the Civil War were never claimed. These are the remainder of 26,000 medals that were authorized in 1866 by the West Virginia legislature. These medals represent those who were honorably discharged, killed in battle, or who died of wounds or diseases incurred while in service. The milled edges of the medals bear the name and regiment of the veteran. A two-volume finding aid titled *Civil War Medals* lists the names of those veterans whose medals are still at this archives, with name, rank (if known), company or battalion, and regiment. Descendants who wish to acquire a medal may file a claim by submitting the form Claim Application for Union Civil War Medals, which is available at the archives.

Military Records of West Virginia State Troops During the Civil War (available when microfilmed—1994-95).

Military Records of West Virginia State Militia During the Civil War (available when microfilmed—1994-95).

Military Description Records of Virginia Volunteers, U.S.A., 1861-63. Officers and enlisted men of various regiments.

Registers of Officers, 1861-65 (militia, 1861-62).

Records of Enlistments, 1861-65. Various regiments.

Descriptive Roll Records, West Virginia Infantry, 1861-64.

Descriptive Roll Records, West Virginia Cavalry, 1861-63.

Civil War—Confederate (1861-65)

NATIONAL ARCHIVES MICROFILM

Index to Compiled Service Records of Confederate Soldiers Who Served in Organizations From the State of Virginia (M382).

Compiled Service Records of Confederate Soldiers Who Served in Organizations From the State of Virginia (M324).

WEST VIRGINIA MICROFILM

Copies of records at the Virginia State Library: *Confederate Soldiers' Service Records of Virginia; and Confederate Navy.*

OTHER RECORDS

Card Catalog (see above) With Names of Soldiers Who Served in Confederate Units of the Artillery, Cavalry, and Infantry. This information is also available in the West Virginia microfilm cited above, *Confederate Soldiers' Service Records of Virginia. . . .*

Card Catalog: Soldiers' Graves—CSA. These cards give name, date and place of birth, brief summary of military service, place of burial with directions to the grave, and names of next of kin. The data on these cards is also available on microfilm: *West Virginia Adjutant General's Office: Burial and Cemetery Records* (see above).

Spanish-American War (1898-99)

Commissioned Officers' Records of Service, 1899-1910. Office of the West Virginia Adjutant General.

Muster Roll Records, West Virginia Infantry, 1898-99.

Statements of Service for Persons From West Virginia Who Served on Active Duty (microfiche). Name, service number, residence, date of enlistment, place of birth, age at enlistment or date of birth, organization, grade and date of discharge. Arranged alphabetically.

World War I (1917-18)

Index Cards Prepared by the Work Projects Administration (WPA): "World War I Casualties"; name, rank, county of residence, nativity, and date and place of wound or death.

Statement of Service for Persons From West Virginia Who Served on Active Duty (microfiche). Name, service number, residence, date of enlistment, place of birth, age at enlistment or date of birth, organization, grade and date of discharge. Arranged alphabetically.

World War II (1941-45)

Armed Forces of the United States Reports of Transfer or Discharge, 1941-45 (microfiche). Arranged alphabetically.

Records Covering Service of Members of the West Virginia State Guard (an organized civilian militia) Who Served in a Civil Defense Role in Order to Replace the National Guard While Serving in a Federal Status Overseas During World War II (microfiche). Arranged alphabetically.

Korean War (1950-53)

Discharge Certificates. Available on microfiche.

Vietnam War (1963-75)

Discharge Certificates. Available on microfiche.

Pay Vouchers and Rosters, Army National Guard, for Quarterly Drill Attendance (1971-75) (microfiche).

Manuscript Collections

Finding Aid

Main-entry Listing of Manuscripts in the Archives. This finding aid lists collections accessioned before the end of 1992, updated annually. Collections with military significance are described below.

Collections

Civil War Collection, 1861-65. In five series: correspondence; official and miscellaneous papers; secondary source materials; roster and muster rolls; and lists of soldiers by geographical area (Ms79.18).

Confederate Veterans: Minute book of Camp Allen Woods (Ms91.2).

Confederate Veterans From Charles Town (Ms80.308).

Lewis, Virgil Anson: Correspondence Concerning Indian Wars in Western Virginia. (Ms79.16)

Carnes, Eva Margaret: Revolutionary War List (Ms80.28).

Revolutionary War Pension Claims, 1820-43 (thirty items) (Ms84.190).

Union Muster Rolls, West Virginia Regiments, 1860-65 (Ms84.188).

United Daughters of the Confederacy, West Virginia Division (includes names of those eligible for the Southern Cross of Honor, 1902-17) (Ms79.19).

Thirty-first Virginia Infantry (Ms79.238).

Virginia Militia (Kanawha Riflemen) pledge record (1838) (Ms79.149).

War Records Collection: In three series: personal papers; military units records; and pension lists. Documents pertain to the American Revolution, War of 1812, Mexican War, and the Spanish-American War; and include day books, annual returns, a penitentiary record, muster rolls, pension claims, and miscellaneous documents (Ms79.20).

West Virginia Civil War Regimental Historical Memoranda (typescript) (Ms79.272).

Confederate States of America Conscript Records (Ms79.239).

Reports, Captain Clinton's Company, Union (Ms88.22).

OFFICE OF THE ADJUTANT GENERAL FOR WEST VIRGINIA

Attn: Personnel Records
1703 Coonskin Drive
Charleston, West Virginia 25311-1085
(304) 341-6300

This facility, located a few miles north of the state archives, has records pertaining to the West Virginia National Guard and West Virginia National Guardsmen who saw federal service in twentieth-century wars. Records pertaining to World War II, the Korean War, and the Vietnam War are considered confidential in accordance with the federal Privacy Act. Although copies of many records cannot be furnished, staff personnel may provide certain information from the records to veterans or their qualified family members. Currently available records consist of the following:

Enlistment Record, West Virginia State Guard. Contains much personal and family data and includes a service record.

Statement of Physical Condition and Oath, West Virginia State Guard. Includes a service record.

Honorable Discharge From the West Virginia State Guard.

Application for Victory Medal (World War I). Contains considerable military service information.

Enlistment Records. A brief statement of enlistment for World War I.

Enlisted Record and Report of Separation—Honorable Discharge. Contains name, rank, serial number, date and place of birth, date and place of discharge from service, and records of service assignments.

Statement of Service, World War II.

PUBLISHED SOURCES—WEST VIRGINIA

General

Felldin, Jeanne R., and Charlotte H. Tucker, comps. *Index to the Soldiers of West Virginia. . . .* Tomball, Tex.: Genealogy Publications, 1976.

Lewis, Virgil A. *Soldiery of West Virginia in the French and Indian War; Lord Dunmore's War; the Revolution; the Later Indian Wars; the Whiskey Insurrection; the Second War with England, the War With Mexico, and Addenda Relating to West Virginia in the Civil War.* Third biennial report of Department of Archives & History, state of West Virginia, 1911. Reprint. Baltimore: Genealogical Publishing Co., 1972.

Pre-1775 (colonial wars)

Lewis, Virgil A. *History of the Battle of Point Pleasant.* Harrisburg, Va.: C.J. Carrier Co., 1974. Appendix A is a roster of companies that fought in the battle.

Poffenbarger, Livia N.S. *The Battle of Point Pleasant: A Battle of the Revolution, October 10th 1774.* Point Pleasant: State Gazette, 1909. Reprint. Charleston (?): Jarrett Print Co. (?), 1936 (?). Contains short biographical sketches of those who participated in the battle.

1775-83 (American Revolution)

Johnston, Ross B., comp. *West Virginians in the American Revolution.* Parkersburg: 1959. Reprint. Baltimore: Genealogical Publishing Co., 1977.

Lang, Theodore F. *Loyal West Virginia From 1861 to 1865. . . .* Baltimore: Deutsch, 1895.

Reddy, Anne W. *West Virginia Revolutionary Ancestors Whose Services Were Non-military and Whose Names, Therefore, Do Not Appear in Revolutionary Indexes of Soldiers and Sailors. . . .* Washington, D.C.: Model Printing Co., 1930. Reprint. Baltimore: Genealogical Publishing Co., 1973.

1861-65 (Civil War)

Dilts, Bryan L., comp. *1890 West Virginia Census Index of Civil War Veterans or Their Widows.* Salt Lake City: Index Publishing, 1986.

Pompey, Sherman L. *Civil War Veteran Burials of the West Virginia Cavalry Units.* Eugene, Oreg.: Western Oregon Genealogical Research Library, 1978. Microfilm 81.1540.

West Virginia. Adjutant General's Office. *Annual Reports, 1864–1865.* Wheeling: Public Printer, 1865–66.

1898-99 (Spanish-American War)

West Virginia. Adjutant General's Office. *Report for 1899–1900. Spanish-American War Roster.* Wheeling: 1900 (?).

Wisconsin

| 1634 | French explorer Jean Nicolet entered Green Bay on Lake Michigan looking for the Northwest Passage. |
| 1673 | Jacques Marquette and Louis Joliet explored the upper Mississippi River system through Wisconsin. |

1763	The Treaty of Paris which ended the French and Indian War transferred Wisconsin from France to Great Britain. (See French and Indian War in the appendix.)
1783	The Treaty of Paris which ended the American Revolution transferred Wisconsin to the United States, but British forts in the area prevented actual American control and provided a source of continued friction between the two countries. (See American Revolution in the appendix.)
1787	Wisconsin became part of the Northwest Territory.
1800	Wisconsin became part of Indiana Territory.
1809	Wisconsin became part of Illinois Territory.
1815	The Treaty of Ghent, which ended the War of 1812, resulted in British abandonment of their forts in the Great Lakes area. (See War of 1812 in the appendix.)
1818	Wisconsin became part of Michigan Territory.
1831-32	The Black Hawk War between Indians and settlers in the Old Northwest spread into Wisconsin. (See Black Hawk War in the appendix.)
1836	Wisconsin became a territory.
1848	Wisconsin became a state.

. . . .

STATE HISTORICAL SOCIETY OF WISCONSIN

Archives Division
816 State Street
Madison, Wisconsin 53706
(608) 264-6400

Finding Aids

Harper, Josephine L. *Guide to the Draper Manuscripts.* Madison: State Historical Society of Wisconsin, 1983.

Paul, William G. *Wisconsin's Civil War Archives.* Madison: State Historical Society of Wisconsin, 1965.

Records

General

Service Record Cards, 1870-1946. A card catalog lists National Guard personnel (yellow cards) and Naval Militia (pale blue cards). Information given includes name of officer or enlisted man, home address, date and place of birth, physical description, date and term of enlistment, military unit, previous military service, date and cause of discharge, and related information; also available on microfilm.

Similar card records pertaining to World War I and World War II personnel are described below.

National Guard (1891-1928)

Descriptive Books, Third Infantry Regiment, Company A, 1891-11. Within each volume names are arranged by rank and thereunder alphabetically. Officers and enlisted men are listed by name; rank; age; physical description; place of birth; occupation; where, when, and by whom enlisted; and name of nearest relative; available in three volumes.

Records, First Cavalry Regiment, 1891-1928. The records consist of letters (partially indexed by name of addressee), roll book, muster book, treasurer's book, and cash books maintained in the orderly room of Troop A. These are available in six volumes.

Military Appointments, 1862-1950. Records from the Wisconsin secretary of state; name, date of commission, military unit, and residence.

An alphabetical graves registration of deceased veterans from the nineteenth century through December 1969 is available at the Department of Veterans Affairs, 77 North Dickinson Street, Madison, Wisconsin 53705. This department also has service records of soldiers of the Spanish-American War, World War I, and World War II.

Indian Wars (Winnebago, 1827, and Black Hawk, 1832)

Since Wisconsin was a part of the Michigan Territory at the time of the Winnebago and Black Hawk Indian uprisings, these records may be found at the National Archives. These incidents resulted in the mobilization into federal service of almost the entire Wisconsin militia and thus reveal the names of most of the area's adult male population of those times. Many veterans of these conflicts, or their dependents, applied later for pensions or bounty lands under the federal acts of 1850 and 1855. The National Archives records may contain those documents.

Civil War—Union (1861-65)

Muster Rolls and Descriptive Rolls of Men Serving in Each Wisconsin Military Unit During the Civil War. Each roll shows name, rank, date and place of commissioning or enlistment, by whom enlisted, term of service, physical description, occupation, residence, date of termination of service, engagements, whether died in service and, if so, date and place of death; occasionally place of burial; arranged by regiment and thereunder by company. These rolls are available in fifty-nine volumes and also on twenty-two reels of microfilm.

Regimental Muster and Descriptive Rolls of Men Serving in Each Wisconsin Military Unit During the Civil War. Each roll contains name; rank; place of birth; age; occupation; marital status; date, place, and by whom enlisted; term of service; physical description; date of residence; and remarks (which include promotions, details, leaves, absences, engagements, whether died in service and, if so, date and place of death; occasionally place of burial); arranged by regiment and thereunder by company. These rolls are available in fifty-seven volumes and also on ten reels of microfilm.

The finding aid *Wisconsin's Civil War Archives* (cited above) contains descriptions of the records. Some representative collections are listed below.

Telegrams, 1861–65. These and similar collections consist of communications to the governor or state adjutant general.

Applications and Recommendations for Military Offices, 1862–64. Includes applications for military commissions—arranged by type of service (field officers, quartermaster officers, medical personnel, nurses, paymasters, chaplains, etc.); indexed.

Applications for Commissions, 1861–65. Similar to the above but also including letters of recommendation.

List of Specially Qualified Applicants for Military Offices, 1861–63 (?). Arranged by congressional district; includes name and residence.

Regimental Roster of Officers, 1861–65. Includes name, military unit, date of appointment, date of rank, and residence.

Military Correspondence. Various types of communications to the office of the governor concerning specific persons and other military matters.

Record of Disposition of Personal Effects of Dead Soldiers, 1863. Included are name of deceased, military unit, date and place of death, and an inventory of personal effects.

Correspondence, General and Outgoing, From the Office of the Wisconsin Secretary of State. Often concerns military commissions and appointments, as well as correspondence from family members of soldiers.

Veterans Reserve Corps Warrants, 1864–65. A record of warrants drawn for volunteer aid payments to dependents of volunteers in the Veteran Reserve Corps. Data includes name of volunteer, town and county of residence, military unit, date mustered in, name of wife or head of family, amount of monthly payment, and often the date of discharge.

Volunteer Aid, 1861–68. A roll of Wisconsin volunteers having dependents entitled to receive five dollars per month. Similar

rolls name individuals who qualified for extra pay for volunteer work.

Paymaster General's Record of Commissioned Officers and Debts, 1861–62. This list was sent by the adjutant general to the paymaster and pertains to pay due officers for the Sixteenth and Eighteenth Infantry Regiments.

Militia Lists, 1861. Lists of individuals between the ages of eighteen and forty-five (recorded by town clerks); name of town, name of individual subject to military duty, and individual's signature.

Desertion Records, 1861–67. Consists of two lists: those who deserted from a military unit and those who did not report for the draft or who deserted after reporting; name, residence, date of desertion, and remarks.

List of Deserters and Deserters Excused, 1866; 1868. Includes information concerning alleged deserters exonerated for various reasons.

Enumeration of Civil War Veterans, 1885; 1895; 1905. Special state censuses were taken using returns from county clerks listing veterans residing in Wisconsin during each of the three years shown above. Included are name, rank, and post office. Also included is name of unit or vessel; arranged alphabetically by county and thereunder by local military unit. The 1905 enumeration arranged the names alphabetically by Wisconsin military unit; organizations of other states; United States regular army; "colored" organizations; sailors; marines. These censuses are available in published volumes.

Soldiers Buried at Madison, 1862–66. Lists Union and Confederate servicemen who died at the United States Post Hospital at Camp Randall and were buried at Madison.

Soldiers' Orphans' Home, 1869–1880. Includes names of soldiers' orphans at the state normal schools, 1871–76.

Iron Brigade Reunion, 1884. A register of members of the Iron Brigade who attended their reunion in 1884; includes signature of each member, company, regiment, and home address.

Allotment Roll, 1862–82. Lists soldiers sending allotments to dependents; date, name of soldier, military unit, name and address of dependent, amount allotted per month, etc.

Soldiers' Orphans' Home Financial Papers. Record of disbursements of funds provided by donors for orphans of soldiers who died in the Civil War; name of orphan, name of father with military unit and date of death, and date orphan reached legal age.

Military Journal (of Wisconsin's adjutant general). These index commissions of officers, discharges, and related information.

Orders for Commissions, 1862–63. These consist of orders from the governor relative to the granting of military commissions.

Persons Liable for Military Duty. Lists of all men between the ages of eighteen and forty-five in each town and by war; prepared by sheriffs of each county. Remarks include exemptions and the reasons therefor.

District Enrollment Board Rolls of Draftees and Substitutes. Provides information in daily muster rolls, including information concerning each individual and facts related to individual's travel, clothing issued, etc.

Book of Local Credits, 1863–65. Lists of recruits from congressional districts in Wisconsin; name of recruit, date mustered in, regiment, and remarks.

Recruit Books, 1864–65. Lists of recruits, including information about the individual and enlistment data.

County Draft Books, 1862–63. Records of draftees by town or ward and county of residence; also name of substitute furnished (if any).

Index to Wisconsin Volunteers, 1862–66. An alphabetical list of soldiers, both draftees and volunteers. It was published as *Wisconsin Volunteers, War of the Rebellion, 1861–65; Arranged Alphabetically. . . .* (Madison: 1914).

Certificates of Service, 1867–90. Copies of certificates of military service issued by the state adjutant general during the Civil War; fourteen volumes, each indexed by name of soldier or officer.

Pension Claims, 1889–90. Correspondence and affidavits pertaining to claims by veterans and widows.

Camp Randall Duty Roster, 1862–64. Lists officers and others stationed at this post. Other records deal with clothing and equipment issuances, as well as services performed by civilian workers.

Claims for Boarding Volunteer Soldiers, 1861–63. Claims by civilians for boarding soldiers. Also available is a collection of certificates for meals furnished to volunteer soldiers, 1862–66.

Records of Various Volunteer Regiments, State Militia and National Guard Companies, and Designated Infantry Regiments. The name or number of the unit must be specified. Data provided includes statistical reports, but there are also several specialized lists of personnel that vary by unit.

County and Local Records. Various records (draft, militia, volunteers, special rolls, etc.) are available from the counties of Dane, Greene, Green Lake, Brown, Buffalo, Sauk, Shawano, and Winnebago. Some of these are available only at one of the research centers located on campuses of the University of Wisconsin and the Northland College at Ashland, Wisconsin.

Spanish-American War (1898–99)

Muster-in and Muster-out Rolls. Rolls for the First–Fourth Infantry Regiments. Each shows name; rank; age; physical description; place of birth; occupation; date, place, and by whom enrolled and mustered into service; valuation of horses and equipment; marital status; name and address of nearest kin; travel distance from residence to rendezvous; and remarks. Arranged by regiment; available in eight volumes.

Regimental Rosters and Indexes, 1875–ca. 1910. Rosters include the following information about officers: name, rank, date of commission, station, date of rank, staff rank, date of discharge, and remarks. Information for enlisted men is as follows: name, age, rank (for band personnel), occupation,

station, term of enlistment, date of enlistment, date of discharge and date discharge approved, and remarks; arranged by regiment; available in eleven volumes; indexes are in volumes 1 and 2.

World War I (1917–18)

Card Catalog of Officers and Enlisted Men in the State Guard (blue cards) and the State Guard Reserve ("peach" cards).

Military Service Records and Bonus Records. Service records of Wisconsin veterans who served during World War I. Each shows name, service number, residence, date and place of birth, unit, grade, dates of service, wounds, decorations, and amount of bonus paid; available only on microfilm (eighty-eight reels).

World War II (1941–45)

Card Catalog of Officers and Enlisted Men in the National Guard During Part of World War II (yellow cards) and the State Guard (pink cards).

Manuscripts

The Draper Manuscripts. The State Historical Society of Wisconsin is the custodian of the vast collections and writings of Lyman Copeland Draper, an itinerant whose mission was the preservation of the records of several eastern states. He made personal notes of his observations and conversations and acquired or borrowed official and personal papers, including memoirs from hundreds of sources, as he traveled across the Allegheny region from western New York to Georgia and all states between during the early and mid-1800s. Among his papers are many accounts of military actions; they also include an extensive set of revolutionary war pension applications.

Some parts of this collection have been published separately and provide supplementary information about military engagements of the era. These and other portions of Draper's collection can be found at several other research libraries nationwide. Some that may provide data for the military researcher are the following.

State Historical Society of Wisconsin. *Calendar of the George Rogers Clark Papers of the Draper Collection of Manuscripts.* Calendar Series, vol. 4. Reprint. Utica, Ky.: McDowell Publications, 1985.

———. *The Preston and Virginia Papers of the Draper Collection of Manuscripts.* Calendar Series, vol. 1. Madison: the society, 1915.

———. *Calendar of the Kentucky Papers of the Draper Collection of Manuscripts.* Calendar Series, vol. 2. Madison: the society, 1925. Reprint. Utica, Ky.: McDowell Publications, 1983 (?).

———. *Calendar of the Tennessee and Kings Mountain Papers of the Draper Collection of Manuscripts.* Calendar Series, vol. 3.

Madison: the society, 1929. Reprint. Utica, Ky.: McDowell Publications, 1983 (?).

PUBLISHED SOURCES—WISCONSIN

1861-65 (Civil War)

Love, William D. *Wisconsin in the War of the Rebellion; a History of All Regiments and Batteries the State Has Sent to the Field, and Deeds of Her Citizens,Governors and Other Military Officers. . . .* Chicago: Church and Goodman, 1866.

Quiner, E.B. *The Military History of Wisconsin: a Record of the Civil and Military Patriotism of the State, in the War for the Union, With . . . Regimental Histories, Sketches of Distinguished Officers . . . Roll of the Illustrious Dead . . . etc.* Chicago: Clarke & Co., 1866.

Rood, Hosea W. *The Grand Army of the Republic.* Menasha (?): 1923.

_____ . *History of Wisconsin Veteran's Home 1886-1926.* Madison (?): Democrat Print Co., 1926.

Soldiers' and Citizens' Album of Biographical Record [of Wisconsin]: Containing Personal Sketches of Army Men and Citizens Prominent in Loyalty to the Union. . . . 2 vols. Chicago: Grand Army Publishing Co., 1888, 1890. Includes some portraits.

Wisconsin. Adjutant General's Office. *Roster of Wisconsin Volunteers, War of the Rebellion, 1861–1865. . . .* 2 vols. Madison: Democrat Print Co., 1886.

_____ . *Wisconsin Volunteers, War of the Rebellion, 1861–1865: Arranged Alphabetically.* Compiled . . . During the Years 1895-1899. Madison: Democrat Print Co., 1914.

Wisconsin. Commission on Civil War Records. *Wisconsin Losses in the Civil War. . . .* Madison (?): Democrat Printing Co., state printer, 1915.

Wisconsin. *Shiloh Monument Commission: Report of the Commission.* Madison (?): issued by the commission, 1909.

Wisconsin Soldiers and Sailors: Reunion Roster. Fond du Lac: 1880.

1898-99 (Spanish-American War)

Immell, Ralph M. *Roster of Wisconsin Troops in the Spanish-American War.* Madison: Soldiers' Rehabilitation Board, n.d. Reprinted from the *Sentinel Almanac and Book of Facts,* 1899.

1916 (Mexican Border Service)

Thisted, Moses N. *With the Wisconsin National Guard on the Mexican Border in 1916-17.* Hemet, Calif.: Alphabet Printers, 1981.

1917-18 (World War I)

Gregory, John Goadby, ed. *Wisconsin's Gold Star List: Soldiers, Sailors, Marines and Nurses From the Badger State. . . .* Madison: State Historical Society of Wisconsin, 1925.

Wyoming

1803 An unexplored part of the French empire, Wyoming was transferred to the United States as part of the Louisiana Purchase.

1824 Although fur trappers working for John Jacob Astor had discovered South Pass in 1812, its effective discovery came in 1824 when Crow Indians showed it to Jedediah Smith and other trappers. It became the route of the Oregon and California Trails.

1867-69 Construction of the Union Pacific Railroad brought the first significant numbers of settlers to Wyoming.

1868 Wyoming became a territory.

1890 Wyoming became a state.

WYOMING STATE ARCHIVES

Barrett Building
2301 Central Avenue
Cheyenne, Wyoming 82002
(307) 777-7826

Records

General

Records of Wyoming National Guardsmen and a few other military records are maintained by the Wyoming State National Guard. These may be obtained from the Office of the Wyoming State Adjutant General, 5500 Bishop Blvd., Cheyenne, Wyoming 82002; telephone: (307) 772-6201.

The William Alexander Carter Manuscript Collection. This is a collection of Carter's business papers and correspondence from the time he served as a civilian sutler (post trader) at Fort Bridger, Wyoming, from 1857 to his death in 1881. Among the papers are documents relating to Lot Smith's Company of Utah (Mormon) militia. The Wyoming State Archives has twelve reels of microfilm copies of the papers, which are housed at the Western Americana Division, Yale University Library, New Haven, Connecticut.

Civilian Payroll Lists (1921–39) and Voucher Lists (1893–1939). Office of the Adjutant General.

List of Men of Co. I, Third Infantry, Wheatland, Wyoming, 1913–16, and Photostatic Copies of a Casualty List of Wyoming Men in World War I, 1920. Arranged chronologically. (RG 0007)

Spanish-American War (1898–99)

Correspondence From the Office of Governor DeForest Richards Concerning Medals Issued to Spanish-American War Veterans.

Spanish-American War Payroll Vouchers, 1898–99. Office of the Adjutant General.

World War I (1917–18)

County Clerks' Records of Military Discharges. Although not required, many veterans registered their discharges with the county clerk in the county where they resided after their military service. Except for Sublette County, where there was no registration, such registration generally began in the other counties in 1919–a few years earlier in two instances: Converse and Fremont counties. Registering of discharges continued at the county level through the post-World War II era. These records were microfilmed and transferred to the state archives. All such World War I registrations are indexed (with the exception of Weston County).

Fremont County Draft Board Records, ca. 1918–19.

The state archives also has lists of Wyoming residents who were killed in World War I.

World War II (1941–45)

Registration of military discharges with county clerks generally continued until after World War II. The records were microfilmed and transferred to the state archives. In the counties of Crook, Laramie, and Sweetwater there were no registrations of World War I veterans, although registration was initiated after the close of World War II. A list of the counties and the years for which registrations of World War I and World War II military discharges are available can be obtained from the state archives. All are indexed except those from Laramie and Weston counties.

PUBLISHED SOURCES—WYOMING

1898–99 (Spanish-American War)

Bartlett, Ichabod S., ed. *History of Wyoming.* 3 vols. Chicago: S.J. Clarke Publishing Co., 1918.

9

Published Sources: Works That Pertain to More Than One State

9

Published Sources: Works That Pertain to More Than One State

The most accurate method of acquiring information concerning a military veteran is to examine the primary records—those created at or near the time the individual was actually present at the event. The collections of official records cited in the preceding chapters will assist researchers in locating such primary records. However, a shortcut toward the same goal, and probably the more efficient initial procedure, is to examine published lists of names of personnel abstracted from official records: perhaps someone has already searched the primary records, abstracted the names, and published them. After finding the information in this form, the researcher can search primary sources to verify the published version and to discover additional data that might not have been abstracted for publication.

It would be practically impossible to discover and list all of the publications applicable to the military researcher's task, but the following titles are cited as an attempt to provide some of the more useful works. Many publications cited in this book are also cited in other bibliographies, and some professional researchers might complain that repeating them here is redundant. However, non-experts often find it difficult to locate the many bibliographies that are available to the more sophisticated librarian or genealogist. Further, new and useful works are published every day, and bibliographies more than a few years old do not contain these more recent works.

A useful category of publications that contain lists of military personnel are the annual or biennial reports of the adjutants general of the states; this is especially true of those reports covering war years. Reports issued between wars normally contain the names of members of the state National Guard. These reports (for selected years) are cited in this volume, but the researcher is encouraged to study others to find names of those who served between wars. These reports may be found in abundance at state libraries, the Library of Congress, the U.S. Army Center for Military History (Washington, D.C.), and the U.S. Army Military History Institute (Carlisle Barracks, Pennsylvania.)

In addition to the books cited here, certain categories of published works are valuable for supplemental research. They are as follows:

1. Histories of regiments or other military units, including ship histories and cruise books. Prime sources for these types of publications are the U.S. Army Military History Institute and the U.S. Army Center for Military History. The New York City Public Library has a large collection of ship cruise books.

2. Orderly books. Many orderly books created during the American Revolution may be seen at the Manuscript Division of the Library of Congress or at the National Archives microfilm room.

3. State and local histories, many of which may contain the names of local residents who served during wartime.

4. Publications by patriotic societies (Daughters of the American Revolution, Sons of the American Revolution, etc.) that contain abstracts of pension lists, headstones, etc. These publications are valuable, but, except for a few of the more important ones, they are too numerous to list here.

5. Articles in periodicals, journals, and other serial publications. An excellent guide to hundreds of such articles may be found in Lois Horowitz's *A Bibliography of Military Name Lists From Pre-1675 to 1900. A Guide to Genealogical Sources* (cited below).

6. Manuscript material such as personal diaries, journals, and narratives, some of which may include names of veterans. Chadwyck-Healey's *Index to Personal Names in the National Union Catalog of Manuscript Collections, 1959–1984* (cited below) may be helpful. State and local historical societies have card catalogs of their manuscript holdings.

7. Biographies of individuals, found in most reference libraries.

8. Academic theses or dissertations.

General Publications

The works cited in this section are those that pertain to more than one military engagement, to more than one state, or to a lengthy time period (war years and non-war years).

Guides and Bibliographies

Arksey, Laura, Nancy Pries, and Marcia Reed. *American Diaries: An Annotated Bibliography of Published American Diaries and Journals.* Detroit: Gale Research Co., 1983.

Baker, Mary Ellen. *Bibliography of Lists of New England Soldiers.* Boston: New England Historic Genealogical Society, 1977.

Deputy, Marilyn, and Pat Barben. *Register of Federal United States Military Records: A Guide to Manuscript Sources at the Genealogical Library, Salt Lake City, and the National Archives in Washington, D.C.* 3 vols. Bowie, Md.: Heritage Books, 1986.

Heitman, Francis B. *Historical Register and Dictionary of the United States Army, From its Organization, September 29, 1789, to March 2, 1903.* 2 vols. Urbana: University of Illinois Press, 1965.

Horowitz, Lois. *A Bibliography of Military Name Lists From Pre-1675 to 1900: A Guide to Genealogical Sources.* Metuchen, N.J.: Scarecrow Press, 1990. This is a monumental work that lists, in great detail, both books and periodicals that contain names of military personnel.

Index to Personal Names in the National Union Catalog of Manuscript Collections, 1959–1984. 2 vols. Alexandria, Va.: Chadwyck-Healey, 1987.

Filby, P. William, comp. *American & British Genealogy and Heraldry: A Selected List of Books.* 3rd ed. Boston: New England Genealogical Society, 1983. Books that include military and pension lists are found on pages 1233–433.

Kirkham, E. Kay. *Some of the Military Records of America, Before 1900: Their Use and Values in Genealogical and Historical Research.* Salt Lake City: Deseret Book Co., 1964. 2nd ed. Provo, Utah: Stevenson's Genealogical Center, 1972.

Lists of Logbooks of United States Navy Ships, Stations, and Miscellaneous Units, 1801–1947. Special List 44. Washington, D.C.: NARS, 1978.

Military Service Records: A Select Catalog of National Archives Microfilm Publications. Washington, D.C.: National Archives Trust, 1985.

Neagles, James C. *The Library of Congress: A Guide to Genealogical and Historical Research.* Salt Lake City: Ancestry, 1990.

Office of the Chief of Naval Operations, Navy Department. *Dictionary of American Naval Fighting Ships.* 9 vols. Washington, D.C.: Government Printing Office, 1959–90.

Seeley, Charlotte P. *American Women and the U.S. Armed Forces.* Revised by Virginia C. Purdy and Robert Gruber. Washington, D.C.: U.S. National Archives and Records Administration, 1992. Describes the records housed at the National Archives and presidential libraries that relate to women involved with military organizations.

Szucs, Loretto D., and Sandra H. Luebking. *The Archives: A Guide to the National Archives Field Branches.* Salt Lake City: Ancestry, 1988.

U.S. Congress. *American State Papers, Class IX (Claims).* Reprints of documents of the 1st Congress, 2nd sess. through the 17th Congress, 1790–1823. Indexed at end of volume. See also McMullin, Phillip W., ed. *Grassroots of America.* Salt Lake City: Gendex, 1972. Indexes all thirty-eight volumes of the *American State Papers.*

U.S. Congress. Senate. *Medal of Honor Awards, 1863–1962.* Washington, D.C.: Government Printing Office, 1964.

U.S. National Archives and Records Administration. *Guide to Genealogical Research in the National Archives.* Washington, D.C.: National Archives Trust Fund Board, 1985.

U.S. Naval History Division. *U.S. Naval History Sources in the United States.* Washington, D.C.: the division, 1979.

Publications With Lists of Names

American Archives: Consisting of a Collection of Authentick Records . . . in 6 Series. "Prepared and Published Under Authority of an Act of Congress . . . by Peter Force." 9 vols. Washington, D.C.: 1837–53 (?). Reprint. New York (?): Johnson Reprint, 1972 (?). Elmsford, N.Y.: Microforms International Marketing Corp., 198- (?). The first, second, and third series have not appeared. The fourth and fifth series have extensive lists of soldiers.

Amos, Preston E. *Above and Beyond in the West: Black Medal of Honor Winners, 1870–1940.* Washington: Potomac Corral, the Westerners, 1974.

Callahan, Edward W., ed. *List of Officers of the Navy of the United States and of the Marine Corps From 1775 to 1900: Comprising a Complete Register of all Present and Former Commissioned, Warranted, and Appointed Officers . . . Regular and Volunteer; Compiled From Official Records of the Navy Department.* Gaithersburg, Md.: Olde Soldier Books, 1988. Also includes midshipmen and cadets at the Naval Academy, 1840–1900.

Cogar, William B. *Dictionary of Admirals of the U.S. Navy.* Annapolis, Md.: Naval Institute Press, 1989–91.

Cullum, George W. *Biographical Register of the Officers and Graduates of the U.S. Military Academy at West Point, N.Y..* 3rd ed. 9 vols. Boston: Houghton, Mifflin, 1891–1950. Registers for the period 1802–1950 include state of birth and place and date of death for each graduate.

Hamersly, Lewis R. *The Records of Living Officers of the U.S. Navy and Marine Corps.* 7 eds., early 1800s–1902. Philadelphia: J.B. Lippincott & Co. New York: J.M. Carroll & Co., 1988 (?).

———. *Records of Living Officers of the United States Army.* Philadelphia: L.R. Hamersly & Co., 1884.

———. *Biographical Sketches of Distinguished Officers of the Army and Navy.* New York: L.R. Hamersly, 1905.

Hamersly, Thomas H.S. *General Register of the United States Navy and Marine Corps, Arranged in Alphabetical Order, For One Hundred Years (1782 to 1882) . . .* Washington, D.C.: T.H.S. Hamersly, 1882.

———. *Complete Regular Army Register of the United States, 1778–1879 . . .* Washington, D.C.: W.K. Boyle, 1882.

Lee, Irvin H. *Negro Medal of Honor Men.* New York: Dodd, Mead, 1967 (?).

Powell, William H. *List of Officers of the Army of the United States from 1779 to 1900, Embracing a Register of All Appointments by the President of the United States in the Volunteer Service During the Civil War and of Volunteer Officers in the Service of the United States, June 1, 1900.* New York: L.R. Hamersly, 1900. Reprint. Detroit: Gale Research Co., 1967.

Reynolds, Clark G. *Famous American Admirals.* New York: Van Nostrand Reinhold, 1978. Includes more than two hundred biographies with portraits.

Schuon, Karl. *U.S. Navy Biographical Dictionary.* New York: F. Watts, 1965.

———. *U.S. Marine Corps Biographical Dictionary: The Corps' Fighting Men, What They Did, Where They Served.* New York: F. Watts, 1965.

Spiller, Roger J., ed. *Dictionary of American Military Biography.* 3 vols. Westport, Conn.: Greenwood Press, 1984.

Stubbs, Mary Lee, and Stanley R. Connor. *Army, Cavalry.* Army Lineage Series. Office of the Chief of Military History, U.S. Army. Washington, D.C.: 1969. Also includes incomplete lineages of regular army, army reserve, and Army National Guard.

U.S. Congress. *Medal of Honor Recipients, 1863–1968.* 93rd Cong., 2nd sess. Washington, D.C.: Government Printing Office, 1968. Rev. ed. 1973.

U.S. Congress. House. *Digested Summary and Alphabetical List of Private Claims . . . 1st to the 31st Congress . . . 1853.* Reprint. Baltimore: Genealogical Publishing Co., 1970. See also publications: 32nd to 41st Cong. (1851–70) and 42nd to 46th Cong. (1871–81).

U.S. Department of the Army. Office of the Chief of Chaplains. By Peter Thompson. *From the Antecedents to 1791: The United States Army Chaplaincy.* Vol. 1. Washington, D.C.: 1978.

———. By Earl F. Stover. *Up From Handymen: The United States Army Chaplaincy, 1865–1922.* Vol. 3. Washington, D.C.: 1977.

U.S. Department of the Army. Public Information Division. *The Medal of Honor of the United States Army.* Washington, D.C.: Government Printing Office, 1948.

U.S. Military Academy. *Official Register of the Officers and Cadets, 1878.* West Point, N.Y.: United States Military Academy, 1878.

———. *Official Register of Officers and Cadets, 1917–1947.* West Point, N.Y.: United States Military Academy, various years.

———. *Register of Graduates and Former Cadets of the United States Military Academy, 1802–1991.* West Point, N.Y.: the Association of Graduates, USMA, 1991.

U.S. Navy Department. *Medal of Honor. The Navy, 1861–1949.* Washington, D.C.: Government Printing Office, n.d.

———. *United States Navy Chaplains, 1778–1945.* Clifford M. Drury, director. Biographical sketches of 3,353 chaplains, including two who served in the Continental Navy.

U.S. Pension Bureau. *Roster of Examining Surgeons Appointed under Authority of the Commissioner of Pensions . . .* Washington, D.C.: Government Printing Office..

U.S. Surgeon General's Office. *The Medical Department of the United States Army From 1775 to 1873.* Washington, D.C.: 1873. Registers of medical officers, including those killed in action since 1789. Name, original entry, date, state of birth and appointment, and remarks, pages 266–300.

Webster's American Military Biographies. Springfield, Mass.: G & C Merriam Co., 1978. Reprint. New York: Dover, 1984.

Wilkes, Laura E. *Missing Pages in American History, Revealing the Services of Negroes in the Early Wars in the United States of America, 1641–1815.* Reprint. Washington, D.C.: 1919 (?).

Witt, Mary E.S. *An Alphabetical List of Navy, Marine and Privateer Personnel and Widows From Pension Rolls, Casualty Lists, Retirement and Dismissal Rolls of the United States Navy Dated 1847.* Dallas: Mew Publishing, 1986.

Pre-1775 (colonial wars)

Guide

Wehmann, Howard H., comp. *A Guide to Pre-federal Records in the National Archives.* Revised by Benjamin L. DeWhitt. Washington, D.C.: NARA, 1989.

Publications With Lists of Names

Blacks in the United States Armed Forces. Basic Documents. Edited by MacGregor, Morris J., and Bernard C. Nalty. 13 vols. Wilmington, Del: Scholarly Resources, 1977. Vol. 1 covers the colonial era.

Bodge, George M. *Soldiers in King Philip's War: Being a Critical Account of That War, With a Concise History of the Indian Wars of New England From 1620–1677.* 3rd ed. Boston: the author, 1906. Reprint. Baltimore: Genealogical Publishing Co., 1976.

Clark, Murtie J. *Colonial Soldiers of the South, 1732–1774.* Baltimore: Genealogical Publishing Co., 1983. Includes militia muster rolls and payrolls for Maryland, Virginia, North and South Carolina, and Georgia; and Colonel Gooch's American Regiment for the War of Jenkins' Ear from the colonies of Massachusetts, Rhode Island, Connecticut, New York, New Jersey, Maryland, and North Carolina.

Coleman, Emma L. *New England Captives Carried to Canada Between 1677 and 1760 During the French and Indian Wars.* 2 vols. Bowie, Md.: Heritage Books, 1989.

Ellis, George W. and John E. Morris. *King Philip's War: Based on the Archives and Records of Massachusetts, Plymouth, Rhode Island and Connecticut. . . .* New York: Grafton Press, 1906. Reprint. New York: AMS Press, 1980.

General Society of Colonial Wars. *An Index of Ancestors and Roll of Members.* 3 vols. New York: the General Assembly, 1922. Hartford, Conn.: 1941. Baltimore: 1977.

McDermott, John Frances, ed. *The Spanish in the Mississippi Valley, 1762–1804.* Urbana: University of Illinois Press, 1974. List of soldiers with places of birth, pages 373–86.

National Society of the Daughters of Colonial Wars. *Membership List and Index of Ancestors.* 2 vols. Somerville, Mass.: the society, 1941.

Swanson, Carl E. *Predators and Prizes: American Privateering and Imperial Warfare, 1739–1748.* Columbia: University of South Carolina Press, 1991. Pertains primarily to Massachusetts, Connecticut, Rhode Island, New York and Pennsylvania. Table 4.1 lists thirty vessels and their commanders. Privateer vessels and their captains are so designated in the index.

Taylor, Philip F. *A Calendar of the Warrants for Land in Kentucky, Granted for Service in the French and Indian War.* Baltimore: Genealogical Publishing Co., 1967.

1775–83 (American Revolution)

Guides and Bibliographies

Eakin, Joyce L. *Colonial America and the War for Independence.* United States Army Military History Research Collection special bibliographic series; no. 14. Carlisle Barracks, Pa.: U.S. Army Military History Research Collection, 1976.

Gephart, Ronald M., comp. *Revolutionary America, 1763–1789: A Bibliography.* 2 vols. Washington, D.C.: Government Printing Office, 1984.

Miles, Lion G., and James L Kochan. *Guide to Hessian Documents of the American Revolution, 1776–1783.* Morristown, N.J.: 1989.

Neagles, James C., and Lila L. Neagles. *Locating Your Revolutionary War Ancestor: A Guide to the Military Records.* Logan, Utah: Everton Publishers, 1983.

Schweitzer, George K. *Revolutionary War Genealogy.* Knoxville, Tenn.: the author, 1982.

White, J. Todd, and Charles H. Lesser, eds. *Fighters for Independence: A Guide to Sources of Biographical Information on Soldiers and Sailors of the American Revolution.* Chicago: University of Chicago Press, 1977.

Publications With Lists of Names

Allen, Gardner W. *A Naval History of the American Revolution.* 2 vols. Boston, 1913. Reprint. Williamstown, Mass.: Corner House, 1970. Appendix includes lists of Continental Navy officers, vessels, and bondsmen.

Bailey, James D. *Some Heroes of the American Revolution.* Spartanburg, S.C.: Band & White, Printers, 1924. Includes biographical sketches of some officers.

Banvard, Joseph. *Soldiers and Patriots of the American Revolution.* Boston: D. Lothrop & Co., 1876.

Barnes, John S. *The Logs of the* Serapis, Alliance, Ariel, *Under the Command of John Paul Jones, 1779–80.* Naval Historical Society, 1911. Contains crew lists of these vessels as well as of the *Bon Homme Richard.*

Billias, George A. *George Washington's Generals.* New York: W. Morrow, 1964.

Bird, Harrison. *March to Saratoga: General Burgoyne and the American Campaign, 1777.* New York: Oxford University Press, 1963. Names of British and German officers, pages 281–85; American officers, pages 187–88.

Bowman, John E. *Some Veterans of the American Revolution in Various Parts of the United States: Items From Newspapers, 1816–1850.* 2 vols. New Ipswich, N.H.: 1923. Also names some veterans of the French and Indian War.

Bradford, James C., ed. *Guide to the Microfilm Edition of the Papers of John Paul Jones, 1747–1792.* Alexandria, Va.: Chadwyck-Healey, 1986.

Brown, Margie G. *Genealogical Abstracts, Revolutionary War Veterans, Scrip Act, 1852.* Oakton, Va.: the author, 1990. Abstracted from the Bureau of Land Management, Record Group 49, National Archives Branch.

Chunn, Calvin E. *Not By Bread Alone.* Valley Forge, Pa.: Society of the Descendants of Washington's Army at Valley Forge, 1981. Biographical data about those who served with George Washington at Valley Forge.

Claghorn, Charles E. *Naval Officers of the American Revolution: A Concise Biographical Dictionary.* Metuchen, N.J.: Scarecrow Press, 1988.

––––––. *Women Patriots of the American Revolution: A Biographical Dictionary.* Metuchen, N.J.: Scarecrow Press, 1991.

Clarke, John. *An Impartial and Authentic Narrative of the Battle Fought on the 17th of June 1775 . . . on Bunker's Hill . . . Near Charles Town, in New England.* London: 1775. Reprint. New York: W. Abbat, 1909. Lists casualties among officers.

Coburn, Frank W. *The Battle of April 19, 1775, in Lexington, Concord, Lincoln, Arlington, Cambridge, Somerville, and Charlestown, Massachusetts.* 2d ed., rev. and with additions. Port Washington, N.Y.: Kennikat Press, 1970 (?). Lists Americans killed, wounded, and missing, pages 157–58; British killed, wounded, prisoners, and missing, pages 159–60.

Coggins, Jack. *Ships and Seamen of the American Revolution.* Harrisburg, Pa.: Stackpole Books, 1975.

Cross, Christopher. *Soldiers of God.* New York: E.P. Dutton, 1945.

Dandridge, Danske B. *American Prisoners of the Revolution.* Baltimore, Md.: Genealogical Publishing Co., 1967.

Daughters of the American Revolution. *DAR Patriot Index.* 3 vols. Washington, D.C.: Daughters of the American Revolution, 1966–86. Lists of patriots identified as members of the DAR; kept up to date by supplements.

Draper, Lyman C. *King's Mountain and Its Heroes: History of the Battle of King's Mountain, October 7th, 1780, and the Events Which Led to It.* Cincinnati: 1881. Reprint. Baltimore: Genealogical Publishing Co., 1967. Supported by data collected from original documents, contemporary narratives, and interviews with survivors and their descendants.

Duncan, Louis C. *Medical Men in the American Revolution, 1775-1783.* Carlisle Barracks, Pa.: 1931. Reprint. New York: A.M. Kelley, 1970. List of medical men who participated in the American Revolution, pages 379-414.

English, William H. *Conquest of the Country Northwest of the River Ohio, 1778-1783, and Life of Gen. George Rogers Clark.* 2 vols. Indianapolis: Bowen-Merrill, 1896. Reprint. New York: Arno Press, 1971. Vol. 1: lists British captured with Lieutenant-Governor Hamilton at Vincennes, 24 February 1779, pages 585-86; vol. 2: roll of officers and soldiers allotted land in George Rogers Clark's Indiana grant for service under him in the reduction of British posts in Illinois, with acreage and descriptive numbers of the land received by each man, pages 839-50.

Frost, John. *The American Generals, From the Founding of the Republic to the Present Time, Comprising Lives of the Great Commanders, and Other Distinguished Officers Who Have Acted in the Service of the United States . . .* Philadelphia: 1848. Reprint. Hartford, Conn.: Case, Lockwood & Co., 1860.

Garden, Alexander. *Anecdotes of the Revolutionary War in America, With Sketches of Character of Persons the Most Distinguished, in the Southern States, for Civilian and Military Services.* 2 vols. Charleston, S.C.: 1822. Reprint. Spartanburg, S.C.: Reprint Co., 1972.

Germain, Aidan H. *Catholic Military and Naval Chaplains, 1776-1917.* Washington, D.C.: 1929. Includes French chaplains in the American Revolution.

Godfrey, Carlos E. *The Commander-in-Chief's Guard, Revolutionary War.* Washington, D.C.: 1904. Reprint. Baltimore: Genealogical Publishing Co., 1972. Rosters of infantry and cavalry guards, biographical sketches with military records of approximately three hundred officers and men.

Greene, Robert E. *Black Courage 1775-1783: Documentation of Black Participation in the American Revolution.* Washington, D.C.: National Society of the Daughters of the American Revolution, 1984. Some twenty-two biographical sketches followed by fourteen appendices listing both military and civilian patriots. Some data garnered from pension applications.

Gumpertz, Sydney G. *Jewish Legion of Valor: The Story of Jewish Heroes in the Wars of the Republic and a General History of the Military Exploits of the Jews Through the Ages.* New York: 1934. Reprint. New York: 1946.

Harding, Margery Heberling, comp. *George Rogers Clark and His Men, Military Records, 1778-1784.* Frankfort: Kentucky Historical Society, 1981. Sources are cited.

Hatcher, Patricia L. *Abstracts of Graves of Revolutionary Patriots.* 4 vols. Dallas, Tex.: Pioneer Heritage Press, 1987-88.

Hayward, Elizabeth M. *Soldiers and Patriots of the American Revolution: A List Compiled From Baptist Periodicals at the Shirk Library, Franklin College.* Ridgewood, N.J.: 1947.

_____, comp. *The Chaplains and Clergy of the Revolution: A List Compiled From Baptist Periodicals at the Shirk Library, Franklin College.* Ridgewood, N.J.: 1947.

Headley, Joel T. *The Chaplains and Clergy of the Revolution.* New York: Charles Scribner, 1864. Reprint. Collingswood, N.J.: 1976. Approximately forty biographical sketches.

Heaton, Ronald E. *Masonic Membership of the General Officers of the Continental Army.* Washington, D.C.: Masonic Service Association, 1960.

Heitman, Francis B. *Historical Register of Officers of the Continental Army During the War of the Revolution, April 1775–Dec. 1783.* Washington, D.C.: 1893. Several eds. Reprint of new, rev., enl. ed. of 1914 with addenda by Robert H. Kelby, 1932. Baltimore: Genealogical Publishing Co., 1967.

Hillard, Elias B. *The Last Men of the Revolution: A Photograph of Each From Life . . . Accompanied by Brief Biographical Sketches.* Hartford, Conn.: N.A. & R.A. Moore, 1864. Reprint. Barre, Mass.: Barre Pub., 1968.

Homans, Benjamin, ed. *Register of the Officers of the Army of the United States.* Washington, D.C.: 18–.

_____, ed. *Register of the Officers of the Navy of the United States, Corrected to the First of July, 1835.* Washington, D.C.: the author, 1835.

Is That Service Right? Washington, D.C.: National Society Daughters of the American Revolution, 1986.

Kaminkow, Marion J., and Jack Kaminkow. *Mariners of the American Revolution: With an Appendix of American Ships Captured by the British During the Revolutionary War.* Baltimore: Magna Carta Book Co., 1967. Includes some four thousand names of those who became prisoners of the British. Data includes name of vessel, date and place imprisoned, and when released (or escaped).

Long, Richard S., comp. *Biographies of Continental Marine Officers.* Washington, D.C.: History and Museum Division, Headquarters, U.S. Marine Corps, 1974.

Lu, Helen M., and Gwen B. Neumann, comps. *Revolutionary War Period: Bible, Family & Marriage Records Gleaned from Pension Applications.* 12 vols. Dallas: the author, 1980–91.

McDermott, John Francis, ed. *The Spanish in the Mississippi Valley, 1762–1804.* Urbana: University of Illinois Press, 1974 (?). List of soldiers and their places of birth, pages 373–86.

McLane, Curren R. *American Chaplains of the Revolution.* Louisville, Ky.: National Society of the Sons of the American Revolution, 1991.

McManemin, John A. *Captains of the Continental Navy.* Ho-Ho-Kus, N.J.: Ho-Ho-Kus Publishing Co., 1981.

_____. *Captains of the Privateers During the Revolutionary War.* Spring Lake, N.J.: Ho-Ho-Kus Publishing Co., 1985.

Mattox, A.H. *A History of the Cincinnati Society of Ex-Army and Navy Officers with the Name, Army Record, and Rank of the Members, Alphabetically Arranged.* Cincinnati: P.G. Thomson, 1880.

Metcalf, Bryce. *Original Members and Other Officers Eligible to the Society of the Cincinnati, 1783–1938.* Strasburg, Va.: Shenandoah Publishing House, 1938.

Miller, Florence H. *Memorial Album of Revolutionary Soldiers, 1776.* Crete, Nebr.: 1958. About 380 biographical sketches with portraits (mostly officers), alphabetically arranged.

Monnette, Orra E. *Spirit of Patriotism: Revolutionary and Ancestral Records of the Society, Sons of the Revolution in the State of California.* Los Angeles: Standard Print Co., 1915. Personnel of American naval vessels from published sources.

Muster and Pay Rolls of the War of the Revolution, 1775–1783. Collections of the New York Historical Society, 1914–15, vols. 47–48. New York: the society, 1916. Vol. 1: Artillery; Canadian troops; Connecticut troops; Continental infantry; Maryland, Massachusetts, New Hampshire, and New Jersey troops; vol. 2: New York, North Carolina, Pennsylvania, Rhode Island, South Carolina, and Virginia Troops. Index.

Neagles, James C. *Summer Soldiers: A Survey & Index of Revolutionary War Courts-martial.* Salt Lake City: Ancestry, 1986. Lists 3,315 accused offenders in courts-martial cases from 168 orderly books at the National Archives and Library of Congress. Includes name, unit, the charge, the court's finding, the punishment (if any), and the source.

Nell, William C. *Services of Colored Americans in the Wars of 1776 and 1812.* Boston: Prentiss & Sawyer, 1976.

Newman, Debra L., comp. *List of Black Servicemen Compiled From the War Department Collection of Revolutionary War Records.* Washington, D.C.: NARS, 1974. Special list, NARS, no. 36.

The Patriots of the Revolution of '76. Sketches of the Survivors. . . . Boston: G.W. Tomlinson, 1864. Biographies of American Revolution veterans who were still receiving pensions during the Civil War.

Paullin, Charles O. *The Navy of the American Revolution: Its Administration, Its Policy, and Its Achievements.* Cleveland: 1906. Reprint. New York: Haskell House, 1971. Lists the officers and vessels of the navy.

Penrose, Maryly B., comp. *Indian Affairs Papers, American Revolution.* Franklin Park, N.J.: Liberty Bell Associates, 1981. Source documents, including "List of Indians to Have Commissions in the American Forces," page 99; petitioners to New York state for payment, pages 314–15. Appendix D lists Indian pension applicants, pages 349–66.

Peterson, Clarence S. *Known Military Dead During the American Revolutionary War, 1775–1783.* Baltimore: 1959. Reprint. Baltimore: Genealogical Publishing Co., 1967.

Pierce's Register: Register of the Certificates Issued by John Pierce, Esquire, Paymaster General and Commissioner of Army Accounts for the United States, to Officers and Soldiers of the Continental Army Under Act of July 4, 1783. Washington, D.C.: Sen. Doc., 63rd Cong., 3rd sess., 1915. Washington, D.C.: National Society of the Daughters of the American Revolution, 17th Report, 1913–14. Reprint. Baltimore: Genealogical Publishing Co., 1973. Lists payments made only to soldiers who served in the Continental Army (not state militias). Opposite blocks of certificate numbers, pages 6–9, are names of particular military units, some commanding officers (sometimes both), and date the certificates were issued. The remainder of the book is an alphabetical list of soldiers, each with a certificate number and dollar amount paid. No rank, regiment, state, or other information is provided. This data was taken from a manuscript copy in the Rare Book Collection, Library of Congress, with printed title page (New York: Printed by Francis Childs, 1786.)

Ploski, Harry A., and James Williams, comp. and ed. *The Negro Almanac: A Reference Work on the African American.* 5th ed. Detroit: Gale Research Co., 1989. Includes nineteen sketches of "Black Patriots in the Era of the American Revolution."

Ray, Alexander. *Officers of the Continental Army Who Served to the End of the War and Acquired the Right to Commutation Pay and Bounty Land: Also Officers Killed in Battle or Died in the Service.* Washington, D.C.: J.& G.S. Gideon, 1849.

Richter, Victor W. *George Washington Leibgarde.* Hoboken, N.J.: Concord Society,1924.

Rouse, J.K. *Another Revolutionary War Hero Dies.* Kannapolis, N.C.: the author, 1978. More than one hundred death notices of revolutionary war veterans from newspapers, alphabetically arranged.

Saffell, William T. R. *Records of the Revolutionary War: Containing the Military and Financial Correspondence of Distinguished Officers; Names of the Officers and Privates of Regiments, Companies, and Corps, With the Dates of Their Commissions and Enlistments . . . General Orders of Washington, Lee, and Greene, at Germantown and Valley Forge . . . a List of Distinguished Prisoners . . . the Time of Their Capture, Exchange, etc.* New York: 1858. Reprint of 3rd ed. Baltimore: C.C. Saffell, 1894. Reprint. Baltimore: Genealogical Publishing Co., 1969.

Smith, Charles R. *Marines in the Revolution: A History of the Continental Marines in the American Revolution, 1775–1783.* Washington, D.C.: History and Museums Division, Headquarters, U.S. Marine Corps, 1975. Biographical data for more than one hundred officers.

Smith, Clifford N. *Federal Land Series: A Calendar of Archival Material on the Land Patents Issued by the United States Government, With Subject, Tract, and Name Indexes.* 4 vols. in 5. Chicago: American Library Association, 1972–86.

Stewart, Margaret. *Black Soldiers of the American Revolutionary War.* Centre, Ala.: Stewart University Press, 1978. Contains biographical sketches.

Toner, Joseph M. *The Medical Men of the Revolution, With a Brief History of the Medical Department of the Continental Army: Containing the Names of Nearly Twelve Hundred Physicians.* Philadelphia: Collins, Printer, 1876.

United States. Yorktown Sesquicentennial Commission. *Proceedings of the United States Yorktown Sesquicentennial Commission in Connection with the Celebration of the Siege of Yorktown, 1781.* Washington: Genealogical Publishing Co., 1932.

Waldenmaier, Nellie P. *Some of the Earliest Oaths of Allegiance to the United States of America.* Lancaster, Pa.: Lancaster Press, 1944. Oaths of 975 military officers including George Washington.

Williams, Eugene F. *Soldiers of God, the Chaplains of the Revolutionary War.* New York: Carlton Press, 1975. Biographical sketches of chaplains who served during the American Revolution.

Who Was Who During the American Revolution. Compiled by Jerry Kail. Indianapolis: Bobbs-Merrill, 1976.

Witt, Mary E. *An Alphabetical List of Navy, Marine and Privateer Personnel and Widows From Pension Rolls, Casualty Lists, Retirement and Dismission Rolls of the United States Navy Dated 1847.* Dallas: Mew Publishing, 1986.

Wolf, Simon. *The American Jew as Patriot, Soldier and Citizen.* Edited by Louis E. Levy. Philadelphia: Levytype Co., 1895. Reprint. Boston: Gregg Press, 1972.

Loyalists–American Revolution

Guides and Bibliographies

Bunnell, Paul J. *Research Guide to Loyalist Ancestors: A Directory to Archives, Manuscripts, and Published Sources.* Bowie, Md.: Heritage Books, 1990. Sources in Canada, United States, England, and the Bahamas.

Palmer, Gregory. *A Bibliography of Loyalist Source Materials in the United States, Canada, and Great Britain.* Westport, Conn.: Meckler Publishing Co., 1982.

Publications With Lists of Names

A List of General and Staff Officers. New York: J. Rivington, 1778.

An Index to Georgia Colonial Conveyances and Confiscated Lands Records, 1750–1804. Atlanta: R.J. Taylor, Jr., Foundation, 1981.

Antliff, W. Bruce. *Loyalists Settlements, 1783–1789: New Evidence of Canadian Loyalist Claims.* Ontario: Ministry of Citizenship and Culture, 1985.

Black List: A List of Those Tories Who Took Part With Great Britain in the Revolutionary War, and Were Attainted of High Treason, Commonly Called the Black List . . . Philadelphia:

1802. Reprint. New York: 1865. Lists of Pennsylvania loyalists.

Brown, Wallace. *The Good Americans: The Loyalists in the American Revolution.* New York: William Morrow and Co., 1969.

Bunnell, Paul J. *The New Loyalist Index.* Bowie, Md.: Heritage Books, 1989. Provides name, vital records (when reported), where from and where settled, regiment and rank, and claim (if any).

Candler, Allen D., comp. *The Revolutionary Records of the State of Georgia. Compiled and Published Under Authority of the Legislature* . . . 3 vols. Atlanta: 1908. Reprint. New York: AMS Press, 1972. Vol. 1 includes sales of confiscated estates: name, date, location, and acreage of property, amount and to whom sold; list of those banished.

The Centennial of the Settlement of Upper Canada by the United Empire Loyalists, 1784–1884. Boston: Gregg Press, 1972.

Clark, Murtie J. *Loyalists in the Southern Campaign of the Revolutionary War.* 3 vols. Vol. 1, *Official Rolls of Loyalists Recruited From North and South Carolina, Georgia, Florida, Mississippi, and Louisiana;* vol. 2, *Official Rolls of Loyalists Recruited From Maryland, Pennsylvania, Virginia, and . . . Other Colonies for the British Legion, Guides and Pioneers, Loyal Foresters, and Queen's Rangers;* vol. 3, *Official Rolls of Loyalists Recruited From the Middle Atlantic Colonies, With Lists of Refugees From Other Colonies.* Baltimore: Genealogical Publishing Co., 1981.

Coke, Daniel P. *The Royal Commission on the Losses and Services of American Loyalists, 1783 to 1785.* Oxford: 1915. Edited by Hugh Edward Egerton. Reprint with new editorial note—New York: B. Franklin, 1971.

Coldham, Peter W. *American Loyalist Claims: Abstracted From the Public Record Office, Audit Office Series 13, Bundles 1–35 & 37.* 1st ed. Washington, D.C.: National Genealogical Society, 1980–.

Corupe, Linda, comp. *Index to the Loyalists of the Eastern Townships of Quebec.* Quebec (?): the author, 1984 (?).

Davis, Robert S., Jr. *Georgia Citizens and Soldiers of the American Revolution.* Easley, S.C.: Southern Historical Press, 1979. List of Georgia claimants from AO 13 (cited below), pages 222–27.

DeMond, Robert O. *The Loyalists in North Carolina During the Revolution.* Durham, N.C.: Duke University Press, 1940. Reprint. Baltimore: Genealogical Publishing Co., 1979. Appendices list officers and men in the Loyal Militia, the Royal North Carolina Militia, refugees, confiscated lands, applicants for claims, and pension rolls.

Dubeau, Sharon. *New Brunswick Loyalists: A Bicentennial Tribute.* Generation Press, 1983.

Dwyer, Clifford S. *Index to Series I of American Loyalist Claims: 2 Series, AO 12, Series 1* (microform, 30 reels). DeFuniak Springs, Fla.: Ram Publishing, 1985.

———. *Index to Series II of American Loyalists Claims: 2 Series, AO 13, Series 2* (microform, 145 reels). Transcribed for Ray Jones by Clifford S. Dwyer and Peter Wilson Coldham. DeFuniak Springs, Fla.: Ram Publishing, 1986.

Eardley-Wilmot, John. *Historical View of the Commission for Enquiring Into the Losses, Services, and Claims of the American Loyalists, at the Close of the War Between Great Britain and Her Colonies in 1783* . . . London: 1815. Reprint. Boston: Gregg Press, 1972.

Edgerton, Hugh E., ed. *The Royal Commission on the Losses and Services of American Loyalists, 1783 to 1785.* Oxford: Roxburghe Club, 1915. Reprint. New York: B. Franklin, 1971.

Fitzgerald, E. Keith. *Loyalist Lists: Over 2,000 Loyalist Names and Families From the Haldimand Papers.* Ontario Genealogical Society, 1984.

Flick, Alexander C. *Loyalism in New York During the American Revolution.* New York: 1901. Reprint. New York: AMS Press, 1970. Appendix lists confiscated property with dates of sale, Loyalist owner, purchases, price, description, and remarks.

Ford, Worthington C., comp. *British Officers Serving in the American Revolution, 1774–1783.* Brooklyn, N.Y.: Historical Print Club, 1897.

Fraser, Alexander, ed. *Second Report of the Bureau of Archives for the Province of Ontario.* Toronto: L.K. Cameron, 1905.

Fryer, Mary B., and William A. Smy. *Rolls of the Provincial (Loyalist) Corps, Canadian Command, American Revolutionary Period.* Toronto: Dundurn Press, 1981.

Gilroy, Marion. *Loyalists and Land Settlement in Nova Scotia.* Baltimore: Genealogical Publishing Co., 1980. Reprint. Halifax, Nova Scotia: Nova Scotia Public Archives, 1990.

Great Britain. War Office. *A List of the General and Staff Officers, and of the Officers in the Several British, Foreign, and Provincial Regiments, Serving in North-America, Under the Command of His Excellency, General Sir Henry Clinton, K.B., With the Dates of Their Commissions as They Rank in Each Corps and in the Army.* New York: 1777. Philadelphia: Macdonald & Cameron, 1778. New York: Macdonald & Cameron, 1779. Reprint. Boston: 1942.

Hammond, Otis G. *Tories of New Hampshire in the War of the Revolution.* Boston, Mass.: Gregg Press, 1972.

Hancock, Harold B. *The Loyalists of Revolutionary Delaware.* Newark: University of Delaware Press, 1977.

Hassam, John T. *The Confiscated Estates of Boston Loyalists.* Cambridge, Mass.: J. Wilson and Son, 1895. Lists name, year, and docket number in Suffolk County probate records.

Hays, Louise F., comp. *Georgia Military Records, 1779–1842.* 9 vols. N.p., 1940. Unpublished typescripts from records at the Georgia State Archives; indexed.

Hill, Isabel L. *Some Loyalists and Others.* Fredericton, New Brunswick: I.L. Hill, 1977. Biographical sketches, many with portraits.

Jones, E. Alfred. *The Loyalists of Massachusetts: Their Memorials, Petitions and Claims.* London: 1930. Reprint. Baltimore: Genealogical Publishing Co., 1969.

_____. *The Loyalists of New Jersey: Their Memorials, Petitions, Claims, Etc. From English Records.* Newark, N.J.: New Jersey Historical Society, 1927. Reprint. Boston: Gregg Press, 1972.

Kelby, William, comp. *Orderly Book of the Three Battalions of Loyalists Commanded by Brigadier-General Oliver de Lancey, 1776–1778; to Which is Appended a list of New York Loyalists in the City of New York During the War of the Revolution.* Originally issued in series in The John Divine Jones Fund Series of Histories and Memoirs, vol. 3. New York: New York Historical Society, 1917. Reprint. Baltimore: Genealogical Publishing Co., 1972. The appended list contains more than one thousand names.

Livinston, Mildred R. *Upper Canada Sons and Daughters of United Empire Loyalists.* Kingston, Ontario: Brown & Martin, 1981.

Maryland Loyalists Regiment. *Orderly Book of the "Maryland Loyalists Regiment."* Brooklyn, N.Y.: Historical Printing Club, 1891.

Maas, David E., comp. *Divided Hearts: Massachussetts Loyalists, 1765–1790, a Biographical Directory.* Boston: Society of Colonial Wars in the Commonwealth of Massachusetts and the New England Historic Genealogical Society, 1980.

Montgomery, Thomas L. *Forfeited Estates Inventories and Sales.* Pennsylvania Archives, 6th series, vols. 12 and 13. Harrisburg, Pa.: Harrisburg Publishing Co., 1907.

New York Mercantile Library Association. *New York City During the American Revolution; Being a Collection of Original Papers From the Manuscripts in the Possession of the Mercantile Library Association of New York City.* New York: 1861.

Norton, Mary B. *The British-American: The Loyalist Exiles in England, 1774–1789.* Boston: 1972. Reprint. London: Constable, 1974.

Palmer, Gregory. *Biographical Sketches of Loyalists of the American Revolution.* Westport, Conn.: Meckler Publishing Co., 1984.

_____. *A Bibliography of Loyalist Source Materials in the United States, Canada, and Great Britain.* Westport, Conn.: Meckler Publishing Co., 1982.

Paltsits, Victor H. *Minutes of the Commissioners for Detecting and Defeating Conspiracies in the State of New York: Albany County Sessions, 1778–1781.* 3 vols. in 2. Boston: Gregg Press, 1972.

Parrish, Lydia. *Records of Some Southern Loyalists.* Unpublished manuscript at Houghton Library, Harvard University. A microfilm copy is at the Georgia State Archives (drawer 12, box 1).

Peters, Thelma P. *The American Loyalist and the Plantation Period in the Bahama Islands.* A microfilm copy is at the Georgia State Archives (drawer 190, box 76).

Peterson, Jean, comp. *The Loyalist Guide: Nova Scotian Loyalists and Their Documents.* Halifax, Nova Scotia: Nova Scotia Public Archives, 1983.

Pruitt, Albert B. *Abstracts of Sales of Confiscated Loyalist Land and Property in North Carolina.* The author, 1989.

Reid, William D. *The Loyalists in Ontario: The Sons and Daughters of the American Loyalists of Upper Canada.* Lambertville, N.J.: Hunterdon House, 1973.

Ryerson, Adolphus E. *Loyalists in East Florida, 1774 to 1785: The Most Important Documents Pertaining Thereto, Edited With an Accompanying Narrative.* 2 vols. Port Washington, N.Y.: Kennikat Press, 1966.

Sabine, Lorenzo. *The American Loyalist, or, Biographical Sketches of Adherents to the British Crown in the War of the Revolution; Alphabetically Arranged; With a Preliminary Historical Essay.* Boston: C.C. Little and J. Brown, 1847. Reprinted as *Biographical Sketches of Loyalists of the American Revolution, With an Historical Essay.* Port Washington, N.Y.: Kennikat Press, 1966. Baltimore: Genealogical Publishing Co., 1979.

Scott, Kenneth, comp. *Rivington's New York Newspaper: Excerpts From a Loyalist Press, 1773–1783.* New York: New York Historical Society, 1973. Tory James Rivington's newspaper, *Rivington's New York Loyal Gazette,* contains numerous items about loyalists, including many in the military.

Sequestration, Confiscation and Sale of Estates. State Papers of Vermont, vol. 6. Edited by Mary Greene Nye. Montpelier, Vt.: secretary of state, 1941.

Siebert, Wilbur H. *Loyalists in East Florida, 1774 to 1785: The Most Important Documents Pertaining Thereto; Edited With an Accompanying Narrative.* 2 vols. DeLand, Fla.: Florida State Historical Society, 1929. Reprint. Boston: Gregg Press, 1972.

Stark, James H. *The Loyalists of Massachusetts and the Other Side of the American Revolution.* Boston: W.B. Clarke Co., 1910. Reprint. Clifton: A.M. Kelley, 1972. Contains many biographical sketches.

Stryker, William S. *'The New Jersey Volunteers (Loyalists) in the Revolutionary War'.* Trenton, N.J.: Narr, Day & Narr, 1887.

Talman, James J., ed. *Loyalist Narratives From Upper Canada.* Toronto: 1946. Reprint. New York: Greenwood Press, 1969.

Tyler, John W. *Connecticut Loyalists: An Analysis of Loyalist Land Confiscations in Greenwich, Stamford, and Norwalk.* New Orleans: Polyanthos, 1977. Appendices list names from tax assessments and confiscated estates.

United Empire Loyalist Centennial Committee (Toronto). *The Old United Empire Loyalists List.* Toronto: 1885. Reprint. Baltimore: Genealogical Publishing Co., 1969. Lists names, places of residence, and descendants.

VanTyne, Claude H. *The Loyalists in the American Revolution.* Bowie, Md.: Heritage Books, 1989.

Wallace, William S. *United Empire Loyalists: A Chronicle of the Great Migration.* Boston, Mass.: Gregg Press, 1972.

Wright, Esther C. *The Loyalists of New Brunswick.* Fredericton, New Brunswick: 1955. Reprint. Hantsport, Nova Scotia: the author, 1981. The end notes and appendix include names of American loyalists, places of their former homes, Revolutionary War service, land grants, and places of residence.

Yoshpe, Harry Beller. *The Disposition of Loyalist Estates in the Southern District of the State of New York.* New York: Columbia University, 1939. Reprint: New York: AMS Press, 1967.

Foreign Combatants— American Revolution

Atwood, Rodney. *The Hessians: Mercenaries From Hessen-Kassel in the American Revolution.* Cambridge, Mass.: Cambridge University Press, 1980. Appendix E lists officers of battalions and Jägercorps serving in America.

Balch, Thomas. *The French in America During the War of Independence of the United States, 1777–1783.* 2 vols. Philadelphia: Porter & Coates, 1891–95. Reprint. Boston: Gregg Press, 1972. Alphabetically arranged biographical sketches.

Benson, Adolph B. *Sweden and the American Revolution.* New Haven, Conn.: Tuttle, Morehouse & Taylor, 1926. Biographical data for about seventy officers who served with the patriots.

Bodinier, Gilbert. *Dictionnaire des Officiers de l'Armee Royale qui ont Combattu aux Etats-Unis Pendant la Guerre d'Independance, 1776–1783 . . .* Vincennes, France (?): Ministere de la Defense, Etat-Major de l'Armee de Terre, Service Historique, 1983.

Burgoyne, Bruce E. *Waldeck Soldiers of the American Revolution.* Bowie, Md.: Heritage Books, 1991.

Contension, Ludovic Guy Marie du Bessey de, Baron. *La Societe des Cincinnati de France et la Guerre d'Amerique, 1778–1783.* Paris: A. Picard, 1934 (?). Names of French officers eligible for membership in the Society of Cincinnati.

DeMarce, Virginia E. *An Annotated List of 317 Former German Soldiers Who Chose to Remain in Canada After the American Revolution.* Arlington, Va: the author, 1981.

_____. *Canadian Participants in the American Revolution: An Index.* Arlington, Va.: the author, 1980.

_____. *Mercenary Troops From Anhalt-Zerbst, Germany, Who Served With the British Forces During the American Revolution.* 2 vols. McNeal, Ariz.: Westland Publications, 1984.

_____. *The Settlement of Former German Auxiliary Troops in Canada After the American Revolution.* Arlington, Va.: the author, 1982.

_____. *The Settlement of Former German Auxiliary Troops in Canada After the American Revolution. Supplement.* Sparta, Wis.: Joy Reisinger, 1984.

Dickore, Marie P., ed. and trans. *Hessian Soldiers in the American Revolution: Records of Their Marriages and Baptisms of Their Children in America Performed by the Rev. G.C. Cöster, 1776–1782, Chaplain of Two Hessian Regiments.* Cincinnati: C. J. Krehbiel Co., 1959.

Dulfer, Kurt. *Hessische Truppen im Amerikanischen Unabhängigkeitskrieg (Hetrina): Index Nach Familiennamen.* 4 vols. Marburg, Germany: Archivschule Marburg, 1976–87. (See Clifford N. Smith, "German Mercenaries of the American Revolution." *National Genealogical Society Quarterly* 65 (1977): 75–81.)

Eelking, Max von. *The German Allied Troops in the North American War of Independence, 1776–1783.* Translated and abridged from the German of Max von Eelking (published Hanover, Germany: 1863) by J.G. Rosengarten. Albany, N.Y: Joel Munsell's Sons, 1893. Reprint. Baltimore: Genealogical Publishing Co., 1969. Lists Hessian officers serving under Generals Howe, Clinton, and Carleton, pages 281–351.

Gardiner, Asa B. *The Order of the Cincinnati in France (L'Ordre de Cincinnatus'): Its Origin and History: With the Military or Naval Records of the French Members Who Became Such by Reason of Qualifying Service in the Army or Navy of France or of the United States in the War of the Revolution for American Independence.* Rhode Island State Society of the Cincinnati, 1905.

Heckert, C.W. *The German-American Diary; Notes of Related Historical Interest, Including Translated Excerpts From the Wiederholdt Diary, American Revolutionary War.* Parsons, W.Va.: McClain Printing Co., 1980. Includes the German (American) Regiment (Pennsylvania Germans); roster of Co. 5, Regiment von Knyphausen; and a list of Hessian prisoners.

Johnson, Amandus. *Swedish Contributions to American Freedom, 1776–1783; Including a Sketch of the Background of the Revolution, Together with an Account of the Engagements in Which Swedish Officers Participated, and Biographical Sketches of These Men.* 2 vols. Philadelphia: Swedish Colonial Foundation, 1953–57. Vol. 2 lists Swedes who served under the British or with the American forces.

Lasseray, Andre. *Les Francais Sous les Treize Etoiles (1776–1783) Cinq Planches Hors Texte.* 2 vols. Mâcon, France: Imprimerie Protat Freres, 1935.

Les Combattants Francais de la Guerre Americaine, 1778–1783. Paris: 1903. Reprints. Washington, D.C.: Sen. Doc. 77, 58th Cong., 2d sess.; Baltimore: Genealogical Publishing Co., 1969. Lists some 45,000 French soldiers who participated in the American Revolution.

Maginniss, Thomas H. *The Irish Contributions to America's Independence.* Philadelphia: Doire Publishing Co., 1913.

Miles, Lion G. *The Hessians of Lewis Miller.* Millville, Pa.: Precision Printers, 1983. Includes portraits of the participants.

Murphy, Charles. *The Irish in the American Revolution.* Groveland, Mass.: Charles Murphy Pub., 1975. Names some officers, gunners, and matrosses (gunners' assistants).

Noailles, Amblard Marie Raymond Amedee, Vicomte de. *Marines et Soldats Francais en Amerique Pendant la Guerre de l'Independance des Etats-Unis (1778–1783).* Paris: Perrin et Cie, 1903. Appendices include names of officers, naval vessels, and fighting units.

O'Brien, Michael J. *A Hidden Phase of American History; Ireland's Part in America's Struggle for Liberty.* Illustrated by Portraits . . . New York: 1919. Reprint. Baltimore: Genealogical Publishing Co., 1973. Appendix lists officers of the American army and navy of Irish birth or descent; noncommissioned officers and men.

_____. *The Irish at Bunker Hill: Evidence of Irish Participation in the Battle of 17 June 1775.* New York: Devin-Adair Press, 1968. Shannon, Ireland: Irish University Press, 1968.

Richards, Henry M. *The Pennsylvania-German in the Revolutionary War, 1775–1783.* Lancaster, Penn.: Pennsylvania German Society, 1908. Reprint. Genealogical Publishing Co., 1978. Includes biographical sketches and lists.

Rosengarten, J.G. *The German Soldier in the Wars of the United States.* Philadelphia: J.B. Lippincott, 1890. Reprint. San Francisco: R and E Research Associates, 1972. Biographical data and list of German officers in the revolutionary army.

Smith, Clifford N. *British and German Deserters, Discharges, and Prisoners of War Who May Have Remained in Canada and the United States, 1774–1783.* McNeal, Ariz.: Westland Publications, 1991.

_____. *Brunswick Deserter-immigrants of the American Revolution.* Thomson, Ill.: Heritage House, 1973. Names, ages, and places of birth of approximately three thousand British deserters who remained in the Unites States and Canada.

_____. *Deserters and Disbanded Soldiers From British, German, and Loyalist Military Units in the South, 1782.* McNeal, Ariz.: Westland Publications, 1991.

_____. *Mercenaries From Ansbach and Bayreuth, Germany, Who Remained in America After the Revolution.* Thomson, Ill.: Heritage House, 1974. Includes more than 1,100 names.

_____. *Mercenaries From Hessen-Hanau Who Remained in Canada and the United States After the American Revolution.* DeKalb, Ill: Westland Publications, 1976. Names and places of birth of almost one thousand soldiers who remained in North America.

_____. *Muster Rolls and Prisoner-of-War Lists in American Archival Collections Pertaining to the German Mercenary Troops Who Served With British Forces During the American Revolution.* 3 vols. DeKalb, Ill: Westland Publications, 1976.

_____. *Notes on Hessian Soldiers Who Remained in Canada and the United States After the American Revolution, 1775–1784.* McNeal, Ariz.: Westland Publications, 1992.

_____. *Some German-American Participants in the American Revolution: The Ratterman Lists.* McNeal, Ariz.: Westland Publications, 1990.

Wytrwal, Joseph A. *Poles in American History and Tradition.* Detroit: Endurance Press, 1969. Includes names of Poles who fought in the American Revolution, pages 30–38.

Pensioners and Bounty Land Recipients— American Revolution

Clark, Murtie J., comp. *The Pension Lists of 1792–1795: With Other Revolutionary War Pension Records.* Baltimore: Genealogical Publishing Co., 1991. Includes certain Revolutionary War pension records predating the War Department and Treasury Department fires of 1800 that survive as congressional reports: invalid claims submitted in 1792, 1794, and 1795 by the secretary of war to Congress and certificates of debt issued to those whose claims, made prior to 1792, were barred because they were filed after the deadline. Data includes name of veteran; branch of service; date, number, and type of certificate; date from which interest accrued; and the amount. From state returns there is a list of Continental Army officers who died prior to 28 May 1778 whose widows and orphans were eligible for seven years' half pay. Also includes abstracts of petitions for individual invalid pensions submitted by the secretary of war to Congress during 1790–1800. The appendix lists "Invalid Pensioners whom Congress approved under the 1798 Act for the Relief of Disabled Soldiers and Seamen."

_____. *Index to U.S. Invalid Pension Records, 1801–1815.* Baltimore: Genealogical Publishing Co., 1991. Names alphabetically arranged by state with rank, page number in original document, and remarks (if any).

_____. *The Pension Roll of 1835.* U.S. Government Document Serial Nos. 249, 250, 251. Washington, D.C.: 1835. Reprint. 1968. Revised edition with name index. Baltimore: Genealogical Publishing Co., 1992.

Closson, Bob, comp. *Register of Invalid Pensions: Revolutionary Service, 1789.* Apollo, Pa.: Closson Press, 1981.

English, William H. *Conquest of the Country Northwest of the River Ohio, 1778–1783, and Life of Gen. George Rogers Clark.* Indianapolis: Bowen-Merrill, 1896. Reprint. New York: Arno Press, 1971. Vol. 1 includes a list of British captured at Vincennes, 24 February 1779, pages 585–86; vol. 2 includes a roll of three hundred men who were allotted land in Clark's Grant (Indiana) for service under Clark in the reduction of the British post in Illinois, with quantity and descriptive numbers, pages 831–50.

Index of Revolutionary War Pension Applications in the National Archives. Special Publication No. 40. Revised and enlarged bicentennial edition. Washington, D.C.: National Genealogical Society, 1976. Revolutionary War pension and bounty land warrant application files, 1800-1900.

McMullin, Phillip W., ed. *Grassroots of America: A Computerized Index to the American State Papers: Land Grants and Claims (1789–1837) With Other Aids to Research (Government Document Serial Set Numbers 28 Through 36).* American State

Papers. Index. Salt Lake City: Gendex, 1972. Master index to claimants and recipients of land grants as they occur in the *American State Papers.* Includes veterans of the American Revolution claiming bounty land in the Northwest Territory under a military bounty provided by the state of Virginia.

Naval Documents of the American Revolution. 9 vols. Edited by William Bell Clark and William James Morgan. Washington, D.C.: Naval Historical Center, 1964–86. Period covered to date is 1774–September 1777; includes both the American and European theaters.

Pensioners of Revolutionary War Struck Off the Roll, With an Added Index to States. Baltimore: Clearfield Co., 1989. Pensioners' names listed by state of residence.

Ray, Alexander. *Officers of the Continental Army Who Served to the End of the War, and Acquired the Right to Commutation Pay and Bounty Land.* Washington, D.C.: J. and G. S. Gideon, Printers, 1849. Library of Congress copy replaced by microfilm 44511.

U.S. Bounty Land Office. *List of the Names of Such Officers and Soldiers of the Revolutionary Army as Have Acquired a Right to Lands from the United States, and Who Have Not Yet Applied Therefore . . .* Sen. Doc. 42, 20th Cong., 1st sess. Serial set 164. Washington, D.C.: 1828.

U.S. Bureau of the Census. *A Census of Pensioners for Revolutionary or Military Services; With Their Names, Ages, and Places of Residence, as Returned by the Marshals of the Several Judicial Districts Under the Act for Taking the Sixth Census.* Sixth Census, 1840. Washington, D.C.: Blair and Rives, 1841. Reprint. Baltimore: Genealogical Publishing Co., 1967. Reprint. Apollo, Pa.: B. Closson and M. Closson, 1979.

U.S. Congress. House. *Digested Summary and Alphabetical List of Private Claims Which Have Been Presented to the House of Representatives From the First to the Thirty-first Congress, Exhibiting the Action of Congress on Each Claim, With References to the Journals, Reports, Bills, &c., Elucidating Its Progress.* Compiled by Order of the House of Representatives. 3 vols. House Misc. Doc., 32nd Cong., 1st sess. Washington, D.C.: 1853. Reprint. Baltimore: Genealogical Publishing Co., 1970.

U.S. Department of the Interior. *Report of the Secretary of the Interior With a Statement of Rejected or Suspended Applications for Pensions.* Washington, D.C.: Government Printing Office, 1852. Reprinted as *Rejected or Suspended Applications for Revolutionary War Pensions, with an Added Index to States.* Baltimore: Genealogical Publishing Co., 1969. Pensions listed by state, with name, town, and county of residence, and reasons for suspension.

U.S. Laws, Statutes, etc. *Resolutions, Laws, and Ordinances, Relating to the Pay, Half Pay, Commutation of Half Pay, Bounty Lands, and Other Promises Made by Congress to the Officers and Soldiers of the Revolution; to the Settlement of the Accounts Between the United States and the Several States; and to Funding the Revolutionary Debt.* Washington, D.C.: 1838. Reprint. New York: Research Reprints, 1970 (?). Detailed index of more than three hundred claimants (memorialists); names of

widows or other heirs, affiants, witnesses, etc., are not included.

U.S. War Department. *Letter from the Secretary of War, Communicating a Transcript of the Pension List of the United States, Showing the Number of Pensioners in the Several Districts, Also, the Amount Allowed to Each Pensioner.* June 1, 1813. Referred to the Committee of Claims. Washington, D.C.: A. & G. Printers, 1813. Includes 1,766 names alphabetically arranged by state with military rank and annual stipend.

_____ . *Letter From the Secretary of War, Communicating a Transcript of the Pension List of the United States.* Vol. 6. Washington, D.C.: A. & G. Printers, 1813. Reprint. St. Paul, Minn.: 1894.

_____ . *Letter From the Secretary of War, Transmitting a Report of the Names, Rank, and Line, of Every Person Placed on the Pension List, in Pursuance of the Act of the 18th March, 1818, &c.* Washington, D.C.: Gales & Seaton, 1820. Reprinted as *The Pension List of 1820. With an Index by Murtie June Clark.* Baltimore: Genealogical Publishing Co., 1991.

_____ . *Register of the Certificates Issued by John Pierce, Esq., Paymaster General and Commissioner of the Army Account of the United States. To Officers and Soldiers of the Continental Army Under Act of July 4, 1783.* 4 vols. New York: F. Childs, 1786. Reprinted as *Pierce's Register.* National Society of the Daughters of the American Revolution, 17th Report, 1913–14. Baltimore: Genealogical Publishing Co., 1973.

_____ . *Report From the Secretary of War, in Obedience to Resolutions of the Senate of the 5th and 30th of June, 1834, and the 3d of March, 1835, in Relation to the Pension Establishment of the United States.* Reprinted as *The Pension Roll of 1835.* 4 vols. Baltimore: Genealogical Publishing Co., 1968. Vol. 1: New England states: Connecticut, Maine, Massachusetts, New Hampshire, Rhode Island, Vermont; vol. 2: mid-Atlantic states: Delaware, New Jersey, New York, Pennsylvania; vol. 3: southern states: Alabama, Arkansas, District of Columbia, Florida, Georgia, Kentucky, Louisiana, Maryland, Mississippi, North and South Carolina, Tennessee, Virginia; vol. 4: midwestern states: Illinois, Indiana, Michigan, Missouri, Ohio.

White, Virgil D. *Genealogical Abstracts of Revolutionary War Pension Files.* 4 vols. Waynesboro, Tenn.: National Historical Publishing Co., 1990–92. Data from the National Archives, the Virginia half-pay claims, and state pension and bounty land records.

1784–1815
(War of 1812)

Guides and Bibliographies

Fredriksen, John C., comp. *Free Trade and Sailor's Rights: A Bibliography of the War of 1812.* Westport, Conn.: Greenwood Press, 1985.

_____ , comp. *Resource Guide for the War of 1812.* Westport, Conn.: Greenwood Press, 1979.

Smith, Dwight L. *The War of 1812. An Annotated Bibliography.* New York: Garland Publishing, 1985.

Publications With Lists of Names

Andrews, Charles. *The Prisoners' Memoirs.* New York: the author, 1815. Reprint. New York, 1852. Names and places of residence of some former Dartmoor prisoners who declared the author's comments "just and true," pages v–vii; names and places of residence of some American prisoners (and the American vessels on which they were captured) who were released from Dartmoor to enlist in the Royal Navy, April 1813–14, pages 252–80.

Biggs, James. *The History of Don Francisco de Miranda's Attempt to Effect a Revolution in South America, in a Series of Letters.* 3rd ed. Boston: E. Oliver, 1811. Several lists of "officers" and men appointed by Miranda for his expedition to Venezuela, pages 19–20, 77–78; those executed or sentenced to hard labor, pages 242–43, 312.

Blizzard, Dennis F., comp. *The Roster of the General Society of the War of 1812.* Mendenhall, Pa.: the society, 1989. Roster of members living in 1892 who were veterans of the War of 1812, pages 15–20; ancestor list, pages 205–41.

Bowen, Abel. *The Naval Monument, Containing Official and Other Accounts of All the Battles Fought Between the Navies of the United States and Great Britain During the Late War.* Boston: 1830. Reprint. Boston: G. Clark, 1840. Includes Naval Register for 1815 with name, rank, and date of commission, following page 315.

Canada Public Archives. *General Entry Book of American Prisoners of War at Quebec.* Hartford, Conn.: National Society of the Daughters of the American Revolution, 1923. Typescript. Information includes prisoner's number and name; by what ship or how taken; date and place; military rank (or citizen); when received into custody and from what ship; place of birth; age; physical description; supplies issued; and whether exchanged, discharged, died, or escaped with dates and basis for discharge.

Carr, Deborah E. *Index to Certified Copy of List of American Prisoners of War, 1812–15.* National Society of the United States Daughters of 1812, 1924.

Clark, Byron N. *A List of Prisoners of the War of 1812.* Burlington, Vt.: Research Publications, 1904.

Clark, Murtie J. *American Militia in the Frontier Wars, 1790–1796.* Baltimore: Genealogical Publishing Co., 1990. Includes militia from Kentucky, Ohio Territory, Southwest Territory, Virginia, New Jersey, Pennsylvania, and Georgia.

_____ . *The Pension List of 1820.* Baltimore: Genealogical Publishing Co., 1991.

Cullum, George W. *Register of the Officers and Graduates of the U.S. Military Academy, at West Point, N.Y., From March 16, 1802, to January 1, 1850.* New York: J.F. Trow, 1850.

Dieffenbach, H.B., comp. *Index to the Brave: Records of Soldiers of the War of 1812.* N.p. 1945.

Evans, Stephen H. *The U.S. Coast Guard, 1790–1815 . . .* Annapolis, Md.: U.S. Naval Institute, 1949.

Fredericksen, John C. *Free Trade and Sailors' Rights: A Bibliography of the War of 1812.* Westport, Conn.: Greenwood Press, 1985.

Galvin, Eleanor S., comp. *1812 Ancestor Indexes, 1892–1970: National Society United States Daughters of 1812.* Norcross, Ga.: Harper Printing, 1970. Names, dates, military service, and wives of approximately 20,000 who served in the military between 1784 and 1815.

Harris, Nancy E., comp. *1812 Ancestor Index, 1903–1986.* Washington, D.C.: National Society of the United States Daughters of 1812, 1986.

Kent, David L. *Foreign Origins. Comprising an Enumeration of Men of Foreign Birth Enlisted in the United States Army From 1798 to 1815; Together With the Dates & Places of Enlistment and Ages of the Men . . . Arranged by State Alphabetically . . . With No Exception the Town or City of Birth Abroad . . .* Arlington, Va.: C.M. Kent, 1981.

Lail, Glady E. *The Guide to Register of Audits, Treasury Department.* Alexandria, Va.: the author, 1981. Names, dates, and index card numbers of individuals who appear in audit accounts at the National Archives for the period 1791–1814.

McKee, Christopher. *A Gentlemanly and Honorable Profession. The Creation of the U.S. Naval Officer Corps, 1794–1815.* Annapolis, Md.: Naval Institute Press, 1991. Includes much biographical data and a number of portraits.

National Society of the United States Daughters of 1812. Polly L. Murphy, trans. *Index to Compiled Service Records of Volunteer Soldiers Who Served During the War of 1812.* The society, 1983.

The Naval War of 1812: A Documentary History. Projected 3-vol. work. Edited by William S. Dudley. Washington, D.C.: Naval Historical Center, Department of the Navy. Government Printing Office, 1985–. Vol. 1: Original documents including "List of Captains, Masters-Commandant, Lieutenants, Acting Lieutenants, and Midshipmen, in the Navy of the United States" in 1805, pages 4–6; American prisoners of war discharged from Halifax and vessels on which they had served, 1812, pages 480–87, etc.

Office of Naval Records and Library. Department of the Navy. *Naval Documents Relating to the United States Wars With the Barbary Powers...1785 Through 1801.* 7 vols. Washington, D.C.: Government Printing Office, 1939–45. Each volume is indexed. Includes many lists; for example, "Muster Roll of U.S. Ship *George Washington* from earliest entry date 30 April 1800 to 4 May 1801," vol. 1, pages 444–47. Vol. 7 is titled *Register of Officer Personnel United States Navy and Marine Corps and Ships Data, 1801–1807.* It includes names of commissioned, warrant, and acting officers alphabetically arranged with date of assignment, rank, vessels in which served, and other comments.

_____. *Naval Documents Related to the Quasi-War Between the United States and France.* 7 vols. Washington, D.C.: Government Printing Office, 1935–38. Lists include, for example, "Pay Roll of U.S. Frigate *United States*, Captain John Barry, U.S. Navy, Commanding," vol. 7, pages 61–66; "Officers of the U.S. Navy and Marine Corps, and in Ships Under the Jurisdiction of the Navy, During the Quasi-War with France, 1797–1801," vol. 7, pages 315–75; "American Armed Merchantmen, 1799–1801," vol. 7, pages 376–438, etc.

Parsons, Usher. *Brief Sketches of the Officers Who Were in the Battle of Lake Erie.* Albany, N.Y.: J. Munsell, 1862.

Peterson, Charles J. *The Military Heroes of the War of 1812: With a Narrative of the War.* Philadelphia: J.B. Smith, 1858. Biographical sketches; illustrated with woodcuts and engravings; bound with *Military Heroes of the War With Mexico...*

Peterson, Clarence S. *Known Military Dead During the War of 1812.* Baltimore: the author, 1955. Names listed with rank, unit, date of death, and, occasionally, place of death.

Scott, Kenneth, comp. *British Aliens in the United States During the War of 1812.* Baltimore: Genealogical Publishing Co., 1979. Names alphabetically arranged by state with age (fourteen years or older), length of time in United States, number of family members, occupation, and sometimes date of arrival, place of birth, physical description, etc. Half-pay British officers and navy personnel are so designated.

Todd, Charles S. *Bounty Lands to the Regular and Volunteer Officers of the War of 1812.* Washington: N.p. ca. 1880.

Tucker, Glenn. *Poltroons and Patriots.* Indianapolis and New York: Bobbs-Merrill, 1954.

White, Virgil D., trans. *Index to Volunteer Soldiers, 1784–1811.* Waynesboro, Tenn.: National Historical Publishing Co., 1987.

_____. *Index to War of 1812 Pension Files.* 3 vols. Waynesboro, Tenn.: National Historical Publishing Co., 1989. Index to applicants eligible for pensions or bounty lands under the acts of 1871 and 1878; list compiled from 102 rolls of microfilm at the National Archives; includes name of pensioner or widow, state from which served, pension or bounty land warrant number, date and place of marriage, place of residence, and date and place of death.

Witt, Mary E.S., comp. *An Alphabetical List of Navy, Marine, and Privateer Personnel and Widows From Pension Rolls, Casualty Lists, Retirement and Dismission Rolls of the United States Navy Dated 1847.* Dallas: MEW, 1986. Includes many War of 1812 veterans.

Young, Bennett H. *The Battle of the Thames: With a List of the Officers and Privates Who Won the Victory.* Louisville, Ky.: John P. Morton & Co., 1903.

Captains of the Old Steam Navy: Makers of the American Naval Tradition, 1840–1880. Edited by James C. Bradford. Annapolis, Md.: Naval Institute Press, 1986. Interpretive biographies of thirteen men "who guided the Navy into the age of steam."

Indian Wars (1790–1898)

Publications With Lists of Names

Altshuler, Constance W. *Cavalry Yellow & Infantry Blue: Army Officers in Arizona Between 1851 and 1886.* Tucson, Ariz.: Arizona Historical Society, 1991. Biographical sketches of eight hundred army officers who "served in Arizona between 1815, when the first American post was established, and 1886 when the Indian Wars officially ended. But most had careers ranging far beyond the [Arizona] Territory. Their collective experience included every major army action from the War of 1812 through World War I . . . Slaked Plains to Wounded Knee, from France to China."

Bledsoe, Anthony J. *Indian Wars of the Northwest. A California and Oregon Sketch.* San Francisco: Bacon & Co., 1885.

Bowden, J.J. *The Ponce de Leon Land Grant.* El Paso, Tex. (?): Western Press, 1969 (?). Includes army casualties of the Second Seminole War, pages 119–80.

Brady, Cyrus Townsend. *Indian Fights and Fighters: The Soldier and the Sioux.* New York: 1904. Reprint with an introduction by James T. King. Lincoln: University of Nebraska Press, 1971.

Downey, Fairfax D. *The Buffalo Soldiers in the Indian Wars. Illus. With Old Remington Prints and Line Drawings by Harold James.* New York: McGraw-Hill, 1969. History of four African-American cavalry regiments created in 1866 specifically to fight in the Indian Wars.

Hafen, Le Roy R. and Ann W. Hafen, eds. *Powder River Campaigns and Sawyers Expedition of 1865: A Documentary Account Comprising Official Reports, Diaries, Contemporary Newspaper Accounts, and Personal Narratives.* Far West and the Rockies Historical Series, 1820–1875, vol. 12. Glendale, Calif.: A.H. Clark Co., 1961.

Hardorff, Richard G. *The Custer Battle Casualties: Burials, Exhumations, and Reinterments.* El Segundo, Calif.: Upton & Sons, 1991.

Kingsbury, David L. *Sully's Expedition Against the Sioux in 1864.* St. Paul, Minn.: 1898.

Peters, Joseph P., comp. *Indian Battles and Skirmishes on the American Frontier, 1790–1898: Comprising Record of Engagements With Hostile Indians Within the Military Division of the Missouri From 1868 to 1882: Chronological List of Actions, etc. With Indians From January 1, 1866 to January 1891: and a Compilation of Indian Engagements From January 1837 to January 1866.* New York: Argonaut Press, 1966.

Record of Officers and Soldiers Killed in Battle and Died in Service During the Florida War. Washington: Government Printing Office, 1882. Second Seminole War, 1835–42.

Webb, George W. *Chronological List of Engagements Between the Regular Army of the United States and Various Tribes of Hostile Indians Which Occurred During the Years 1790 to 1898, Inclusive.* St. Joseph, Mo.: Wing Printing and Publishing Co., 1939. Reprint. New York: AMS Press, 1976.

White, Virgil D. *Index to Indian War Pension Files, 1892–1926.* Waynesboro, Tenn.: National Historical Publishing Co., 1987.

Force, Peter. *Register of the Army and Navy of the United States, 1830.* Washington, D.C.: the author, 1830.

Peterson, Charles J. *The Military Heroes of the War With Mexico.* Philadelphia: 1848. Reprint. Philadelphia: J.B. Smith, 1858.

Peterson, Clarence S. *Known Military Dead During the Mexican War, 1846–48.* Baltimore: the author, 1957.

Robarts, William H. *Mexican War Veterans. A Complete Roster of the Regular and Volunteer Troops in the War Between the United States and Mexico, From 1846 to 1848.* Washington, D.C.: Brentano's, 1887. Includes names, ranks, dates and places of death or injury (if applicable).

Troxel, Navena H., and Susan M. Warner, comp. *Mexican War Index to Pension Files, 1886–1926.* 10 vols. Gore, Okla.: VT Publications. Reprint. Plano, Tex.: Fifth Wheel, 1983–86. Names alphabetically arranged with application number (veteran or widow); state from which served or residence of widow; bounty land warrant; military unit; and dates served.

U.S. Adjutant General's Office. *Official Army Register for 1835.* Washington, D.C.: Adjutant General's Office, January 1835.

U.S. Congress. House. Committee on Pensions. *Pensions to Certain Enlisted Men and Officers Who Served in the Civil War and the War With Mexico.* Washington: Government Printing Office, 1907.

U.S. Revenue-cutter Service. *Register of the Officers and Vessels of the Revenue-cutter Service of the United States.* Washington, D.C.: Government Printing Office, 1914.

White, Virgil D. *Index to Mexican War Pension Files.* Waynesboro, Tenn.: National Historical Publishing Co., 1989.

_____ , trans. *Index to Old Wars Pensions Files, 1815–1926.* 2 vols. Waynesboro, Tenn.: National Historical Publishing Co., 1987. Compiled from microfilm records held by the National Archives. Name of veteran (or widow), rank, file designation, war in which served, and state in which veteran or widow filed a claim. Includes rejected applications.

Wolfe, Barbara Schull, trans. *Index to Mexican War Pension Applications.* Indianapolis: Heritage House, 1985. Created from records held by the National Archives.

1816–60 (Mexican War)

Bibliographies

Snoke, Elizabeth R. *The Mexican War: A Bibliography of MHRC Holdings for the Period 1835–1850.* Carlisle Barracks, Pa.: 1973.

Tutorow, Norman E., comp. and ed. *The Mexican-American War: An Annotated Bibliography.* Westport, Conn.: Greenwood Press, 1981.

Publications With Lists of Names

Daughters of the Republic of Texas. *Muster Rolls of the Texas Revolution.* Austin, Tex.: Daughters of the Republic of Texas, 1986.

1861–65 (Civil War)

Guides and Bibliographies

Allen, Desmond Walls. *Where to Write for Confederate Pension Records.* Bryant, Ark.: Research Associates, 1991. Briefly describes pension files, date of earliest pension legislation, available indexes, addresses of file locations in each Southern state, and other sources of information.

Amann, William F. *Personnel of the Civil War.* 2 vols. New York: Thomas Y. Yoseloff, 1961.

Atlas to Accompany the Official Records of the Union and Confederate Armies. Washington, D.C. Government Printing Office, 1891–95. Reprint. New York: Fairfax Press, 1983.

Broadfoot, Tom, ed. *Civil War Books. A Priced Checklist.* Wendell, N.C.: Avers Press, 1978.

Dornbusch, Charles E. *Military Bibliography of the Civil War.* 4 vols. New York: New York Public Library, 1971–87.

Dyer, Frederick H. *Compendium of the War of the Rebellion.* 2 vols. Des Moines, Iowa: the author, 1908. Reprint. New York: Thomas Y. Yoseloff, 1959.

Evans, Clement A., ed. *Confederate Military History. . . .* 12 vols. Atlanta, Ga.: Confederate Publishing Co., 1899. Reprint. Dayton, Ohio: Morningside Bookshop, 1975. Includes biographical sketches.

Groene, Bertram H. *Tracing Your Civil War Ancestors.* Rev. ed. Winston-Salem, N.C.: John F. Blair Publisher, 1980.

Hill, Walter. "Exploring the Life and History of the 'Buffalo Soldiers.'" *The Record.* National Archives and Records Administration. March, 1998.

Meredith, Lee W. *Guide to Civil War Periodicals.* Vol. 1. Twentynine Palms, Calif.: Historical Indexes, 1991.

Moebs, Thomas T. *Confederate States Navy Research Guide: Confederate Naval Imprints . . . Marine Corps and Naval Officer Biographies, Description and Service of Vessels, Subject Bibliography . . .* Williamsburg, Va.: Moebs Publishing Co., 1991.

Neagles, James C. *Confederate Research Sources: A Guide to Archive Collections.* Salt Lake City: Ancestry, revised 1996.

Nevins, Allen, James I. Robertson, and Wiley I. Bell. *Civil War Books, A Critical Bibliography.* 2 vols. Baton Rouge, La.: Louisiana State University Press, 1967–69.

O'Quinliven, Michael. *An Annotated Bibliography of the United States Marines in the Civil War.* Washington, D.C.: U.S. Marine Corps, 1968.

Schweitzer, George K. *Civil War Genealogy.* Knoxville, Tenn.: the author, 1982.

Stephenson, Richard W., comp. *Civil War Maps in the Library of Congress, An Annotated List.* Washington, D.C.: Library of Congress, 1961.

Tancig, William J., comp. *Confederate Military Land Units 1861–65.* New York: Thomas Y. Yoseloff, 1967.

U.S. Army Military History Research Collection. *Bibliography of the Era of the Civil War, 1820–76.* Edited by B. Franklin Cooling. Carlisle Barracks, Pa.: 1974.

U.S. Navy Department. *Official Records of the Union and Confederate Armies in the War of the Rebellion.* 128 vols. Washington, D.C: Government Printing Office, 1880–1900. Reprint. Gettysburg, Pa.: National Historical Society, 1971.

U.S. Navy Department. *Official Records of the Union and Confederate Navies in the War of the Rebellion.* 31 vols. Washington, D.C.: Government Printing Office, 1894–1927.

U.S. War Department. War College Division. *Bibliography of State Participation in the Civil War, 1861–66.* Washington, D.C.: Government Printing Office, 1913.

Publications With Lists of Names—Union

Blacks in the United States Armed Forces: Basic Documents. Edited by Morris J. MacGregor and Bernard C. Nalty. 13 vols. Wilmington, Del.: Scholarly Resources, 1977. Vols. 2 and 3 cover the Civil War.

Cogar, William B. *Dictionary of Admirals of the U.S. Navy.* Annapolis, Md.: Naval Institute Press, 1989. Contains illustrated biographies. Vol. 1: 1862–1900.

Larson, Carl V., comp. and ed. *A Data Base of the Mormon Battalion: An Identification of the Original Members of the Mormon Battalion.* Providence, Utah: Keith W. Watkins & Sons, 1987.

Leckie, William H. *The Buffalo Soldiers.* U. of Oklahoma Press, 1993.

Lord, Francis A. *Civil War Sutlers and Their Wares.* New York: Thomas Y. Yoseloff, 1969. An appendix lists names of sutlers arranged by unit to which assigned; also lists manufacturers and dealers in merchandise.

Powell, William H. *Officers of the Army and Navy (regular) Who Served in the Civil War.* Philadelphia: L.R. Hamersly, 1892.

Roll of Commanderies . . . . Register of the Military Order of the Loyal Legion of the United States. Boston: n.p., 1906.

Roll of Honor: Names of Soldiers Who Died in Defense of the American Union. 27 vols. Washington, D.C.: Government Printing Office, 1865–71. Records are arranged by burial place. Entries include name, rank, regiment, company, and date of death.

Sifakis, Stewart. *Who Was Who in the Union: A Comprehensive, Illustrated Biographical Reference to More Than 1,500 of the Principal Union Participants in the Civil War.* New York: Facts on File, 1988.

Wright, Edward N. *Conscientious Objectors in the Civil War.* New York: A.S. Barnes & Co., 1961.

U.S. Adjutant General's Office. *Official Army Register of the Volunteer Force of the United States Army for the Years 1861, '62, '63, '64, '65.* Washington, D.C.: Government Printing Office, 1865. Reprint. Gaithersburg, Md.: Ron R. Van Sickle Military Books, 1987. Vol. 1: New England states; vol. 2: New York, New Jersey; vol. 3: Pennsylvania, Delaware, Maryland, District of Columbia; vol. 4: West Virginia, Virginia, North Carolina, South Carolina, Georgia, Florida, Alabama, Mississippi, Louisiana, Texas, Arkansas, Tennessee, Kentucky; vol. 5: Ohio, Michigan; vol. 6: Indiana, Illinois; vol. 7: Missouri, Wisconsin, Iowa, Minnesota, California, Kansas, Oregon, Nevada; vol. 8: territories of Washington, New Mexico, Nebraska, Colorado, Dakotas, Veteran Reserve Corps, U.S. Veteran Volunteers, U.S. Volunteers, U.S. Colored Troops. Lists all commissioned officers for state volunteer regiments.

_____ . Shiloh National Military Park Commission. *The Battle of Shiloh and the Organizations Engaged.* Washington, D.C.: Government Printing Office, 1909.

U.S. Pension Bureau. *List of Pensioners on the Roll, January 1, 1883, Giving the Name of Each Pensioner, the Cause for Which Pensioned, the Post Office Address, the Rate of Pension per Month, and the Date of Original Allowance as Called for by Senate Resolution of December 8, 1882.* 5 vols. Reprint. Baltimore: Genealogical Publishing Co., 1970.

Publications With Lists of Names— Confederate

Brock, R.A. *The Appomattox Roster: Paroles of the Army of Northern Virginia . . . .* Richmond, Va. Reprint. New York: The Antiquarian Press, 1962.

Brown, Dee A. *The Galvanized Yankees.* Urbana, Ill.: Urbana Press, 1963.

Confederate Medical and Surgical Journal. 14 vols. January 1864–February 1865. Reprint. Metuchen, N.J.: Scarecrow Press, 1976.

Confederate Roll of Honor. Mattituck, N.Y.: J.M. Carroll & Co., 1885.

Confederate Veteran (Nashville, Tennesee). *Confederate Veteran.* 40 vols. Nashville, Tenn.: Confederate Veteran, 1893–1932. *Cumulative Index to the Confederate Veteran Magazine, 1893–1932.* 3 vols. Wilmington, N.C.: Broadfoot, 1986. Publication of this journal resumed in September 1984. It is now published bimonthly in Houston, Texas, as the official journal of the Sons of Confederate Veterans.

Crute, Joseph H., Jr. *Confederate Staff Officers, 1861–1865.* Powhatan, Va.: Derwent Books, 1982.

Dickinson, Sally B. *Confederate Leaders.* Staunton, Va.: McClure Co., 1935.

Donnelly, Ralph M. *Biographical Sketches of the Commissioned Officers of the Confederate States Marine Corps.* Alexandria, Va.: the author, 1979.

_____ . *Service Records of Confederate Enlisted Marines.* Washington, D.C.: the author, 1979.

Dotson, Claude, comp. *List of Field Officers, Regiments and Battalions in the Confederate States Army, 1861–1865.* Washington, D.C.: Government Printing Office, 1899. Reprint. Macon, Ga.: J.W. Burke Co., 1912. Reprint. Mattituck, N.Y.: J.M. Carroll & Co., 1983.

Krick, Robert K. *Lee's Colonels: A Biographical Register of the Field Officers of the Army of Northern Virginia.* 2d rev. ed. Dayton, Ohio: Morningside Bookshop, 1984. "Confederate field officers, other than Army of Northern Virginia," pages 357–462.

Meredith, Lee W., comp. *Civil War Times and Civil War Times Illustrated, 30 Year Comprehensive Index.* Twentynine Palms, Calif.: the author, 1990.

Mills, Gary B. *Civil War Claims in the South: An Index of Civil War Damage Claims Filed Before the Southern Claims Commission, 1871–1880.* Laguna Hills, Calif.: Aegean Park Press, 1990.

Pardons by the President: Final Report of the Names of Persons Who Lived in Alabama, Virginia, West Virginia, or Georgia, Were Engaged in Rebellion and Pardoned by the President, Andrew Johnson. Bowie, Md.: Heritage Books, 1986.

Register of Officers of the Confederate States Navy, 1861–1865. Washington, D.C.: Government Printing Office, 1931. Reprint. Mattituck, N.Y.: J.M. Carroll & Co., 1983.

Sifakis, Stewart. *Compendium of the Confederate Armies.* 5 vols. New York: Facts on File, 1992. This work is a companion to Dyer's Compendium (see above). It is being published in a multi-volume series. Now available for several southern states. Data includes organizational and battle history of each unit, including names of officers.

_____ . *Who Was Who in the Confederacy.* New York: Facts on File, 1988. A biographical encyclopedia of more than one thousand Confederate participants, including some civilians.

U.S. Adjutant General's Office. Shiloh National Military Park Commission. *The Battle of Shiloh and the Organizations Engaged.* Washington, D.C.: Government Printing Office, 1909.

U.S. War Department. *General Officers Appointed . . . Confederate States, 1861–1865.* Washington, D.C.: Government Printing Office, 1908. Reprint. Mattituck, N.J.: J.M. Carroll Co, 1983.

U.S. War Department. *List of Staff Officers of the Confederate States Army.* Washington, D.C.: Government Printing Office, 1891. Reprint. Mattituck, N.Y.: J.M. Carroll & Co., 1983.

Wakelyn, Jon L. *Biographical Dictionary of the Confederacy.* Westport, Conn.: Greenwood Press, 1977.

Warner, Ezra J. *Generals in Gray: Lives of the Confederate Commanders.* Baton Rouge: Louisiana State University Press, 1959.

Wilson, Beverly E. *General Officers of the Confederacy, 1861–1865.* Typescript. Baytown, Tex.: the author, n.d.

Wright, Marcus J. *General Officers of the Confederate Army.* New York: Neal Publishing Co., 1911. Reprint. Mattituck, N.Y.: J.M. Carroll & Co., 1983.

Foreign Combatants

Lonn, Ella. *Foreigners in the Confederacy.* Chapel Hill, N.C.: 1940. Reprint. Gloucester, Mass.: P. Smith, 1965. Appendices II and III are lists of foreign-born officers.

_____ . *Foreigners in the Union Army and Navy.* Baton Rouge, La., 1951. Reprint. New York: Greenwood Press, 1969. Appendices list captains of Swedish birth; Polish officers; Swedish knights-errant and soldiers of fortune; German surgeons; and Hungarian officers of high rank.

Vasvary, Edmund. *Lincoln's Hungarian Heroes: The Participation of Hungarians in the Civil War, 1861–65.* Washington, D.C.: 1919. Includes a roster.

Wytrwal, Joseph A. *Poles in American History and Tradition.* Detroit: Endurance Press, 1969. Contains a list of names from the "Polish Legion," pages 152–53, note 13.

Confederate Exiles in South America

Griggs, William C. *The Elusive Eden: Frank McMullan's Confederate Colony in Brazil.* Austin: University of Texas Press, 1987. Refers to the Vila Americans in the Iguape region, province of São Paulo. Includes three appendices with censuses of the McMullan-Bowan Colony, pages 149–55.

Hanna, Alfred J., and Kathryn A. Hanna. *Confederate Exiles in Venezuala.* Tuscaloosa, Ala.: Confederate Publishing Co., 1960.

Harter, Eugene C. *The Lost Colony of the Confederacy.* Jackson: University Press of Mississippi, 1985. An appendix includes surnames of more than three hundred Confederate exiles who settled in Brazil, pages 126–28.

Hill, Lawrence F. *The Confederate Exodus to Latin America.* Austin, Tex.: N.p. 1936.

———. *Confederate Exiles in Brazil.* Durham, N.C.: 1927.

Oliveira, Betty A. *North American Immigration to Brazil: Tombstone Records of the "Campo" Cemetery, Santa Barbara d'Oeste, São Paulo State, Brazil.* Brasilia, Brazil: Grafica do Senado Federal, 1978. Lists some 450 gravestone inscriptions.

Werlich, David P. *Admiral of the Amazon: Randolph Tucker, His Confederate Colleagues and Peru.* Charlottesville: University Press of Virginia, 1990. Index includes names of many exiles.

Prisoners, Casualties, Deceased— Union and Confederate

Berry, Chester D. *Loss of the* Sultana *and Reminiscences of Survivors: History of a Disaster Where Over One Thousand Five Hundred Human Beings Were Lost, Most of Them Being Exchanged Prisoners of War on Their Way Home After Privation and Suffering from One to Twenty-three Months in Cahaba and Andersonville Prisons.* Lansing, Mich.: D.D. Thorp, 1892. Reprint: Nashville: Tennessee State Library and Archives, 1954.

Busey, John W. *These Honored Dead: The Union Casualties at Gettysburg.* Highstown, N.J., 1982.

Ericson, Carolyn R., and Frances T. Ingmire. *Confederate Soldiers Buried at Vicksburg, Feburary (sic) 15, 1862–July 4, 1863.* Nacogdoches, Tex.: the authors, 1981.

Harris, William C. *Prison-life in the Tobacco Warehouse at Richmond.* Philadelphia: G.W. Childs, 1862. List of the Richmond Prison Association (officers and civilians), with rank, name, regiment, where captured, residence, and remarks (date removed, paroled, escaped, exchanged, died, etc.).

Isham, Asa B. *Prisoners of War and Military Prisons: Personal Narratives of Experience in the Prisons at Richmond, Danville, Macon, Andersonville, Savannah, Millen, Charleston and Columbia . . . With a List of Officers Who Were Prisoners of War From January 1, 1864.* Cincinnati: Lyman & Cushing, 1890.

Jeffrey, William H. *Richmond Prisons 1861–1862: Compiled from the Original Records Kept by the Confederate Government, Journals Kept by Union Prisoners of War, Together with the Name, Rank, Company, Regiment and State of the Four Thousand Who Were Confined There.* St. Johnsbury, Vt.: Republican Press, 1893.

Krick, Robert K. *The Gettysburg Death Roster: The Confederate Dead at Gettysburg.* Dayton, Ohio: Morningside Bookshop, 1981.

Murray, J. Ogden. *The Immortal Six Hundred: A Story of Cruelty to Confederate Prisoners of War.* Winchester, Va.: The Eddy Press Corporation, 1905. Reprint. Little Rock, Ark: Eagle Press, 1986. List of six hundred prisoners by state, with rank, regiment, date and place captured, and residence; some portraits.

Ransom, John L. *John Ransom's Andersonville Diary.* Introduction by Bruce Catton. Originally published privately as *Andersonville Diary. . . .* Auburn, N.Y.: 1881. Reprint. Middlebury, Vt.: P.S. Erickson, 1986. Includes "List of the Dead" by state with grave number, name, regiment, company, and date of death, pages 273–381.

Register of Confederate Soldiers and Citizens Who Died in Federal Prisons and Military Hospitals in the North. Nacogdoches, Tex.: Ericson Books, 1984.

U.S. Quartermaster General. *Roll of Honor. Names of Soldiers Who Died in Defence of the American Union Interred in the National and Public Cemeteries.* Washington, D.C.: Government Printing Office, 1865–69.

1866–1900 (post-Civil War, Spanish-American War)

Bibliography

Venzon, Anne C. *The Spanish-American War: An Annotated Bibliography.* New York: Garland, 1990.

Publications With Lists of Names

Admirals of the New Steel Navy: Makers of the American Naval Tradition, 1880–1930. Edited by James C. Bradford. Annapolis, Md.: Naval Institute Press, 1990. Biographical sketches of thirteen officers who guided the U.S. Navy into the modern era.

Carroll, John M., ed. *The Medal of Honor: Its History and Recipients for the Indian Wars.* Bryan, Tex.: 1979. Covers the years 1866–95.

Coston, William H. *The Spanish American War Volunteer.* Freeport, N.Y.: Books for Libraries Press, 1971. Lists African-American soldiers.

Fort D.A. Russell, Wyoming. *Roster of Commissioned Officers of the Second Regiment of Infantry, United States Army, Who Participated in the Campaign Against Santiago de Cuba, and Who Were Present With the Army at Anytime Between June 2d and July 17th, 1898.* N.p. 1904.

_____. *Roster of Enlisted Men of the Second Regiment of Infantry, United States Army, Who Participated in the Campaign Against Santiago de Cuba, and Who Were Present With the Army at Anytime Between June 2d and July 17, 1898.* N.p., 1904.

List of Members of Various State Societies of the Sons of the American Revolution Who Served in the War With Spain. New York: the society, 1900.

Military Album, Containing Over One Thousand Portraits of Commissioned Officers Who Served in the Spanish-American War. New York: L.R. Hamersly & Co., 1902.

National Society Daughters of the American Revolution. "Roster of Women Nurses Enlisted for Spanish-American War and the Philippine Insurrection, 1898–1901." *Third Annual Report (1898–1900).* Provides names of about 1,200 nurses, with residence and place of service, pages 227–83.

O'Neal, Bill. *Fighting Men of the Indian Wars: A Biographical Encyclopedia of the Mountain Men, Soldiers, Cowboys, and Pioneers Who Took Up Arms During America's Westward Expansion.* Stillwater, Okla.: Barbed Wire Press, 1991.

Peterson, Clarence S. *Known Military Dead During the Spanish-American War and the Philippines Insurrection.* Baltimore: N.p. 1958.

Princeton in the Spanish-American War, 1898. Princeton, N.J.: Princeton Press, 1899. Contains a roll of honor of the USS *Maine.*

Society of Colonial Wars. *Register of Members of the Society of Colonial Wars Who Served in the Army or Navy of the United States During the Spanish-American War. . . .* New York: the society, 1899.

U.S. Adjutant General's Office. *Officers of Volunteer Regiments Organized Under the Act of March 2, 1899.* Washington, D.C.: Government Printing Office, 1899.

U.S. Congress. House Commission on War Claims. *Officers and Soldiers . . . War With Spain . . . Held in Service in the Philippine Insurrection.* Washington, D.C.: Government Printing Office, 1937.

U.S. Congress. House Committee on Pensions. *Pensions to Veterans of the Spanish-American War.* Washington, D.C.: Government Printing Office, 1935.

_____. *Pensions for Widows of Spanish-American War Veterans.* Washington, D.C.: Government Printing Office, 1929.

1901–40 (World War I)

Guides and Bibliographies

Controvitch, James T., comp. *United States Army Unit Histories: A Reference and Bibliography.* Manhattan, Kans.: Kansas State University, 1983. Refers primarily to units since 1900.

Dornbusch, Charles E. *Histories of American Army Units, World Wars I and II and Korean Conflict.* Washington, D.C.: Office of the Adjutant General, Special Services Division, 1956.

Pappas, George S. *United States Army Unit Histories: A Bibliography.* Carlisle Barracks, Pa.: U.S. Army Military History Institute, 1971–1978. Refers to both World War I and World War II units.

U.S. National Archives. *Federal Records of World War II.* NARS. Reprint. Detroit: Gale Research Co., 1982.

Publications With Lists of Names

Haulsee, W.M., F.G. Howe, and A.C. Doyle, comp. *Soldiers of the Great War.* 3 vols. Washington, D.C.: Soldiers Record Publishing Association, 1920. By state, lists of those killed in action or who died of disease or wounds or by accident, or who were wounded in action; includes many photographs. Vol. 1: Alabama–Maine; vol. 2: Massachusetts–Ohio; vol. 3: Oklahoma–Wyoming, followed by a supplement with additional photographs.

Navy Directory of Officers of the United States Navy and Marine Corps, Also Including Officers of the U.S. Naval Reserve Force (active), Marine Corps Reserve (active), and Foreign Officers Serving With the Navy. Washington, D.C.: Government Printing Office, various years.

Officers and Enlisted Men of the United States Navy Who Lost Their Lives During the World War From April 6, 1917 to November 11, 1918. Washington, D.C.: Government Printing Office, 1920. Lists sailor's name; rank; date, place, and cause of death; and name of next of kin.

Strait, Newton A. *Roster of All Regimental Surgeons and Assistant Surgeons in the Late War: With Their Service, and Last-known Post-office Address: Compiled From Official Records . . .* Washington, D.C.: N.A. Strait, 1882.

Trimble, Clifford R. *The Honor Roll, 1917, 1918, 1919.* Princeton, Ill: the author, 1920.

U.S. Congress. House. *Retirements From the Active List of the Navy.* Washington, D.C.: Government Printing Office, 1914.

U.S. Department of the Army. *United States Army Register, 1900-1980.* Washington, D.C.: Government Printing Office, various years. Lists names of regular army personnel, active duty and retired.

U.S. Bureau of Naval Personnel. *Officers and Enlisted Men of the United States Navy Who Lost Their Lives During the World War, From April 6, 1917 to November 11, 1918.* Washington, D.C.: Government Printing Office, 1920.

U.S. Navy Department. *Retirements on Account of Age of the Commissioned Officers, Warrant Officers and Mates of the Navy of the United States, and of the Marine Corps, to January 1, 1911.* Washington, D.C.: Government Printing Office, 1899 (?).

1941-45 (World War II)

Guides and Bibliographies

Esner, A.G.S. *A Subject Bibliography of the Second World War.* Boulder, Colo.: Westview Press, 1977.

Contravitch, James T., comp. *United States Army Unit Histories: A Reference and Bibliography.* Manhattan, Kans.: Kansas State University, 1983. Refers primarily to units since 1900.

Dornbusch, Charles E. *Histories of American Army Units, World Wars I and II and Korean Conflict.* Washington, D.C.: Office of the Adjutant General, Special Services Division, 1956.

_____ . *Unit Histories of the United States Air Forces; and United States Air Force History.* New York: Arno Press, 1980.

Maurer, Maurer, ed. *Combat Squadrons of the Air Force, World War II.* Washington, D.C.: Office of Air Force History, Headquarters, United States Air Force, and Government Printing Office, 1967. Revised edition 1982. Revised edition 1992.

Pappas, George S. *United States Army Unit Histories.* Carlisle Barracks, Pa.: U.S. Army Military History Institute, 1971-78. Refers to both World War I and World War II units.

U.S. Army Military History Collection. Roy Barnard, William Burns, and Duane Ryan. *The Era of World War II.* Carlisle Barracks, Pa.: 1977. Contains general reference works, biography.

U.S. Navy Department Library. *Guide to United States Naval Administrative Histories of World War II.* Compiled by William C. Heimdahl and Edward J. Marolda. Washington, D.C.: Naval History Division, Department of the Navy, 1976. Lists unpublished histories of the Department of the Navy, shore establishments, and operating forces maintained in the collections of the Navy Department Library.

U.S. Naval History Division, Operational Archives. *World War II Histories and Historical Reports in the U.S. Naval History Division. Partial Checklist.* Washington, D.C.: the division, 1973.

Waves National. *A Pictorial History of Navy Women, 1908-1988.* N.p., 1990. Consists of photographs with biographical summaries.

Publications With Lists of Names

American Prisoners of War During the Japanese Occupation of the Philippines During World War II. A collection of materials, chiefly from the Santa Tomas (Manila) and Los Banos internment camps, assembled by R.E. Cecil, a former prisoner of war. Includes rosters of staff and inmates and other information concerning camp operations.

Blair, Marion E. *Principal Officials and Officers, Navy Department and United States Fleet, Sept. 1, 1939-June 1, 1945.* Washington, D.C.: Records Administration Division, Administrative Office, Navy Department, 1945.

Francis, Charles E. *The Tuskegee Airmen: The Men Who Changed a Nation.* The author, 1988.

Motley, Mary P., comp. and ed. *The Invisible Soldier: The Experience of the Black Soldiers, World War II.* Detroit: Wayne State University Press, 1975. Oral histories of more than fifty black servicemen and their units.

Murphy, Edward F. *Heroes of World War II.* Novato, Calif.: Presidio, 1990.

Schuon, Karl. *U.S. Navy Biographical Dictionary.* New York: F. Watts, 1965.

Tunney, Christopher. *A Biographical Dictionary of World War II.* London: Dent, 1972. Short sketches of soldiers, sailors, airmen, secret agents, politicians, and others of the World War II era.

U.S. Army Medical Service. *Personnel in World War II. Washington. Office of the Surgeon General, Dept. of the Army.* Washington, D.C.: Government Printing Office, 1963. Includes some portraits.

U.S. Bureau of Medicine and Surgery. *The History of the Medical Department of the United States Navy in World War II.* 2 vols. Washington, D.C.: Government Printing Office, 1953-. Vol. 2 contains a list of medical corps personnel who were killed in action. Provides name, rank or rate, date, activity (name of ship or unit), and place of death. Also contains names of prisoners of war, those wounded in action, and recipients of medals.

U.S. Bureau of Naval Personnel. *War Casualties; Officers, U.S. Navy and U.S. Naval Reserve, Dec. 7, 1941 to July 1, 1942.* Washington, D.C.: 1942.

U.S. Bureau of Ships. *Directory of Engineering Duty Officers.* Washington, D.C.: 1955.

U.S. Congress. House. 27th Cong., 2d Sess. *Register of the Commissioned and Warrant Officers of the United States Navy and Marine Corps, and Reserve, 1942–1968.* Washington, D.C.: Government Printing Office, 1968.

U.S. Department of the Air Force. Daniel B. Jorgenson. *Air Force Chaplains.* 4 vols. Washington, D.C.: Government Printing Office, 1961. Contains names of chaplains from World War II through the Vietnam War.

U.S. Department of the Air Force. *Air Force Register, 1949–1972.* 2 vols. Washington, D.C.: Government Printing Office, 1972.

U. S. National Guard Bureau. *General Officers of the Army and Air National Guard.* Washington, D.C.: the bureau, 1972.

U.S. Navy. *List and Station of the Commissioned and Warrant Officers of the Navy of the United States, and of the Marine Corps, on the Active List, and Officers on the Retired List Employed on Active Duty.* Washington, D.C.: Government Printing Office, various years.

U.S. Navy. Office of Information. *Combat Connected Naval Casualties, World War II, by States.* 2 vols. Washington, D.C.: Government Printing Office, 1946. Includes those who were killed in action, who died of wounds, or who lost their lives as a result of operations or movements in war zones; lists those on active duty 7 December 1941 through the end of the war; includes wounded prisoners of war; provides name, rank, name of family members, home address; does not include casualties in the U.S. area or deaths by natural causes in any area.

U.S. Office of the Chief, Army Reserve. *General Officers of the United States Army Reserve.* Washington, D.C.: 1963.

U.S. Secretary of the Army. *Official Army and National Guard Register, 1936–1990.* 1 vol. for each year. Washington, D.C.: the bureau, various years.

U.S. War Department. *World War II Honor List: Dead and Missing.* The department, 1946. One volume for each state: Alabama through Wyoming.

Who Was Who in World War II. Edited by John Keegan. New York: T.Y. Crowell, 1978. London: Arms and Armour Press, 1978. Consists primarily of photographs, some with text.

1946–53 (Korean War)

Bibliography

Dornbusch, Charles E. *Histories of American Army Units, World Wars I and II and Korean Conflict.* Washington, D.C.: Office of the Adjutant General, Special Services Division, 1956.

Publications With Lists of Names

Murphy, Edward F. *Korean War Heroes.* Novato, Calif.: Presidio, 1992.

U.S. Department of the Army. *Unit Citations and Campaign Participation Credit Registers.* Washington, D.C.: 1952.

U.S. Department of Defense, Office of Public Relations. *Korean War Dead Returns.* Washington, D.C.: 1952.

1954–75 (Vietnam War)

Guides and Bibliographies

Bergma, Herbert L. *Chaplains With Marines in Vietnam, 1962–1971.* Washington, D.C.: U.S. Marine Corps, History and Museum Division, 1985. An appendix lists names, ranks, denominations, dates arrived in Vietnam, and first unit to which assigned.

Burns, Richard D., and Milton Leitenberg. *The Wars in Vietnam, Cambodia, and Laos, 1945–82.* Santa Barbara, Calif.: ABC-Clio Information Service, 1984.

Groh, John E. *Air Force Chaplains, 1971–1980.* Office, Chief of Air Force Chaplains. Washington, D.C.: 1986.

Leitenberg, Milton, comp. *The Vietnam Conflict.* Santa Barbara, Calif.: ABC-Clio Information Service, 1984.

Stanton, Shelby L. *Vietnam Order of Battle.* Millwood, N.Y.: 1981. Updated and reprinted 1982 by Kraus Reprint. Contains unit histories.

Sugnet, Christopher L. *Vietnam War Bibliography.* Lexington, Mass.: Lexington Books, 1983.

U.S. Marine Corps, History and Museums Division. *The Marines in Vietnam, 1954–73*. Washington, D.C.: the division, 1974.

Publications With Lists of Names

Magner, George J., George R. Hoak, and T.O. Jacobs. *Interviews on Small-unit Combat Actions in Vietnam*. 11 vols. Washington, D.C.: George Washington University, Human Resources Research Office, 1966. Contains interviews with 471 members of 29 rifle companies, arranged by company.

Murphy, Edward F. *Vietnam Medal of Honor Heroes*. New York: Ballantine Books, 1987.

U.S. Congress. Senate. *Vietnam Era Medal of Honor Recipients, 1964–1972*. Washington, D.C.: Government Printing Office, 1973.

U.S. Department of Defense. *List of Casualties Incurred by United States Military Personnel in Connection with the Conflict in Vietnam; Deaths From 1 January 1961 Through 30 September 1975*. Washington, D.C.: the department, ca. 1975. One volume for each state: Alabama through the U.S. Virgin Islands.

U.S. National Guard Bureau. *General Officers of the Army and Air National Guard, 1966–1985*. Washington, D.C.: the bureau, various years.

Vietnam Veterans Memorial. *Directory of Names*. Washington, D.C.: Vietnam Veterans Memorial Fund, 1984. An alphabetical index to the names inscribed on the memorial; includes name, rank, branch of service, date of birth, date of casualty, city and state of residence, panel number, and line number where inscribed.

APPENDIX

America's Military Conflicts: A Brief History

APPENDIX

America's Military Conflicts: A Brief History

This appendix is based on the assumption that researchers using military records will profit from understanding the historical context of the military units and conflicts they are studying. American history is a story of almost constant armed conflict of one type or another, including frontier skirmishes, civil disturbances, and foreign wars, and ranging in seriousness from Utah's "Posey War" of 1923, in which only two people were killed, to the Civil War of 1861 to 1865, in which more than a half-million Americans lost their lives. American military history is thus an immense subject, and this appendix is neither comprehensive in considering all significant armed conflicts, nor exhaustive in its narrative of individual incidents. Rather, its purpose is to provide a helpful historical context for the episodes of greatest likely interest to researchers. Those needing more information on a specific incident, or information on conflicts not included here, may consult T. Harry Williams' *History of American Wars From 1745 to 1918* or any of the more specific works cited at the end of this appendix.

Warfare was a constant fact of American life long before the arrival of Europeans, for intertribal conflict was a part of most Indian cultures. But such wars were limited in their devastation because of primitive technology, sparse population, and the Indian concept of war as a chivalric test of honor, rather than a means of exterminating the enemy. The arrival of Europeans drastically changed the nature of American warfare, for the settlers brought a superior technology featuring steel, horses, and firearms; they came in rapidly increasing numbers, encroaching upon the Indians and increasing the frequency of conflict; and they brought a concept of total war often based upon racist assumptions that considered extermination of the Indians a necessary step toward progress. The Europeans also brought a global perspective that the Indians lacked, and thus conflicts originating on other continents often spread to America.

The establishment of American independence in 1783 changed this picture very little. In spite of Americans' desire for isolation from European affairs (expressed in such documents as George Washington's Farewell Address and the Monroe Doctrine), their need for foreign trade and expansion kept alive the need for diplomatic, and sometimes military, contact with Europe. And the westward movement of settlers brought them into continued violent contact with Indians. Finally, during the latter half of the nineteenth century, Americans became increasingly involved—economically, politically, and militarily—in Latin America, the Pacific islands, and the Far East, leading to repeated participation in global conflicts during the twentieth century. Increasing economic ties with the rest of the world, linked with rapid transportation and electronic communication, have kept global considerations in the forefront of contemporary American life.

This appendix summarizes selected conflicts involving American forces at home and abroad. Most civil disturbances, such as industrial strikes, riots, and civil rights demonstrations involving militias or regular troops, are omitted, as are natural disasters, such as hurricanes, floods, or fires, in which military units provided security and relief. Two general criteria have governed the selection process: the event was major enough to have been covered in several published histories, and there is a good chance that a significant quantity of records pertaining to it exist either in national or state archives.

Jamestown Conflicts
Virginia: 1622-44

The settlers at England's first permanent American colony had the misfortune to take up residence at one of the few places on the continent where the Indians were well organized. The Powhatan Confederation (part of the larger Huron Confederation) was well able to resist the Europeans' encroachment. Although conflicts waned from time to time as Englishmen like John Smith and John Rolfe established temporary good relations with the chieftains Powhatan and Opechancanough, constant encroachment and attempts to force European culture upon the Indians led to tensions that erupted in a general war in 1622. On 22 March, a well-coordinated Indian assault on Jamestown resulted in the deaths of 347 settlers and came close to destroying the entire colony. The English retaliated with a genocidal policy that nearly exterminated the Powhatan Indians over the next ten years. During a final revolt of the Indians in 1644, Opechancanough was captured and murdered in Jamestown. English authority in the region was not again seriously challenged (Bridenbaugh 1980).

Pequot War
Connecticut: 1636-38

Although initial relations between the Puritan colonists in New England and their Indian neighbors were generally peaceful, Puritan expansion into the interior brought them into contact with the Pequot tribe, which had recently established hegemony over other Indians in the Connecticut Valley and wished to keep the Europeans out. A treaty of 1634 failed to keep peace, and acts of hostility by the Pequots against Puritan frontier settlers led to war in 1636. The culmination of the war was the Puritan attack on the Pequots' Mystic Fort at dawn on 26 May 1637, in which several hundred Indians were killed and the village inside the fort burned. By the fall of 1638 most of the Pequots had been killed, including their chief, Sassacus. The Treaty of Hartford on 21 September ended the existence of the Pequot tribe as an entity, prohibited its former members from living within the old tribal territory, and placed many Pequots as slaves with other tribes allied with the Puritans (Vaughan 1965).

King Philip's War
Massachusetts, Rhode Island: 1675-76

Although resistance to Christian conversion was the immediate issue of King Philip's War, the conflict in fact was the culmination of Indian frustration over nearly a half-century of white encroachment. In terms of percentage of population killed and property destroyed, it ranks as the most costly war in American history. It marks the ultimate defeat of New England Indians and the onset of uncontested white domination of the region.

Philip was a son of the Wampanoag chief Massasoit, with whom the original Puritan colonists had established friendship, but by 1675 the basis of that friendship had worn thin. When three Wampanoags were executed for the murder of a Christian Indian, war broke out. Under Philip's leadership, Indians destroyed white settlements throughout New England. By the time Philip was killed in August 1676, several thousand colonists had died, over a dozen towns destroyed, and the total colonial expense was an estimated £100,000. Indian casualties were even greater, in addition to almost complete loss of their land, which was given as bonuses to colonial veterans of the war (Leach 1958).

Bacon's Rebellion
Virginia: 1676

Both an Indian war and a popular uprising, Bacon's Rebellion was a grave test of the stability of the Virginia government in the seventeenth century. When settlers on the Virginia frontier became frustrated at the unwillingness of Governor William Berkeley to provide military assistance against Indian harassment, they elected a youthful and impetuous newcomer to the colony, Nathaniel Bacon, to lead such an expedition. Bacon's Rebellion quickly became more than an Indian war, although its main impetus was always the desire of Virginia frontiersmen for Indian lands. In June 1676, Bacon's followers in the colonial assembly introduced laws designed to curb the governor's authority and to bring a greater degree of democracy to Virginia politics. During the ensuing civil conflict, Bacon's forces twice drove Berkeley out of Jamestown and burned the community on the latter occasion. The rebellion ultimately collapsed after Bacon died of dysentery on 26 October (Bridenbaugh 1980; Craven 1968).

King William's War
New England, New York: 1689-97

The Glorious Revolution of 1688, which brought the Protestant William of Orange to the English throne, was followed in 1689 by a declaration of war on France that lasted until the Peace of Ryswick in 1697. One phase of that war was a struggle for dominance in North America. The French Count Frontenac began a grand scheme of invasion of New York from Montreal in 1689. In February 1690, a French force of 210 men, including 96 Indians, attacked Schenectady, killing sixty settlers and burning the town. The force then proceeded into the area of modern New Hampshire and Maine.

To counter the French, England's Sir William Phips advanced on Port Royal, Acadia (later Nova Scotia), with seven ships and approximately five hundred militiamen, taking it without resistance. In August he sailed to Quebec, which he subjected to a naval artillery barrage, but he was driven off. Although the war ended with the Peace of Ryswick, tension between France and Great Britain continued in Europe and America, breaking out again in King George's War in 1740. This tension were not resolved until the French were driven out of North America in the French and Indian War (Craven 1968).

Queen Anne's War
Massachusetts, South Carolina, Florida, Canada: 1702-13

When Louis XIV of France attempted to install his grandson on the Spanish throne as Philip V, he encountered resistance from an alliance of English, Austrians, and Dutch who were seeking to avoid the threat of French domination of Europe. The resulting war spread to include conflicts among English and French colonies in North America. French and Indian raids on border towns in northern New England in 1703 led to repeated land and sea expeditions from Massachusetts against Acadia.

In 1710, Port Royal was attacked by English troops and surrendered, thus making Acadia British territory. A naval expedition against Quebec in 1711 resulted in shipwreck and failure.

The war also provided an opportunity for the Carolinas to strike at the Spanish in Florida, but invasions in 1702 and 1704 produced only minor damage around St. Augustine. French naval retaliation against Charleston in 1706 was equally ineffectual. The Treaty of Utrecht in 1713 ceded much of northeastern Canada to the British, and the coveted *assiento*, the right to provide slaves to the Spanish colonies in Central America, was given to the English (Craven 1968).

Yamasee War
South Carolina, Georgia: 1715-16

In 1715, Indians outside Port Royal, South Carolina, conspired to drive all white people from the coast from St. Augustine to Cape Fear. War broke out on April 15, Easter Sunday, with an Indian attack on Port Royal. Most of the three hundred colonists fled by ship, but those who remained were tortured and killed. Yamasee Indians killed approximately one hundred colonists at St. Bartholomew's Parish. Eventually a military force routed the Indians at the Combahee River, and permanent garrisons were established for protection of the colonists (Jones, 1969).

War of Jenkins' Ear
Georgia, Florida: 1739-42

Having consumed most of the wealth that it had gained from Mexico and Peru by the beginning of the eighteenth century, the Spanish Empire began to decline. Lacking enough ships and sailors to supply its vast colonial population, Spain was forced to depend increasingly upon Britain's commercial fleet. This dependency increased tension between the two countries, whose relations had never been amicable in any event.

This tension led to hostilities during an encounter between a Spanish ship and an English vessel, of which Robert Jenkins was captain. The Spanish captain cut off Jenkins' ear while pirating the Englishman's cargo. Jenkins displayed his severed ear in England upon his return, and on 19 October 1739 England declared war on Spain. The fighting in America was inconclusive. Although a force from Georgia attacked St. Augustine in 1740, it was repulsed, and a Spanish reprisal at St. Simon's Island in Georgia was similarly driven back.

When the Holy Roman Emperor Charles VI died in 1740, war erupted in Europe over who would succeed him (the War of Austrian Succession). England's attention was diverted from the Spanish war in America to the greater issues of the European war, and the English abandoned the earlier conflict in 1742 (Dorn 1940).

King George's War
Canada, Northern New England, New York: 1740-48

This war, known in European history as the War of Austrian Succession, in America took the form of several half-hearted conflicts between English and French colonists and their Indian allies, but it produced no permanent changes. A force of 4,200 untrained volunteers from New England, led by an evangelistic preacher named William Pepperell, laid siege to the French city of Louisburg in Canada on 18 April 1745, finally forcing its surrender on 16 June. Other fighting against the French and their Indian allies occurred through northern New England and New York. The Treaty of Aix-la-Chappelle of 1748 returned Louisburg to the French (Ivers 1874; Leckie 1968).

French and Indian War
Northern Colonies and Canada: 1754-63

Known as the Seven Years' War (1756 to 1763) in European history, the conflict lasted longer than that in America, for it began there two years earlier in border disputes between the English and French colonists. Based on the exploits of a succession of intrepid explorers and missionaries during the seventeenth and eighteenth centuries, France claimed the St. Lawrence River, the Great Lakes, and the interior country drained by the Ohio and Mississippi Rivers. The English colonists felt restricted in their Atlantic Seaboard settlements; they wished to expand westward into country the French were utilizing lightly, if at all.

This friction resulted in war in 1754, when a mixed force of 150 British regulars and Virginia militiamen under the command of Lt. Col. George Washington unsuccessfully contested control of Fort Duquesne (now Pittsburg) against a French force. In a battle at nearby Great Meadows, where Washington had quickly erected a fort called Fort Necessity,

he and his men were defeated on 4 July by nine hundred Frenchmen. In 1755, Gen. Edward Braddock arrived in America with instructions to lead another assault on Fort Duquesne, but his force of 1,400 British regulars and 450 militia was defeated in the Battle of the Wilderness on 9 July, and Braddock was killed. Washington led the remnants of his force back to Fort Cumberland, and the main theater of the conflict shifted to Canada. British naval forces entered the Bay of Fundy and secured Nova Scotia. French-speaking residents (Acadians) who refused to take an oath of loyalty to the British crown were expelled on 8 October, thus beginning their famous exile and dispersion among the lower thirteen colonies and eventually to Louisiana, where they became known as Cajuns.

The war spread to Europe in 1756, and war between France and England was declared on 15 May. Most of the fighting occurred in the Great Lakes area. Exceptions included a bloody and unsuccessful English assault on Fort Carillon (later Fort Ticonderoga) in 1758, George Washington's capture of Fort Duquesne (rebuilt as Fort Pitt after the evacuating French blew it up), and the capture of Louisburg by a combined English land and naval assault in 1759. Quebec then came open to attack, and Gen. James Wolfe moved against it in September 1759. Wolfe's ill-advised ascent of the steep cliffs from the river to the Plains of Abraham, where effective retreat was impossible, was answered by the Marquis de Montcalm's even more ill-advised decision to leave the fortress and give battle. The British victory at the Battle of Quebec on 18 September cost both Wolfe and Montcalm their lives, but it also cost the French their Canadian empire, which they surrendered to the British on 8 September 1760.

The Treaty of Paris of 1763 ended the war. It made permanent the French cession of Canada and all territory east of the Mississippi to the British. France had already ceded the Louisiana country to Spain by the Treaty of Fontainebleu in 1762. The effect of the war was to drive France, for all practical purposes, out of North America, but its significance did not end there. The war doubled Britain's national debt and gave the British a vast new territory to administer, leading to the taxation crisis that precipitated the American Revolution (Lawson, 1972; Leach 1973).

Cherokee Uprising
Carolinas: 1760-61

During the French and Indian War, friction between Cherokee Indians and settlers in Virginia and the

Carolinas increased. In 1760 an Indian attack prompted an invasion of Cherokee country by a combined force of 1,500 Carolinians, but the invaders were beaten back by an ambush that killed eighty of them. The following year, a militia force of 2,600 launched a punitive expedition that forced the Cherokee to ask for peace (O'Donnell 1973).

Pontiac's Rebellion
Michigan, New York, Pennsylvania: 1763

Frustrated by British trading practices in the Great Lakes area when British colonists replaced the French at the end of the French and Indian War, and motivated by apocalyptic religious ideas, a chief named Pontiac orchestrated a massive campaign to drive the British out of the West. Of the British western forts, only Detroit and Pitt withstood the siege. Fort Pitt was relieved in August by a force under Col. Henry Bouquet, which defeated the Indians at the Battle of Bushy Run, and Pontiac lifted the siege of Detroit in November. A peace treaty of 1766 concluded the affair. Pontiac was murdered in 1769 by another Indian, who may have been bribed to do so by an English trader (Jacobs 1972).

War of the Regulators
North Carolina: 1771

Frontiersmen in the western portions of North Carolina had become incensed over inequitable taxation. Organized into groups called Regulators, they petitioned Governor William Tryon for relief and tax reform, but Tryon met their pleas with accusations of sedition, arrested two of their leaders, and ordered them to disperse.

Although the Regulators won some electoral victories in 1770, the reforms they sought continued to elude them. In September they shut down the courts at Hillsborough and burned the house of a hated tax official. In May 1771, the governor recruited a force of 917 men from among affluent families in the eastern part of the colony, and such poorer men as he could bribe to join because none of the regular militia would enlist. This force routed some two thousand Regulators in a battle at Alamance. One Regulator leader was executed on the battlefield, and six others were later tried and executed. Many of the defeated Regulators remained defiant, refusing to take an oath of loyalty to the government and retreating further into the mountains to avoid government control (Hofstadter and Wallace 1970).

Lord Dunmore's War
Virginia, Pennsylvania, Ohio: 1774

Captain Michael Cresap, an Indian trader and fighter on the Ohio River, was mistakenly charged in April 1774 with murdering the family of an Indian chief, and Indians began a series of raids against white traders and settlers. Military forces under the command of John Murray, Earl of Dunmore, who was the royal governor of Virginia, moved down the Ohio River and defeated the Shawnee at the Battle of Point Pleasant in October. A treaty was signed thereafter to end hostilities (Thwaites and Kellogg 1905).

American Revolution
American Colonies: 1775–1783

Causes of the War
To finance administration of the far-flung North American empire that England had acquired in the French and Indian War, Parliament in 1764 began imposing taxes directly upon the colonists, rather than requesting money indirectly from the colonial assemblies through the royal governor. The colonists regarded this practice as unfair because it deprived them of the veto power long enjoyed and cherished by the colonial assemblies. During the following decade, the colonists resisted a succession of such taxes with ever-increasing violence that eventually involved various colonial militias in armed encounters with British regular forces sent to impose order. As hopes and even desire for accommodation diminished, the Second Continental Congress issued its Declaration of Independence on 4 July 1776.

Military Organization
Counties and towns had always maintained local militias to defend themselves against Indian attacks. These local units, augmented by forces from the colonies, eventually comprised the Continental Army. Some militia and colonial troops fought only within the borders of their own colonies, while others fought under the command of the Continental Army, led by the Virginian Gen. George Washington. Each colony was requested to provide for the Continental Army a specified number of regiments according to its population, for an eventual total of eighty-eight regiments. This goal was never reached because of an inability to pay and supply such a large force. A Continental Navy, subordinate to the army, was formed in 1775, but it never had more than thirty vessels at any one time. Continental Marines were stationed aboard the ships to

engage in close combat at sea. Private ship owners were awarded bounties for capturing British vessels and otherwise interrupting British commercial shipping.

The Battles

Three of the war's most important battles occurred before the new nation came into being on 4 July 1776. The first shots fired between opposing military forces were exchanged at Lexington, Massachusetts, on 19 April 1775, when seven hundred British regulars from Boston under the command of Col. Francis Smith encountered armed resistance on their way to destroy arms stored at Concord and to arrest Samuel Adams and John Hancock. Skirmishes pressed by local forces produced heavy British casualties on the return march. On 10 May 1775, a combined force under Benedict Arnold and Ethan Allen achieved surprise at Fort Ticonderoga and captured it with little bloodshed, thus ensuring that the strategic border between Vermont and New York would remain in American hands and that New England would not be cut off from the other colonies. Finally, on 17 June 1775, British troops drove Boston's defenders from their fortifications on Breed's Hill across the harbor (the battle became known improperly as the Battle of Bunker Hill) but incurred heavy casualties, revealing that Americans could hold their own even in formal battles.

The war spread to the Middle Colonies and the South as well. After defending New York City during the summer and fall of 1776, Washington was eventually driven into New Jersey and then to Pennsylvania. Before the Continental Army retired to its infamously miserable winter quarters at Valley Forge, however, Washington struck back in the brilliant Battle of Trenton on 26 December 1776, routing unsuspecting Hessian mercenaries who were still recovering from Christmas celebrations. In 1777 the British attempted to sever the links between New England and the other colonies by sending a large force under Gen. John Burgoyne south from Canada to Fort Ticonderoga, then down the Hudson River to New York. On 17 October, the Americans entrapped a British army at Saratoga, New York, and forced surrender of the entire army. This battle was a turning point in the war, for the French were inspired by it to sign a commercial and military treaty with the United States, and French land and naval forces assumed a major part of the fighting thereafter.

Moved by rumors of many British sympathizers in the South, British efforts in the later years of the war shifted to that region, where the British attempted to establish a base from which to recover the North. In fact, the British met vigorous opposition in the South and suffered some serious setbacks after a few initial victories. The end of the war came in the South, when the British general Lord Cornwallis attempted to quash resistance in Virginia. He was met by a combined force of American and French armies and French naval support which trapped him at Yorktown and forced his surrender on 19 October 1781.

The Battle of Yorktown was the last major confrontation of the revolutionary war. In 1783, the Treaty of Paris recognized American independence and ceded to the United States all British lands east of the Mississippi River and from Canada to the Gulf of Mexico (Alden 1954; Morris 1976).

Shays' Rebellion
Massachusetts: 1786–87

Economic depression following the American Revolution, particularly in western Massachusetts, forced many people into debtors' jails for inability to pay their debts and taxes. When the legislature failed to ease the tax burden, revise the court system, or print paper money, the impoverished citizens regarded their situation as hopeless. Because property ownership was a requirement for the vote, they were unable to effect changes in the political system.

On 29 August 1786, after the legislature had been unsuccessfully petitioned to close the courts, Daniel Shays of Pelham, a veteran of the revolution, led an armed group of farmers to Northampton. They demanded that debtors no longer be indicted by the courts and insisted that the courts cease to meet. The militia was called out, but violence was avoided and both groups dispersed. The following January, Shays' army of one thousand reassembled and attempted to obtain supplies from the Springfield arsenal but was repulsed by artillery fire. In February some of the rebels were captured at Petersham, but Shays escaped to Vermont. The captive insurgents were offered clemency, and a newly elected legislature moved to alleviate their hardships. Shays was never captured; he died in poverty in New York. The episode pointed to the need for an effective central government to regulate the currency and other economic matters, and it contributed to pressure that prompted the convening of the Constitutional Convention of 1787 (Morris 1976).

Whiskey Rebellion
Pennsylvania: 1794

In 1791,the federal government placed excise taxes on whiskey, an obligation that became burdensome for rural families who made the product for barter. Those charged with noncompliance were ordered to appear at court in Philadelphia or New York, a trip that was financially ruinous for frontier farmers. A rebellion against the tax broke out in the western counties of Pennsylvania in 1794.

A military force under George Washington marched toward the rebellious counties in the summer of that year—the only instance to date in which the commander-in-chief of the armed forces of the United States has actually led an army in the field. Although some arrests were made, the cases resulted in pardons or were dismissed for lack of evidence. The Whiskey Rebellion demonstrated that the new federal government was determined to enforce its laws, even to the extent of invoking military action (Baldwin 1939).

Quasi-War With France
Atlantic Coast, West Indies: 1798-1800

Following the American Revolution, the French became unhappy with the United States for apparently violating the terms of the treaty of 1778, which required a French presence at any treaty negotiations with Great Britain. However, the Treaty of Paris of 1783, which formally ended the American Revolution, had been solely between the United States and its former colonial ruler. Also, during the Federalist Era of the 1790s in the United States, pro-British sentiments seemed repeatedly to operate against French interests. Bad feelings between the two nations grew as a result of American repudiation of the French ambassador in 1793, the apparently pro-British Jay's Treaty of 1794, and the abortive XYZ Affair of 1797, in which treaty negotiations between the two countries broke down.

French harassment of American shipping along the Atlantic coast and in the Caribbean, a perennial feature of the postwar relations between the two countries, increased in 1798 in informal hostilities known as the Quasi-War. In 1800, the two countries signed a convention releasing the United States from the obligations of the 1778 treaty, and an uneasy peace resulted (Morris 1976; Miller 1960).

Barbary Wars
North Africa: 1801-05

Four North African states—Algiers, Morocco, Tripoli, and Tunis—were accustomed to charge other nations "tribute," an extortion for the privilege of undertaking commerce in the Mediterranean. European nations and the United States were accustomed to paying the extortion to avoid what seemed to be needless conflict that would be necessary to eliminate it. However, in 1801 the Pasha of Tripoli increased the tribute and declared war on the United States; President Thomas Jefferson had little choice but to fight. Jefferson, no believer in a permanent navy, had poorly prepared the United States for this encounter, and it proved embarrassing when such American naval forces as did exist were unable to subdue the Barbary pirates.

The war featured two dramatic engagements: In 1804, Lieutenant Stephen Decatur boldly burned the American frigate *Philadelphia*, which had been taken by Tripoli after running aground and was being held for ransom. The following year, marine Lt. Presley N. O'Bannon, with seven other marines, led a motley force of Greeks and discontented Arabs on a long march from Alexandria to take the city of Derna and force Tripoli to negotiate. The resulting treaty only returned tribute rates to their former level, and the issue of Barbary piracy was not finally eliminated until an agreement was reached in 1816 (Morris 1976; Smelser 1968).

War of 1812
Great Lakes, Maryland, New Orleans: 1812-15

The roots of the War of 1812 lay in the unsuccessful commercial relations between the United States and Great Britain that had continued since the American Revolution. Locked in war with Napoleonic France, Parliament issued Orders in Council that authorized British naval vessels to board American ships and seize alleged deserters to augment their own crews. Also, a group of expansionists from the South and West known as "War Hawks" wished to take advantage of Britain's preoccupation with France to invade Canada.

It was perhaps the most curious war in American history. Poor communication prevented the Americans from knowing that the obnoxious Orders in Council had been repealed before the American declaration of war on 18 June 1812. Although American naval forces won impressive victories on Lake Erie, the land forces were largely untrained and ineptly led, so the Canadian invasion was unsuccessful. Eventually, even Washington, D.C., was lost to British forces. Finally, the Battle of New Orleans, the most dramatic American military success of the war, was fought some two weeks after the peace treaty had been signed.

American frigates built for the Quasi-War With France and other ships built subsequently took part in naval engagements. The sea duels enhanced the prestige of the U.S. Navy but did little to influence the outcome of the war. More helpful were the privateers—private ships, the owners of which had obtained "letters of marque" from President James Madison, which authorized them to capture British ships and divide the proceeds among the capturing crew. This practice, however, made it more difficult for the navy to recruit seamen, who naturally preferred the potential profits of this kind of adventure to the fixed pay of navy service.

Lake Erie was dominated by American naval forces. Commodore Oliver Hazard Perry built a flotilla and trained sailors to sail it up the Niagara River to the lake, where he overcame British naval forces in a series of bloody battles.

The American invasion of Canada failed, for the untrained and poorly led American troops were no match for the enemy. The unruly and reluctant militias provided by some of the states failed to fight or even to cross their own state borders to prevent British victory in neighboring states. Although the Americans did reach the Canadian capital of York (now Toronto), burning the parliament building and library, most of the battles resulted in heavy American casualties and ignoble surrenders. American forces lost battles at Fort Dearborn, on the Niagara River, at Lake George, and in Ohio, though Gen. William Henry Harrison and his Kentucky volunteers won at the Thames River. In August the British invaded Maryland and captured Washington, D.C., as President Madison and his cabinet fled. The British burned the Capitol, the Library of Congress, and the White House.

On 22 November 1814, Gen. Andrew Jackson was dispatched to New Orleans to resist a planned British invasion up the Mississippi, in Florida, and other parts of the South. He augmented his force of several hundred army regulars with volunteers from Kentucky, Tennessee, and Louisiana and with a few gunboats. On 8 January 1815, Jackson successfully defended the city of New Orleans against a British land force, both sides unaware that the Peace of Ghent had ended the war on 24 December 1814. The United States ratified the treaty on 17 February (Smelser 1968; Morris 1976; Horsman 1969).

Indian Wars (1811–58)

Although the conflicts between Indians and whites had a multitude of causes, white encroachment on Indian lands was by far the most common one. Competition for land was the inescapable issue; the whites' practices of cutting down forests, plowing up grasslands, and fencing in domestic animals rendered the land unusable for the Indians. As the white population increased, the search for new land increased along with it, and conflict with Indians intensified.

This conflict was particularly dramatic in the south, where cotton cultivation began to dominate the economy during the early nineteenth century. Since the largest returns on cotton came from large plantations worked by slaves, the need for land among southern whites was great. Federal troops were sometimes used to put down Indian resistance, but the government found its final solution in the Indian removal program of the 1830s, under which most of the remaining Indians in the southeast were forcibly driven to the Indian Territory (Oklahoma) west of the Mississippi.

Conflicts between Indians and American settlers were often fueled during the early nineteenth century by Europeans as well—the British in the northwest and the Spanish in Florida. American diplomacy eventually ended those problems. The Treaty of Ghent, which ended the War of 1812, resulted in the removal of British forts in the Great Lakes region, and the Adams-Onis Transcontinental Treaty of 1819 purchased Florida for the United States.

Battle of Tippecanoe (Indiana: 1811)

Concerned with the westward encroachment of settlers into Ohio and beyond, the great Shawnee chief Tecumseh and his twin brother Tenskwatawa urged hostility toward American frontiersmen who threatened their hunting lands. Tecumseh forged an alliance among the tribes in the Great Lakes area. In November 1811, William Henry Harrison, recently appointed governor of the Indiana Territory, led 300 regular soldiers and approximately 650 militiamen into northern Indiana to confront Tenskwatawa. He built a fort near Tippecanoe Creek, intending to hold a conference with Tenskwatawa. However, the Indians assaulted Harrison before dawn on the day of the planned conference. The Indians attacked three times but each time were thrown back. When they eventually fled, Harrison burned the Indians' village. This incident stiffened Tecumseh's resolve and solidified his support for the British, who had courted his assistance (Morris 1976).

First Seminole War (Florida: 1817-19)

In 1817, apparently with the backing of the Spanish, who then governed Florida, the Seminole Indians (formerly Lower Creeks) residing there conducted raids against American settlers near the Florida-Georgia border. When the United States began building forts on the Georgia side, the Indian forays became more numerous and were conducted with more intensity. The United States appealed to Spanish officials in Florida to control the Indians and to help stem the tide of Negro slaves who were fleeing into Florida from Georgia.

Andrew Jackson and Gen. Edmund Gaines were ordered to put down the incursions, but they expanded their mission by raising, without authorization, a force of almost 2,500, more than half of whom were Creek Indians, the others being American volunteers from Georgia, Kentucky, and Tennessee. Contrary to general orders from the secretary of war, they invaded Florida, where for three months they burned and pillaged. They also captured and executed one of two Englishmen who had been trading and conspiring against the Americans with the Seminole leader, Billy Bowlegs. Bowlegs and most of his people escaped into the Everglades. Before departing the area, Jackson and Gaines bombarded the Spanish capital of Pensacola, seized it, raised the American flag, and garrisoned it with soldiers.

The U.S. Senate was in a furor over Jackson's violation of the Constitution and the resultant friction between Spain and the United States, since the disposition of Florida was then being negotiated. A compromise was worked out with Spain and captured Spanish forts were returned. Two weeks later, on 22 February 1819, the United States acquired from Spain all of Florida, extending to the Mississippi River, through the Adams-Onis Treaty (Dangerfield 1965; Lamar 1977).

Black Hawk War (Illinois, Wisconsin: 1831-32)

In 1804, a group of Saux and Fox Indians, claiming to represent their tribes, ceded some 50 million acres in northwestern Illinois, southwestern Wisconsin, and eastern Missouri. Saux Chief Black Hawk, living near Rock Island, Illinois, and other Saux and Fox disavowed this action. In 1831, when some white squatters appropriated Black Hawk's village and met with Indian resistance, the Illinois militia was called out to put down the insurrection,

whereupon Black Hawk withdrew across the Mississippi River to Iowa.

Internecine hostilities broke out between tribes of Saux, Fox, Winnebago, Sioux, and Chippewa. The Illinois governor called out his militia and asked the War Department for reinforcements to control the warfare and to counter Black Hawk's attempts to forge a hostile confederation, so elements of the U.S. Sixth Infantry were moved into place.

Black Hawk had recently returned to Illinois. When the military ordered him to leave, fighting broke out. Black Hawk offered a peace plan, which was rejected. After receiving reinforcements from local garrisons and some of the U.S. First Infantry, the soldiers defeated the Indians at the Battle of Wisconsin Bluffs (near the present city of Madison) and again at the Bad Axe River on 3 August 1831, killing many as they forded the river. Black Hawk was taken to Washington, D.C., where he met with President Andrew Jackson. When released, he returned to Iowa and spent the remainder of his life in peace.

A month after the battle at the Bad Axe, Gen. Winfield Scott forced the Winnebago to cede their Wisconsin lands, and the Saux and Fox ceded lands in eastern Iowa in exchange for money and a promise of annuity payments (Hassler 1982; Merk 1978).

Second Seminole War (Florida: 1835-42)

At a conference in 1835, Seminole Chief Osceola refused to agree to two earlier treaties of 1832 and 1833 that provided for the removal of the Seminoles from Florida to the West. Soon thereafter, in December 1835, Seminoles assaulted and massacred almost all of a detachment of 109 American soldiers at Wahoo Swamp. On the same day, Osceola and a party of sixty ambushed other soldiers, killing all of them. In response, Col. Duncan Clinch, with more than 230 soldiers, most of them regular U.S. Army, defeated a group of Seminoles at the Withlacoochee River, killing 107 of them.

Gen. Winfield Scott was ordered to proceed to Florida to remove the Seminoles. In April 1836, General Scott made his move, but after several battles the Indians simply disappeared into the swamps. Scott then retired from the area and three other generals, in succession, replaced him. They led raids into Seminole territory for several years, burning and destroying villages and crops. From 1835 to 1842, a total of 60,691 militiamen, volunteers, and regulars fought in the campaign; forty-one percent of them became casualties.

Most of the Seminoles remained in Florida with Osceola, where they lived in peace on a temporary reservation near Pease Creek. Some Seminoles and members of other tribes, particularly the Choctaw, Cherokee, Creek, and Chickasaw, were removed to federally designated Indian territory in the 1830s. Traveling by way of Missouri and Arkansas, about four thousand Indians walked the "Trail of Tears" from Georgia and North Carolina to Oklahoma. They were accompanied by military personnel who guided them on their long trek; many of them died en route (Hassler 1982; Merk 1978; Lamar 1977).

Navajo Wars (New Mexico, Arizona: 1846-68)

After the outbreak of the Mexican War in 1846, American troops occupied Santa Fe and continued a tradition of violence against the Navajo Indians that had been a major theme of Spanish and Mexican dominance in the Southwest. A succession of treaties with various Navajo leaders followed, but none produced lasting peace because the Americans, like their Spanish and Mexican predecessors, failed to realize that Navajo politics was a highly localized entity and that no single headman could speak for more than his own band. In 1863, Col. Kit Carson led Federal troops against the Indians, forcing them, through a brutal scorched earth policy of economic as well as military depredation, to surrender. Although some Navajo bands never capitulated, fleeing instead into the Utah canyon country, the bulk of the Navajo population agreed to enter a Federal concentration camp at Bosque Redondo (Fort Sumner) in eastern New Mexico, where they remained until their return in 1868 to a reservation roughly approximating their traditional homeland (McNitt 1972; Trafzer 1982; Locke 1989).

Third Seminole War (Florida: 1848-58)

At the close of the Second Seminole War, it was agreed that the Seminoles could remain in the Everglades if they did not molest the white settlers. The peace was kept until July 1848, when approximately seventy Seminoles and about thirty Indians from other tribes attacked a plantation at New River, Florida. Although Seminole chief Billy Bowlegs promised this would be the end of Indian violence, the U.S. government negotiated Seminole relocation over the next few years. In 1856 there were at least three minor skirmishes with casualties, but there was no general uprising among the Indians. With the Civil War looming, the government abandoned attempts at Seminole relocation (Peters 1979; Lamar 1977).

Yakima Wars (Washington, Oregon, Idaho: 1855-58)

In 1855, the Yakima Indians joined the Klickitects and other tribes to wage war in the Pacific Northwest. A group of white prospectors passing through the region was attacked, and in August 1855 the Indians killed an Indian agent. A U.S. Army detachment attempted to arrest the agent's murderers but retreated when threatened by superior forces.

In November and December, regular army soldiers and a group of volunteers invaded the region and pushed out the Indians. Later in December, other regular solders fought a four-day battle against Indians in the Walla Walla Valley. After a defeat at the hands of Indians in Spokane country in May 1858, the military stepped up its campaign, and by year-end the Indian threat had passed (Fuller 1931; Schwantes 1989; Lamar 1977).

Utah War
Utah: 1857-58

Persecution and violence were part of the history of The Church of Jesus Christ of Latter-day Saints (Mormons) almost from its founding by Joseph Smith in western New York in 1830. Moving first to Ohio, then to Missouri, the Mormons found themselves met with increasing jealousy, prejudice, and violence. Eventually gathering at Nauvoo, Illinois, on the Mississippi River, the Mormons swelled the community with a constant stream of converts, making Nauvoo the largest city in the state. Fears of Mormon power backed by the Nauvoo Legion, a Mormon militia, led to Smith's arrest and jail-house murder in 1844. His successor, Brigham Young, announced that he would move the Mormons to the far West in 1846. The exodus ended in the valley of the Great Salt Lake.

Suspicions of the Mormons continued, however, and, after Utah gained territorial status in 1850, the Utah Mormons were accused of treating Federal judges roughly and of disobeying Federal laws. Accordingly, 2,500 soldiers under Col. Albert Sidney Johnston were dispatched in 1857 to restore order in Utah. The force met guerilla resistance from the Mormons in Echo Canyon in northern Utah, and spent the winter at Fort Bridger, Wyoming. When the soldiers finally entered Salt Lake City in the spring, negotiations wi h the Mormons produced an agreement that they would establish a military compound, which was later called Camp Floyd, in the hills west of

Utah Lake. There the soldiers remained until the outbreak of the Civil War.

An ugly sidelight of the Utah War was the Mountain Meadows Massacre. Mormons and Indians attacked a wagon train of California emigrants at Mountain Meadows in southern Utah, killing more than one hundred of them. The leader of the attackers, John Lee, was eventually tried, found guilty, and executed (Furniss 1960; Brooks 1950).

Aroostook War
Maine: 1839

In 1830, land disputes erupted between Canadian lumbermen and American settlers who had been granted lands within the Madaueskan area of Maine. A posse of Maine citizens, joined by some ten thousand Maine militiamen, was authorized to eject the lumbermen. The federal government authorized an additional 50,000 men if needed, but no blood was shed in the dispute.

Gen. Winfield Scott was sent to negotiate with the Canadians, and a boundary commission was established. The result was the Webster-Ashburton Treaty of 1842, which, among other things, settled the international boundary question (Burrage 1919; Morris 1976; Van Deusen 1959).

War of Texas Independence
Texas: 1836

The Republic of Mexico, which included the territory of Texas, encouraged Americans to settle in that area during the early 1800s. The republic granted American settlers large tracts of land in return for a promise (seldom kept) to become Catholics and to obey the laws forbidding slavery. Southern frontiersmen rushed in to claim land, and by 1834 a colony headed by Stephen Austin numbered 20,000 whites and 2,000 Negro slaves, outnumbering the native Mexicans in the area by four to one. President John Quincy Adams, and later President Andrew Jackson, offered to buy the territory, but Mexico refused.

When the Americans in Texas numbered 30,000, the president of Mexico, Gen. Antonio López de Santa Anna, proclaimed a new constitution that abolished states' rights and imposed heavy-handed controls over the Americans

north of the Rio Grande River. In reply, the Americans in the territory declared their independence on 2 March 1836, set up a provisional government, and expelled the Mexican garrison at San Antonio.

At this turn of events, Santa Anna, with an army of three thousand, marched on San Antonio. Some Americans, under the leadership of William Travis, Jim Bowie, and Davy Crockett, took refuge in a walled Franciscan monastery known as the Alamo. They held out for ten days, after which they were overwhelmed and slain by the Mexican troops. It is estimated that 200 Americans were killed in the massacre that day; the Mexicans lost 1,544. Three weeks later, 350 defending Americans were killed when the Mexicans assaulted the town of Goliad.

Gen. Sam Houston waited with a small army at San Jacinto, where he routed the Mexicans after a brief battle. Santa Anna was captured there, but he was released under a promise to return to Mexico and to support an independent Texas. He did not keep this promise, and his broken promise was a factor in the Mexican War a decade later (Leckie 1968; Van Deusen 1959).

Dorr Rebellion
Rhode Island: 1841

The Rhode Island state constitution, passed in 1663 and still in effect in the mid-nineteenth century, restricted suffrage to freeholders and their eldest sons. These made up only half of the white male adult population, and sentiment grew in favor of scrapping the old constitution. A schism developed when, in 1842, Gov. Samuel W. King was reelected and inaugurated at Newport. The liberal popular party, which controlled the northwestern section of the state and much of the legislature, held a separate election and named Thomas W. Dorr governor. They based themselves in Providence and prepared to maintain their position by force.

President John Tyler was asked for military assistance to put down the Providence rebels. Tyler admonished both sides to come to a peaceful agreement, but when Dorr's advocates seized the state arsenal, they were brought under control by the state militia. In 1844, Dorr was sentenced to life imprisonment for treason but was released the following year (Morris 1976).

Mexican War
Mexico, Texas, New Mexico, California: 1846–48

After Texas won its independence from Mexico in 1836, it engaged in several border skirmishes in attempts to settle ownership of disputed lands, particularly the 100- to 150-mile-long strip lying between the Rio Grande and Neuces rivers. Gen. Zachary Taylor was dispatched to the area with a force of four thousand soldiers to control Mexican incursions. When eleven Americans were killed, President James K. Polk recommended to Congress that war be declared; Congress complied on 13 May 1846. Taylor's troops included about two thousand regular army soldiers of the Fifth Infantry, augmented by large numbers of untrained, undisciplined militia and volunteer units. Many had enlisted for terms of three to twelve months and had to be replaced by new recruits the following year. They came from many states of the Union, but especially from the southern states.

In September 1846, Taylor invaded Mexico and was met with strong but futile resistance from the forces of Mexico's governor and war hero of the battles of the Alamo and Goliad, Antonio López de Santa Anna. Taylor went on to achieve victories in Monterey, Saltillo, and Buena Vista.

The war was also used as an opportunity to take over the territories of New Mexico and California. Col. Stephen W. Kearney was dispatched from Fort Leavenworth, Kansas, for this purpose, and on 18 August 1846, he took Santa Fe without a fight. Leaving a small force there, Kearney continued to San Diego and Los Angeles. U.S. Navy Commodore John D. Sloat landed at Monterey in northern California on 7 July 1846 and claimed it for the United States.

Gen. Winfield Scott relied heavily on the U.S. Navy to launch an attack at Vera Cruz, Mexico, on 9 March 1847. The Mexican defenders refused to capitulate, so the Americans unleashed a siege bombardment that lasted until 27 March, when the Mexicans surrendered. Within days, Scott's army of approximately 20,000 battled Santa Anna, achieving victories at Cerro Gordo, Puebla, Chapultepec, and finally at Mexico City on 14 September 1847.

The Treaty of Guadalupe-Hidalgo, signed on 2 February 1848, ceded California and the New Mexico territory to the United States and established the Rio Grande River as the border between Texas and Mexico (Smith 1919; Singletary 1960).

American Civil War
Southern and Border States, Pennsylvania: 1861–65

The roots of the American Civil War are in the phenomenon of sectionalism, which can be traced as far back as the colonial period. During the first half of the nineteenth century, it became increasingly apparent that the Northern and Southern states were developing in significantly different directions: the North toward industrialization, commerce, urbanization, and political liberalism, and the South toward plantation agriculture based on slave labor. Largely through the efforts of great statesmen like Daniel Webster, John C. Calhoun, and especially Henry Clay, the political system was able to contain the centrifugal impulses of sectionalism, but the deaths of those men in the early 1850s left the country vulnerable to the call for states' rights and, ultimately, secession. The election of Abraham Lincoln in 1860 on a platform of commercial development and containment of slavery left those in the South feeling isolated as the nation seemed to be in wholesale pursuit of Northern interests. Accordingly, Southern states began leaving the Union even before Lincoln's inauguration. Ultimately, eleven Southern states seceded, though four border slave states— Missouri, Kentucky, Maryland, and Delaware—remained loyal.

The new Confederate States of America elected Jefferson Davis president and set about the difficult task of coercing the states to provide soldiers while adhering to a states' rights constitution. The Union also experienced difficulty in recruitment, and both sides were eventually forced to employ conscription laws.

Since the Confederacy was operating without European diplomatic recognition and without an effective navy, the North had a considerable advantage at sea, immediately imposing a blockade of Southern ports. Although the blockade did place pressure on the Southern economy, it was never completely effective, and the naval aspect of the war—with the exception of the Union naval efforts that opened up the Mississippi River in 1862—was relatively unimportant.

The land war occurred in three theaters: the East, the West, and the Trans-Mississippi region. In the East, the fighting was largely concentrated in northern Virginia because of the proximity of the two capitals: Washington, D.C., and Richmond, Virginia. The first Battle of Bull Run, near Manassas, Virginia, on 21 July 1861, deflated Northern assumptions about a quick end to the war. Confederate Gen. Thomas Jackson earned his *nom de guerre*, "Stonewall," as he held his position against Union troops commanded by Irvin MacDowell until reinforcements from the Shenandoah Valley under Joseph Johnston arrived, when the Union lines broke and a rout ensued. Only the fact, as Johnston later observed, that the Confederates were more disunited in victory than the Union forces were in defeat prevented the Southerners from overrunning nearby Washington, D.C. Nor was the Union army of 130,000 under George McClellan any more successful in its repeated assaults toward Richmond during the Peninsular Campaign of 1862.

Gen. Robert E. Lee, assuming command of the Confederate armies in 1862, made two attempts to carry the war to the North. In Maryland, McClellan stopped him at Sharpsburg, or Antietam Creek, but McClellan's costly and uncoordinated attacks allowed Lee to withdraw to Virginia. Bolstered by victories at Fredericksburg and Chancellorsville, Lee invaded Pennsylvania in 1863. The turning point of the war occurred on the third day of the Battle of Gettysburg, 3 July 1863, when well-entrenched Union troops under Gen. George Meade beat back an ill-advised Confederate infantry assault. However, Meade failed to counterattack against Lee's disadvantageous position and allowed him to withdraw once again to Virginia.

In the Western theater, Ulysses S. Grant emerged as a resourceful and relentless leader, taking forts Henry and Donelson in Tennessee, then winning a major victory at Shiloh. The Confederate fortifications at Vicksburg, Mississippi, fell to Grant's protracted siege in 1863, allowing Union land forces to link up with gunboats on the river and effectively split the Confederacy in two.

Fighting in the Trans-Mississippi region focused largely on Southern attempts to separate Missouri from the Union, but battles at Wilson's Creek, Missouri, in 1861 and Pea Ridge, Arkansas, on the Missouri border failed in that aim. Eventually, the conflict reached as far as New Mexico, where Confederate forces were defeated at the Battle of Glorieta Pass, near Albuquerque, on 28 March 1862.

In 1864, Grant and his cohort, Gen. William T. Sherman, took the war into the Eastern theater. Through the summer of 1864, Sherman's 112,000 troops marched across the heart of the South from Chattanooga, Tennessee, to Atlanta, Georgia, and on to the coast, leaving behind them an immense swath of destruction. Grant moved toward Richmond, which was defended by Lee. Recognizing the Union's vast numerical superiority, Lee eventually abandoned the Southern capital in an attempt to link his forces with those of his lieutenant, Joseph Johnston, who was pinned down by Sherman. Failing in that attempt, Lee

surrendered to Grant at Appomattox Courthouse, Virginia, on 9 April 1865 (Randall and Donald 1961).

Indian Wars (1865–1900)

From the close of the Civil War until the end of the nineteenth century, the U.S. Army was called upon to protect the hordes of settlers rushing into western territories. The army was dissatisfied with the work of Indian agents under the Department of the Interior and wanted authority to keep the Indians on their reservations. There were approximately 250,000 Indians among ninety-nine tribes in the Rocky Mountain region and in the Great Plains, through which the settlers had to pass on their way West. The Dawes Act of 1887 provided for the eventual dissolution of the tribes as entities and the distribution of their lands to their constituent members.

Regular army forces, often cavalry regiments, were stationed at forts and stockades throughout the West and were on call for times of need. Between 1865 and 1891, the army engaged in thirteen campaigns against the Indians that involved more than a thousand engagements. It is impossible to describe all this activity, but below are brief summaries of some of the more important conflicts engaged in by military forces during the balance of the nineteenth century (Utley 1974; Lamar 1977).

Sioux and Cheyenne Wars (Dakotas and Montana: 1866–90)

With the exception of the 1862 Minnesota Uprising, in which members of the Santee tribe of the Sioux murdered about seven hundred whites in retaliation for corrupt Indian administration and the arrogance of encroaching white settlers, most of the violence between the Sioux and white Americans was carried out by the Teton tribe. Frequent violent encounters with the Tetons began in 1864, when the Indians began harassing whites who invaded their hunting grounds. The army retaliated with the Powder River expedition in 1865, but the Sioux annihilated Lt. Col. W. J. Fetterman's command of eighty men sent to punish them in 1866.

An uneasy peace ensued as the government ineptly attempted to confine the Sioux to a system of reservations and to teach them to live a sedentary agricultural life. However, poor administration, inadequate provisions, harassment by white neighbors, and a series of agricultural disasters bred deep discontent among the Indians. In 1875, when gold prospectors entered the Sioux reservation in the Black Hills despite agreements not to do so, the Indians rose up to drive them out. Army forces were dispatched to drive the Indians back onto the reservations. In three separate campaigns, the army learned that the Indians were well able to resist. On 1 March 1876, several cavalry and infantry units were driven back in the Powder River country. On 17 June, Chief Crazy Horse and a force of 1,500 Sioux engaged another column of troops at the indecisive Battle of Rosebud. And on 25 June, Lt. Col. George Armstrong Custer suffered the famous disaster on the Little Big Horn River when he and 211 men attacked an encampment of at least 2,500 Sioux and Cheyenne. In response, Gen. Phil Sheridan led punitive expeditions against the Sioux and Cheyenne and forced most of them back onto the reservations.

The final conflict between the U.S. Army and the Sioux took place at Wounded Knee, South Dakota, on 29 December 1890. Inspired by a new apocalyptic religion, the Ghost Dance, which promised a messiah who would bring back the buffalo and the traditional ways of life and drive out the white men, a group of Sioux left the reservation. Intercepted by the army at Wounded Knee, they refused to give up their weapons. Two hundred men, women, and children were massacred by overzealous troops (Utley 1974; Lamar 1977).

Apache Wars (Arizona, New Mexico, Mexico: 1870–86)

Few, if any, Indian tribes resisted white settlement more implacably than the Apaches, from their first encounter with the Spanish in the early seventeenth century to the imprisonment of Geronimo in 1886. Conflicts with Americans began when gold was discovered in central Arizona in 1863 and prospectors began moving into the area. Although Gen. George Crook succeeded in getting many Apaches to settle on the San Carlos Reservation in 1875, the next decade saw repeated rebellions against reservation life and a succession of raiding campaigns led by such famous leaders as Geronimo, Cochise, and Mangas Coloradas.

Geronimo was especially troublesome to the whites. After Mexican soldiers killed his mother, wife, and children in 1858, Geronimo developed a hatred for all whites that motivated repeated raids in the Southwest and Mexico during the 1870s and 1880s. A succession of arrests and escapes led to Geronimo's final imprisonment in 1886 in Florida. After five years there, he was released and spent his final years as an army scout and tourist attraction at Ft. Sill, Oklahoma (Lamar 1977).

Modoc War (California: 1872–73)

As white settlers moved into southern Oregon and northern California, the Modoc Indians were placed on a reservation with their traditional enemies, the Klamaths. The arrangement was predictably unsuccessful, and, in 1872, a Modoc chief named Captain Jack led his people off the reservation and back onto their traditional lands, where they clashed with recent white settlers. The army dispatched Gen. Edward R. S. Canby, a Civil War hero, to return the Modocs to the reservation. At a conference with Captain Jack on 11 April 1873, the Indians killed Canby and a minister companion. War broke out, and the Indians were defeated at a battle at Dry Lake and surrendered on 22 May 1873. Captain Jack and several other Indian leaders were hanged, and the Modocs returned to the Klamath Reservation (Lamar 1977).

Nez Perce Wars (Idaho and Montana: 1877)

Most of the Nez Perce tribe had moved into a reservation in Idaho, near Oregon and Washington, but some who had not agreed to a previous treaty stayed outside the reservation. In mid-June 1877, when their leaders were discussing whether to obey an order to go into the reservation, Indians murdered four white men, and fifteen more whites were killed in the ensuing hostilities.

This conflict prompted a long trek by the Nez Perce to escape the army, which pursued the Indians and their leader, Chief Joseph, for 1,700 miles over a three-month period. The parties engaged in battle a number of times, and several Indians and soldiers were killed at each confrontation. The Nez Perce attempted to reach Canada, where they might be safe, but they were overtaken just before they reached the border. Some women, children, and ninety-eight braves made it safely across the border before Chief Joseph proclaimed "I shall fight no more forever" and surrendered to the army on October 1877. The Nez Perce were first taken to Fort Leavenworth and then to Indian Territory before some were allowed to go back to the Idaho reservation. Others were sent to a Washington reservation, where Joseph died on 21 September 1904 (Beal 1963).

Spanish-American War
Cuba, Philippine Islands: 1898

The Spanish, who had been in the West Indies since Christopher Columbus arrived, began to lose their influence in the area during the nineteenth century, and Spain's colonies began to leave her. Spanish Cuba rose against her in 1868 but was put down after a ten-year war. Following heavy repression from Spanish authorities, the Cubans revolted again in 1895 and called upon the United States for assistance.

While negotiations were going on, the USS *Maine* mysteriously exploded on 15 February 1898, killing 250 men. The ship was in Havana's harbor at the time, having been sent there during a Cuban riot. The cause of the explosion was never discovered, but it formed the basis for a rally cry to free Cuba from Spain. War was declared on 20 April 1898.

Immediately, U.S. Commodore George Dewey took a fleet of warships to the Pacific and made for Manila in the Philippines. The seven Spanish ships in the harbor were repeatedly raked by Dewey's ships, and the next morning Manila was taken with no loss of life and little damage among the American ships.

In the Atlantic the U.S. Navy sought out Spanish ships, and marines occupied Cuba's Guantanamo Bay on 7 June 1898. Land warfare on Cuba followed, with troops sent from Tampa, Florida. Santiago was the first objective. During the ensuing weeks, an inept American army, composed of thousands of volunteers and relatively few regular army men and led by Lieut. John J. Pershing, battled the Spaniards until the Americans eventually won at San Juan Hill, where Lt. Col. Theodore Roosevelt, recently resigned as secretary of the navy, was in command. The U.S. Navy prevailed in the seas around Santiago, shelling Spanish ships and the shoreline until Spain surrendered its fleet and the land forces took Santiago. An armistice on 12 August 1898 led to peace negotiations that produced the Treaty of Paris on 10 December. The treaty's major provisions included Cuban independence, transfer of Puerto Rico and Guam to the United States, and cession of the Philippine Islands to the United States for a payment of twenty million dollars (Morris 1976).

Philippine Insurrection
Philippine Islands: 1899-1902

At the beginning of the Spanish-American War, the United States supported Philippine independence fighter Emilio Aguinaldo in raising an army against the Spanish. Aguinaldo assumed the United States would reward this assistance with Philippine independence. When the Treaty of Paris gave control of the Philippines to the United States,

Aguinaldo appealed for independence but was turned down. He then turned against the United States, and war broke out between a Filipino army of approximately 70,000 and an American force almost as large. Although the Filipinos had been largely defeated by the end of 1899, sporadic resistance to American rule continued until 1902, when the Philippine Government Act passed by Congress granted the Philippines a high degree of self government (Morris 1976).

Boxer Revolt
China: 1900

During the late 1890s, various European powers began dividing China into "spheres of influence" in which they enjoyed special trading privileges and a high degree of political control. In 1899, American Secretary of State John Hay issued the first of two "Open Door Notes" stating American opposition to such dismemberment of China. A revolt in the spring of 1900 by a group of antiforeign Chinese called the Boxers was an attempt to expel all foreigners from China. The Boxers occupied Peking and laid siege to the various foreign legations there. On 14 August, Peking was relieved by an international military force that included American troops (Morris 1976).

Tampico and Vera Cruz Incidents
Mexico: April 1914

Hostilities between the United States and Mexico almost came to war in April 1914. Crew members of the USS *Dolphin* were arrested on 9 April by forces of the Mexican dictator Victoriano Huerta. Although the Americans were later released, Huerta insulted the United States by failing to honor a request to salute the American flag in apology. Still pursuing an apology, American forces bombarded the port of Vera Cruz on 21 April. The tensions helped cause Huerta's abdication on 15 July (Link 1954).

Mexican Punitive Expedition
Mexico: 1916-17

Francisco "Pancho" Villa, a notorious Mexican bandit who opposed the Mexican president, headed an outlaw gang and precipitated border incidents with the United States. Villa raided Columbus, New Mexico, killing fifteen

Americans. In retaliation, 75,000 National Guardsmen led by Gen. John J. Pershing were sent into Mexico to track down the bandit. Unsuccessful, the force was recalled in January 1917 for service in the European war (Link 1954).

World War I
Europe: 1917-18

The unification of Germany in 1870, with its rapidly developing industrialization and militarism, upset the balance of power that had characterized European diplomacy since the Peace of Westphalia in 1648. The resulting fear of war led the smaller nations to sign (usually secret) defense treaties with the larger nations so that, by the early twentieth century, Europe was divided into two hostile and heavily armed blocs grouped around ancient enemies France and Germany. In such circumstances, a trivial incident was capable of triggering an immense war. Such an incident occurred on 28 June 1914, when a Serbian nationalist murdered the heir to the Austrian throne in Sarajevo. Serbia, though part of the Austro-Hungarian Empire, was an ally of Russia, which came to Serbia's defense upon Austria's threat to retaliate for the murder. This brought additional nations into the conflict and, by the end of the summer, all Europe was at war.

Although President Woodrow Wilson admonished Americans to "remain neutral in fact as in name," American sympathies came to rest heavily with the Allies—led by France and Great Britain—as the war developed. There were strong financial ties, for Americans loaned more money to the Allies than to the Germanic Central Powers. Germany's frank militarism and employment of the U-boat—the submarine, whose deadly stealth seemed immoral to many Americans—also turned the tide of American sympathies. Several developments brought America into the war. The U-boat sinking of the British passenger liner *Lusitania* on 7 May 1915, with the deaths of 128 Americans, led Wilson to demand the first of what became a series of German pledges to restrict submarine warfare. Finding it could not compete with the British navy without the U-boat, Germany announced resumption of unrestricted submarine warfare on 31 January 1917. Turmoil in Russia threatened to remove that country from the war, thus freeing German forces from the eastern front and seriously jeopardizing Allied fortunes. Finally, the intercepted Zimmermann Note of 1 March 1917, in which Germany offered Mexico restoration of its territorial losses of 1848 in turn for a declaration of war upon the United States, enraged Americans. On 6 April 1917, Congress issued a declaration of war on Germany.

A Selective Service Act provided for drafting young American men, and Gen. John J. Pershing was placed in charge of the American Expeditionary Force, which would reinforce the Allied armies that had been mired in bloody stalemate in the trenches of northern France since 1914. Although American troops participated in only two major campaigns—Belleau Wood and the Argonne Forest—and a few other isolated battles, their contribution was enough to shift the initiative decisively to the Allies.

When President Wilson issued his famous Fourteen Points in January 1918, it was apparent that they were far more than a simple peace proposal, and were in fact a plan for the reconstruction of Western civilization. They included such ideas as the abolition of secret treaties, freedom of the seas, free trade, disarmament, national self-determination, and liquidation of colonial empires. Point Fourteen was crucial, for it proposed a League of Nations, an international congress for negotiation and redress of future frictions. Tempted by the promise of an easy peace, the Germans signed an armistice on 11 November 1918.

Wilson himself led the American delegation to the treaty negotiations at Versailles in 1919, only to learn the hard lesson that the Allies intended to impose a harsh peace. "Moses gave us ten commandments, and we broke every one," Georges Clemenceau of France observed. "Now Wilson gives us fourteen. We shall see." Germany was not even allowed to participate in the talks, as point after point of the fourteen was rejected or eviscerated. Germany was burdened with war guilt, stripped of its army and industrial regions, and forced to make reparation payments to the Allies. Finally, even though Wilson insisted upon his League of Nations, he returned to a hostile Senate that would not ratify the treaty, and the United States never joined the world's first permanent international congress, a congress the American president had created. In its vindictiveness, the Treaty of Versailles sowed the seeds of World War II: Adolf Hitler rose to power in the 1930s on the strength of the claim that Germany had been cheated out of its destiny and lured to destruction by an international Jewish conspiracy using the bait of middle-class democracy in the form of the Fourteen Points (Link 1955).

World War II
Europe, Asia, the Pacific, Africa: 1939-45

Despite the tensions that remained in Europe after the Treaty of Versailles, the first act of aggression that led to World War II occurred not there but in the Far East. In 1931, Japan, still smarting from the second-rate naval status accorded her ten years before at the Washington Conference on arms limitation, and desiring a foreign empire that would raise her status in the international community, invaded Manchuria. Although Japan placed a veneer of legitimacy on the act by setting up a puppet regime headed by Henry Pu-yi, the deposed Manchurian emperor of China, it was clearly an act of aggression in violation of the Kellogg-Briand Pact of 1928 and was so identified by the Lytton Commission sent by the League of Nations to investigate the episode in 1932. Still, the league did nothing, having no troops at its disposal and, indeed, no real coercive power. The lesson was clear: aggression would not be punished, and ambitious heads of state in other parts of the world—among them Germany's Adolf Hitler and Italy's Benito Mussolini—were quick to learn it.

Japan invaded China in 1937. The United States became alarmed at Japanese expansionism, for it was now a Pacific power as well, particularly since the acquisition of Hawaii and the Philippine Islands in 1898. As Japan continued to move southward through east Asia, the United States exercised its own sanctions, first through refusing to sell Japan such raw materials as petroleum and scrap metal, then through freezing all Japanese assets in the United States. On 7 December 1941, Japan retaliated in a devastating air attack on the U.S. naval base at Pearl Harbor in Hawaii. The next day, the United States entered the war.

Despite having entered the war, as it were, through the back door, the United States regarded the European theater as of primary importance and fell back to a holding position for the time being in the Pacific. German aggression in Europe had paralleled that of Japan during the 1930s. Adolf Hitler's rise to power was based on a determination to recover the empire denied his country by the Treaty of Versailles. Desiring peace, the other major European powers accepted his annexations of Austria, the Rhineland, and Czechoslovakia as adjustments to the balance of power, but when Germany invaded Poland on 1 September 1939, Great Britain and France declared war.

America's first military involvement in the western theater was to help the British drive the Germans out of North Africa, the point of German occupation closest to America and the place where the opponent seemed most vul-nerable. The campaign began on 8 November 1942 and was successful. The following year the Allies invaded Sicily, then Italy, forcing Italian surrender and gaining time to prepare for opening a second front in France. That event occurred on D-Day, 6 June 1944, when Americans joined a total Allied force of a million soldiers in a bold cross-channel invasion from England to the beaches of Normandy. The Allied push across France and into Germany followed, crossing the Rhine River and eventually entering Berlin itself. Hitler committed suicide when the situation became hopeless, and representatives of his government surrendered on 7 May 1945.

Though America's primary commitment was to the European theater during the early years of the war, important turning points occurred in the Pacific in 1942 with the American naval victories at the battles of Coral Sea and Midway. Some of the bloodiest fighting of the war ensued as American marine and army units moved from one island to the next, dislodging deeply entrenched Japanese forces. As American forces moved west, aerial attacks on Japan itself became possible. When Americans reached Okinawa, south of Japan, in 1945, the fighting became especially brutal as fire-bomb assaults on Tokyo were met by desperate *kamikaze* attacks on American naval vessels. Finally President Harry Truman, who had succeeded to the presidency after President Franklin Roosevelt's death on 12 April 1945, ordered the dropping of atomic bombs on strategic Japanese sites, hoping to drive the Japanese to desperation and shorten the war. The first bomb fell on Hiroshima on 6 August and the second on Nagasaki on 9 August leading to Japanese surrender on 14 August.

World War II ended with no comprehensive treaty like the Treaty of Versailles, though separate treaties were signed to resolve specific situations. In Europe, Germany became the scene of an armed stalemate through joint occupation by the former allies: the western democracies—France, Great Britain, and the United States—and the communist Soviet Union. The resulting maneuvering for position and control on the part of democracy and communism took place in the East as well and became known as the Cold War (Keegan 1989).

Korean War
Korea: 1950-53

Although the Soviet Union entered the war against Japan only days before the Japanese surrender, it was given a major role in shaping the postwar world. One aspect of this role was the occupation of the northern portion of

Korea, a former Japanese possession that was divided into occupation zones at the thirty-eighth parallel, with the United States occupying the southern portion. Elections supervised by the United Nations were scheduled for 1948, after which Korea was to be reunited and self-governed. Although the Soviet Union refused to allow United Nations supervisors into the north, the elections in the south went ahead as scheduled After a democratic government was established in the south, the United States withdrew in 1949, announcing that Korea was henceforth outside the American defensive perimeter, though economic assistance would be provided.

On 25 June 1950, North Korean forces invaded the south and by September had driven the South Korean defenders (supported by United Nations forces) into a narrow perimeter around Pusan, on the southeastern coast of the peninsula. On 15 September, United Nations forces under Gen. Douglas MacArthur launched a counteroffensive at Inchon, on the western coast near Seoul, quickly driving the North Korean army northward almost to the Yalu River, the border between North Korea and China. On 26 November, Chinese troops entered the war and by the first of the year had driven the United Nations forces back into South Korea. A famous altercation occurred early in 1951 between MacArthur and President Harry Truman, MacArthur arguing for the necessity of carrying the war into Chinese territory and Truman ordering him to avoid such a widening of the conflict. The altercation led to MacArthur's removal from command on 11 April 1951.

During the summer of 1951, an armistice and peace negotiations began, but the negotiations enjoyed little progress for the next two years. President-Elect Dwight Eisenhower fulfilled a campaign pledge by visiting Korea in December 1952, but the stalemate continued until the death of the intransigent Joseph Stalin in 1953. A treaty signed on 26 July 1953 made permanent the partition of Korea between a communist north and a democratic south, with a demilitarized zone between (Morris 1976; Link 1955).

Vietnam War
Vietnam: 1954–75

Motivated by Cold War anti-communist fervor, most Americans after World War II were unable to distinguish between the issue of Vietnamese independence from French colonial administration and the communism of the movement's primary advocates, Ho Chi Minh and his Viet

Minh followers in the northern part of the country. Consequently, in the civil war that broke out after World War II between the Viet Minh communists and the supporters of French colonialism in the south, the United States supported the French. After the partition of Korea in 1953, advocates of a similar solution in Vietnam gained increasing support, but President Eisenhower refused to support the idea until representatives of the United States, France, and the Vietnamese communists met at a conference in Geneva in 1954. The French arrived at the conference in a poor bargaining position because of their recent military disaster at the hands of communist forces at Dien Bien Phu. The French relinquished their claims to Vietnam immediately after the conference, leaving the United States as the advocate of democracy in the country.

The Geneva Accords temporarily partitioned the country at the seventeenth parallel pending United Nations-supervised elections in 1956. When that date arrived, the United States supported Ngo Dinh Diem, the noncommunist dictator in the south, in refusing the elections, realizing that Ho Chi Minh and the communists would decisively carry the election; the United States did not want another communist regime in Asia. Civil war resumed, and the United States had placed a total of 16,600 military advisors in Vietnam to shore up the shaky democracy in the south by the time of President John F. Kennedy's death in 1963.

President Lyndon B. Johnson, wishing to succeed in every area in which his predecessor had failed, required a rationale for massive military involvement in Vietnam. The incident he sought occurred in August 1964 in alleged North Vietnamese assaults on American naval vessels in the Tonkin Gulf off Vietnam. Congress passed the Tonkin Gulf Resolution in response, granting the president virtual *carte blanche* to counter aggression against American forces. In the summer of 1965, American combat troops entered the country at Da Nang.

In the United States, an antiwar movement broke out and gained momentum after the Tet Offensive of January-February 1968, in which American gains of the past three years seemed to be wiped out almost immediately. The massacre of 347 Vietnamese civilians by American soldiers at the village of My Lai in March 1968 led to serious questioning of the moral value of the American presence. During the Democratic primary races of that year, President Johnson yielded to the antiwar challenge of Sen. Eugene McCarthy and Robert Kennedy and removed himself from contention.

Richard Nixon emerged as the victor in that presidential race, largely upon the strength of his promise that he had a plan to end the Vietnam war. That plan turned out to be "Vietnamization," the process of training and equipping South Vietnamese forces to defend their country. That process continued until 29 April 1975, when the American withdrawal was completed and the last of 58,000 Americans died in the war. South Vietnam's capital fell to invading communist forces the following day (Karnow 1983; Fitzgerald 1972).

Sources Cited in the Appendix

Alden, John Richard. *The American Revolution, 1775–1783.* New York: Harper & Row, 1954.

Baldwin, Leland W. *Whiskey Rebels.* Pittsburg: University of Pittsburg Press, 1939.

Beal, Merrill D. *"I Will Fight No More Forever": Chief Joseph and the Nez Perce War.* Seattle: University of Washington Press, 1963.

Bridenbaugh, Carl. *Jamestown, 1544–1699.* New York: Oxford University Press, 1980.

Brooks, Juanita. *The Mountain Meadows Massacre.* Stanford: Stanford University Press, 1950.

Burrage, H. S. *Maine and the Northeastern Boundary Controversy.* Portland: state of Maine, 1919.

Craven, Wesley Frank. *The Colonies in Transition, 1660–1713.* New York: Harper & Row, 1968.

Dangerfield, George. *The Awakening of American Nationalism, 1815–1828.* New York: Harper & Row, 1965.

Dorn, Walter L. *Competition for Empire.* New York: Harper & Row, 1940.

Fitzgerald, Frances. *Fire in the Lake: The Vietnamese and the Americans in Vietnam.* New York: Random House, 1972.

Fuller, George W. *A History of the Pacific Northwest.* New York: Alfred A. Knopf, 1931.

Furniss, Norman F. *The Mormon Conflict, 1850–1859.* New Haven: Yale University Press, 1960.

Hassler, Warren W. *With Shield and Sword.* Ames: Iowa State University Press, 1982.

Hofstadter, Richard, and Michael Wallace. *American Violence.* New York: Alfred A. Knopf, 1970.

Horsman, Reginald. *The War of 1812.* New York: Alfred A. Knopf, 1969.

Ivers, Larry E. *British Drums on the Southern Frontier: The Military Colonization of Georgia, 1733–1749.* Chapel Hill: University of North Carolina Press, 1874.

Jacobs, Wilbur R. *Dispossessing the American Indian.* New York: Scribner's, 1972.

Jones, Katharine M. *Port Royal Under Six Flags.* Indianapolis: Bobbs Merrill, 1969.

Karnow, Stanley. *Vietnam: A History.* New York: Viking, 1983.

Keegan, John. *The Second World War.* New York: Viking Penguin, 1989.

Lamar, Howard R. *The Reader's Encyclopedia of the American West.* New York: Crowell, 1977.

Lawson, Don. *The Colonial Wars–Prelude to the American Revolution.* New York: Abelard-Schuman, 1972.

Leach, Douglas E. *Arms For Empire: A Military History of the American Colonies in North America, 1607–1763.* New York: Macmillan, 1973.

_____ . *Flintlock and Tomahawk: New England in King Philip's War.* New York: Macmillan, 1958.

Leckie, Robert. *The Wars of America.* New York: Harper & Row, 1968.

Link, Arthur S. *American Epoch: A History of the United States Since the 1890s.* New York: Alfred A. Knopf, 1955.

_____ . *Woodrow Wilson and the Progressive Era, 1910–1917.* New York: Harper & Row, 1954.

Locke, Raymond Friday. *The Book of the Navajo.* Los Angeles: Mankind Publishing Co., 1989.

McNitt, Frank. *Navajo Wars.* Albuquerque: University of New Mexico Press, 1972.

Merk, Frederick. *History of the Westward Movement.* New York: Alfred A. Knopf, 1978.

Miller, John C. *The Federalist Era, 1789–1801.* New York: Harper & Row, 1960.

Morris, Richard B. *Encyclopedia of American History.* New York: Harper & Row, 1976.

O'Donnell, James H., III. *Southern Indians in the American Revolution.* Knoxville: University of Tennessee Press, 1973.

Peters, Virginia B. *The Florida Wars.* Hamden, Conn.: Archon Books, 1979.

Randall, J. G., and David Donald. *The Civil War and Reconstruction.* Boston: Heath, 1961.

Schwantes, Carlos A. *The Pacific Northwest: An Interpretive History.* Lincoln: University of Nebraska Press, 1989.

Singletary, Otis A. *The Mexican War*. Chicago: University of Chicago Press, 1960.

Smelser, Marshall. *The Democratic Republic, 1801–1815*. New York: Harper & Row, 1968.

Smith, Justin. *The War With Mexico*. New York: Macmillan, 1919.

Thwaites, Reuben Gold, and Louise P. Kellogg, eds. *Documentary History of Dunmore's War, 1774*. Madison: Wisconsin Historical Society, 1905.

Trafzer, Clifford E. *The Kit Carson Campaign: The Last Great Navajo War*. Norman: University of Oklahoma Press, 1982.

Utley, Robert M. *Frontier Regulars: The United States Army and the Indians*. New York: Macmillan, 1974.

Vaughan, Alden T. *New England Frontier: Puritans and Indians, 1620–1675*. Boston: Little, Brown, 1965.

Van Deusen, Glyndon. *The Jacksonian Era, 1828–1848*. New York: Harper & Row, 1959.

Williams, T. Harry. *The History of American Wars From 1745 to 1918*. New York: Alfred A. Knopf, 1981.

Index

A

Aachen, battle of, 127
Absentees, 15, 46
Abstract cards, 21
Academies, military, 52, 98
   See also each branch of military service
Acadia
   See also Nova Scotia
   Port Royal, 395
Acadians, 396
Adams
   Ansel, photographs, 182
   John Quincy (President), 403
   Samuel, 398
Adams-Onis Transcontinental Treaty, 220, 343, 400–401
Adjutant General, 17, 29, 34, 91, 108, 146
   state-level reports, 369
Admiralty laws, 120
Aeronautics, Military School of, 133
Africa, 409
African-American(s), 215, 277, 309, 317
   American Revolution, 373, 375
   Army, 174
   bounty numbers, 271
   cavalry regiments, 382
   Civil War, 109, 122, 240, 273, 343, 384
   claims for back pay and bounty, 304
   colored troops, 299
   draft substitutes, 249

   early wars, 371
   enlisted men, 305
   Fourth Regiment, 215
   free Negroes, 310
   Indian Wars, 387
   Medal of Honor, 96, 371
   Michigan, 279
   Military Academy, U.S., 99, 175
   military service, 175, 214
   military service 1639–1886, 89, 133, 225, 240, 298, 309, 340
   military units, 23
   NAACP, 175
   pensions, 341
   Revolutionary war, 275, 312, 333, 374
   slaves, 403
   troops, 152
   veterans' home, 311
   War of 1812, 374
   World War I, 332, 336
   World War II, 388
Agent Orange, 162
Agents
   American prisoners of war, for, 108
   Indian, 405
   Naval Intelligence, 43, 118
   secret, 92, 388
   special, 97, 110
Aguinaldo, Emilio, 407
Aides-de-camp, 95
Ainsworth List, The, 98

Air Corps Units, 105
Air Force, 21, 105, 113, 175, 177
   See also Army Air Force
   Commands, 144
   engineering personnel, 152
   Fifth Fighter Command, 98
   history, 178
   Library of Congress collection, 165
   Medical Services, 152
   Oral History Catalog, 152
   personnel, 131, 177
   records, 125, 131, 140
   register 1949–75, 153
   squadron intelligence, 98
   units, 152
Air Force Academy, 182
Air Force Historical Research Agency, 40, 98, 152, 177–178
Air Force History Office, 152
Air Force Journal, 181
Air Force Register, 158, 181, 389
Air National Guard Register, 158
Air operations (navy), 120
Air Service Units, 105
Air Stations, 134, 140–141
   Norfolk Naval (Virginia), 136
Aircraft, 105, 156, 177
   carriers, 153
Aircraft Production, Bureau of, 105
Airfields, 105
Airplanes, 40, 158

For Reference

Not to be taken from this room